D1341095

MARK RYAN
WITH CONTRIBUTIONS FROM
STEVE FOSTER

UNLOCKING
CONSTITUTIONAL &
ADMINISTRATIVE LAW

SERIES EDITORS:
JACQUELINE MARTIN & CHRIS TURNER

Withdrawn

NY

Orders, please contact Bookpoint Ltd, 130 Milton Park, Abingdon, Oxon OX14 4SB. Telephone: (44) 01235 827720. Fax: (44) 01235 400454. Lines are open from 9.00–5.00, Monday to Saturday, with a 24-hour message answering service. You can also order through our website www.hoddereducation.co.uk

If you have any comments to make about this, or any of our other titles, please send them to educationenquiries@hodder.co.uk

British Library Cataloguing in Publication Data
A catalogue record for this title is available from the British Library

ISBN: 978 0 340 81606 6

First Edition Published 2007

Impression number   10   9   8   7   6   5   4   3
Year   2012   2011   2010   2009

Cover photo © Wild Country/Corbis
Typeset by Phoenix Photosetting, Chatham, Kent
Printed in Malta for Hodder Education, An Hachette Livre UK Company, 338 Euston Road, London NW1 3BH

CONTENTS ∎

UNLOCKING
CONSTITUTIONAL
& ADMINISTRATIVE LAW

ACKNOWLEDGEMENTS ■

The books in this series are a departure from traditional law texts and represent one view of a type of learning resource that we feel is particularly useful to students. The series editors would therefore like to thank the publishers for their support in making the project a reality. In particular we would also like to thank Alexia Chan for her continued faith in the project from its first conception.

Jacqueline Martin & Chris Turner

I would like to thank Gibson Fairnie (for his assistance in proof-reading the text), Donna Shannon, Vicki Mcgeown and Steve Foster, for their support during the writing of this text.

This book is dedicated to my mother and my siblings.

Mark Ryan

The authors and publishers would like to thank the following for permission to reproduce copyright material: extracts on pages 5, 64, 105–106, 192, 554 and 559 reproduced by permission of Taylor & Francis Books (UK); extract on page 119 reproduced by permission of The Constitution Unit; extracts on pages 237, 242 and 243 reproduced by permission of The Electoral Commission. © Crown copyright material is reproduced with permission of the Controller of HMSO.

The publishers apologise if inadvertently any sources remain unacknowledged and will be glad to make the necessary arrangements at the earliest opportunity.

PREFACE

The *Unlocking the Law* series is an entirely new style of undergraduate law textbook. Many student texts are very prose dense and have little in the way of interactive materials to help a student feel his or her way through the course of study on a given module.

The purpose of this series, then, is to try to make learning each subject area more accessible by focusing on actual learning needs, and by providing a range of different supporting materials and features.

All topic areas are broken up into 'bite-size' sections, with a logical progression and extensive use of headings and numerous sub-headings. Each book in the series will also contain a variety of charts, diagrams and key facts summaries to reinforce the information in the body of the text. Diagrams and flow charts are particularly useful because they can provide a quick and easy understanding of the key points, especially when revising for examinations. Key facts charts not only provide a quick visual guide through the subject but are useful for revision purposes also.

The books have a number of common features in the style of text layout. Important cases are separated out for easy access and have full citation in the text as well as in the table of cases for ease of reference. The emphasis of the series is on depth of understanding much more than breadth. For this reason, each text also includes key extracts from judgments, where appropriate. Extracts from academic comment from journal articles and leading texts are also included to give some insight into the academic debate on complex or controversial areas. In both cases these are indented to make them clear from the body of the text.

Finally, the books also include much formative 'self-testing', with a variety of activities ranging through subject-specific comprehension, application of the law, and a range of other activities to help the student gain a good idea of his or her progress in the course.

Symbols used in this series:

This is a small extract from a judgment in a case. It may follow a case example or the case may be identified immediately above.

This is a section from an Act or a reference to an Act.

This is an Article of the EC Treaty or of the European Convention on Human Rights. In this text, this symbol also denotes an aspect of a national constitution.

Q	This is a quote from an official report or parliamentary/government paper.

Where a paragraph is indented, this is an extract from an academic source such as an article or a leading textbook.

Note also that for all incidental references to 'he', 'him', 'his', we invoke the Interpretation Act 1978 and its provisions that 'he' includes 'she' etc.

Chapters 1–15 and 18–22 were written by Mark Ryan, and Chapters 16–17 were written by Steve Foster.

The law is stated as we believe it to be on 1 January 2007, although where space permits some material has been added after this date.

Mark Ryan
Steve Foster

TABLE OF CASES ■

TABLE OF STATUTES AND OTHER INSTRUMENTS ■

International Legislation

chapter 1 INTRODUCTORY CONCEPTS ■

1.1 The distinction between public law and private law

In general, the term 'law' can be broadly divided into two branches: public law and private law. Constitutional and administrative law form part of public law.

1.1.1 Private law

In essence, private law is that branch of the law that is concerned with the relationship that individuals have with one another. For example:

- An individual forms a legally binding contract with a work colleague when he agrees to purchase a three-piece settee from him (see further *Unlocking Contract Law*).

- An individual sues a neighbour in the law of defamation for making untrue slanderous accusations about his past (see further *Unlocking Torts*).

- Two adjoining land owners legally dispute the location of a boundary fence between their land (see further *Unlocking Land Law*).

- A pedestrian sues the driver of a car in the law of negligence after being badly injured in an accident caused by his careless driving (see further *Unlocking Torts*).

1.1.2 Private law involving other than private individuals

It is also worth noting at this point that it is possible for individuals to have private law transactions or legal relations with the state (in this context and for present purposes, the state means simply the government, public authorities, local authorities, etc). For example, an individual may form a legally binding contract with a local authority, or indeed may even sue that same body in the law of negligence if it has acted carelessly and caused harm. Although in one sense such

1

relations would appear to form part of contract and tort law respectively (with the defendant in these cases being the state, rather than a private individual), such actions could also have a public law dimension. This is because as these actions in contract and negligence involve the state they will be governed by special rules and principles which have the effect of treating the state differently from an ordinary private individual defendant. This point serves to indicate at this early stage that in the United Kingdom the distinction between private and public law is not absolute and so it is not always easy to draw the line between them with complete precision. For example, in this context Lord Wilberforce in *Davy v Spelthorne Borough Council* [1984] 1 AC 262 commented:

> **J** 'The expressions "private law" and "public law" have recently been imported into the law of England from countries which, unlike our own, have separate systems concerning public law and private law. No doubt they are convenient expressions for descriptive purposes. In this country they must be used with caution.'

1.1.3 Public law

Public law (which subsumes both constitutional and administrative law – see section 1.2) is that branch of the law that focuses on the power of the state. In essence, public lawyers are concerned with the location of state power, how that power is exercised and controlled, and how it impacts on the individual. At a very basic level, public law is concerned with the following questions:

- Who and what bodies/institutions/individuals exercise state/public power?
- What is the nature and extent of these powers?
- Why do these bodies/institutions exercise power?
- How do these bodies relate to each other?
- How is power used?
- How is the use of power regulated?
- How are these bodies/institutions/individuals made accountable?
- What protection is given to the individual from the power of the state?

In other words, the study of public law is concerned with the identification of public power, the institutions that exercise it and how these institutions relate to one another and to the individual. Most importantly, it is concerned with how the use of public power is regulated and controlled. Thus, the constitutional principle of the accountability of the state (whether it be in a legal or political form), is a major theme that underpins the subject of public law and consequently, therefore, this text.

In summary, in contrast to private law which is concerned essentially with individual/private legal relations, public law focuses on the structure and organisation of the state and how the individual relates to the state.

1.1.4 Public law and criminal law

At this point, it is pertinent to note that the broad term public law also technically embraces criminal law, as crimes are termed as offences against the state, and so punishable by it. Although criminal law clearly has a public law dimension, historically the substantive subject of criminal law (eg offences against the person, theft, etc) has nevertheless been taught as a separate subject (see further *Unlocking Criminal Law*). Notwithstanding this, certain aspects of criminal law (for example the breadth and extent of police powers for arresting and detaining individuals) will necessarily be subsumed within the field of public law as they raise issues concerning basic human rights and civil liberties. In particular, the substantive criminal law offences which involve restricting freedom of expression, for example: the laws of blasphemy, obscenity and indecency, will be considered as part of Chapter 18.

1.1.5 Public law and politics

Public law, more so than any other substantive law subject, is intimately and inextricably linked with the disciplines of political science and government. As a consequence, it is an advantage to have a background interest in, and awareness of, general British politics when studying public law as the subject necessarily draws upon some of these principles. In fact, as we will see in Chapter 4, some of the sources of the British constitution are actually political practices (constitutional conventions).

For example, in the context of the government's relations with Parliament, government ministers are both collectively and individually responsible to Parliament for their actions and yet this accountability is not legal, but essentially political in nature, determined by predominately political factors. Furthermore, the connection and overlap between politics and constitutional law is evident in the context of civil liberties which involves the basic human rights and freedoms of the individual. These rights – which include, for example, the right to life – raise the issue of whether such rights should be enjoyed, and whether they are actually political/moral/religious questions which happen to be dressed up as legal questions which are determined by (unelected) judges in a courtroom (whether domestically or in Europe).

Public law is highly topical and an ever-changing and dynamic subject. In studying public law, therefore, it is advisable to keep abreast of recent developments through the daily broadsheet newspapers. Thus, every day there will be, invariably, something with a public law dimension and therefore of interest to public lawyers. Hypothetical examples could include the following:

- A government minister resigns over a scandal.
- A local authority acts illegally by abusing its powers.

- The European Court of Human Rights in Strasbourg makes a judgment against the United Kingdom for breaching the European Convention on Human Rights.

- The Queen approves the appointment of 10 new life peers to sit in the House of Lords.

- Parliament passes a law which restricts freedom of expression.

- The European Court of Justice in Luxembourg declares that the United Kingdom has failed to follow European Community law.

- The Administrative Court declares that the Home Secretary has breached the Human Rights Act 1998.

ACTIVITY

Problem solving

Read one week's issues of a national daily newspaper and try to identify articles which you think have relevance to the study of public law.

1.1.6 Public law and European Community law

As a result of the enactment of the European Communities Act 1972 (see Chapter 15), in recent decades both public law and private law have been significantly affected by, and subject to, European Community (EC) law. Although the main substantive subjects of EC law (eg the free movement of goods, workers, services, etc) are studied separately (see further *Unlocking EU Law*), certain aspects of it, such as the primacy of EC law have had such a profound effect on the constitution of the United Kingdom that they have to be considered in the context of public law. In particular, the reception of EC law (which has now overriding legal effect) into the United Kingdom has resulted in, *inter alia*, the restriction of the power of the United Kingdom Parliament to pass any law that it chooses (see Chapter 7 in conjunction with section 15.6).

KEY FACTS

Public law embraces both constitutional and administrative law and is essentially concerned with the organs of the state, together with how they relate to the individual and to themselves.

Public law is concerned with the use and regulation of public power.

1.2 The distinction between constitutional and administrative law

Although both constitutional and administrative law form part of the generic term public law, a distinction, albeit a fine one, can be made between them.

1.2.1 Constitutional law

At a very basic level constitutional law can be described simply as the law relating to the constitution. Although the term constitution will be considered in Chapter 2, for present purposes a constitution represents a set of basic rules and principles which govern the government/state.

A more detailed definition is provided by Barnett who defined constitutional law in the following terms:

> 'Constitutional Law is concerned with the role and powers of the institutions within the state and with the relationship between the citizen and the state'.

> H Barnett, *Constitutional and Administrative Law* (6th edn, Routledge–Cavendish, 2006), p 3.

In other words, constitutional law concerns, among others, the following elements (all of which will be considered in this text):

- The principal institutions of the state, viz., Parliament (see Chapters 8 to 10), the government (see Chapter 11), the courts (see Chapter 13) and devolved/decentralised state bodies (see Chapter 14).
- The specific roles and functions conferred on these institutions, together with the nature and extent of their powers (for example, see Chapter 11 on the powers of the executive).
- The procedures and mechanisms used to oversee, regulate and check these powers (for example, see Chapter 12 in relation to the parliamentary controls over the government).
- The ways in which these institutions relate to one another (for example, see Chapter 10 on how the House of Lords and Commons relate to one another).
- The ways in which these institutions relate to the individual (for example, see Chapter 9 on parliamentary elections).
- The basic and fundamental rights of the individual (for example, the right to life and free speech) and how – and to what extent – these rights and freedoms can be protected from infringement by the state (see Chapters 16 and 17 on the European Convention on Human Rights and Chapter 18 on freedom of speech).

1.2.2 Administrative law

In general terms, administrative law (in contrast to constitutional law above) is concerned with, simply, the law relating to the administration/government. It is thus a separate branch of constitutional law relating to the executive (those who execute or carry out the law). Wade and Forsyth defined it in the following terms:

> 'administrative law may be said to be the body of general principles which govern the exercise of powers and duties by public authorities'.

> H Wade and W Forsyth, *Administrative Law* (9th edn, Oxford University Press, 2004), p 5.

The government, its officers and agencies are invested with extensive powers to provide services (eg administering welfare benefits) and to carry out specific government functions (eg making regulations). Administrative law, therefore, is focused specifically on the various powers that the government exercises and how these powers are controlled and regulated to ensure that the administration acts strictly within its limits. This branch of the law is concerned with both the legal control of the government through the mechanisms of judicial review (see Chapters 19 and 20) and tribunals (see Chapter 21), as well as extra judicial means of control in the form of inquiries (see Chapter 21). In addition, it also embraces parliamentary/political controls in the form of the Parliamentary Ombudsman (see Chapter 21).

It is clear that in the United Kingdom the distinction between administrative law and constitutional law is not, necessarily, easy to draw. At a general level it could be said that whereas constitutional law tends to consider the whole apparatus of the state, administrative law, in contrast, is more specifically focused on how the executive/administration uses and misuses its powers. For practical purposes, this text considers each branch separately through a collection of various chapters: constitutional law is considered in Chapters 1–14 and 16–18 whilst administrative law is detailed in Chapters 19–21. In addition, a general introduction to European Community law is covered in Chapter 15. As such, it will be plain that constitutional law will form the major component of this book.

KEY FACTS

Constitutional law is the law relating to the constitution, the state institutions, their powers, together with how they relate to the individual.

Administrative law is concerned specifically with the law relating to the administration/executive/government and its control.

ACTIVITY

Question

How can one define and recognise constitutional law?

chapter 2 CONSTITUTIONS ■

AIMS AND OBJECTIVES

At the end of this chapter you should be able to:

■ Define a constitution

■ Appreciate the nature and content of constitutions

■ Appreciate the purpose of constitutions

■ Distinguish between different types of constitution

■ Understand the concept of constitutionalism

2.1 Definition

All organisations – whether a university chess club or a state – have a constitution of some description, as society requires rules in order to function and ensure order. These rules are simply known as the constitution (constitutional rules). Bradley and Ewing have noted that a constitution can be defined in two ways: with a narrow or a wide meaning. In a narrow sense they have described a constitution as:

> 'a document having a special legal sanctity which sets out the framework and the principal functions of the organs of government within the state and declares the principles by which those organs must operate'.

A Bradley and K Ewing, *Constitutional and Administrative Law* (14th edn, Pearson/Longman, 2007), p 4.

In a broader sense of the term, they refer to, and quote, Wheare:

> 'it is used to describe the whole system of government of a country, the collection of rules which establish and regulate or govern the government'.

K Wheare, *Modern Constitutions* (2nd edn, Oxford University Press, 1966), p 1.

In its first report in July 2001, the House of Lords Select Committee on the Constitution recognised the difficulty in defining the term constitution and put forward the following definition:

> **Q** 'Our working definition of a constitution is that it is the set of laws, rules and practices that create the basic institutions of the state and its component and related parts, and stipulate the powers of those institutions and the relationship between the different institutions and between those institutions and the individual'.
>
> First Report of Session 2001–02 of the House of Lords Select on the Committee on the Constitution, *Reviewing the constitution: Terms of reference and method of working* HL Paper 11 (2001), p 16.

For present purposes, therefore, we may conclude that a constitution is simply a set of rules and principles that govern the organisation and structure of the state which the governing institutions must, or should, adhere to. As will be indicated below, these constitutional rules almost invariably will be found in a single written document entitled 'The Constitution', although sometimes – as in the United Kingdom – these rules are located other than in a specific constitutional document (see Chapter 4 on the sources of the constitution of the United Kingdom).

ACTIVITY

Question

Using the above definitions, how would you define a constitution in your own words?

2.2 The contents of a constitution

What will a constitution contain? The exact contents of a state constitution will differ from state to state. It must be remembered that constitutions exist in both democratic and non-democratic countries, although by their nature, democratic constitutions should follow the principles of constitutionalism (see section 2.6.2).

As an introduction or foreword, a preamble is found in many state constitutions. It tends to be declaratory in nature and identifies the people as the constituent (sovereign) power from which the moral authority of the constitution derives. For example, in the Irish constitution (1937) it is stated at the outset that:

 We the people . . . do hereby adopt, enact and give to ourselves this constitution.

In general, the main text of a constitution will contain the following elements.

2.2.1 The establishment of the institutions of government together with their roles, powers and functions

A constitution will set out the basic ground rules of the state which will include the establishment of these institutions (and so their legitimacy – see section 2.4.2). In short, it will locate and establish the principal institutions of the state together with their roles/functions:

- The law-making institution which passes legislation (Parliament/Congress/Assembly).

- The executive/government institution which enforces the law and makes policy decisions (Prime Minister/Cabinet/President).

- The judicial institution which interprets and declares the law (the courts/Constitutional Court/Supreme Court).

For example, the constitution of the United States of America (1789) states the following:

- Art I, s 1. All legislative powers herein granted shall be vested in a Congress of the United States, which shall consist of a Senate and House of Representatives.

- Art II, s 1. The executive power shall be vested in a President of the United States of America.

- Art III, s 1. The judicial power of the United States shall be vested in one Supreme Court, and such inferior courts as the Congress may from time to time ordain and establish.

In this way the constitution of the United States sets out the three key institutions of the state.

The constitution will also set out the specific powers of each institution. For example, again with reference to the constitution of the United States, Art II, s 2 states that the President shall have the power (with the consent of the Congress) to make Treaties and to nominate (also with congressional consent) the judges of the Supreme Court. Similarly, Art I, s 8 states that Congress shall have the power to lay and collect taxes and declare war. In short, a constitution will establish the key institutions of the state and allocate them constitutional roles and responsibilities and equip them with public powers.

2.2.2 The establishment of the relationship between the different institutions of the state

The constitution will also set out the constitutional relationship between the various institutions established under it. This relationship will necessarily involve the principle of the system of checks and balances between the institutions (see Chapter 5). For example, as seen above, the constitution of the United States stipulates that Congress is the body responsible for passing legislation;

however, Art I, s 7 states that before a Bill becomes law it must be presented to the President for approval. If the latter rejects the Bill, it can still become law providing that Congress reconsiders it and both congressional chambers pass the Bill with a two-thirds majority. This therefore sets out the constitutional relationship between the President and Congress in the context of the passage of legislation.

In the German constitution (1949), Art 67 states that the Bundestag (the lower House of the German Parliament) can express a lack of confidence in the Federal Chancellor by electing (with a majority of its members) a successor to replace him. Thus, a major theme of public law is how the state institutions relate to and complement one another, and most importantly, how these institutions check and balance one another.

2.2.3 The establishment of the relationship between the state institutions and the individual

As noted above, constitutional law is partly concerned with how the individual relates to the state (ie what powers can the state exert over the individual). For example, in what circumstances can the individual be arrested and detained or have their freedom of expression interfered with? A democratic constitution, however, will constitutionally ring-fence and safeguard certain basic rights of the individual which the state institutions cannot interfere with (or can only do so with compelling justification). In other words, this means that the rights of the individual are put beyond the reach of the state. In one sense, this can be seen as part of the social contract (see section 2.4.2) which the citizen makes with the state. This in turn confers legitimacy on the state institutions to rule.

One of the most famous declarations of basic and fundamental human rights is the first 10 amendments of the constitution of the United States which collectively are known as 'The Bill of Rights'. As an example, Art IV of the Bill of Rights is set out below:

 The right of the people to be secure in their persons, houses, papers, and effects, against unreasonable searches and seizures, shall not be violated, and no warrants shall issue, but upon probable cause, supported by oath or affirmation, and particularly describing the place to be searched, and the persons or things to be seized.

Similarly, Part III of the Indian constitution sets out the fundamental rights of the individual which include, among others:

- the right to equality
- the right to freedom of religion
- the right to freedom of speech, assembly, association, etc
- the right against exploitation.

By setting out the basic rights of the individual in the constitution in this way, these fundamental rights and freedoms are accorded special protection from infringement by the state.

2.2.4 The methods and procedures to change the constitution

Although constitutions are (generally) documents which embody the framework of the state, they are not necessarily meant to be documents which are incapable of amendment and improvement. Indeed, the contents of a state constitution which could not be altered in any way in order to adapt to changing times would make the citizens of that state a prisoner of their constitution, as a constitution may have been drafted decades, if not centuries, before. A constitution will typically, therefore, stipulate the method and procedures that must be complied with in order to alter its provisions.

For example, amendments to the constitution of the United States can be made provided two-thirds of both Houses of Congress, together with three-quarters of the state legislatures, approve such changes. In fact, there have been 27 such amendments made in the past two centuries – one notable example was the 22nd Amendment in 1951 when the constitution was altered to prevent a President being elected to serve more than two terms in office. Similarly, in France under Art 89 of the constitution of the Fifth Republic (1958), an amendment can be made when a proposal has passed – in identical terms – both Houses of the French Parliament and has subsequently been approved by the people in a referendum. In 2005 the French people, in a referendum, rejected the Treaty establishing a constitution for Europe.

KEY FACTS

A constitution will contain the principal institutions of the state, their functions and powers.

A constitution will establish the relationship between each of the state institutions together with how these institutions relate to the citizen.

A constitution will also indicate how (or if) it can be altered and the process that must be undertaken to do so.

2.3 Entrenching constitutional law

Due to the nature of its subject matter (establishing the structure and institutions of the state), a constitution and its laws ideally should be of a higher/fundamental status. In other words the law relating to the constitution (ie 'constitutional law') should in legal terms be superior and more fundamental than other 'ordinary' or 'non-constitutional' law (eg private laws such as contract and trust law). Thus, as the constitution represents the basic framework of the government, it should necessarily have a greater legal and moral authority than other ordinary laws in the legal system. This reflects the comparative importance and significance of constitutional law. Indeed, it could be contended that in a jurisprudential sense, constitutional law is more significant and important than all the other laws, which of course only exist because of the existence of a constitution and constitutional law.

Typically therefore the constitutional document embodying the constitutional law of the state will invariably be a form of law which is superior/higher than other laws in the legal system. For example, s 2 of the South African constitution of 1997 states that:

 This Constitution is the supreme law of the Republic; law or conduct inconsistent with it is invalid, and the obligations imposed by it must be fulfilled.

Similarly, Art 98 (Chapter X: *Supreme Law*) of the Japanese constitution (1947) states that:

 This Constitution shall be the supreme law of the nation and no law, ordinance, imperial rescript or other act of government or part thereof, contrary to the provisions hereof, shall have legal force or validity.

As constitutional law will be accorded a higher and fundamental legal status, this inevitably means that it will more difficult to alter than other 'ordinary' laws which can be amended, or even abolished, through the ordinary legislative process (see section 2.2.4 for the special procedures that may be necessary in order to amend a constitution).

The notion of constitutional law being of a superior status will be reconsidered in Chapter 3 in the context of the United Kingdom's very unusual constitutional arrangements (see section 3.4.4).

KEY FACTS

Constitutional laws are typically given a higher and more fundamental legal status than other non-constitutional rules/laws (eg private laws governing the formation and enforcement of contracts made between private individuals – contract law).

2.4 The purpose of a constitution

Why do countries have constitutions? There are many reasons for creating a constitution and these are set out below.

2.4.1 To ensure stability and order

As noted above, all countries (and organisations) have a constitution of some description because all societies require rules and organisation in order to ensure stability. Without a set of basic rules there would be no structure or organisation and chaos would ensue. Constitutions, therefore, provide a set of basic ground rules and principles which establish and regulate the basic framework of the state. A constitution helps ensure that a state – or indeed even a social club – achieves its primary purpose and objectives.

For example, if one object of a people is to safeguard the basic rights of the individual in society (particularly vulnerable minorities), this can be achieved with a constitution setting up a mechanism such as a declaration of human rights, together with a Supreme/Constitutional Court to safeguard and protect such rights from infringement. Similarly, how can undergraduates who wish to play chess regularly and on an orderly basis do so unless they establish a constitution, which in turn creates bodies which will organise, oversee and regulate subscriptions, room bookings, the entering of local/national chess tournaments/events, etc?

2.4.2 To ensure that government operates by consent and has constitutional and moral legitimacy

Thomas Paine, writing in the eighteenth century, stated that:

> 'A constitution is not the act of a government, but of a people constituting a government, and a government without a constitution is power without right ... A constitution is a thing antecedent to a government; and a government is only the creature of a constitution.'

Rights of Man in *The Complete Works of Thomas Paine,* cited in M Allen and B Thompson, *Cases & Materials on Constitutional & Administrative Law* (8th edition, Oxford University Press, 2005) p1.

What Paine meant was that a constitution ensures that the governing institutions (Congress/Parliament, President/government and courts) should have constitutional legitimacy and so govern with the consent of the people over whom they govern. In other words, by agreeing to and endorsing the constitution, the people confer legitimacy on it and the institutions created under it. For example, this was done in the Republic of Ireland where the constitution was approved by the people in a national referendum. Art 6, s 1 of the constitution specifically states that:

All powers of government, legislative, executive, and judicial, derive, under God, from the people, whose right it is to designate the rulers of the state.

This in turn confers moral and constitutional authority on those institutions created under the constitution to govern the state and regulate the lives of the citizens. As noted above, this can be likened to a social contract between the governed (the citizen) and the governing institutions (Parliament, government and the courts). As part of this social bargain, the governing institutions are conferred with the constitutional and legal powers to rule and govern the people. In return, these institutions ensure stability and order in the state/society and are (largely) prevented from interfering with the basic human rights of the individual which are typically enshrined in a Bill/Charter of Rights.

A democratic constitution ensures (at least in theory) that government is with the consent of the people. For example, in Iraq in January 2005, the Iraqi people voted for a transitional National Assembly, which would draft a new constitution. This draft constitution was in turn approved by the people in a national referendum in October 2005, and subsequent to this the new democratically elected Iraqi Government was formed. Having said this, the approval of the people can, in practice, be somewhat nominal as demonstrated by the Indian constitution. Although it was approved by a constitutent Assembly (representing the people), the terms of the constitution were not actually directly approved by the Indian people themselves.

In short, if the constitution – and as a consequence the state institutions created under it – has the consent of the people (nominal or otherwise), this means that the institutions have the constitutional legitimacy to carry out their prescribed functions and exercise their powers stipulated in the constitution. In other words, the constitution, the state apparatus and its institutions have a badge of legitimacy. In this context see Art 1 of the Brazilian constitution (1988):

 All power emanates from the people, who exercise it by means of elected representatives or directly, as provided by this constitution.

2.4.3 To represent a constitutional watershed

A state constitution is generally founded to represent a break with the past and so represent a watershed in terms of the history, politics and institutional structure of that particular state. For example, the creation of a constitution may well follow:

- A revolution: the United States of America (1789)
- Independence following colonial rule: Malawi (1966)
- The removal of a dictatorship: Spain (1978)
- A war: West Germany (1949), Japan (1947).

The creation of a new constitution will enable that country to draw a clear line under its past and give it the opportunity to establish a new state apparatus with new institutions governed by principles which have the clear approval of the people. See for example, the new constitution of Iraq, which represents a clear break with its historical and authoritarian past.

2.4.4 A constitutional limit and control on governmental power

As a constitution establishes institutions and invests them with public powers and responsibilities, it is the hallmark of a democratic constitution that these institutions are controlled, regulated and checked by the constitution itself (which, of course, embodies the consent of the people, nominal or otherwise – see section 2.4.2). In other words, a constitution will set out the limitations of governmental power (this can be done in various ways, in particular see section 2.6.2 on the notion of constitutionalism). A constitution must therefore not only allocate and distribute public power, but must also ensure that the use of that power is checked; otherwise public power will be misused and abused at the expense of the citizen. For example, the Swedish constitution (the Instrument of Government of 1975 (Ch 1)) states boldly that:

Public power shall be exercised under law.

2.4.5 To affirm particular values and goals

All constitutions are by their nature man-made and so drafted with certain underlying principles and goals in mind. These could be, for example, the promotion of democratic values, open government, the welfare and public good of the citizen or the attainment of religious aims. For example, the Irish constitution of 1937 (as originally drafted) made specific reference to the special position of the Roman Catholic Church, thereby reflecting the importance attached to the church in society as a whole. It is of interest to note, however, that as a result of the divisive nature of this provision, in an amendment to the constitution in 1973 (the Fifth Amendment), this special position of the Catholic Church was removed. Similarly, the Brazilian constitution is not concerned solely with the organisation of the state institutions, but also extends to economic and social reforms in society as a whole. In particular, Art 3 sets out that one objective of the constitution is to eradicate poverty.

KEY FACTS

The rationale behind a constitution is to ensure the following:

- order and stability

- the legitimacy of the governmental institutions

- to mark a watershed

- the limitation of governmental power

- to affirm specific goals considered important for that society.

ACTIVITY

Problem solving

In July 2010, a country obtains its independence after occupation by a foreign power for over 30 years. You are asked to advise the drafters of its new constitution as to how it should be drawn up. In particular,

- What needs to go into the constitution?

- What does not need to go into the constitution?

- How can you ensure that the constitution achieves both what (a) the citizens and (b) the envisaged governing institutions, desire from the constitution?

2.5 Different types of constitutions

There are various types of constitutions in existence around the world and noted below are the principal ways in which they can be (very broadly) categorised and classified.

2.5.1 Written and unwritten constitutions/codified and uncodified constitutions

Historically, one major way of classifying and distinguishing between constitutions is through the labels of written and unwritten constitutions. A written constitution was one in which the rules of the constitution were located in a written document entitled 'The Constitution'. For example, the constitution of the United States can be found in the document called the United States

Constitution, which contains seven Articles along with their various amendments. Similarly, the Indian constitution can be found in a document which comprises almost 400 Articles and nine accompanying schedules. In contrast, an unwritten constitution would be one in which the major constitutional rules of the state could not be found in a single document – as in the United Kingdom.

Care, however, has to be taken with this particular method of classifying constitutions:

- Firstly, it is clear that not every single principle and rule relating to a constitution will be detailed in a single written constitutional document. For example, as constitutional rules are not necessarily self-explanatory or cover every constitutional eventuality, these rules have to be interpreted by the courts (Supreme/Constitutional or otherwise). As a consequence, these judgments interpreting the constitution will also form part of the constitutional rules which govern the country. In addition, the rules of a written constitution will be invariably supplemented by unwritten political practices and conventions which have grown up around it (on constitutional conventions see section 4.13).

- Secondly, even in the United Kingdom (which has historically been labelled as having an unwritten constitution in the absence of a single constitutional document called 'The United Kingdom Constitution'), it is nevertheless clear that many of its constitutional rules are actually written down: for example in parliamentary legislation.

As a consequence, in recent years it has become fashionable to classify constitutions on the basis of being codified or not, rather than on the basis of the written/unwritten dichotomy. In this way the constitution of the United States would be rightly defined as a codified constitution with its major rules being codified largely (but not exclusively) in its seven Articles and subsequent amendments. In contrast, the United Kingdom can be described as uncodified in the sense that its constitutional rules and principles are located in a multitude of different sources which have not been brought together and codified in a single document (see further Chapter 4).

2.5.2 Rigid and flexible constitutions

Historically, constitutions have also been classified according to whether or not there is a special procedure which must be followed in order to change the constitutional text (and therefore constitutional law). In order to alter the content and provisions of a rigid constitution, a procedure is stipulated which requires specific legal/constitutional obstacles to be overcome. For example, a proposed amendment may require the approval of the people in a national referendum and/or the use of special majorities in the Parliament/Assembly. By way of illustration, Chapter 8 of the 1901 Constitution of Australia stipulates that a proposed amendment to the provisions of the constitution must be initiated and approved in the Australian Parliament and thereafter approved by the Australian people in a referendum.

In contrast, a flexible constitution is one in which the content and principles of the constitution can be amended by the ordinary legislative process which is used to alter, or abolish, other 'ordinary' (ie non-constitutional laws). Flexible constitutions are much less common than rigid constitutions because constitutional rules, by their very nature, are viewed as being fundamental, and so should be more difficult to change than other laws. Israel, New Zealand and the United Kingdom provide examples of flexible constitutions. An example of a recent change to the constitutional arrangements of the United Kingdom is illustrated by the enactment of the Constitutional Reform Act 2005 which creates a separate Supreme Court which is scheduled to come into effect in 2009. This legislation was passed by the United Kingdom Parliament through the ordinary channels of the law-making process: the consent of both the House of Commons and the House of Lords, together with the Royal Assent.

It should be noted that just because a constitution is labelled as rigid (owing to its prescribed method of amendment), it does not necessarily follow that the constitution is never amended or that in practice it is actually very difficult to alter. In reality changes to a constitution are driven by, and dependent upon, the political will in that particular state. As noted above, the constitution of the United States has been altered on 27 occasions, even though there are significant obstacles to be overcome in order to change it. In contrast, a flexible constitution may not necessarily be changed frequently in practice, even though it is possible to do so. Although the United Kingdom constitution has traditionally been labelled as flexible, there are certain aspects which have not actually been altered for generations. Two examples will suffice at this stage:

- In Parliament, the House of Commons (as the elected House) has dominance over the House of Lords (see section 10.10).

- The monarch will always confer her Assent to a Bill in order to make it law. This consent has not been refused for centuries (see section 11.9.2).

2.5.3 Federal and unitary constitutions

A federal constitution (such as in the United States, Australia and Germany) is one where the powers and responsibilities of the institutions of the state are constitutionally divided between the centre (federal institutions) and the regions/states/provinces. For example, in the United States the federal (national) Congress has specified powers and responsibilities under the constitution (eg in relation to national and international affairs). In contrast, the legislatures of the various states (eg Florida, California, etc) have powers and responsibilities which relate specifically to the regulation and government of that particular state. In essence the rationale behind a federal constitution is twofold:

- Firstly, to reduce further the power of the state (and so minimise the exercise of arbitrary power) by separating and dividing power and responsibilities between central and local institutions.

- Secondly, to safeguard and constitutionally ring-fence the powers of the local states/provinces/ regions to enable them to determine their own local laws which are tailored to local needs.

In a unitary constitution (found for example in the United Kingdom and the Republic of Ireland), power is focused in the main and central law-maker (in the United Kingdom this is Parliament). Although, as we shall see in Chapter 14, there exist a number of other decentralised bodies in the United Kingdom, namely local authorities and the Scottish Parliament, this does not however, make the United Kingdom a federal state, as these bodies are necessarily subordinate to, and ultimately dependent on, the United Kingdom Parliament in Westminster. For example, for five decades until the 1970s Northern Ireland had its own Parliament, but this was abolished by the Westminster Parliament which had established it in the first place. In short, these institutions do not have express constitutional protection, unlike the legislatures in Florida, California, etc, as under the constitution of the United States, Congress could not simply pass a law abolishing these state legislatures.

ACTIVITY

Question

Explain the main ways in which constitutions can be classified. Are these useful or definitive?

2.6 Constitutionalism and acting 'constitutionally'

2.6.1 Introduction

Although commentators appear to find it difficult to define the term constitutionalism, in essence it means government (or the institutions of the state) acting in accordance with the rules and principles enshrined in the constitution, thereby resulting in limited constitutional government. Generally anything allowed by a constitution would be considered as 'constitutional' (ie conforming to, and acting strictly within, the parameters permitted by the constitution). In countries which adhere to the ideas of limited government, however, constitutionalism would demand that there is sufficient control on the power of the government. In other words, a constitution should not merely be descriptive – simply describing the powers of the governing institutions – but must also control and check that power through the constitution. The rationale behind constitutionalism is to prevent an abuse of public power by the state institutions.

Consider the following imaginary constitution which details the following provision:

(A) Art X. The President may, if in his personal opinion he deems it appropriate to do so, order the arrest, detention, torture and execution of any citizens considered undesirable. This power, and the exercise of it, cannot be challenged in any court of law under any circumstances.

Suppose a President acted under this provision and used his conferred powers to torture 'undesirable' citizens of this state. In a very technical sense, the President could claim to be acting simply in accordance with what the constitution expressly permits him to do, and therefore, technically he could claim to be acting 'constitutionally' (at least in a bare legal sense). Public lawyers, however, would not regard the exercise of this power, and the content and nature of Art X itself, as following the basic precepts of constitutionalism. In short, this provision gratuitously – and unnecessarily – interferes with the basic and fundamental rights of the citizen. Moreover, Art X (and therefore the constitution) does not permit any effective regulation or legal check on the exercise of this arbitrary and exceptionally wide power which violates the basic fundamental human rights of the individual.

2.6.2 The basic principles of constitutionalism

The principles of constitutionalism (particularly in the context of the constitution of the United Kingdom) will be referred to continuously throughout this text, but for present purposes, it should be noted that in order to comply with constitutionalism, a constitution should control the use of public power in the following ways (as adapted from Barnett):

- The governing institutions should be separated in terms of personnel and functions (see Chapter 5 on the separation of powers).
- The basic rights of the individual should be safeguarded and protected (see Chapters 16 and 17).
- In exercising public power, state institutions must act strictly within their limits (see Chapter 6 on the rule of law together with Chapters 19 and 20 on judicial review).
- There must exist an independent court system staffed by impartial judges to check the use of public power (see Chapter 13 on the judiciary).
- Basic democratic and other principles and values must be adhered to (eg see Chapter 9 for democratic elections to the House of Commons).

In addition, owing to the unusual constitutional arrangements that pertain in the United Kingdom, the terms acting 'constitutionally' and 'unconstitutionally' have specific meanings in our constitution (see section 4.15).

ACTIVITY

Essay writing

What government conduct or law would you consider to be (a) constitutional and (b) unconstitutional? Revisit this question after you have completed section 4.15 and again at the end of this text.

KEY FACTS

A constitution is a body of rules (usually enshrined in a formal document) which sets out the main framework of the state.

A constitution is a set of laws, rules and practices that create the basic institutions of the state, and its component and related parts, and stipulate the powers of those institutions and the relationship between the different institutions and between those institutions and the individual (working definition of the House of Lords Select Committee on the Constitution).

Constitutionalism is concerned with limiting governmental power through the rules and values of the constitution.

Acting constitutionally means acting in accordance with the rules of the constitution, whereas acting unconstitutionally means to breach and infringe these constitutional rules.

Further reading

Barnett, H, *Constitutional and Administrative Law* (6th edn, Routledge–Cavendish, 2006), Chapter 1.

Barendt, E, *An Introduction to Constitutional Law* (Oxford University Press, 1998), Chapter 1.

Bradley, A and Ewing, K, *Constitutional and Administrative Law* (14th edn, Pearson/Longman 2007), Chapter 1.

Finer, S, Bogdanor, V and Rudden, B, *Comparing Constitutions* (Clarendon Press, 1995), Chapters 1 and 2.

Maddex, R, *Constitutions of the World* (2nd edn, CQ Press, 2001). This text sets out in very brief terms the main elements of one hundred constitutions of the world.

Wheare, K, *Modern Constitutions* (2nd edn, Oxford University Press, 1966), Chapters 1 to 4.

THE NATURE OF THE BRITISH CONSTITUTION ■

AIMS AND OBJECTIVES

At the end of this chapter you should be able to:

■ Explain what is meant by the term the British constitution

■ Identify and explain the main features of the British constitution

3.1 Introduction and terminology

The aim of this chapter is to provide a general overview of the main characteristics of the United Kingdom constitution. All of the features and themes detailed below will be developed, to a greater or lesser extent, throughout the rest of this text.

At this stage it is appropriate to note that the United Kingdom is an unusual state in international law as it is composed of four distinct countries, namely:

• England

• Scotland

• Wales and

• Northern Ireland.

Moreover, there are three distinct legal jurisdictions and three systems of law, namely:

• England and Wales (as a single jurisdictional entity)

• Northern Ireland and

• Scotland.

As there is a single constitutional framework which governs the whole of the United Kingdom, strictly speaking, it is correct to refer to *the United Kingdom constitution* (however, the exact constitutional arrangements pertaining in each jurisdiction may on occasions differ). In order to illustrate the workings of the constitution, throughout this text examples will be drawn from all three jurisdictions.

Furthermore, for ease of reference, hereafter in the text, the term *the United Kingdom constitution* will be replaced by the term *the British constitution*.

3.2 Does the United Kingdom have a constitution?

3.2.1 The absence of a codified constitutional document

Before considering the nature and sources of the British constitution, we must first consider the question of whether the United Kingdom has a constitution at all. This is because the United Kingdom lacks a formal codified document called 'The British Constitution'. In short, there is no single document which has special legal status and which embodies the principal rules concerning the government of the country. If we refer to the definition of a constitution (at section 2.1) it is clear that the United Kingdom does not possess a constitution in terms of the first definition (ie a constitutional document or code setting out the framework of the state with 'special legal sanctity' attached to it) as it lacks a formal constitutional document. The United Kingdom does, however, have a constitution in the second sense of the term (ie 'a collection of rules' which govern the governing institutions) as it clearly has rules and practices (albeit derived from disparate sources) which govern the state. There are rules, for example, governing:

- How the various state institutions are composed.

- The scope of the powers exercised by the monarch.

- How the government is legally controlled.

- How legislation is passed.

Wheare has defined the United Kingdom constitution in the following terms:

> 'The British Constitution is the collection of legal rules and non-legal rules which govern the government in Britain'.

> K Wheare, *Modern Constitutions* (2nd edn, Oxford University Press, 1966), p 1.

3.2.2 The factors which indicate a British constitution

It could be argued that the following factors indicate (and presuppose) that the United Kingdom clearly has a constitution of some sort:

- If the United Kingdom had no constitution there would necessarily be no government, Prime Minister, Parliament or police force. Indeed, there would be no apparatus of the state of any kind.

- United Kingdom cases and statutes make specific reference to constitutional issues (an example of the latter is the Constitutional Reform Act 2005).

- Numerous books and papers have been written about 'The British Constitution' and the constitutional law of the United Kingdom.

- British commentators may on occasions speak of a 'constitutional crisis' (for example, commentators spoke of a constitutional crisis with the break up of the Prince of Wales' first marriage).

- There was (until 2007) a department called the Department for Constitutional Affairs headed by the Lord Chancellor and Secretary of State for Constitutional Affairs. In addition, the Cabinet has a Constitutional Affairs sub-committee which considers constitutional issues.

- In recent years the House of Lords has established the House of Lords Select Committee on the Constitution with the specific remit to:

  (i) consider the constitutional implications of all public Bills, and

  (ii) to keep under review the operation of the constitution.

Although the United Kingdom may lack a single authoritative constitutional document, this does not mean that we do not have a constitution. The United Kingdom has a constitution in the broader sense of the term used above as it has rules and principles that regulate the government of the country. There is a clear framework of rules, both legal and political, from which we can identify:

- the key institutions of the state

- the composition and powers of these institutions

- how these institutions interrelate and check and balance one another

- how these institutions relate to the individual

- how the rights and freedoms enjoyed by the individual are safeguarded.

3.2.3 The five tenets of the British constitution

The United Kingdom, therefore, has a constitution, albeit different in form from other states that have a codified written document. It is highly pertinent to note that the House of Lords Select Committee, in setting out its remit, identified five tenets of the British constitution which are as follows:

- The sovereignty of Parliament (see Chapter 7).

- The rule of law (see Chapter 6) and the protection of the individual (see Chapters 16 and 17).

- The Union of the United Kingdom (see Chapter 14).

- Responsible government (see Chapter 12).

- Membership of the Commonwealth, European Union and other international bodies (see Chapters 15 and 16).

ACTIVITY

Problem solving

Can you think of any factors that might suggest that the United Kingdom has a constitution? Revisit this question after you have completed Chapter 3 and again at the end of this text.

3.2.4 A system of government rather than a constitution?

Some commentators such as Ridley, however, have questioned whether the United Kingdom has a constitution in any meaningful sense of the term given that it lacks the following characteristics. These features are as follows:

- 'It establishes, or constitutes, the system of government.' A constitution establishes (and so is necessarily prior to) the system of government and its institutions. In short, the constitution is a constituent act.

  In the United Kingdom the system of government and state institutions have not been specifically created by a single authoritative constitutional document or code; instead, they have developed and evolved over the years. By way of example, the Scottish Parliament, a major institution of the state, was only created in 1998. It is of interest, however, to note that the legislation creating the Scottish Parliament was preceded by a national referendum in Scotland.

- 'It therefore involves an authority outside and above the order it establishes.' A constituent power (namely the people) ratifies the constitution, thereby conferring it and the institutions established under it with constitutional legitimacy (see section 2.4.2).

  In the United Kingdom the people in a referendum have never formally ratified the 'constitution'. Notwithstanding this, as we have a parliamentary democracy, the people do at least periodically elect the House of Commons which, in turn, gives democratic legitimacy to the laws that Parliament passes. Furthermore, these elections also confer legitimacy (albeit in an indirect sense) on the government to govern and determine major policy issues (see Chapter 11).

- 'It is a form of law superior to other laws.' The laws of the constitution are supreme and a higher form of law in relation to other ordinary or non-constitutional laws.

  In the United Kingdom, historically, the laws of the constitution have not assumed a higher legal status than other 'ordinary' laws. In this context, however, now see the comments of Laws LJ at section 4.4.5.

- 'It is entrenched.' Owing to their content and importance, constitutional laws should be entrenched, thereby making it difficult (in some cases impossible) to repeal or alter them.

As a consequence of the principle of parliamentary sovereignty, historically, laws in the United Kingdom could not be legally entrenched and so protected from subsequent repeal or amendment. In this context, however, now see the comments of Laws LJ at section 4.4.5.

In the absence of these characteristics Ridley has argued that the United Kingdom does not have a constitution, but instead merely has a system of government (F Ridley, 'There is no British Constitution: A Dangerous Case of the Emperor's Clothes' (1988) 41 Parliamentary Affairs 340).

ACTIVITY

Question

Do you agree with Ridley's arguments that the United Kingdom does not have a constitution? Revisit this question after you have completed Chapter 3 and again at the end of this text.

3.3 The nature of the British constitution

3.3.1 An uncodified constitution

As noted above, the United Kingdom lacks a single authoritative constitutional text entitled 'The British Constitution'. Instead, the constitutional rules which regulate the government of the state are located elsewhere in a variety of sources which include, *inter alia*, Acts of Parliament, case law and binding political practices (see Chapter 4).

In this sense, therefore, the United Kingdom has an uncodified constitution which sets it apart from most other states which have codified documents (eg the United States, France, Canada and the Republic of Ireland). As a result, the British constitution has been described by Finer, Bogdanor and Rudden as indistinct and indeterminate. In short, the exact boundaries of the British constitution are less easy to identify and pinpoint than in a state with a formal codified constitution. Indeed, even within the United Kingdom, academics and commentators may disagree over what is and what is not part of the constitution and even what is and what is not a constitutional issue (see section 4.2.2).

3.3.2 Why does the United Kingdom not have a codified constitution?

As noted in section 2.4.3, state constitutions are generally founded to represent a political watershed and a clear break with the past. The catalyst for this watershed could have been, for instance:

- a political upheaval

- an invasion
- a revolution.

In simple terms, the United Kingdom/Britain (with the exception of the period of 1649–60 with Oliver Cromwell as Lord Protector overseeing a non-monarchial government under the 1653 Instrument of Government) has not experienced such momentous events as being invaded or colonised. As a consequence, it has not been necessary to create a new codified constitution to mark a watershed. In fact, it has been pointed out by the Institute for Public Policy Research that the reality is that very few constitutions are actually conceived as a result of a sober and measured reflection on the perceived shortcomings of existing, functioning arrangements. Instead, they are drafted in the context of other factors such as political upheaval, independence, etc (R Blackburn (ed), *A Written Constitution for the United Kingdom* (Mansell Publishing Limited, 1993) p 5).

It is of interest to point out that in 1991 the Institute for Public Policy Research produced a draft '*Constitution for the United Kingdom*' and although this constitution has not been implemented, it does serve as a useful blueprint should there come a time that the United Kingdom decided that it required a written codified, entrenched constitution.

3.3.3 The incremental development of the British constitution

Most countries have a clear date indicating the origin of their constitution; for example, the Indian constitution was passed in 1949 and came fully into force in January 1950. In contrast, in the absence of a single constitutional text, the British constitution lacks a clear and single identifiable origin. Instead, the constitution has gradually developed over the centuries. Indeed, one hallmark of the United Kingdom is that constitutional change has traditionally tended to be somewhat measured and incremental. As the British constitution has historically developed in an *ad hoc* fashion, it is clear that there has been no great and overall grand design behind it. Instead, it has grown organically to meet the needs required at the time and this is particularly the case in respect of, for example, the development of constitutional conventions (see section 4.13).

In recent years, however – since the election of the Labour Government in 1997 – the form of our constitutional arrangements has been radically reshaped by the passage of a raft of constitutional statutes passed in very quick succession (see section 3.4.5).

KEY FACTS

The United Kingdom, unlike most states, has an uncodified constitution. It lacks a single authoritative constitutional text/document in which the main rules and principles governing the framework and organisation of the state are set out.

CONTINUED ▶

KEY FACTS

Constitutions are typically established, for instance, in the aftermath of a war or gaining independence from a former colonial/foreign power. The United Kingdom has not historically experienced such momentous events, and therefore not found it necessary to mark a watershed by drafting a written codified document called 'The British Constitution'.

In the absence of a single constitutional text, the British constitution lacks a clear and single identifiable origin, and instead its constitutional rules and principles have developed incrementally over the centuries through, among other things, statute and common law.

3.4 The key features of the British constitution

The key features of the United Kingdom constitution are set out below. By identifying and highlighting these features at this stage, students will be provided with a snapshot of the essential elements which make up the British constitution

3.4.1 An unwritten constitution?

As noted at section 2.5.1 above, constitutions historically, have been classified as either written or unwritten, with the United Kingdom traditionally falling within the latter category. Notwithstanding this, it must be remembered that many of the United Kingdom's constitutional rules are written down and therefore are found in documentary form. For example, the legal and constitutional principle that parliamentary legislation (Acts of Parliament) can be enacted without the consent of the upper chamber is set out in the Parliament Acts of 1911 and 1949 (see section 10.10.1). The description of the British constitution as unwritten does not therefore appear to be strictly accurate. A more apposite label would be to describe the constitution as uncodified as the constitutional rules have not been brought together in one single authoritative document or constitutional code.

3.4.2 Law and convention as sources (see Chapter 4)

The sources of the British constitution embrace both legal and non-legal sources.

The legal sources include, among others, Acts of Parliament, case law and international treaties. The non-legal sources include binding political rules known as constitutional conventions.

It should be noted that the United Kingdom is not unique in having constitutional rules that are in effect political practices (for example, United Kingdom government ministers are constitutionally responsible to Parliament for their actions). Other countries also have political rules which supplement the legal rules detailed in their constitution. For example, in the United States of America, by convention congressional committees reflect the composition of Congress. What is significant in the United Kingdom, however, is the extent to which these political rules arguably play a more significant role in the context of our constitutional arrangements than they do in other countries with codified constitutions.

3.4.3 The legislative supremacy of Parliament (see Chapter 7)

In essence, the legislative supremacy of Parliament (parliamentary sovereignty) means that, in law, Parliament (technically the Queen in Parliament) can pass any law that it chooses. In short, historically there has been no legal limitation on the legislation that Parliament can pass. This feature is the foundation of, and underpins, the British constitution. This is in contrast to the vast majority of other constitutions. For example, the legislature of the United States (Congress) or the Republic of Ireland (the Oireachtas) cannot pass any law that they choose. Instead, they are legally limited by their formal codified documentary constitutions.

As parliamentary sovereignty is the cornerstone of the British constitution it is considered in detail in Chapter 7. Moreover, as the United Kingdom's membership of the European Community has challenged the traditional conception of parliamentary sovereignty, the principle will be revisited in Chapter 15 in the context of the study of the European Community.

3.4.4 No special legal and higher status

As noted at section 2.3, constitutional laws (owing to their fundamental character and substance) typically possess a higher and fundamental status in relation to other 'ordinary' or 'non-constitutional' laws such as contract or tort laws. In the United Kingdom, however, historically no clear and sharp distinction has been made between:

- constitutional (or fundamental) laws and
- ordinary or 'non-constitutional' laws.

In the United Kingdom, therefore, historically both laws have had equal legal standing. This point, however, has to be reconsidered in the context of the comments made by Laws LJ in *Thoburn v Sunderland City Council* [2002] EWHC 195 (Admin) where he drew a distinction between constitutional statutes and non-constitutional statutes (see section 4.4.5).

Historically, therefore, the United Kingdom has been characterised as having no special higher constitutional law and has lacked a clear hierarchy of laws which distinguishes constitutional laws from ordinary laws. As noted above, for commentators such as Ridley, one fundamental prerequisite of a constitution is that, owing to their fundamental nature, its constitutional laws should have a higher and superior legal status to other laws. The United Kingdom, however, has historically lacked such a hierarchy of laws.

3.4.5 A flexible constitution

Following on from the fact that the United Kingdom has an uncodified constitution, together with the fact that its main characteristic is that Parliament can pass any law that it chooses, the constitution is also described as being flexible (see section 2.5.2). In other words, unlike many other countries, there are no legally entrenched constitutional laws that cannot be repealed or are legally more difficult to repeal than ordinary non-constitutional laws. In essence, there is no aspect of the British constitution that cannot, in law, be altered. As Parliament theoretically can pass any law, this means that it can legally amend any legal rule or alter any aspect of our constitutional arrangements. For example:

The Constitutional Reform Act 2005

Section 18 of this Act creates (in principle, as the section has yet to come into force) a separate Supreme Court to replace the existing Appellate Committee of the House of Lords, which as the highest domestic court sits within Parliament [see section 5.7.4]. The new Supreme Court, in contrast, will be legally and constitutionally separate from Parliament.

The House of Lords Act 1999

This Act reduced the number of hereditary peers (these were peers who assumed a place in the House of Lords by virtue of inheriting their seat) from 759 to 92. In effect, at a stroke this Act reduced the size of the upper chamber by over one half [see section 10.6.3].

In short, the United Kingdom has been characterised as having a flexible constitution since its constitutional laws and rules can in theory be amended relatively easily (but note the point made at section 2.5.2). This is in contrast to other countries such as the United States whose constitution (Art V) stipulates a special procedure which must be complied with in order to amend the rules of the codified constitution.

As noted above, the flexibility of our constitution has been graphically demonstrated since the Labour government came to power in 1997 and proceeded to radically reshape the constitutional landscape of the United Kingdom (see Chapter 22). These changes include, among others:

- The Human Rights Act 1998 conferring positive human rights on individuals.
- The Government of Wales Act 1998 which created the National Assembly for Wales.
- The European Parliamentary Elections Act 1999 which introduced a party list in respect of the election of the British Members to the European Parliament.

- The House of Lords Act 1999 which removed the majority of hereditary peers from the House of Lords.

- The Freedom of Information Act 2000 which enabled individuals access to information held by public authorities.

- The Constitutional Reform Act 2005 which makes provision for a Supreme Court and reformed the office of the Lord Chancellor and the system of judicial appointments.

- The Electoral Administration Act 2006 which reduced the minimum age of candidates to be elected to the House of Commons from 21 to 18 years.

- The Terrorism Act 2006 which created a criminal offence of encouraging terrorism (including statements which glorify the commission or preparation of acts of terrorism).

This collective raft of reforms arguably represents the most significant reshaping of the United Kingdom constitution for centuries and demonstrates the highly flexible nature of our constitution. All this legislation, however, was passed through the ordinary parliamentary legislative process without the need for special majorities in either House (in this context see section 4.2.4) or the support of the people in a referendum. In fact, referenda were held in Scotland, Wales and Northern Ireland prior to the creation of the devolved institutions for these regions. These referenda, however, were not strictly (ie legally) necessary in order to pass the relevant legislation (see Chapter 14).

ACTIVITY

Questions

1. Why were the above reforms implemented?

2. Are you are aware of any other constitutional reforms which have been made since the election of the Labour Government in 1997? Revisit this question after you have completed Chapter 22.

3.4.6 A unitary constitution (see Chapter 14)

The United Kingdom has a unitary constitution (as opposed to a federal one) in the sense that ultimate legal and political power is focused centrally in the Westminster Parliament. In essence, Parliament has the legal power to enact laws for all parts and legal jurisdictions (ie Scotland, Northern Ireland, England and Wales) that make up the United Kingdom. Under Parliament there exist the following layers of decentralised government:

- Local authorities.

- The Scottish Parliament.

- The National Assembly for Wales.

- The London Assembly.
- The Northern Ireland Assembly (in 2007 this was reactivated).

However, these layers of decentralised/devolved government only exist (and in fact are permitted to exist) by virtue of Parliament in Westminster. In other words, they are all creatures of statutes passed by the Westminster Parliament and could ultimately be legally abolished by such an Act. These tiers of government, therefore, lack the constitutional status and legal/constitutional protection that they would enjoy under a federal constitution.

As noted at section 2.5.3, in a federal system of government such as the United States, the federal constitution divides the power of the state horizontally between the centre (federal institutions, Congress, President, etc) and the local regions (state legislatures, eg the State Legislature of Florida). In contrast, in the United Kingdom, Parliament could in legal theory abolish any local authority or devolved institution. Moreover, this could be achieved through an ordinary Act of Parliament, thereby reinforcing the flexibility of the United Kingdom constitution (see section 3.4.5).

3.4.7 A limited monarchy (see 11.1.2)

The Head of State in the United Kingdom is the monarch, although her role in the constitution is typically ceremonial. Historically, the monarch formerly enjoyed extensive personal legal powers and even today the Queen, in legal theory, still has considerable legal power vested in her. For example, legally the monarch can:

- dissolve Parliament
- dispense the prerogative of mercy
- appoint Lords of Appeal in Ordinary (law lords).

These powers are, however, exercised by the monarch strictly in accordance with constitutional convention; that is, she acts on the advice of her ministers. For example, although the monarch formally and legally dissolves Parliament, it is the Prime Minister of the day that seeks a general election who will request that she do so. In other words, although these powers continue to be legally vested in the monarch, they are in effect practically exercised by her government ministers. In this sense the powers of the monarchy are constitutionally limited (limited by constitutional convention: see section 4.13) and thus the United Kingdom is characterised as having a limited constitutional monarchy.

3.4.8 No strict separation of powers (see Chapter 5)

The United Kingdom historically, has been characterised as failing to adhere to a strict separation of powers whereby the three organs of state, namely the legislature, executive and judiciary, are separate and distinct from each other in terms of their functions and personnel. Instead, owing to the various overlaps of personnel and functions, the United Kingdom exhibits a weak separation of powers.

The Constitutional Reform Act 2005, however, provides a recent example of Parliament attempting to realign our constitutional arrangements so as to accord with a stricter concept of the separation of powers. This Act, *inter alia,* constrains the role of the executive in the appointment of the judiciary and creates (in principle) a Supreme Court separate from Parliament.

3.4.9 An independent and impartial judiciary (see Chapter 13)

Although the United Kingdom does not have a strict separation of powers, historically, the judicial arm of the state (with the clear exception of the law lords sitting in Parliament – see section 5.7.4) has been largely separate from the other two organs. Indeed, in constitutional terms it is of paramount importance that the judges are independent of both the executive and the legislature and that they are protected from political pressure.

A related characteristic of the British constitution is the limited role of the judiciary. In the United Kingdom the judiciary are constitutionally limited in the sense that they do not exercise the constitutional power enjoyed by many of their judicial counterparts elsewhere in the democratic world. For example, in the United States the Supreme Court has the power to declare 'unconstitutional', and invalidate, Acts of Congress if they contravene the written, entrenched constitution (*Marbury v Madison* (1803) 1 Cranch 137). This principle is known as the constitutional or judicial review of legislation. In contrast, in the United Kingdom, historically the judiciary has consistently reiterated that they were not constitutionally empowered to strike down and challenge Acts of Parliament. This point will be revisited in the context of both European Community law (see Chapter 15) and the Human Rights Act 1998 (see Chapter 17).

3.4.10 A parliamentary executive (see sections 5.7.1 and 11.6.1)

The United Kingdom has a parliamentary executive whereby the executive (the government) is drawn from the legislature (Parliament). Far from being separated as required by a strict doctrine of the separation of powers (see Chapter 5), the executive and legislature are actually fused. This can be contrasted with the presidential system of government in, for example, the United States, where the executive (President) is constitutionally and legally separate from the legislature (Congress). Parliamentary executives, however, are not uncommon. For example, the Republic of Ireland also has a parliamentary executive; however, unlike the United Kingdom, it has a codified constitution.

3.4.11 Responsible and accountable government (see Chapter 12)

A constitutional principle linked directly to the parliamentary executive is that of responsible government. This principle entails the government being politically and constitutionally accountable to Parliament (and ultimately therefore to the electorate) for its actions and decisions. In recent decades, however, there has been concern that the balance between the executive and the legislature has shifted far too much in favour of the former, thereby undermining the principle of accountable government. In short, the modern executive is in a position to dominate and largely control the legislature amounting to what Lord Hailsham described as an 'elective dictatorship' (see section 9.8).

3.4.12 A bicameral legislature (see Chapters 8–10)

Parliament (the legislature) is the principal law-making body within the constitution and is bicameral as it is composed of two houses:

- The House of Commons.
- The House of Lords.

This is common to many major democracies whose legislatures comprise two chambers (eg the United States, France, Germany, Spain, etc). In contrast, it is generally the case that smaller states have unicameral legislatures with only one chamber (eg Denmark, Sweden and New Zealand – the latter abolishing their second chamber in 1950). In terms of the principle of constitutionalism bicameral legislatures disperse power, though not necessarily equally, between two competing sources of power/chambers.

3.4.13 A representative democracy (see section 9.4)

The United Kingdom has a parliamentary democracy whereby the composition of the legislature (or at least the House of Commons) is determined by the people through periodic and free national elections.

3.4.14 An acceptance of the rule of law and respect for human rights (see Chapters 6 and 16–18)

A major characteristic of the British constitution is the acceptance of the rule of law, which is a foundation of a democratic state (see Chapter 6). This is the constitutional principle that all organs, institutions and state officials are under the law. The rule of law is inextricably linked to an independent and impartial judiciary (see Chapter 13) as it is, in effect, the judiciary that legally enforce the principles underpinning it.

The United Kingdom is also hallmarked by its historic general respect for basic human rights and freedoms. In other words, certain underlying democratic values are inherent within our constitutional arrangements such as:

- The freedom of political action (Chapters 16–17).
- The right to vote (see section 9.6).
- Freedom of expression (see Chapter 18).

ACTIVITY

Essay writing

Explain the nature of each of the characteristics of the British constitution.

- Which features do you consider to be particularly important?

- Which features set the United Kingdom apart from other countries?

Revisit this activity at the end of this text.

KEY FACTS

The principles of the British constitution

- An uncodified constitution (although it is largely collected from written sources).
- A largely flexible constitution.
- In legal theory Parliament can pass any law that it chooses (parliamentary sovereignty).
- The sources of the constitution are both legal (eg Acts of Parliament) and non-legal (eg constitutional conventions).
- Historically, constitutional law has not had a fundamental, higher legal status.
- There is no strict separation of powers.
- An acceptance of the rule of law and respect for human rights.

The principles of the constitution which affect particular state institutions

Parliament	• Parliamentary sovereignty. • A representative democracy. • A bicameral legislature. • A unitary constitution.
The government/executive	• A parliamentary executive. • Responsible and accountable government. • A limited monarchy.
The judiciary	• An independent and impartial judiciary. • Upholds the rule of law and respect for human rights.

Further reading

Barendt, E, *An Introduction to Constitutional Law* (Oxford University Press, 1998), Chapter 2.

Blackburn, R (ed), *A Written Constitution for the United Kingdom* (Mansell Publishing Limited, 1993). This book rather usefully sets out a proposed blueprint for a written codified constitution for the United Kingdom.

Finer, S, Bogdanor, V and Rudden, B, *Comparing Constitutions* (Clarendon Press, 1995), Chapter 3.

Hood Phillips, O, Jackson, P and Leopold, P, *Constitutional and Administrative Law* (8th edn, Sweet & Maxwell, 2001), Chapter 2.

Ridley, F, 'There is no British Constitution: A Dangerous Case of the Emperor's Clothes' (1988) 41 Parliamentary Affairs 340.

Munro, C, *Studies in Constitutional Law* (2nd edn, Butterworths, 1999), Chapter 1.

chapter
4 THE SOURCES OF THE
BRITISH CONSTITUTION

AIMS AND OBJECTIVES

At the end of this chapter you should be able to:

- Appreciate the difficulties in ascertaining the sources of the British constitution

- Identify and explain the different domestic legal sources that make up the British constitution

- Identify and explain the different international legal sources that make up the British constitution

- Identify and explain the different domestic non-legal sources that make up the British constitution

4.1 Introduction

In the United States and the Republic of Ireland, the laws of the constitution can be found in their respective documentary constitutions. In contrast, as the United Kingdom has no codified constitutional document entitled: 'The British Constitution', this necessarily raises the question of where the laws and rules of the constitution are to be found. The answer is that these rules are gleaned from consulting a wide range of sources. As indicated in Chapter 3, these disparate sources embrace, among others, legislation, case law and international Treaties together with constitutional conventions.

Notwithstanding this, as noted at section 2.5.1, the point needs to be made that even in countries with a codified constitution, not all aspects of the constitution will be explicitly set out in that constitutional documentary text. The legal rules contained in the documentary constitution will have to be interpreted by a Supreme or Constitutional Court and therefore these judicial interpretations will also form part of the constitutional rules. Furthermore, the legal rules of the constitution will be supplemented by binding political rules and practices.

4.2 The difficulties associated with the sources in the United Kingdom

The United Kingdom has a constitution of multiple sources. There are, however, a number of difficulties in locating these sources.

4.2.1 What is a constitutional issue?

In the British constitution it is not necessarily easy to determine what is, and is not, a constitutional principle, rule or issue. In the Republic of Ireland, for example, the principal constitutional laws and rules are set out in its formal constitutional text. In contrast, in the United Kingdom, in the absence of such a document, the task of identifying a law of (or issue relating to) the constitution is inevitably more difficult. Instead of consulting an authoritative constitutional text, the main rules and laws of the British constitution are found by consulting, *inter alia*, various statutes and case law and deciding whether the statute or case in question encapsulates a constitutional principle or rule. Indeed, in terms of the former, Hazell has commented that:

> 'There is no clear classification of what is a constitutional Bill and what is not, and with our unwritten constitution it is impossible to devise one'.

> R Hazell, 'Time for a New Convention: Parliamentary
> Scrutiny of Constitutional Bills 1997–2005' [2006] PL 247.

4.2.2 The lack of a clear demarcation between constitutional and ordinary laws

The above difficulty is exacerbated by the fact that constitutional law in the United Kingdom has not assumed a legally higher or fundamental status (but see Laws LJ at section 4.4.5). In fact, constitutional law in the United Kingdom is not even clearly segregated so as to demarcate it from other 'ordinary' non-constitutional laws. Dicey noted that:

> 'There is under the English constitution no marked or clear distinction between
> laws which are not fundamental or constitutional and laws which are fundamental
> or constitutional'. (sic)

> A Dicey, *Introduction to the Study of the Law of the Constitution* (10th edn, Macmillan, 1959), p 89.

In this way, as indicated earlier, the United Kingdom constitution is somewhat indeterminate, as its parameters are not necessarily clear. Indeed, in giving evidence before the House of Lords Select Committee on the Constitution, Lord Irvine (the then Lord Chancellor) stated that the government not only did not have a definition of the United Kingdom constitution, but that it took a pragmatic view as to whether a Bill should be termed a constitutional Bill or not.

Accordingly, the student of the British constitution needs to consult various statutes and decide on an Act by Act basis whether the legislation expounds a rule of the constitution. Compare, for example the following two statutes:

S **The Sale of Goods Act 1979**

This Act details the selling of goods, for example, their quality and being fit for their purpose, etc.

S **The Scotland Act 1998**

This Act established the Scottish Parliament together with the Scottish Executive (see Chapter 14).

The Sale of Goods Act 1979 is a non-constitutional statute as it is part of the private law of contract and is essentially concerned with individual contractual relations (therefore, generally speaking, not of interest to a public/constitutional lawyer). In contrast, the Scotland Act 1998 is clearly a constitutional statute as it creates a major institution of the state: the Scottish Parliament which has the power to pass legislation (Acts of the Scottish Parliament). Very occasionally an Act may actually refer to the constitution in its title as with the recent passing of the Constitutional Reform Act 2005.

4.2.3 A sub-division of constitutional law

A proposal was put to the House of Lords Select Committee on the Constitution that in terms of parliamentary scrutiny of constitutional legislation it was possible to divide such Bills into the following:

- Bills of major (first class) constitutional significance and
- Bills of less than first class constitutional significance (legislation which represents a minor amendment to the constitution).

The rationale behind the proposal was to enable Bills of first class constitutional importance to receive greater and more effective scrutiny. The Committee recognised the problems with such a division as although Bills such as the House of Lords Bill 1999 and European Communities Bill 1972 would clearly fall within the first category, it questioned which category legislation such as the Political Parties, Elections and Referendums Bill 2000 would fall into. As such it would prove impossible to provide a watertight definition of a first class constitutional Bill (Fourth Report of Session 2001–02 of the House of Lords Select Committee on the Constitution, *Changing the constitution: The process of constitutional change*, HL Paper 69 (2002), p 17).

4.2.4 All statutes passed in essentially the same manner

Constitutional statutes cannot be identified simply by how they were enacted by Parliament. In essence there is a single passage for legislation and therefore constitutional statutes are passed in the same way through Parliament as non-constitutional statutes. In other words, no special majority is needed in the two Houses of Parliament in order to enact a statute that alters an established constitutional principle or abolishes a previous constitutional statute.

Moreover, historically, these statutes (such as the Scotland Act 1998) have the same legal standing as other ordinary/non-constitutional statutes (such as the Sale of Goods Act 1979) which do not raise constitutional issues. Even though the former established a key institution of the state, historically in law this Act does not have higher legal status than the Sale of Goods Act 1979. In fact, Dicey asserted that Acts such as the Union with Scotland Act (which established the Parliament of Great Britain) were not supreme over a statute like the Dentists Act 1878, as both could be repealed in the same way. In short, the Scotland Act 1998 can be repealed legally and amended in the same way as the Sale of Goods Act 1979 in the sense that no special majority of votes in either House is required.

This general point above, however, now has to be revisited in the light of Laws LJ's comments in the *Thoburn* (2002) case in which he stated that constitutional statutes, unlike non-constitutional statutes, cannot be impliedly repealed (see section 4.4.5).

In any event, it is worth noting that even though there is a single passage for legislation, a constitutional convention exists in the House of Commons that Bills of constitutional importance (however these are determined) are considered in a Committee of the Whole of the House, rather than a general committee (formerly known as a standing committee) (see section 12.7.3).

4.2.5 No definitive list of statutes of a constitutional nature

What is clear is that there is no exhaustive list of statutes deemed to be of constitutional status as noted by the House of Lords Select Committee on the Constitution:

Q	'The constitution is said to be in flux, and the sense of what it is constantly evolving. The constitution is uncodified and although it is in part written there is no single, accepted and agreed list of statutes which form that part of the constitution which is indeed written down'. First Report of Session 2001–02 of the House of Lords Select Committee on the Constitution, *Reviewing the constitution: Terms of reference and method of working*, HL Paper 11 (2001), p 8.

4.2.6 No Constitutional or Supreme Court to specifically resolve issues of a constitutional nature

In terms of constitutional case law, the student must consider, on a case by case basis, whether or not it raises a constitutional issue or expounds a particular constitutional rule. The difficulty in the United Kingdom is the lack of a special Constitutional or Supreme Court which has the responsibility to process constitutional cases *per se*, as for example, the Irish or United States Supreme Courts do. Such courts authoritatively and definitively interpret the documentary constitution and will necessarily process cases that raise constitutional issues. Instead, the United Kingdom extracts its constitutional principles from case law drawn from all courts (both criminal and civil jurisdictions). Indeed, a case which *prima facie* appears to deal with a matter of private law (eg the law of trespass) may also have a constitutional dimension to it by raising a constitutional issue. For example:

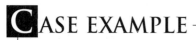ASE EXAMPLE

Entick v Carrington (1765) 19 St Tr 1030 (for details see section 4.8.2)

At one level this case may appear to deal with the private law of trespass, namely the King's messengers trespassing on Entick's property. In fact, the case has a clear constitutional resonance as it is also concerned with protecting the individual from the state and restricting the powers of the executive.

CASE EXAMPLE

Derbyshire County Council v Times Newspapers Ltd and Others [1993] 1 All ER 1011 (for details see section 4.8.2)

This case dealt with the private law of defamation, but it necessarily raised the constitutional issues of free expression and the freedom to criticise state/governmental institutions (see also section 18.4.1).

It should be noted, however, that although the United Kingdom lacks a special Constitutional or Supreme Court which specifically resolves constitutional issues *per se*, cases that form part of the jurisdiction of the Administrative Court (part of the High Court) will necessarily raise constitutional issues. This court is specifically responsible for applying judicial review principles to public authorities/government bodies so as to ensure that they exercise their legal public powers strictly in accordance with the law (see Chapters 19 and 20).

In contrast, it is pertinent to remember that when the new Supreme Court is activated, despite its title, cases coming before it will not necessarily be of interest to public/constitutional lawyers. In short, as the Supreme Court will essentially function as the House of Lords does at present, it will process appeals concerning all aspects of law including private law cases. In one respect at least, the new court will resolve constitutional issues as its jurisdiction will involve processing 'devolution' issues which concern the actions of the devolved institutions (see Chapter 14).

ACTIVITY

Problem solving

Explain the difficulties in trying to locate the sources of the British constitution.

Using your knowledge gained from the first three Chapters, how would you decide whether something was a constitutional issue?

4.3 The classification of the sources of the British constitution

4.3.1 The classification of legal and non-legal sources

The aim of this section is to identify the variety of sources that make up the British constitution. A number of examples will be given to illustrate each particular constitutional source.

With the difficulties identified at section 4.2 in mind, set out below are some of the main rules and principles of the constitution extracted from a wide variety of sources. These sources can be broadly divided into:

- Legal sources:

    (a) Domestic primary legislation (see section 4.4)

    (b) Domestic delegated legislation (see section 4.5)

    (c) Legislation of local authorities and the devolved institutions (see section 4.6)

    (d) European Community legislation (see section 4.7)

    (e) Domestic case law – the common law (see section 4.8.2)

    (f) Domestic case law – interpreting statutes (see sections 4.8.3 and 4.8.4)

    (g) Domestic case law – the royal prerogative (see section 4.9)

    (h) European Community case law (see section 4.10.1)

    (i) European Convention case law (see section 4.10.2)

    (j) The law and custom of Parliament (see section 4.11)

    (k) Treaties and international law (see section 4.12)

- Non-legal sources:

    (a) Constitutional conventions (see section 4.13)

    (b) Academic writings (see section 4.14)

The above information is also illustrated in the form of a table at the end of the chapter.

4.4 Domestic primary legislation

4.4.1 Acts of Parliament

Domestic primary legislation is legislation passed by the Queen in Parliament. These Acts of Parliament will have passed through both the House of Commons and the House of Lords (unless the Parliament Acts apply – see section 10.10.1) and have received the Royal Assent. These Acts are mostly piecemeal and *ad hoc* measures which have been passed over time to address a particular issue.

4.4.2 Acts of Parliament affecting the organs of the state

Primary legislation (as well as domestic delegated legislation) may have constitutional importance if it defines the powers of the state or government organs or regulates the procedure of those organs.

Below is a list of selected (but not exhaustive) statutes which illustrate a particular constitutional principle or rule. The first authority concerns the limitation of an institution of the state, the monarch:

The Magna Carta 1215 (affirmed as a statute in 1297)

This historic document is of constitutional significance as it represented a legal limitation and curb on the power of the monarch. It also concerns the constitutional relationship between the individual and the state. In essence, the Magna Carta set out, among other things,

- the church's freedom;

- the protection of the liberties of 'freemen' not to be imprisoned:

    'No freeman shall be taken or imprisoned, or be disseised of his freehold, or liberties, or free customs, or be outlawed, or exiled, or any other wise destroyed; nor will we not pass upon him, nor condemn him, but by lawful judgment of his peers, or by the law of the land' (sic) (clause 29). In short, this is an embronic constitutional statement concerning an individual's right to a fair trial.

The following statute concerns the constitutional relationship between two institutions of the state, namely, the monarch and Parliament:

The Bill of Rights 1689

S In brief, in historic terms the Bill of Rights sets out the conditions on which William of Orange (William III) ascended the throne as monarch. The Act altered the constitutional relationship between Parliament and the monarch, by expanding the power of the former at the expense of the latter. It included, among other things:

- Art 1 prohibiting the monarch from suspending laws without parliamentary consent (a constitutional limitation on the power of the monarch);

- Art 6 prohibiting the monarch from keeping a standing army without parliamentary consent (a constitutional limitation on the power of the monarch);

- Art 9 stated 'that the freedom of speech and debates or proceedings in Parliament ought not to be impeached or questioned in any court or place out of Parliament'. In essence, this meant that parliamentary members enjoyed legal immunity in respect of their words used in Parliament (see section 8.6.1).

One function of a constitution is to establish institutions of the state as illustrated by the following two statutes:

The Union with Scotland Act 1706

S This Act relates directly to the creation of the Parliament of Great Britain (the legislature which existed until 1800). Before this legislation, England (together with Wales) and Scotland had separate independent Parliaments and the effect of the Union legislation was to dissolve these and replace them with a single Parliament, namely, the Parliament of Great Britain.

The Union with Ireland Act 1800

S This legislation provided for the unification of Great Britain and Ireland and created the Parliament of the United Kingdom of Great Britain and Ireland (replacing the Parliament of Great Britain above).

The following Act set out the legal and constitutional relationship between two institutions of the state, the House of Commons and the House of Lords:

Parliament Act 1911 (as amended in 1949)

S This Act established the legal domination of the elected House of Commons over the unelected House of Lords. Prior to this Act a Bill required the consent of both Houses in order to become law. Thereafter, certain Bills only technically required the consent of the House of Commons alone as the House of Lords could only delay the enactment of such legislation, but not veto it (see section 10.10.1).

The Act is also constitutionally significant as it reduced the maximum length of a Parliament from seven to five years. It is of interest to contrast this provision with other countries with codified constitutions. For instance, Art I of the United States constitution states that Senators serve for six years and members in the House of Representatives for two years.

The following Act is an example of Parliament formally incorporating international law obligations into the United Kingdom's domestic legal system:

The European Communities Act 1972

This Act is undoubtedly the most important statute passed in the past few hundred years. This Act legally incorporated European Community law and principles into the law and legal system of the United Kingdom. European Community law has had a profound effect on our uncodified constitutional arrangements. In particular, it has affected the classic doctrine of parliamentary sovereignty (as expounded by Dicey) as since 1973 Parliament cannot now simply pass any law that it chooses if that law will violate European Community law. It has affected the constitutional role of the judges in relation to legislation and has conferred Community law rights on individuals that they can enforce in their domestic courts (see Chapter 15).

The following Act concerned the limitation of the power of the executive:

The House of Commons Disqualification Act 1975

This Act is concerned with the constitutional relationship and balance between the executive and the House of Commons. Section 2 specifies that only 95 government ministers (ministerial offices) can sit in the House of Commons, thereby ensuring (at least in constitutional theory) that the executive ministers, by virtue of their limited numbers, do not dominate the rest of the chamber (see section 11.6.3 below).

The following Act refers to the establishment of a new state institution:

The Government of Wales Act 1998

This Act devolved power to Wales by establishing a National Assembly for Wales. This legislation had been preceded by a referendum in Wales, which, albeit very narrowly, endorsed the creation of this Assembly. This demonstrates participatory democracy whereby the people who would be affected by the legislation were specifically consulted as to whether they approved of its proposals. As noted above, however, such a referendum was not technically legally necessary, but was considered politically appropriate (see section 14.5).

The following Act altered the composition of an institution of the state, namely, the second chamber in Parliament:

The House of Lords Act 1999

This Act removed the vast majority of hereditary peers from the House of Lords. The existence of hereditary peers (members who inherited their seats in the House of Lords) has always marked out the United Kingdom's constitutional arrangements as being very unusual in a democracy. The Act demonstrates graphically the power of Parliament to pass any law that it chooses. In short, the House of Lords Act 1999 effectively halved the size of the House of Lords (see section 10.6.3).

The following Act reformed various aspects of the constitution:

The Constitutional Reform Act 2005

As its title indicates, this Act is a quintessential constitutional measure. Its constitutional impact is as follows:

- It makes provision for a new Supreme Court, which will replace the existing House of Lords court that currently forms part of Parliament (see section 22.2.1).

- It reformed the way in which judges are appointed (see section 13.3.1 below).

- It remodelled the historic role of the Lord Chancellor, who is a major state official (see sections 5.7.9 and 22.2.2).

ACTIVITY

Select a number of the Acts of Parliament set out above and explain in each case why the statute is considered to be constitutionally significant. Find other Acts which relate to the organs of the state.

4.4.3 Acts of Parliament conferring rights on the individual

Legislation may also have constitutional importance if it contains provisions, which directly or indirectly affect the rights and liberties of the individual. A statute may therefore have ramifications for human rights or fundamental freedoms either by conferring special rights on individuals, or by restricting their freedoms.

The following four Acts confer rights on individuals:

The Sex Discrimination Act 1975

This Act is an example of Parliament passing a law to protect individuals by providing them with legal redress and rights in the event of discrimination. In short, the Act makes it illegal to discriminate against men or women on the grounds of sex in the context of education, work, housing or providing goods or services. If an individual has been discriminated against he or she has the right to seek legal redress.

S **The Race Relations Act 1976**

This Act relates to discrimination on the grounds of race (whether this is at work, renting accommodation, etc). If an individual has been racially discriminated against he or she has the right to seek legal redress.

In both these statutes the state has recognised that one function of the state is to ensure that all individuals are treated with equal respect, and providing them with a remedy if discrimination occurs.

S **The Human Rights Act 1998**

Along with the European Communities Act 1972, this statute is arguably the most constitutionally significant statute of the twentieth century. The Act gives further effect in domestic law to the fundamental rights and freedoms set out in the European Convention on Human Rights. This legislation represents a constitutional sea change in the way in which human rights are protected in the United Kingdom, as with the implementation of this Act individuals are permitted to raise alleged breaches of these rights directly before domestic courts (see Chapter 17).

S **The Representation of the People Act 1983**

This Act consolidates earlier Representation of the People Acts, which conferred the legal right on individuals to vote in elections to the House of Commons. It is of constitutional importance as it directly relates to the foundation of (participatory) democracy and the constitutional relationship between the individual and the State: the right of the people to elect and determine the composition of the legislature, and indirectly, the executive.

It should be noted that under the doctrine of parliamentary sovereignty, all of the above statutes (even though they detail important principles underpinning our constitution) could be repealed or amended. No special procedure (or special majority in Parliament) is required to alter or repeal them. Notwithstanding this, these legislative measures contain fundamental constitutional principles which the courts will assume are not to be varied as they lie at the heart of the basis of our constitution. In short, they would not be amended without substantial constitutional upheaval.

4.4.4 Acts of Parliament restricting the freedoms of the individual

It is important to note that Parliament will frequently pass statutes that will restrict the actions and freedoms of individuals. The following four Acts illustrate this:

S **The Perjury Act 1911**

Under this Act it is a criminal offence for a person sworn in as a witness in court proceedings to make a statement which he knows to be false or not believe to be true. This legislation protects the administration of justice.

The Public Order Act 1986

This legislation is concerned, *inter alia*, with the control and limitation of public processions and assemblies in order to protect public order.

The Prevention of Terrorism Act 2005

The objective of this Act is to prevent terrorism-related activity. The Act aims to achieve this by providing for the issuing of two types of 'control orders' which impose obligations on individuals who are suspected of being involved in terrorism-related activities. The obligations imposed would be tailored to the risk posed by the suspect concerned and could include, for example, restricting movement, prohibiting the possession of specified items or restricting communication and association. Owing to its draconian nature and restriction on human rights, the Act proved to be highly contentious but nevertheless passed expeditiously through Parliament.

The Serious Organised Crime and Police Act 2005

Section 132 of this Act makes it a criminal offence (unless police authorisation has been granted) for any person to take part in or organise a demonstration in a public place which is situated in a designated area. The Secretary of State has deemed the exclusion zone to extend to 1,000 yards from Parliament itself. The rationale behind this is to control demonstrations around Parliament Square.

ACTIVITY

Exercise

Select a number of the Acts of Parliament set out above and explain in each case what constitutional significance the statute has for the individual and individual rights. Find other Acts which have a constitutional impact on the individual.

4.4.5 Laws LJ and Acts of Parliament with constitutional status

As indicated above, historically the United Kingdom has been characterised as not having higher fundamental, entrenched laws. In recent years this orthodoxy has been questioned. For example, Laws LJ in *Thoburn v Sunderland City Council* [2002] EWHC 195 (Admin) (albeit *obiter*) argued that:

'We should recognise a hierarchy of Acts of Parliament: as it were "ordinary" statutes and "constitutional" statutes. The two categories must be distinguished on a principled basis.'

He added that these 'constitutional statutes' should embrace, among others, the following:

- The Magna Carta.
- The Bill of Rights.
- The Union with Scotland Act.
- The Human Rights Act.
- The Scotland Act.
- The European Communities Act.

Furthermore, he commented that whereas ordinary statutes could be impliedly repealed by a later inconsistent Act, constitutional statutes such as the ones listed above are not subject to implied repeal.

ACTIVITY

Question

What is the significance of Laws LJ's comments for our understanding of the sources of the British constitution?

4.5 Domestic delegated legislation

4.5.1 The nature of delegated legislation

Delegated legislation can also have direct constitutional significance. Delegated legislation is subordinate or secondary legislation made under the authority of a primary statute (the enabling Act of Parliament). This legislative power is conferred on the executive, for example a government minister. In doing so, it represents a clear breach of the separation of powers, but is constitutionally justified on the basis of practical necessity (see section 5.7.2).

4.5.2 Examples of delegated legislation

A recent example of the Prime Minister using a delegated legislative power is as follows:

The Secretary of State for Constitutional Affairs Order 2003 (SI 2003 No 1887)

This order transferred specified functions of the Lord Chancellor (whom at that point the government anticipated would be abolished under the impending Constitutional Reform Bill) to the newly created post of the Secretary of State for Constitutional Affairs. This order was passed under the aegis of the Ministers of the Crown Act 1975.

A further example, the Supreme Court Fees (Amendment) Order 1996, is detailed below in *R v Lord Chancellor, ex parte Witham* [1997] 2 All ER 779 (see section 4.8.3).

4.6 Legislation of local authorities and the devolved institutions

4.6.1 Local authorities and delegated legislation

Local authorities enjoy a delegated legislative power. As local authorities technically form part of the executive, this is also a breach of the separation of powers, although this power is justified on the basis of practical necessity. An example is detailed below.

The Warwick District Council Off Street Parking Places Order 2006

Under the aegis of the Road Traffic Regulations Act 1984 (the primary/parent Act), Warwick District Council (part of Warwickshire County Council – an executive body) made the above delegated legislation which updated the existing charges for local council car parks.

4.6.2 Legislation and the devolved institutions

The devolved institutions also have the power to pass legislation (both secondary and primary in nature – see Chapter 14). For example, in the case of Scotland the Scottish Parliament has the power to pass Acts of the Scottish Parliament as illustrated by the following example:

S **The Scottish Parliamentary Standards Commissioner Act 2002**
This Act established the office of a Parliamentary Standards Commissioner for the Scottish Parliament to investigate complaints concerning Members of the Scottish Parliament (MSPs) as to whether they had breached, for example, parliamentary Standing Orders or the Code of Conduct.

4.7 Legislation of the European Community

As a result of the European Communities Act 1972 European Community law (both primary and secondary) now forms an ever burgeoning and important part of United Kingdom law (see Chapter 15). In broad terms there are two types of European Community law:

- primary sources and
- secondary sources.

4.7.1 Primary sources

These include the founding Treaty of Rome 1957 together with its subsequent amendment over the years (eg the Single European Act 1986 which, *inter alia*, extended the powers of the European Parliament).

4.7.2 Secondary sources

European Community legislation is passed by the European Community institutions. Typically the European Commission will draft a proposal which has to be adopted by the Council (The Council of Ministers), sometimes acting in concert with the European Parliament. In brief, European legislation comes in a number of forms:

- Regulations
- Directives
- Decisions.

Regulations

The constitutional significance of regulations is that they are of general application and are self-executing as they do not require a Member State to formally implement them. In other words, the United Kingdom Parliament (or any other Parliament or Assembly in the Community) does not need to pass a law to incorporate the regulation as it will automatically form part of domestic law. An example of a regulation which was passed shortly after the United Kingdom joined the Community is detailed below:

Regulation 1365/75

This created a European Foundation for the improvement of living and working conditions of workers, which relates to individual social and economic rights.

Directives

In contrast to regulations above, directives do not have general application (instead they are addressed to particular Member States) and they require Member States to implement them through the passage of domestic legislation. In the United Kingdom directives can be implemented through either the passage of an Act of Parliament (see below) or by the means of delegated legislation in the form of a Statutory Instrument.

Council Directive 95/46/EC

The Data Protection Act 1998 was passed by the United Kingdom Parliament in order to implement the above European directive. This directive was aimed at protecting the rights of individuals in respect of personal data held about them. This issue relates directly to an individual's right to privacy.

Decisions

A decision does not have general application, but is addressed to particular parties (undertakings/companies) or Member States. Decisions can be used to implement a policy as illustrated by the example below:

> **Council Decision laying down the Procedures for the Exercise of Implementing Powers Conferred on the Commission 99/468 [1999] OJ L184/23**
>
> This Council decision, known as the 'Comitology decision', set out the procedure to be followed when the Council confers a law-making power on the European Commission.
>
> This delegation of legislative power is analogous to the United Kingdom Parliament (as the legislature) delegating a law-making power to the government (the executive) – see section 5.7.2).

Non-legally binding secondary sources

Opinions and recommendations are measures which do not have legally binding effect. For example, the European Commission can issue a 'reasoned opinion' in the context of enforcement proceedings against a Member State for violating European Community law. The opinion would set out the ways in which the Commission considered the Member State to have breached the law, for example, by failing to implement a directive.

KEY FACTS

Legislation may have constitutional importance if it:

- establishes a state institution/organ of government;
- defines the powers of a state institution;
- regulates the functions of a state institution;
- regulates the procedure of a state institution;
- regulates the relationship between state institutions;
- regulates how the state relates to the individual by either conferring rights on the individual or by restricting their freedoms.

4.8 Domestic case law

4.8.1 The role of the courts

The courts play an important role in respect of constitutional rules. This is true also in countries where these rules are codified in a documentary constitutional text. This is because all constitutional rules (whether contained in a codified document, or not) need to be interpreted and clarified. As noted earlier, even in the United States the rules and principles set out in the constitution need to be interpreted, and this is performed by the United States Supreme Court (see *Marbury v Madison* (1803) 1 Cranch 137 at section 5.7.10).

In the United Kingdom, in the absence of a single authoritative constitutional text, the courts play a particularly important role as many of our constitutional rules are to be found in court decisions (ie judicial decisions made in legal disputes brought before them for adjudication). For example, the most important principle of our constitution, namely, the legislative sovereignty of Parliament, is a court-based doctrine. This principle exists because the courts have declared it so in various decisions. Similarly, the separation of powers and the rule of law are underpinned by judicial decisions. Indeed, Dicey writing at the turn of the twentieth century referred to England as having a court-based constitution (a common law constitution). Indeed, more recently it has been suggested that:

> 'our constitutional law remains a common law ocean dotted with islands of statutory provision'.
>
> S Sedley, 'The Sound of Silence, Constitutional Law Without a Constitution'
> (1994) 110 LQR 270.

It is certainly the case, however, that since the election of the Labour Government in 1997, many more statutes affecting the constitution have been enacted. In addition, it must be remembered that the courts are necessarily reactive as they must wait for a legal dispute to be brought before them in order to declare the law.

Not every court decision, of course, will illustrate or expound a constitutional principle or clarify a particular constitutional rule. Therefore it is necessary (as in the case of statutes), to examine each court decision on a case by case basis to ascertain whether the ruling has constitutional significance, and consequently whether it forms part of the constitutional law of the United Kingdom.

In the United Kingdom the courts may make decisions of constitutional importance either by:

- declaring the common law; or
- interpreting statutes in the light of certain constitutional principles.

4.8.2 The common law

Many of our constitutional rules are derived from the judiciary declaring the common law.

The following two cases declare that the government/state must act within the law:

CASE EXAMPLE

***Entick v Carrington* (1765) 19 St Tr 1030**

Under a warrant issued by the Secretary of State, the defendants (the King's messengers) were required to search for John Entick and deliver him together with his papers before the Secretary of State. The allegation against Entick was that he was suspected of seditious libel. As the King's messengers broke into his house and seized his papers, Entick successfully sued them in the tort of trespass. As the trespass had not been justified by any legal authority (in other words a valid warrant to enter Entick's premises), a tort had been committed. The case, though superficially concerned with the private law of trespass, has a clear constitutional dimension as it is concerned with the limitation of the power of the state, and protecting the individual from the exercise of arbitrary state power. In other words, in order for the state to enter a person's property, it must have appropriate legal authority or it will be deemed unlawful.

CASE EXAMPLE

***M v Home Office* [1994] 1 AC 377** (for details see section 6.7.6)

This case stated that government ministers were subject to the jurisdiction of the courts and their orders. It reiterated that government must act under the law.

The following case concerns the protection of the constitutional principle of free expression and the freedom to express criticism of governmental institutions:

CASE EXAMPLE

***Derbyshire CC v Times Newspapers Ltd and Others* [1993] 1 All ER 1011**

In this case Derbyshire County Council wished to sue *The Sunday Times*, its editor and two journalists in defamation for articles concerning alleged share dealings of the council. The House of Lords held that in the common law of defamation, Derbyshire County

CONTINUED ▶

Council did not have the right to sue for damages as such a right would have been contrary to the public interest.

Although this case is in the context of the private law of defamation, it necessarily raises the constitutional issue of freedom of speech to criticise the government (see section 18.4.1).

The following case indicates that criminal offences (which restrict the freedom of the individual) can originate from the common law.

CASE EXAMPLE

Shaw v DPP [1962] AC 220

Shaw had been convicted, *inter alia*, of a common law conspiracy to corrupt public morals as he had conspired with advertisers and others to debauch and corrupt the morals of the youth and other subjects. Shaw had published a 'Ladies Directory' that contained the names and addresses of prostitutes. Shaw appealed and contended, *inter alia*, that there was no such offence. The House of Lords held that the courts had a residual power to supervise such offences that were prejudicial to public welfare. Viscount Simonds stated that:

> J '...there remains in the courts of law a residual power to enforce the supreme and fundamental purpose of the law, to conserve not only the safety and order but also the moral welfare of the State.'

The following case concerns freedom of expression and the protection of specified religious beliefs:

CASE EXAMPLE

R v Chief Metropolitan Stipendiary Magistrate, ex parte Choudhury [1991] 1 All ER 306

The High Court confirmed that the common law offence of blasphemy was confined to the Christian religion. The case concerned freedom of speech and the protection of religious beliefs (see section 18.3.1) and the court was concerned about the impact on freedom of speech and setting clear limits to the offence if it were extended to other religions.

The following case reaffirms the fundamental principle concerning the judicial arm of the state:

CASE EXAMPLE

R v Bow Street Metropolitan Stipendiary Magistrate, ex p Pinochet Ugarte (No 2)
[2000] 1 AC 119 (for details see section 13.4.2)

In order to reiterate the fundamental importance of the principle of the independence of the judiciary and the right of individuals to a fair trial, the House of Lords set aside their previous decision in relation to a warrant for General Pinochet's extradition. The decision was set aside as one of the judges, Lord Hoffmann, had had a connection with Amnesty International who were seeking the extradition of Pinochet.

4.8.3 Statutory interpretation

The courts in interpreting statutes may do so in the light of certain constitutional principles. In particular, as the United Kingdom has historically lacked a Bill of Rights, the courts have used these principles in order to protect the individual. Accordingly, where a statute is unclear or ambiguous the courts can draw upon certain constitutional principles which include the assumption that surely Parliament would never have intended to:

- legislate contrary to international law and Treaty obligations
- legislate retrospectively
- legislate so as to interfere with a person's right of access to the courts
- create taxes in the absence of clear authority.

The following case illustrates the first two presumptions:

CASE EXAMPLE

Waddington v Miah **[1974] 2 All ER 377**

In this case the House of Lords interpreted the Immigration Act 1971 so that it did not have retrospective criminal effect. Lord Reid stated that 'it is hardly credible that any government department would promote or that Parliament would pass retrospective criminal legislation'. He also noted that Art 7 of the European Convention on Human Rights prohibited the imposition of retrospective criminal offences. In other words, the courts will assume that Parliament intended to legislate in accordance with the United Kingdom's international obligations.

The following case illustrates the third presumption:

CASE EXAMPLE

R v Lord Chancellor, ex parte Witham [1997] 2 All ER 779

Under the authority of section 130 of the Supreme Court Act 1981 the Lord Chancellor made the following delegated legislative provision: the Supreme Court Fees (Amendment) Order 1996. Art 3 of this Order removed from litigants in person who received income support their (previously enjoyed) exemption from such fees. Witham, who was unemployed and on income support, was unable to institute proceedings in person for defamation as the exemption had been removed by the 1996 Order. Witham sought judicial review of Art 3 of the Order as *ultra vires* and so beyond the legal powers of the Lord Chancellor.

It was held by the High Court that access to the courts was in effect a constitutional right recognised by the common law and that this right could only be restricted by clear and specific statutory authority. The court interpreted s 130 as not empowering the Lord Chancellor to issue Art 3, the effect of which had been to deny Witham access to the courts and legal redress (a common law constitutional right). This case demonstrates the courts protecting the rights of individuals to access the courts and to seek justice.

The fourth presumption is demonstrated by *Attorney-General v Wilts United Dairies Ltd* (1921) 37 TLR 884.

4.8.4 Statutory interpretation and the Human Rights Act 1998

In recent years the role of the courts in interpreting legislation has been heightened by the passage of the Human Rights Act 1998. The Act is in effect an interpretative one in that s 3 requires all courts and tribunals to interpret all legislation in accordance with the rights and freedoms enshrined in the European Convention on Human Rights. If the relevant statute cannot be read in line, the courts cannot strike down primary legislation; instead the higher courts can issue a declaration of incompatibility (see Chapter 17).

The following case is an example of the operation of the Human Rights Act:

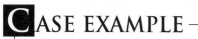
CASE EXAMPLE

Bellinger v Bellinger [2003] UKHL 21

Mrs Bellinger was a transsexual who had been born male. In 1981 she went through a ceremony of marriage with a man. Section 11 of the Matrimonial Causes Act 1973 states

CONTINUED ▶

a marriage is valid only if the parties are male and female. Mrs Bellinger sought, and was denied, a declaration that her marriage was valid notwithstanding that she was born male. The House of Lords stated that the terms male and female in the Act were to be given their ordinary meaning and referred to the respective biological gender at birth. Accordingly, within the meaning of s 11, as the parties were not male and female, the marriage was not valid. The court did, however, issue a declaration of incompatibility that s 11 was incompatible with Art 8 of the European Convention on Human Rights (the right to respect for private and family life) and Art 12 (the right to marry). This did not mean that the 1973 Act was invalidated. However, in response to this declaration, Parliament passed the Gender Recognition Act 2004 which recognised the reassigned gender of a person who has undergone gender reassignment.

For further examples see Chapter 17.

4.9 The royal prerogative

The royal prerogative is power that derives from the common law. Historically these powers would have resided personally in the monarch/Crown but today they are effectively exercised in the name of the Crown by the government of the day (see section 11.9).

The following two cases demonstrate the role of the courts in demarcating the legal parameters of the royal prerogative:

CASE EXAMPLE

The case of Proclamations (1611) 12 Co Rep 74

In this case the court declared that the King cannot by proclamation create a new criminal offence and that the King only enjoyed the prerogatives that the law of the land permitted him. In other words, the powers under the royal prerogative were limited.

CASE EXAMPLE

Burmah Oil Company Ltd v Lord Advocate [1965] AC 75

This case concerned the destruction of the oil installations of Burmah Oil (a group of four companies). During the Second World War these installations were destroyed by the British Army in Burma under the direction of the British government in order to deny

CONTINUED ▶

industrial resources which could be useful to the advancing Japanese. The House of Lords held that although the action had been carried out lawfully under the royal prerogative, a payment had to be made for the destruction of the property. The court further held that the Crown would only be immune from such payment if the destruction had been as a result of battle damage. Here the British Army had not actually been fighting the enemy as the Japanese had been advancing. This case demonstrates that the courts will determine the parameters of the Crown's common law powers.

ACTIVITY

Exercise

Select a number of the domestic case law decisions above and explain in each case why the case is considered to be constitutionally significant. Can you find any more constitutional cases?

4.10 European case law

Decisions made by the courts in Europe (both in Luxembourg and in Strasbourg) have had an impact on our constitution.

4.10.1 The European Court of Justice in Luxembourg

Decisions and rulings made by this European Court can have an impact on our law and legal system and its case law and principles are known as a tertiary source of European Community law. The functions of the European Court of Justice are to ensure that Community law is upheld against Member States and the other European institutions (known as direct actions/the contentious jurisdiction) and to provide the definitive interpretation of European Community law (indirect actions/the non-contentious jurisdiction).

In terms of the latter jurisdiction, where a court of a Member State is faced with a provision of Community law which is unclear, Art 234 of the Treaty of Rome 1957 allows that court to refer the point directly to the European Court for it to interpret. This interpretation which clarifies the law is known as a preliminary ruling which, once delivered, is binding (see section 15.4.2). Preliminary rulings can involve either:

- a court/tribunal of another Member State making a reference to the European Court. In the example below, the reference was made by an Italian court:

CASE EXAMPLE

Costa v ENEL Case 6/64 [1964] ECR 585

In 1962 Italy nationalised its electricity industry and Costa claimed that this breached the Treaty of Rome (the founding Treaty of the European Economic Community as it was known then). The issue in the case was whether national domestic legislation took precedence over European Community law. On an Art 234 reference the European Court affirmed that the creation of the EEC had created a new legal order whereby Member States had restricted their sovereign rights. In short, Community law took precedence over inconsistent domestic law thereby firmly establishing the principle of the primacy of European Community law. This principle, although in the context of a ruling involving Italy, has a direct impact on all Member States (including the United Kingdom who joined 10 years after this ruling was issued).

* a United Kingdom court/tribunal making a reference to the European Court:

CASE EXAMPLE

R v Secretary of State for Transport, ex parte Factortame Ltd (No 2) [1991] 1 AC 603

This seminal case is of profound constitutional importance and will be considered in detail at section 15.6.4. In brief, the European Court of Justice ruled that rights enjoyed under European Community law must be given full effect in a domestic legal system even whilst a domestic court is waiting for a preliminary ruling to be given by the European Court of Justice. In response to this ruling the House of Lords – for the first time – disapplied an Act of Parliament (the Merchant Shipping Act 1988), thereby compromising the principle of parliamentary sovereignty (see section 15.6.5).

Through preliminary rulings the European Court has developed major principles underpinning European Community law, for example, the doctrines of direct effect and the primacy of Community law.

4.10.2 The European Court of Human Rights in Strasbourg

Judgments made by the European Court of Human Rights also have an impact on the United Kingdom. The function of the European Court is to interpret and provide the authoritative interpretation of the articles of the European Convention. The effects of these judgments are not as immediate as with the judgments and rulings of the European Court of Justice above (see Chapter 16).

CASE EXAMPLE

Dudgeon v United Kingdom (1982) 4 EHRR 149

Dudgeon was a homosexual who resided in Northern Ireland, which in the 1970s still criminalised homosexual activity between adult males (ss 61 and 62 of the Offences Against the Person Act 1861). Dudgeon contended that these provisions interfered with Art 8 of the European Convention (the right to respect for private life). The European Court of Human Rights held that this legislation violated Art 8. Under international law the United Kingdom is bound to adhere to the decisions of the European Court of Human Rights, for example, where necessary by desisting from a particular practice or by introducing legislation to remove the incompatibility. In response to this judgment, the Homosexual Offences (NI) Order 1982 was passed which decriminalised homosexual activity between adult males in Northern Ireland.

ACTIVITY

Question

Why do you think decisions in the European Courts (the European Court of Justice and the European Court of Human Rights) are relevant to the study of the British constitution? Revisit this activity after completion of Chapters 15 to 17.

4.11 The law and custom of Parliament

Parliament (both the House of Commons and the House of Lords) regulates its own internal proceedings and determines its own standards of behaviour. This is done through laws and rules which are unique to it, known as the law and custom of Parliament (see section 8.5). These privileges (known as parliamentary privileges) are regarded as necessary in order to ensure that Parliament and its members can carry out and discharge its constitutional functions. These laws/privileges comprise both:

- statutory sources (Art 9 of the Bill of Rights which guarantees freedom of speech and debates or proceedings in Parliament) and

- common law sources whereby the courts recognise that, for example, Parliament has the right to determine and regulate its own membership and proceedings. This includes how legislation proceeds through Parliament as demonstrated in the following case:

CASE EXAMPLE

British Railways Board v Pickin [1974] AC 765

Pickin sought to claim that Parliament had been fraudulently misled into passing the British Railways Act 1968. The House of Lords held that the role of the courts was merely to consider and apply enactments of Parliament and not to challenge the British Railways Act 1968. In essence, the courts would not question the internal proceedings within Parliament as to how the Bill came to be on the parliamentary roll (see sections 7.8.1 and 8.7.2).

KEY FACTS

Judicial decisions in case law may have constitutional importance if they:

- define the powers of a state institution (*Burmah Oil Company Ltd v Lord Advocate* (1965));

- regulate the relationship between state institutions; or

- regulate how the state relates to the individual by either conferring rights onto the individual (see *Entick v Carrington* (1765)) or by restricting their freedoms.

4.12 Treaties and international law

International Treaties such as:

- the Universal Declaration of Human Rights 1948 and

- the International Covenant on Civil and Political Rights 1966

also act as an indirect influence on the United Kingdom constitution. Moreover, case law from other national Supreme and Constitutional Courts may also prove to indirectly influence and shape our law. For example, in the *Derbyshire County Council* case (see sections 4.8.2 and 18.4.1), in the context of the importance attached to safeguarding freedom of speech, Lord Keith made reference to a decision issued by the United States Supreme Court (*New York Times Co v Sullivan* (1964) 376 US 254). This Supreme Court decision had endorsed the public policy interest in allowing a citizen to criticise an ineffectual or corrupt public official without fear of legal impediment.

4.13 Constitutional conventions

As noted above, the rules of the constitution can be divided into legal rules (above) and political rules, with the latter being constitutional conventions which are effectively binding political constitutional rules.

4.13.1 Definition of a constitutional convention

Dicey defined conventions in the following terms:

> 'conventions, understandings, habits or practices which, though they may regulate the conduct of the several members of the sovereign power, of the Ministry, or of other officials, are not in reality laws at all since they are not enforced by the courts. This portion of constitutional law may, for the sake of distinction, be termed the "conventions of the constitution", or constitutional morality.' (*sic*)

> A Dicey, *Introduction to the Study of the Law of the Constitution* (10th edn, Macmillan, 1959), p 24.

More recently Barendt defined them as:

> 'Constitutional conventions may be defined as principles of political or constitutional morality which are regarded as binding, but which are not legally enforceable'.

> E Barendt, 'Fundamental Principles' in D Feldman (ed), *English Public Law* (Oxford University Press, 2004), p 14.

Furthermore, Barnett has provided a fuller definition:

> 'A constitutional convention is a non-legal rule which imposes an obligation on those bound by the convention, breach or violation of which will give rise to legitimate criticism; and that criticism will generally take the form of an accusation of "unconstitutional conduct"'.

> H Barnett, *Constitutional and Administrative Law* (6th edn, Routledge-Cavendish, 2006), p 30.

From these definitions we can see that constitutional rules can be distinguished between legal rules, which are enforced in a court of law, and political rules which are considered simply politically or morally binding. Barnett has contended, however, that the breach or blatant disregard of a convention would be considered to be (morally) unconstitutional (see section 4.15.2).

4.13.2 Preliminary points to note about constitutional conventions

It should be noted that:

- Firstly, constitutional conventions are not actually laws and yet they are studied as part of constitutional law. They are a very important part of the constitution and in fact may actually assume more constitutional significance than the legal rules that they supplement (see for example, the convention that the monarch will give her consent to a Bill presented to her – see further section 4.13.6).

- Secondly, constitutional conventions are not confined to the United Kingdom as they are also found in other countries such as the United States and Canada. These countries have codified constitutions and yet their constitutional text is supplemented by political conventional practices. For example, in Canada it is the practice that the federal Cabinet comprises representatives of all the Canadian provinces.

- Thirdly, constitutional conventions regulate key aspects of the British constitution and in particular, the government and the monarch. Some of the most important conventions are detailed below. It should be noted, however, that this is not an authoritative list (nor could it be, as inevitably there would be no universal agreement as to what it should include).

- Fourthly, in terms of their nature it should be noted that constitutional conventions are rules which are not necessarily prescribed with absolute precision (this gives them flexibility to develop and evolve) and there may be disagreement over their existence. It should also be noted that, unlike laws which are ultimately clarified in a court, there is no definitive authority or body which rules upon conventions. For example, although we are fairly clear in general terms about the rule governing the granting of the Royal Assent, other constitutional conventions are much less clear and definitive. For instance, it is a less well-established convention that one law lord should be drawn from Northern Ireland. Furthermore, in terms of ministerial responsibility, is it a modern day convention that ministers should resign for major mistakes in their government departments, as opposed to resigning for personal misadventures? (see section 12.3.5).

4.13.3 Constitutional conventions in respect of Parliament

These include, *inter alia*, the following:

- Committees of the House of Commons should reflect the party representation in the chamber (see section 12.6.4).

- Money Bills originate in the House of Commons.

- In the House of Lords, lay peers (ie non-judicial peers) do not sit in the Appellate Committee of the House of Lords (see section 5.7.4).

- Parliament must meet at least once a year. It is of interest to compare this rule with the United States constitution, Art 1, s 4 of which states that, legally, Congress shall assemble at least once in every year.

4.13.4 Constitutional conventions in respect of the monarch/executive

These include, *inter alia*, the following:

- The monarch assents to a Bill passed by both Houses of Parliament (see section 11.9.2).

- Following a general election the monarch will appoint as Prime Minister the MP who is the leader of the political party who can command a majority of support in the House of Commons.

- Many of the legal powers formally vested in the monarch are in fact exercised in practice by the government of the day in the name of the Crown (see section 11.9.4).

- Government ministers are collectively responsible to Parliament for the overall operation of government policy (see section 12.2).

- Government ministers are individually responsible to Parliament for their actions and the policy and actions of their government department (see section 12.3).

- In the event of the government losing a motion of no confidence in the House of Commons, the Prime Minister must either recommend the dissolution of Parliament or offer his resignation with that of the government (see section 12.2.1).

- The Prime Minster should be drawn from, and sit in, the House of Commons (see section 11.2.2).

- Government ministers must sit in one of the Houses of Parliament (see section 11.6.1).

- Cabinet discussions should remain secret (see section 12.2.3).

4.13.5 Constitutional conventions in respect of the judiciary

These include, *inter alia*, the following:

- Law lords do not get involved in overtly party political matters when the House performs its legislative and deliberative functions (see section 5.7.4).

- Two of the 12 law lords should be Scottish.

- The judiciary in general do not involve themselves in overtly party political issues (see section 13.4.4).

- In historical terms, the Lord Chancellor, when acting as judge, would not take part in cases involving the government.

4.13.6 The significance of constitutional conventions

The importance of constitutional conventions, particularly in the British constitution, cannot be underestimated as these political rules and principles form a major aspect of our constitution. In fact, if we were to view the British constitution by simply examining the legal rules, then we would have a very jaundiced and imbalanced perception of the constitution. For example, in relation to the Royal Assent, although under the royal prerogative the monarch can legally refuse to give her consent to a Bill, in practice it has become a long-established convention that this consent is always granted on the advice of her ministers. If we were, however, to simply consider the legal rule concerning the Royal Assent in isolation without reference to the convention supplementing it, we would have a much distorted view of the realities of the modern monarch's powers and of the constitution.

4.13.7 The purpose of constitutional conventions

Sir Ivor Jennings noted that constitutional conventions:

> 'provide the flesh which clothes the dry bones of the law; they make the legal constitution work; they keep it in touch with the growth of ideas'.

I Jennings, *The Law and the Constitution* (5th edn, Hodder and Stoughton, 1959) pp 81–82.

In short, constitutional conventions supplement the legal rules of the constitution. Their purpose is to ensure that the constitution can develop and adapt to ever changing contemporary principles and values. For example, the constitutional conventions regulating the legal powers of the monarch ensure that these powers are generally exercised by her government ministers on her behalf and in her name. This is consistent with democratic values as executive ministers are politically responsible to Parliament (through the convention of ministerial responsibility) whereas the monarch is unelected. It also illustrates the nature of the constitutional monarchy whereby the powers of the monarch are limited and controlled by binding political rules. Similarly, although the monarch formally undertakes the legal dissolution of Parliament, by convention she acts on the advice of the Prime Minister.

Constitutional conventions ensure that the constitution can develop on an incremental basis to address contemporary needs. For example, a constitutional convention (the Sewel Convention – named after Lord Sewel) has arisen as a result of the creation of the Scottish Parliament. In effect it states that the Westminster Parliament will not normally legislate in respect of 'devolved matters', except with the consent of the devolved legislatures (eg the Scottish Parliament). This convention, therefore, regulates the constitutional and political relationship between the major state institutions (see section 14.3.12).

ACTIVITY

Questions

How would you define a constitutional convention?

What constitutional purposes do they serve?

4.13.8 Why are constitutional conventions followed?

Constitutional conventions affect the main individuals and institutions in our constitution: the monarch, Prime Minister, Cabinet ministers, law lords and members of the House of Commons and Lords, but given that they are merely political rules, why are they followed? Indeed, constitutional conventions are not justiciable (ie not suitable for resolution before judicial proceedings) and so not enforced in a court. In fact, according to the Joint Committee on Conventions, constitutional conventions, owing to their nature, are 'unenforceable' (First Report of Session 2005–06 of the Joint Committee on Conventions, *Conventions of the UK Parliament*, HL Paper 265-I, HC 1212-I (2006), para 279).

As political rules, constitutional conventions are considered by those bound by them to be a constitutional and political obligation. In addition, political repercussions would result from their breach which, as observed by Barnett, would involve allegations of unconstitutional behaviour (eg acting contrary to the spirit and political principles underpinning the constitution – see section 4.15.2). For example, if the government were to lose a vote of no confidence in the House of Commons and yet refused to resign and carried on in office regardless, this would result in criticism. Furthermore, ministers will generally resign for major and embarrassing personal errors and misadventures (but less so for departmental errors) because of the resulting criticism that would follow if they did not (for examples, see section 12.3.4).

4.13.9 The flexibility of constitutional conventions

It should be noted that on occasions, owing to their flexible nature, constitutional conventions can at times be set aside. For example, in the mid-1970s the convention of collective Cabinet responsibility was temporarily set aside in relation to the 1975 EEC national referendum. The Labour Cabinet at the time was divided over the issue of the referendum, which concerned whether the United Kingdom should remain in the EEC (as it was then known). The Labour Prime Minister at the time, Harold Wilson, set aside this convention on this issue. It is also worth considering the current debate over the relevance of the Salisbury-Addison Convention to the contemporary House of Lords (see section 10.11).

4.13.10 What are the origins of constitutional conventions?

The origins of the laws and legal rules of the constitution (whether it be in the form of a statute or a constitutional principle extracted from a case) can be located relatively easily. In contrast, the point at which a mere accepted practice has crystallised into a political constitutional rule with an obligation to follow it is much more problematic. This is because constitutional conventions develop piecemeal over time on an *ad hoc* basis to supplement the legal rules by adjusting and adapting the constitution to reflect contemporary political principles and needs.

Sir Ivor Jennings suggested a three-part test to determine the existence of a constitutional convention:

1. What are the precedents for the convention?

2. Do those connected with this rule believe that they ought to act in a certain constitutional way (ie follow this rule)?

3. Is there a constitutional reason for the rule?

I Jennings, *The Law and the Constitution* (5th edn, Hodder and Stoughton, 1959) p 136.

It should be noted, however, that sometimes constitutional conventions can be created by agreement. An example of this is the Sewel Convention in respect of the Scottish Parliament (see section 14.3.12).

4.13.11 The distinction between laws and constitutional conventions

What is the difference between laws (legal rules) and constitutional conventions (non-legal/political rules)?

* Firstly, in general, laws are enforced in a court, whereas constitutional conventions are not.

* Secondly, as Alder has commented:

'A law does not fall into desuetude, yet a convention can disappear if it is not followed for a significant period, or if it is broken without objection'.

J Alder, *Constitutional and Administrative law* (5th edn, Palgrave/Macmillan, 2005), p 51.

In other words, Alder is making the point that, unlike a law, a convention depends upon regular and consistent use for its validation.

4.13.12 The judicial recognition of constitutional conventions

Although the courts do not enforce constitutional conventions, they have at times recognised their existence and made specific reference to them. An illustration of where a court made direct reference to the convention of collective responsibility is in the following case:

CASE EXAMPLE

Attorney-General v Jonathan Cape Ltd [1976] 1 QB 752

The Attorney-General sought an injunction to restrain publication of a book detailing the diaries of the late Richard Crossman, who died in 1974. The diaries detailed discussion in the Cabinet in the 1960s and the legal action was based on an alleged breach of

CONTINUED ▸

confidence. The law of confidence concerns the situation where an individual has received information in circumstances that the information should remain confidential. Collective ministerial responsibility includes the rule that Cabinet discussions are secret, so as to allow ministers to discuss issues freely before a collective decision is agreed upon and thereafter defended publicly (see section 12.2.3).

The court held that under the law of confidence it could restrain the publication of politically confidential information where the public interest required restraint and here the convention was relevant to assessing the balance between the public interest and confidentiality. There was, however, a time limit after which the confidential nature of the information would lapse and on the facts an injunction to restrain the publication in 1975 of discussion 10 years earlier (1964–66) was not justified.

Moreover, in the following case in the context of a Canadian constitutional convention, the Canadian Supreme Court recognised and acknowledged its existence, but affirmed that as political rules, conventions cannot be enforced in a court of law:

CASE EXAMPLE

Reference Re Amendment of the Constitution of Canada (1982) 125 DLR (3d) 1

This case considered whether the consent of the Canadian provinces was necessary before the Canadian legislature requested the United Kingdom Parliament to amend the Canadian constitution in a way which affected the federal/provincial relationship. At this time, in order for the Canadian constitution to be altered, it required legislation from the Westminster Parliament in London. The Canadian Supreme Court held that as a matter of constitutional convention, the consent of the Canadian provinces was required, thereby recognising the existence of the convention. As a matter of law, however, such consent was not legally necessary. The court stated that in respect of the constitution's 'conventional rules':

J 'In contradistinction to the laws of the constitution, they are not enforced by the courts. One reason for this situation is that, unlike common law rules, conventions are not judge-made rules. They are not based on judicial precedents... Nor are they in the nature of statutory commands which it is the function and duty of the courts to obey and enforce. Furthermore, to enforce them would mean to administer some formal sanction when they are breached.'

In the following case, the Court of Appeal in determining the legal powers of a government minister made its decision in the context of the fact that the minister (under the convention of ministerial responsibility) was constitutionally, and politically, accountable to Parliament for his actions:

CASE EXAMPLE

Carltona Ltd v Commissioners of Works and Others [1943] 2 All ER 560

Carltona Ltd challenged the requisition of their factory by the Commissioners of Works. The power to requisition this property was made under the Defence (General) Regulations 1939. Carltona argued that the requisition was invalid as the decision had in practice been taken by a civil servant, an Assistant Secretary who was not a competent authority, instead of the Commissioners of Works. The Court of Appeal held that the order was valid, as it would not be practical for the minister to take every decision personally; accordingly an official can make decisions on the authority of the minister so that the official acts in the name of the minister. Strictly speaking the official becomes the alter ego of the minister. Lord Greene MR stated that:

J 'Constitutionally, the decision of such an official is, of course, the decision of the minister. The minister is responsible. It is he who must answer before Parliament for anything that his officials have done under his authority, and if for an important matter he selected an official of such junior standing that he could not be expected competently to perform the work, the minister would have to answer for that in Parliament.

Similarly, in the controversial case of *Liversidge v Anderson* [1942] AC 206 the court was influenced by the convention of ministerial responsibility in reaching its decision concerning the exercise of the legal powers of a government minister to detain an individual during wartime (see section 6.7.10).

4.13.13 Converting constitutional conventions into laws

It is of course possible for a constitutional convention to be converted into statutory form, thereby making it a legal rule and so legally enforceable. In fact, this has already been achieved in the British constitution and is illustrated by the following two statutes.

The Parliament Act 1911

S Codification may be considered necessary if a constitutional convention is flagrantly breached. Before the Parliament Act 1911, it had been a convention that the House of Commons was the dominant chamber and that the House of Lords would ultimately give way to it. The House of Commons was of course elected although at this point it did not involve universal suffrage. In 1909 the Finance Bill containing Lloyd George's budget was rejected by the House of Lords and this resulted in the passage of the 1911 Act, which effectively placed on a statutory basis the principle that the upper chamber was legally subordinate to the lower House (see section 10.10.1).

The Statute of Westminster 1931

S Section 4 of this Act codified (ie enacted in statutory form) the constitutional convention that the United Kingdom Parliament would not legislate for a Dominion (eg Canada, New Zealand and Australia) without their consent.

Moreover, during the passage of the Constitutional Reform Bill an unsuccessful attempt was made to codify the historic constitutional convention that the Lord Chancellor must be both a peer in the House of Lords and a lawyer. It is also of interest to remember that other countries have also enacted constitutional conventions in a legal form. For example, the 22nd Amendment to the constitution of the United States codified the convention that limited the President to two terms of office.

Although it is possible for constitutional conventions to be converted into legal rules, is this necessarily desirable? At least two basic objections can be raised:

- Firstly, there inevitably would be debate over defining these conventions and their precise ambit.

- Secondly, new constitutional conventions in any event would develop so as to supplement those conventions which had been codified.

Finally, it is pertinent to point out that in 2006 the Joint Committee on Conventions was established to consider the practicality of codifying the constitutional conventions which regulate the relationship between the House of Commons and the House of Lords. Its conclusions are set out at section 22.6.2, although for present purposes it is worth noting the following passage:

> **Q** 'In our view the word "codification" is unhelpful, since to most people it implies rule-making, with definitions and enforcement mechanisms … It would raise issues of definition, reduce flexibility, and inhibit the capacity to evolve. It might create a need for adjudication, and the presence of an adjudicator, whether the courts or some new body, is incompatible with parliamentary sovereignty'.
>
> First Report of Session 2005–06 of the Joint Committee on Conventions, *Conventions of the UK Parliament*, HL Paper 265-I, HC 1212-I (2006), para 279.

The Committee observed that codification of conventions in a broad sense could mean an authoritative statement of conventions, or in a narrower sense, the reduction of them 'to a literal code or system'. In any event, the Committee made it very clear that there was universal opposition to legislating on these matters (as this would, for example, affect their flexibility and inhibit their evolution). Furthermore, the courts should have no role in adjudicating on them.

KEY FACTS

- 'Constitutional conventions may be defined as principles of political or constitutional morality which are regarded as binding, but which are not legally enforceable' (Barendt).

- Constitutional conventions regulate key aspects of the British constitution; in particular, the monarch and the government.

- They supplement the legal rules of the constitution and help to ensure that the constitution can develop and adapt to ever changing contemporary principles and values.

- Political repercussions would result from their breach which would lead to allegations of unconstitutional behaviour (acting in a morally unconstitutional way).

4.14 Authoritative writers

Historic writers on the British constitution include, for example, the works of Blackstone and Dicey. Indeed, Dicey's work (A Dicey, *Introduction to the Study of the Law of the Constitution* (10th edn, Macmillan 1959)), has informed our understanding of the constitutional principles of, *inter alia:*

- the rule of law (Chapter 6)
- constitutional conventions (see section 4.13.1)
- parliamentary sovereignty (Chapter 7).

Today distinguished contemporary academics (eg the texts of Feldman *Civil Liberties and Human Rights in England and Wales* (2nd Edition, Oxford University Press, 2002) or Wade and Forsyth's *Administrative Law* (9th Edition, Oxford University Press, 2004)) will also be referred to in order to assist the court in applying the constitution.

It should also be noted that senior judges, serving or otherwise, will write occasionally in legal academic journals and deliver extra-judicial speeches. For instance, in 2004 the then Lord Chief

Justice, Lord Woolf, delivered a speech on the rule of law at Cambridge University (Lord Woolf, 'The rule of law and a change in the constitution' [2004] CLJ 317).

4.15 Acting unconstitutionally in the United Kingdom

4.15.1 The difficulties associated with the term unconstitutional in the United Kingdom

As noted at section 2.6, acting unconstitutionally means to act contrary to the constitutional rules, spirit and principles underpinning the constitution. In the United Kingdom in the absence of a codified document, the use of the term *unconstitutional* is problematic as the rules of the constitution have not been codified. In fact, these rules have not even been universally and definitively agreed upon and consequently, as indicated earlier at section 4.2, there is no universal agreement on what is, and what is not, a constitutional issue. In light of this, it is difficult to gain universal agreement on what is *unconstitutional.*

In addition, in the absence of a codified constitutional document which has fundamental status, the courts in the United Kingdom (unlike a number of Supreme or Constitutional Courts in other countries with a codified constitution) cannot declare Acts of Parliament to be legally unconstitutional. In other words, they cannot declare that an Act is invalid as being contrary to the principles set out in the constitution. This is because there is no fundamental, codified constitutional text and instead, owing to the principle of parliamentary sovereignty, Parliament can legally pass any law that it chooses as the courts are (traditionally at least) unable to challenge or question it (see Chapter 7).

4.15.2 Examples of acting unconstitutionally in the United Kingdom

In the United Kingdom we would consider the following to be unconstitutional:

- A violation of the rule of law (see Chapter 6).

- The arbitrary use of power without restraint (see Chapters 19 and 20).

- The departure from and interference with fundamental principles including, for example, the right of access to the courts (see *Chester v Bateson* at section 5.7.2) or the presumption of innocence (*ex parte Khawaja* at section 6.7.10).

- A breach or disregard of a constitutional convention (see section 4.13).

- A breach of European Community law (see Chapter 15).

- A breach of the European Convention (either through an adverse ruling of the European Court of Human Rights, or in the context a declaration of incompatibility made by the domestic courts under the Human Rights Act 1998 (see Chapters 16 and 17 respectively)).

Some more examples are detailed below.

Firstly, suppose the monarch refused to give the Royal Assent to a Bill, despite having been specifically requested to do so by the government. It is a constitutional convention that the monarch confers her assent to a Bill and, as indicated above, a breach of a constitutional convention leads to an accusation of unconstitutional conduct. The failure to give assent to the Bill would, however, not be illegal as the disregard of a constitutional convention is not enforced in a court of law. We could argue, therefore, that although this behaviour was *legally constitutional* (ie lawful), it would nevertheless, be *morally unconstitutional* (as being contrary to the fundamental political principles underpinning the constitution).

Secondly, according to parliamentary sovereignty, Parliament can legally pass any law that it chooses and so the courts are unable to declare an Act of Parliament *legally unconstitutional* as being repugnant to the British constitution (but in this context see section 7.7). In theory, therefore, suppose Parliament chooses to pass the (imaginary) Elections Act 2010, s 1 of which deprives all individuals with an income of less than £5,000 a year of the right to vote in general elections. Commentators would undoubtedly consider this legislation to be unconstitutional, at least from a moral perspective (*morally unconstitutional*), as it interferes with basic democratic principles, namely participatory democracy and the right to vote. The Act, however, would in legal theory be technically enforceable and therefore *legally constitutional*, as Parliament under the British constitution can legally pass any Act that it chooses.

CASE EXAMPLE

Madzimbamuto v Lardner-Burke [1969] 1 AC 645

Lord Reid in the Privy Council made the point that under the principle of parliamentary sovereignty, Parliament can in legal theory pass any law (eg the Southern Rhodesia Act 1965), even if that statute contravened a well established constitutional principle (eg that the UK Parliament would not legislate for Southern Rhodesia without its consent). In this context he commented that:

J 'It is often said that it would be unconstitutional for the United Kingdom Parliament to do certain things, meaning that the moral, political and other reasons against doing them are so strong that most people would regard it as highly improper if Parliament did these things. But that does not mean that it is beyond the power of Parliament to do such things. If Parliament chose to do any of them the courts could not hold the Act of Parliament invalid.' (See also section 7.6.4.)

It is worth noting that the (imaginary) Elections Act 2010 inevitably would be challenged by aggrieved individuals under the European Convention on Human Rights:

- Initially, in the domestic courts under the Human Rights Act 1998 by seeking a declaration that the Act contravenes Protocol 1, Art 3, in effect, the right to vote. Notwithstanding this, Parliament and the government could politically ignore any such declaration and the Act would remain in force (see Chapter 17).

- Thereafter, aggrieved individuals could petition the European Court of Human Rights in Strasbourg. The European Court would inevitably declare that the (imaginary) Elections Act 2010 violated the European Convention and require that the United Kingdom remove this offending legislation. The United Kingdom Parliament could in legal theory ignore such a ruling, however, for political reasons it would implement the European Court's ruling.

Thirdly, an example of Parliament passing a statute which was arguably *morally unconstitutional* (but perfectly legal and enforceable) is the War Damage Act 1965 which, in effect, reversed a ruling of the House of Lords that proved to be financially inexpedient (see sections 6.7.9 and 7.5.1). It is a fundamental principle of the constitution that the role of the courts and the administration of justice is safeguarded. Similarly, it could conceivably be argued that s 20C of the Taxes Management Act 1970 was *morally unconstitutional* as it conferred exceptionally wide sweeping powers on the executive at the expense of the individual (see *Rossminster Ltd and Others* at sections 6.7.5 and 6.7.9). Both statutes infringe major principles which are fundamental to the constitution.

Finally, as the term unconstitutional is necessarily a somewhat indistinct term, commentators inevitably will disagree over whether legislation or government action is *morally unconstitutional.* For example, is the Prevention of Terrorism Act 2005 *morally unconstitutional* as it interferes with the fundamental liberties of the individual, or is it a necessary response to an emergency threatening the life and safety of the public?

ACTIVITY

Essay writing

What is meant by acting unconstitutionally in the British constitution?

KEY FACTS

Legal sources:		Non-legal sources:
Domestic legislation	• Acts of Parliament • Delegated legislation • Legislation of local authorities and the devolved institutions	• Constitutional conventions • Academic writings
European Community legislation	• Primary sources • Secondary sources	
Domestic case law	• The common law • Interpreting statutes • The royal prerogative	
European case law	• European Court of Justice • European Court of Human Rights	
The law and custom of Parliament	• Parliamentary privilege	
Treaties and international law	• Universal Declaration of Human Rights 1948	

Further reading

Alder, J, *Constitutional and Administrative Law* (5th edn, Palgrave/Macmillan, 2005), Chapter 2.

Barnett, H, *Constitutional and Administrative Law* (6th edn, Routledge-Cavendish, 2006), Chapter 2.

Bradley, A and Ewing, K, *Constitutional and Administrative Law* (14th edn, Pearson/Longman, 2007), Chapter 2.

Ellis, E, 'Sources of Law and the Hierarchy of Norms' in Feldman, D (ed), *English Public Law* (Oxford University Press, 2004), p 44.

Turpin, C, *British Government and the Constitution* (5th edn, Cambridge University Press, 2002), Chapter 2, Pts 1 and 2.

chapter 5 THE SEPARATION OF POWERS ■

At the end of this chapter you should be able to:

■ Explain what is meant by the principle of the separation of powers

■ Identify and explain the aspects of the British constitution that violate the separation of powers

■ Identify and explain the aspects of the British constitution that accord with the separation of powers

■ Assess the overall significance of the separation of powers in the British constitution

5.1 Introduction

In the context of the Chapter on constitutions we noted the importance of ensuring that state/governmental power is limited by the constitution. One way in which state power can be controlled is through the principle of the separation of powers. In essence, under this doctrine public/state power is divided and dispersed between separately constituted institutions, each with a distinct function to perform. This is in accord with the principle of constitutionalism, namely, that the power of the state should be limited. The aim of this Chapter is to consider the constitutional doctrine of the separation of powers and examine its significance in the context of the British constitution.

5.2 Definition

5.2.1 Introduction

The separation of powers has been described in the following terms:

'in a nation which has political liberty as the direct object of its constitution no
one person or body of persons ought to be allowed to control the legislative,
executive and judicial powers, or any two of them'.

Lord Lester and D Oliver (eds), *Constitutional Law and Human Rights* (Butterworths, 1997) p 21.

The doctrine of the separation of powers is typically associated with the French commentator
Montesquieu writing in the eighteenth century. He was concerned with avoiding a concentration
of state power and ensuring that this power was limited. Although the principle of dividing the
various functions and powers of the state power predates Montesquieu, his description of the three
branches of government namely, the legislature, executive and judiciary, has a modern resonance.

In very general terms, the separation of powers denotes that in order to avoid an unnecessary
concentration of state power, the following three state functions should be separate from one
another:

- The legislative function (the law-making function).
- The executive function (the governmental function).
- The judicial function (the adjudicative and interpretative function).

In short, these functions should be separate and there should also be no duplicity of personnel. The
definition of the separation of powers, however, is a somewhat elastic concept which is subject to
different interpretations. These range from a very strict separation of powers, through to
graduations of the principle, whereby the functions and institutions interrelate and check and
balance each other.

5.2.2 A pure separation of powers

A pure separation of powers would insist that the three organs of government be completely
separated and constitutionally isolated from each other. This would entail that the three elements
of the state are institutionally separate from each other with each organ performing a specific and
exclusive constitutional function. Furthermore, individuals should only form part of one organ.
This therefore prohibits, for instance, a judge from sitting in the legislature as this would represent
an overlap in terms of personnel. The three organs should be separated in terms of their functions
so that each performs its own constitutional function and does not purport to exercise the specified
function of another. This prohibits, for example, the courts making legislation and thereby
performing a legislative function. Similarly, the legislature is prohibited from interfering with the
courts' adjudicative and interpretative function.

In summary, under a pure separation of powers there should be no overlap in terms of:

- Functions (eg the judiciary should not exercise a legislative function or interfere with the
  executive function).
- Personnel (eg a judge should not form part of the executive body).

- Institutions (eg the executive body should not form part of another institution such as the legislature).

5.2.3 A less than pure separation of powers

In contrast to a pure separation of powers, there are various graduations of the doctrine whereby the functions/organs of government may be largely separate (to varying degrees), but interrelate and check and balance each other (eg the judiciary checks and balances the legislative power). This less than pure separation of powers – a weaker and partial separation – acknowledges the political reality that the machinery and practice of government require that state institutions have to work with one another. In fact, Barnett has argued that a pure separation of powers could prove to be unworkable in practice, as it could lead to constitutional deadlock between the institutions. Under a weaker version of the separation of powers, the tensions and checks and balances between the three state institutions aim to ensure that state power is not abused, by ensuring that it is not all concentrated in, and controlled by, one particular state organ. This necessarily makes it more difficult for each branch of the state to carry out its particular function, as it is checked and balanced by the other branches.

ACTIVITY

Essay writing

Explain the difference between a pure separation of powers and a less strict version of the principle.

KEY FACTS

The separation of powers is an internal method of institutionally controlling state power.

Under the doctrine of the separation of powers, public/state power is divided and dispersed between separately constituted institutions, each with a distinct function to perform.

The separation of powers is an important aspect of constitutionalism.

5.3 The different powers of the state

The functions/powers of the state can, in effect, be divided into three. It should be noted however, that this division into three clearly defined state functions is not without controversy. Some commentators have questioned whether it is really possible to definitively and clearly separate these functions/powers.

5.3.1 The legislative function

This function is performed by the legislature and it involves the enactment of general laws. In the United Kingdom the Queen in Parliament represents the law-maker (ie a Bill passes through both Houses of Parliament and receives Royal Assent in order to become an Act of Parliament). Similarly, in the Republic of Ireland the Oireachtas is the law-maker (Art 15.2 of the Irish constitution) and in the United States it is Congress (Art 1). We will see later, however, that in the United Kingdom (as in a number of other countries) the legislative role is not performed solely by the legislature.

5.3.2 The executive function

The executive (or governmental) function is performed by the government or administration. The executive administrates (carries out) the functions, powers and duties contained in general legislative provisions. The executive is the most difficult of all three organs to define, and it has been described simply as the residual functions/roles of the state that exist once the legislative and judicial functions have been outlined and demarcated (Lord Lester and D Oliver (eds), *Constitutional Law and Human Rights* (Butterworths,1997), p 22).

In general terms, the executive executes the law as it carries out and implements it. In the United Kingdom not only does the executive initiate policy (including the drafting of parliamentary legislative proposals), but it implements the resulting legislation. The executive also determines and executes public policy in terms of both domestic and foreign affairs. In the United Kingdom the term executive can include the following bodies:

* The Sovereign as the nominal head of the executive (see section 11.1.2).

* Her Majesty's Government comprising the Prime Minister, Cabinet, junior government ministers (in effect the political executive), supported by government departments staffed by civil servants (see Chapter 11).

* Local authorities. It should be noted that it is possible for the two branches of the executive function (ie central and local government) to be of different political colours. For example, in the 1980s when central government (the political executive) was Conservative, and many local authorities were controlled by the Labour Party, this led to friction and litigation between the branches of the executive. This led to what has been described as the *juridification* of their constitutional relationship. This meant that the courts were used in order to demarcate the boundary between central and local government (see section 14.2).

- The armed forces and the police who carry out and implement the law on a practical basis (see section 11.4).

In the United States the political executive is the President and in the Republic of Ireland it is the government (ie Taoiseach and Cabinet).

5.3.3 The judicial function

The judicial function is performed by the judiciary and it involves the determination of the law laid down in statutes or in the common law in relation to disputes arising from that law. It is a forum for resolving legal conflicts. The judicial arm of the state, therefore, settles legal disputes by interpreting and applying the law to a particular case before it. In the United Kingdom this function is performed by an array of judges (both senior and junior, full-time and part-time, legally qualified and those lacking formal legal qualifications, eg magistrates). As we shall see later, however, the judicial function is not exclusively performed by the judiciary alone.

In the United States Art III of the constitution confers judicial power on the judges and the Supreme Court. In the Republic of Ireland Art 34.1 stipulates that the exclusive responsibility to administer justice is performed by the judiciary (including the Irish Supreme Court).

KEY FACTS

In general terms:

- The legislative function involves enacting law.
- The executive function involves the implementation of that law as well as making policy decisions.
- The judicial function involves settling legal disputes arising from the law.

5.4 The relationship between the three powers in the United Kingdom

In the United Kingdom the three functions of the state are not isolated and completely separate from one another. Instead, they interrelate with each other. This is illustrated in the context of the creation and enforcement of primary legislation. Detailed below are three examples of how the various state functions would combine with each other in the context of (imaginary) legislation.

5.4.1 The (imaginary) Crime Act 2010

The policy behind this legislation is that the government (the political executive) responded to a perceived public need for a new criminal offence to be introduced. After a White Paper on the policy had been issued, the provisions of the Bill were set out by departmental lawyers and then sent to parliamentary draftsmen who composed the proposed legislation: The Crime Bill. This is an example of the executive formulating policy by initiating new legislative proposals in order to create a new criminal offence.

As part of the Queen's Speech in November 2009 (the beginning of the 2009–10 parliamentary session), the government presented the Crime Bill to Parliament for it to approve. Parliament as the legislature is responsible for enacting legislation and both Houses (House of Commons and the House of Lords) considered the measure and the Bill was amended to remedy some minor drafting inaccuracies. Once the Crime Bill passed successfully through both Houses of Parliament it received the Royal Assent (as we saw at section 4.13.4, by constitutional convention, such assent is always given by the monarch) and it became the Crime Act 2010.

Once in force, the Crime Act 2010 would be enforced by the police (the executive in practical terms), who would bring before the Crown Prosecution Service (a department which is responsible for the prosecution of offenders) cases of individuals who are alleged to have committed the new criminal offence enshrined in the Act. In court the offender would be tried and the court process would determine whether the offence contained within the Crime Act 2010 had been breached and if so, decide what punishment is appropriate (the parameters of the punishment available being stipulated in the Act).

5.4.2 The (imaginary) Tax Act 2010

The government wanted to introduce a new tax and this policy was encapsulated in the Tax Bill. This Bill was then presented to Parliament (with the House of Commons having special responsibility for financial measures) for it to accept (with or without amendments) or reject. After Parliament approved the Tax Bill it was given the Royal Assent and it became the Tax Act 2010. This Act would then be enforced (ie the new tax would be collected by HM Revenue & Customs – a government department) and in the event of a dispute arising concerning the interpretation of this measure (ie what payment is due in law), ultimately the courts would adjudicate on this (although a tax tribunal – the General Commissioners of Income Tax – would initially process the issue).

5.4.3 The (imaginary) Public Order Act 2010

In 2010 Parliament passed, and the Royal Assent was given to, the Public Order Bill making it the Public Order Act 2010. Section 1 of the Act stated that the Home Secretary may pass such regulations (in the form of a Statutory Instrument) as he thinks fit in order to protect public order. This is an example of Parliament delegating a legislative power to a government minister which would enable him/her to pass delegated/secondary legislation (see section 5.7.2).

In constitutional terms, the reality is that the executive, which typically controls the House of Commons, has drafted a Bill which, after it has been made law, confers a legislative power back onto itself, that is onto a government minister: in the case of the Public Order Act 2010, the Home Secretary.

ACTIVITY

Problem solving

Identify an Act of Parliament that has been passed recently by Parliament, and consider how the three state institutions have interacted in the context of that legislation.

5.5 What is the rationale behind the separation of powers?

The separation of powers is central to a democratic constitution.

5.5.1 To avoid a concentration of public power in one body/institution

As noted above, Montesquieu argued that state power should be divided and separated in order to avoid a concentration of power which otherwise could lead to tyranny and oppression:

> 'When legislative power is united with executive power in a single person, or in a single body of the magistracy, there is no liberty … Nor is there liberty if the power of judging is not separate from legislative power and from executive power. If it were joined to legislative power, the power over the life and liberty of the citizens would be arbitrary, for the judge would be the legislator … All would be lost if the same man or the same body of principal men, either of nobles, or of the people, exercised these three powers: that of making the laws, that of executing public resolutions, and that of judging the crimes or the disputes of individuals'.

> C Montesquieu, *The Spirit of the Laws* (1748), cited in A Bradley and K Ewing,
> *Constitutional and Administrative Law* (14th edn, Pearson/Longman 2007), pp 84–85.

Thus, if one person performed two or more state functions this would inevitably lead to oppression and tyranny. For example, if a person making the laws (a legislative role) also enforced and implemented these legislative provisions (an executive role) and then determined whether a person had violated that law in a case before them (a judicial role), this person would in effect enjoy excessive and tyrannical powers. If all state power was concentrated in one body, therefore, it would inevitably be abused.

5.5.2 To provide a system of checks and balances between the branches of government

Under a partial separation of powers the objective is to avoid a concentration of power. This is achieved not by an absolute separation and isolation of the three functions, but instead through the creation of a number of checks and balances between them. In other words, one institution may well interfere with the (constitutional) functions of another. For example, in the Republic of Ireland, the Oreachtas as the legislature is responsible for enacting laws. Under Art 34 of the Irish constitution, however, the Irish Supreme Court may declare legislation legally unconstitutional and therefore null and void. Moreover, under Art 26 the President of Ireland (a formal and typically ceremonial aspect of the executive) may refer a Bill that has not yet been signed (and so yet to become an Act) to the Supreme Court to determine whether or not it is unconstitutional. If the Bill, or any part of it, is deemed unconstitutional, the Bill cannot become law. This therefore frustrates the legislature in its function of law-making.

Similarly, the doctrine of the separation of powers is clearly evident in the United States constitution, although it is based on a subtle set of checks and balances. For instance, the President (executive) can, initially at least, check the legislature in the context of legislation by vetoing proposed legislation which has successfully passed through Congress. Ultimately, however, the latter can overturn the presidential veto by a two-thirds majority in each House. In addition, in terms of appointments to the Supreme Court, the Senate (the second chamber of Congress) must confirm a Presidential nomination (an executive decision) of a proposed Justice to the court.

5.5.3 To provide an efficient government

At one level the doctrine of the separation of powers helps to achieve efficient government. In short, by specifically allocating definite functions to specific institutions staffed with particular expertise (eg judges who are expert at assessing evidence and judging), this necessarily provides efficient government.

5.5.4 To safeguard the independence of the judiciary

The separation of powers subsumes the fundamental notion that the judiciary should be constitutionally independent. In other words, in a democratic constitution it is of paramount importance that the judges – who form part of the court system – are independent, impartial and free from interference from the other branches of government (particularly the executive). The principle of the independence of the judiciary embraces, *inter alia*, the notion that the judiciary must be free to determine disputes before them strictly in accordance with the law (see Chapter 13).

KEY FACTS

The reasoning behind the separation of powers includes the following:

- To avoid an abuse of state power by preventing a concentration of public power in one body/institution.

- To provide a system of checks and balances between the branches of government.

- To safeguard the independence of the judiciary.

- To provide efficient government.

5.6 The separation of powers in the United Kingdom

The question as to whether or not the United Kingdom adheres to the principles underpinning the separation of powers is somewhat controversial as there is no clear agreement on this point. It does depend, of course, in which sense the term is being used.

5.6.1 The separation of powers as part of the British constitution

For example, in *R v Her Majesty's Treasury, ex parte Smedley* [1985] 1 QB 657 Sir John Donaldson MR stated that:

> J 'Although the United Kingdom has no written constitution, it is a constitutional convention of the highest importance that the legislature and the judicature are separate and independent of one another.'

Similarly, Lord Diplock in *Duport Steels Ltd and Others v Sirs and Others* [1980] 1 All ER 529 has commented that:

'it cannot be too strongly emphasised that the British constitution, though largely unwritten, is firmly based on the separation of powers: Parliament makes the laws, the judiciary interpret them.'

Further, Lord Templeman in *M v Home Office and others* [1994] 1 AC 377 has noted that:

 'Parliament makes the law, the executive carry the law into effect and the judiciary enforce the law.'

5.6.2 The separation of powers not being part of the British constitution

In contrast, the academic writer de Smith has dismissed the separation of powers in the context of the United Kingdom by arguing that:

> 'No writer of repute would claim that it is a central feature of the modern British constitution'.

> S de Smith and R Brazier, *Constitutional and Administrative Law* (8th edn, Penguin, 1998), p 18.

Moreover, Lord Lloyd (an ex law lord), speaking in a debate on the proposed Supreme Court and speaking specifically in the context of the law lords sitting in Parliament (an overlap of the legislature and the judiciary), commented that:

> **Q** 'The theory of the separation of powers requires that they be kept separate. The answer is that the separation of powers is not part of our constitution'.
>
> *Hansard*, HL Vol 665, col 57.

5.6.3 Initial observations on the separation of powers and the British constitution

What is clear is that:

- Firstly, the British constitution does not follow a pure separation of powers with each branch of the state completely separated from each another in terms of functions and personnel. Instead, to the extent that it does adhere to the separation of powers, it follows a partial/modified version involving checks and balances.

- Secondly, even where the United Kingdom does depart from the doctrine of the separation of powers, these departures may well be driven by practical necessity. In any event, they may well be governed by constitutional conventions.

The issue of the separation of powers in the British constitution is inevitably less clear cut than in other countries. This is because in other democracies with a codified constitution the principle of the separation of powers has been specifically written into, and so is structurally part of, the constitutional text (eg France and the United States). In contrast, the British constitution has developed incrementally and organically over hundreds of years. It is perhaps worth remembering that the modern expression of the separation of powers is found in Montesquieu writing in the eighteenth century (and subsequently incorporated into the constitution of the United States). Yet a number of our constitutional rules and principles predate this, for instance, the office of the Prime Minister dates back to the first part of the eighteenth century. Finally, it is of interest to note that the institutional structure of the European Community does not exhibit a clear separation of powers (see section 15.2.2).

5.7 Aspects of the British constitution not in accord with the separation of powers

Detailed below are the main ways in which the constitution does not follow the separation of powers (pure or otherwise).

5.7.1 The parliamentary executive (an overlap of the legislature and the executive)

One of the main characteristics of the British constitution is that it has a parliamentary executive, as, by constitutional convention the executive (the political executive) is drawn from the legislature (Parliament). In general, the political executive (the government) comprises over 100 members, most of whom are drawn from the elected House of Commons. The remainder are peers in the House of Lords (see section 11.6). For example, in March 2007, the government comprised 113 members, 91 of whom were MPs from the House of Commons and 22 peers from the House of Lords.

In terms of personnel, therefore, it is clear there is an overlap between members of the executive and the legislature with members of the government enjoying both executive and legislative functions. Indeed, Bagehot writing in the nineteenth century noted that:

'The efficient secret of the English Constitution may be described as the close
union, the nearly complete fusion of the executive and legislative powers'.

W Bagehot, *The English Constitution* (Oxford University Press, re-printed 2001), p 11.

The parliamentary executive and accountable government

One clear advantage of a parliamentary executive is that the government is directly accountable and
responsible to Parliament, and in fact, this is a major principle of the constitution (see ministerial
responsibility at section 12.1). As government ministers are drawn from within Parliament, this
provides the opportunity for them to be accountable on a daily basis through the following
parliamentary mechanisms:

- written and oral questions (see section 12.4);
- debates (see section 12.5);
- select committees (see section 12.6.2).

In addition, s 2 of the House of Commons Disqualification Act 1975 specifically limits the
number of government ministers (ministerial offices) who can sit in the House of Commons to 95
MPs out of a total of 646 MPs. This, at least in constitutional theory, prevents the government
from dominating the House of Commons.

Notwithstanding the above, it is certainly the case that in the last few decades the parliamentary
executive has generally ensured dynamic government whereby the government has been able to
influence heavily the parliamentary legislative programme. A widely perceived difficulty, however, is
that due to the electoral system, the government generally speaking (though not at all times),
secures office following a general election with the support of a clear (and sometimes substantial)
majority of seats in the House of Commons. This in turn means that the government can
dominate the Commons to such an extent that it has led to the suggestion that the balance
between the executive and the legislature has swung too heavily in favour of the former. In fact,
Lord Hailsham writing in the 1970s suggested that our electoral system produced a government
which was akin to an 'elective dictatorship' (see section 9.8).

Although Parliament, in the context of the separation of powers, is the supreme legislative/law
making body, the question has to be asked as to whether in practice Parliament actually legislates or
whether it merely legitimises and 'rubber stamps' the Bills initiated by the government of the day.
Each year most Bills enacted as Acts of Parliament are government sponsored Bills. Few Bills which
become Acts have been drafted and initiated by members of Parliament themselves acting as
parliamentarians (known as Private Members' Bills).

The parliamentary executive and the devolved institutions

It is also worth noting that the devolved institutions in Scotland, Wales and Northern Ireland
exhibit a form of a parliamentary executive. For example, in Scotland the Scottish Executive

(effectively the Scottish Cabinet) is drawn from the Scottish Parliament (Members of the Scottish Parliament – MSPs).

The position in other countries

The feature of a parliamentary executive is not, of course, restricted to the United Kingdom. The Republic of Ireland with its written, entrenched codified constitution also has a parliamentary executive whereby the Irish Government (comprising the Taoiseach and Cabinet ministers) is drawn from, and constitutionally accountable to, the Irish Parliament (the Oireachtas).

In contrast, in the United States the President does not form part of the legislature as it is a presidential system of government with the President sitting separately from Congress. In France, Cabinet ministers do not sit in the French Parliament as Art 23 of the French constitution (Fifth Republic) states that membership of government is incompatible with that of Parliament. Both the United States and France reflect a greater degree of separation of powers between the executive and legislature than the United Kingdom.

ACTIVITY

Question

What do you think are the dangers of having a parliamentary executive, particularly in the context of the British constitution?

5.7.2 Delegated legislation (an overlap involving the executive performing a legislative function)

Introduction

Under the separation of powers, the constitutional function of the legislature is to enact law, and the role of the executive is to execute and apply it. The practice of delegated legislation, however, entrusts a law-making power onto a member of the executive (eg a government minister or a local authority). The process of delegated legislation involves Parliament passing an Act (the 'enabling' or 'parent' Act), which in turn confers a power on a minister to make delegated legislation (also known as secondary/subordinate legislation) which generally takes the form of a Statutory Instrument (see the example at section 5.4.3).

The rationale behind delegated legislation

The rationale behind delegating a legislative power onto the executive is partly one of practical necessity. In practice it would be impossible for Parliament to legislate all the details of all the laws that are necessary in a modern society. The general principle governing delegated legislation is that the enabling Act encapsulates the general principles/policies of the legislation, whilst the secondary legislation – made under the authority of that Act – supplements these general broad principles with detailed provisions. Thus, it fills in the fine details of legislation.

Delegated legislation also has practical uses, as it allows the law to be flexible and be responsive, for example, updating levels of fines. An example of a local authority enjoying a delegated legislative power to alter local car parking charges was illustrated at section 4.6.1.

Even though there is a widespread view endorsing the practical necessity for the continued use of delegated legislation (although not necessarily in the volume in which it is used), it still represents a violation of the separation of powers. It should also be remembered that the vast majority of domestic legislation which is passed is delegated, not primary Acts of Parliament.

There are however, both political and legal controls over the use of this type of legislation.

Parliamentary control of delegated legislation

This is covered at section 12.7.5.

Legal control of delegated legislation

Delegated legislation is also subject to scrutiny and control by the courts. It is a general legal principle that a minister can only pass delegated legislation that is authorised and envisaged by the parent Act. The executive must, therefore, pass legislation which is *intra vires* (within the legal powers conferred by the Act). If the legislation made is outside the powers conferred, and so beyond the purpose for which the delegated power was given, it can be declared *ultra vires* by the courts and invalidated. In this way, the courts minimise the practice of delegated legislation being a violation of the separation of powers. The courts ensure that the executive uses its conferred delegated legislative powers strictly for its envisaged purpose so that it is not abused. It also ensures that parliamentary sovereignty is upheld by ensuring that Parliament's will is not thwarted, for example, by a minister passing legislation which had not been specifically envisaged by Parliament. An example of the legal control exercised by the courts over the use of delegated legislation is illustrated by the following case:

CASE EXAMPLE

Chester v Bateson [1920] 1 KB 829

Section 1 of the Defence of the Realm Consolidation Act 1914 conferred the power on the Minister of Munitions to issue regulations (delegated legislation) to prevent the successful prosecution of the war being endangered. Under the Act, the minister issued reg 2A(2) which stated that 'no person shall, without the consent of the Minister of Munitions take … any proceedings for the purpose of obtaining an order or decree for the recovery of possession of, or for the ejectment of a tenant of, any dwelling house' in which a munitions worker was living.

CONTINUED ▶

Chester (a landlord) served on Bateson (a tenant employed in a shell shop) notice of his intention to recover possession of his property as Bateson's tenancy had expired. Bateson challenged this by contending that Chester had not obtained the consent of the minister before commencing proceedings. Chester contended that the Regulation was *ultra vires* the Defence of the Realm Consolidation Act 1914 and the court agreed. The court held that the Regulation effectively prevented the landlord from having access to the courts in order to recover his property without first obtaining the consent of the minister. Avory J stated that:

> **J** 'In my opinion there is not to be found in the statute [1914 Act] anything to authorise or justify a regulation having that result; and nothing less than express words in the statute taking away the right of the King's subjects of access to the Courts of Justice would authorise or justify it.'

Delegated legislation in other countries

The use of delegated legislation, of course, is not confined to the British constitution. In the Republic of Ireland, for example, although Art 15.2 of the Constitution states that only the Oireachtas may create laws, the Irish Parliament does, however, regularly delegate a power to make ministerial orders on government ministers. These legislative instruments are also supervised by the courts.

5.7.3 The Crown/monarch is formally involved in all three branches of government (an overlap of the legislature, executive and judiciary)

In the United Kingdom the term Crown can denote either the government/executive or the monarch. As noted at section 3.4.7, the United Kingdom has a monarchical constitution and the monarch is constitutionally involved (to a greater or lesser extent) in all three functions of government.

The monarch and the legislative function

The Queen is formally part of the legislature (Parliament) and involved in the legislative process as a Bill requires the granting of the Royal Assent in order for it to become an Act of Parliament. In fact, the supreme legislative power in the United Kingdom is technically known as the Queen in Parliament. The role of the monarch is reflected in the enacting formula of a typical public Bill:

BE IT ENACTED by the Queen's most Excellent Majesty, by and with the advice and consent of the Lords Spiritual and Temporal, and Commons, in this present Parliament assembled, and by the authority of the same, as follows ...

A slightly revised version is used where the Parliament Acts of 1911 and 1949 have been used (see section 10.10.1).

In practical reality, the role of the monarch in the legislative process is a purely formal one as by constitutional convention the monarch will grant her assent to a Bill unless her government ministers advise her not to do so. Similarly, in the Republic of Ireland the Head of State (President of Ireland) signs Bills passed by the Oireachtas to give them the force of law. In the United States, the President signs Bills passed by Congress (although he approves them, he can also veto them).

In addition, as part of the legislature, the Queen opens each new parliamentary session and delivers the 'Queen's Speech' which details the government's proposed legislative programme for the ensuing parliamentary session. By constitutional convention, the speech is, of course, written by the government of the day and represents the Bills which they anticipate will become law.

The monarch and the executive function

The monarch is constitutionally part of the executive as she is the Head of State and the political executive is known as Her Majesty's Government. The monarch appoints the Prime Minister together with other government ministers, although these appointments are in practice a formal process, as they are governed by constitutional convention. Although the monarch will formally appoint these ministers, this is done on the recommendation of the Prime Minister of the day and so the political reality is that it is the latter who actually chooses which individuals will occupy which particular ministerial office. The monarch is also Head of the armed forces and is in fact technically the Commander-in-Chief of the armed forces (the executive in practical terms).

The monarch and the judicial function

The monarch is also formally part of the judiciary in the sense that she is the source and font of all justice. In fact, judicial appointments are made in the name of the Crown (hence 'Her Majesty's Judges' who operate and dispense justice in the 'Royal Courts of Justice'). Although the monarch formally makes these judicial appointments, by constitutional convention, she will act on the basis of ministerial advice. From April 2006 the independent statutory Judicial Appointments Commission (created under the Constitutional Reform Act 2005) has been responsible for recommending judicial appointments for the Lord Chancellor to approve or reject. It is of constitutional interest to note that historically the judicial oath of allegiance sworn by judges is not to the British constitution or to the people, but instead to the Crown.

5.7.4 The House of Lords has both legislative and judicial functions (an overlap involving the judiciary performing a legislative function)

The dual constitutional function of the House of Lords

- Firstly, the House comprises part of the legislature as it is the upper chamber in Parliament. Thus, it plays an integral part in the law-making process.

- Secondly, the House, or more specifically a committee of the House known as the Appellate Committee of the House of Lords, acts as the highest domestic court in the United Kingdom (with the exception of Scottish criminal matters which proceed to the High Court of Justiciary). The judges in the Appellate Committee are technically known as the Lords of Appeal in Ordinary, but are commonly referred to as the law lords. In legal theory the law lords can perform two different constitutional functions:

  (i) A judicial function – they resolve legal disputes as part of the the Appellate Committee.

  (ii) A legislative function – they can engage in debate and vote on proposed legislation during the passage of a Bill in the second chamber.

The constitutional conventions which have regulated this breach of the separation of powers

In spite of this breach of the separation of powers, historically it has been mitigated by two constitutional conventions:

- Firstly, although technically any peer (legally trained or otherwise) could sit in the Appellate Committee, by constitutional convention only serving Lords of Appeal in Ordinary do so.

- Secondly, it became an established constitutional convention that law lords did not get involved in controversial political matters when taking part in the legislative functions of the House as a parliamentary chamber. In fact, in June 2000 the senior law lord, Lord Bingham issued the following self-denying ordinance as to when it would be constitutionally inappropriate for serving law lords to engage in the legislative proceedings of the chamber:

> **Q**
>
> 'As full members of the House of Lords the Lords of Appeal in Ordinary have a right to participate in the business of the House. However, mindful of their judicial role they consider themselves bound by two general principles when deciding whether to participate in a particular matter, or to vote: first, the Lords of Appeal in Ordinary do not think it appropriate to engage in matters where there is a strong element of party political controversy; and secondly the Lords of Appeal in Ordinary bear in mind that they might render themselves ineligible to sit judicially if they were to express an opinion on a matter which might later be relevant to an appeal to the House'.
>
> *Hansard*, HL Vol 614, col. 419.

The European Convention on Human Rights

It is worth pointing out that although it is unusual for judges to sit in a parliamentary body, under the European Convention on Human Rights, it appears that the United Kingdom does not have to comply with a pure separation of powers. This is illustrated in the following case decided by the European Court of Human Rights in 2004:

CASE EXAMPLE

Pabla Ky v Finland (2006) 42 EHRR 34

In 1997 an MP of the Finnish Parliament acted as an expert member of a panel of the Finnish Court of Appeal which rejected Pabla Ky's appeal concerning a rent contract. Pabla Ky contended that the dual constitutional function of the MP (ie as part of the legislature and the Court of Appeal) violated Art 6 of the European Convention protecting the right to a fair trial before an independent and impartial court.

A chamber of the European Court held by a majority that there had been no violation of Art 6 as the MP in the case had not previously participated in the passing of the legislation (Act on Commercial Leases 1993) which was at issue as he had not been part of Parliament at this time. The Court stated that:

> **J**
>
> 'The Court is not persuaded that the mere fact that the MP was a member of the legislature at the time when he sat on the applicant's appeal is sufficient to raise doubts as to the independence and impartiality of the Court of Appeal. While the applicant relies on the theory of separation of powers, this principle is not decisive in the abstract.' (*sic*)

A new Supreme Court

In any event, under the Constitutional Reform Act 2005, the law lords are scheduled to be removed from Parliament in 2009 and reconstituted as a separate Supreme Court (see section 22.2.1). This aspect of the Act is governed by a *sunrise* provision (s 148) which has the effect that the new Supreme Court will not come into force unless the Lord Chancellor is satisfied that the court would be provided with suitable accommodation. The court is scheduled to be activated in 2009, and until that time the law lords will continue to sit within the legislature. For a summary of the arguments for and against the creation of the Supreme Court see section 22.2.1.

ACTIVITY

Question

What do you think are the advantages and disadvantages of the present law lords having a dual constitutional role in the House of Lords? Revisit this activity after you have completed Chapter 22.

5.7.5 Parliament exercises functions other than legislative (an overlap involving the legislature performing a judicial function)

The nature of the law and custom of Parliament

Although Parliament is the legislature, it is also responsible for regulating, controlling and disciplining its members which are effectively judicial functions. These privileges are unique to the two Houses of Parliament and its members, and are derived from the law and custom of Parliament. The law and custom of Parliament, includes the following privileges:

- Freedom of speech.

- Freedom from arrest.

- To provide for its own composition.

- To regulate its own proceedings (including determining the legislative process).

- To compel witnesses to attend and give evidence.

These privileges are regulated by both Houses of Parliament. Each House exercises its own jurisdiction and can punish those individuals who disregard its rules or who commit a contempt of Parliament, for example, obstructing Parliament in its functions. This can include interfering with a witness or a Member of Parliament.

The High Court of Parliament

In these circumstances each House of Parliament acts as a constituent part of the High Court of Parliament, thereby performing a judicial function. In 2003, for instance, the House of Commons temporarily suspended an MP for breaching parliamentary rules. In effect, Parliament acts as a self-regulating body and the 'ordinary' courts exercise no jurisdiction over these matters.

Parliamentary law in other countries

The notion that the legislature regulates its own composition and proceedings is not confined to the United Kingdom. For example, in the Republic of Ireland, Art 15.10 of the constitution expressly authorises the two Houses of the Oireachtas to decide their own rules in terms of the rights of the Houses and their members. Further, if these rules are violated, each House may impose penalties. Similarly, Art I, s 5 of the United States constitution states that each Chamber of Congress determines its own internal rules of procedure.

5.7.6 Historically, the executive has exercised a judicial function (an overlap involving the executive performing a judicial function)

Ministers have, historically, been given powers which were, in effect, judicial in nature. For example, under s 35 of the Criminal Justice Act 1991 Parliament conferred a power on the Home Secretary to determine the period of imprisonment (the 'tariff') to be served by discretionary life prisoners. The constitutional rationale behind this power was that the Home Secretary has a general responsibility for public order and maintaining public confidence in the criminal justice system. The use of this power, however, was controlled legally by the courts in judicial review proceedings (see Chapters 19 and 20) as illustrated by the following case:

CASE EXAMPLE

R v Secretary of State for the Home Dept, ex parte Venables and Thompson **[1997] 3 All ER 97**

Venables and Thompson were convicted of the murder of two year old James Bulger. The trial judge stated that in his view the minimum period of detention necessary to satisfy retribution and deterrence was a tariff of eight years. The Lord Chief Justice advised a tariff of 10 years, but the Home Secretary, in exercising his powers under s 35 of the Criminal Justice Act 1991, imposed 15 years. In reaching this decision the Home Secretary indicated that he had had regard for the public concern regarding this case. A public petition including 278,300 signatures, over 5,000 letters and 20,000 'coupons' from a newspaper had demanded that Venables and Thompson should be detained for life.

CONTINUED ▶

Venables and Thompson challenged the use of the Home Secretary's discretion and the House of Lords held, *inter alia*, that he had acted unlawfully as he had misdirected himself by giving weight to irrelevant considerations (namely, the public protest directed to the detriment of these two particular individuals). Lord Steyn stated that:

> **J** 'In fixing a tariff the Home Secretary is carrying out, contrary to the constitutional principle of the separation of powers, a classic judicial function ... the power to fix a tariff is nevertheless equivalent to a judge's sentencing power. Parliament must be assumed to have entrusted the power to the Home Secretary on the supposition that, like a sentencing judge, the Home Secretary would not act contrary to fundamental principles governing the administration of justice.'

Thus, as the Home Secretary was exercising a sentencing power (a judicial function) he was required to remain detached from the pressures of public opinion (see also *R (Anderson) v Secretary of State for the Home Department* [2002] UKHL 46 at section 13.2.1). As a postscript to the *Venables* case, Venables and Thompson subsequently petitioned the European Court of Human Rights (*V & T v UK* (2000) 30 EHRR 121) and successfully contended that their right to a fair trial under Art 6 had been breached. In brief, the setting of the tariff (which was tantamount to a judicial sentence) had not been performed by an independent and impartial figure, as the Home Secretary was part of the executive. After this European ruling, Parliament enacted s 60 of the Criminal Justice and Courts Services Act 2000 which now requires that the tariff to be served by young offenders is to be determined by the trial judge. As a result, this realigned the British constitution more in accord with a stricter separation of powers. Nevertheless, today the executive still retains and exercises some recall and release powers in respect of specified serious offenders.

KEY FACTS

The following aspects of the British constitution are infringements of the separation of powers:

- The parliamentary executive whereby the executive is drawn from the legislature. Although this allows government ministers to be accountable directly to Parliament, there has been the concern that this overlap permits the executive to control the legislature.

CONTINUED ▸

KEY FACTS

- The practice of delegated legislation entrusts a law-making power on a member of the executive. In constitutional theory it is controlled by both parliamentary and legal means.
- The monarch is constitutionally involved (to a greater or lesser extent) in all three functions of government.
- The House of Lords has both legislative and judicial functions by acting as the second legislative chamber and as the highest domestic court of appeal.
- Parliament exercises functions other than legislative as it can act as the High Court of Parliament.
- Government ministers have historically exercised a judicial function in terms of sentencing, although this has been controlled by legal means.

5.7.7 The Privy Council (an overlap involving the executive performing legislative and judicial functions)

The Privy Council (which is part of central government and so continues to be part of the executive today) historically has acted as the chief advisory body to the monarch. Its importance, in modern times, however, has been superseded by the development of the Cabinet. In fact, the Privy Council has been described as:

'today little more than an organ for giving formal effect to certain acts done under prerogative or statutory powers'.

O Hood Phillips, P Jackson and P Leopold, *Constitutional and Administrative Law*
(8th edn, Sweet & Maxwell, 2001), p 334.

The Privy Council numbers around 500 members who comprise individuals of high rank. It includes, among others, the following:

- The Prime Minister.
- Cabinet ministers.
- The Leader of the Opposition.
- Senior judges (both from the United Kingdom and the Commonwealth).
- Other senior public figures.

Meetings of the Privy Council normally comprise:

- Meetings involving the monarch together with (typically) four selected Cabinet ministers (Her Majesty in Council) at which formal validity will be given to instruments/orders previously agreed at a Cabinet meeting.

- Meetings without the monarch (a Committee of the Privy Council).

The role of the Privy Council is to advise the Queen in carrying out her responsibilities as monarch. These responsibilities and acts comprise Orders in Council or proclamations. The latter are used, for example, to dissolve Parliament prior to a general election, or to declare war.

The legislative function of the Privy Council

The Privy Council has a legislative function as it can make orders, known as Orders in Council, which comprise:

- Statutory Orders in Council (a form of delegated legislation) – where the power to make the orders has been delegated by Statute onto Her Majesty. By constitutional convention she acts on the advice of her ministers. Such orders have been used to transfer government responsibilities between government departments (Ministers of the Crown Act 1975).

- Non-statutory orders – derived from the common law royal prerogative. Such orders have been used to regulate the Civil Service (see the *GCHQ* case at section 11.9.6).

As pointed out by Hood Phillips, the nature of an Order in Council can be legislative, executive or judicial.

The judicial function of the Privy Council

One committee of the Privy Council has a judicial function: the Judicial Committee of the Privy Council. This was established under the Judicial Committee Act 1833 and acts as the final court of appeal for various Commonwealth countries (eg Barbados), together with Guernsey, Jersey and the Isle of Man. In addition, the Privy Council also hears 'internal' devolution cases (for example, whether the Scottish Parliament has exceeded its legal powers under the Scotland Act 1998 – see Chapter 14).The members of the Judicial Committee comprise serving and retired law lords together with other senior United Kingdom judges. In addition, members of the court also include judges from the Commonwealth. When the new Supreme Court is activated it will assume responsibility for devolution issues.

5.7.8 The law officers (an overlap involving members of the government sitting in the legislature and performing a quasi-judicial function)

The Attorney General and Solicitor General are members of the government, but not the Cabinet (although the Attorney General can attend the latter). The Solicitor General acts as the deputy to the Attorney General. These law officers are chosen from MPs or peers and so are part of the legislature (they form part of the parliamentary executive). In March 2007, the Attorney General was drawn from the House of Lords and the Solicitor General from the House of Commons. The Attorney General is responsible for a number of bodies which include the Crown Prosecution Service and Serious Fraud Office and in line with the convention of ministerial responsibility is accountable to Parliament for them.

The law officers are the legal advisers to the government and can represent government departments in court. As noted by Bradley and Ewing, they perform a quasi-judicial role in relation to, for example, contempt of court proceedings. Moreover the Attorney-General's consent is required for the prosecution of specific criminal offences (although in this context, he should act independently of the government and not take instructions from it). He can also enforce public rights by suing on behalf of the public and referring a question of law to the Court of Appeal, as well as unduly lenient criminal sentences.

5.7.9 The Lord Chancellor (historically, an overlap of the legislature, executive and judiciary)

The office of the Lord Chancellor has traditionally been cited as a classic example of the way in which the United Kingdom violates the separation of powers. The Lord Chancellor, historically, has formed part of all three state institutions with his main responsibilities detailed below:

The legislature

The Lord Chancellor sat in the upper chamber as the impartial *ex officio* Speaker of the House of Lords and presided over the House. This role encompassed a number of ceremonial roles (eg the State opening of Parliament). He also exercised a limited power to keep order within the chamber and represented the House both domestically and internationally.

The executive

As a minister of the Crown, the Lord Chancellor was a senior member of the Cabinet and head of a major government department: the Lord Chancellor's Department. In June 2003 this department was replaced with the Department for Constitutional Affairs which had responsibility for, *inter alia*, the administration of legal aid. The Lord Chancellor was also a spokesman for the government in the House of Lords.

The judiciary

The Lord Chancellor could sit as a senior judge in the Court of Appeal, the Privy Council or the Appellate Committee. This judicial function was governed and regulated by a constitutional convention that the Lord Chancellor would not sit in clearly political cases or in which the government was a party. The Lord Chancellor was also Head of the Judiciary in England and Wales and President of the Supreme Court of Judicature (the collective term for the Court of Appeal,

High Court and Crown Court and not to be confused with the new Supreme Court under the Constitutional Reform Act 2005). The Lord Chancellor was also involved in the appointment of a wide range of judicial posts. For example, in respect of the law lords, by constitutional convention the Prime Minister would consult him on suitable candidates (these appointments would then be formally appointed by the monarch). In addition, the Lord Chancellor was responsible for processing complaints against judges and administering judicial discipline.

ACTIVITY

Question

What do you think were the dangers of the Lord Chancellor exercising all three functions indicated above?

Changes to the office of the Lord Chancellor made by the Constitutional Reform Act 2005

In June 2003, in pursuance of modernising the constitution and realigning it with the separation of powers, the government announced the abolition of the office of the Lord Chancellor. Simultaneously, the post of Secretary of State for Constitutional Affairs was established which it was envisaged would eventually supersede the office of the Lord Chancellor. However, the Constitutional Reform Bill proved to be highly contentious in the House of Lords and was amended so as to retain, and so merely modify, the office of the Lord Chancellor, rather than abolish the post outright. This explained the subsequent adoption the dual title of *Secretary of State for Constitutional Affairs and Lord Chancellor*. In essence, the changes effected by the Act in respect of the Lord Chancellor are as follows:

The legislature

- **The Speaker of the House of Lords**

In the context of reforming the office of the Lord Chancellor, it was necessary to reform his position as Speaker of the House of Lords. For one thing, s 2 of the Constitutional Reform Act 2005 made it clear that a future Lord Chancellor may not even be a peer (it had been a longstanding constitutional convention that he sat in the upper chamber). In 2006 the House of Lords agreed to the Report of the Select Committee on the Speakership of the House (First Report, HL Paper 92 (2005)). This report recommended that the House elect a Speaker for five years to replace the Lord Chancellor. In July 2006 the House elected Baroness Hayman as Lord Speaker.

- **The Lord Chancellor as a peer**

One issue raised by the Constitutional Reform Bill was whether a future Lord Chancellor/Secretary of State for Constitutional Affairs should continue to be drawn exclusively from the House of Lords. The House of Lords attempted to amend the Bill by codifying the constitutional convention that the Lord Chancellor should be a peer and therefore be unable to sit in the House of Commons. In the end, a compromise was reached between the government and the House of Lords with the effect that s 2 of the Act states that a person can not be recommended for appointment by the Prime Minister as Lord Chancellor unless he was qualified by experience which could include, for example, experience as a member of either House. As a result, a future Lord Chancellor may not necessarily be drawn from the second chamber: in June 2007 Jack Straw MP was appointed as Lord Chancellor and Secretary of State for Justice. In any event, his position as a government minister (and so part of the parliamentary executive) will still continue, of course, to represent a breach of the separation of powers.

The executive

- **The Lord Chancellor as a government minister**

The Lord Chancellor/Secretary of State will continue to act as a minister and head the Department for Constitutional Affairs (replaced in May 2007 by the Ministry for Justice) with responsibility for, *inter alia*, the administration of the courts. Although he inevitably will continue to form part of the Cabinet, with a dilution of his responsibilities, it remains to be seen how senior a figure he will be viewed in future. Indeed, his constitutional responsibilities within the Cabinet will continue to include protecting the independence of the judiciary and ensuring that the principles underpinning the rule of law are not infringed by government legislative proposals. In this context, s 17 of the Act sets out the oath to be sworn by the Lord Chancellor:

'I will respect the rule of law, defend the independence of the judiciary and discharge my duty to ensure the provision of resources for the efficient and effective support of the courts for which I am responsible.'

The judiciary

- **The appointment of judges**

In the event of a vacancy in England and Wales, since April 2006 the new statutory Judicial Appointments Commission (established under the Act) selects one candidate and presents that selection to the Lord Chancellor who can then either accept or reject the nomination. Although the Act reduces the discretion of the Lord Chancellor in making judicial appointments, it still retains him as part of the process (on whether the executive should be involved in judicial appointments see section 13.3).

- **The Lord Chancellor as a judge**

In terms of sitting as a judge, even before the Constitutional Reform Bill had been introduced into Parliament, Lord Falconer had already announced in the government's September 2003 consultation paper on the reform of the Lord Chancellor that he did not intend to sit as a judge as:

> **Q** 'It can no longer be appropriate for a senior judge to sit in Cabinet or for a Government Minister to be our country's senior judge. I have myself made it clear that I shall not sit judicially.'
>
> *Constitutional reform: reforming the office of the Lord Chancellor* CP 13/03 (2003), pp 5–6.

The Act now prohibits the office-holder of the Lord Chancellor from holding judicial office.

- **The Head of the Judiciary**

The Lord Chief Justice will assume the office of the President of the Courts of England and Wales and the Act gives effect to a *concordant* which sets out the constitutional relationship between the Lord Chancellor (representing the executive) and the Lord Chief Justice (representing the judiciary).

ACTIVITY

Essay writing

Compare and contrast the legislative, executive and judicial roles exercised by the Lord Chancellor before and after the enactment of the Constitutional Reform Act 2005.

5.7.10 Judges as legislators (an overlap involving the judiciary performing a legislative function)

In the British constitution the judicial function involves:

- resolving legal disputes
- determining the law laid down in (a) statutes and (b) the common law and
- providing relevant remedies.

This necessarily raises the question of where the constitutional line exists between the act of interpreting and the act of legislating, and whether the courts ever exercise a *de facto* legislative function.

The interpretation of statutes

In interpreting statutes, the constitutional role of the courts is to ascertain the intention of Parliament when it passes legislation. The obvious difficulty is that words may have a variety of different possible meanings, and in order to circumscribe the role of the courts when determining the meaning of legislative provisions, the judiciary have developed a number of self-limiting principles of statutory interpretation which assist them. For example, the literal rule requires j to give words their ordinary and natural meaning.

In addition, judges will construe unclear ambiguous legislation in the light of certain constitutional principles such as the right of access to the courts. These constitutional presumptions are, of course, judicial creations and determined by the judiciary themselves. For instance, in *Chester v Bateson* at section 5.7.2, Avory J made it clear that nothing less than express words in the Defence of the Realm Consolidation Act 1914 would justify a regulation passed under it which denied a person access to the courts and the administration of justice.

The common law

The common law involves the courts declaring points of law in the context of cases that come before them for their resolution. The gradual development of the common law (which is achieved by the courts making decisions in the context of case law) necessarily permits a degree of flexibility in allowing common law principles to develop and adapt to changing circumstances (social or moral). This is illustrated particularly in the context of the private law of negligence which has progressively developed during the twentieth century.

In *Duport Steels Ltd and Others v Sirs and Others* [1980] 1 All ER 529 Lord Scarman noted that society had permitted the judges in the context of the common law and equity 'to formulate and develop the law'. Furthermore, in *Malone v Metropolitan Police Commissioner* [1979] Ch 344 Sir Robert Megarry VC made it clear that at times judges do legislate, albeit only interstitially, and he specifically distinguished between 'The extension of the existing laws and principles' and the creation of wholly new rights, for example in the instant case, a tort of privacy (see section 6.7.9). In short, it is Parliament's role to create such new rights.

In the context of judges and the legislative function, it is pertinent to repeat the point that Dicey made a century ago:

> 'A large proportion of English law is in reality made by our judges ... the adhesion by our judges to precedent, that is, their habit of deciding one case in accordance with the principle, or supposed principle, which governed a former case, leads inevitably to the gradual formation by the courts of fixed rules for decision, which are in effect laws'.

A Dicey, *Introduction to the Study of the Law of the Constitution* (10th edn, Macmillan, 1959), p 60.

Also, some judges perform a legislative function when they make rules of procedure, practice rules and directions for the courts to follow. For example, when the new Supreme Court is activated, s 45 of the Constitutional Reform Act 2005 will confer a power on the President of the Supreme Court to make Supreme Court Rules which will govern the practice and procedure to be followed in court.

In 1966 Lord Gardiner issued on behalf of the law lords the following seminal practice statement which enabled the House of Lords to depart from its previous decisions (*Practice Statement* [1966] 1 WLR 1234):

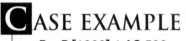

> 'Their Lordships nevertheless recognise that too rigid adherence to precedent may lead to injustice in a particular case and also unduly restrict the proper development of the law. They propose, therefore, to modify their present practice and, while treating former decisions of this House as normally binding, to depart from a previous decision when it appears right to do so.'

In terms of whether the judges perform a legislative/law-making function, Barnett has argued that:

> 'it is artificial to deny that judges "make law". Every new meaning conferred on a word, every application of a rule by a new situation, whether by way of statutory interpretation or under common law, "creates" new law. Judges have themselves abandoned the fiction of the "declaratory theory" which asserts that they do not "make" law, but merely discover its true meaning. From the separation of powers perspective, judicial law making should cause disquiet only if judges display overtly dynamic law making tendencies'.

> H Barnett, *Constitutional and Administrative law* (6th edn, Routledge–Cavendish, 2006), p 109.

An interesting example of the judiciary effectively 'making' the law is illustrated by the following case.

CASE EXAMPLE

R v R [1992] 1 AC 599

In this case the House of Lords set aside the long-standing common law rule that a husband could not rape his wife. Even though this historic rule was viewed as anachronistic, the ruling nevertheless represents a *de facto* use of law making power. In constitutional terms, the process must necessarily be seen as *de facto* legislative, with the courts developing/creating the law.

In addition, at times some members of the judiciary may perform a quasi-executive function. For instance, magistrates (who from part of the judicial arm of the state) control the granting of certain types of licences.

Judicial law making outside the United Kingdom

It should be noted that the notion that judges are *de facto* lawmakers is not confined to the British constitution. For example, it is also illustrated in the following judicial decision in the context of the United States constitution:

CASE EXAMPLE

Marbury v Madison (1803) 1 Cranch 137

In this case, the United States Supreme Court enunciated a major principle underpinning the American constitution by declaring that the Supreme Court had the constitutional power to declare an Act of Congress to be unconstitutional (and so invalid) where it was repugnant to the written constitution. This case illustrates the powerful position of the judiciary in relation to a constitution, as the power to declare congressional legislation legally unconstitutional had not been specifically and expressly stated in the text of the constitution, but instead had been deemed implicit by the Supreme Court.

Similarly, in the context of the European Community, the European Court of Justice in Luxembourg has developed fundamental principles of European law, which have not been expressly or explicitly spelt out in the 1957 Treaty of Rome. For example, neither of the following principles were expressly written in the text of the EC Treaty, but were nevertheless deemed implicit:

- The principle of direct effect which conferred European Community law rights on individuals which could be enforced in the domestic courts of Member States.

- The principle of the primacy of European Community law which required that where Community law and domestic law were inconsistent, the former must prevail.

ACTIVITY

Essay writing

To what extent do judges ever perform a legislative function and what are the constitutional implications of this?

5.7.11 Administrative tribunals (a tribunal with a judicial function having a link with the executive)

Many legal disputes that an individual will have with the state will be resolved not by the ordinary courts of law, but instead by an administrative tribunal. These tribunals will be staffed by experts and act in a judicial manner and apply law to the facts before them. Historically, however, there has been concern that in terms of the separation of powers these bodies were effectively associated with the administration over which they were adjudicating (see section 21.1.3).

KEY FACTS

The following aspects of the British constitution are infringements of the separation of powers:

- The Privy Council is an executive body which has legislative and judicial functions.

- The Attorney General is part of the government (ie the parliamentary executive) and has a quasi-judicial function.

- The judges inevitably perform a *de facto* legislative function in interpreting statutory provisions and developing common law principles.

- Tribunals perform a judicial function, but historically there has been concern of their close relationship with the administration (the executive).

- The Lord Chancellor has historically had a significant role to play in all three state institutions, although these breaches were partly regulated by constitutional convention.

5.8 Aspects of the British constitution in accord with the separation of powers

5.8.1 Introduction

Although the above examples indicate the ways in which the United Kingdom infringes the doctrine of the separation of powers, these violations may be driven by practical considerations (eg delegated legislation and judges making practice rules). In any event, the breaches of the separation of powers may well be governed by constitutional conventions. For example we have already noted the following:

- The parliamentary executive (see section 5.7.1) – although government ministers are drawn from Parliament, they are governed by the conventions of collective and individual ministerial responsibility.

- The law lords (see section 5.7.4) – although the law lords have dual constitutional functions, they are regulated by the convention not to become involved in politically controversial matters.
- The role of the monarch (see section 5.7.3) – although the monarch is involved in all three state institutions, these are largely formal overlaps as she is governed by convention (eg in respect of the Royal Assent).
- The Attorney General (see section 5.7.8) – by convention, acts independently of the government in granting consent in respect of prosecutions for specific criminal offences.
- The Lord Chancellor (see section 5.7.9) – historically for example, when about to speak for the government in the House of Lords, by convention he would physically move from the woolsack to indicate that he was no longer acting as the impartial Speaker of the House.

The existence of these constitutional conventions, therefore, serves to mitigate the fact that there is a notional or apparent breach of the separation of powers.

5.8.2 The existence of three state institutions

It is also clear that (at least descriptively) it is possible to identify the three state institutions in the British constitution as follows:

- The legislature (the United Kingdom Parliament).
- The executive (the United Kingdom Government comprising the Prime Minister, government ministers, government departments, civil servants together with local authorities).
- The judiciary (the judges in the various different jurisdictions of the United Kingdom).

It is also worth noting that in terms of dividing state power:

- The legislative branch is divided into two chambers (the House of Commons and the House of Lords). Parliament, therefore, does not necessarily act as a single cohesive force (see section 10.12).
- The executive branch is divided into central and local government. As indicated earlier, there can be tension and conflict between these two branches of the executive.

Both of the above divisions ensure that there are competing power sources within the legislative and executive state institutions.

- The judicial branch of state is divided into a formal hierarchical court structure and a system of tribunals.

The following examples illustrate how the British constitution, to varying degrees, respects the doctrine of the separation of powers (whether a pure or weaker version of the principle):

5.8.3 The legislature and judiciary

- **Historically there has been no judicial review of parliamentary legislation**

Parliamentary Sovereignty is the foundation of the British constitution with the result that the courts (at least historically) could not strike down an Act of Parliament. This respects the pure doctrine of the separation of powers with the courts recognising the constitutional function of Parliament which is to enact primary legislation (Parliament is, of course, democratically elected). The role of the courts, accordingly, is simply to interpret Acts of Parliament and not to question or challenge them (but now see the impact of European Community law at section 15.6).

In countries such as the United States and the Republic of Ireland, however, their respective Supreme Courts can invalidate legislation passed by the legislature (as part of the checks and balances of the separation of powers and the constitution). In contrast, France exhibits a purer separation of powers as the French courts lack the constitutional authority to judicially review legislation passed by the French Parliament. However, the French Constitutional Council can consider the 'constitutionality' of legislation before it becomes law. If such a measure is declared 'unconstitutional' (as being contrary to the constitution) it cannot be promulgated.

- **The *sub judice* resolution**

Parliament recognises the respective constitutional roles of the court and the legislature through the use of the *sub judice* resolution. This prohibits parliamentary members commenting on 'live' or pending cases before the courts. This rule protects the role of the judiciary in carrying out its judicial business free from interference (see section 13.4.3).

- **Parliamentary criticism of the judiciary**

By constitutional convention, parliamentary members refrain from criticism of individual judges except on a substantive motion, for example supporting an address to remove him. This prevents interference with the judicial function.

- **Internal parliamentary proceedings**

The judiciary will refrain from trespassing upon the constitutional province of Parliament in respect of the law and custom of Parliament. For example, they will refuse to investigate the internal proceedings of Parliament, even if specifically invited to do so in litigation. In *British Railways Board v Pickin* [1974] AC 765 the House of Lords held that if it is alleged that Parliament had been 'deceived' into passing a particular piece of legislation, then this is a matter for Parliament to rectify, and not the courts (see sections 7.8.1 and 8.7.2).

- **Judicial appointments**

There is a degree of separation between the legislature and the judiciary in that the former has no part to play in the appointment of judges, although Parliament can remove the senior judiciary (see section 13.4.1). In contrast, in the United States putative Justices of the Supreme

Court have to undergo a congressional hearing before the Senate (the upper chamber in Congress), who are required to approve these appointments.

- **Judicial disqualification**

  Section 1 of the House of Commons Disqualification Act 1975 prohibits full-time members of the judiciary from sitting in the House of Commons thereby achieving a degree of separation between the judiciary and the legislature.

- **The law lords**

  As noted at section 5.7.4, although the law lords currently still form part of the House of Lords, historically this violation of the separation of powers has been mitigated by the 2000 self-denying ordinance. In fact, it should be noted that some law lords (such as the senior law lord, Lord Bingham) have effected a complete practical separation by specifically refraining from engaging in either debates or voting on legislation. In July 2004 the House of Lords Select Committee on the Constitutional Reform Bill (Volume 1: Report, HL Paper 125-I (2004), Appendix 8) supplied a table which indicated that up to the time of its Report (July 2004), eight out of the then 12 serving law lords had made no interventions in debates in the chamber.

  In any event, the Constitutional Reform Act 2005 paves the way for the establishment of a new and separate Supreme Court. This court will be physically, institutionally and legally separate from Parliament and will bring the British constitution more into line with a stricter separation of powers. It is scheduled to be activated in 2009.

- **Statutory interpretation**

  In terms of interpreting legislation, the courts have consistently reiterated the constitutional role of the judge in relation to statute law. This is illustrated by the House of Lords in the following case, where they effectively rebuked the Court of Appeal in terms of how they had interpreted a statutory provision:

CASE EXAMPLE

Duport Steels Ltd and Others v Sirs and Others **[1980] 1 All ER 529**

The case concerned the very restrictive interpretation which the Court of Appeal had given to s 13 of the Trade Union Labour Relations Acts 1974 (as amended in 1976) which, in effect, conferred an immunity in tort in respect of acts done by a person in contemplation or furtherance of a trade dispute.

On 2 January 1980 the Iron and Steel Trades Confederation (ISTC) called a strike of its members employed by the British Steel Corporation with which it was in dispute concerning wage rates for 1980. In an effort to exert pressure on the government to provide British Steel with extra public funds so that it could make a more acceptable offer

CONTINUED ▸

to ISTC, by 17 January the latter had resoved to extend the strike to its union members in the private sector of the steel industry.

Duport Steels Ltd together with other private companies sought injunctions against Sirs (general secretary of ISTC) and others against inducing private employees to break their contracts of employment and come out on strike. Although at first instance the injunctions were refused, they were granted by the Court of Appeal on the basis that the dispute on 17 January was a second dispute, this time involving the government, and therefore did not fall within a trade dispute (as the government was not an employer). The court also considered the injustice to employers and workers in the private sector and the economic consequences for the country as a whole of the extension of the strike.

The House of Lords, however, reversed this decision and stated that the test was subjective in that, provided Sirs and others honestly believed at the time that their action might help one of the parties to the trade dispute achieve their objectives, then they would be entitled to immunity in tort under s 13. The action of Sirs and others, therefore, had been taken in furtherance of the trade dispute with British Steel. Lord Diplock reaffirmed that the role of the courts in relation to statutory provisions was to give effect to the words that Parliament had approved:

> J 'Where the meaning of the statutory words is plain and unambiguous it is not for the judges to invent fancied ambiguities as an excuse for failing to give effect to its plain meaning because they themselves consider that the consequences of doing so would be inexpedient, or even unjust or immoral. In controversial matters such as are involved in industrial relations there is room for differences of opinion as to what is expedient, what is just and what is morally justifiable. Under our Constitution it is Parliament's opinion on these matters that is paramount.'

Similarly, Lord Scarman noted that his criticism of the Court of Appeal was:

> J '... that in their desire to do justice the court failed to do justice according to law.'

It should also be pointed out that under s 3 of the Human Rights Act 1998, all courts and tribunals are now required to interpret all legislation in line with the rights detailed in the European Convention on Human Rights where it is possible to do so. It is clearly the case that this statutory obligation has inevitably given the judges a more dynamic and purposive approach to statutory interpretation. Nevertheless, Lord Woolf CJ in *Poplar Housing and Regeneration*

Community Association Ltd v Donoghue [2001] EWCA Civ 595 made it very clear that the constitutional role of the judiciary in relation to the Human Rights Act 1998 (and the constitution in general) was to interpret legislation and not to legislate:

> **J** 'It is difficult to overestimate the importance of s 3 ... When the court interprets legislation usually its primary task is to identify the intention of Parliament. Now, when s 3 applies, the courts have to adjust their traditional role in relation to interpretation so as to give effect to the direction contained in s 3 ... [but] ... s 3 does not entitle the court to *legislate* (its task is still one of *interpretation*, but interpretation in accordance with the direction in s 3).'

A case, however, in which the House of Lords arguably crossed the line between interpreting and legislating was in *R v A (Complainant's sexual history)* [2001] UKHL 25 (see section 17.6.1).

KEY FACTS

The following aspects of the British constitution are in accord with the principles underpinning the separation of powers (a pure version or otherwise) in respect of the legislature and judiciary:

- The *sub judice* resolution ensures that Parliament does not interfere with the constitutional role of the court which is to resolve cases free from influence or interference.

- By constitutional convention, parliamentary members refrain from criticising individual judges, as this could undermine their perceived independence.

- The courts do not interfere with the internal proceedings of Parliament.

- Parliament is not involved in the appointment of judges.

- Full-time judges are precluded from sitting in the House of Commons.

- In 2009 under the Constitutional Reform Act 2005 the serving law lords are scheduled to be removed from Parliament and reconstituted in a separate Supreme Court.

- The judges have consistently reiterated their limited constitutional role in respect of interpreting statutory provisions.

5.8.4 The judiciary and executive

- **Judicial independence of the executive**

It is a fundamental constitutional principle that the judiciary must remain independent of the executive (see Chapter 6). Indeed, s 3 of the Constitutional Reform Act 2005 specifically requires ministers of the Crown to uphold judicial independence and prohibits them from having special access to the judiciary. Moreover, the Act put on a statutory footing the *concordat* which had been agreed between the Lord Chief Justice and the Lord Chancellor. The *concordat* spelt out the constitutional relationship (and demarcated the boundaries) between the executive and the judicial arms of the state.

- **Executive criticism of judges**

By constitutional convention, members of the executive do not criticise individual judges.

- **The removal of senior judges**

Senior judges are not removable by the government of the day, but instead by Parliament. This means that the executive cannot simply remove a judge who has proved to be troublesome for the government in court.

- **Judicial review (adhering to the separation of powers?)**

Judicial review involves the courts reviewing the actions of the executive to ensure that ministers/executive officials act lawfully and strictly with their legal powers when they, for example:

- Enact delegated legislation.
- Make a public law decision.
- Exercise a public law discretion.

In constitutional terms, on the one hand, judicial review could be seen as a violation of a pure separation of powers as the judiciary is effectively interfering with the actions of another state institution: the executive. Conversely, on the other hand, the process of judicial review could be viewed as part of a modified version of the separation of powers, with the courts checking and balancing the executive, thereby avoiding an abuse of executive power.

In the United Kingdom, the courts are conscious of their constitutional position in supervising the activities of the executive. For instance, in the context of an alleged abuse of power by a local authority in respect of how it exercised a particular public law discretion (eg in terms of the allocation of financial resources), the judges will act with restraint in ensuring that they do not substitute their judicial view of how a particular public law discretion should have been exercised with that of the local authority. Instead, they ensure that the discretion exercised was within the legal limits of the local authority. Judicial review is essentially a procedural mechanism which is aimed at the decision-making process, rather than the decision itself *per se* (see section 19.2.2).

In the context of the relationship between the separation of powers and judicial review, Craig has noted that the principle of the separation of powers:

'operates as a source of judicial legitimacy, with the courts defending their role as the rightful interpreters of legislation, and of the legality of executive action. It serves also as the foundation for judicial restraint, with the courts being mindful of not substituting their view on matters of discretion for that of the body to whom Parliament has granted the power'.

P Craig 'Fundamental Principles of Administrative Law' in D Feldman (ed),
English Public Law (Oxford University Press, 2004), p 707.

- **The reform of the Lord Chancellor**

As indicated earlier, under the Constitutional Reform Act 2005 the Lord Chancellor will no longer be the Head of the judiciary in England and Wales and will share the administering of judicial discipline with the Lord Chief Justice. Moreover, the Lord Chancellor will no longer sit as a judge thereby making a clearer separation between the judiciary and the Lord Chancellor (who still remains a member of the political executive).

KEY FACTS

The following aspects of the British constitution are in accord with the principles underpinning the separation of powers (a pure version or otherwise) in respect of the executive and judiciary:

- Section 3 of the Constitutional Reform Act 2005 specifically requires ministers of the Crown to uphold judicial independence and prohibits them from having special access to the judiciary.
- By constitutional convention, members of the executive do not criticise individual judges.
- The senior judiciary are protected from removal by the executive.
- The process of judicial review could be viewed as part of a modified version of the separation of powers, with the courts checking and balancing the executive, thereby avoiding an abuse of executive power.

CONTINUED ▶

KEY FACTS

- The Lord Chancellor's historic judicial functions have been curtailed under the Constitutional Reform Act 2005. In particular, he will no longer be the Head of the Judiciary in England and Wales or sit as a judge.

5.8.5 The executive and legislature

- **The House of Commons Disqualification Act 1975**

Section 1 of the House of Commons Disqualification Act 1975 prohibits specified non-elected members of the executive, ie members of the armed forces, civil servants and the police from sitting in the lower House, thereby achieving a degree of separation between the executive and the House of Commons. In addition, as indicated earlier, the Act specifically limits the number of government ministers who can sit in the House of Commons to 95 MPs thereby, in constitutional theory, preventing the government from dominating the House of Commons.

- **Lord Chancellor**

As the Lord Chancellor is no longer the Speaker in the House of Lords, this has severed the historic connection between the Speaker and the government (although historically the Lord Chancellor, despite being a member of the executive, was of course supposed to act impartially when acting as Speaker). The new elected Lord Speaker of the House of Lords is not a member of the Cabinet and is politically impartial.

KEY FACTS

The following aspects of the British constitution are in accord with the principles underpinning the separation of powers (a pure version or otherwise) in respect of the executive and legislature:

- The House of Commons Disqualification Act 1975 prohibits specified non-elected members of the executive from sitting in the House of Commons.

- The Speaker of the House of Lords is no longer a member of the Cabinet.

ACTIVITY

Essay writing

Do you think that the British constitution adheres to the principle of the separation of powers? Do you think that any departures are justified?

5.9 Conclusion

Even before the advent of the Constitutional Reform Act 2005, Munro had made the following concluding observation concerning the separation of powers in the British constitution:

> 'In a variety of important ways, ideas of the separation of powers have shaped constitutional arrangements and influenced our constitutional thinking, and continue to do so. The separation in the British constitution, although not absolute, ought not to be lightly dismissed'.

C Munro, *Studies in Constitutional Law* (2nd edn, Butterworths, 1999), p 332.

Table 5.1: The separation of powers in the British constitution

	Legislature/ Legislative function	Executive/ Executive function	Judiciary/ Judicial function
Parliament	**Constitutional function to pass primary legislation**		• The High Court of Parliament – regulates its own proceedings
Executive	• Passes delegated legislation • Forms the parliamentary executive	**Constitutional function to determine and initiate policy. Implements and carries out the law**	• Historically, given a judicial function in the context of sentencing
Judiciary	• Develops the common law • Law lords sit in Parliament until 2009 (CRA 2005)		**Constitutional function to resolve legal disputes and interpret the law**

CONTINUED ▶

	Legislature/ Legislative function	Executive/ Executive function	Judiciary/ Judicial function
The monarch	• Queen in Parliament • Royal Assent	• Her Majesty's Government ministers	• Her Majesty's judges and the Royal Courts of Justice
The Lord Chancellor	• Part of the parliamentary executive • Historically, was Speaker of the House of Lords • Historically, major government spokesman in the House	• Senior Cabinet minister and head of a government department • Approves judicial appointments	• Historically, used to sit as a judge and act as the Head of the judiciary (now see CRA 2005)
The Privy Council	• Orders in Council	• Precursor to the Cabinet and advises the monarch	• Judicial Committee of the Privy Council

Further reading

Alder, J, *Constitutional and Administrative Law* (5th edn, Palgrave/Macmillan, 2005), Chapter 6.

Barber, N, 'Prelude to the Separation of Powers' [2001] 61 CLJ 59.

Barendt, E, 'Separation of Powers and Constitutional Government' [1995] PL 599.

Bradley, A and Ewing, K, *Constitutional and Administrative Law* (14th edn, Pearson/Longman, 2007), Chapter 5.

Munro, C, 'The Separation of Powers: Not such a Myth' [1981] PL 19.

Munro, C, *Studies in Constitutional Law* (2nd edn, Butterworths, 1999), Chapter 9.

chapter 6

THE RULE OF LAW ■

AIMS AND OBJECTIVES □□□

At the end of this chapter you should be able to:

■ Explain what is meant by the rule of law

■ Explain Dicey's conception of the rule of law

■ Explain the criticism of Dicey's conception of the rule of law

■ Assess the application of the rule of law to the British constitution

6.1 Definition

'For my part two core meanings of the rule of law are essential to an understanding of our public law. The first is not a legal concept. The rule of law is a term of political philosophy or institutional morality. It conveys the idea of government not under men but under laws. It eschews the instrumentalist conception of law that enables an oppressive regime to attain its aims by the use of law, as happened in South Africa in the apartheid era. It addresses the moral dimension of public power …

In its second sense the rule of law is a general principle of constitutional law. Its central focus is to constrain the abuse of official power. It protects a citizen's right to legal certainty in respect of interference with his liberties. It guarantees access to justice. It ensures procedural fairness over much of the range of administrative decision-making by officials'.

Lord Steyn, *The Constitutionalisation of Public Law* (The Constitution Unit, 1999), p 4.

In essence, the rule of law means that government and its officials, together with private citizens, must act under the law. The rationale behind it is to control the exercise of public power by the state by ensuring that it is exercised strictly within legal limits. As such, the courts play a central role in upholding the rule of law and therefore, this principle is inextricably linked with the independence of the judiciary (see Chapter 13).

The rule of law does not have one clear fixed meaning, but instead has been subject to a number of different interpretations. It is a key component of the principle of constitutionalism, namely, governmental action must be subject to limitation in order to avoid an abuse of power.

The rule of law is not a modern concept, but is of ancient origin as it was Aristotle (*The Politics*) (Penguin, 1962) p 143) who stated that:

> 'It is preferable that that law should rule rather than any single one of the citizens.'

In other words, under the rule of men, citizens are governed by men (or a group of individuals) who are capable of acting in an irrational, capricious and vindictive manner. In contrast, under the rule of law, citizens are governed by an overarching universal law. Moreover, 'the law', unlike the rule of men, is not applied in a capricious or irrational fashion and governs the actions of private individuals and state officials alike. In short, all are under the law. In this context, Lord Denning MR in the Court of Appeal in *Gouriet v Union of Post Office Workers* [1977] 1 QB 729 commented that:

> **J** 'To every subject in this land, no matter how powerful, I would use Thomas Fuller's words over 300 years ago: "Be you ever so high, the law is above you".'

In the United Kingdom, in the absence of a written codified constitution legally restraining the actions of the government, the rule of law assumes a particularly important position.

In modern parlance, the rule of law can be interpreted in different ways. For example, Bradley and Ewing (*Constitutional and Administrative Law* (14th edn, Pearson/Longman, 2007), pp 99–103) identified the following three elements of the rule of law today that they consider to be particularly worth noting:

- Law and order is better than anarchy.

- There should be government according to the law.

- The rule of law as a political doctrine.

6.2 The rule of law as a legal principle

6.2.1 A legal principle and procedural mechanism

In this interpretation, the rule of law is seen as a procedural mechanism (Barnett referred to it as a procedural device) controlling and limiting the exercise of governmental/public power. The actions of state officials (eg government ministers or police officers) which impact on the individual should have a clear foundation in law. As noted by Bradley and Ewing this is the principle of legality.

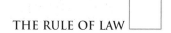

For example, Art 5(2) of the European Convention on Human Rights states that:

 'Everyone who is arrested shall be informed promptly, in a language which he understands, of the reasons for his arrest and of any charge against him.'

These requirements ensure that an arrested person understands why, and on what grounds (ie legal basis), he has been arrested and detained by the state. It also makes state officials legally accountable for their actions, as when they interfere with individual freedoms, they are required to justify legally their actions. The rule of law in this sense is a procedural mechanism (the principle of legality) which ensures that government and its officials act under the law. An interesting example of the principle of legality is illustrated by the following case.

CASE EXAMPLE

R (Jones) v Chief Constable of Cheshire Constabulary, Police [2005] EWHC 2457 (Admin)

Jones had been issued a pedlar's certificate under the Pedlars Act 1871, and when arrested and interviewed by the police on suspicion in relation to an offence of dishonesty (although he was never charged), his certificate was seized. The court granted a declaration (in judicial review proceedings) that the police had no lawful power to seize or revoke the certificate as the Pedlars Act 1871 had contained no provision to that effect.

In other countries, the principle that government action must be in accordance with the law will be specifically set out in the written codified constitutional text. For example, as noted at section 2.4.4, in Sweden Chapter 1 of the 1975 Instrument of Government states that 'Public power shall be exercised under law'. Similarly, Art 20 of the German constitution states that:

 'the executive and the judiciary are bound by the law.'

Thus, in the United Kingdom, in the absence of a written codified document legally and constitutionally restraining the power of government, the rule of law is of paramount importance. The judiciary uphold the constitutional principle that all individuals (both private and state officials) are under the law. In particular, they ensure that government and its officials are accountable to the law through the procedural mechanism of judicial review (see Chapters 19 and 20). In brief, the judiciary supervises the actions of the executive to ensure that it acts strictly within its legal powers.

6.2.2 The limitation of the procedural mechanism

As noted by Bradley and Ewing, the rule of law should not simply be confined to the consideration of the principle of legality. In other words, if the rule of law is viewed exclusively as a procedural mechanism which asks simply (and only) whether a government official possessed for example, the requisite legal power to arrest an individual (ie had the state official followed the law?), then this in itself does not necessarily fully protect the individual (see the imaginary Detention Act 2011 detailed at section 6.4). This is because it is possible – in the British constitution at least – for exceptionally wide and extensive powers of arrest and detention to be conferred legally on state officials. Such powers could in effect be used almost at will and to the clear detriment of the individual. Notwithstanding their impact on individual freedoms, if these powers had a legal basis to them, under the principle of legality (which requires state action to have a legal foundation), the use of them would be lawful as these powers would necessarily be legitimised by the law. In strict procedural terms, therefore, these state officials would be acting 'according to the law'.

The rule of law, accordingly, may also embrace a broader meaning with a substantive content which would, among other things, critically evaluate laws that have been made in terms of their impact on human rights and other fundamental principles (see section 6.4).

KEY FACTS

The rule of law as a legal principle ensures that government acts under the law.

In this sense it is a procedural mechanism which protects the individual from an unlawful use of state power as it requires state officials to justify their actions.

ACTIVITY

Essay writing

What is the difference between the rule of law and the rule of men?

6.3 The rule of law as a political ideal/theory

6.3.1 A formal view of the rule of law

This interpretation of the rule of law is concerned with the form that the law takes. In other words, once a law has been passed in the requisite constitutional manner (eg in the United Kingdom this would involve the Queen in Parliament passing an Act of Parliament), the law itself should exhibit particular characteristics.

6.3.2 Raz and the rule of law

law quarterly review

Raz is a major exponent of a formal conception of the rule of law (J Raz, 'The Rule of Law and its Virtue' (1977) 93 LQR 195). In essence, he stated that the rule of law is a political ideal which means that individuals should be ruled by the law and that the law must be able to guide individuals if they are to obey the law. As a consequence, this allows individuals to plan their lives accordingly.

In particular Raz argued that the making of laws should be guided by, *inter alia*, the following principles:

'(1) All laws should be prospective, open and clear'.

Prospective laws – Laws should be prospective so that laws look forward rather than punishing behaviour retrospectively. Such retrospective laws are objectionable because, of course, the individual has no control over their past conduct. By their nature, they do not permit the law to guide and influence an individual's behaviour. In this context, Willes J in *Phillips v Eyre* (1870–71) LR 6 QB 1 has noted:

> **J** 'Retrospective laws are, no doubt, prima facie of questionable policy, and contrary to the general principle that legislation by which the conduct of mankind is to be regulated ought, when introduced for the first time, to deal with future acts and ought not to change the character of past transactions carried on upon the faith of the then existing law ... Accordingly, the Court will not ascribe retrospective force to new laws affecting rights, unless by express words or necessary implication it appears that such was the intention of the legislature.'

Moreover, Art 7 of the European Convention on Human Rights specifically outlaws retrospective criminal offences:

> **A** 'No one shall be held guilty of any criminal offence on account of any act or omission which did not constitute a criminal offence under national or international law at the time when it was committed.'

Open laws – Laws should be open so that individuals are able to access them. Laws should not be secret or difficult to locate as this would not enable the individual to be guided by the law.

One result of secret laws is that as individuals will necessarily be unaware of them, they will inevitably be in a state of apprehension. For example, if an individual was unsure as to whether it was a criminal offence (punishable by a term of imprisonment) to hold a political demonstration, in order to err on the side of caution, he would in all likelihood not demonstrate in case the demonstration violated the law. Significantly, this demonstration could have been a protest about, for instance, the policies of the incumbent government.

Clear laws – Laws should be clear and intelligible so that the individual can understand them. Ambiguous, imprecise or unclear laws will inevitably confuse the individual and prevent the law guiding and influencing their actions.

In the context of open and clear laws, in *Merkur Island Shipping Corporation v Laughton and others* [1983] 2 AC 570 Sir John Donaldson MR in the Court of Appeal stated that:

> J
>
> 'The efficacy and maintenance of the rule of law, which is the foundation of any parliamentary democracy, has at least two pre-requisites. First, people must understand that it is in their interests as well as in that of the community as a whole, that they should live their lives in accordance with the rules and all the rules. Second, they must know what those rules are. Both are equally important.'

     '(2) Laws should be relatively stable'.

Raz

Laws should remain relatively stable and not change too frequently as otherwise individuals could be fearful that the law may have changed in the intervening period, and so therefore they would be unable to plan their lives effectively for fear that the law had in fact changed. .

     '(3) The making of particular laws (particular legal orders) should be guided by open, stable, clear and general rules'.

Raz

For example, particular laws of an ephemeral status (eg administrative law-making/delegated legislation) should be enacted in the context of 'detailed ground rules laid down in framework laws' (eg parent legislation).

Thus, Raz views the above characteristics as not in themselves concerned with the substance of the law itself (see section 6.4), but instead with the form of the law. Raz accepts that these characteristics (open, clear, stable, prospective laws) could, of course, be met by a non-democratic state. He included within the principles underpinning the rule of law that the independence of the judiciary must be guaranteed. It is the courts that apply the law and they should do so free from external interference. The judiciary, in ensuring the correct application of the law should also apply the principles of natural justice/the duty to act fairly (see Chapter 20) and ensure that they are observed. In addition, the courts should be accessible to an aggrieved individual (so that the judiciary can provide an effective remedy), and that the judges should have power of review over both primary and subordinate legislation and administrative actions to ensure conformity with the principles underpinning the rule of law.

KEY FACTS

Raz states that the following principles comprise a formal conception of the rule of law:

Laws should possess the following characteristics in order to conform to a particular standard which should enable it to guide individual behaviour:

- Open
- Clear
- Stable
- Prospective.

The following principles concern the legal machinery for enforcing the rule of law:

- The independence of the judiciary must be guaranteed as the judges ensure that the law is correctly applied and followed. In ensuring the correct application of the law they will apply the principles of natural justice/the duty to act fairly.

- The courts should be accessible to individuals so that the judiciary can provide an effective remedy, and the judges should have power of review over legislation and administrative actions to ensure conformity with the principles underpinning the rule of law.

6.4 The rule of law as a substantive concept

This interpretation of the rule of law is concerned in particular with the substantive content of laws passed. In essence, laws passed should encapsulate and contain certain fundamental values for example, the respect for basic constitutional principles such as the protection of basic human rights.

In this context, consider the following imaginary statute:

The (Imaginary) Detention Act 2011

Section 1 permits a police officer to arrest, and detain for 10 days, any individual who criticises the economic policy of the incumbent government.

In February 2011, Gibson is arrested and detained for 10 days for criticising the Chancellor of the Exchequer's Budget proposals.

In relation to the rule of law as a substantive concept, the questions are not simply:

- Does the state official (eg police officer) possess the legal power to detain Gibson? (ie is Gibson's detention authorised by law/Act of Parliament?) – see the principle of legality at section 6.2.

  and

- Has this law (the (Imaginary) Detention Act 2011) been promulgated in the constitutionally correct manner by the appropriate body? (ie was it passed by the Queen in Parliament)?

  and

- Does this law exhibit certain characteristics? (ie is the (Imaginary) Detention Act 2011 open, clear, stable, general and prospective so as to be capable of guiding Gibson's behaviour?) – see the formal conception of the rule of law at section 6.3.2.

In addition, the rule of law as a substantive concept is concerned with the question relating to the substance and moral character of the law:

- Should state officials (eg the police) have been conferred with the wide and extensive powers of detention in respect of individuals who merely criticise a government's economic policy? In other words, should Parliament have passed the (Imaginary) Detention Act 2011 in the first place?

In this sense the rule of law embraces a substantive concept as it evaluates laws made according to a set of fundamental constitutional principles which include the protection of individual freedoms. In this way, this interpretation of the rule of law effectively has a moral dimension which would, for example, question whether the state really required the (Imaginary) Detention Act 2011. This would be on the basis that it is draconian legislation which unnecessarily violated the principles underpinning the rule of law (ie it is an excessive interference with an individual's right to freedom of expression and the right of personal liberty). Ironically, therefore, the (Imaginary) Detention Act 2011 – although it was a law itself – would inevitably be considered to be a violation of the rule of law (as a substantive concept). Although such legislation would undoubtedly be considered *morally unconstitutional* (see section 4.15), owing to the doctrine of parliamentary sovereignty, it would nevertheless be legally enforceable (though subject to a declaration of incompatibility by the courts under section 4 of the Human Rights Act 1998 – see section 17.7).

The inherent problem with the substantive conception of the rule of law is that the principles which underpin it (ie including the basic rights of the individual and the balancing of these rights against other competing interests such as public order/safety and national security, etc), are not universally agreed upon. For example, there is no universal agreement on the legitimate scope of police powers or on the morality of abortion and the respective rights of mother and unborn child. To some extent, therefore, the substantive conception of the rule of law is necessarily subjective and in essence depends upon a personal conception of human rights. In short, it depends to a great extent upon one's personal judgement of what is a 'good law' (morally right because it protects the rights you favour) and what is a 'bad law' (morally wrong because it infringes rights that you favour).

For example, returning to the example given at section 4.15.2, does the Prevention of Terrorism Act 2005 breach the rule of law because it interferes with the fundamental liberties of the individual? Or, is it consistent with the rule of law as an unfortunate, but necessary, response to an emergency threatening the life and safety of the public? In fact, is the Act aimed at actually protecting the rule of law itself by dealing with elements that threaten to undermine the existence of the state itself? (See section 6.5.)

ACTIVITY

Problem solving

Distinguish between the rule of law as:

- A procedural mechanism.
- A political ideal.
- A substantive concept.

6.5 The rule of law as the antithesis of anarchy and chaos

This (rather basic) interpretation of the rule of law emphasises the need for social order within the state as apposed to anarchy and chaos. In other words, the rule of law requires an ordered state comprising, *inter alia*, a functioning legal system and independent judges through which citizens' disputes can be resolved and settled by peaceful and consensual means, as opposed to having to resort to armed force. This interpretation would be in contrast to a country which was, in effect, administered by state officials who acted arbitrarily and in a completely unregulated and capricious fashion. In short, a state governed by the rule of men.

An inextricable aspect of an ordered legal system is the principle of the independence of the judiciary and court system. In order to hold the government to account, ensure that legal disputes are resolved fairly and according to the law and that citizens will have confidence in the administration of justice, judges must be impartial and independent from the government and state officials.

6.6 The rule of law in international terms

As noted above, the concept of the rule of law is of some antiquity and is also used in an international context, although its meaning may differ.

6.6.1 The rule of law and the Universal Declaration of Human Rights

The preamble to the Universal Declaration of Human Rights (1948) adopted by the General Assembly of the United Nations confirms respect for fundamental human rights and states:

'whereas it is essential, if man is not to be compelled to have recourse, as a last resort, to rebellion against tyranny and oppression, that human rights should be protected by the rule of law.'

In effect, this emphasises that the state should protect basic individual rights and not undermine them. Implicit within this is that should such rights be infringed by the state, then the individual should have access to legal machinery (ie the courts) in order to challenge it.

6.6.2 The rule of law and the European Convention on Human Rights

The European Convention sets out the basic rights and freedoms of the individuals and seeks to ensure that these rights enjoyed by each individual are protected by their respective state and domestic legal system. The European Court of Human Rights, in interpreting the rights of the Convention, draws upon the concept of the rule of law. In fact, the preamble makes reference to the rule of law as being part of the common heritage of the signatory states.

Most of the rights (eg the right to freedom of expression) in the European Convention are conditional rights, rather than being absolute (see Chapter 16). In brief, conditional rights can be legitimately interfered with by the state for specified and limited purposes. For example, Art 10 confers on everyone the right to freedom of expression. This right is, however, conditional and can be legitimately interfered with in order to, *inter alia*, protect health or morals (see section 18.2.4). Moreover, any legitimate interference with the Convention rights has overtones of the terminology of the rule of law. This is illustrated by the following case:

CASE EXAMPLE

Handyside v United Kingdom (1976) 1 EHRR 737

Handyside was a publisher of the *Little Red Schoolbook* (a reference book aimed at children and adolescents aged 12–18 which had a section concerning sex, including topics on masturbation, contraceptives, pornography, etc). He was prosecuted under the Obsence Publications Act 1959 (as amended in 1964), as the book was adjudged to be obscene. Handyside argued (unsuccessfully) in the European Court of Human Rights that this criminal conviction and the destruction of his books violated Art 10 (the right to freedom of expression).

In essence, any interference with Art 10 had to be consistent with the main elements of the rule of law. In other words, the restriction/interference had to have a legitimate aim and be 'prescribed by law' which, in effect, concerned the form and nature of the law purporting to restrict the Convention right (ie the Obscene Publications Acts 1959 and 1964). The reasoning of the court in the case was as follows:

The court noted at the outset that the action taken against Handyside (ie his conviction and destruction of his books) was an interference with his right to freedom of expression under Art 10(1). However, the question was: could it be justitied?

- Firstly, any interference with Handyside's right to freedom of expression had to have a legitimate aim. Art 10(2) permits interference in the interests of the aim of protecting morals. In the case the court held that the interference with Handyside's right was in the interests of the protection of morals (ie the children who would be exposed to the book) and so had a legitimate purpose under Art 10(2).

- Secondly, any interference with Handyside's right had to be 'prescribed by law'. In other words, the interference had to have a clear legal foundation in domestic law so that it was accessible and intelligible to Handyside. The court held that the Obscene Publications Acts 1959/1964 were clearly set out in domestic law.

- Thirdly, any interference with Handyside's right also needed to be proportionate and so not excessive, thereby ensuring that restrictions did not unnecessarily infringe the rights of the Convention. In this case the restriction on Handyside's right to freedom of expression had not been disproportionate and so was necessary in a democratic society.

In short, the European Court of Human Rights held that the interference with Handyside's right to freedom of expression under Art 10 was legitimate, prescribed by law and justified. The reasoning employed by the court clearly draws upon the various principles underpinning the rule of law.

ACTIVITY

Problem solving

Re-read the *Handyside* case example above and link the reasoning and tests employed by the European Court with the principles underpinning the rule of law that you have already covered in this chapter.

6.6.3 The Declaration of Delhi

In 1959 the Declaration of Delhi was issued by the International Commission of Jurists. Although the Declaration is not legally binding, it noted that the obligations imposed by the rule of law included, *inter alia*, the right to a representative government, an independent judiciary and a fair trial including due process.

6.6.4 The European Community/Union

In the context of the European Union, the 1997 Treaty of Amsterdam made it clear that the Union itself was founded on respect for democratic principles, human rights and the rule of law. It is also pertinent to note that the preamble to the draft 2004 European Constitution (which has not come into force) made specific reference to drawing upon the inheritance of the European States, which included the rule of law.

Furthermore, in performing its function of interpreting European Community law, the European Court of Justice uses a number of principles to assist it. One of these principles is that of legal certainty which is essentially based on the rule of law. For example, in reviewing the acts/legislation made by the political institutions (ie the Council/Commission/European Parliament), the European Court in *Commission v France* Case C–30/89 [1990] ECR 1-691 has noted that:

> **J** 'It must be remembered that the Court has repeatedly held that certainty and forseeability are requirements which must be observed all the more strictly in the case of rules liable to entail financial consequences.'

KEY FACTS

- The rule of law is a concept of some antiquity that has been subject to a number of different interpretations and meanings.

CONTINUED ▶

KEY FACTS

- In general terms it means that all are subject to the law, rather than being subject to the whims of man (the rule of men).

- It is a key element of constitutionalism which is aimed at ensuring that government and its officials act under the law and strictly within their legal powers.

- It can be interpreted as a principle of legality, a political ideal and as a substantive concept.

- At a basic level it emphasises the need for social order within the state as apposed to anarchy and chaos.

- The principle is also used in an international context.

6.7 The rule of law in the British constitution

6.7.1 Introduction to the rule of law in the United Kingdom

The rule of law is a central aspect of the British constitution. In fact, it assumes a particular significance in the absence of a written codified document which legally and constitutionally sets out the limits of the government (particularly in the context of human rights). Jowell has noted that in countries with a written constitution, a Bill of Rights typically will disable the government and elected Parliaments from abusing their power, whilst in the United Kingdom the rule of law as an unwritten principle of the constitution 'performs a similar disabling function' ('The Rule of Law Today' in J Jowell and D Oliver, *The Changing Constitution* (5th edn, Oxford University Press, 2004), p 19). It should be remembered, however, that the British courts have been traditionally unable to challenge primary legislation (see Chapter 7).

In the United Kingdom, therefore, the rule of law denoting the fundamental principle that government is under the law takes on a particular significance. Indeed, Lord Woolf in a lecture on the rule of law reaffirmed the constitutional significance of the principle:

'One of the most important of the judiciary's responsibilities is to uphold the rule of law, since it is the rule of law which prevents the Government of the day from abusing its powers'.

Lord Woolf, 'The rule of law and a change in the constitution' [2004] CLJ 317.

In the United Kingdom, the rule of law (at least historically) has been closely associated with Dicey. This classic conception of the rule of law in his book *Introduction to the Study of the Law of the Constitution* represented an early attempt at explaining the rule of law in the context of the 'English' constitution (today Dicey would mean the British constitution). In particular, Dicey argued that the constitution rested upon the twin pillars of parliamentary sovereignty and the rule of law.

Although Dicey's conception has been criticised (and these criticisms are considered below), his principles arguably still have resonance today,

6.7.2 Dicey and the rule of law

Dicey highlighted three aspects (or conceptions as he described them) of the rule of law:

- That an individual would only be punished for a distinct breach of the law and that there was a predominance of regular law over arbitrary power (see sections 6.7.3 to 6.7.5).
- The principle of equality under the law (see sections 6.7.6 and 6.7.7).
- The principles of the constitution are the result of the ordinary law of the land (see sections 6.7.8 and 6.7.9).

6.7.3 Dicey's first aspect

Dicey stated that the rule of law meant:

> 'that no man is punishable or can be lawfully made to suffer in body or goods except for a distinct breach of law established in the ordinary legal manner before the ordinary courts of the land. In this sense the rule of law is contrasted with every system of government based on the exercise by persons in authority of wide, arbitrary, or discretionary powers of constraint.
>
> It means, in the first place, the absolute supremacy or predominance of regular law as opposed to the influence of arbitrary power, and excludes the existence of arbitrariness, of prerogative, or even of wide discretionary authority on the part of the government. Englishmen are ruled by the law, and by the law alone; a man may with us be punished for a breach of the law, but he can be punished for nothing else'.

A Dicey, Introduction to the Study of the Law of the Constitution
(10th edn, Macmillan, 1959), pp 188 and 202 respectively.

This first aspect effectively can be broadly broken down into two elements:

- An individual is only punished for a breach of the law.
- The predominance of regular law.

Element 1 – An individual is only punished for a breach of the law

In short, Dicey argued that a punishment would only be imposed on an individual if he violated the law as established in ordinary legal proceedings before a court. In other words, the individual was not subject to the whims of a state official.

Element 2 – The predominance of regular law

In essence, Dicey argued that the rule of law denoted the predominance of regular law as opposed to the exercise of arbitrary power. As regular law had a clear legal origin and was reasonably precise in its ambit, the use of regular law can be controlled. Regular law did not involve the granting of arbitrary or wide discretionary powers on state officials as such powers could be used to the detriment of the individual. As Dicey asserted 'wherever there is discretion there is room for arbitrariness'. Regular law, therefore, necessarily limited and controlled the use of state power.

In contrast to regular law (which has a clear legal origin and clear legal limits), wide discretionary powers on the other hand, lacked clear ascertainable legal parameters (the rule of men). As a consequence, if an individual contended that a government official had abused his wide discretionary powers, it would be difficult to challenge. Arbitrary power, of course, is characterised by the lack of clear legal limits and it in effect permits state officials to act in an unregulated and effectively unchallengeable manner. This in turn makes it difficult to make these bodies legally accountable for their actions which adversely and unfairly affect the individual.

Legal accountability, therefore, benefits the individual as it gives certainty in terms of the limits and parameters of state power. It has been argued that from an administrative/governmental perspective, regular law (with the absence of wide discretionary powers) benefits state officials as it makes the use of their powers more efficient.

6.7.4 Critique of Dicey's first aspect (element 1)

In terms of the first element of Dicey's first aspect, it is worth noting the following examples which indicate that an individual could 'suffer in body or goods' without having violated a law as established before the ordinary courts.

- **Remand**

Consider the following scenario: Carl, an unconvicted defendant with no previous criminal convictions, has been remanded in custody (in a remand wing of a prison) prior to his criminal trial for murder. He has been refused bail under the Bail Act 1976 because the court has substantial grounds for fearing that he will fail to surrender to the court for his trial. At his subsequent trial, Carl is found not guilty. In this scenario Carl has suffered in body (through his enforced detention) though it has not been established that he has breached any criminal law. Moreover, Carl would not be entitled to automatic compensation from the state for the duration of his detention.

There are, of course, sound public policy reasons for the authorisation of the detention of such an individual and these are indicated in the Bail Act itself:

S **The Bail Act 1976, Sched 1 Pt 1(1)**

Although there is a general presumption for the court to grant bail, under para 2 the defendant need not be granted it if the court is satisfied that the defendant if released on bail would:

(a) fail to surrender to custody (eg abscond); or

(b) commit an offence while on bail; or

(c) interfere with witnesses or otherwise obstruct the course of justice.

Although it could be argued that Carl's detention is authorised by the law (Sched 1, Pt I, para 2 of the Bail Act 1976), the point needs to be made that the Bail Act does not require the court to be satisfied that the above events actually would occur, merely that there were substantial grounds for believing that they would occur (P Murphy (ed), *Blackstone's Criminal Practice 2007* (17th edn, Oxford University Press, 2007) p 1340). In any event, as Carl has been found not guilty, he has suffered in body whilst waiting for his trial to commence.

- **Search powers** – Section 1 of the Police and Criminal Evidence Act 1984 authorises a police officer to stop and search a person or vehicle for stolen or prohibited articles provided the officer has reasonable grounds for suspecting that he will find such articles. The officer may detain the person or vehicle in question for the purpose of the search. Suppose David is detained and searched in the street under this provision: provided the police officer had reasonable grounds for suspecting that he would find stolen/prohibited articles on David's person, the detention and search would be lawful even though no such articles were actually found. David has suffered in body in the absence of a violation of the law.

- **Indefinite detention of suspected international terrorists** – Below is an interesting example of how Parliament can pass a law which authorises the indefinite detention of non-United Kingdom nationals suspected of terrorism. In summary, foreign nationals were detained without either charge or trial and so were made to 'suffer in body' even though no charge was brought against them.

CASE EXAMPLE

A and others v Secretary of State for the Home Department **[2004] UKHL 56**

Section 23 (Pt 4) of the Anti-terrorism, Crime and Security Act 2001 authorised the indefinite detention without charge or trial (ie detention without trial) of foreign nationals suspected of being international terrorists, but who could not be deported (whether temporarily or indefinitely). These detainees could not be charged before a court as, *inter alia,* the exposure of the evidence against these individuals could compromise the intelligence services who had gathered it. Further, these individuals could not be deported

CONTINUED ▶

as under Art 3 of the European Convention, a state cannot deport an individual to a country where there is a real risk that the deportee will be subjected to torture or inhuman or degrading treatment (see section 16.10.4). As a consequence, the detainees were not prosecuted for any criminal offences, nor were they deported, which left the suspects detained indefinitely without charge or trial. These individuals could, however, leave the United Kingdom voluntarily to a country which would accept them.

Under Art 5 of the Convention deportation proceedings of individuals must be pursued with due diligence (*Chahal v UK* (1997) 23 EHRR 413) and so in 2001 the government made the Human Rights Act 1998 (Designated Derogation) Order in respect of this obligation (ie an official departure from Art 5). Such derogations are permissible under Art 15 in times of war or other public emergency threatening the life of the nation (eg the threat of terrorism).

Detainees held under the Act challenged this terrorism legislation and derogation Order under the Human Rights Act 1998. The House of Lords declared that s 23 of the Act was incompatible with Arts 5 (right to liberty and security of person) and 14 (right not to be discriminated against) and the derogation made by the government was quashed. In brief, the court held that s 23 of the Act was disproportionate and discriminatory against non-UK nationals.

It should be noted, however, that owing to the doctrine of parliamentary sovereignty, this decision of the court did not disapply the 2001 Act (see section 17.7), it merely alerted Parliament and the government that the Act violated the European Convention.

- **Compulsory purchase powers** – Local authorities typically have powers of compulsory purchase which empowers them to compulsorily purchase private property, for example to make way for a new road. In these circumstances, the home owner will suffer in goods without having breached a law.

6.7.5 Critique of Dicey's first aspect (element 2)

This aspect of Dicey's first conception has been subject to some criticism.

The first point to ask is are there any wide discretionary powers which are open to abuse in the modern British constitution? Although there are laws which are relatively precise, there are examples where exceptionally wide powers have been conferred on the executive by legislation. It should be remembered that under the principle of parliamentary sovereignty, Parliament can simply pass whichever law it chooses. For instance, the following case is a good example of Parliament passing a law which conferred an exceptionally wide power on state officials:

CASE EXAMPLE

Inland Revenue Commissioners and Another v Rossminster Ltd and others [1980] AC 952

Section 20C of the Taxes Management Act 1970 stated that a judicial authority could issue a warrant authorising Inland Revenue officers to enter and search premises if satisfied that 'there is reasonable ground for suspecting that an offence involving any form of fraud in connection with, or in relation to, tax has been committed and that evidence of it is to be found on premises specified in the information'.

A senior revenue officer suspected some tax fraud had been committed, and sought and obtained a warrant to search premises of Rossminster Ltd, and to seize anything the officers had reasonable cause to believe as evidence of a tax fraud. The revenue officers (accompanied by the police) entered Rossminster Ltd's premises and seized anything believed to be evidence of a tax fraud. As Rossminster Ltd had not been informed of the specific offences suspected, or the person suspected of committing them, they sought judicial review to quash the search warrant as illegal.

The Court of Appeal granted such a declaration. In particular Lord Denning MR commented that 'The trouble is that the legislation is drawn so widely that in some hands it might be an instrument of oppression'. He noted further that an offence involving fraud in relation to tax could include a number of different kinds of offences and so in pursuance of the traditional role of the courts to protect the liberty of the individual, the warrant must particularise the specific offence.

The House of Lords, however, reversed the decision of the Court of Appeal and held that the warrants were lawful as they had been issued strictly in accordance within the legal authority of s 20C. Lord Scarman commented regrettably that even though the warrant had not been particularised, the requirements of the Act had nevertheless been complied with. He stated that although the provision was lawful, it represented 'a breath-taking inroad upon the individual's right of privacy and right of property'.

In this context, it is of course worth remembering that as a consequence of the parliamentary executive, it is invariably the case that it is the government which drafts the Bill which in turn confers a wide statutory power on the executive (see sections 5.7.1 and 5.4.3). Indeed, as indicated at section 4.15.2, it was suggested that the Taxes Management Act could well be construed by some commentators to be *morally unconstitutional.*

In addition, delegated legislation confers a law-making power on the executive to enact law, and there is inevitably an element of discretion in carrying out this function. The courts will, however, imply certain limits in respect of the use of this power (see in context of judicial review, Chapters 19 and 20) as illustrated by the following example:

CASE EXAMPLE

Commissioners of Customs and Excise v Cure & Deeley Ltd [1962] 1 QB 340

Section 33 of the Finance (No 2) Act 1940 conferred a power on the Commissioners of Customs and Excise to 'make regulations providing for any matter for which provision appears to them to be necessary for the purpose of giving effect to the provsions of this Part of this Act and enabling them to discharge their functions'. In pursuance of this power, the Commissioners made reg 12 of the Purchase Tax Regulations 1945 which, in essence, stated that if a person failed to return a tax return – or an incomplete one – the Commissioners may determine the amount of tax appearing to them to be due and demand this payment and that this shall be deemed the proper tax due.

The Queen's Bench Division held that reg 12 was *ultra vires* s 33 of the Finance Act. The court held that although s 33 (ie *appears to them to be necessary*) appeared to confer a discretion on the Commissioners, it did not necessarily make that body the sole judge of what its powers were, as well as to how it could exercise those powers.

The court held that the effect of reg 12 purported to confer on the Commissioners the powers of a judge and it tried to oust the jurisdiction of the court. The consequence of the regulation was to substitute the figure which the Commissioners deemed to be due, for the figure that was lawfully and actually due under the law. As Sachs J noted:

> **J** 'In the result this attempt to substitute in one segment of the taxpayer's affairs the rule of tax collectors for the rule of law fails.'

A recent example of Parliament (largely controlled, of course, by the government) proposing to confer wide discretionary powers on the state (in the form of the police) was the Terrorism Bill of 2005 (which became the Terrorism Act 2006):

The Terrorism Act 2006

This legislation, as originally drafted, sought to introduce a provision which would permit the police to detain terrorist suspects for up to a maximum of 90 days without charge. It was argued that such a time limit was necessary in order to allow the prosecuting authorities to acquire and analyse the evidence against those detained under the legislation. In the event, the House of Commons voted for the reduced period of 28 days. During the passage of the Bill, a number of commentators argued that the period of detention initially proposed was excessive and contrary to the traditions of the rule of law. It must be remembered that the detention relates to the period before the detainee has even been charged with committing an offence.

Such was the criticism of the draconian and excessive nature of the proposed powers (which would have conferred extensive and wide-ranging powers on the police), that it represented the first defeat in the House of Commons for the Labour Government since assuming office in 1997.

The advantages of state discretion

In terms of discretionary powers, it is clear that in a complex modern state, discretion is a necessary tool for the modern day administrator. In fact, far from adversely affecting the individual, discretionary power in the hands of a state official can be used for their advantage and benefit. In other words, if 'regular, clear and precise laws' are applied rigorously to all individuals at all times and in all circumstances, this in itself can cause injustice and unfairness to a particular individual. Accordingly, discretion can be used by an administrator to mitigate the rigidity and harshness of the law, particularly for example in the context of providing welfare benefits.

Thus, far from being a disadvantage, discretion is a necessary and unavoidable tool as the following examples demonstrate:

- Local authorities (an executive body) with limited and finite financial resources need the power to make decisions as to how best to deploy those limited resources. The use of the discretion is, however, controlled through the process of judicial review so that its exercise is legal, rational and procedurally fair (see Chapter 20). In this way, the use of the discretion is regulated in order to avoid an abuse of power.

- The Crown Prosecution Service (which takes over prosecutions instigated by the police) has a discretion not to prosecute in an appropriate case. This decision is taken with consideration of The Code for Crown Prosecutors in mind. This means that even if there is sufficient evidence for a realistic conviction of a defendant, the prosecution will not be pursued if it is contrary to the public interest.

- The courts, in dispensing punishment to convicted offenders may have a degree of discretion, within specific parameters, as to which sentence to impose. This is determined according to the facts and circumstances of the particular case. In brief, it would be manifestly unfair to stipulate exactly the same penalty on all defendants convicted of the same offence (eg theft under the Theft Act 1968), as the circumstances, nature, impact and significance of the offence (together with the circumstances of the convicted defendant) will necessarily vary.

Although judicial discretion is considered to be a central part of the practice of sentencing, there is inevitably a risk of disparity between sentences imposed. In effect, therefore, this discretion is to some extent 'structured' by the establishment of general sentencing principles. In fact, the Magistrates' Association has produced the Magistrates' Courts' Guidelines (2004) which details the types of offences typically dealt with by magistrates. For example, the guidelines indicate the characteristics which would make the offence an average one, and those characteristics which would make it more or less serious than the average.

The control of discretion

If discretion is considered a necessary tool, its use needs to be controlled and circumscribed, otherwise the unregulated use of a discretionary power could be tantamount to the use of arbitrary power.

This regulation can be achieved through the courts via the process of judicial review (see Chapters 19 and 20). For example, a statute may confer a discretionary power on a government minister to:

1. 'act as he thinks fit'/'act when it appears to him to be necessary',

or

2. 'pass such regulations as he thinks fit', in order to achieve a particular public purpose.

The courts, however, will necessarily imply that the use of such power is not without its legal limits. Although Parliament has conferred a discretionary power, it is assumed that Parliament envisaged the minister exercising that discretion/power to use it:

- Legally.
- Rationally.
- In a procedurally fair manner.
- Consistently with the rights set out in the European Convention (now required under the Human Rights Act 1998).

In this way the courts can control and 'structure' the use of discretionary power. We saw that in *Cure & Deeley* (see section 6.7.5) (and previously in *Witham*, section 4.8.3 and *Chester v Bateson*, section 5.7.2) that the courts will make it plain that notwithstanding the power to enact delegated legislation 'which appears to them to be necessary', this is not an absolute power.

Dicey specifically disapproved of, and referred to, 'wide discretionary authority'. Today in a modern-day complex state, discretion is inevitable and practically unavoidable. Moreover, the principle of discretion can benefit the individual by mitigating the harshness of the law provided that the discretion is exercised within clear legal parameters and subject to review by the courts to ensure that it is not abused or misused.

ACTIVITY

Question

What do you think are the advantages and disadvantages of the use of executive or other discretion?

KEY FACTS

Dicey's first aspect of the rule of law

Dicey's first aspect is that a punishment would only be imposed on an individual if he violated the law as established in the ordinary legal proceedings before a court. It also denoted the predominance of regular law as opposed to the exercise of arbitrary power.

It is clear that at times individuals can suffer without violating the law (eg remand, stop and search powers of the police etc).

Discretion is inevitable and necessary in a modern state and can be used to the advantage of the individual in order to mitigate the harshness of the 'regular' law. This discretion, however, has to be regulated.

6.7.6 Dicey's second aspect

In terms of equality before the law, Dicey stated that:

> '…with us no man is above the law, but (what is a different thing) that here every man, whatever be his rank or condition, is subject to the ordinary law of the realm … In England the idea of legal equality, or of the universal subjection of all classes to one law administered by the ordinary courts, has been pushed to its utmost limit. With us every official, from the Prime Minister down to a constable or a collector of taxes, is under the same responsibility for every act done without legal justification as any other citizen

> … equality before the law, or the equal subjection of all classes to the ordinary law of the land administered by the ordinary law courts; the "rule of law" in this sense excludes the idea of any exemption of officials or others from the duty of obedience to the law which governs other citizens or from the jurisdiction of the ordinary tribunals'.

> A Dicey, *Introduction to the Study of the Law of the Constitution*
> (10th edn, Macmillan, 1959), pp 193 and 202–203 respectively.

Dicey argued that all individuals (both private citizens and state officials) are under the ordinary law. As a consequence, if a state official breached the law, he would be treated in the same way as an ordinary private individual would be if they had violated the same law: the same law would be applied to both before the ordinary courts. In other words, state officials did not enjoy special immunities from the law nor were they given special protection from the reaches of the 'ordinary' law.

In particular, Dicey contrasted our system with that which existed in France, whereby disputes with the government or state officials were processed in specific courts/tribunals (*tribunaux administratifs*). These tribunals processed administrative law (*droit administratif*), which was distinct from the ordinary court system. This meant that in France, there was a clear and separate system of administrative law which regulated the constitutional relationship between the individual and the state. Dicey perceived that these tribunals afforded the state and its officials a degree of protection which meant that these officials were not fully accountable as a private citizen would be before the ordinary court system. In fact, the *tribunaux administratifs* were staffed by specialists in public administration who were able to determine and assess the liability of public officials.

Dicey's principle of equality under the law is neatly illustrated by *Entick v Carrington* (1765) (see section 4.8.2). In this case, officials of the state were sued in the law of trespass for unlawfully entering Entick's property and seizing his papers. A private individual would have been treated in the same way had they entered and seized Entick's property. This illustrates the state being held to account to the ordinary law of the land before the ordinary court system.

A further example is demonstrated by the police exceeding their legal powers of detention:

Section 41 of PACE 1984 requires that a suspect may not be held in police detention beyond 24 hours without being charged (unless this has been extended under s 42 by a superintendent or above). If they exceed this time limit without lawful authority, then they (typically the Chief Constable) are liable to be sued in the tort of false imprisonment in the same way that an individual would be if they detained another individual without lawful authority.

An interesting judicial affirmation of the principle that everyone is equal under the law, in particular government ministers, is illustrated by the following case:

CASE EXAMPLE

M v Home Office [1994] 1 AC 377

M, a citizen of Zaire, was unsuccessful in seeking political asylum in the United Kingdom. On the day he was to be removed from the country, he applied for leave to move for judicial review of this rejection. The judge in chambers thought M might have an arguable point and therefore required M's deportation to be postponed pending the application. The judge thought that counsel for the Secretary of State had, in effect, given an undertaking that M would not be removed pending the hearing of his case. In any event,

CONTINUED ▶

M was removed from the United Kingdom to Paris bound for Zaire. Later that evening the judge issued a mandatory 'without notice' order which required the Home Secretary to return M to the jurisdiction of the court. The Home Secretary successfully challenged this order on the basis that the judge had had no jurisdiction to make it. Nevertheless, M's lawyers issued contempt proceedings against the Secretary of State for failing to comply with the court order while it was in force.

The House of Lords held, firstly that the court did have the jurisdiction to make coercive orders against ministers of the Crown (whilst they were acting in their official ministerial capacity). Secondly, if a government minister ignored an injunction made against him in his official capacity as a minister, the court possessed the jurisdiction to make a finding of contempt of court against him or his government department. Lord Templeman stated that:

> **J** 'the argument that there is no power to enforce the law by injunction or contempt proceedings against a minister in his official capacity would, if upheld, establish the proposition that the executive obey the law as a matter of grace and not as a matter of necessity, a proposition which would reverse the result of the Civil War.'

6.7.7 Critique of Dicey's second aspect

The rule of law and judicial review

Although Dicey disapproved of the French administrative law system, in the last few decades it is arguable that the United Kingdom has developed a separate form of administrative law which in some ways is akin to the French system. In fact, judicial review proceedings in which the courts supervise the actions of the executive to ensure that they act lawfully, are hallmarked by special features which are not present in the ordinary court system (see Chapter 19, and in particular section 19.2.5). For example:

- A claimant must seek permission to apply for judicial review (there is no right *per se*).

- A claimant must act promptly and not later than three months (in contrast, litigants suing in tort have six years – three if it involves personal injuries (Limitation Act 1980)).

- The claim must be made against a public body (or a body treated as such).

- The claim must also concern a public law issue (for example, how a public body misused its public law powers).

- The remedies which the court can issue are discretionary, and not automatic. As a consequence, even if the claimant can demonstrate that a public authority has acted unlawfully by misusing its public law powers, the court may take the view that it is not in the interest of public administration to grant relief.

- Judicial review proceedings are heard before specialist judges in the Administrative Court.

- These judges apply special public law principles (eg the public body must act rationally, in a procedurally fair way and respect the requirements of the European Convention on Human Rights).

In this way the state and its officials are not being treated in the same way as ordinary individuals. Instead, they are subject to a specialist court applying special public law principles. In this sense, in many ways the Administrative Court is not too dissimilar to the French administrative law system which Dicey disapproved of. In fairness to Dicey, however, the process of judicial review is an area of judicial activity which has only really exploded in the second half of the twentieth century.

The system of administrative tribunals

Today many disputes between the individual and the state (for example, in relation to the processing of welfare benefits and immigration) are resolved not through the ordinary courts, but instead by specialist tribunals (see section 21.1). These tribunals are staffed by experts, apply judicial principles and are effectively judicial in nature, but historically they have had a connection with the government department with which the dispute was concerned.

Main exceptions to the principle of equality

Although there should be general equality under the law, this does not mean that there should be no immunities at all or that all should be treated the same in all circumstances. There are a number of exceptions to the general principle of equality before the law and these include:

- Article 9 of the Bill of Rights 1689 states that the freedom of speech, debates or proceedings in Parliament ought not to be questioned in a court. The constitutional rationale behind this legal immunity for parliamentarians is to ensure that they can exercise their functions without fear of litigation. This immunity is regulated by Parliament itself so that if a member abuses this immunity (eg gratuitously defames a constituent), this will be investigated and punished by Parliament (see section 8.7.3).

- The Sovereign, together with foreign Heads of State/Sovereigns enjoy legal immunity from criminal liability: s 20 of the State Immunity Act 1978. However, following the passage of the Crown Proceedings Act 1947, Crown government departments could thereafter be sued in contract law as of right.

- Diplomatic agents enjoy immunity under s 2(1) of the Diplomatic Privileges Act 1964.

- In relation to the courts, judges of the superior courts are not liable for anything said or done whilst carrying out their judicial function (*Anderson v Gorries* [1895] 1 QB 668) (see section 13.4.2). This is based on the protection of judicial independence and the administration of justice so that judges can perform their constitutional functions of adjudication and apply the law independently, without fear of litigation. This benefits the wider public whose cases will be processed by the courts.

143

- For public policy reasons, specified classes of individuals are treated differently. For example, employers and employees as a group or class of individuals, have different obligations imposed upon them by the law which reflect the imbalance of power in their relationship. This is also the case in respect of landlords and tenants.

- In respect of equality it should be remembered that the police and public authorities exercise particular functions (eg the police investigating and combating crime), that individuals do not. The exercise of these powers, therefore, have no real parallel in the private world of individuals. As a result, it is argued that these bodies should, therefore, be subject to additional legal controls.

The consequences of treating 'unequal' entities (ie state officials and private individuals) equally, is that it can give rise to constitutional difficulties as illustrated in *Malone v Metropolitan Police Commissioner* [1979] Ch 344. In brief, Malone alleged that the tapping of his telephone conversations in order to obtain evidence in criminal proceedings was unlawful. The court held, however, that there was no law against it. Sir Robert Megarry VC stated that:

> **J** 'England, it may be said, is not a country where everything is forbidden except what is expressly permitted; it is a country where everything is permitted except what is expressly forbidden ... if such tapping can be carried out without committing any breach of the law; it requires no authorisation by statute or common law; it can lawfully be done simply because there is nothing to make it unlawful.'

In this case the tapping of Malone's telephone took place on the premises of the Post Office and so no breach of the law of trespass had taken place (contrast *Entick* see section 4.8.2). This case demonstrated the danger in treating constitutional unequals (here the police and a private individual – the latter would not have access to post office premises) equally, as in these circumstances, in pursuance of protecting the individual, the actions of the police should be subject to extra controls and regulation.

ACTIVITY

Problem solving

Should the government be equally bound by the law? Can you think of reasons why government should be (a) immune under the law and (b) have more duties under the law?

KEY FACTS

Dicey's second aspect of the rule of law

Dicey contended that all individuals (both private individuals and state officials) are equal under the ordinary law. This meant that if a state official breached the law, he would be treated in the same way as an ordinary private individual. Under the principle of equality, state officials did not enjoy special immunities from the law.

It is clear that there are a number of exceptions to the principle of equality before the law:

- The Sovereign, foreign Heads of State, diplomats and parliamentarians enjoy immunity from the law.

- Judges of the superior courts are not liable for anything said or done whilst carrying out their judicial function.

- In terms of their rights and responsibilities, certain classes of people, for instance, landlords and tenants will be treated differently under the law.

6.7.8 Dicey's third aspect

Dicey stated that:

> 'We may say that the constitution is pervaded by the rule of law on the ground that the general principles of the constitution (as for example the right to personal liberty, or the right of public meeting) are with us the result of judicial decisions determining the rights of private persons in particular cases brought before the courts ... with us the law of the constitution, the rules which in foreign countries naturally form part of a constitutional code, are not the source but the consequence of the rights of individuals, as defined and enforced by the courts'.

> A Dicey, *Introduction to the Study of the Law of the Constitution*
> (10th edn, Macmillan, 1959), pp 195 and 203 respectively.

Dicey was making the point that Britain had a court-based constitution (in effect, a common law constitution) in the sense that the principles of the constitution, concerning the rights of the individual, were the direct consequence of decisions made by judges. In this way, Dicey contrasted the English (British) constitution with constitutional arrangements pertaining elsewhere, in which the rights and freedoms of the individual derived from a written codified constitutional document embracing a Bill or Charter of Rights.

For example, Entick (see section 4.8.2) successfully sued the King's messengers (state officials) in the ordinary law of trespass. Entick did not need to rely on a constitutional guarantee set out in a Bill of Rights. Instead, Entick relied on the common law to equip him with a practical remedy which could be enforced in the ordinary courts. For Dicey, these practical remedies gave the individual better protection than guarantees enshrined in a written constitution (typically in a Bill of Rights) which were not necessarily enforceable in practice by aggrieved individuals. In other words, although a Bill of Rights may in legal theory pledge to protect a panoply of human rights and freedoms, it lacks value for the individual if he cannot actually enforce those rights in practice before an independent court and secure a practical remedy for their infringement.

ACTIVITY

Question

How did Dicey think that liberty should be protected?

Do you agree with him?

6.7.9 Critique of Dicey's third aspect

The courts have clearly fashioned a number of common law remedies for the individual which include the following:

- Trespass to person.

- Trespass to land.

- Trespass to property.

- False imprisonment.

- Assault.

- Battery.

These remedies, accordingly, can be used against state officials, as well as other individuals. For example, if an individual is unlawfully detained by the police they can sue in an action for false imprisonment. These remedies are in addition to any statutory rights and remedies which have been specifically conferred by an Act of Parliament (eg the right not to be discriminated against on the grounds of sex under the Sex Discrimination Act 1975). The courts, however, can only protect the individual if in fact a particular right has been recognised either by the common law or by statute.

This point was neatly illustrated in the *Malone* case at section 6.7.7, as one of Malone's submissions against the Metropolitan Police Commissioner in respect of the tapping of his telephone was that it violated his right to privacy. Sir Robert Megarry VC countered this by indicating that no tort of privacy existed as Parliament had not legislated to create one and the courts in developing the common law had not fashioned one. In fact, in terms of the separation of powers, he noted that it was not the constitutional function of the judiciary to 'legislate in a new field' and create this new right of privacy:

'No new right in the law, fully-fledged with all the appropriate safeguards, can spring from the head of a judge deciding a particular case: only Parliament can create such a right.'

The courts, therefore, have been selective as to which tortious remedies an aggrieved individual can employ.

In any event, the capacity of the courts to protect the individual from the power of the actions of the state are necessarily curtailed by the central element of the constitution, namely, parliamentary sovereignty. Although Parliament can pass legislation conferring legal remedies on an individual (eg in the context of sexual and racial discrimination), it can conversely, pass laws which excessively interfere with the liberties and freedoms of the individual. In these circumstances, the courts are effectively rendered powerless if this excessive interference is expressly authorised and legitimised in the provisions of an Act.

For instance, it is worth recalling Lord Scarman's comments in *Rossminster Ltd* (1980) in relation to s 20C of the Taxes Management Act 1970 which conferred sweeping powers on Inland Revenue officers (see section 6.7.5). According to Lord Scarman although the Act represented a 'breath-taking inroad into the right of individual privacy', it was not the constitutional responsibility of the court to set it aside.

In fact, Parliament has on occasions passed retrospective law to negate and reverse the ruling of the courts. The most famous example being the enactment of the War Damage Act 1965 which in effect overruled the decision in the *Burmah Oil* case (see sections 4.9 and 7.5.1). This legislation was arguably *morally unconstitutional* (see section 4.15.2) as it interfered with the ruling of the highest court on the grounds of financial expediency.

In short, the courts:

* can develop the common law so as to provide practical remedies if an individual's (selected) freedoms have been violated, and

* will also interpret unclear legislative provisions in the light of constitutional principles which protect the individual (eg the presumption that Parliament did not intend to interfere with a person's right of access to the courts – see section 4.8.3).

Ultimately, however, Parliament can simply override the protection provided by the judges by passing legislation which clearly and explicitly authorises an interference with the freedoms of the individual. In contrast, under a codified constitution with an entrenched Bill of Rights, such legislation – all things being equal – would be rendered legally (and morally) unconstitutional and declared invalid by a Constitutional/Supreme Court.

For Dicey, however, as Parliament is elected by the people (or at least the dominant House of Commons is) it is answerable to the people and so this in itself necessarily restrains Parliament from passing draconian laws. In short, the constitutional theory is that parliamentarians will not pass laws which would unnecessarily and gratuitously infringe individual rights and freedoms, as the electorate have political sovereignty (see section 7.2.2). In other words, MPs must face the public at the time of re-election at a general election and so are ultimately answerable to the people for the laws that they pass. The problem with this, of course, is that draconian legislation which only affects a certain section of society (eg prisoners, terrorist suspects and paedophiles) may in reality be popular with the public at large. This serves to illustrate that democracy should not be necessarily equated simply with majority rule as it may be necessary to ring-fence the rights of 'unpopular' individuals and protect them from the 'tyranny of the majority' (the relationship between the rule of law and parliamentary sovereignty will be considered at section 7.13).

Another point to note is that this element of Dicey's conception of the rule of law is now subject to the passage of the Human Rights Act 1998. This Act, in effect, gives further effect in the law of the United Kingdom to the rights enshrined in the European Convention on Human Rights. Under s 3 of the Act all courts and tribunals have the responsibility of interpreting all legislation consistently 'so far as it is possible to do so' in line with the rights of the European Convention. The effect of s 6 of the Act is that the courts and tribunals themselves, in effect, constitute a public authority for the purposes of the Act and so when interpreting or developing the law, they must act consistently with the European Convention. The Human Rights Act represents a significant shift in terms of 'rights protection' in the British constitution, and in some ways is akin to a Bill or Charter of positive rights (albeit a weak one) whereby positive and lawful justification is now needed for the state to interfere with the rights of the individual.

Although the Human Rights Act would appear to be at odds with Dicey's suspicions of written constitutional guarantees of rights, the articles of the Convention are enforced by individuals before the courts (in fact, any court or tribunal and not necessarily the Administrative Court). The role of the court, accordingly, will continue to remain central to the protection of individual rights. Under the Human Rights Act 1998 the function of the court is to uphold the protection afforded by these rights by construing all legislation in line with the Convention and ensuring that public authorities fully respect these rights and freedoms.

ACTIVITY

Question

What impact do you think that the Human Rights Act 1998 has had on Dicey's third aspect of his conception of the rule law?

KEY FACTS

Dicey's third aspect of the rule of law

Dicey contended that our constitution was in effect a court-based constitution in the sense that the rights and freedoms of the individual were the direct consequence of decisions made by judges.

In this way, Dicey contrasted the English (United Kingdom) constitution with the constitutional arrangements elsewhere, in which the rights and freedoms of the individual were derived from the written codified constitutional document embracing a Bill or Charter of Rights.

Dicey's third aspect now has to be re-evaluated in the light of the passage of the Human Rights Act 1998 which in effect represents a list of basic positive rights of the individual which can be enforced in the domestic courts.

6.7.10 The role of the United Kingdom courts and the rule of law

The following cases are examples where the principles underpinning the rule of law have been invoked in the courts.

The rule of law as a basis for the control of *de facto* arbitrary powers

In *Entick v Carrington* (see section 4.8.2) one of the arguments used by the defendants (ie the state) as a justification for the use of the warrant was that this power was essential to 'government and state necessity' and moreover that such warrants had been issued before and had not been questioned. Lord Camden CJ stated:

> **J** 'This power, so claimed by the secretary of state, is not supported by one single citation from any law book extant ... According to this reasoning, it is now incumbent upon the defendants to shew the law, by which this seizure is warranted. If that cannot be done, it is a trespass.' (sic)

The court also rejected the argument based on state necessity. In short, this case tells us that it is not the constitutional function of the judiciary to equip the government with new powers. If the government required these powers, then Parliament would need to pass the requisite legislation. In fact, the *Entick* case neatly demonstrates all three of Dicey's propositions:

- **The government/state must act within the law and not exercise arbitrary powers** – The state tried (unsuccessfully) to use a power in the form of a warrant which had no legal foundation or origin. As a result, the state could not 'trump' or lawfully negate the common law right (as expressed in the law of trespass) not to be trespassed against without lawful justification.

- **Equality under the law** – The state was held to account according to the ordinary law (trespass) before the ordinary courts.

- **A court-based constitution** – The ordinary courts provided Entick with a practical remedy against the state in the law of trespass.

More recently in *Webb v Chief Constable of Merseyside Police* [2000] 1 All ER 209 the Court of Appeal reiterated the principle that government is under the law. In this case the court made it clear that it was unlawful for a public authority (eg the police) to expropriate money or property from an individual without authorisation in a statute.

The House of Lords also reiterated the rule of law in the following ruling by refusing to countenance an abuse of public power by the executive:

CASE EXAMPLE

R v Secretary of State for the Home Department, ex parte Fire Brigades Union [1995] 2 All ER 244

The Criminal Injuries Compensation Scheme was established in 1964 under the royal prerogative to provide compensation to victims of crimes. In 1988 the Criminal Justice Act codified the scheme, but under s 171 it would not come into force until a day to be determined by the Secretary of State. This section therefore conferred a power on the minister to decide exactly when the statutory scheme should come into force. In December 1993 a government White Paper indicated that the compensation provisions of the Act would not be implemented, but would in due course be repealed. Instead, in March 1994 the government announced (under the royal prerogative) that a new tariff scheme would take effect from April 1994 (the flat-rate tariff scheme was in effect a cheaper scheme as it would compensate victims on the basis of the category that they fell into, rather than on an individual basis).

Trade Unions (whose members were susceptible to violent crime in their work) sought judicial review of the decision and sought a declaration, *inter alia*, that the Secretary of State had acted unlawfully by failing to bring into force the above provisions of the 1988 Act.

CONTINUED ▶

The House of Lords held that the Home Secretary had a power to act as he had been conferred with a discretion as to when it was appropriate to bring the scheme into force and that this was a matter for him to decide. Accordingly, it would not be constitutionally appropriate for the courts to interfere to require the Home Secretary to bring those provisions into effect. This statutory discretion, however, was not unlimited and the Home Secretary was required (whilst the sections were not in force) to keep under review the question of whether these provisions should be brought into force. It was, therefore, unlawful and an abuse of power to use royal prerogative power inconsistently with that responsibility. As a result, the Home Secretary's decision not to implement the provisions of the Act and that a tariff scheme would be implemented in their place, was unlawful. Lord Browne-Wilkinson stated that:

> J 'It does not follow that, because the Secretary of State is not under any duty to bring the section into effect, he has an absolute and unfettered discretion whether or not to do so ... the Secretary of State comes under a clear duty to keep under consideration from time to time the question whether or not to bring the section (and therefore the statutory scheme) into force. In my judgment he cannot lawfully surrender or release the power contained in section 171(1) so as to purport to exclude its future exercise either by himself or by his successors.'

Similarly, in *Cure & Deeley* (1962) (see section 6.7.5) the courts demonstrated that they will limit the scope of wide discretionary powers conferred on executive authorities.

CASE EXAMPLE

R v Horseferry Road Magistrates' Court, ex parte Bennett [1994] 1 AC 42

Bennett was a New Zealand citizen who claimed that he had been kidnapped from South Africa and brought to England where he was arrested to face criminal charges. The Magistrates' Court refused his request to adjourn the committal of his case to the Crown Court. Bennett sought judicial review of the decision, but the High Court refused his application.

The House of Lords held that the courts should take cognisance of the circumstances which led to the defendant to appear before the court and refuse to try him. In this case, Bennett had been brought back to the United Kingdom without regard to the available extradition process and in violation of international law. The High Court could inquire into

CONTINUED ▸

the circumstances that led an individual to be brought before the court and stay the prosecution if it was satisfied that extradition proceedings had been disregarded. Lord Griffiths stated that:

> **J** 'The judiciary accept a responsibility for the maintenance of the rule of law that embraces a willingness to oversee executive action and to refuse to countenance behaviour that threatens either basic human rights or the rule of law.'

Judicial deference

In contrast to *Bennett* above, however, the courts have (in pursuance of preserving the separation of powers/functions between the executive and judiciary) on occasions given excessive deference to the executive. This is illustrated in the following historic case:

CASE EXAMPLE

Liversidge v Anderson [1942] AC 206

Under reg 18B of the Defence (General) Regulations 1939, the Secretary of State could make an order to detain a person if he *had reasonable cause* to believe that the person was of hostile origin or associations.

The House of Lords held that under this emergency legislation (in the context of the Second World War) a court could not inquire as to whether in fact the minister had reasonable grounds for his belief that the person be of hostile associations. In other words, this was an issue of executive discretion for the minister concerned and that the court could not require the minister to give the particulars of the grounds on which he had had reasonable cause to believe the detainee to be of hostile associations.

This is a highly controversial case as it effectively conferred a considerable power onto the executive. Indeed, as Lord Atkin said in his dissenting opinion, 'I protest, even if I do it alone, against a strained construction put on words with the effect of giving an uncontrolled power of imprisonment to the minister'.

In this case the court was aware that the minister was politically accountable for his actions to Parliament under the constitutional convention of ministerial responsibly (see section 4.13.12).

The controversial majority decision in this case was rejected in subsequent case law: see Lords Diplock and Scarman in *Inland Revenue Commissioners and Another v Rossminster Ltd and others* [1980] AC 952.

A more recent example of the courts adopting a 'hands off approach' in order to avoid trespassing on the constitutional role of the executive (eg to determine public policy) is the following case. This case demonstrates the courts showing deference to executive decision-making (ie decisions which were in effect politically sensitive) in order to avoid infringing the principle of the separation of powers. In short, the executive has been charged with making these decisions. This in turn, however, gave the individual little legal protection from the exercise of state power.

CASE EXAMPLE

R v Secretary of State for Home Affairs, ex parte Hosenball **[1977] 1 WLR 700**

Hosenball was an American journalist and in the interests of national security the Home Secretary issued a deportation order against him under s 3 of the Immigration Act 1971. It was alleged that Hosenball had obtained for publication information harmful to the security of the United Kingdom. He was informed that he could make representations to an individual panel in respect of his deportation, but could not appeal. Despite a request by Hosenball's solicitors, the Secretary of State declined to provide further information (ie the relevant particulars of what was alleged against him).

The panel subsequently conducted a hearing at which Hosenball called witnesses and made representations. Shortly afterwards the Secretary of State made the deportation order which Hosenball sought to quash on the grounds that the rules of natural justice had been violated as he had been denied the particulars of the allegations made against him.

The Court of Appeal held that the principles underpinning natural justice were modified when issues of national security were involved. Here public policy necessitated the protection of the confidentiality of security information. On the facts of the case, the Secretary of State had considered personally Hosenball's request for further particulars of the allegations (but that this had been refused as it was not in the interests of national security to provide further information) and there was nothing to suggest that he had acted unfairly. The court also noted that under the convention of ministerial responsibility the Secretary of State was politically answerable to Parliament for his decision. Lord Denning MR observed that:

> J 'There is a conflict here between the interests of national security on the one hand and the freedom of the individual on the other. The balance between these two is not for a court of law. It is for the Home Secretary, he is the person entrusted by Parliament with the task. In some parts of the world National Security has on occasions been used as an excuse for all kinds of infringements of individual liberties. But not in England.'

ACTIVITY

Question

What is wrong with the approach taken by the majority in *Liversidge* (1942) and the Court of Appeal in *ex parte Hosenball* (1977)?

The rule of law in the defence of fundamental constitutional principles

As noted at section 4.8.3, in construing legislative provisions, the courts will do so in the light of certain constitutional principles and presumptions. In this way, the courts recognise and uphold the principles which underpin the rule of law.

Retrospective legislation

One constitutional principle is the presumption against retrospective legislation (see sections 4.8.3 and 6.3.2). In *Waddington v Miah* [1974] 2 All ER 377 the House of Lords construed the Immigration Act 1971 so as not to have retrospective criminal effect. Lord Reid drew upon the presumptions that surely Parliament would never pass retrospective criminal legislation or knowingly legislate contrary to international law/Treaties as he stated that:

> **J** 'there has for a very long time been a strong feeling against making legislation, and particularly criminal legislation, retrospective'.

Lord Reid then referred to Art 11 of the Universal Declaration of Human Rights and Art 7 of the European Convention. In this light, he argued:

> **J** 'So it is hardly credible that any government department would promote or that Parliament would pass retrospective criminal legislation'.

Similarly, the House of Lords in *R v Secretary of State for the Home Department, ex parte Pierson* [1998] AC 539 ensured that the Home Secretary's powers of reviewing a tariff to be served by a mandatory life sentence prisoner (s 35 of the Criminal Justice Act 1991), did not, in effect, retrospectively increase a sentence. Lord Steyn noted that:

> **J** 'unless there is the clearest provision to the contrary, Parliament must be presumed not to legislate contrary to the rule of law. And the rule of law enforces minimum standards of fairness, both substantive and procedural.'

These cases, of course, do not mean that Parliament cannot explicitly pass laws which are retrospective or even contrary to the European Convention. In terms of the former, in 1991

Parliament passed the War Crimes Act which is clearly retrospective legislation as it relates to atrocities committed during the Second World War in Germany or territories occupied by Germany. Moreover, it is of interest to note that this Act was enacted under the Parliament Acts of 1911 and 1949, as the House of Lords refused to pass it and therefore it was passed without their consent (see section 10.10.2).

The principle of legality

In order to protect the individual, the courts use the doctrine of legality. This precludes statutory interference with the rights/freedoms of citizens unless this is expressly provided for with specific words (this means that general words will be insufficient to achieve this aim). This is illustrated in the following case:

CASE EXAMPLE

R v Secretary of State for the Home Department, ex parte Simms and another [1999] 3 All ER 400

O'Brien and Simms had been convicted of murder and claimed to have been the victims of a miscarriage of justice and they sought to reopen their cases through oral interviews with journalists. Under paras 37 and 37A of the Prison Service Standing Order 5A (made under s 47(1) of the Prison Act 1952 and r 33 of the Prison Rules 1964), the prison authorities refused to permit these interviews unless the journalists concerned signed an undertaking not to publish any part of the resulting interviews. The journalists refused to do so and O'Brien and Simms challenged the lawfulness of the above prison policy.

The House of Lords held that a blanket ban on interviews of prisoners by journalists was unlawful. The purpose of the interviews was, in effect, to enlist the investigative resources of the journalists to help the prisoners gain access to justice, with the eventual aim of demonstrating that there had been a miscarriage of justice. The court held that a blanket ban, therefore, deprived a prisoner of a basic and fundamental right, that of gaining access to justice. Paragraphs 37 and 37A were to be interpreted in line with the principle of legality, which meant that ambiguous or general words did not override fundamental rights such as the right to gain access to justice (which was in effect a constitutional right). Although the paragraphs themselves were not *ultra vires*, the above policy was unlawful. Lord Steyn noted that:

> J 'The starting point is the right of freedom of expression. In a democracy it is the primary right: without it an effective rule of law is not possible ... They wish to challenge the safety of their convictions. In principle it is not easy to conceive of a more important function which free speech might fulfil.'

The presumption of innocence

One constitutional principle underpinning the rule of law is the presumption of innocence (ie the burden/standard of proof). In *R v Secretary of State for the Home Department, ex parte Khawaja* [1984] 1 AC 74, the House of Lords stated that in relation to an application for judicial review of an order detaining an individual under the Immigration Act 1971, it was for the executive/state to prove to the court on the balance of probabilities the facts relied upon by an immigration officer as justifying the determination that the person *was* an illegal entrant.

KEY FACTS

The British courts and the rule of law

The constitutional function of the judiciary is to uphold the principles underpinning the rule of law.

The courts control the *de facto* use of arbitrary powers by the state (*ex parte Fire Brigades Union* (1995) and *ex parte Bennett* (1994)).

The courts also interpret law in light of certain constitutional principles:

- Prospective legislative (*Waddington v Miah* (1974)).
- The principle of legality (*ex parte Simms and another* (1999)).
- The presumption of innocence/standard of proof (*ex parte Khawaja* (1984)).

6.7.11 Conclusion

The rule of law is a central aspect of the British constitution as it is an essential element of constitutionalism, namely, the principle that government and state power must be limited, regulated and controlled. The rule of law is also inextricably linked with the independence of the judiciary as one of the constitutional responsibilities of the judiciary is to uphold the various principles underpinning the rule of law. In particular, a practical demonstration of the rule of law is illustrated each time a judge in judicial review proceedings in the Administrative Court holds the executive and public bodies legally to account for the misuse of their public law powers. This reaffirms the principle that all bodies, and in particular the government, are under the law.

In fact, the importance attached to the principle of the rule of law was recently given statutory recognition in s 1 of the Constitutional Reform Act 2005:

This Act does not adversely affect–

   (a) the existing constitutional principle of the rule of law , or

   (b) the Lord Chancellor's existing constitutional role in relation to that principle.

For example, traditionally the Lord Chancellor would try to ensure that the principles underpinning the rule of law (eg safeguarding the presumption of innocence) were respected when, for example, draft legislative measures were being considered in Cabinet.

Finally, in considering the rule of law, the following comments of Lord Woolf are worth noting:

> 'Ultimately, it is the rule of law which stops a democracy descending into an elected dictatorship'.

Lord Woolf, 'The rule of law and a change in the constitution' [2004] CLJ 317.

ACTIVITY

Essay writing

What do you understand by the rule of law and what is its constitutional value?

What is the significance of the principle in the context of the British constitution?

Further reading

Barnett, H, *Constitutional and Administrative Law* (6th edn, Routledge-Cavendish, 2006), Chapter 4.

Lord Bingham, 'Dicey Revisited' [2002] PL 39.

Bradley, A and Ewing, K, *Constitutional and Administrative Law* (14th edn, Pearson/Longman, 2007), Chapter 6.

Craig, P, 'The Rule of Law' in Feldman, D, (ed), *English Public Law* (Oxford University Press, 2004), p 697.

Jowell, J, 'The Rule of Law Today' in Jowell, J and Oliver, D, (eds) *The Changing Constitution* (5th edn, Oxford University Press, 2004), p 5.

Majid, A, 'Do we care about the rule of law?' (2005) 155 NLJ 1561.

Raz, J, 'The Rule of Law and its Virtue' (1977) 93 LQR 195.

Lord Steyn, 'Democracy, the Rule of Law and the Role of Judges' [2006] EHRLR 243.

Lord Woolf, 'Droit Public-English Style' [1995] PL 57.

chapter 7 PARLIAMENTARY SOVEREIGNTY ■

At the end of this chapter you should be able to:

■ Define the term parliamentary sovereignty

■ Identify and explain Dicey's conception of parliamentary sovereignty

■ Identify and explain the different aspects of parliamentary sovereignty

■ Explain how parliamentary sovereignty relates to other aspects of the British constitution

■ Explain the constitutional importance of parliamentary sovereignty

7.1 Introduction

Parliamentary sovereignty is the central element of the British constitution and it is impossible to understand the nature and mechanics of the constitution without an appreciation of this principle. In fact, this doctrine sets the British constitution apart from the vast majority of other democratic states. For example, although the legislative bodies of the United States' Congress and the Republic of Ireland's Oireachtas are law-making bodies which pass primary legislation, these legislatures do not have unlimited law making powers as they are constitutionally and legally constrained by their written codified constitutions. For example, Art 15.4 of the Irish constitution states that the Oireachtas shall not enact legislation 'which is in any respect repugnant' to the constitution. In other words, if these bodies were to pass legislation which was inconsistent with the rules laid down in their codified constitutions, it would be subject to judicial review (constitutional review) by their respective Supreme Courts and declared illegal, that is to say legally unconstitutional (contrast with section 4.15) and so invalid.

In contrast, in the United Kingdom the Queen in Parliament (or Crown in Parliament) can in legal theory pass any law and the legislation which is enacted is not subject to judicial review by the courts. This is because Parliament historically has not been constrained by a higher set of legal rules enshrined in a written constitution. In other words, Acts of Parliament (unlike Acts of the United States Congress) could not be tested or questioned against an overriding codified constitution (however, the position in the context of European Community law will be considered at section 15.6).

Although in the United Kingdom the courts historically have not subjected Acts of Parliament to judicial review, they do review and invalidate delegated legislation made by the executive. This is because this type of legislation (eg Statutory Instruments) does not enjoy the sovereign status of primary legislation as it has not been passed by the legislature, but rather by the executive (see section 5.7.2). Finally, although the principle of a legislature with the legal power to make any law that it chooses is very unusual, it is not unique. New Zealand also has an uncodified constitution which contains a Parliament (a unicameral legislature comprising the House of Representatives) which possesses the constitutional characteristic of sovereignty and, as in the United Kingdom, it is able to pass any law that it chooses.

7.2 Terminology

The term parliamentary sovereignty (which denotes that the Queen in Parliament has unlimited legislative power) is arguably apt to mislead, because the term 'sovereignty' can have another meaning. For example, it is used in the context of international law, relations and politics to indicate that a state is independent and sovereign (for example, France or Italy). As a consequence, a number of legal academics prefer to use the term the legislative supremacy of Parliament. Notwithstanding this, as parliamentary sovereignty (at least in historic terms) is closely associated with Dicey, and as he used this term, this book will do likewise. This should not be problematic providing we understand the sense in which the term is being used, namely to denote the legal principle that Parliament can in theory pass any law that it chooses.

As indicated earlier, Dicey argued that the constitution was founded on the following twin pillars:

- The rule of law and
- Parliamentary sovereignty.

In respect of the term sovereignty, he specifically differentiated between:

- Legal sovereignty and
- Political sovereignty

7.2.1 Legal sovereignty

In essence, legal sovereignty is concerned with the legislative power of the Queen in Parliament (the principle that any legislation can be made on any subject). Legal sovereignty is concerned with the constitutional relationship between the courts and the legislature (hence it is therefore necessarily an issue of constitutional significance). It is with legal sovereignty that this chapter is specifically concerned with. Legal sovereignty relates to Bills which have been consented to (and therefore have become Acts of Parliament) by the following three constitutional elements:

- The House of Commons.

- The House of Lords (providing the Parliament Acts of 1911 and 1949 do not apply –
  see section 10.10.1 below).

- The monarch (Royal Assent).

Legal sovereignty is not concerned with the political machinations within Parliament which led to the passing of the Act. It is not therefore concerned with the scenario, for example, whereby a highly controversial Bill only narrowly passed through both Houses.

7.2.2 Political sovereignty

In contrast, political sovereignty rests with the people (the electorate), for as Dicey noted the electorate can 'always enforce their will'. By this he meant that politically, Parliament (or more specifically the House of Commons and so by extension the government) is accountable directly to the people at every general election. In a sense, therefore, this is analogous to a social contract between the governed (specifically the electorate) and the state, whereby the people at a general election confer power and constitutional legitimacy on Parliament to legislate. Such authority can, of course, be revoked by the people at the next general election.

Logically therefore, as Parliament can legally pass any law it chooses, this could include a draconian law which breaches the basic rights and freedoms of the individual. Such legislation, however, would be unlikely to be passed as, ultimately, parliamentarians serving in the House of Commons would have to face the electorate at some point within the next five years. Political sovereignty, therefore, places external, political restraints on the legislation that the Queen in Parliament will actually enact in practice.

KEY FACTS

- Legal sovereignty is concerned with the legal relationship between Parliament and the courts.

- Political sovereignty is concerned with the political relationship between Parliament (specifically the House of Commons and by extension the government) and the people (the electorate).

7.3 The meaning and scope of legal sovereignty

7.3.1 Introduction

Parliamentary sovereignty means simply that the Queen in Parliament can legally pass any law (with one exception – see section 7.9) as the courts do not have the constitutional power to invalidate laws and declare them to be legally unconstitutional (see section 4.15) or even illegal (but see in the context of European Community law at section 15.6).

In essence, as made clear by Lord Diplock in *Duport Steels Ltd and Others v Sirs and Others* [1980] 1 All ER 529: 'Parliament makes the laws, the judiciary interpret them'. In fact, this constitutional interaction between the two arms of the state has been described by Lord Bridge in *X Ltd v Morgan-Grampian (Publishers) Ltd* [1991] 1 AC 1 in terms of a 'twin sovereignty':

> 'In our society the rule of law rests upon twin foundations: the sovereignty of the Queen in Parliament in making the law and the sovereignty of the Queen's courts in interpreting and applying the law.'

7.3.2 The origins of parliamentary sovereignty

In view of the fact that parliamentary sovereignty is the key element of the British constitution, it is perhaps surprising that the exact origin of the principle is not clear. In other countries, citizens can date accurately the origin and promulgation of their written codified constitution (eg the Indian constitution was declared passed in November 1949 and came into force on 26 January 1950). What is clear is that parliamentary sovereignty is a common law doctrine. In other words, it is the courts that have for centuries in their judgments accepted that the Queen in Parliament can pass any law. In this context, Wade has made the following point:

> 'The rule of judicial obedience is in one sense a rule of common law, but in another sense – which applies to no other rule of common law – it is the ultimate *political* fact upon which the whole system of legislation hangs. Legislation owes its authority to the rule: the rule does not owe its authority to legislation'.

> H Wade, 'The basis of legal Sovereignty' [1955] CLJ 172.

More recently, in terms of the origin of the principle of parliamentary sovereignty, Lord Steyn in *R (Jackson) v Attorney General* [2005] UKHL 56 reaffirmed that:

> 'It is a construct of the common law. The judges created this principle.' (But see his further comments at section 7.7).

In short, parliamentary sovereignty exists because judges have, for centuries, consistently stated that they do not have the constitutional power to review or question Acts of Parliament and that the judicial function was limited to interpreting legislation in order to ascertain the intention of Parliament in passing it. The case below illustrates the principle:

CASE EXAMPLE

Cheney v Conn [1968] 1 WLR 242

Cheney was assessed for income tax under the Finance Act 1964. Part of the receipts from those taxes for these years (1963–65) were allocated to the construction of nuclear weapons. Cheney challenged his tax assessments on the basis that part of the proposed use of the taxes (ie the construction of nuclear weapons) was contrary to international law: the Geneva Convention (scheduled to the Geneva Conventions Act 1957).

The High Court (Chancery Division) held that the charge to tax under the Act and the tax assessments were not invalidated. Even if there was a conflict between international law and statute, where the latter's provisions were clear and unambiguous, it would prevail. Ungoed-Thomas J stated that:

> **J** 'If the purpose for which a statute may be used is an invalid purpose, then such remedy as there may be must be directed to dealing with that purpose and not to invalidating the statute itself. What the statute itself enacts cannot be unlawful, because what the statute says and provides is itself the law, and the highest form of law that is known to this country. It is the law which prevails over every other form of law, and it is not for the court to say that a parliamentary enactment, the highest law in this country, is illegal.'

ACTIVITY

Problem solving

Why do you think that it is logically impossible for the principle of parliamentary sovereignty to be established in an Act of Parliament?

7.3.3 What constitutes an Act of Parliament?

As the principle of parliamentary sovereignty necessitates that the courts obey and apply Acts of Parliament, this in turn begs the question as to what exactly is an Act of Parliament.

In identifying what constitutes an Act of Parliament, historically the courts have applied the 'enrolled Bill rule' as stated by Lord Campbell in the following case:

CASE EXAMPLE

Edinburgh and Dalkeith Railway Co v Wauchope (1842) 8 C1 & F 710

Wauchope unsuccessfuly argued that a statute (a private Act of Parliament) should be disapplied because the standing orders of the House of Commons had not been complied with. These orders had required that individuals affected by the proposed legislation were to be consulted. In terms of a Bill's passage through Parliament, Lord Campbell in the House of Lords noted (*obiter dictum*) that:

> 'all that a court of justice can look to is the parliamentary roll; they see that an Act has passed both Houses of Parliament, and that it has received the Royal Assent, and no court of justice can inquire into the manner in which it was introduced into Parliament, what was done previously to its being introduced, or what passed in Parliament during the various stages of its progress through both Houses of Parliament.'

Thus, the judges will simply look to the 'parliamentary roll' to ascertain whether or not a Bill had become an Act of Parliament. The judiciary will not be concerned with the internal process and passage of that Bill within Parliament as that would inevitably contravene parliamentary privilege which dictates that Parliament has the constitutional right to determine and monitor its own proceedings (see section 8.7.2). In referring to the parliamentary roll, historically the procedure adopted by the courts would be as follows:

The enrolled Bill rule

- Has the Bill received the consent of the House of Commons?
- Has the Bill received the consent of the House of Lords?
- Has the Bill been granted Royal Assent?

If the answer to all three questions is yes, the Bill is treated as an Act of Parliament. The courts, therefore, are not concerned with how (or more pertinently, why) the Bill came to be on the parliamentary roll (on this point, see also *Pickin* at section 7.8.1). As noted by Bradley, however, today the courts do not need to consult the parliamentary roll as the the words of enactment at the beginning of a statute will indicate this information (House of Lords Select Committee on the Constitution, Seventh Report of Session 2005–06, *Constitutional aspects of the challenge to the Hunting Act 2004*, HL 141 (2006), Appendix 3).

ACTIVITY

Question

What constitutional problems would arise (if any) if the courts were to investigate how a Bill proceeded through Parliament?

As it is the Queen in Parliament that makes Acts of Parliament, it is clear that a 'mere' resolution of the House of Commons is not an Act of Parliament – it does not alter the law nor does it have sovereign status (*Stockdale v Hansard* (1839) 9 Ad and El 1; *Bowles v Bank of England* [1913] 1 Ch 57). Thus, it should be remembered that technically it is an Act of Parliament enacted by Parliament which is sovereign, rather than Parliament itself.

KEY FACTS

- Parliamentary sovereignty means that in legal theory the Queen in Parliament can legally pass any law.

- Parliamentary sovereignty is a construct of the common law, although its precise origins are not clear.

- In determining what constitutes an Act of Parliament, historically the judges would look to the 'parliamentary roll' to ascertain whether or not a Bill had become an Act of Parliament. The judiciary would not be concerned with the internal process of the Bill through Parliament (*Edinburgh and Dalkeith Railway v Wauchope* (1842)).

7.4 Dicey and parliamentary sovereignty

Dicey viewed the principle of parliamentary sovereignty as the cornerstone of the constitution and described it in the following terms:

'The principle of Parliamentary sovereignty means neither more nor less than this, namely, that Parliament thus defined has, under the English constitution, the right to make or unmake any law whatever; and, further, that no person or body is

recognised by the law of England as having a right to override or set aside the
legislation of Parliament'.

A Dicey, *Introduction to the Study of the Law of the Constitution* (10th edn, Macmillan, 1959), pp 39–40.

Dicey viewed parliamentary sovereignty as having both positive and negative elements.

- The positive aspect was that the Crown/Queen in Parliament can legally pass any law it chooses
  (with one exception – see principle 3 below).
- The negative aspect was that no court or other body can question a statute.

Dicey's conception is considered below in the following three interconnected elements/principles:

- The Queen in Parliament can legally pass any law (principle 1 – see section 7.5).
- The courts do not challenge the authority of an Act of Parliament (principle 2 – see section
  7.8).
- Parliament cannot bind its successors or be bound by its predecessors (principle 3 – see section
  7.9).

7.5 Principle 1: The Queen in Parliament can legally pass any law

This in essence embodies the positive element of parliamentary sovereignty, namely, the Queen in
Parliament can in legal theory pass any law (including the repeal or modification of any existing
primary legislation). Parliament can pass any law it considers necessary because under the British
constitution there is legally nothing to stop Parliament from doing so.

7.5.1 Parliamentary sovereignty and the common law

In the United Kingdom's three legal systems (see section 3.1) there is a hierarchy of laws as Acts of
Parliament (statutory sources) are higher in legal status than the common law. In short, where the
content of the common law and a statute are inconsistent, the latter will prevail. This means that
should Parliament decide to do so, it can legislate to override (or codify) the common law as
illustrated in the context of the law of tort when in 1987 Parliament passed the Consumer
Protection Act. In fact, the Act was passed in order to comply with a European Community
directive, thereby also demonstrating the influence European law has had, and continues to have,
on the British constitution (see Chapter 15).

Similarly, in the context of the royal prerogative (a power which the government derives from the
common law – see section 11.9), Parliament can, if it chooses to do so, legislate in an area already
covered by the royal prerogative. In these circumstances, the resulting statutory provisions will take
precedence over the royal prerogative and thereafter the government would be required to act in

accordance with the new statutory provision rather than the pre-existing royal prerogative. As Lord Dunedin stated in *Attorney-General v De Keyser's Royal Hotel Ltd* [1920] AC 508 (see section 11.9.5):

> 'if the whole ground of something which could be done by the prerogative is covered by the statute, it is the statute that rules.'

In addition, as noted at section 4.9, in *Burmah Oil Co Ltd* (1965) the House of Lords had determined that although the destruction of the oil installations in Burma during the Second World War was permissible under the royal prerogative, it nevertheless necessitated compensation for the damage caused. In direct response to this judgment, Parliament in 1965 passed the War Damage Act which in effect nullified the above decision of the House of Lords. In short, therefore, the common law can be overridden by an Act of Parliament at any time. This in itself raises an interesting issue, as, if the principle of parliamentary sovereignty is a 'construct' and rule of the common law, can Parliament legislate to change the common law rule espousing parliamentary sovereignty? (see section 7.10).

7.5.2 Parliamentary sovereignty and the law-making process

Parliament has legislated to alter the law-making process for passing primary legislation, thereby changing the legal and constitutional relationship between the two Houses of Parliament. As will be explored in more detail at section 10.10.1, the combined effect of the Parliament Acts of 1911 and 1949 is that the House of Lords can delay the enactment of a Bill for approximately one year. As a result, after 1911 a Bill can become an Act of Parliament without the consent of one of the constituent elements of the 'Crown in Parliament': the House of Lords. The Parliament Acts, therefore, have altered the passage of primary legislation within Parliament and rendered the consent of the House of Lords theoretically unnecessary in respect of those Bills passed under its provisions.

In addition, through the Parliament Acts, Parliament has altered the judicial perception of what amounts to an Act of Parliament for when the Parliament Acts are involved (which in itself is rare), the consent that the courts require in order to be satisfied that a Bill has become an Act is simply that it has received the consent of the following two elements:

* The House of Commons.

* The monarch (via the granting of the Royal Assent).

7.5.3 Parliamentary sovereignty and the interpretation of legislation

One constitutional role of the judiciary is to interpret Acts of Parliament with a view to ascertaining the intention of Parliament. The judges have historically, developed certain judicial guidelines in construing legislative provisions. In addition, Parliament has given statutory guidance to the courts as to how to construe legislative provisions. For example, s 6(a) of the Interpretation Act 1978 states that unless the contrary intention is indicated in a statute: 'words importing the masculine gender include the feminine'.

More recently Parliament passed the Human Rights Act 1998 which, in effect, is an interpretation Act governing how all legislation (pre- and post-1998) should be interpreted. It expressly directs the judiciary to interpret wherever possible all legislation in line with the articles of the European Convention on Human Rights:

Interpretation of legislation

Human Rights Act 1998, s 3(1)

> So far as it is possible to do so, primary legislation and subordinate legislation must be read and given effect in a way which is compatible with the Convention rights.

This mandatory provision imposes a new statutory obligation on the judiciary instructing them how to interpret legislation affecting human rights. In effect, it requires the judiciary to ensure that the interpretation of the legislation before them is consistent and compatible with the articles of the European Convention (unless the words of the legislation cannot bear such a meaning and a declaration of incompatibility may be given under s 4 (see section 17.7). As a consequence of this 'new' statutory instruction, the judiciary may have to depart from a previous judicial interpretation of a provision of an Act which had been made prior to the enforcement of the Human Rights Act 1998 (this former judicial interpretation would not, of course, have necessarily been made with the articles of the Convention in mind).

This raises the extent to which s 3 has affected the constitutional role of the judiciary, whereby judges have construed legislation in such a way as to blur the constitutional line between interpretation and legislation. For a case in which it is arguable that the judges may well have crossed this boundary and legislated, see s 41 of the Youth Justice and Criminal Evidence Act 1999 in *R v A (Complainant's sexual history)* [2001] UKHL 25 (see section 17.6.1).

Moreover, s 2 of the Human Rights Act 1998 states that a court in the context of applying a Convention right must take into account, *inter alia*, any judgment of the European Court of Human Rights. This provision, therefore, specifically directs the judiciary to consider the jurisprudence of the European Convention in Strasbourg when, *inter alia*, interpreting legislation.

The Human Rights Act 1998 has clearly altered the way in which the judiciary interpret United Kingdom legislation. Indeed, in *R v A* Lord Hope has described s 3 as:

> J   'quite unlike any previous rule of statutory interpretation. There is no need to identify
>   an ambiguity or absurdity. Compatibility with convention rights is the sole guiding
>   principle ... But the rule is only a rule of interpretation. It does not entitle the judges
>   to act as legislators.'

Parliament could, of course, also legally repeal this Act thereby relieving the judiciary of this statutory interpretative obligation. As indicated at section 7.12, however, it would appear that the Act could only be repealed on an express basis, and not on an implied one.

7.5.4 Parliamentary sovereignty and the constitution

As Parliament can, in law, pass any primary legislation that it chooses, this necessarily means that it can also pass any law which alters, whether incrementally or radically, the nature of the United Kingdom's uncodified constitution. As noted earlier at section 3.4.5, the United Kingdom has a flexible constitution. In other countries with a codified rigid constitution (eg the United States), in order for the constitution to be altered a special procedure stipulated in the constitution has to be complied with (see section 2.5.2).

In contrast, in the United Kingdom the rules of the constitution do not have special or entrenched legal status and can therefore be altered by Parliament at will. As a consequence, Parliament can simply amend the British constitution by passing a Bill through the ordinary parliamentary legislative process like any non-constitutional Bill (although by constitutional convention, constitutional Bills in the House of Commons are considered on the Floor of the House – see section 12.7.3). Even though a Bill may have profound, far reaching constitutional implications, no special majority is needed within Parliament (or even to be supported by the people in a referendum) for the Bill to become an Act. Moreover, even though the resulting Act may radically reshape the United Kingdom's constitutional arrangements, and no matter how politically controversial it is, the courts are legally disabled from challenging or invalidating the Act. In legal theory, therefore, Parliament can reform the constitution in any way it sees fit.

A few examples will suffice to demonstrate the principle that Parliament can alter any aspect of the British constitution and it is pertinent to note the comments in 2000 of the Royal Commission on the reform of the House of Lords that stated that, in relation to the 1997 Labour Government's initial batch of constitutional reforms such measures:

> 'would have been impossible under the laborious systems required to amend the
> written constitutions of many other countries'.

A House for the Future Cm 4534 (The Stationery Office, 2000) para 5.2.

Some key constitutional changes since 1997:

- **The Scotland Act 1998** (this Act devolved power to Scotland – see section 14.3).

- **The House of Lords Act 1999** (this Act removed most of the hereditary peers from the House of Lords – see section 10.6.3).

- **The European Parliamentary Elections Act 1999** (this Act altered the electoral system used to elect MEPs to the European Parliament from the 'first past the post' system to one in which elections took place on the basis of a proportional party list system).

In effect, therefore, no aspect of the constitution is technically unalterable (but see section 7.7). In fact, in 1996 Parliament (rather controversially) amended Art 9 of the Bill of Rights Act 1689 by the enactment of s 13 of the Defamation Act 1996 (see section 8.6.2). A further example of a major constitutional change being effected by statute is the following legislation:

S **The Local Government Act 1985**

This Act abolished the Greater London Council (the GLC) and metropolitan councils in London. It demonstrated graphically that local government in the context of the British constitution does not enjoy 'constitutional status' in the sense that it does not have any special constitutional or legal protection from the legislature.

In addition, Parliament can choose to lengthen or shorten the life of a Parliament. For example, the Septennial Act 1715 stipulated that the maximum length of a parliamentary term was seven years (it had previously been three years under the Triennial Act 1694). At the beginning of the twentieth century, s 7 of the Parliament Act 1911 reduced this period to five years. Although five years is the current maximum length of term for modern Parliaments, this period could be either shortened or lengthened by another Act of Parliament.

Thus, as Parliament can (at least in legal theory) seemingly alter any aspect of the British constitution, this begs the question as to whether parliamentary sovereignty is consistent with constitutionalism (see sections 7.6 and 7.13).

ACTIVITY

Question

What are the advantages and disadvantages of Parliament being able to reform the constitution through the passage of a simple Act of Parliament?

7.5.5 Parliamentary sovereignty and international law

Parliament can pass legislation which breaches international law. This was illustrated earlier in *Cheney v Conn* (1968) (see section 7.3.2) and the following case illustrates the same point:

CASE EXAMPLE

Mortensen v Peters (1906) 14 SLT 227

A by-law was passed (by the Fishery Board for Scotland) under s 7 of the Herring Fishery (Scotland) Act 1889 which prohibited trawling within the Moray Firth (part of the Moray Firth is an area beyond British territorial waters). Mortensen (a Danish captain of a Norwegian trawler) was convicted in a Scottish Sheriff Court for violating the above by-law. Mortensen's appeal was based, *inter alia*, on international law which permits a state to regulate fishing within its territorial waters, however, Mortensen had been arrested in that part of the Moray Firth which was outside British territorial waters.

The High Court of Justiciary held that the intention of Parliament in the 1889 Act was to allow by-laws to be passed covering the Moray Firth even if this was contrary to the rules of international law as part of this area is in international waters. It should be recalled that there is a statutory presumption that Parliament does not intend to legislate contrary to international law (see section 4.8.3).

J 'For us an Act of Parliament duly passed by Lords and Commons and assented to by the King is supreme, and we are bound to give effect to its terms.'

The Lord Justice-General

Even in the context of the European Convention of Human Rights, and irrespective of the Human Rights Act 1998, Parliament can in legal theory if it chooses to do so (though politically unlikely), legislate contrary to the articles enshrined in the European Convention.

Notwithstanding the general rule above, Parliament is constrained (in the context of international law) by the international Treaties which the United Kingdom has signed. For example, in respect of the European Convention, Art 1 states that:

(A) 'The High Contracting Parties shall secure to everyone within their jurisdiction the rights and freedoms defined in Section I of this Convention.'

As a result, historically Parliament has tried to avoid passing legislation which violates the rights set out in the Convention, thereby honouring (in international law) the United Kingdom's international obligations in respect of this Treaty. Although in strict legal theory Parliament could deliberately and flagrantly legislate contrary to these Articles (irrespective of its obligations in international law to protect such rights), the political consequences of such legislation would involve criticism of the United Kingdom in the Council of Europe together with possible expulsion (see section 4.15.2).

In addition, in terms of European Community law, Parliament could (in legal theory) pass legislation which clearly and expressly contravenes and repudiates European Community law principles (see section 15.6.5).

It is worth noting that although Parliament passes laws on its own volition (albeit invariably under the impetus and direction of the executive), it will also pass legislation in order to fulfill its international obligations. For example, when the European Court of Human Rights has declared that United Kingdom law is inconsistent with the Convention, Parliament will invariably introduce legislation in order to remedy this defect as in international law it is required to fulfill the requirements set out by the court in Strasbourg. The following statute is an example of this:

The Contempt of Court Act 1981

This legislation regulates freedom of expression (eg the press) pending and during a court hearing. It was passed in response to a ruling of the European Court that the common law of contempt of court had unnecessarily infringed freedom of speech (*Sunday Times v UK* (1979) 2 EHRR 245).

In short, Parliament passed this legislation as a direct result of external pressure, namely the United Kingdom's international obligation to comply with a ruling of the European Court of Human Rights (in the context of prisoners' voting rights – see also section 22.5.2). Similarly, in the context of European Community law, Parliament will pass laws in response to European Directives. For example, the Data Protection Act 1998 was enacted as a result of a Directive.

7.5.6 Parliamentary sovereignty and extra territorial jurisdiction

In legal theory, Parliament can enact legislation which purports to have extra-territorial effect. In other words, it could legislate outside the legal jurisdiction of the United Kingdom (see *Mortensen* (1906) section 7.5.5). The classic example to illustrate this is put forward by Sir Ivor Jennings (*The Law and the Constitution* (5th edn, Hodder and Stoughton, 1959), pp 170–171). He theorised that Parliament could, in legal theory, pass legislation banning smoking on the streets of Paris (in the Health Act 2006 Parliament did legislate to ban smoking in United Kingdom public houses). In fact, Parliament has legislated for territory outside of the United Kingdom:

The War Crimes Act 1991

This Act has extra-territorial effect as it concerns murder committed by a British citizen (or resident in the United Kingdom) in Germany or an area under German occupation between 1939–45. The Act was passed under the Parliament Acts 1911 and 1949 as the House of Lords refused to pass it. In particular, they were concerned that the Act had criminal retrospective effect (see section 6.3.2) and there were reservations about the reliability of evidence dating back 50 years.

The Sex Offenders Act 1997

Section 7 of this Act permits the United Kingdom courts to have legal jurisdiction over specified sexual offences committed overseas.

ACTIVITY

Question

Could the United Kingdom Parliament legislate for the Republic of Ireland?

7.5.7 Parliamentary sovereignty and the conferring of powers onto the executive

Parliament can legislate to confer wide discretionary powers on the executive. As noted earlier in *Inland Revenue Commissioners and Another v Rossminster Ltd and others* [1980] AC 952 (see section 6.7.5), s 20C of the Taxes Management Act 1970 conferred very wide powers on Inland Revenue officers to search premises. In this case Lord Scarman lamented that as the Act had been complied with:

> J 'It is therefore with regret that I have to accept that, if the requirements of section 20C of the Taxes Management Act 1970 … are met, the power exists to enter, and search premises, and seize and remove things there found and that the prospect of an immediate judicial review of the exercise of the power is dim.'

Today such a provision may be challenged under the Human Rights Act 1998 (see Chapter 17).

In fact, Parliament often confers law-making powers on the executive in the form of an enabling Act. For example, s 1 of the Export Control Act 2002 conferred a power on the Secretary of State to make an order (delegated legislation in the form of a Statutory Instrument) in connection with imposing export controls in respect of goods. As indicated earlier (see section 5.7.2), therefore, Parliament can legislate to violate the separation of powers by conferring a discretionary law-making power on the executive.

The Legislative and Regulatory Reform Act 2006

This Act conferred a power on a minister to make an order (delegated legislation) to reform legislation or implement the recommendations made by the Law Commissions (see section 22.2.3).

In the context of Parliament conferring duties and powers on the executive, it is pertinent to note that, at least in recent decades, the executive has to a large extent dominated the House of

Commons. By extension, therefore, the executive has largely controlled Parliament as a whole (see Chapter 12), which in turn determines the legislation that it passes.

7.6 Non-legal restraints on Parliament

7.6.1 Political restraints

Although Parliament can, in legal theory, pass any law that it chooses, this does not necessarily mean that Parliament will pass any such law. This is because although there may be an absence of legal limitations on Parliament, there are, of course, political restraints on it. As indicated earlier, political sovereignty rests with the people as the people elect Parliament and therefore the electorate act as a political restraint on the laws that Parliament passes.

In other words, if Parliament passed a highly controversial, objectionable and draconian law, at the following general election these parliamentarians (specifically the elected MPs) would have to face the wrath of the electorate as they sought to be re-elected. In short, as Dicey noted: 'The electors can in the long run always enforce their will' (A Dicey, *Introduction to the Study of the Law of the Constitution* (10th edn, Macmillan, 1959) p 73). As such, Parliament is limited politically as it will inevitably refrain from passing legislation which the electorate would find unacceptable.

One obvious difficulty with this analysis, of course, is that the draconian legislation in question may only affect, or be directed at, a minority of the population who, as a group may not necessarily be popular (eg prisoners). As a result, such legislation may in fact be acceptable to (and indeed popular with) the majority of the population who would be unaffected by its consequences.

That said, at least since the operation of the Human Rights Act 1998, all legislation must now be interpreted in light of the Articles of the European Convention (see Chapter 17).

ACTIVITY

Question

How effective do think political sovereignty is as a political restraint on parliamentary sovereignty?

7.6.2 Political entrenchment

Although according to Dicey legislation cannot be *legally entrenched* and protected from repeal, nevertheless, it may well be the case that certain Acts of Parliament (owing to their content and political importance) become *politically entrenched* in the sense that Parliament may lack the political will (eg support of the electorate) to repeal them.

One example could be the Human Rights Act 1998. In strict legal terms, Parliament could expressly repeal this legislation (on implied repeal of this Act see sections 4.4.5 and 7.12).

Politically, however, it may be very difficult for Parliament to muster the support from the electorate to repeal this legislation. In short, once the Human Rights Act conferred positive rights on individuals which they can enforce against the state in a court, it may prove to be very difficult *politically* (and *internationally*) to revoke them. In other countries the rights of the individual are contained in a Bill or Charter of Rights which will, typically, form part of a legally entrenched constitution. These rights, therefore, will be difficult to alter or abolish as they are legally entrenched.

Similarly, the Scotland Act 1998 establishing a Scottish Parliament in Edinburgh can in legal theory be expressly repealed (on implied repeal see sections 4.4.5 and 7.11), but in political terms it may prove to be very difficult to repeal. Indeed, the Scottish Parliament had been preceded by a referendum in Scotland in which the Scottish people endorsed the principle of a new Scottish Parliament.

7.6.3 Practical restraints

In respect of parliamentary sovereignty, it is important to distinguish between what is legally possible (which in legal theory is limitless) and what is actually possible in practice. For example, in 1931 Parliament passed the Statute of Westminster which stated in s 4, that no United Kingdom statute passed after the commencement of this Act shall extend to the law of a Dominion (in 1931 these Dominions included Australia, Canada, New Zealand, the Irish Free State and Newfoundland), unless the Dominion in question requested and consented to that legislation.

In strict legal theory, however, the United Kingdom Parliament could simply repeal this provision and proceed to legislate for one of the above Dominions against their consent. This point was made by Viscount Sankey LC in the Privy Council in *British Coal Corporation v The King* [1935] AC 500, who stated that:

> J   'It is doubtless true that the power of the Imperial Parliament to pass on its own initative any legislation that it thought fit extending to Canada remains in theory unimpaired: indeed, the Imperial Parliament could, as a matter of abstract law, repeal or disregard s 4 of the Statute. But that is theory and has no relation to realities.'

In other words, even if the United Kingdom Parliament were to pass such legislation, it would not be effective or enforceable in the relevant Dominion (unless that state decided to adopt it), thereby demonstrating a practical restraint on Parliament.

Similarly, should Parliament legislate to repeal the grants of independence to former dependent territories with the intention of revoking their independent status, the mere legal passage of such legislation would not, of course, affect the actual independence of that particular state.

As Lord Denning MR in *Blackburn v Attorney General* [1971] 2 All ER 1380, commented:

J 'Take the Statute of Westminster 1931, which takes away the power of Parliament to legislate for the dominions. Can anyone imagine that Parliament could or would reverse that statute? Take the Acts which have granted independence to the dominions and territories overseas. Can anyone imagine that Parliament could or would reverse those laws and take away their independence? Most clearly not. Freedom once given cannot be taken away. Legal theory must give way to practical politics.'

Moreover, to take the example used above concerning Parliament legislating to ban smoking on the streets of Paris (see section 7.5.6), Sir Ivor Jennings has pointed out that such a law would not be effective within Paris itself as it is outside the jurisdiction of the United Kingdom courts. In strict legal theory the legislation in question would be legally valid, but not practically enforceable in France.

7.6.4 Constitutional conventions

Parliament can choose to legislate contrary to a constitutional convention. For example, since the establishment of the Scotland Act 1998 a convention has been established to the effect that the United Kingdom Parliament will not legislate in the context of a devolved matter for Scotland without the consent of the Scottish Parliament (the *Sewel Convention*). As a constitutional convention, it is simply a political rule of the constitution and as such, in legal theory, Parliament could choose to ignore it and proceed to pass legislation for Scotland in the absence of the consent of the Scottish Parliament. The political ramifications of such action, however, would inevitably prevent Parliament from passing such legislation.

Constitutional conventions, therefore, do not legally bind Parliament and this point was reiterated by Lord Reid in the Privy Council in the following case:

CASE EXAMPLE

Madzimbamuto v Lardner-Burke [1969] 1 AC 645

In 1965 it was a well established constitutional convention that the United Kingdom Parliament did not legislate for Southern Rhodesia (now Zimbabwe) without the consent of the government of the legislative Assembly of Southern Rhodesia. In 1965, however, the Prime Minister of Southern Rhodesia issued a declaration of independence to the effect that Southern Rhodesia was now an independent sovereign state and no longer a crown colony. The United Kingdom nevertheless passed legislation purporting to apply to Southern Rhodesia in contravention of the above convention.

CONTINUED ▶

Lord Reid noted that although the constitutional convention was an important principle, it had no legal effect, which limited the legal powers of Parliament to pass legislation (see the full quotation at section 4.15.2). In fact, in reality the legislation in question did not have any impact on Southern Rhodesia and illustrates the practical limitations on Parliament (analogous to legislating to ban smoking on the streets of Paris).

ACTIVITY

Problem solving

Can the Queen in Parliament legally pass the following laws and if so, what would be their effect?

- The House of Lords Bill (which proposes to reinstate the expelled hereditary peers).

- The Mexico Bill (which proposes to make it a criminal offence for anyone to eat chewing gum on the streets of Mexico City).

- The Elections Bill (which proposes to abolish elections to the House of Commons).

- The Finance Bill (which proposes to exclude anyone earning less than £25,000 a year from voting in local government elections).

- The Prime Minister Bill (which proposes to override the constitutional convention that the Prime Minister must be drawn from within Parliament).

- The Courts Bill (which proposes to abolish jury trial for all criminal offences).

Revisit your answers after reading section 7.7.

7.7 Is there a limitation on the laws that Parliament can pass?

Dicey noted that there was one clear limitation on Parliament, namely that Parliament cannot bind its successor, or be bound by its predecessor (see section 7.9). In addition, the judiciary (both in a judicial and an extra judicial context) have suggested that there are in fact limits to Parliament's legislative power. For example, recently in the House of Lords Lord Steyn noted (albeit *obiter*) in *R (Jackson) v Attorney General* [2005] UKHL 56, that owing to the fact that parliamentary sovereignty was a common law construct, accordingly:

> **J** 'it is not unthinkable that circumstances could arise where the courts may have to qualify a principle established on a different hypothesis of constitutionalism. In exceptional circumstances involving an attempt to abolish judicial review or the ordinary role of the courts, the Appellate Committee of the House of Lords or a new Supreme Court may have to consider whether this is a constitutional fundamental which even a sovereign Parliament acting at the behest of a complaisant House of Commons cannot abolish.'

In other words, if Parliament passed legislation which abrogated certain fundamental principles of the constitution, then the courts, in applying the common law principle of parliamentary sovereignty, may decide that even Parliament (notwithstanding the sovereignty of Parliament) could not make such legislation. It is of interest to note that in his evidence to the House of Lords Select Committee on the Constitution in November 2005, the Lord Chancellor disagreed with Lord Steyn's comments that, aside from Europe, Parliament was prevented from legislating in respect of certain principles of the constitution. The Lord Chancellor considered himself to be 'on the side of the conventional constitutional thinkers' on this issue (Sixth Report of the House of Lords Select Committee on the Constitution, *Meeting with the Lord Chancellor* (HL Paper 84 (2005), Q15).

Similarly, Lord Woolf writing extra judicially in 1995 commented that there might be limits on Parliament's legislative powers as enforced by the courts if Parliament passed legislation fundamentally undermining the rule of law (in particular, by removing or substantially impairing the constitutional role of the courts in the context of judicial review):

> 'if Parliament did the unthinkable, then I would say that the courts would also be required to act in a manner which would be without precedent. Some judges might chose to do so by saying that it was an unrebuttable presumption that Parliament could never intend such a result. I myself would consider there were advantages in making it clear that ultimately there are even limits on the supremacy of Parliament which it is the courts' inalienable responsibility to identify and uphold. They are limits of the most modest dimensions which I believe any democrat would accept. They are no more than are necessary to enable the rule of law to be preserved.'

> Lord Woolf, 'Droit Public-English Style' [1995] PL 57.

The above examples are, of course, highly unlikely to occur in practice and so these potential limitations are somewhat theoretical.

ACTIVITY

Question

What do the above judicial comments tell us about the constitutional relationship between the judiciary and the legislature?

KEY FACTS

Parliament can in legal theory pass a law which:

- Abolishes or alters the common law.
- Infringes international law.
- Alters (either marginally or radically) the uncodified constitution.
- Has extra territorial jurisdiction.
- Alters the law-making process or the judicial rules of statutory interpretation.
- Is retrospective in nature.
- Abrogates a constitutional convention.
- Confers wide discretionary powers on the executive.

There are, however, political and practical restraints on parliamentary sovereignty.

7.8 Principle 2: The courts do not challenge the authority of an Act of Parliament

7.8.1 Introduction

Dicey stated that:

> 'no person or body is recognised by the law of England as having a right to override or set aside the legislation of Parliament'.

A Dicey, *Introduction to the Study of the Law of the Constitution* (10th edn, Macmillan, 1959), p 40.

This principle represents the negative side of parliamentary sovereignty, namely, that no body (court or otherwise) can challenge an Act of Parliament. This is, of course, inextricably linked to the first principle that the Crown in Parliament can in law pass any law that it chooses because once the legislation is enacted, no court can invalidate it.

In essence, therefore, parliamentary sovereignty concerns the constitutional relationship between the United Kingdom's courts and the United Kingdom Parliament, with the former being legally subordinate to the latter. Thus, irrespective of the content of the statute, the courts' constitutional responsibility is simply to interpret and apply the legislation passed by Parliament.

 CASE EXAMPLE

R v Jordan [1967] Crim LR 483

Jordan had been convicted and sentenced to imprisonment for offences committed under the Race Relations Act 1965. He contended that the Act was invalid on the basis that it curtailed freedom of expression and sought legal aid to apply for a writ of *habeas corpus* on this ground.

The Queen's Bench Division of the High Court held that the courts did not have the power to question the validity of primary legislation. Jordan's claim was dismissed as completely unarguable.

Similarly, in *Duport Steels Ltd and Others v Sirs and Others* [1980] 1 All ER 529 Lord Scarman reiterated that the constitutional relationship between the judge and parliamentary legislation was that the former:

 'must not deny the statute. Unpalatable statute law may not be disregarded or rejected, merely because it is unpalatable.'

The following case illustrates a number of principles relating to sovereignty and the constitutional relationship between the courts and Parliament.

 CASE EXAMPLE

British Railways Board v Pickin [1974] AC 765

In 1968 a private Act of Parliament (The British Railways Act 1968) was passed with the effect of nullifying the effect of an earlier private Act of 1836. The latter had established a railway line and provided that if such a line should be abandoned, the lands on which the line was built should vest in the owners of the adjoining lands. Instead, under s 18 of the later 1968 Act, such land would now vest in the British Railways Board.

CONTINUED ▸

Pickin owned land adjoining a track and instituted an action against the British Railways Board claiming ownership of the adjoining land to the centre line of the track. The Board argued that under the 1968 Act the land vested in the Board. In reply, Pickin alleged that the Board (in promoting the British Railways Bill) had misled Parliament by a false recital in the preamble to the 1968 legislation. It was argued accordingly that the Board could not rely on the 1968 Act to deprive Pickin of title to this land. The Court of Appeal reversed a decision to strike out Pickin's above argument and the Board appealed to the House of Lords which allowed its appeal.

The court held that the function of the court was to apply Acts of Parliament. It was not lawful to impugn the validity of legislation by seeking to establish that Parliament in passing such legislation had been misled by fraud.

> J 'The idea that a court is entitled to disregard a provision in an Act of Parliament on any ground must seem strange and startling to anyone with any knowledge of the history and law of our constitution' (Lord Reid).

Further, Lord Morris noted:

> J 'When an enactment is passed there is finality unless and until it is amended or repealed by Parliament. In the courts there may be argument as to the correct interpretation of the enactment: there must be none as to whether it should be on the Statute Book at all'.

The *Pickin* case illustrates the following principles concerning our constitution:

- Firstly, the court reiterated that the courts do not have the constitutional authority to impugn or challenge the validity of an Act. This applied whether the statute was a public or private Act of Parliament (the case concerned a private Act).

- Secondly, Lord Reid dismissed the notion that the modern courts could disregard an Act of Parliament on the basis that: 'it was contrary to the law of God or the law of nature or natural justice but since the supremacy of Parliament was finally demonstrated by the revolution of 1688 any such idea has become obsolete'. This was a clear reference to, and repudiation of, the earlier historic case of *Dr Bonham's Case* (1610) 8 Co Rep 114 in which Coke CJ had stated that the common law would control and adjudge to be void an Act of Parliament which was 'against common right and reason, or repugnant, or impossible to be performed'.

It should be remembered that although the courts will not impugn the validity of an Act of Parliament, this does not preclude them from questioning and invalidating secondary legislation. In fact, the courts regularly judicially review the content and exercise of delegated legislation by the executive and other bodies (see Chapters 19 and 20). Although the term judicial review is used in the British constitution, this is in relation to delegated legislation rather than primary legislation (but in the context of European Community law see section 15.6.4).

ACTIVITY

Problem solving

Can you envisage any circumstances in which Parliament passed an Act where it would be (a) morally, or (b) constitutionally appropriate for the courts to question it?

7.8.2 The courts may assume that Parliament did not intend to act unconstitutionally

Although the courts do not question an Act of Parliament, it must be remembered that it is in fact the judiciary who interpret statutes and extract and apply their meaning. As Dicey noted:

> 'Parliament is supreme legislator, but from the moment Parliament has uttered its will as lawgiver, that will becomes subject to the interpretation put upon it by the judges of the land'. (sic)

A Dicey, *Introduction to the Study of the Law of the Constitution* (10th edn, Macmillan, 1959), p 413.

Moreover, as indicated earlier at section 4.8.3, in construing legislation the courts have developed a number of principles as aids to their construction. For example, one historic constitutional role of the United Kingdom judges is to safeguard the freedom of the individual. As a result, where legislation appears to be ambiguous or capable of a number of interpretations, the courts will apply certain constitutional fundamentals in interpreting that legislation.

These 'constitutional presumptions' include, *inter alia*, that surely Parliament would never have intended the following results:

- An interference with the human rights and liberties of the individual.

- A restriction of an individual's access to the courts.

- To legislate contrary to an international Treaty or international obligations.

These presumptions are justified on the constitutional basis that if Parliament did intend to achieve any of the outcomes indicated above, it would have made this very clear in the relevant statutory provision. As pointed out at section 4.8.3, the last presumption was demonstrated in *Waddington v*

Miah [1974] 2 All ER 377 where the House of Lords interpreted the Immigration Act 1971 in line with Art 7 of the European Convention (which outlaws the imposition of retrospective criminal legislation). In other words, the courts assume that Parliament intends to act consistently, and so legislate in line with its international obligations, unless the statute clearly indicates this not to be the case (in the context of European Community law see section 15.6.5).

In the Republic of Ireland, the Irish constitution also uses an analogous presumption, namely, the *presumption of constitutionality*. Article 15.4 of the Irish constitution states that the Oireachtas shall not pass legislation inconsistent with the written codified constitution. As a result of this, unless the contrary is proved, the courts will assume that legislation passed by the Oireachtas is 'constitutional', and so in accordance with the constitution.

Dicey summarised the first two principles underpinning parliamentary sovereignty in the following way:

> 'Parliamentary sovereignty is therefore an undoubted legal fact. It is complete both on its positive and on its negative side. Parliament can legally legislate on any topic whatever which, in the judgment of Parliament, is a fit subject for legislation. There is no power which, under the English constitution, can come into rivalry with the legislative sovereignty of Parliament'.

> A Dicey, *Introduction to the Study of the Law of the Constitution* (10th edn, Macmillan, 1959), pp 68–70.

7.8.3 The surrender of parliamentary sovereignty?

Although there are no limits on the laws that it can pass, this does not mean that Parliament cannot, ultimately, surrender its sovereignty forever. In other words, Parliament could in legal theory simply dissolve itself. On this point Dicey has noted that Parliament:

> 'may simply put an end to its own existence. Parliament could extinguish itself by legally dissolving itself and leaving no means whereby a subsequent parliament could be legally summoned'.

> A Dicey, *Introduction to the Study of the Law of the Constitution* (10th edn, Macmillan, 1959), p 69.

In this sense, Parliament could legally terminate itself – which is likened to a suicide, and is, of course, irreversible.

In the albeit unlikely event of the United Kingdom adopting a codified entrenched constitution containing constitutional laws which had a higher special legal status, Parliament would need to divest itself of the principle of parliamentary sovereignty. This is because the United Kingdom could not have a legally entrenched codified constitution which would legally control the laws which the new legislature could pass, whilst simultaneously retaining the principle of parliamentary sovereignty.

KEY FACTS

- Historically, the courts cannot question Acts of Parliament (*R v Jordan* (1967), *British Railways Board v Pickin* (1974)). This is in contrast, for example, to the Supreme Court in the United States or the Republic of Ireland

- The constitutional function of the judiciary is limited simply to interpreting and ascertaining the meaning of an Act of Parliament. In construing legislation, however, the courts will apply certain constitutional fundamentals and assume that Parliament did not intend to legislate 'unconstitutionally' (*Waddington v Miah* (1974)).

7.9 Principle 3: Parliament cannot bind its successors

7.9.1 Introduction

The third aspect of parliamentary sovereignty involves the following two interrelated principles:

- Parliament cannot bind its successors. For example, the Parliament in 2010 cannot restrict the laws that could be passed by the Parliament of 2011.

- Parliament cannot be bound by its predecessor. For example, the Parliament of 2011 cannot be bound or restricted by the 2010 Parliament.

In summary, it has been argued traditionally that Parliament cannot entrench legislation. Dicey stated that on the occasions that language had been used in an Act of Parliament which purported to imply that a particular statute could not be altered or repealed by a subsequent Parliament, 'the endeavour has always ended in failure'. Thus, one Parliament cannot be bound by its predecessors.

This principle ensures that each new Parliament retains its sovereign power to pass whatever legislation is deemed necessary at the time. If one Parliament could tie the hands of its successor, the later Parliament would not enjoy full legislative power to pass any legislation that it chooses, as it would be restrained by this former Parliament. Today this principle can be justified on the basis that each new Parliament should enjoy full sovereign legislative power as each new Parliament represents the latest will of the people as reflected in the latest general election (see political sovereignty at section 7.2.2). It also means that laws can adapt to new developments and that one Parliament does not become a prisoner of the views (as embodied in legislation) of a previous Parliament (perhaps of centuries before).

This principle means that in the United Kingdom, Acts of Parliament cannot be legally (as opposed to being politically) entrenched, that is to say that they cannot legally be protected from repeal by a subsequent Parliament at a later date. As Herbert CJ noted centuries ago in *Godden v Hales* (1686) 11 St Tr 1165:

> 'if an Act of Parliament had a clause in it that it should never be repealed, yet without question, the same power that made it may repeal it.'

Indeed, this would even apply to two Acts passed within the same parliamentary term, whereby an Act passed in the first session of a Parliament could be repealed by a later Act in the second session of the same Parliament, although this would be highly unlikely to happen in practice.

ACTIVITY

Question

Distinguish between the legal and political entrenchment of legislation.

The principle that Parliament cannot bind its successors is achieved through the twin doctrines of:

- Express repeal.
- Implied repeal.

7.9.2 Express repeal

This is the principle that a later Act of Parliament expressly and explicitly repeals an earlier inconsistent Act (or section of it). Parliament can *unmake* any law that it chooses. In fact, an Act of Parliament will detail in its Schedule the legislation (or provisions of such) that is to be specifically repealed. For example, s 49(1) of the Inquiries Act 2005 expressly repeals the Tribunals of Inquiry (Evidence) Act 1921 and s 49(2) makes reference to Sched 3 which details the extent of other provisions of statutes which are repealed or revoked. The doctrine of express repeal means that even if, as Herbert CJ indicated above, an Act stated that it was exempt from repeal, it could nevertheless be expressly repealed by a later Act (see further section 7.10.1).

7.9.3 Implied repeal

The doctrine of implied repeal comes into operation when two Acts of Parliament dealing with the same subject matter are inconsistent with each other, but the later Act does not expressly repeal the earlier one. In these circumstances the doctrine of implied repeal would ensure that the provisions of the later Act prevailed, by impliedly repealing the earlier Act to the extent that it was inconsistent. In short, this means that two inconsistent Acts stating two different things on the same subject matter cannot stand together. In this way, the courts give effect to the latest will of Parliament (as reflected at the last general election). The doctrine is illustrated by the following two cases:

CASE EXAMPLE

Vauxhall Estates Limited v Liverpool Corporation [1932] 1 KB 733

Section 2 of the Acquisition of Land Act 1919 provided for the assessment of compensation in respect of land acquired compulsorily by a government department or local authority. Section 7 of the Act provided that: 'The provisions of the Act or order by which the land is authorised to be acquired, or of any Act incorporated therewith, shall, in relation to the matters dealt with in this Act, have effect subject to this Act, and so far as inconsistent with this Act those provisions shall cease to have or shall not have effect'.

In 1925 s 46 of the Housing Act provided for the assessment of such compensation for land acquired compulsorily on a less generous basis. The Corporation of Liverpool proposed a scheme under the 1925 Act for the improvement of Liverpool which included lands owned by Vauxhall Estates Ltd who contended that the amount of compensation should be assessed under s 2 of the 1919 Act. This was because the assessment of compensation under the 1925 Act differed materially from the 1919 Act and so s 7 of this Act rendered the later Act of no effect. Counsel for Vauxhall had argued that s 7 of the 1919 Act purported, in effect, to prevent the implied repeal of its provisions (thereby purporting to tie the hands of a successor Parliament).

The Divisional Court held that the 1925 Act repealed by implication (ie impliedly repealed) the earlier Act of 1919, to the extent that it was inconsistent. The court held that even if the 1919 Act had purported to apply to future Acts, s 46 of the 1925 Act would prevail. On the facts, Avory J concluded that on its true construction, s 7 applied only to existing Acts in 1919 and not to future Acts (the other two judges did not decide this issue).

> **J** 'Speaking for myself, I should certainly hold, until the contrary were decided, that no Act of Parliament can effectively provide that no future Act shall interfere with its provisions.' (Avory J)

185

CASE EXAMPLE

Ellen Street Estates Limited v Minister of Health [1934] 1 KB 590

In this case the Court of Appeal approved of, and followed, the decision in *Vauxhall Estates* (see above). It is of interest to note that counsel for Vauxhall appeared for Ellen Street Estates and submitted that the Divisional Court decision in *Vauxhall Estates* had been wrongly decided and that it was possible for Parliament to state that an Act could be repealed in express terms only, and not by implication. Since s 46 of the 1925 Act was inconsistent with the 1919 Act, and the 1925 Act had not expressly repealed it, accordingly, this later provision (s 46 of the 1925 Act) should have no legal effect. The Court of Appeal rejected this contention in the following terms by Maugham LJ:

> 'The Legislature cannot, according to our constitution, bind itself as to the form of subsequent legislation, and it is impossible for Parliament to enact that in a subsequent statute dealing with the same subject-matter there can be no implied repeal. If in a subsequent Act Parliament chooses to make it plain that the earlier statute is being to some extent repealed, effect must be given to that intention just because it is the will of the Legislature.'

Thus, even if a Parliament in 2010 stated in an Act that it could not be repealed, according to the above doctrines a later Parliament could either:

* expressly repeal this legislation with an Act of Parliament specifically stating this (express repeal); or

* impliedly repeal this legislation by passing an Act of Parliament which was plainly inconsistent with the provisions of the earlier Act (implied repeal), but without expressly repealing (or even referring to) the earlier 2010 Act.

Notwithstanding the points made above, the doctrine of implied repeal needs to be reconsidered in the context of the following:

* European Community law (see section 15.6).

* The Human Rights Act 1998 (see section 7.12).

* Other constitutional statutes (see Laws LJ at section 4.4.5).

KEY FACTS

Parliament cannot bind its successors or be bound by its predecessors. This is achieved through the following doctrines:

- Express repeal is the principle that a later Act of Parliament expressly and explicitly repeals an earlier inconsistent Act (or section of it).

- Implied repeal is the principle that when two Acts of Parliament dealing with the same subject matter are inconsistent with each other (but that later Act does not expressly repeal the earlier one), the later Act impliedly repeals the earlier one to the extent that it is inconsistent (*Vauxhall Estates Limited v Liverpool Corporation* (1932) and *Ellen Street Estates Limited v Minister of Health* (1934)).

These doctrines taken together indicate that Parliament cannot entrench legislation against subsequent repeal by a later Parliament.

7.10 Is legal entrenchment possible?

Is it at all possible for Parliament to bind its successors and legally entrench legislation?

In essence, academic commentators have traditionally distinguished between two types of entrenchment:

- Entrenchment in terms of subject matter.
- Entrenchment in terms of the manner and form of later legislation (this relates to the procedure for making legislation).

One argument typically levelled in favour of entrenchment is that since the principle of parliamentary sovereignty is a common law rule, and since statutes have a superior status to the common law, logically therefore, why cannot Parliament simply legislate to alter this common law rule relating to sovereignty and entrenchment? According to Wade, however, as indicated at section 7.3.2, although the recognition of parliamentary sovereignty is a rule of the common law, it is in essence the one common law rule that cannot be altered (in the absence of a legal revolution – but see the 'revolution' in the context of European Community law at section 15.6.5).

7.10.1 Entrenchment in terms of subject matter

Democratic constitutions generally protect certain subject matters (such as fundamental basic human rights or other fundamental principles) from legal infringement or revocation by later legislation. Thus, such rights are typically 'constitutionally ring-fenced' in a Bill or Charter of Rights and are thereby placed out of the reach of the legislature and the 'ordinary' legislative process.

In contrast, in the United Kingdom as a result of parliamentary sovereignty, even if such basic rights were embodied in statutory form which stated that owing to their nature they could never be repealed (eg an entrenched British Charter of Rights), a future Parliament could simply legislate to revoke them at a later date (on the Human Rights Act 1998 see section 7.12). According to Herbert CJ (see section 7.9.1) under the traditional conception of parliamentary sovereignty, such a Charter could nonetheless be repealed. Indeed, Lord Scarman in 1974 commented that:

> 'It is the helplessness of the law in face of the legislative sovereignty of Parliament which makes it difficult for the legal system to accommodate the concept of fundamental and inviolable human rights'.

Lord Scarman, English Law: The New Dimension (1974), p 15.

Dicey's theory is known as the continuing theory of sovereignty, whereby each Parliament has full legislative sovereignty.

Acts of Union

It is commonly suggested, however, that owing to their content and fundamental importance, one category of statutes – the Union Acts – cannot be subsequently repealed. The two Union Acts are:

- The Union with Scotland Act 1706 – which united England and Wales with Scotland to form the Parliament of Great Britain; and

- The Union with Ireland Act 1800 – which united England, Wales and Scotland with Ireland to form the Parliament of the United Kingdom.

The argument is that these Acts have a special legal status. In other words, they are legally entrenched against repeal and the Acts themselves indicate as much. For example, in relation to the 1706 Act, Art 25 states:

S 'That all Laws and Statutes in either Kingdom, so far as they are contrary to, or inconsistent with the Terms of these Articles, or any of them, shall, from and after the Union, cease and become void, and shall be so declared to be, by the respective Parliaments of the said Kingdoms.'

In fact, Dicey made specific reference to the Union Acts. In respect of the 1706 Act which had enacted, *inter alia,* that Scottish university professors should acknowledge, profess and subscribe to the Confession of Faith (a protestant doctrine), he noted that the Act 'in substance enacts that this provision shall be a fundamental and essential condition of the treaty of union in all time coming'. Notwithstanding this, as he pointed out, this provision was subsequently partly repealed by the Universities (Scotland) Act 1853. Furthermore, more recently s 37 of the Scotland Act 1998 states that the Union with Scotland Act 1706 has effect subject to this later Act.

Similarly, Art 5 of the Union with Ireland Act 1800 stated:

'that the Doctrine, Worship, Discipline, and Government of the said United Church (United Church of England and Ireland) shall be, and shall remain in full force for ever ... [and] ... that the Continuance and Preservation of the said United Church, as the established Church of England and Ireland, shall be deemed and taken to be an essential and fundamental Part of the Union.'

The Irish Church Act 1869 subsequently disestablished the Irish Church. In summary, Dicey stated that:

'the history of legislation in respect of these very Acts affords the strongest proof of the futility inherent in every attempt of one sovereign legislature to restrain the action of another equally sovereign body'.

A Dicey, *Introduction to the Study of the Law of the Constitution* (10th edn, Macmillan, 1959), p 65.

These examples indicate that even if an Act stated that because of its subject matter, its provisions are 'fundamental and unalterable', they could, nevertheless, be repealed by a subsequent Parliament.

ACTIVITY

Question

What would be the constitutional advantages and disadvantages of Parliament being able to entrench the subject matter of legislation against subsequent repeal by a later Parliament?

7.10.2 Entrenchment in terms of the manner and form of later legislation

This type of entrenchment refers to entrenching legislation in terms of the manner and form of later legislation (that is to say the procedure for making legislation). In other words, it is concerned with the following type of scenario:

The (imaginary) British Charter of Rights Act 2010

Section 1: the rights detailed in this Act can only be repealed by a future Parliament with the support of 80 per cent of both Houses of Parliament.

The above Act purports to entrench the human rights detailed in it by providing that these rights cannot be repealed by a later Parliament, unless it has the support of 80 per cent of both Houses of Parliament. Unlike the first type of entrenchment (see section 7.10.1), this Act is not stating that its provisions can never be repealed under any circumstances in the future. Rather, by stipulating that 80 per cent support of both Houses is required, it is purporting to make it *difficult* for a subsequent Parliament to repeal its provisions. In other words, it is purporting to entrench those rights by requiring a specified 'manner and form' of later legislation in order to repeal them (the manner and form here being the support of 80 per cent of both Houses of Parliament).

The question is what would happen if a 2011 Parliament passed an Act revoking the human rights that were enshrined in the British Charter of Rights Act 2010, but it did so through the ordinary parliamentary process (ie the Bill passed through with a simple majority vote in both chambers and not the 80 per cent as stipulated by the Act). Would the 2011 Act be legal?

There is no absolute answer to this question. Under the traditional conception of parliamentary sovereignty the 2011 Act would prevail, notwithstanding that it had not complied with the manner and form provision stipulated in s 1 of the 2010 Act. Indeed, if we recall the enrolled Bill rule (see section 7.3.3), the courts would simply look to see if the 2011 Bill was on the parliamentary roll and as stated in *Pickin* (1974), the courts would not investigate the internal proceedings of Parliament (as this risks breaching the separation of powers). On this traditional basis, therefore, it could be argued that providing the 2011 Bill was on the parliamentary roll having obtained the consent of both Houses, the courts would not investigate further as to whether the Bill had obtained the support of 80 per cent of both Houses. In this context, see the comments of Maugham LJ in *Ellen Street Estates* (1934) (see section 7.9.3).

There is, however, some support for the proposition that legislation (for example the 2011 Act) would not be enforced (or even constitute an Act) where a previous Act (for example the 2010 Act) had, in effect, entrenched its provisions by specifically stipulating the 'manner and form' that had to be followed by later legislation in order to repeal it. Three standard cases are used to support this argument:

CASE EXAMPLE

Attorney-General for New South Wales v Trethowan **[1932] AC 526**

The Colonial Laws Validity Act 1865 (a United Kingdom statute) conferred power on the New South Wales legislature to make laws in respect of the constitution of that state. Section 5 of the Act stated that every representative legislature shall have full power to make laws respecting the constitution providing such laws 'shall have been passed in such manner and form as may from time to time be required by any Act of Parliament'.

The Constitution Act 1902 as amended in 1929 (s 7A) stated that no Bill abolishing the Legislative Council of New South Wales (the upper chamber) should be presented to the Governor (for royal consent) until it had been approved by a majority of the electors. The same procedure was needed to repeal s 7A.

In 1930 both Houses of the New South Wales legislature passed two bills (to abolish the Legislative Council and repeal s 7A), however, neither Bill had been approved by the electorate. Two members of the Legislative Council (which was purportedly being abolished) sought a declaration that the two Bills could not be presented to the Governor for assent until approved by the electors, together with an injunction to prevent the Bills being presented for assent.

The Privy Council (on an appeal from the High Court of Australia) confirmed that the Bills needed to comply with the 'manner and form' as stipulated in s 7A. Thus the Bills required the support of the electors before they could lawfully be presented to the Governor.

CASE EXAMPLE

Harris v The Minister of the Interior **(1952) (2) SA 428**

Section 152 of the South Africa Act 1909 stipulated that a Bill which amended section 35 of the Act (concerning the de-registering of individuals for voting purposes on the basis of their colour) required the consent of two-thirds of both Houses (sitting together) of the South African Parliament.

The Supreme Court of South Africa held that in order to pass the 1951 Separate Representation of Voters Act (which had been passed by the two Houses separately and not sitting together) the 'manner and form' stipulated by s 152 of the South Africa Act 1909 had to be followed. As a consequence the 1951 Act was null and void.

CASE EXAMPLE

The Bribery Commissioner v Pedrick Ranasinghe [1965] AC 172

Section 29(4) of the Ceylon (Constitution) Order in Council 1946 stated that the Ceylon Parliament may amend or repeal any of the provisions in this Order, but that no Bill be presented for Royal Assent unless it had endorsed on it a certificate stating that it had been passed by not less than two-thirds of the House of Representatives.

The Privy Council affirmed the judgment of the Supreme Court of Ceylon that as the Bribery Amendment Act 1958 (which in effect altered the constitution) had no such certificate, the orders made by the Bribery Tribunal (under the 1958 Act) against Ranasinghe were null and inoperative. In short, in amending the Ceylon constitution, the Speaker's certificate was a necessary part of the legislative process and so any Bill not complying with s 29(4) was invalid and *ultra vires*. The Bribery Amendment Bill, therefore had to follow the 'manner and form' set out in s 29(4).

Although these cases demonstrate that in each case the legislature was required to follow the stipulated 'manner and form' for later legislation, as Commonwealth authorities they are not strictly analogous with the sovereign United Kingdom Parliament. As Barnett has commented, the cases indicate that:

> 'legislative bodies do not necessarily enjoy full sovereign power, and that some form of "higher law" may control their powers. In each of these cases, the powers of the legislatures of New South Wales, South Africa and Ceylon (as it then was) had been established under an Act of the sovereign United Kingdom Parliament. That being so, the legislative bodies had to comply with the constitutional laws in force.'

H Barnett, *Constitutional and Administrative Law* (6th edn, Routledge-Cavendish, 2006), p 178.

In fact, Dicey clearly distinguished between sovereign legislatures (eg the United Kingdom) and non-sovereign law-making bodies (subordinate legislatures). In particular, judicial persons would have the 'authority to pronounce upon the validity or constitutionality of laws' which had been passed by non-sovereign law-making bodies. What is clear, therefore, is that although as a constitutional principle, all legislatures pass laws, this does not mean that they are all sovereign as with the United Kingdom. For example, the Scottish Parliament is a legislature with the power to pass Acts of the Scottish Parliament (see section 14.3), however, it is necessarily a limited legislature with limited law-making powers as it is governed, and legally controlled, by the legislation which established it: the Scotland Act 1998. In this way the Scottish Parliament should be contrasted with the sovereign United Kingdom Parliament in Westminster which has neither been established, nor had its powers delegated or controlled, by a prior constitutional document.

The redefinition theory

A variant of the *manner and form* argument in favour of entrenching legislation is the so-called *redefinition theory of sovereignty*. In general an Act of Parliament is passed by a combination of all of the following:

- The House of Commons.
- The House of Lords.
- The monarch (in the form of the Royal Assent).

Under the redefinition theory it is possible for legislation to, in effect, be entrenched by specifying an additional element to the above constituent parts in order to amend or repeal specified (important) legislation. In this way Parliament is redefining itself in relation to certain legislation, making it more difficult to repeal, as an *extra* element has been added to the legislative process. This extra element will typically be the support of the people in a referendum.

Consider the following provision of the Northern Ireland Act 1998 which states that:

> **S** s 1: It is hereby declared that Northern Ireland in its entirety remains part of the United Kingdom and shall not cease to be so without the consent of a majority of the people of Northern Ireland voting in a poll held for the purposes of this section

What is the legal meaning of this provision? Could a later Parliament simply legislate to sever Northern Ireland from the rest of the United Kingdom without the consent of the people in the province? A traditional view of sovereignty would be that a later Act, following the enrolled Bill principle, could sever Northern Ireland without the consent of the people as stated in s 1 of the 1998 Act. In other words, the courts would not look beyond the parliamentary roll to ascertain whether an additional element had been satisfied (ie the consent of the people of Northern Ireland).

In contrast, one theory is that s 1 of the 1998 Act has redefined Parliament for the purposes of the future status of Northern Ireland. In other words, any Bill attempting to sever the province would require the consent of the following elements in order to be a valid Act:

- The House of Commons.
- The House of Lords (though technically not needed if the Parliament Acts of 1911 and 1949 are used).
- The consent of the people of Northern Ireland voting in a poll.
- The monarch (in the form of the Royal Assent).

It is certainly true that Parliament has already redefined how it passes legislation which is accepted and recognised by the courts. As we shall see (section 10.10.1) under the Parliament Acts of 1911 and 1949 the consent of the House of Lords is no longer needed – all that is required is the

Speaker of the Commons to indicate that a Bill has passed under the Parliament Acts. Accordingly, why is it not possible to add an extra element (eg consent of the people in a referendum)? In this context, consider the following case:

CASE EXAMPLE

Manuel v Attorney-General [1983] 1 Ch 77

Canadian Indian Chiefs sought a declaration that the Canada Act 1982 was *ultra vires* as it was inconsistent with the safeguards provided by the Statute of Westminster Act 1931. Section 4 of the 1931 Act stated that no statute shall extend to a Dominion (eg Canada) without its express consent (the argument was that the Indian peoples had not given their consent). The Court of Appeal refused the declaration on the basis that the Canada Act 1982 was valid as its preamble stated that Canada had expressly requested and consented to this legislation, thereby satisfying s 4 of the 1931 Act.

The court did, however, state *obiter* (making it clear that they were not purporting to decide the issue) that it was content to assume that the following proposition was correct: 'that Parliament can effectively tie the hands of its successors, if it passes a statute which provides that any future legislation on a specified subject shall be enacted only with certain specified consents' (Slade LJ).

According to Ellis this:

> 'contains a tiny judicial hint that English courts might consider a future UK Parliament bound by a stipulation as to manner and form, although under what conditions this might be so it is difficult to predict'.

> 'The Legislative Supremacy of Parliament and its Limits' in D Feldman (ed),
> *English Public Law* (Oxford University Press, 2004), p 147.

The *Jackson* case

It is worth noting the recent House of Lords decision in *R (Jackson and Others) v Attorney General* [2005] UKHL 56. For the facts of this case see section 10.10.3). For present purposes, the case concerned the 1911 Parliament Act (as amended in 1949) which allows legislation to be passed without the consent of the House of Lords. Section 2(1) of the 1911 Act, however, expressly excludes from its ambit a Bill purporting to extend the life of Parliament. Accordingly, legislation proposing to extend the life of Parliament required the express consent of the House of Lords.

In the *Jackson* case, according to Bradley and Ewing (*Constitutional and Administrative Law*, 14th Edn, Pearson/Longman, 2007, p 68), their Lordships were of the opinion (albeit *obiter*) that:

- Legislation purporting to extend the maximum duration of Parliament beyond five years required the express consent of the House of Lords (as required by the 1911 Parliament Act). Their Lordships were unanimous on this point.

- By a majority, their Lordships considered that the Parliament Acts *themselves* could not be used to delete the exception set out in s 2(1). In other words, they were of the opinion that a Bill purporting to delete the requirement in s 2(1) (that a Bill to extend the life of Parliament was excluded from the Parliament Acts), could not *itself* be pushed through under the Parliament Acts. Instead, it would need the express consent of the House of Lords. Conversely, it is noteworthy that the senior law lord, Lord Bingham, indicated that the special procedure under the Act theoretically could be used to delete this exception in s 2(1).

For an interesting analysis of the implications for sovereignty of this case, see A Young, 'Hunting sovereignty: *Jackson v Her Majesty's Attorney-General*' [2006] PL 187.

Conclusion

Notwithstanding the continuing debate concerning *legal entrenchment*, it is undoubtedly the case that a number of legislative enactments (particularly those which confer rights and remedies such as the Sex Discrimination Act 1975 and Race Relations Act 1976) are in fact *politically entrenched* in the sense that although legally these Acts could be repealed, the practical reality is that the political will to do so would be lacking. As a result, even if the traditional and orthodox view of parliamentary sovereignty is taken that legal entrenchment is not possible, political entrenchment of certain legislation is possible. Thus the practical distinction between legal and political entrenchment becomes less important.

ACTIVITY

Essay writing

Do you think that Parliament can entrench legislation in terms of the manner and form of later legislation? What would be the constitutional advantages and disadvantages of being able to do so?

KEY FACTS

It is traditionally stated that in terms of subject matter Parliament cannot entrench legislation against subsequent repeal.

There is disagreement over whether Parliament can entrench itself in terms of the manner and form of later legislation:

- The orthodox view (Dicey's continuing theory of sovereignty) is that one Parliament cannot bind another in terms of the manner and form of later legislation (Maugham LJ in *Ellen Street Estates Limited v Minister of Health* (1934)).

- A more modern view is that it is possible for one Parliament to bind itself in this way (*Attorney-General for New South Wales v Trethowan* (1932), *Harris v The Minister of the Interior* (1952)).

- A variant of the manner and form argument is the *redefinition theory of sovereignty* which states that Parliament can redefine its constituent elements to include an extra element such as the consent of the people (or a section of it) in a referendum (Slade LJ in *Manuel v Attorney-General* (1983)).

- The majority (*obiter*) view in *Jackson* (2005) was that s 2(1) of the Parliament Act 1911 could not be removed without the consent of the House of Lords.

7.11 Parliamentary sovereignty and devolution

In 1998 Parliament passed three devolution Acts which delegated powers to the regions:

- Scotland (Scotland Act 1998).

- Wales (Government of Wales Act 1998).

- Northern Ireland (Northern Ireland Act 1998).

These bodies have been established by the Westminster Parliament and so are legally subordinate to it. For example, s 28(7) of the Scotland Act 1998 states that the Westminster Parliament can still legislate for Scotland:

This section does not affect the power of the Parliament of the United Kingdom to make laws for Scotland.

Strictly speaking, of course, in legal theory such a provision is not necessary as Parliament can in any event pass any law that it chooses, including legislation for Scotland.

In legal theory, these devolved bodies could be simply extinguished by the Westminster Parliament passing legislation expressly repealing the above devolution Acts. Indeed, in the early 1970s Parliament revoked the Northern Irish Parliament which had operated for 50 years (see section 14.4.1). In terms of the implied repeal of this legislation, however, in *Thoburn v Sunderland City Council* (2002), Laws LJ indicated that the above Acts fell within the definition of 'constitutional statutes', and as such, would not be susceptible to implied repeal (see section 4.4.5). In any event, as indicated earlier, in political terms it might prove difficult to repeal these Acts (this is certainly the case in respect of the Scotland Act 1998 (see section 14.3.12)).

7.12 Parliamentary sovereignty and the Human Rights Act 1998

In terms of the link between parliamentary sovereignty and the Human Rights Act, two points need to be made.

Firstly, the Human Rights Act 1998 does not enable the courts to invalidate Acts of Parliament which are plainly inconsistent with any of the Articles of the European Convention. Although s 4 of the 1998 Act enables the higher courts to issue a declaration of incompatibility in such circumstances, such a declaration in itself does not invalidate the offending legislation. The Act, therefore, maintains parliamentary sovereignty. The government's White Paper which preceded the Human Rights Act 1998, made it plain that under the Act the judiciary would not have the power to strike down Acts of Parliament as this would be likely to bring the courts into constitutional conflict with the legislature. Furthermore, it was noted there was no evidence that such constitutional power was sought either by the judges themselves or by the public (Rights Brought Home: The Human Rights Bill, Cm 3782, Home Office (1997), para 2.13).

In short, as noted by Lord Steyn in *R v DPP exp Kebilene and others* [1999] 3 WLR 972:

> **J** 'It is crystal clear that the carefully and subtly drafted Human Rights Act 1998 preserves the principle of Parliamentary sovereignty.'

The Human Rights Act, therefore, is unlike Charters or Bills of Rights in other countries which typically have fundamental legal status. Indeed, the Act was passed through the ordinary parliamentary legislative process and can in fact (at least in legal theory), be expressly repealed at anytime by a future Parliament. It can be argued, however, that the Act is at least politically entrenched as it would prove difficult to revoke the Act and remove these positive individual rights (see section 7.6.2).

Second, the Human Rights Act in one respect is not an 'ordinary statute' as it is, in effect, an 'interpretative Act' setting out how the judiciary are to interpret legislation. As such, it is clear that the rule of implied repeal does not apply to the Act in the sense that:

- The Human Rights Act 1998 does *not* impliedly repeal any Act (or provision of it) passed before 1998 which is inconsistent with one of the Articles of the European Convention (given further effect by the 1998 Act). On this point the White Paper stated that the Act was 'intended to provide a new basis for judicial interpretation of all legislation, not a basis for striking down any part of it' (para 2.14).

- The Human Rights Act 1998 itself is not *impliedly* repealed by legislation passed after 1998 which is inconsistent with the Articles of the European Convention. During the parliamentary passage of the Bill the Lord Chancellor – who introduced the Bill – made it clear that the doctrine of implied repeal could have no application to the Act (*Hansard* HL Vol 583, col 509). It should be remembered that Laws LJ (see section 4.4.5) has argued that the Human Rights Act, together with the devolution Acts above, are 'constitutional statutes', and so not subject to implied repeal.

7.13 Parliamentary sovereignty and the rule of law

Dicey noted that parliamentary sovereignty and the rule of law pervaded the whole of the constitution, and that parliamentary sovereignty favoured the supremacy of the law of the land. He also pointed out that the independent position of the judiciary under the constitution (who of course uphold the rule of law) was secured by Parliament (it should be remembered that judges are not removed by the executive (see section 13.4.1)).

Although Parliament can pass any law it chooses, the courts will construe legislation in the light of the political/moral precepts underpinning the rule of law which respect basic constitutional principles (the protection of rights, access to the courts, etc). Writing extra-judicially, Lord Woolf noted that our parliamentary democracy is based on the rule of law:

> 'As both Parliament and the courts derive their authority from the rule of law so both are subject to it and can not act in a manner which involves its repudiation. The respective roles do not give rise to conflict because the courts and Parliament each respects the role of the other.

Lord Woolf, 'Droit Public-English Style' [1995] PL 57

This raises the issue of constitutionalism and parliamentary sovereignty. As defined earlier (see sections 2.6 and 4.15), constitutionalism is the principle that state power is effectively limited by constitutional rules (typically contained in a written codified constitutional document). Under the principle of parliamentary sovereignty, however, there are no legal limits restraining the laws that Parliament can pass, as there is no codified constitution constraining it as in other countries. Is parliamentary sovereignty, therefore, consistent with constitutionalism?

One response to this is that although in legal theory Parliament can pass any law that it chooses, in reality it does not. It is an unwritten maxim of the British constitution generally that those in power (parliamentarians and ministers) do not use their full powers to the maximum. In other words, Parliament is restrained politically and morally by the precepts underpinning the rule of law, and generally does not legislate contrary to them.

This is not to say that Parliament has not legislated in breach of the rule of law, as demonstrated by the War Damage Act 1965 which overruled a judicial ruling of the House of Lords, for economic expediency (see sections 4.9, 6.7.9 and 7.5.1). Although the British constitution is based on the twin pillars of parliamentary sovereignty and the rule of law, morally, the latter will typically restrain the former. In legal terms, however, ultimately, they are unequal pillars as Parliament can (if it so chooses) legislate to undermine the principles underpinning the rule of law. It is also pertinent to remember that owing to the electoral system, as the government of the day typically has dominance over the House of Commons, this has led to the argument that in practice we have 'executive sovereignty' rather than parliamentary sovereignty (see section 9.8).

In the final analysis, it is of interest to note that recently the Lord Chancellor commented that we must trust Parliament to understand the basis of our constitution so as not to violate the rule of law (Sixth Report of Session 2005–06 of the House of Lords Select Committee on the Constitution *Meeting with the Lord Chancellor* HL Paper 84 (2005), Q20).

ACTIVITY

Exercise

Revisit Chapter 6 and explain how the rule of law relates to and restrains parliamentary sovereignty.

Further reading

Allan, T, 'Parliamentary sovereignty: law, politics, and revolution', (1997) 113 LQR 443.

Barnett, H, *Constitutional and Administrative Law* (6th edn, Routledge-Cavendish 2006), ch 7.

Bingham, Lord, 'Dicey Revisited' [2002] PL 39.

Bradley, A, 'The Sovereignty of Parliament – Form or Substance?' in Jowell, J and Oliver, D, *The Changing Constitution* (5th edn, Oxford University Press, 2004), p 26.

Burns, S, 'When is an Act of Parliament not an Act of Parliament?' (2006) 156 NLJ 191.

Wade, HWR, 'The basis of legal sovereignty' [1955] CLJ 172.

Young, A, 'Hunting sovereignty: Jackson v Her Majesty's Attorney-General' [2006] PL 187.

chapter 8 PARLIAMENT I: NATURE, FUNCTIONS AND PRIVILEGE ■

AIMS AND OBJECTIVES □□□

At the end of this chapter you should be able to:

■ Identify and explain the different functions of Parliament

■ Explain the nature and significance of parliamentary privilege

8.1 Introduction and terminology

The United Kingdom Westminster Parliament is bicameral as it is composed of two Houses. It is also tripartite as it is composed of three constituent elements. These elements are as follows:

• The Queen in Parliament (a largely ceremonial role).

• The House of Commons (a wholly elected chamber).

• The House of Lords (a largely appointed chamber with a residual hereditary element).

8.1.1 Parliamentary terms

A parliamentary term is the period which exists between national general elections. Each Parliament lasts for a term which is divided up into a number of sessions. The United Kingdom Parliament, unlike some other legislatures such as the Scottish Parliament, does not have a fixed parliamentary term as it is variable and can last up to five years. Section 7 of the Parliament Act 1911 states that the maximum length of a parliamentary term is five years.

In fact, even the maximum length of a parliamentary term (which in other countries will be specifically stipulated in its written codified constitutional document) can be altered by statute. For example, the Parliament Act 1911 reduced the maximum length of a parliamentary term to five years (the previous Septennial Act 1715 had set the length at seven years). Moreover, since 1911 the length of the parliamentary term has, out of practical necessity, been extended during both World Wars, for example, the 1911 Parliament was extended to after the First World War and the 1935 Parliament to 1945.

In contrast to other countries with fixed term Parliaments where the date of a general election has been stipulated by the constitution, in the United Kingdom it is effectively the executive (specifically the Prime Minister) that determines the length of the parliamentary term by deciding when to call a national general election for the House of Commons. In essence, an election will be called when it is most advantageous to the executive (ie when they are most likely to win it). The United Kingdom is not unique in this sense, as in the Republic of Ireland, the Taoiseach (the Irish Prime Minister) also determines the timing of the next general election.

A parliamentary term ends when Parliament is dissolved by a proclamation issued by the Crown (the monarch) under the royal prerogative. By constitutional convention this power to dissolve Parliament will be exercised on the advice of the Prime Minister. In this way the latter determines the length of a parliamentary term and when a general election will be called. In general, parliamentary terms in modern times tend to be around four years. The dissolution of one Parliament leads to the summoning of the next one which will be established after the general election.

8.1.2. A vote of no confidence

Although in general it is the Prime Minister that effectively determines the timing of a general election, there is, however, one circumstance when this will be decided for him. In the event of a government losing a vote of no confidence in the House of Commons, in general terms the constitutional convention is that the Prime Minister should request a dissolution of Parliament from the monarch, thereby precipitating a general election. This is somewhat rare, although in 1979 the Labour Prime Minister James Callaghan lost a vote of no confidence by one vote, as a result of which he requested a dissolution. Mrs Thatcher won the resulting general election and became Prime Minister in May 1979 (see further section 12.2.1).

8.1.3 The summoning of a Parliament

After a general election, the Crown (the monarch), under the royal prerogative, summons a new Parliament. Following the general election of 2005 a new Parliament was summoned and it became the 54th Parliament (each Parliament is numbered). Directly after a general election the monarch will appoint the Prime Minister and by constitutional convention the monarch will appoint the person who commands the support of the majority of MPs in the House of Commons. As a consequence of our electoral system, this is, in general terms, a mere formality. When a Prime Minister has won a second or third successive general election victory (as with Tony Blair in 2001 and 2005), the monarch does not appoint the Prime Minister as he is still the Prime Minister and by constitutional convention he will be asked to form the next government.

Under the Meeting of Parliament Act 1694, Parliament, by law, must be summoned to meet at least once in every three years. The practical reality is that after a general election, the next Parliament will be summoned quickly. This is because in practice, Parliament will be held annually as the machinery of government necessitates this (for example, income tax for the following year needs to be authorised by Parliament).

8.1.4 Parliamentary sessions

Every parliamentary term is subdivided into parliamentary sessions consisting of approximately one year each. Each parliamentary session (which typically begins in November and ends the following October) will be opened by the State Opening of Parliament and the Queen's Speech. The Queen's Speech is written by the government of the day and outlines its proposed legislative programme for the ensuing session.

Parliamentary sessions tend to be approximately one year. This is because of constitutional convention and not because of any legal statutory requirement. These sessions can, however, be longer immediately following a general election. For example, the general election of 2005 meant that the first session of the new Parliament ran from June 2005 to October 2006 (a period of almost 18 months). A typical Parliament will comprise four sessions before the Prime Minster calls a general election, although under the Parliament Act 1911, it could run to five sessions.

8.1.5 Prorogation

At the end of each parliamentary session Parliament is prorogued (ie suspended). The effect of this is that if a Bill introduced in one parliamentary session has not passed through Parliament and received the Royal Assent by the end of that session, it is lost and the Bill would have to be re-introduced (as a new Bill) in the following session. In recent years, however, it has been possible to 'carry over' Bills from one parliamentary session to the next. For example, the Constitutional Reform Bill 2003-04 was carried over in the House of Lords (where it had not completed its stages owing partly to the fact that very unusually, it was sent to a select committee for detailed consideration) to the 2004-05 parliamentary session. In fact, this arrangement in respect of the Constitutional Reform Bill was specifically referred to in the Queen's Speech of November 2004.

During the prorogation of Parliament all business in both Houses ceases (including work in parliamentary committees), with the exception of the judicial work performed by the law lords.

KEY FACTS

- The period between Parliaments is known as a term and each term is subdivided into a maximum of five sessions.
- Each session is approximately one year and at the end of each session, Parliament is suspended (prorogued).
- Before a general election Parliament is dissolved by the monarch and after each general election each new Parliament is summoned by the monarch.

8.2 A bicameral legislature

8.2.1 Bicameralism

The United Kingdom Parliament is bicameral consisting of two chambers (namely, the elected House of Commons and non-elected House of Lords). The majority of legislatures/assemblies in the world are, however, unicameral consisting of only one chamber. For example:

- New Zealand (House of Representatives).
- Denmark (Folketing).
- Sweden (Riksdag).

Unicameral legislatures tend to be found in smaller states (with one clear exception being China) with relatively homogenous populations. In contrast, the United Kingdom, together with most large democracies such as the United States, Canada, France, Italy and Spain, has two chambers. Indeed, a bicameral system tends to be found particularly in federal states such as Australia and the USA where the upper House can represent the interests of the various different regions and peoples. Moreover, most lower chambers tend to be more powerful than their corresponding upper chambers (excluding the United States Senate).

8.2.2 Arguments in favour of bicameralism

- Two chambers disperse the power to make law between two (rival) power centres. By dispersing and dividing it, the power to make legislation is necessarily constitutionally limited.

- Two chambers can ensure that legislative proposals are examined and scrutinised more effectively than in a unicameral legislature, as legislation must (generally speaking) pass through both chambers in order to become law. In particular, a second chamber can look afresh at and revise legislative proposals which have passed through the lower House.

- A second chamber can act as constitutional safeguard and protector of the constitution from the wishes of the (more generally powerful) lower chamber.

8.2.3 Arguments in favour of unicameralism

- Unicameral legislatures tend to be more decisive.

- Unicameral systems avoid inter-chamber constitutional conflict which is necessarily inherent in a bicameral system where two chambers compete with each other.

In any event, in respect of recent attempts at reforming the House of Lords (see section 22.6.1), in February 2003 the House of Commons (on a free vote) overwhelmingly defeated a motion in favour of abolishing the upper chamber altogether in order to become a unicameral state by 390 votes to 172. More recently, in March 2007 the Commons voted to retain a bicameral system by 416 votes to 163. As a result, it is clear that any future reform of the House of Lords will necessarily involve retaining the second chamber. Historically, some countries such as Denmark and New Zealand have abolished their second chambers (1953 and 1950 respectively), although in both cases, the populations are comparatively small (5 and 4 million respectively).

ACTIVITY

Question

Do you think that the United Kingdom should have a bicameral legislature? Revisit this question after you have completed Chapter 10 (the House of Lords).

8.3 The Queen in Parliament

It is the Queen in Parliament (Crown in Parliament) which passes primary legislation, and so the monarch is a constituent element of Parliament. Her main constitutional roles include:

- Summoning Parliament after a general election.
- Proroguing Parliament at the end of a parliamentary session.
- Dissolving Parliament prior to a general election.
- Opening each parliamentary session with the State Opening and the delivery of the Queen's Speech.
- Granting assent to a Bill in order for it to become an Act of Parliament.
- Appointing the Prime Minister who is drawn from Parliament.
- Appointing government ministers who are drawn from Parliament.

The above constitutional duties are performed by the monarch but, generally speaking, in accordance with constitutional convention she acts on the advice of her government ministers.

The monarch is not allowed in the House of Commons to observe debates (a consequence of the English Civil War), which is why Members of Parliament (MPs) go to the House of Lords to hear the delivery of the Queen's Speech. The monarch is, however, permitted to listen to debates in the Lords. The monarch will be considered again in the context of Chapter 11.

8.4 The functions of Parliament

The principal functions of Parliament are set out below, but they do, of course, necessarily blend with the individual constitutional functions of the two Houses. Although Parliament is the legislature, it will be noted that its constitutional responsibilities are not confined to simply passing legislation. In 2006 the parliamentary website (www.parliament.uk) identified the following seven functions of Parliament.

8.4.1 A legislative function (examining and passing proposals for law)

The passing of legislation is the principal constitutional function of a legislature. In the United Kingdom the Queen in Parliament is the supreme domestic law-making body. As Parliament is elected by the people and composed of elected representatives (at least in terms of the House of Commons), in a sense, the resulting laws made represent the will of the people.

Although in constitutional theory it is the Queen in Parliament that passes the law, the practical reality is that Parliament to a large extent passes laws which have been drafted and initiated by the government of the day. Indeed, such is this dominance, it could be argued that, generally speaking, Parliament rubberstamps or legitimises the legislative proposals sought by the government. One of the constitutional functions of the executive in the British constitution is that of developing policy and initiating proposed legislation (eg the Legislative and Regulatory Reform Bill, the Prevention of Terrorism Bill and the Identity Card Bill).

Notwithstanding the above, some legislative proposals are initiated by parliamentary members in the form of Private Members' Bills of which there are a number of different types. These can be initiated by members in either House, but the likely success of these measures becoming law are, to a large extent, dependent upon support from the government, as it dominates the parliamentary timetable. During the session of 2003–04 out of 38 public Bills which obtained the Royal Assent, 33 were government Bills and five were Private Members' Bills (Fact sheet L2, *Private Members' Bill Procedure*, House of Commons Information Office (Parliamentary Copyright, 2004), p 2). In addition to the above Bills, Parliament also processes private Bills (sponsored by, for example, local authorities) and hybrid Bills (a mixture of public and private elements).

In general terms, Bills require the consent of both Houses of Parliament in order to become law. In exceptional cases, however, only the consent of the House of Commons is necessary in the event of the Parliament Acts 1911 and 1949 being used (see section 10.10.1).

8.4.2 A deliberate function (the scrutiny of executive policy and administration)

Parliament acts as a constitutional check on the exercise of executive power. In short, Parliament scrutinises executive policy, administration and actions thereby ensuring that the government of the day is constitutionally accountable and responsible to Parliament (which, of course, represents the people). In constitutional theory, accountability is secured through the following parliamentary mechanisms:

- The scrutiny of legislative proposals.
- Debates.

- Questions.
- Select committees.

For a detailed consideration of the nature and effectiveness of these mechanisms, see Chapter 12. As John Stuart Mill noted in the nineteenth century:

> 'Instead of the function of governing, for which it is radically unfit, the proper office of a representative assembly is to watch and control the government.'

Considerations on Representative Government (1861) cited in C Turpin, *British Government and the Constitution* (5th edn, Cambridge University Press, 2002), p 448

The constitutional function of Parliament (particularly in the context of a parliamentary executive) therefore, is to hold the government to account, make it explain and justify its polices and actions/decisions. In doing so, Parliament acts as a constitutional restraint on the executive and may influence its actions. In this way Parliament acts as a forum for influencing executive policy. By scrutinising the actions of the executive, Parliament confers constitutional legitimacy on executive actions.

Both Houses scrutinise the actions of the executive, and it is particularly important in the absence of a written entrenched codified constitution that the executive is effectively scrutinised by Parliament. Effective and meaningful scrutiny, of course, necessarily depends upon the government providing accurate and full information. Historically, in the United States Freedom of Information provisions have permitted access to government information and in the United Kingdom in 2000, Parliament passed the Freedom of Information Act which (subject to certain conditions and exceptions) equips individuals with access to governmental information and records.

8.4.3 A forum for debate (debating the major issues of the day)

Both Houses of Parliament act as forums for debate on matters of public importance and interest. One interesting development which has taken place in recent years is the use of a parallel chamber known as Westminster Hall. Due to the congested nature of the timetable in the House of Commons, debates can now take place in this 'parallel' chamber. Such debates might otherwise have found little space on the Floor of the House of Commons.

8.4.4 To provide for taxation/finance

By voting for taxation, Parliament enables the administration of government to be carried out. In order for the government of the day to spend/raise money it must have the express permission of Parliament. In particular, it is the House of Commons (which is directly elected by the people) which has control over such financial matters (eg scrutinising expenditure and authorising spending as well as taxation. On the latter, see the annual Budget – the Finance Bill).

8.4.5 To safeguard the rights of individuals

This is a function performed by both Houses. In particular, every MP in the House of Commons has a specific constituency with a responsibility to help redress constituents' grievances (see section 9.3.1). In terms of protecting the rights of the individual, the House of Lords has a particular role to act as a constitutional safeguard and watchdog of civil liberties when considering legislative proposals which threaten to undermine the basic rights of the individual (see section 10.9.9). In addition, Parliament has established the Joint Committee on Human Rights to consider matters relating to human rights and to consider remedial orders made under the Human Rights Act 1998 (see Chapter 17).

8.4.6 The examination of proposed European legislation

As a member of the European Community, laws can be made in Europe (principally in the Council of Ministers which is the Community's legislature), which directly affect the United Kingdom. In fact, these laws can override the domestic law (including Acts of Parliament) of the United Kingdom (see section 15.6). Parliament, through committees in both Houses, supervises proposed legislative measures in Europe (see section 12.9).

8.4.7 A judicial function

The Appellate Committee of the House of Lords performs the role of the highest domestic court in the United Kingdom. As indicated earlier (section 5.8.3), this is a function which is currently being reformed. Both Houses also perform a judicial function in the context of enforcing parliamentary privilege and disciplining members who act in contempt of Parliament (see section 8.5).

In addition the following functions could be added:

- **The recruitment of the government**

As the United Kingdom has a parliamentary executive, the executive is necessarily drawn from Parliament. By constitutional convention, members of the government must sit in either House of Parliament (except the Prime Minster who must sit in the Commons). Parliament, therefore, provides the pool from which the government is drawn and accountable to. Although ministers are drawn from both Houses, they predominately come from the House of Commons.

- **The removal of specified personnel**

Both Houses of Parliament acting in concert with each other are constitutionally responsible for removing key personnel. For example, the senior judges (see section 13.4.1) and the Parliamentary Commissioner for Administration (see section 21.3.6).

KEY FACTS

The functions of Parliament	Performed by
Legislative	Both Houses, although ultimately the House of Commons is dominant
The control of finance	The House of Commons (exclusively)
Safeguarding rights	Both Houses, although the House of Lords has a particular responsibility for this
Scrutiny of the executive	Both Houses, although the House of Commons is typically dominated by the government of the day
Judicial	Both Houses enforce parliamentary privilege. The Appellate Committee of the House of Lords is the final court of appeal (until 2009)
Scrutiny of European legislation	Both Houses
Debate	Both Houses
Recruitment of the government	Both Houses, though largely from the House of Commons
Representative	The House of Commons as it is elected, although life peers in the Lords to some extent can reflect society at large

8.5 Parliamentary privilege

8.5.1 Definition and types of privilege

Erskine May defines the privileges of Parliament in the following way:

'Parliamentary privilege is the sum of the peculiar rights enjoyed by each House
collectively as a constituent part of the High Court of Parliament, and by
Members of each House individually, without which they could not discharge their
functions, and which exceed those possessed by other bodies or individuals. Thus

privilege, though part of the law of the land, is to a certain extent an exemption from the general law'.

E May, *Parliamentary Practice* (23rd edn, LexisNexis Butterworths, 2004), p 75.

According to Erskine May, at the commencement of each new Parliament, the Speaker of the House of Commons lays claim to the following rights/privileges known as the four petitions (it is taken that similar privileges also apply in the Lords):

- **Freedom of speech**

(see section 8.6).

- **Freedom from arrest**

The freedom of members not to be arrested within Parliament was established at a very early date and the constitutional rationale behind it was to enable members to attend the chamber so that they could perform their constitutional functions as part of Parliament. This privilege was confined to arrest in the context of civil matters (not criminal ones) and, as noted by the Joint Committee on Parliamentary Privilege (see below), since the almost practical abolition of imprisonment for debt (Debtors Act 1869), it seems to have little modern relevance (with the exception of an immunity from arrest for disobeying a court order in civil proceedings – *Stourton v Stourton* [1963] 1 All ER 606). In 1999 the Joint Committee recommended its abolition (Joint Committee on Parliamentary Privilege, *Report, Volume 1 – Report and Proceedings of the Committee*, HL Paper 43-I HC 214-I (1999), p 85).

- **Free access to the monarch**

Both Houses have access to the Sovereign (although peers have access as individuals) and MPs attend the Lords to hear the Queen's Speech.

- **The most favourable construction be placed upon the proceedings in the House**

According to Erskine May, today this is simply 'a formal courtesy'.

In addition to the above, Parliament also enjoys, *inter alia*:

- the right to determine and regulate its own membership and internal proceedings (see sections 8.7.1 and 8.7.2)
- the right to administer punishments in the form of a contempt of Parliament in the event of a privilege being breached (see section 8.7.3).

8.5.2 The origins, sources and constitutional rationale of parliamentary privilege

Parliamentary privilege forms part of the law and custom of Parliament. The sources of privilege are found in Acts of Parliament (eg Art 9 of the Bill of Rights 1689), practices within Parliament and court decisions which have identified the existence of privileges and rights. Parliament, through the enactment of a statute can:

- Create new privileges.

- Amend or modify an existing privilege. For example, see s 13 of the Defamation Act 1996 (section 8.6.2).

- Abolish a privilege. For example, the Criminal Justice Act 2003 abolished the immunity and privilege of members to be excused *as of right* from jury service.

The constitutional reason that parliamentary members (of both chambers) enjoy the above privileges, immunities and rights is to ensure that they can carry out their constitutional functions as part of Parliament. Members need to be able to air grievances and call to account the government. Moreover, Parliament itself must be able to regulate its own composition and affairs without interference from either the ordinary courts or the government.

Parliamentary privileges and immunities, in particular freedom of speech, is not unique to the United Kingdom. For example, Art 15.10 of the Irish Republic's constitution permits both chambers of the Oireachtas to make their own internal rules and standing orders regulating each House. These internal rules and procedures cannot be challenged by the Irish courts.

8.6 Freedom of speech

8.6.1 Article 9 of the Bill of Rights 1689

Members of Parliament in both Houses enjoy an absolute immunity in respect of freedom of speech within Parliament:

 'the freedom of speech and debates or proceedings in Parliament ought not to be impeached or questioned in any court or place out of Parliament'.

Article 9, the Bill of Rights 1689

The constitutional rationale behind this is to enable parliamentary members to have freedom of speech so as to be able to discuss whatever subject they choose ('freedom of speech and debates'). The legal immunity is absolute and includes immunity from both civil and criminal liability as proceedings 'ought not to be impeached or questioned'. This enables members freely to perform their parliamentary functions and duties (raising issues of public concern, etc) without the fear of legal repercussions. In *A v United Kingdom* (2003) (see below) the European Court of Human Rights accepted that the justification for this absolute immunity was twofold:

- Firstly, it permitted free debate.

- Secondly, it ensured a constitutional separation between the judiciary and the legislature, as the former could not interfere with debates and speeches in the latter.

Similarly, in the Republic of Ireland, Art 15.12 of the constitution protects members of both Houses of the Oireachtas for what they say in the legislature, with all official reports and 'utterances' being privileged.

As Art 9 confers an absolute immunity on members this would appear to contravene one of the principles underpinning the rule of law, namely, equality under the law with no immunities from its ambit (see section 6.7.6). As a result, it is imperative that parliamentary members use this right/immunity in a responsible way and do not abuse it. In the event of abuse, as recognised by the European Court in *A v United Kingdom* (2003), one safeguard is that internal disciplinary proceedings can be taken against the member involved (see section 8.7.3).

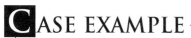

CASE EXAMPLE

A v United Kingdom (2003) 36 EHRR 51

In a parliamentary debate, an MP referred specifically to A and her family in the context of anti-social behaviour and 'neighbours from hell'. A denied the truth of these allegations, but she was prohibited from suing the MP in defamation owing to Art 9 of the Bill of Rights 1689. She petitioned the European Court of Human Rights and argued that this immunity violated, *inter alia*, Art 6 (the right of access to a court) and Art 8 (the right to respect for private life).

The European Court held that there had been no violation as the immunity pursued the legitimate aims of protecting free speech and maintaining a separation of powers. It noted that all Contracting States had some system of parliamentary immunity. In fact, the court pointed out that the immunity in the United Kingdom was narrower than in some countries, as for example the immunity did not extend to an MP's statement made outside of Parliament (see section 8.6.3).

ACTIVITY

Question

Do you think that from a constitutional perspective parliamentary members should enjoy immunity from the law with respect to free speech?

8.6.2 Section 13 of the Defamation Act 1996

Before 1996 one consequence for MPs of Art 9 of the Bill of Rights was that they would be prevented from suing in defamation if the defendant wished to adduce in his defence evidence of an MPs behaviour in Parliament (thereby 'questioning' parliamentary proceedings). In two separate actions initiated by MPs in the mid-1990s (*Allason v Haines, The Times*, 14 July 1995 and the *Hamilton* case where Neil Hamilton had wanted to sue *The Guardian*), both cases were stayed by the court as the respective defendants wished to rely, in effect, on proceedings in Parliament in their defence. It was held that it would have been unjust to permit the actions to continue if the defendants could not raise this information to defend their case. The courts in both cases relied on the following Privy Council decision:

CASE EXAMPLE

Prebble v Television New Zealand **[1995] 1 AC 321**

Prebble instituted defamatory proceedings against Television New Zealand who wished to rely on statements made by him in the New Zealand Parliament. The Privy Council held that it was an infringement of parliamentary privilege (and contrary to the Bill of Rights 1689) for a party in legal proceedings to question words spoken in Parliament (ie suggesting that they were untrue, misleading or instigated for improper motives) and, therefore, those particulars of the defence relating to it had rightly been struck out. Notwithstanding the exclusion of these particulars, the action should not have been stayed, however, as the defendant could still allege the majority of matters on which it wished to rely in order to justify the alleged libel.

The effect of this meant that, although on the one hand an MP could not be sued in respect of comments made in Parliament, on the other, it meant that an MP could not sue in defamation to clear his name if the defence wished to use words used in Parliament in their defence. As a result of this type of scenario, s 13 of the Defamation Act 1996 was (rather controversially) passed. This provision permits a member of either House to waive his right to parliamentary privilege if he is instituting an action for defamation and the defendant wishes to raise evidence of parliamentary statements and questions of that MP in their defence. This provision was criticised by the Joint Committee on Parliamentary Privilege:

> 'A fundamental flaw is that it undermines the basis of privilege: freedom of speech
> is the privilege of the House as a whole and not of the individual member in his
> own right, although an individual member can assert and rely on it'.

Joint Committee on Parliamentary Privilege, *Report, Volume 1 – Report and Proceedings of the Committee*,
HL Paper 43-I HC 214-I (1999), para 68.

Instead, it recommended its replacement with a provision whereby each House could collectively waive privilege.

In the event, Neil Hamilton subsequently (and unsuccessfully) sued Mohamed Al Fayed for defamation after waiving parliamentary privilege under s 13. During the litigation Al Fayed unsuccessfully sought to have the action struck out on the basis of being, *inter alia*, an abuse of process as the matter at issue had already been determined in Parliament by the Committee on

Standards and Privileges and the Parliamentary Commissioner for Standards (the former had concluded that Hamilton's conduct had fallen below the standards expected in the House).

The House of Lords held that s 13 nevertheless applied and was a complete answer to the case as Hamilton's individual protection under parliamentary privilege was waived (this did not infringe the privilege of Parliament as a whole). Although the court noted that in the absence of s 13 waiving parliamentary privilege, the court should have stayed the trial as otherwise it would have been impossible for Al Fayed to have a fair trial (*Hamilton v Al Fayed* [2000] 2 All ER 224).

ACTIVITY

Question

What are the advantages and disadvantages of s 13 of the Defamation Act 1996?

8.6.3 What are 'proceedings' in Parliament?

As noted by the Joint Committee on Parliamentary Privilege, unfortunately no comprehensive definition has been provided by either Parliament or the courts as to the meaning of proceedings in Parliament. According to the Joint Committee, 'proceedings' would include *inter alia*:

- Debates and proceedings on Bills.

- Questions.

- Proceedings within committees (this could include a select committee sitting outside Parliament).

- Parliamentary votes.

The following cases illustrate what is meant by proceedings in Parliament:

CASE EXAMPLE

Dillon v Balfour (1887) 20 LR Ir 600

Dillon wished to sue Balfour (a government minister) in defamation for comments made by him about her during the course of the passage of a Bill through the House of Commons (she contended that it undermined her professional reputation as a midwife). The action was struck out because the comments were part of the proceedings in Parliament and so the court had no constitutional jurisdiction in respect of the matter.

CASE EXAMPLE

George Strauss **HC Vol 568, Col 814**

This case concerned an allegedly defamatory letter sent by Strauss MP to a government minister concerning the London Electricity Board (which then threatened to sue Strauss for libel). Strauss argued in Parliament that this legal action would represent a breach of parliamentary privilege. However, a resolution of the House of Commons decided that this letter was not a 'proceeding in Parliament'. In doing so they rejected a recommendation of the Committee of Privileges that it should be covered by parliamentary privilege.

Parliamentary privilege does not apply where an MP repeats outside Parliament words which he has used in a speech made earlier in the House of Commons. This explains why MPs may be willing to make comments within Parliament which they will not repeat outside the chamber for fear of legal repercussions.

8.6.4 'Proceedings in Parliament ought not to be impeached or questioned in any court'

Under the Bill of Rights the courts cannot question proceedings in Parliament. However, since the *Pepper v Hart* (1993) decision (below) the courts can make reference to parliamentary materials as an aid to the construction of legislation.

CASE EXAMPLE

Pepper v Hart **[1993] 1 All ER 42**

The House of Lords held that in order to give effect to the true intention of Parliament in interpreting legislation, the court could refer to parliamentary materials where the legislation in question was:

- ambiguous, obscure or absurd;

CONTINUED ▶

> - the material relied on consisted of statements made by the minister or promoter of the Bill together (if needed) with other such parliamentary material necessary to understand these statements and these statements were clear.
>
> The court made it clear that this reference to parliamentary material would not infringe Art 9 of the Bill of Rights as it was not 'questioning' the freedom of speech within Parliament, rather the court was merely trying to give effect to the intention of Parliament.

In the context of the Human Rights Act 1998 the House of Lords has held that in evaluating the compatibility of Acts of Parliament with European Convention rights, the court if necessary could have regard to relevant background material (ie explanatory departmental notes and ministerial statements when the Bill was progressing through its parliamentary stages, but not to debates) in order to identify the policy objective of the legislation (*Wilson v First County Trust Ltd (No 2)* [2003] UKHL 40).

Publication of proceedings outside Parliament

Section 1 of the Parliamentary Papers Act 1840 conferred an absolute privilege against criminal or civil actions to a person who publishes a paper printed by order of, or under the authority of Parliament (correct copies were covered by s 2). This Act had been passed in the context of (and in response to) litigation involving Stockdale suing Hansard for defamation for publishing a report ordered by the House of Commons (*Stockdale v Hansard* (1839) 9 Ad & E1). In this case, although Lord Chief Justice Denman accepted that the House had exclusive jurisdiction over its proceedings, it could not by resolution simply declare the material to be privileged.

In terms of extracts/abstracts by the press of a parliamentary paper (attracting qualified privilege) s 3 of the 1840 Act was subsequently amended by the:

- Defamation Act 1952 (in respect of reports on radio).
- Broadcasting Act 1990 (in respect of television).

In terms of reporting parliamentary proceedings, s 15 of the Defamation Act 1996 gives qualified privilege to a fair and accurate report of these proceedings.

KEY FACTS

Article 9 of the Bill of Rights 1689 protects MPs from civil and criminal liability from things said in Parliament.

It protects proceedings in Parliament which would include, *inter alia*:

- Debates and proceedings on Bills.
- Questions.
- Proceedings within committees (this would include a select committee sitting outside Parliament).
- Parliamentary votes.

From a constitutional perspective Art 9:

- Permits free debate and enables parliamentary members to discuss whatever subject they choose without the fear of legal ramifications.
- Ensures a clear constitutional separation between the judiciary and the legislature.

8.7 Other privileges

Other privileges enjoyed by both Houses are:

- The right to determine their own composition.
- The right to regulate their own internal proceedings.
- The right to punish individuals for contempt of Parliament.

8.7.1 The right to determine their own composition

The House of Commons will, for example, determine who is entitled to be a member of the House and decide if a person is unfit to serve. The House will also determine the timing of by-elections.

8.7.2 The right to regulate their own internal proceedings

As pointed out by Evans (*Handbook of House of Commons Procedure* (5th edn, Dod, 2004), p 35), this is known as the 'exclusive cognisance' of its proceedings. Each House will make standing orders to regulate its proceedings including in relation to the passage of legislation. As indicated earlier (see section 7.3.3), the courts will not look beyond the parliamentary roll and question the manner of parliamentary proceedings as this would violate the separation of powers between the judiciary and the legislature. As a consequence, Parliament will determine its own internal proceedings and decide if it has been interfered with. As pointed out by Lord Reid:

> **J** 'The court has no concern with the manner in which Parliament or its officers carrying out its Standing Orders perform these functions. Any attempt to prove that they were misled by fraud or otherwise would necessarily involve an inquiry into the manner in which they had performed their functions in dealing with the Bill which became the British Railways Act 1968.'
>
> *British Railways Board v Pickin* [1974] AC 765

In this case, Lord Morris added that it would be both undesirable and impracticable for the courts to embark upon such an inquiry. In fact, as illustrated by the following two cases, the courts have historically made it very clear that the internal administration of the House of Commons is not subject to control by the courts.

CASE EXAMPLE

Bradlaugh v Gossett (1884) 12 QB 271

The House of Commons passed a resolution excluding Bradlaugh from the chamber (even though he had been elected to the House of Commons) 'until he shall engage not further to disturb the proceedings of the House'. Bradlaugh unsuccessfully sought a declaration that this order was void together with an order restraining the Serjeant-at-Arms from preventing him from entering the House. The court held that it could not inquire into the propriety of a resolution of the House (this was a matter relating to the internal proceedings of the House).

CASE EXAMPLE

Chaffers v Goldsmid [1894] 1 QB 186

The court stated that no action would lie in the event of a member of the House of Commons refusing to present a petition (to redress certain grievances) to the chamber presented to him by a constituent.

More recently the Court of Appeal has made it clear that as the activities of the Parliamentary Commissioner for Standards (see section 8.8.2) were in essence concerned with the proceedings of the House, they were beyond the supervisory powers of the courts to control what she does in relation to an investigation (*R v Parliamentary Commissioner for Standards, ex parte Al Fayed* [1998] 1 All ER 93).

In regulating its own proceedings, the Houses can, for example:

- Exclude disorderly strangers.
- Resolve to sit in a secret session.
- Debate any matter it chooses (subject to the *sub judice* resolution – see section 13.4.3).

8.7.3 The right to punish individuals for contempt of Parliament

Erskine May defined contempt of Parliament as:

> 'Generally speaking, any act or omission which obstructs or impedes either House of Parliament in the performance of its functions, or which obstructs or impedes any Member or officer of such House in the discharge of his duty, or which has a tendency, directly or indirectly, to produce such results'.

> E May, *Parliamentary Practice* (23rd edn, LexisNexis Butterworths, 2004), p 128.

Thus, contempt of Parliament is broader than simply a breach of privilege (which in itself is a contempt), because it embraces behaviour which is not necessarily an infringement of privilege. Erskine May points out that contempt covers, *inter alia*, the following:

- Misconduct in the presence of the House or a committee.
- Disobeying a rule or order.
- Misconduct of members (eg an MP accepting a bribe).
- Premature disclosure of committee proceedings.
- Obstructing or molesting members.
- Obstructing officers of the House or witnesses.

The procedure in respect of contempt of Parliament (by a member)

A member will raise the issue with the Speaker who will decide if it takes precedence over business. If so, the member can table a motion for the next day proposing that the matter is referred to the Select Committee on Standards and Privileges. The Committee in considering the matter has the power to send for persons, records and papers. Unlike in ordinary criminal or civil cases, the accused member is (generally) not allowed representation by counsel. If the Committee decides that a serious breach has occurred, a debate on the Committee's report will ensue. The House then decides whether or not to accept the report and recommendations of the Committee (on occasions it may not), and will determine a punishment. In the upper chamber, the House of Lords Committee for Privileges investigates if a breach of privilege or contempt has taken place and reports to the House, who in turn, will determine what action (if any) to take.

The punishments in the event of a contempt of Parliament

Both Houses have their own penal jurisdiction and punishments which are separate from the ordinary courts. These are as follows:

- Imprisonment (seemingly obsolete as it has not been used for some time).

- Fines (no longer in the House of Commons).

- Censure by the Speaker (a reprimand or admonishment by the Speaker).

- Expulsion.

- Suspension.

In this context, it is pertinent to note that Parliament is specifically excluded from the ambit of the Human Rights Act 1998 as under it, Parliament does not have to follow legally the requirements of the European Convention (including Art 6 – the right to a fair trial). Notwithstanding this, as pointed out by the Joint Committee on Parliamentary Privilege, Parliament in exercising its internal disciplinary powers could theoretically be challenged under Art 6 of the Convention before the European Court of Human Rights in Strasbourg, if its proceedings are not fair. As a result, it indicated that Parliament should adopt (at least) minimum requirements of fairness in its internal disciplinary procedures (Joint Committee on Parliamentary Privilege, *Report, Volume 1 – Report and Proceedings of the Committee*, HL Paper 43-I HC 214-I (1999), para 284). The Joint Committee also recommended the enactment of a Parliamentary Privileges Act which would codify parliamentary privileges.

ACTIVITY

Question

Do you think that the way in which Parliament disciplines those who commit a contempt of Parliament is consistent with the right to a fair trial under Art 6 of the European Convention? Revisit this question after having completed Chapter 16 on the European Convention.

KEY FACTS

The main privileges of Parliament are:

- Freedom of speech.

- Freedom from arrest.

- Free access to the monarch.

- The most favourable construction be placed upon the proceedings in the House.

- The right to determine and regulate its own membership.

- The right to determine its internal proceedings.

- The right to administer punishments in the form of a contempt of Parliament.

8.8 Members' interests and standards

8.8.1 The Register of Members' Interests

In 1975 the House of Commons established a compulsory Register of Members' Interests, which required MPs to declare their financial interests with the outside world (ie payments, remunerated directorships or trades, etc). In addition, MPs should declare interests when participating in debates. The House of Lords also has a Register of Lords' Interests in respect of consultancies, remunerated directorships, etc.

8.8.2 Standards in Public Life

As a result of the 'cash for questions' affair in 1994, the then Prime Minister established the Committee on Standards in Public Life 'to examine current concerns about standards of conduct of all holders of public office'. This committee (the Nolan Committee) issued its report in 1995 (First Report of the Committee on Standards in Public Life, *Standards in Public Life, Volume 1: Report*, Cm 2850-I (1995)) and led to:

- **The creation of the Select Committee on Standards and Privileges** (to replace the Committee of Privileges).

  Its responsibilities involve considering matters of privilege and contempt, overseeing the Parliamentary Commissioner for Standards (see below) and considering breaches of the Code of Conduct (see below) together with complaints relating to the Register of Members' Interests.

- **The establishment of a Parliamentary Commissioner for Standards**

  The responsibility of this officer involves maintaining the Register of Members' Interests (and advising members in respect of it) and investigating complaints about a number of parliamentary registers. The Commissioner also monitors the Code of Conduct (see below).

  In terms of investigation, the Commissioner would undertake an initial investigation and report to the Select Committee on Standards and Privileges which may investigate the matter and report to the House. It is the House itself that will determine the penalty. As indicated earlier (see section 8.7.2), the investigations of the Commissioner are not subject to judicial review.

- **The establishment of a Code of Conduct for Members of Parliament**

Q	'1. The purpose of this Code of Conduct is to assist Members in the discharge of their obligations to the House, their constituents and the public at large by: a) Providing guidance on the standards of conduct expected of Members in discharging their parliamentary and public duties, and in so doing b) Providing the openness and accountability necessary to reinforce public confidence in the way in which Members perform those duties. 2. The Code applies to Members in all aspects of their public life. … 7. In carrying out their parliamentary and public duties, Members will be expected to observe the following general principles of conduct identified by the Committee on Standards in Public Life in its First Report as applying to holders of public office.' Source: www.publications.parliament.uk.

Q 'The seven principles of conduct

- Selflessness

- Integrity

- Objectivity

- Accountability

- Openness

- Honesty

- Leadership.'

First Report of the Committee on Standards in Public Life, *Standards in Public Life,*
Volume 1: Report, Cm 2850-I (1995), p 14.

Among other things, the Code of Conduct states that:

- Members should conscientiously register their interests.
- Members shall not act as a paid advocate.
- Members shall not accept a bribe (as being contrary to the law of Parliament).

The House of Lords by way of a resolution in 2001 adopted the House of Lords Code of Conduct which set out the rules on Lords' Interests. A sub-committee of the House of Lords Committee for Privileges monitors the operation and investigates breaches of the code. It should be made clear that the Parliamentary Commissioner for Standards does not operate in the House of Lords.

Further reading

Alder, J, *Constitutional and Administrative Law* (5th edn, Palgrave Macmillan, 2005), Chapter 9.

Carroll, A, *Constitutional and Administrative Law* (3rd edn, Pearson/Longman, 2003), Chapters 8 and 10.

Factsheet G06 'Disciplinary and Penal Powers of the House of Commons' (House of Commons, Parliamentary Copyright, 2003).

First Report of the Committee on Standards in Public Life, *Standards in Public Life, Volume 1: Report,* Cm 2850-I (1995).

Joint Committee on Parliamentary Privilege, *Report Volume I – Report and Proceedings of the Committee,* HL Paper 43-I, HC 214-I (1999).

Loveland, I, *Constitutional Law, Administrative Law, and Human Rights* (4th edn, Oxford University Press, 2006), Chapter 8.

Oliver, D, 'The Powers and Privileges of Parliament' in Feldman, D, (ed), *English Public Law* (Oxford University Press, 2004), p 112.

Website

www.parliament.uk

chapter 9 PARLIAMENT II: THE HOUSE OF COMMONS ■

AIMS AND OBJECTIVES □ □ □

At the end of this chapter you should be able to:

■ Identify and explain the different functions of the House of Commons

■ Explain the composition of the House of Commons

■ Explain the nature and significance of the electoral system

9.1 The functions of the House of Commons

The House of Commons is the lower, but pre-eminent chamber of Parliament. This is in common with other bicameral legislatures where the lower chamber is dominant (a clear exception to this is the House of Representatives in the United States which in some respects is not as powerful as the upper chamber: the Senate).

9.1.1 Bagehot and the functions of the House of Commons

The specific functions of the House of Commons overlap and blend with those of Parliament as a whole, and these are considered in brief below. Before considering them, it is of interest to set out the functions of the Commons identified by Bagehot in the nineteenth century (W Bagehot, *The English Constitution* (Oxford University Press, 2001), Chapter 6). He set out the following five roles:

- **An elective function (the electoral chamber).**
- **An expressive function.**
- **A teaching function.**
- **An informing function.**
- **A legislative function.**

These will be referred to in the context of a modern formulation of the functions of the House of Commons below.

9.1.2 Modern functions of the House of Commons

Today the functions of the House of Commons can be defined as follows:

A representative role to represent and reflect the will of the people

As each MP is directly elected by his own constituents, the House of Commons performs a representative function reflecting the will of the people. How accurately that will is reflected is determined by the electoral system (see section 9.4.4). In the context of the representative function, in 2004 the House of Commons Select Committee on Modernisation of the House of Commons issued a report entitled: 'Connecting Parliament with the Public'. It opened its report in the following manner:

> **Q**
>
> 'The legitimacy of the House of Commons, as the principal representative body in British democracy, rests upon the support and engagement of the electorate. The decline in political participation and engagement in recent years, as well as in levels of trust in politicians, political parties and the institutions of State should be of concern to every citizen. But it should be of particular concern to the House of Commons.'
>
> First Report of Session 2003–04, *Connecting Parliament with the Public*, HC 368 (2004), p 9.

In particular, the report set out recommendations to:

- Make the building more accessible to people.
- Make greater effort to engage young people.
- Encourage better use of information and communication technology, in order to re-connect the public with Parliament.

Bagehot commented that the House of Commons can 'express the mind' of the people on issues before it (the expressive function). In other words, the chamber reflects and expresses the will of the people and is the sounding board of the nation.

To make laws

In particular, the House of Commons has a dominant role in the passage of legislation as the most important Bills are commenced there and the consent of the House of Lords is not always necessary (see section 10.10.1). Bagehot subsumed within the legislative function the financial function (eg the authorisation of finance).

To provide the personnel of the government

It is the House of Commons that is largely responsible for providing government ministers (this is also the case in other parliamentary executives). In fact, it is the House of Commons which chooses the government as it is periodically elected and represents the will of the people. In effect, the government is determined by the outcome of the general election, as the leader of the political party that secures the majority of seats in the House of Commons will, by constitutional convention, be appointed Prime Minister by the monarch. For example, in May 1997 Tony Blair's Labour Party secured the majority of seats in the House of Commons and he was appointed Prime Minister. Bagehot described this function as the elective function with the House of Commons as the 'electoral chamber'.

To provide the Official Opposition

The House of Commons also (largely) provides the opposition to the government (known as Her Majesty's Official Opposition). The main Official Opposition in the 2007 Parliament was the Conservative Party as they had the second largest number of seats in the Commons. They act as the 'government in waiting' and their responsibility is to scrutinise and examine government actions and policy.

To scrutinise the executive

In constitutional terms, a major role of the House of Commons is to hold the government to account to the elected representatives of the people.

To maintain the government

As noted at section 5.3.2, it is the constitutional function of the government to govern. The role of the House of Commons is somewhat contradictory as it should constitutionally sustain the government (while the government has the support and confidence of the lower House) allowing it to govern and carry on the business of government. At the same time, the House simultaneously must scrutinise the actions and policy of the government and withdraw support from it if it loses confidence in it (in other words, if the government has lost the confidence of the people). On rare occasions, such as in 1979, the government has lost a vote of no confidence, thereby symbolically losing the support of the people as represented in the House of Commons (see section 12.2.1).

To legitimise government actions

In scrutinising government actions, the House of Commons effectively legitimises it, if it passes this scrutiny. This could be in the form of a particular government policy or in a Bill drafted by the government. In this context it is important to bear in mind the political composition of the House of Commons which is dictated by the nature of the electoral system (see section 9.5).

A judicial function

The House of Commons also performs, in effect, a judicial function when it enforces parliamentary privilege (see section 8.7.3).

In addition, according to Bagehot the teaching function of the House of Commons involved it teaching 'the nation what it does not know' (arguably this could occur, for example, in the context of a debate). The informing function involved the House making 'us hear what otherwise we should not' (it could be argued that this function would be performed in the context of questions to government ministers and also in the course of debates).

KEY FACTS ☐☐☐☐☐☐☐

The key functions of the House of Commons

Representative
Each MP is elected and collectively they express the will of the nation.

Recruitment of government
The government is drawn largely from the lower chamber.

To maintain the government and legitimise its actions
The chamber sustains and maintains the government. The latter needs the support of the chamber to survive.

To redress grievances and scrutinise the executive
MPs try to resolve the grievances of their constituents and the chamber as a whole holds the government to account (which can include a vote of no confidence in it).

Legislative
Bills pass through both chambers with the most important Bills beginning in the lower chamber.

Judicial
The House enforces parliamentary privilege and disciplines members.

9.2 The size and composition of the House of Commons

9.2.1 The number of seats in the House of Commons

Although the size of the House of Commons is set out in statute, it can be altered by ordinary legislation. The size of the last four House of Commons is set out below:

- 1992/1997   – 651 MPs

- 1997/2001   – 659 MPs

- 2001/2005   – 659 MPs

- 2005/to date   – 646 MPs

The reason the 54th Parliament (the current Parliament which began in 2005) has 13 seats less than the 53rd Parliament (2001–05) is as a result of the recommendations of the Boundary Commission for Scotland, whereby Scotland lost 13 MPs. This reduction takes account of the fact that Scotland now has its own Parliament and can legislate for itself on specified matters and arguably addresses (to some extent) the so called 'West Lothian question' (see section 22.9.1). In addition, Scotland – along with Wales and Northern Ireland – has traditionally enjoyed more favourable representation at Westminster (the so called 'Celtic preference') for political reasons.

In comparison to other democracies, with 646 MPs the House of Commons is a large lower chamber in relation to its population. In contrast, for example, the United States has 435 members in the House of Representatives and the French National Assembly has 577.

9.2.2 The House of Commons as a representative body?

The regions

The House of Commons is part of the United Kingdom Parliament and so MPs represent all parts of the state as indicated below:

The 2005 Parliament

- England   – 529 MPs
- Wales   – 40 MPs
- Scotland   – 59 MPs (in the previous
                       Parliament there were 72)
- Northern Ireland – 18 MPs
                      646 MPs

Source: www.parliament.uk

Ethnic minorities

In the 2005 general election 15 black and minority ethnic MPs (standing for mainstream political parties) were elected. The Electoral Commission has pointed out that proportionately:

> 'while this figure still falls well short of the total required for the House of Commons to mirror the UK population (51), it is more than twice that in 1992 and nearly four times that in 1987.'

Election 2005: turnout. How many, who and why? (Electoral Commission, 2005), p 18.

Women

The number of female MPs in the past five Parliaments is as follows:

Women MPs

- 1987 Parliament   –   41 MPs
- 1992 Parliament   –   60 MPs
- 1997 Parliament   –   120 MPs
- 2001 Parliament   –   118 MPs
- 2005 Parliament   –   128 MPs

Factsheet M 4 'Women in the House of Commons' (Parliamentary Copyright, 2006), p 6.

Even though 128 female MPs were returned in 2005, proportionately this is still less than 20 per cent of all MPs in the House of Commons. The longstanding concern about the under-representation of women in the House of Commons led to the passage of the Sex Discrimination (Election Candidates) Act 2002. This Act enabled political parties to take positive action (affirmative action) to encourage the election of female MPs by permitting political parties to draw up an 'all-female shortlist' for the selection of their official parliamentary constituency candidate for a general election. This legislation amended the Sex Discrimination Act 1975 as detailed in the following case:

CASE EXAMPLE

Jepson and Dyas-Elliott (applicants) v The Labour Party [1996] IRLR 116

Jepson and Dyas-Elliott were not considered for selection as Labour Party candidates in parliamentary constituencies because these particular constituencies were required to have all-women shortlists. The policy behind this was to increase the number of women elected to Parliament.

CONTINUED ▸

Jepson and Dyas-Elliott contended that they had been unlawfully discriminated against on the grounds of their sex (they were male and so prevented from forming part of the shortlist) contrary to s 13 of the Sex Discrimination Act 1975.

The tribunal upheld their complaints that the policy of all-women shortlists contravened the Sex Discrimination Act. This was because the endorsement of a prospective parliamentary candidate was an 'authorisation' under the Act which facilitated 'engagement in a particular profession', that is the public office of an MP.

Age

MPs tend to be middle-aged, although the 2005 Parliament included two MPs aged 25 and 26 years of age. It should be pointed out that although individuals can vote at 18, until the passing of the Electoral Administration Act 2006 they could not become MPs until 21 years of age to ensure that MPs had a minimum of experience. The 2006 Act now reduces the minimum age to 18.

ACTIVITY

Exercise

Do you think that the House of Commons is sufficiently representative of the population? In terms of its constitutional legitimacy, does this matter?

9.3 The Member of Parliament

9.3.1 The role of a Member of Parliament (MP)

The United Kingdom has a representative democracy. Although MPs are elected representatives of the people, this does not mean that they are simply their delegates who mechanically act on instructions from the electorate. MPs clearly serve their constituents, represent their concerns and redress their grievances, but they also exercise independent mature judgement by themselves.

Carroll (*Constitutional and Administrative Law* (3rd edn, Pearson/Longman, 2003), p 113) has identified five competing factors ('constituencies') which a modern MP has to consider, namely:

- **The political party**

The overwhelming majority of MPs are members of an organised political party with official policies. Political parties ensure discipline through a 'whip' system which compels MPs within that party to vote for the official party line. As a consequence, MPs can be ultimately deselected as the parliamentary candidate for their constituency in a future general election if they behave (and vote) in a way which is detrimental to the official party line and interests.

- **The constituency**

As a constituency MP, he has to be sensitive to the needs of his constituents. MPs will typically have surgeries to meet constituents and will also receive written correspondence from them. According to the House of Commons Information Office, an MP has a number of different methods of resolving grievances which include writing to the relevant department or minster and/or making an appointment to meet the minister in person (Factsheet M1 'You and Your MP' (Parliamentary Copyright, 2005), p 4). In addition, an MP may refer the issue to the parliamentary Ombudsman (see section 21.3).

In fact, an MP may have a constituency which has particular circumstances (eg a government proposal to site a chemical plant there) which will require the MP to articulate and raise in Parliament in the interests of his constituents (whether or not this happens to be against the official party political line).

- **An MP's own conscience**

As indicated by Edmund Burke writing in the eighteenth century, MPs are not mere delegates of the people, but are also charged with exercising their personal judgement on a matter. Indeed, some issues which come before Parliament are defined as 'free vote issues' which are above party political divisions. These will typically be on moral issues such as the death penalty. Interestingly, the debate and votes in February 2003 and March 2007 on the future reform of the House of Lords were officially on the basis of a free vote, free from party political pressure.

- **An interest group**

An MP may have a close relationship with certain interest groups, for example a trade union or a charity/business organisation. Under the Register of Members' Interests (see section 8.8.1) MPs have to declare their financial interests with the outside world.

- **Acting in the public interest**

An MP is a parliamentarian and as such one of his constitutional roles is to hold the government to account. It would appear that MPs perform this role most effectively when they sit in select committees scrutinising government departments. Select committee reports tend to produce a cross-party consensus and it seems that MPs in this context act in a less partisan way than they do when they return to the Floor of the House (see section 12.6.6).

9.3.2 The qualifications required to be an MP

In essence any individual is eligible to become an MP provided:

- they are 18 years of age or older; and
- are a citizen of the United Kingdom, the Commonwealth or the Irish Republic.

The vast majority of MPs belong to a recognised political party. In fact, in 2005 only two independent MPs were elected. Accordingly, the practical reality is that in order to become an MP, a person will need to be selected by a political party as its prospective parliamentary candidate for a constituency.

Prospective parliamentary candidates need to provide a deposit of £500 in order to take part in an election which is lost in the event of a candidate securing less than 5 per cent of the total votes cast in a constituency. The rationale behind the deposit is to prevent frivolous candidates standing for election. From a constitutional perspective, however, it could be argued that the use of the deposit actively discourages individuals from standing for election (putting oneself up for election is part of a participatory democracy). It may also impact adversely on smaller parties who may wish to field candidates in all or most constituencies.

9.3.3 The factors which disqualify a person from becoming an MP

Erskine May (*Parliamentary Practice* (23rd edn, LexisNexis Butterworths, 2004), Ch 3) identified the following factors which disqualify a person from becoming an MP and sitting in the House of Commons:

- **Under age**

Although individuals can vote at 18 years of age (see section 9.6.2), historically they could not stand for parliamentary elections until they were 21 (Parliamentary Elections Act 1695). Under the Electoral Administration Act 2006, the age has now been reduced to 18. In the House of Lords, peers must be at least 21 years of age to take their seat.

- **Aliens**

Aliens (ie non-British citizens) under the Act of Settlement 1700 are disqualified from membership of either House. The British Nationality Act 1981 states that this does not apply to individuals who are Commonwealth citizens or from the Republic of Ireland.

- **Peers**

Members of the House of Lords cannot sit in both parliamentary chambers. It is pertinent to point out, however, that those hereditary peers removed from the House of Lords under the House of Lords Act 1999 (see section 10.6.3) are eligible to be elected as MPs. Indeed, in 2001 one hereditary peer (Viscount Thurso), who formerly sat in the House of Lords until 1999, was elected as an MP (John Thurso). He was re-elected at the 2005 general election.

233

- **Those suffering from mental illness**

Those detained under mental health legislation (ie Mental Health Act 1983) will be disqualified. Under s 141 of the 1983 Act there is a procedure to vacate the seat of an MP who is of 'unsound mind' and the seat will become vacant.

- **Treason**

Those convicted of treason under the Forfeiture Act 1870.

- **Bankruptcy**

In relation to England and Wales, individuals who have bankruptcy orders in effect against them are disqualified (s 266 of the Enterprise Act 2002). In Northern Ireland it is where they are declared bankrupt and in Scotland against whom a sequestration of estate is awarded (s 427 of the Insolvency Act 1986).

- **Those convicted of crimes**

Under the Representation of the People Act 1981, an individual serving a prison sentence of more than a year for any offence is disqualified. This was passed in the context of the election of Bobby Sands as a Westminster MP (who at the time was a prisoner on hunger strike in Northern Ireland).

- **Corrupt/illegal practices**

Under the Representation of the People Act 1983 (as amended) an individual convicted of corrupt practices (eg bribery) at an election is disqualified for five years. Those convicted of illegal practices (eg excessive expenditure) are disqualified for three years

- **Religious representation**

In recent years a disqualification in relation to the clergy has been removed. The House of Commons (Removal of Clergy Disqualification) Act 2001 provides that no ministers of any religious denomination (eg Roman Catholic priests) are disqualified from membership of the House of Commons. The exceptions to this are the Archbishops and Bishops in the House of Lords (see section 10.3).

- **The House of Commons Disqualification Act 1975**

This Act constitutionally and legally prohibits certain elements of the executive (civil servants, police officers, etc) from sitting in the House of Commons as part of the legislature (see section 11.6.3). It is interesting to note that s 1(1)(a) of the Act excludes full-time judges from sitting in the House of Commons. This preserves a degree of separation between the judiciary and the legislature; however, Justices of the Peace are eligible to sit as MPs.

- **Other legislatures**

In addition, s 1(1)(e) of the House of Commons Disqualification Act 1975 disqualifies members of other legislatures outside the Commonwealth (except the Republic of Ireland). In contrast, MPs can be members of, for example, the Scottish Parliament, National Assembly for Wales and the Northern Ireland Assembly. Indeed, in 2007 Alex Salmond, the leader of the Scottish National Party, was a member of both the House of Commons and the Scottish Parliament (in terms of the latter, he was the First Minister).

9.3.4 By-elections

In the event of an MP dying (or being disqualified) his seat becomes vacant and a by-election will ensue. For example, when the Labour MP Robin Cook died in August 2005, a by-election was held in that constituency in September 2005. On this occasion another Labour MP was elected in his place, although it is not always the case that the same political party will win back the seat. For example, when Rachel Squire, a Labour MP, died in January 2006, at the ensuing by-election in February 2006 her seat was taken by a Liberal Democrat candidate.

KEY FACTS

The Role of the MP

An MP has to consider the following competing interests:

- party political pressure from the political party that he belongs to;

- his constituents who elect (and re-elect) him into office as a constituency MP;

- his own conscience on moral matters (eg on the death penalty);

- an interest group with which he has a close relationship (eg a trade union);

- acting as a parliamentarian in the public interest.

9.4 The electoral system

9.4.1 The system of voting

The United Kingdom uses a single member constituency, simple majority system. It is commonly referred to as the 'first past the post' system. The mechanics of the system are detailed below:

- The whole of the United Kingdom is divided up into single member constituencies (for the 2005 general election there were 646 parliamentary constituencies).

- In each constituency political parties will put forward one candidate as a prospective MP. Political parties do not, however, have to contest each seat. For example, in Northern Ireland the main political parties have not traditionally put up candidates owing to the historically idiosyncratic political make-up of the province.

- Each registered voter who chooses to vote (many choose not to vote) puts a cross on the ballot paper next to the chosen candidate.

- Once polling has closed, all the votes cast will be counted. The winning candidate (and so the elected Member of Parliament for that consistency) will be the person who has secured more votes than any other candidate. For example:

Constituency of Birmingham Erdington general election 2005.		
Electorate of 64,951 – 48.9% turnout (31,746 voted)		
Party candidate	**Votes cast in favour**	**% of vote**
Labour (elected as MP)	16,810 (a majority of 9, 575)	53%
Conservative	7,235	23%
Liberal Democrat	5,027	16%

It is imperative to point out that this does not mean that the winning candidate has to obtain a majority of votes cast. In fact, in most cases the winning candidate will not do so.

It is in this way that the United Kingdom's electoral system has been described as the 'first past the post' system as it has been likened to a horse race. In short, the horse that crosses the line first – irrespective of how wide or narrow the margin – is declared the winner. In this sense, the only horse (or candidate) that matters is the winner.

- As the United Kingdom Parliament has single member constituencies, each constituency returns one MP. In some other countries, constituencies are multi-member constituencies whereby a number of representatives are returned for a particular constituency. This scenario is not totally unfamiliar to the United Kingdom as, for example, large multi-member constituencies are used when electing United Kingdom Members of the European Parliament owing to the European Parliamentary Elections Act 1999.

Although only one MP is returned for each constituency, that MP represents the whole of the constituency irrespective of whether a particular constituent voted for them or not (or even if that constituent was ineligible to vote, eg he was under 18 years of age at the time of the election). Moreover, by constitutional convention one MP will not act for the constituent of another MP unless the latter is unwilling or unable to act.

- All constituencies return their MP (either a newly elected MP or an MP who has been re-elected) to the House of Commons. By constitutional convention, the leader of the party with the majority of seats in the House of Commons will be formally appointed Prime Minister by the monarch and asked to form Her Majesty's Government.

9.4.2 Election turnouts

The turnout of the population eligible to vote at the last five general elections is indicated below:

Election turnouts 1987–2005

1987	–	75.3% (of those registered to vote)
1992	–	77.7%
1997	–	71.4%
2001	–	59.4%
2005	–	61.4%

Source: *Election 2005: turnout. How many, who and why?*
(Electoral Commission, 2005), p 20)

It is in this context that the 2004 report of the Select Committee on Modernisation of the House of Commons (see section 9.1.2) should be seen. In short, the 2001 general election turnout (ie 59.4 per cent) by those registered to vote was the lowest since 1918. The general decline in voting necessarily means a reduction in participatory democracy, whereby voters are disconnected with the electoral and parliamentary process.

Although the percentage of voters who voted in the 2005 election was a marginal improvement on the 2001 election, the Electoral Commission indicated that 17 million people who were registered to vote did not cast a vote. It identified the following factors which contributed to people not voting in the 2005 general election:

- A general disillusionment with politics.
- An ignorance about politics.
- A perception that voting made no real difference.
- The difficulty in deciding which political party to vote for.
- The nature of the election campaign.

In terms of the constitutional and political significance of elections the Commission made the following comment:

> 'Elections underpin our democracy, ensuring that our representative institutions are both accountable to public opinion and legitimised by it. They provide an opportunity for politicians and political parties to outline their ideas and to defend their performance. Elections can interest, inform and empower people and, by doing so, can help to build political engagement.'

Election 2005: turnout. How many, who and why? (Electoral Commission, 2005), p 53.

One highly revealing statistic concerning the 2005 general election is that nationally the Labour Party polled less votes (9,552,436) than those electors who were registered to vote, but chose not to exercise their franchise (17 million).

In recent years in order to address voter apathy, there have been attempts to engage with voters by using different forms of voting methods. For example, local government elections have experimented with polling booths located in supermarkets as well as universal postal votes. The Electoral Administration Act 2006 is particularly concerned with increasing the highest possible turnout at elections. For example, Part 4 provides a framework for local authorities to review their polling stations to ensure that they are properly accessible to voters (see section 22.5.2).

ACTIVITY

Question

Why do you think there is a relatively poor turnout for general elections? In terms of the legitimacy of the House of Commons, does this matter?

9.4.3 The advantages of the 'first past the post' electoral system

The United Kingdom's electoral system is somewhat controversial in certain aspects (see 9.4.4), but it has a number of distinct advantages:

- **Simplicity**

  In contrast to other systems available (and in particular to the one recommended by the Jenkins Commission in 1998 – see section 22.5.2), the current electoral system is comparatively simple. It is relatively straightforward for the public to understand as only one box on the ballot paper needs to be ticked. In contrast, in some other systems such as the Single Transferable Vote, candidates are ranked in order of preference. It is also straightforward to administer and provides an efficient method of voting and of forming a parliamentary chamber. It is also a relatively inexpensive system of voting because it is easy to administer.

- **Single member constituencies**

  The system uses single member constituencies, which has the advantage that every constituency in the United Kingdom has one single, identifiable Member of Parliament who represents the interests of that particular constituency. In this way it constitutionally links each MP with one specific geographical area of the state.

- **Produces strong government**

  In general terms, and certainly in the last few decades, the electoral system produces an electoral result which confers one political party (historically either Labour or Conservative) with a majority of seats in the House of Commons. In fact, for six out of the last seven general elections (the exception being 1992), the electoral system has produced a government with a substantial working majority of seats. For example, in 1983 the Conservative Government had a majority of 143 seats, whilst in 1997 the Labour Government enjoyed a majority of 178 seats. It is argued that such majorities allow the government to be decisive and to govern by translating its legislative programme, as set out in its general election manifesto, into laws. Moreover, a strong decisive government is an advantage in a crisis (international or domestic) and is generally regarded as preferable to a weak government typically found in coalition governments consisting of an amalgamation of rival and competing political parties.

In this context it is pertinent to note that although Italy has historically been hallmarked by its coalition and unstable governments, in the 1990s they reformed their electoral system from a proportional one to a mainly 'first past the post' system. This appeared to usher in a period of more stable government. In 2006, however, the system was reformed reverting back to a proportional system which in turn resulted in the general election of April 2006 producing a somewhat inconclusive result.

9.4.4 The disadvantages of the 'first past the post' electoral system

There are at least four major problems with the system as detailed below:

- **A disproportionate system**

One clear difficulty with the electoral system is that it is possible for an MP to be elected on a minority of the vote. The following example from the 2005 general election makes this point:

Birmingham Sparkbrook and Small Heath constituency.
Electorate 73,721 – 51.8% turnout (38,192 voted)

Party candidate	Votes cast in favour	% of vote
Labour	13,787	36.1%
Respect	10,498	27.5%
Liberal Democrat	7,727	20.2%
Conservative	3,480	9.1%

This example shows that the Labour candidate who won this constituency to become its MP did so with less than 50 per cent of the total votes cast (in fact on the basis of only 36 per cent). Indeed, more people voted against the Labour candidate, than in favour of him. This illustrates the nature of the 'first past the post' system: in order to become an MP, all that has to be achieved is to secure more votes than any other candidate. In fact, in Crawley the Labour candidate won with 39.1 per cent of the votes cast (16,411) which represented only 37 more votes than her nearest

(Conservative) rival who came second (16,374 votes/39.01 per cent) (*The Times*, 7th May 2005, p 72).

If the above scenario is replicated in many constituencies across the United Kingdom, then it is possible to see how a government can become elected with a majority of seats in the House of Commons, but with only a minority of the votes cast nationwide in their favour. At the 2005 general election the Labour Party secured 55 per cent of the seats in the House of Commons and yet secured only 35.2 per cent of the total votes cast nationwide. In contrast, the Conservative Party polled 32.4 per cent of the votes cast and secured only 198 seats, representing just over 30 per cent of the House of Commons. This in turn raises the question of whether a government elected on this basis has political legitimacy. Indeed, in the second half of the twentieth century, no government (Labour or Conservative) has assumed office with a majority of the votes cast.

- **Voter apathy**

One possible reason for poor turnouts at general elections (as pointed out by the Electoral Commission) is the perception that that voting 'makes no difference'. In fact, a number of constituencies in the United Kingdom are considered 'safe seats' in the sense that one particular political party traditionally has always won the seat. As a result of this, voting for a candidate of a different political party in such a 'safe' constituency would appear to be fruitless. It must be remembered that under the electoral system the 'winner takes all' and the votes cast for the losing candidates are disregarded. These votes are, in effect, wasted votes.

- **Variations in constituencies**

As the United Kingdom uses the single member constituency system, this inevitably results in some regional variations. The average size of the electorate in a constituency is around 67,000 (Factsheet M1 'You and Your MP' (Parliamentary Copyright, 2005), p 3). Some constituencies, however, such as the Isle of Wight had an electorate of 109,046 at the 2005 general election whereas, in contrast, the constituency of Na h-Eileanan an Iar in Scotland had an electorate of only 21,576. In other words, the value of a vote cast in the latter constituency will have more significance (in terms of determining who wins the seat) than in the former, much larger constituency. In essence, a vote in a smaller constituency – in proportionate terms – is more significant than a vote in a larger constituency. This necessarily raises the issue of whether all votes have equal value.

- **Third parties**

One clear disadvantage of the 'first past the post' system is that it is essentially designed to accommodate a two-party system and so smaller third parties are penalised. For example, at the 2005 election, although the Liberal Democrats polled 5,985,454 votes nationally (roughly two-thirds of those polled for the Conservative Party), they obtained only about one-third of the number of parliamentary seats as the Conservatives (see section 9.5).

9.4.5 Parliamentary constituency boundaries

The review of constituency boundaries due to population movement has historically been carried out by four Boundary Commissions, one for each of the countries of the United Kingdom, and they were governed by the Parliamentary Constituencies Act 1986. On receipt of a report of a Boundary Commission, a government minister would lay a draft order before Parliament for it to approve, giving effect to the Commission's recommendations. The four Boundary Commissions were scheduled to be subsumed under the aegis of the Electoral Commission once the fifth boundary review in 2007 had been completed.

The redrawing of constituency boundaries inevitably has an impact on one or more political parties (eg they either gain or lose potential seats). The redrawing of such constituencies can, therefore, be controversial and in the early 1980s the Leader of the Labour Party sought to challenge one of these proposed changes:

CASE EXAMPLE

R v Boundary Commission for England, ex parte Foot [1983] 1 QB 600

Michael Foot, the leader of the Labour Party and Leader of the Opposition, unsuccessfully sought in judicial review to prohibit the Boundary Commission for England from submitting to the Home Secretary its revised parliamentary constituencies. The Court of Appeal noted that the Commission's duty did include giving effect to, *inter alia*, r 5 (Sched 2 to the House of Commons (Redistribution of Seats) Act 1949), which provided that 'the electorate of any constituency shall be as near the electoral quota as is practicable' (this was designed to ensure the principle of equal representation for electors). It was held, however, that the rule (as a result of s 2 of the House of Commons (Redistribution of Seats) Act 1958), had the status of a guideline and that Foot had failed to discharge the heavy onus of showing that the recommendations of the Boundary Commission were conclusions which no reasonable Commission could have come to.

Constituency boundaries are reviewed and re-adjusted periodically and in 2007 they were scheduled to be reviewed again (this will be the fifth boundary review following those in 1954, 1969, 1982 and 1994).

ACTIVITY

Essay writing

Compare and contrast the advantages and disadvantages of the 'first past the post' electoral system.

KEY FACTS

- The United Kingdom uses the 'first past the post' system which comprises 646 single member constituencies.

- Political parties put forward one candidate as a prospective MP for each constituency.

- The elected Member of Parliament for each constituency will be the person who has secured more votes than any other candidate.

- The leader of the political party that gains the majority of seats in the House of Commons will become Prime Minister.

9.5 The current political composition of the House of Commons

The main political parties polled the following votes at the 2005 general election:

Party	Votes cast	% of votes
Labour	9,552,436	35.2 %
Conservative	8,784,915	32.4%
Liberal Democrat	5,985,454	22%

Source: *Election 2005: turnout. How many, who and why?*

(Electoral Commission, 2005), p 17.

The political breakdown of the House of Commons immediately following the 2005 general election was as follows:

Party	Seats
Labour	355
Conservative	198
Liberal Democrat	62
Scottish National Party	6
Democratic Unionist	9
Sinn Fein (historically did not take their seats for political reasons)	5
Social Democratic Labour Party	3
Ulster Unionist	1
Plaid Cymru	3
Others • Respect Party – G Galloway • Independent – P Law • Independent Kidderminster Hospital and Health Concern – R Taylor	3
Speaker	1
TOTAL	646 MPs

Source: *Election 2005: turnout. How many, who and why?*
(Electoral Commission, 2005), p 17.

On the basis of these figures, after the general election the Labour majority was 65 (if the Speaker is not considered) which meant that the Labour Party (and so by logical extension, the Labour Government – see section 9.9) had 65 more MPs than all of the other political parties put together.

Three points are worth remembering about the political composition of the House of Commons.

- Firstly, the House of Commons is not one single entity that acts as a single unit. Instead, it is composed of a variety of different political parties vying with each other (although it tends to be dominated by one political party).

- Secondly, the overwhelming majority of MPs are members of political parties and therefore very few independent MPs are elected. In 2005, excluding the Speaker of the House, only two independent MPs were elected (see 'Others' in the table above). In this way the House of Commons differs from the House of Lords which is composed of a number of independent peers known as cross benchers (see section 10.7.3).

- Thirdly, the political composition of the House of Commons will change inevitably (albeit marginally) over the course of a parliamentary term. This necessarily has an impact on a government's majority (which may be highly significant if its majority is slim). There are two main reasons for this:

(i) By-elections will be held in the wake of the death of an MP. By-elections are not rare events; for example, in the 1992–1997 parliamentary session, there were 18 by-elections which resulted in nine seats changing political hands (Factsheet M 14 'By-election results: 1992–97' (Parliamentary Copyright, 2003), p 2).

(ii) Change of allegiance – it is also possible for an MP to change political party. For example, in 1999 Shaun Woodward changed parties from Conservative to Labour. This is known as 'Crossing the Floor' of the Commons.

Finally, it has been suggested that the current composition of the House of Lords is more representative of the strength of political parties than the House of Commons (see section 10.7.1). Indeed, in March 2007 the Labour Party had just under 30 per cent of the total seats in the House of Lords in contrast with 55 per cent of seats in the Commons, but had secured only 35 per cent of the votes cast at the 2005 general election.

ACTIVITY

Problem solving

Compare the votes cast for each main political party at the 2005 general election and correlate this with the number of seats that they obtained in the House of Commons. What does this tell you about the electoral system?

9.6 The electorate

9.6.1 The constitutional significance of voting

In a representative democracy it is a prerequisite that democracy is a participatory democracy. This means that, *inter alia*, citizens regularly determine who should represent them in Parliament and who should govern the country. In the United Kingdom the people do not *directly* elect the government/executive, rather they elect representatives (MPs) from whom the government is drawn (see Bagehot's elective function, section 9.1.2).

The constitutional significance of the electorate voting in elections has been clearly recognised by the European Convention:

'The High Contracting Parties undertake to hold free elections at reasonable intervals by secret ballot, under conditions which will ensure the free expression of the opinion of the people in the choice of the legislature.'

Art 3, Protocol No 1.

The European Court in *Mathieu-Mohin and Clerfayt v Belgium* (1988) 10 EHRR 1 has regarded this provision as a very important free-standing right as well as a prerequisite for the enjoyment and protection of other European Convention rights:

'Since it enshrines a characteristic principle of democracy, Article 3 of Protocol No. 1 is accordingly of prime importance in the Convention system.'

In the case of *Matthews v UK* (1999) 28 EHRR 361, the European Court of Human Rights declared that the United Kingdom had violated Art 3, Protocol No 1 when Matthews (a British citizen) resident in Gibraltar (which was not part of the United Kingdom, but a dependent territory), had been denied the right to vote in elections to the European Parliament. As Gibraltar had not been included in the franchise for European parliamentary elections, Matthews had been denied any opportunity to express her opinion as to who should be elected as an MEP.

9.6.2 Who can vote in parliamentary elections?

This is set out in the Representation of the People Act 1983 (as amended). A person can vote who is:

- Of voting age: 18 years or over at the date of the poll (the Family Law Reform Act 1969 reduced the voting age from 21 years of age to 18 and the government has considered the possibility of lowering further the age to 16).

- Registered in the register of parliamentary elections for that particular constituency. Electoral registration officers have a responsibility to produce an electoral register which is compiled on the basis of returns made by householders. Students are permitted to vote in either their permanent constituency address or in their university constituency *Fox v Stirk* [1970] 2 QB 463. In recent years the electoral register has been reformed with the effect that it is now a 'rolling register' which is amended continuously. In addition the term 'residency' has been amended so as to include the homeless, allowing them to vote (as amended by the Representation of the People Act 2000).

- Not disqualified from voting (see section 9.6.3).

- A British, Irish or Commonwealth citizen who is resident in the United Kingdom.

- A person who is a British Citizen resident outside the United Kingdom and qualified as an overseas elector (Representation of the People Act 1985 as amended).

A general election will be held on one day so that all the polls are held simultaneously. An individual can vote only once in one single constituency and cannot vote in more than one constituency in a parliamentary election. It is possible to vote by post (eg if a voter is overseas) or proxy (eg if the voter has a physical disability).

Voting is by secret ballot, although voting is not compulsory as in some countries such as Australia. This necessarily has an impact on electorate turnouts at general elections and in 2005 the then Leader of the House of Commons put forward the suggestion of introducing compulsory voting in order to increase turnout.

9.6.3 Who is disqualified from voting?

The following factors disenfranchise a person from voting at general elections as set out in the Representation of the People Act 1983 (as amended):

- Peers in the House of Lords (however, members of the House of Lords who were removed under the House of Lords Act 1999 are eligible to vote).

- Persons under the age of 18 years on the day of the election – on this point it is worth noting that the electorate for each constituency does not equate to the population of that constituency, as it necessarily excludes anyone under 18.

- Historically, a common law rule of incapacity to vote by reason of a person's mental state (but see s 73 Electoral Administration Act 2006 which abolished any common law rule which provided that a person was subject to a legal incapacity to vote by reason of his mental state).

- Persons guilty of corrupt or illegal practices at elections (within the past five years).

- Citizens of the European Union and other countries (except citizens from the Republic of Ireland or the Commonwealth).

- Those detained in mental hospitals as authorised by statute.

- Convicted prisoners during the term of their detention. Section 3 of the Representation of the People Act 1983 states that:

A convicted person during the time that he is detained in a penal institution in pursuance of his sentence ... is legally incapable of voting at any parliamentary or local government election.

This is a blanket exclusion on prisoners from voting which means that even if the prisoner was scheduled for release a week after polling day at a general election, they would legally still be precluded from voting at it. The Act, however, does not apply to:

- persons imprisoned for contempt of court;

- those imprisoned for default in paying a fine;

- persons on remand and unconvicted mental patients (as amended by the Representation of the People Act 2000).

In the *Hirst* case (see below) in the European Court of Human Rights, the government tried to justify the disenfranchisement of prisoners on the basis that it pursued the following legitimate aims, namely 'of preventing crime and punishing offenders and enhancing civic responsibility and respect for the rule of law, by depriving those who have breached the basic rules of society of the right to have a say in the way such rules are made for the duration of their sentence' (para 33). The blanket disenfranchisement of United Kingdom prisoners to vote was tested in this case.

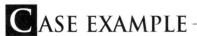

CASE EXAMPLE

Hirst v United Kingdom (No 2) (2004) 38 EHRR 825

Hirst had been serving a sentence of life imprisonment and as a convicted prisoner was legally disqualified from voting (s 3 Representation of the People Act 1983). In the United Kingdom domestic courts he unsuccessfully sought a declaration under the Human Rights Act 1998 that such a provision violated Art 3, Protocol No 1 (the right to free elections). He subsequently petitioned the European Court of Human Rights.

A Chamber of the European Court held that there had been a breach of Art 3 of Protocol No 1. The court reaffirmed that elections were the foundation of an effective democracy. Although the right to vote was not absolute, any limitations had to be proportionate. Even though 13 other countries like the United Kingdom prevented prisoners from voting, 18 countries permitted them to vote and so there was no universal approach taken by states on this issue. The court held that as the ban applied automatically to convicted prisoners whilst in prison and irrespective of the length of sentence or the offence committed, it amounted to an indiscriminate and disproportionate restriction of Art 3 of Protocol No 1.

This decision was subsequently upheld by the Grand Chamber (by 12 to 5 votes) who confirmed that voting was not a privilege, but a right (*Hirst v United Kingdom (No 2)* (2006) 42 EHRR 849).

The United Kingdom was left to decide on the choice of means for securing the above right which had been infringed and in December 2006 the government initiated a consultation process on the issue (see section 22.5.2).

KEY FACTS

Voting at general elections

Voters must be:

- 18 years or over at the date of the poll.

- Registered in the register of parliamentary elections for that particular constituency. An electoral register is compiled on the basis of returns made by householders.

- A British, Irish or Commonwealth citizen (the latter two must be resident in the United Kingdom). Note: a person who is a British citizen resident outside the United Kingdom can qualify as an overseas elector (Representation of the People Act 1985 as amended).

Those currently disqualified from voting at general elections are:

- Peers in the House of Lords.

- Persons under the age of 18 years.

- Persons guilty of corrupt or illegal practices at elections.

- Citizens of the European Union and other countries (except citizens from the Republic of Ireland or the Commonwealth).

- Those detained in mental hospitals as authorised by statute.

- Convicted prisoners during the term of their detention (but reforms to alter this are currently under consideration).

ACTIVITY

Question

What is the democratic importance of elections? In particular, do you think that prisoners should vote in elections?

9.7 The supervision and conduct of elections

9.7.1 The supervision and conduct of elections

Under the Political Parties, Elections and Referendums Act 2000, the functions of the Boundary Commissions were scheduled to be transferred to the Electoral Commission (established in 2000 as an independent public body under the above Act). According to its website, the aim of the Electoral Commission 'is integrity and public confidence in the democratic process' (www.electoralcommission.org.uk).

In terms of general election campaigns the Electoral Commission under the 2000 Act has, among others, the following responsibilities:

- It supervises the registration of political parties. In effect, in order to contest a general election a political party needs to be registered and the Commission can refuse to register a party.

- It supervises the financing of political parties including the publication of financial information and accounts (for example money spent on electoral campaigns). In short, political parties are subject to audit requirements and they must record donations and expenditure. The Commission, therefore, monitors and publishes donations. The Electoral Administration Act 2006 now provides for the regulation of loans and credit facilities.

  It is pertinent to note that in 2006 the Electoral Commission announced a programme whereby it would examine the accountability, regulation and openness of political party funding. Moreover, in 2006 the House of Commons Constitutional Affairs Committee issued its inquiry into the system of the funding of political parties. It argued that the present system of party funding was unstable and this needed to be addressed and *inter alia*: 'We recommend that within a stronger and more robust regulatory framework there be a package of changes to the system of party funding to include: an overall cap on spending, both at local and national level; greater transparency about the sources of all elements of party funding; a voluntarily agreed binding framework for the limiting of all large donations leading to an increase in state funding for political parties' (House of Commons Constitutional Affairs Committee, First Report of Session 2006–07, *Party Funding*, HC 163-I (2006), p 59).

- It is charged with overseeing electoral law and practice.

- It is responsible for promoting the awareness of the electoral process. This educative function is particularly important in the light of poor electorate turnouts at recent elections, not just parliamentary, but also local and European elections.

In January 2007 the Committee on Standards in Public Life issued its report of its review of the Electoral Commission. It recognised the importance that the Commission played in the 'institutional architecture needed to support and maintain' our democracy. However, it recommended that the remit of the Commission be refocused and its powers increased in relation to overseeing elections and the regulation of political party funding. In particular, in terms of the principal role of the Commission, the Committee recommended that the Commission's duties should be refocused so that its principal duties were:

<table>
<tr>
<td>

Q

</td>
<td>

'as regulator of political party funding and campaign expenditure in the United Kingdom, and as regulator of electoral administration in Great Britain with the aim of ensuring integrity and public confidence in the system of political party funding and campaign expenditure and in the administration and conduct of elections'.

Eleventh Report of the Committee on Standards in Public Life, *Review of The Electoral Commission*, Report, CM 7006 (2007)

</td>
</tr>
</table>

It is also of interest to note that the Committee recommended that the Commission should not be involved in electoral boundary setting functions (Recommendation 17).

9.7.2 Election broadcasts

During general elections political parties are able to broadcast party political broadcasts in pursuance of persuading the electorate to vote for their prospective parliamentary candidates. This does not mean that all broadcasts will be screened as illustrated by the following case.

CASE EXAMPLE

R (ProLife Alliance) v British Broadcasting Corporation [2003] UKHL 23

ProLife Alliance was a political party (opposed to abortion) which was entitled to a party election television broadcast at the 2001 general election. The BBC, however, refused to transmit their election broadcast video on the grounds of taste and decency (they had a duty under their Charter to preserve good taste and decency) as it depicted the abortion process (although the video had been an honest and unsensationised account). The party sought judicial review of this decision.

The House of Lords held that the principles underpinning freedom of speech under Art 10 of the European Convention on Human Rights required that access to a public medium of

CONTINUED ▸

communication (ie a television broadcast) should not be refused on an unreasonable, arbitrary or discriminatory basis. The BBC had to justify restricting the content of a programme produced by a political party promoting its aims, but it was for the broadcasters and not the court to apply the appropriate standard. The court held that there was nothing in the reasoning or the overall decision of the BBC to suggest that they had used an inappropriate standard in determining whether the transmitting of ProLife's pictures was likely to be offensive to public opinion. It is of interest to note that in the Court of Appeal (whose decision was reversed by the Lords) Laws LJ had particularly emphasised the constitutional importance of free speech at election times.

9.8 The constitutional significance of the electoral system

The 'first past the post' electoral system has had a profound impact on the British constitution. As noted earlier, the system generally (at least in recent decades) results in one political party having a clear majority of seats in the House of Commons, thereby allowing it to form a government. In some cases, it can equip a party with an overwhelming and almost insuperable majority, for example, after the 1997 general election the Labour Government enjoyed a commanding majority of 178 seats. It must be reiterated that most of the dominant political party's MPs will not formally be part of the government, but through a combination of party loyalty and the whip system, they will generally support its policies and legislative proposals.

The constitutional consequences of the electoral system include the following:

- It alters the constitutional balance between the executive and the House of Commons in favour of the former at the expense of the latter. In particular, with a commanding majority of seats in its favour, it would be very unlikely for a government to be defeated on its proposed legislation.

- Similarly, it would be very unlikely that a government would suffer the defeat of a vote of no confidence. Although in constitutional theory the motion of no confidence is the key parliamentary mechanism to remove a government during a parliamentary term, it is rarely successful. The last occasion that it was successful was in 1979, which triggered the 1979 general election (see section 12.2.1).

- It affects the composition of committees in the House of Commons as by constitutional convention, such committees reflect the party composition of the chamber. As a result, the governing party will necessarily have a majority of MPs of the same political persuasion serving in these committees.

- Lord Hailsham has argued that our electoral system results in what he termed 'an elective dictatorship' (Elective dictatorship, *Listener*, 21st October 1976, pp 496–500). In short, a government with the comfortable support of a majority of MPs in the House of Commons can, in effect, push through whatever legislation it deems necessary. In this way the House of Commons merely legitimises the wishes of the government, who in turn have generally been elected on the basis of a minority of the votes cast.

- Finally, as an adjunct to the above point, it raises the issue of whether such a government is truly politically legitimate with the moral right to carry out its electoral mandate. Indeed, since 1935, no government either Labour or Conservative, has secured more than half of the votes cast in a general election (although in 1955 Anthony Eden's Conservative Party secured 49.7 per cent of the votes cast). All of these administrations (excluding the war-time coalition), therefore, were acting on the basis of the wishes of a minority of the electorate. In this sense it could be argued that the electoral system – to some extent – distorts the will of the electorate by, generally speaking, conferring an inordinate amount of power on one political party that forms the government.

In fact, as a result of the Labour Party securing only 35 per cent of the votes cast at the 2005 election (and yet securing 55 per cent of the seats in the Commons), in the House of Lords the Liberal Democrats have questioned the maintenance of the Salisbury-Addison Convention (see section 10.11). This convention dictates that the House should not oppose at second reading a government Bill which has been foreshadowed in the governing party's most recent general election manifesto. The Liberal Democrat argument is that in such circumstances the government lacks the electoral mandate to pursue its policies on the basis of the percentage of the national vote that it obtained at the 2005 general election.

ACTIVITY

Essay writing

Do you think that we should reform our electoral system?

9.9 An overview of the main elements of the House of Commons – a snapshot at March 2007

In brief, the House of Commons in March 2007 contained the following elements:

- **Her Majesty's Government**

  This consisted officially of 91 Labour MPs who were ministers. A minority of these sat in the Cabinet, but most ministers were outside it. These ministers were also supplemented by a number of unpaid members. All of Her Majesty's Government ministers were supported (at least in theory) by the remainder of the Labour MPs (government backbenchers).

- **Her Majesty's Official Opposition**

    The main Official Opposition was the Conservative Party (the second largest party) headed by the Leader of the Opposition. The Liberal Democrats with 63 MPs acted as the second main Opposition. The remaining MPs from other parties (other than Labour), together with the independent MPs, also constituted part of the Opposition.

- **Government front and backbenchers**

    The Labour Party's frontbenchers were government ministers, whereas their backbenchers (known as government backbenchers) were not technically in the government *per se,* but being of the same political party as the government, generally speaking, supported the government.

- **The Official Opposition's frontbenchers**

    These were composed of shadow spokespersons of government departments collectively known as the shadow Cabinet. For example, the Conservative Shadow Home Secretary shadowed and opposed the Home Secretary. The Conservative Party's backbenchers were Conservative MPs who were not in the shadow Cabinet. Similarly, the Liberal Democrats had shadow spokespersons as frontbenchers, with backbenchers not being in their shadow Cabinet.

- **Party Whips**

    Each political party had party whips to ensure discipline within the ranks of the party and ensure that MPs voted in accordance with official party allegiance and interests. Party whips also helped to keep their respective MPs informed about the parliamentary timetable and business.

- **The Speaker of the House of Commons**

    The Speaker of the House was elected by MPs and as Speaker he put aside party loyalty and acted with complete impartiality and integrity. His constitutional roles included, among others:

    - To chair debates and proceedings (including calling members to speak).
    - To deal with the administration of the House.
    - To call members to order and keep order within the chamber.
    - To act as the representative of the House of Commons in state events.

    The Speaker was assisted by three Deputy Speakers.

- **The Leader of the House**

    This was a member of the government who sat in the Cabinet. The responsibilities of this post included arranging and supervising government business in the chamber (in particular, the legislative programme).

Further reading

Barnett, H, *Constitutional and Administrative Law* (6th edn, Routledge-Cavendish, 2006), Chapters 13 and 14.

Carroll, A, *Constitutional and Administrative Law* (3rd edn, Pearson/Longman, 2003), Chapters 6 to 8.

Election 2005: Turnout. How many, who and why? (The Electoral Commission, 2005).

Factsheet M1 'You and Your MP' (Parliamentary Copyright, 2005).

Factsheet M4 'Women in the House of Commons' (Parliamentary Copyright, 2006).

Factsheet M7 'Parliamentary elections' (Parliamentary Copyright, 2006).

Loveland, I, *Constitutional Law, Administrative Law, and Human Rights* (4th edn, Oxford University Press, 2006), Chapter 7.

Sear, C, 'Electoral franchise: who can vote?' (House of Commons Library, 2005).

White, I, 'The Electoral Commission' (House of Commons Library, 2007).

Websites:

www.parliament.uk
www.electoralcommission.org.uk

PARLIAMENT III: THE HOUSE OF LORDS ■━━━

AIMS AND OBJECTIVES ▢▢▢

At the end of this chapter you should be able to:

■ Identify and explain the different types of membership of the House of Lords

■ Explain the political composition of the chamber

■ Identify and explain the various different functions of the House of Lords

■ Identify and explain the legal and political powers of the House of Lords

10.1 Introduction and size of the House of Lords

The House of Lords has evolved over many hundreds of years and, in fact, pre-dates the House of Commons. It is the second chamber of Parliament and is, by both law and constitutional convention, subordinate to the House of Commons. The House of Lords is an unusual and distinctive House in a number of ways. For example:

• There is no legal or constitutional cap on the size of its membership. Indeed, the size of the House is ultimately in the hands of the executive (specifically the Prime Minister).

• The composition of the House is very different to that of the House of Commons, as not only do a number of independent members sit in the upper House, but unique in a democracy, it comprises a number of individuals who have inherited their seat.

The House of Lords, historically, has been an exceptionally large House in comparison with other upper chambers. Indeed, before it was reformed in 1999, its membership was almost twice the size of the House of Commons. It is generally the case that where states have bicameral legislatures, the upper House will be smaller than the lower chamber. According to research undertaken by Russell, the second chamber of other states, on average, tends to be 60 per cent of the size of the lower one (M Russell, *Second Chambers Overseas: A Summary* (The Constitution Unit, 1999), p 3). Before the enactment of the House of Lords Act 1999, the House of Lords comprised almost 1,300 members, although not all regularly attended the House. In contrast, the House of Commons had 659 MPs (the 1997–2001 Parliament).

The size of upper chambers in other democracies is comparatively smaller. For example, the United States Senate has 100 members and Canada's Senate has 104. Moreover, there is no legal cap on the size of the House of Lords (there is a statutory cap in respect of the House of Commons, but this can be altered). This is not unique, however, as there is no fixed number of members in respect of, for example, Spain's Senato or Belgium's Sénat. In this respect, therefore, the size of the House of Lords constantly fluctuates as peers die and new life peers are created.

10.2 The Composition of the House of Lords

The following table indicates the composition of the House of Lords in March 2007:

Figure 10.1

Members of the House of Lords (Total: 744)

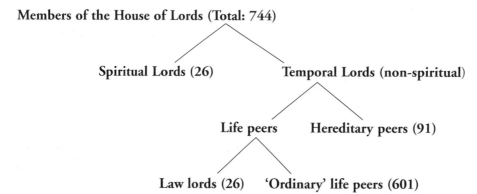

Source: Parliament website: www.parliament.uk

The House of Lords and gender

In March 2007, only 142 members of the House of Lords were female. This included one (recently appointed) female law lord (Baroness Hale) and three hereditary peeresses. The overwhelming majority of female members have been appointed there as life peers. As one-fifth of the House is female this is comparable to the elected House of Commons where, after the 2005 general election, 128 MPs out of 646 were female.

In broad terms, members of the House can be divided into Lords Spiritual and Lords Temporal.

10.3 Lords Spiritual

The Lords Spiritual are, technically speaking, not peers at all, but Lords of Parliament. They are further subdivided into 24 Bishops and two Archbishops of the established church: the Church of England. They represent the link between the church and State – the sovereign is, of course, the Supreme Governor of the Church of England and swears an oath on coronation as monarch to preserve the church. The spiritual members sit as 'independents' as they are independent of any political party. They are *ex-officio* members of the House and when they retire from their religious office they leave the House (although it is possible for them subsequently to be appointed as life peers). All the current Lords Spiritual are male, and will remain so until the ordination of female bishops is realised.

The United Kingdom is in fact the only democracy in Europe that specifically reserves spiritual seats in its law-making body. Nevertheless, the 2000 Royal Commission on the Reform of the House of Lords (*A House for the Future*, Cm 4534 (The Stationery Office, 2000), Ch 15) specifically recommended the retention of such explicit religious representation. It further recommended that the designated religious element of the reformed House should be broadened to include other Christian denominations (eg Roman Catholicism), together with other non-Christian faiths (eg Islam, Judaism, etc). The Royal Commission noted the contribution the current Spiritual Lords made in The House. Indeed, it is certainly the case that they contribute to ethical and religious matters (eg the highly contentious 2006 Assisted Dying for the Terminally Ill Bill). It is of interest to note that in the 2007 White Paper on reforming the House of Lords, the government suggested retaining this category of members (see section 22.6.1).

In addition, a number of members of both parliamentary chambers have a religious affiliation to various different faiths and are therefore able to contribute to debates with a religious dimension.

ACTIVITY

Question

What are the advantages and disadvantages of having religious representation in the legislature?

As indicated by the table at section 10.2, the Lords Temporal are sub-divided into the following elements:

- Law lords.
- 'Ordinary' life peers.
- Hereditary peers.

10.4 The law lords

10.4.1 Appellate Committee of the House of Lords

The Lords of Appeal in Ordinary are more commonly known as the law lords. They are appointed to the House of Lords as life peers under the Appellate Jurisdiction Act 1876. In fact, they represented the first life peers in the House almost a century before the passing of the Life Peerages Act 1958 (see section 10.5.1). Although there are only 12 law lords that are fully judicially active, the remaining 14 have retired as full-time law lords and, unlike the Bishops above, automatically remain as members of the House.

The law lords, whilst sitting as the Appellate Committee of the House of Lords, perform the judicial function of the House (they also sit in the Judicial Committee of the Privy Council). The Appellate Committee is the highest domestic court in the United Kingdom in civil matters – it hears appeals from the following legal jurisdictions:

- England and Wales
- Scotland
- Northern Ireland.

In respect of criminal matters, however, although the Appellate Committee is the highest court for the jurisdiction of England and Wales and Northern Ireland, it is not the highest appellate criminal court in Scotland, as this is the High Court of Justiciary.

The law lords are specifically appointed to carry out the judicial function of the House and under the Judicial Pensions and Retirement Act 1993 they retire at 70 years of age.

10.4.2 A breach of the separation of powers

As indicated earlier (see section 5.7.4), the presence of the law lords in the House of Lords violates a strict interpretation of the separation of powers (namely, judicial members forming part of the legislature). This is mitigated by the following factors:

- Law lords sit as independent cross benchers.
- Law lords are constrained by the self-denying ordinance issued by Lord Bingham in 2000 not to take an active part in politically controversial matters (see section 5.7.4).
- A number of law lords take no part in the parliamentary – as opposed to the judicial – aspects of the House of Lords. One law lord, however, by constitutional convention, will chair Committee E (Law and Institutions) of the European Union Select Committee.

In any event, it is envisaged under Part 3 of the Constitutional Reform Act 2005, that this judicial function will cease with the creation of a new Supreme Court which is scheduled to take place in 2009.

Quite apart from the judicial function of the Appellate Committee, the House of Lords as a whole performs a general judicial function when enforcing the internal rules of parliamentary privilege (see section 8.5).

ACTIVITY

> ### Question
>
> What are the advantages and disadvantages of having the law lords in the legislature?

10.5 Life peers

10.5.1. The Life Peerages Act 1958

Under the Life Peerages Act 1958 the Crown (for practical purposes, the Prime Minister) is conferred with the power to award life peerages to individuals so that they can sit in the House of Lords. They now represent the largest single category of peers. There are at least three clear advantages to the creation of life peerages:

- Firstly, it means that distinguished individuals in different fields (such as medicine, commerce, academia, journalism, etc) can bring their particular skills, expertise and experience to bear in the workings of the House. This is particularly useful in the context of a debate or when scrutinising legislative proposals in these fields.

  The 2000 Royal Commission recognised the importance of this experience in respect of the workings of the House as 'many can offer expertise and experience outside politics. Many are men and women of distinction in their own right'. Indeed, the Royal Commission noted that these characteristics were ones which they envisaged should ideally be in any reformed second chamber.

- Secondly, as life peerages by their nature only exist for the life of the recipient, this means the awarding of life peerages does not permanently and constantly enlarge the size of the chamber. This would be the case with the continual creation of hereditary peers (at least prior to their reform in 1999 – see section 10.6.1).

- Thirdly, the creation of life peerages ensures that the House can be more representative of society. In particular, it specifically allows women and individuals from ethnic minorities to be appointed to the House. In fact, the vast majority of women sitting in the House of Lords have been appointed there under the Life Peerages Act 1958.

10.5.2 The creation of life peerages

The Life Peerages Act 1958 permits the Prime Minister of the day to create new life peers and is therefore a form of patronage. In theory, the Prime Minister under the Act could technically recommend to the monarch that hundreds of new life peers of the same political colour as the governing party be appointed. This scenario raises an interesting issue as to whether it would be constitutional for the monarch to refuse to approve these peerages (see section 4.15). In any event, it is the Prime Minister who determines the size of the upper chamber as he decides how many life peerages to create. By constitutional convention, however, this power of the Prime Minister is not abused. Indeed, the Labour government's justification for creating a significant number of Labour life peers since 1997 was on the basis of ensuring a level of parity with the Conservative Party in the chamber.

10.5.3 The appointment of party political peers

Historically, the position has been that the Prime Minister would determine the overall number of life peerages that are to be created and how many each party should receive, for example:

- 10 for Party A,
- 12 for Party B,
- 4 for Party C, etc.

Although the Prime Minister would determine the list of names for his own political party, the respective leaders of the other parties would decide their own list of names. These names would then be placed before the monarch to approve, and, by constitutional convention, she would act on the advice of the Prime Minister.

10.5.4 The appointment of non-party political peers (independent peers)

In terms of the appointment of non-party political peers (ie independent peers who sit as crossbenchers – see 10.7.3), historically it was the Prime Minister who determined how many crossbench peers should be created. In 1999, the government announced in its White Paper (*Modernising Parliament, Reforming the House of Lords*, Cm 1183 (1999)) that in the transitional phase of reforming the House it would establish a non-statutory body to make these non-party political appointments. In essence, this independent body would determine the names of the non-party political peers. The Prime Minister would, however, still determine the number of crossbench peers required.

The House of Lords Appointments Commission

The House of Lords Appointments Commission is a non-statutory public body and was established in 2000. In 2007 it comprised the following:

- a chairperson (Lord Stevenson)
- two non-party political members
- three members who have been nominated from the three main political parties (Labour, Conservative and Liberal Democrats).

The Appointments Commission has two principal functions:

- Firstly, it determines the individuals who are to be recommended for nomination as non-party political peers. The Commission submits the required number of peers sought by the Prime Minister. On receipt of the nominations from the Appointments Commission, the Prime Minister will then put forward these recommendations to the monarch for approval.

- Secondly, it scrutinises all nominations for life peerages before they are appointed. This applies to both non-party political peers as well as the party political peers submitted by the leaders of the political parties through the conduit of the Prime Minister.

According to the Commission:

Q	'The Commission must be assured that those recommended for political or non party-political peerages meet the highest standards of propriety. Nominations put forward by the political parties will include a statement as to any donations made to the Party concerned by an individual nominee'. House of Lords Appointments Commission Information Pack, *Nominations for non-party political members of the House of Lords*, para 28

This function of the Appointments Commission's work did not prove to be controversial until 2006 when it declined to approve a handful of nominations for party political peerages (in the event, these nominees were not appointed).

The Appointments Commission set out the assessment criteria that it would use in selecting non party-political peers to be as follows:

- An outstanding record of personal success and achievement in a person's chosen field.
- Integrity and independence.
- A commitment to the highest standards of public life.
- The ability to contribute effectively to the work of the House.

House of Lords Appointments Commission Information Pack,
Nominations for non-party political members of the House of Lords, para 6

The Commission stated that all appointments would be on the basis of individual merit and that they wished to attract as wide a range of nominees as possible from all parts of the state.

The Appointments Commission has made the following appointments:

- **2001** – 15 peers were recommended. Before they were announced they were dubbed by the press as the 'peoples peers' (on the basis that ordinary people from ordinary backgrounds would be recommended), although this term was not endorsed by the Commission itself. In the event, the list of this first batch of peers was criticised as it comprised, for example, seven Knights and three Professors and only one candidate under 40 years of age. In other words, they were comparable to individuals already in the House. In fairness to the Commission, four women and four from the ethnic minorities were appointed.

- **2004** – seven peers were recommended.

- **2005** – seven peers were recommended.

- **2006** – seven peers were recommended (this included a female ex senior judge).

- **2007** – six peers were recommended.

In total, by March 2007 the Appointments Commission had therefore appointed 42 peers which hitherto would have been, formerly, effectively within the power of the Prime Minister.

ACTIVITY

Essay writing

What are the advantages and disadvantages of having appointed life peers in the legislature? How do they differ from elected MPs in the House of Commons?

10.6 Hereditary Peers

10.6.1 The position before the House of Lords Act 1999

Prior to the enactment of the House of Lords Act 1999, there were 759 hereditary peers and peeresses who inherited their seat in the Lords. Although there were 759 hereditary peers, this did not mean that they all necessarily attended (the same point can also be made in respect of appointed life peers).

10.6.2 The arguments for the removal of the hereditary peers

In 1997 the Labour government was elected on a manifesto commitment to remove the right of hereditary peers to sit and vote in the House of Lords. In its subsequent White Paper of 1999 the government asserted that:

> **Q** 'the right of hereditary peers to sit and vote in the House of Lords is a significant factor in the lack of political effectiveness and balance of the House. We believe no individuals should have the right to be Members of Parliament solely on the basis of the actions or position of their ancestors. A place in the legislature should be reserved for those who achieve it on their own merits. The continuing right of the whole hereditary peerage to sit and vote has been accepted as an anomaly for most of this century'.
>
> *Modernising Parliament, Reforming the House of Lords,*
> Cm 4183 (The Stationery Office, 1999) p 8.

The government, in its 1999 White Paper, identified the following reasons for their removal:

- Hereditary membership of a legislature was an anachronism – particularly in a democracy. It is of interest to note that, according to Russell (*Second Chambers Overseas: A Summary*, p 5), only one country in the world, Lesotho in Africa, uses the hereditary principle as the main basis for determining its second chamber.

- The hereditary element was unrepresentative of society (for example, only 16 of the hereditaries were female).

- Almost half of the hereditary peers (excluding those on leave or without a writ of summons to enter the House) were identified with the Conservative Party. The result of this was that – as a whole – the Conservative Party had an in-built party bias in the House of Lords.

In due course the Labour Government introduced legislation to remove the hereditary element from the House: The House of Lords Bill (which became the House of Lords Act 1999).

ACTIVITY

Question

Can you think of any arguments in favour of retaining the hereditary principle in the House of Lords?

10.6.3 The House of Lords Act 1999

This legislation ended the right of hereditary peers from sitting and voting in the House of Lords.

S 'No-one shall be a member of the House of Lords by virtue of a hereditary peerage.'

s 1 of the House of Lords Act 1999.

Whilst the House of Lords Bill was being considered in the upper chamber, an amendment was made to it (the Weatherill amendment named after Lord Weatherill) which enabled 92 (approximately 10% of the total) of the existing hereditary peers to remain in the chamber.

The government was prepared to accede to this compromise for two main reasons:

- Firstly, it meant that the Bill would pass through the House of Lords and that at least the majority of hereditary peers (the other 667) would be removed. These individuals would thereafter be entitled to become MPs. In fact, in 2001 an ex-peer, Viscount Thurso (Liberal Democrat), was elected as an MP.

- Secondly, the retention of a rump of hereditary peers was meant to be only ever a temporary arrangement pending long-term full reform of the House, at which point they would ultimately be removed.

The removal of the remaining hereditary peers?

In terms of long-term reform, the hereditary element is still present in the House. Although the Labour Government's 2001 general election manifesto reaffirmed the commitment to remove the remaining hereditaries, a House of Lords Bill scheduled in the Queen's Speech in 2003 was subsequently abandoned. In fact, the Bill was never published. The 2005 Labour Party general election manifesto reaffirmed its commitment to Lords reform:

'As part of the process of modernisation, we will remove the remaining hereditary peers'.

Britain *forward* not back, The Labour Party Manifesto 2005 (The Labour Party, 2005), p 110.

It is inevitable that full reform of the Lords will continue to be a protracted business. Indeed, although the House of Lords Act 1999 was supposed to be an interim measure pending long-term reform of the House, it is worth remembering that the 1911 Parliament Act was also supposed to be a temporary measure pending future reform being implemented. It is pertinent to note that in March 2007 the House of Commons voted in principle to remove the remaining hereditary peers by 391 votes to 111 (see section 22.6.1).

The remaining hereditary peers

Section 2 of the House of Lords Act 1999 retained 92 hereditary peers as follows:

- 2 holding Great Offices of State (Lord Great Chamberlain – the Queen's representative and the Earl Marshal – responsible for ceremonies).

- 75 (in total) elected by each respective political party or group. The number of peers each party received was in direct proportion to the number of hereditary peers each party had at the time of the Act. As the Conservatives had the most hereditaries, they elected the most hereditary peers. The results were as follows:

42 Conservative

2 Labour

3 Liberal Democrat

28 Cross bench (independent peers)

- 15 office holders (for example, Deputy Speakers and Committee Chairs) elected by the whole of the House of Lords.

Source: House of Lords Briefing, Reform and Proposals for Reform since 1900
(Parliamentary Copyright, House of Lords, 2006) p 8

Overall, 92 hereditary peers were retained, three of whom were female. As a result of the House of Lords Act 1999 we have the rather paradoxical situation in which the remaining peers – by virtue of their election – could in one sense claim to be more constitutionally legitimate than their life peer counterparts who have been simply appointed. The point, however, must be made that the electorate was very limited: the 15 office holders were elected by the whole House and the 75 party and cross bench peers were elected by their respective members. In any event, they were not elected by the people outside of the House.

The death of an (elected) hereditary peer

The House of Lords Act 1999 was meant to represent a staging post on the way to full long-term, reform of the chamber. Full reform of the House has to date not been realised (see section 22.6.1) and consequently the 'transitional' House would have to deal with the situation when one of the remaining hereditary peers died. From the end of 2001–02 parliamentary session, vacancies due to death would be filled by a by-election. Candidates for the by-election would be filled, in essence, by peers expelled in 1999. For example, one such by-election was held in March 2007.

As a result of the political impasse over Lords' reform, the retention of the rump of hereditary peers has proved to be more than a transient arrangement. Indeed, it has led to the paradoxical scenario of 'House of Lords' by-elections', which will inevitably become more frequent as the peers age.

ACTIVITY

Question

What are the advantages and disadvantages of having 'elected' hereditary peers in the House of Lords?

10.6.4 Renouncing a peerage

Under the Peerage Act 1963 it has been possible for hereditary peers to renounce their peerages. This represented an irrevocable renunciation for the duration of their lifetime, although their successors would not be affected by it. Under this legislation two major political figures renounced their hereditary peerages:

- Tony Benn – on the death of his father in 1960 he automatically succeeded to the hereditary peerage of the Viscountcy of Stansgate with an entitlement to sit in the House of Lords. At the time he was an MP and he wanted to renounce this peerage and continue to serve in the House of Commons. As an individual cannot sit in both Houses, his Bristol seat became vacant and a by-election was held. Although Benn won the by-election, the Election Court disbarred him from assuming his seat in the House of Commons. After the passing of the Peerage Act 1963, Benn renounced his peerage and was thereafter elected as an MP.

- In October 1963 Harold Macmillan resigned as Prime Minister. This resulted in the Earl of Home disclaiming his hereditary peerage under the 1963 Act to succeed Macmillan as Prime Minister (he became Sir Alec Douglas-Home). This was necessary as by constitutional convention a Prime Minister must be a member of the House of Commons (see section 4.13.4), thereby being directly accountable to the elected representatives of the people.

ACTIVITY

Essay writing

Compare and contrast the different types of members in the House of Lords.

KEY FACTS

Spiritual Lords	**Archbishops and Bishops** – they represent the link between the established church and the state. They provide a religious/moral dimension to the chamber. A very unusual category of members in a democratic legislature.
Temporal Lords	**Hereditary peers** – originally they inherited their seat in the chamber, although after the 1999 reforms they were 'elected' by their counterparts. A unique category of members in a democratic legislature.

CONTINUED ▸

KEY FACTS

Life peers:
- **Law lords** – appointed under the Appellate Jurisdiction Act 1876. It is very unusual in a democracy to have judges in the legislature. Scheduled to be removed under Pt 3 of the Constitutional Reform Act 2005.
- **'Ordinary' life peers** – appointed under the Life Peerages Act 1958. They provide the chamber with expertise and specialism. A number of legislatures, including Canada, have appointed members.

10.7 The party political composition of the House

10.7.1 Political breakdown of the composition of the House of Lords

In common with the House of Commons, members in the House of Lords are organised into political parties and take a party whip. The House of Lords, however, is a less partisan chamber and members are more likely to defy their party whips and official political party largely on the basis that they are not subject to re-election. The main political parties, are therefore, represented in the Lords, although in contrast to the Commons, they are supplemented by a significant independent element.

In March 2007 the political breakdown of the House was as follows:

Political composition of the House of Lords

Party	Number of peers
Conservative	203
Labour	211
Liberal Democrat	77
Independent/crossbenchers	202
Others	12
These figures exclude 13 members on leave of absence from the chamber and the 26 Bishops	

Source: Parliament website: www.parliament.uk.

The above figures indicate that no one political party controls the House of Lords as the two main political parties now have approximate parity with each other. This has been achieved by two factors:

- The removal of the hereditary peers expelled a significant number of peers who identified themselves with the Conservative Party.

- A number of Labour life peers have been created since the election of the Labour Government in 1997.

Before the 1999 reforms, the Conservative Party were the clear dominant grouping within the House. In March 2007 the Labour Party was (albeit marginally) the largest party in the House. It is pertinent to note that Russell and Sciara have argued that in light of the distribution of seats between the main parties that:

> 'Despite being unelected, the notion that the House of Lords is now a "representative" chamber – perhaps even more representative than the House of Commons – has thus grown in currency.'

M Russell and M Sciara, *The House of Lords in 2005: A More Representative and Assertive Chamber?*
(The Constitution Unit, 2006), p 8.

ACTIVITY

Problem solving

Compare and contrast the party political composition in the two Houses of Parliament.

10.7.2 Government ministers in the House of Lords

As will be considered at section 11.6.2, a number of government ministers, including a few Cabinet ministers, sit in the House of Lords. In March 2007 there were 22 ministers in the upper chamber including two members of the Cabinet. Historically, the most prominent figure was of course the Lord Chancellor; however, as stated in s 2 of the Constitutional Reform Act 2005, a future Lord Chancellor may be drawn from either chamber. Until the passage of this Act, by constitutional convention, in modern times the Lord Chancellor has traditionally resided in the upper chamber.

The constitutional advantage of ministers sitting in the House of Lords is that it ensures that the government has representatives in the upper chamber to act as spokespersons and to pilot Bills through it.

10.7.3 Independent/crossbench peers

The House of Lords is hallmarked in terms of its composition by virtue of the fact that a significant number of its members are classed as independents (crossbenchers). In essence cross-benchers can be defined as those peers who do not take a party political whip and have no specific allegiance to one of the three main political parties. This category of peers can include individuals with no definite political affiliations together with some politicians from minority parties with no organised party system.

In any event, crossbenchers sit as individual members and do not constitute a party. They do, however, regularly meet under the aegis of the Convener of crossbench peers where issues of common interest are raised and discussed. Crossbenchers are noted for their independent, non-party political stance on matters.

The importance of having an independent (non-politically aligned) element in the second chamber was emphasised strongly by the 2000 Royal Commission. In particular, it recommended that a fully reformed House should contain a strong crossbench element amounting to around 20 per cent of the total membership of the House. In terms of House of Lords reform, therefore, one of the consequences of the widely supported proposal of a wholly elected chamber, inevitably, would be the loss of this independent element. In short, elected members will invariably be associated with one of the major political parties. As we saw in respect of the House of Commons, very few politicians are elected as an 'Independent'.

In 2002 the Joint Committee on House of Lords Reform underlined the importance of the existing independent element of the House:

<table>
<tr><td rowspan="3">Q</td><td>'The role of Crossbenchers is often particularly significant in relation to participation in debates and committees and the quality they bring to these deliberations'.</td></tr>
<tr><td>House of Lords Reform: First Report, HL Paper 17, HC 171 (2002), p 17.</td></tr>
</table>

The other advantage of having a sizeable independent non-party political element is that it helps to ensure that, in terms of numbers, no one political party dominates the second chamber (see the following table).

Breakdown of the composition of the political and non-political elements in March 2007

	Conservative	Labour	Liberal Democrat	Crossbencher
Life peers	156	207	72	169
Hereditary peers	47	4	5	33
Total	203	211	77	202

Figures adapted from www.parliament.uk and do not include 26 Bishops,

13 peers on leave of absence and 12 'others'.

10.7.4 Other key personnel of the House

The Speaker of the House

Traditionally the Speaker of the House of Lords has been the Lord Chancellor, however, following the Constitutional Reform Act 2005 which radically reformed the nature of this office, the House has had to make alternative arrangements in respect of the post of Speaker. Under s 2 of the Act a future Lord Chancellor may sit in either House and so may not necessarily be a peer. As indicated at section 5.7.9, in this context the chamber resolved to elect a speaker for five years. He would be known as the Lord Speaker and would be expected to give up party politics and occupy the Woolsack (the seat on which, historically, the Speaker of the House sits on). In July 2006 the House of Lords elected Baroness Hayman to act as Lord Speaker.

The Office of the Speaker of the Lords is not an exact parallel of the Speaker of the House of Commons, as the former has fewer responsibilities and is less powerful than her counterpart in the House of Commons. In fact, although she presides over proceedings, her role is in practice a symbolic one.

- As the House of Lords is a self-regulating body (by virtue of their unelected status, the atmosphere is less partisan or politically charged), the responsibility for maintaining order rests not with the Speaker, but with the House collectively.

- The Speaker does not call members to speak and neither does she curtail debate in the chamber.

In common with the House of Commons, however, the Speaker is assisted by a number of Deputy Speakers. Moreover, the Speakers in both Houses represent each respective House abroad and on ceremonial occasions.

The Leader of the House

The Leader of the House is a member of the Cabinet and is responsible for the conduct of government business in the chamber – this is a similar function to the Leader of the House of Commons.

10.8 Disqualification of membership of the House of Lords

There are a number of factors which disqualify individuals from membership of the House of Lords and to some extent these parallel those relating to the House of Commons (see section 9.3.3). According to Erskine May (*Parliamentary Practice* (23rd edn, LexisNexis Butterworths, 2004), Chapter 3) the following are disqualified from membership:

- **Individuals under 21 years**

  (Standing Order No 2, 1685). This partly explains why historically some peers have been absent from the chamber as when they inherited their seat, they may have been too young to enter the House.

- **Aliens**

  Act of Settlement 1700 (as amended by the British Nationality Act 1981). See also section 9.3.3 in respect of the House of Commons.

- **Bankrupts**

  In England and Wales disqualification will apply if a bankruptcy restrictions order has been issued (the Insolvency Act 1986, as amended by the Enterprise Act 2002). In Scotland it applies where the peer's estate is sequestered.

- **Treason**

  Those convicted of treason under the Forfeiture Act 1870. See also section 9.3.3 in respect of the House of Commons.

- **Mental Health**

  Unlike the House of Commons, the Mental Health Act 1983 does not specifically apply to the Lords. The House of Lords Committee for Privileges (HL 254, 1983–84) has recommended that in order to resolve this issue, future legislation should make it clear that such mental health provisions applied to peers.

10.9 The functions of the House of Lords

In the absence of a written codified constitutional text there is no authoritative and constitutionally definitive statement which sets out the powers of the House of Lords (or for that matter, the House of Commons). In 1968, however, the government White Paper on House of Lords reform identified the following functions:

Functions of the House of Lords

Apart from providing the supreme court of appeal, the House of Lords at present performs the following main functions:

(a) the provision of a forum for full and free debate on matters of public interest;
(b) the revision of public bills brought from the House of Commons;
(c) the initiation of public legislation, including in particular those government bills which are less controversial in party political terms and private members' bills;
(d) the consideration of subordinate legislation;
(e) the scrutiny of the activities of the executive; and
(f) the scrutiny of private legislation.

House of Lords Reform, Cmnd 3799 (1968), para 8

More recently the House of Lords Information Office has effectively subsumed these functions into four:

- Making laws.
- Holding the government to account.
- Providing a forum of independent experts.
- Judicial work as the highest court.

The Work of the House of Lords 2005–06 (Parliamentary Copyright House of Lords, 2007), p 1.

In addition, it provided a useful breakdown of the time typically spent by the House of Lords on its various functions:

Breakdown of the workload of the House of Lords

- 60% legislation (55% Bills, 5% Statutory Instruments)

- 40% scrutiny (22% Debates
        14% Questions
        4% Statements)

10.9.1 The judicial role of the House

As indicated earlier, the Appellate Committee of the House of Lords is the highest domestic court in respect of civil and criminal appeals, with the exception of Scottish criminal matters. As a result, the law lords form part of both the legislature and the judiciary and so violate a pure interpretation of the separation of powers (see sections 5.2.2 and 5.7.4). It is of interest to note that the 2000 Royal Commission stated that it could see no reason as to why (in the interim) this judicial function should not continue to be performed by the law lords. The Constitutional Reform Act 2005, however, provides that a new separate free-standing Supreme Court will be established in due course, pending appropriate arrangements for its accommodation (s 148(4)).

Until the law lords are finally removed from the House, the Appellate Committee will continue to operate. Furthermore, those law lords who choose to participate in the legislative and deliberative functions of the House will continue to do so with Lord Bingham's 2000 self-denying ordinance in mind. In general, law lords (serving and retired) have made useful contributions in the context of scrutinising legislation (particularly technical drafting points), as well as contributing to debates by drawing upon their extensive legal and judicial knowledge. In addition, law lords serve on committees as participants and chairs.

It should also be remembered that in a very general sense the House – as a whole – performs a judicial function when it regulates and enforces internal rules of parliamentary privilege (see section 8.5).

10.9.2 A forum for debate

The House of Lords is a debating chamber in which matters of public interest are examined and considered. As in the House of Commons, debates can take place either:

- in the context of the passage of legislation by debating the principles and details of a Bill; or
- as free-standing general debates.

Although both parliamentary chambers hold debates, it is generally argued that debates in the House of Lords are qualitatively better than in the House of Commons for three reasons:

- Firstly, there is a broader range of experience and expertise in the upper chamber which arguably allows debates to be richer and more informed than in the Commons. Much of this experience and knowledge has been appointed under the Life Peerages Act 1958, but some of it is drawn from the ranks of the hereditaries. It must also be remembered that peers are unsalaried and (if working) can continue with their careers in parallel with their duties in the House. Rogers and Walters have noted: 'the fact remains that the House of Lords as currently composed is a knowledgeable place in a way that distinguishes it from most other parliamentary assemblies in the world' (R Rogers and R Walters, *How Parliament works* (5th edn, Pearson/Longman, 2004), p 280).

- Secondly, the atmosphere of the chamber is less partisan. The 2000 Royal Commission made particular reference to the non-polemic style of the House.

- Thirdly, as an adjunct to the point above, a significant number of peers are crossbenchers in any event and so are not aligned to the major political parties.

10.9.3 The revision of public Bills brought from the House of Commons

The House of Lords spends over half of its time examining legislative proposals. This indicates that a major constitutional function of the House of Lords is to act as a 'revising chamber'. Most important Bills, as well as controversial ones, tend to begin in the House of Commons where the government is dominant.

In considering and scrutinising public Bills which have passed through the Commons, the House of Lords can revise, propose and make amendments (with the exception of money/financial Bills – see section 10.10.1). Such amendments can be:

- technical drafting amendments to remedy unclear, imprecise or sloppily drafted provisions, or

- policy amendments based on aspects or provisions of the Bill considered objectionable, unsatisfactory, unnecessary, etc. For example, in 2001 the Anti-Terrorism, Crime and Security Bill was amended by the Lords in order, *inter alia*, to provide individuals with an appellate mechanism against deportation.

Although the procedure and nature of passing legislation is largely similar for both Houses, there are some key differences and these are considered at section 12.7.4.

10.9.4 The initiation of public legislation

In order to spread the legislative workload between the two parliamentary chambers, Bills can begin in either House. In fact, this practice is consistent with other countries such as France and the Republic of Ireland. Two recent examples of highly significant constitutional Bills which commenced in the House of Lords are as follows:

- The Human Rights Bill (introduced in 1997).
- The Constitutional Reform Bill (introduced in 2003).

In each case the Lord Chancellor, as a government minister, was responsible for piloting the Bill through the House.

In contrast to the above, money Bills must begin in the House of Commons as it is the pre-eminent chamber. Similarly, in Australia financial legislation must also be introduced in the House of Representatives (the lower House).

10.9.5 The consideration of subordinate legislation

As indicated at section 5.7.2, subordinate legislation is a clear violation of the separation of powers as it involves the executive performing a legislative function: making legislation (albeit subordinate legislation). In view of this breach, from a constitutional perspective it is imperative that subordinate legislation is subject to adequate scrutiny. As we shall see at section 12.7.5, it is generally agreed that parliamentary supervision of this type of legislation is insufficient, however, the House of Lords performs a useful role in providing some supervision of it. It does so through the following committees:

- The House of Lords Select Committee on Delegated Powers and Regulatory Reform.
- The Joint Committee on Statutory Instruments.
- The House of Lords Select Committee on the Merits of Statutory Instruments.

10.9.6 The scrutiny of the activities of the executive

As Parliament as a whole is constitutionally responsible for supervising the actions of the executive, this means that it is the responsibility of both the House of Commons and the House of Lords to hold the government to account (this is considered in Chapter 12). It should be remembered that the House of Lords contains a number of ministers who can be questioned and scrutinised directly by peers. Russell (*Second Chambers Overseas: A Summary* (The Constitution Unit, 1999), p 11) has noted that it is generally the case that upper chambers have more limited powers in holding the government to account than lower Houses. In this respect, therefore, the House of Lords is comparable with these other legislatures.

In essence, the House of Lords will scrutinise the actions and policy of the executive in the following ways:

- general debates
- debates on legislative proposals
- questions
- debates on government statements
- the committee system.

The 2000 Royal Commission argued that the second chamber needed to be authoritative because, together with the Commons, it must scrutinise effectively the work of the government. After all, a 'more accountable Government is better Government' (*A House for the Future*, Cm 4534 (The Stationery Office, 2000), p 80).

The importance of the House of Lords supervising and checking the actions of the government have been heightened in recent decades in light of the executive's general dominance in, and control over, the lower chamber (see section 9.8).

10.9.7 The scrutiny of private legislation

Private Bills affect particular groups or individuals, rather than having general application like public Bills. Both Houses scrutinise and process private legislation.

In addition to the functions listed above, two other functions should be mentioned:

10.9.8 The scrutiny of proposed European legislation

One function not referred to in the 1968 White Paper (owing to the fact that the United Kingdom did not join the European Community until 1973) is the useful role that the House plays in respect of proposed European Community/Union legislation. This consists of the House of Lords European Union Select Committee examining draft European legislative proposals and documents which are being considered by the Council (the main legislative body in Europe – see section 15.2) and the European Commission, and drawing to the attention of the House those measures warranting further scrutiny.

10.9.9 A guardian of the constitution and watchdog of civil liberties and human rights

One function commonly attributed to the House of Lords is that of the guardian and protector of the constitution: a constitutional long-stop. It has been has commented that this is a classic function performed by second chambers:

> 'The origins of second chambers, either as a representative of "establishment" interests or as a representative of regional territories in a federal system, has made them natural bulwarks against impulsive or politically-motivated action taken by the lower house'.

A Reidy and M Russell, *Second Chambers as Constitutional Guardians & Protectors of Human Rights*
(The Constitution Unit, 1999), p 2.

Such a role (ie acting as a 'natural bulwark') is particularly important in the context of the United Kingdom, which lacks an entrenched codified constitution which acts as a restraint on the government, or indeed Parliament itself (on this point, see Chapter 7). As specifically pointed out by the 2000 Royal Commission:

> 'The risk, however, is that a Government with a secure majority in
> the House of Commons, even if based on the votes of a minority of
> the electorate, could in principle bring about controversial and ill-
> considered changes to the constitution without the need to secure
> consensus support for them.'
>
> *A House for the Future*, Cm 4534 (The Stationery Office, 2000), p 48.

In other constitutions, the upper House will typically have special legal powers over legislation
altering the constitution. In France, for example, the upper chamber (Senat) has a veto over
constitutional amendments as they must pass both Houses. It is interesting to point out that the
Royal Commission specifically refused to recommend that a reformed second chamber should have
extra powers over 'constitutional legislation'. For one thing, it would be very difficult to definitively
identify a 'constitutional Bill' (as noted at section 4.2).

In the following circumstances, however, various statutes have specifically recognised the
constitutional role of the House of Lords as a 'constitutional long-stop'. The consent of the House
is expressly required in order to:

* Extend the life of Parliament (Parliament Act 1911).

* Remove senior judges (Act of Settlement 1700, Supreme Court Act 1981 and Constitutional
  Reform Act 2005).

* Remove the Parliamentary Ombudsman – see section 21.3.6 (The Parliamentary Commissioner
  Act 1967).

In addition, the recently created House of Lords Select Committee on the Constitution has the
following remit:

> 'To examine the constitutional implications of all public bills coming
> before the House; and to keep under review the operation of the
> constitution'.
>
> First Report of the House of Lords Select Committee on the Constitution,
> *Reviewing the constitution: Terms of reference and method of working*
> HL Paper 11 (2001), p 5.

ACTIVITY

Essay writing

Compare and contrast the different functions of the House of Lords. Do you think that some of these functions are more important than others?

KEY FACTS

Function	
Judicial	• Law lords act as the highest court of appeal. • The House as a whole enforces parliamentary privilege.
Legislative	• Can initiate and revise private Bills. • Can initiate and revise public Bills – except money Bills. • Examines subordinate legislation. • Examines proposed European legislation
Scrutiny of the executive	• Debates. • Questions. • Committee work. • Legislation (see above, except private Bills).
Debating chamber	• General forum for debate on matters of public interest (see also in the context of scrutiny of the executive).
Protector of the uncodified constitution	• Acts as a constitutional long-stop and watchdog of civil liberties.

10.10 The legal powers of the House of Lords

The powers of the upper chamber are limited by both law (Parliament Acts – see section 10.10.1) and constitutional convention (see section 10.11).

10.10.1 Legal limitations

Before the Parliament Act 1911, historically the two Houses of Parliament had equal legal power over legislation. In essence, the House of Lords could block/veto Bills passed by the Commons. A constitutional convention, however, developed to the effect that on financial matters (ie money Bills) the upper House would not oppose such Bills passed by the Commons. Notwithstanding this, in 1909 the House of Lords rejected the government's Finance Bill (the Budget) which the House had the power to do in law, but not by constitutional convention. This eventually led to the passage of the Parliament Act 1911 which legally limited the powers of the House of Lords.

The Parliament Act 1911 achieved the following things:

- The House of Lords lost the legal power to delay money Bills (as certified by the Speaker in the House of Commons) for more than one month. After this period, they could be passed without the consent of the upper House (s 1).

- Any public Bill passed by the House of Commons in three successive parliamentary sessions with at least two years between the second reading in the Commons in the first session and the third reading in the Commons in the third session, could become law without the consent of the Lords (s 2). In short, this meant that in future, the House of Lords could only delay legislation (effectively for two years). It thereafter had a temporary 'suspensory veto' over proposed legislation. In summary, although it could reject and oppose legislation, ultimately it could not veto it and stop it from becoming law.

The following were excluded from the ambit of the Parliament Act 1911:

- A Bill proposing to extend the life of Parliament beyond five years.
- A public Bill commenced in the House of Lords.
- A public Bill sent to the House of Lords less than a month before the end of the session.
- A private Bill.
- Subordinate/delegated legislation.

Source: House of Lords Briefing: *The work of the House of Lords – its Role, Functions and Powers*
(Parliamentary Copyright, House of Lords 2002), p 4.

Although legally the House of Lords could have refused to pass the 1911 Parliament Bill, it seems clear that if they had done so the Prime Minister would have (in effect via the Monarch) created sufficient new peers to ensure its passage. Indeed, in 1949 the 1911 Parliament Act was amended so as to further reduce the delaying power of the House of Lords. In fact, the Labour government of the day used the Parliament Act of 1911 itself to force through the Parliament Act of 1949 against the wishes of the House of Lords (see the challenge to this in *Jackson* (2005) at section 10.10.3).

The change introduced by the Parliament Act 1949 was, in effect, to reduce the delaying power of the Lords to one year (ie the three successive sessions were reduced to two and the minimum period in the Commons reduced from two years to one).

As Russell has commented, it is relatively common for upper chambers to have the constitutional and legal power to delay legislation passed by the lower House (the 'suspensive veto'), although ultimately, as in the United Kingdom, generally speaking the lower chamber has the final decisive say (M Russell, *Resolving Disputes between the Chambers* (The Constitution Unit, 1999), p 3).

10.10.2 The use of the Parliament Acts

The Parliament Acts historically, have been rarely invoked; however, the Labour Government has used them three times since 1997. In total the use of the Acts has been as follows:

- Welsh Church Act 1914 (disestablishment of the Church in Wales).

- The Government of Ireland Act 1914 (Irish home rule).

- Parliament Act 1949 (to reduce further the legal powers of the House of Lords).

- War Crimes Act 1991 (concerned with atrocities committed in Germany and German-occupied territories during the Second World War).

- European Parliamentary Elections Act 1999 (establishing a 'closed party' list for candidates for elections to the European Parliament).

- Sexual Offences (Amendment) Act 2000 (reduced the homosexual age of consent to 16).

- Hunting Act 2004 (bans fox hunting – see section 10.10.3)

It is interesting to point out that the provisions in relation to money Bills have not been invoked.

10.10.3 Is the Parliament Act 1949 legal?

In 2005, in one of the most important constitutional cases in recent times, the Appellate Committee of the House of Lords had to determine whether the 2004 Hunting Act and the 1949 Parliament Act had been lawfully passed as Acts of Parliament.

CASE EXAMPLE

R (Jackson and Others) v Attorney-General [2005] UKHL 56

The Hunting Act 2004 made the hunting of wild animals with dogs (ie fox hunting) illegal. This Act had been passed without the consent of the House of Lords under the Parliament Acts of 1911 and 1949. Jackson sought, unsuccessfully (in both the Divisional Court and the Court of Appeal), a declaration that:

- the Parliament Act 1949 was of no legal effect as it had been passed without the consent of the House of Lords; and

- as a consequence, the Hunting Act 2004 was of no legal effect and not an Act of Parliament.

CONTINUED ▸

The House of Lords dismissed Jackson's appeal and affirmed that the Parliament Act 1949 had been lawfully passed under the Parliament Act 1911 (notwithstanding the lack of consent from the Lords). As a result, the Hunting Act 2004 was a lawful Act of Parliament with full legal effect.

The House of Lords noted that after 1911 there were two routes to passing legislation:

- with the consent of the House of Lords; and

- without the consent of the House of Lords (under the Parliament Act).

As a matter of statutory construction, the 1911 Act did not preclude the use of the s 2 procedure (ie, rendering the consent of the upper House unnecessary) to amend itself (ie to create the 1949 Act). Logically, therefore, on the basis of this judgment, it would appear that the Parliament Acts could be amended again to reduce further the power of the House to delay legislation, for example to only six months.

One of the arguments advanced in favour of Jackson was that the 1949 and 2004 Acts were, in effect, *delegated legislation* as they were derivative of the 1911 Act. In short, they owed their validity to a prior enactment (the 1911 Act) and consequently with the status of delegated, rather than primary legislation, they could be reviewed by the court. The court dismissed this argument. As pointed out by Lord Bingham, the 1911 Act referred to legislation complying with the provisions of this Act becoming 'an Act of Parliament on the Royal Assent being signified thereto' (s 2(1)). This clearly denoted primary (and not delegated) legislation. As Lord Bingham stated:

'The 1911 Act did, of course, effect an important constitutional change, but the change lay not in authorising a new form of sub-primary parliamentary legislation but in creating a new way of enacting primary legislation.'

10.11 Limitations imposed by constitutional conventions

Quite apart from the legal limitations outlined above, the House of Lords traditionally has recognised that the House of Commons, as the elected House to which the government is accountable, is the pre-eminent chamber in Parliament. As a consequence, it adheres to the following three constitutional conventions in its dealings with the House of Commons. By convention the House of Lords:

- Should not oppose at second reading a government Bill which has passed through the House of Commons and which has been foreshadowed in the governing party's most recent general election manifesto (the Salisbury-Addison Convention). This is on the basis that if a government has been elected on specified manifesto commitments, it would be constitutionally inappropriate and essentially undemocratic for the Lords to thwart the will of the people as expressed and represented in the House of Commons. In recent times the relevance of this convention has been questioned by the Liberal Democrats in the House. In the debate on the 2005 Queen's Speech, the Leader of the Liberal Democrats, Lord McNally, argued that: 'I do not believe that a convention drawn up 60 years ago on relations between a wholly hereditary Conservative-dominated House and a Labour Government who had 48 per cent of the vote should apply in the same way to the position in which we find ourselves today' (*Hansard*, HL Vol 672, cols 20-21).

The point that is effectively being made is that the Labour Party's share of the vote at the 2005 general election was 35 per cent of the votes cast and yet the party (from whom the government was drawn) obtained 55 per cent of the seats in the House of Commons (see section 9.5).

- Should consider government business within a reasonable time. It was on this basis that Lord Carter objected to the Constitutional Reform Bill being sent to a special select committee for detailed consideration (*Hansard*, HL Vol 658, col 999).

- Does not reject statutory instruments – although in law they are entitled to. Russell and Sciara (*The House of Lords in 2005: A More Representative and Assertive Chamber?* (The Constitution Unit, 2006), p 14) have pointed out, however, that in 2005 there was considerable tension between the government and the House of Lords over two delegated orders under the aegis of:

  1. The Licensing Act 2003 (the Lords voted on a motion to condemn an order expanding drinking hours, though they did not defeat the order itself).

  2. The Criminal Justice Act 2003 (an order – subsequently dropped – to restrict a defendant's right to jury trial in complex fraud trials).

Finally, regard should be had to the 2006 report of the Joint Committee on Conventions which had been established to examine the practicality of codifying the constitutional conventions which regulated the relationship between the two Houses (see section 22.6.2).

ACTIVITY

Essay writing

Compare and contrast the legal and political powers of the House of Lords.

KEY FACTS

Legal powers Parliament Acts 1911 and 1949	• No power to delay money Bills beyond one month. • Only has the power to delay a public Bill for approximately one year. • Retains full legal power to veto: (a) secondary legislation (b) a public Bill initiated in the House of Lords (c) a public Bill designed to extend life of Parliament (d) a private Bill
Political powers Constitutional conventions	• The Salisbury–Addison Convention. • Government business to be considered within a reasonable time. • Does not veto secondary legislation.

10.12 The relationship between the House of Lords and the House of Commons

In general, the two Houses of Parliament co-operate with each other efficiently, otherwise parliamentary business would become unworkable. Indeed, in respect of Lords' amendments made to legislative proposals, in many cases these are accepted by the House of Commons (or, more specifically the government). For its part, the House of Lords has traditionally accepted that it is the subordinate chamber, although on occasions it will force the Commons to reconsider issues/policies, thereby acting as a watchdog and protector of the constitution.

Since its election in 1997, the Labour Government has suffered one defeat on a Bill in the House of Commons (the Terrorism Bill in November 2005, although the legislation was eventually passed and became the Terrorism Act 2006), whereas it has suffered a number of defeats in the Lords. Whether this indicates the dominance that the executive typically has in the Commons, or whether it indicates a more forceful Lords (or whether it is probably both), is an interesting point. What does appear to be the case is that since the removal of most of the hereditary peers in 1999, the House of Lords now sees itself as more constitutionally legitimate than before, and so appears more willing to challenge the wishes of the lower chamber (which is largely controlled by the government). Indeed, the calendar year of 2005 appears to have been a watershed in terms executive/House of Lords relations:

> '2005 witnessed the biggest row between the government and the peers since the start of the twentieth century, leading to the biggest defeats in the Lords since Labour came to power … These and other events suggested that the chamber was growing increasingly assertive.'

> M Russell and M Sciara, *The House of Lords in 2005: A More Representative and Assertive Chamber?*
> (The Constitution Unit, 2006), p 5.

The authors are referring to the major controversy of that year which was the passage of the Prevention of Terrorism Act 2005. The Bill had been introduced as a response to a ruling of the Appellate Committee of the House of Lords (*A and Others v Secretary of State for the Home Department* [2004] UKHL 56, see section 6.7.4) which had declared that it was unlawful to detain terrorist suspects under the Anti-terrorism, Crime and Security Act 2001.

In respect of the Bill, as noted by Russell and Sciara, two particularly significant developments occurred due to the scrutiny in the House of Lords, as a result of which:

> 'The final outcome was a compromise, whereby there was some judicial involvement in issuing all control orders, and the government promised to review the law within a year and bring in a more considered bill. Whilst not being written into the bill this was seen as a victory for its opponents.'

> M Russell and M Sciara, *The House of Lords in 2005: A More Representative and Assertive Chamber?*
> (The Constitution Unit, 2006), p 10.

ACTIVITY

Essay writing

What is the constitutional relationship between the House of Lords and the House of Commons? Do you think that the House of Lords should ever obstruct the wishes of the lower (elected) chamber?

The differences between the House of Commons and the House of Lords

	House of Commons	House of Lords
Composition	• Exclusively elected with constituency responsibilities.	• Unelected – although there are, in a technical sense, 'elected' hereditary peers. • No constituents.
Type of Member	• Elected politicians. • Few independents.	• Appointed politicians. • Sizeable element of independents.
Expertise	• Full-time politicians.	• A wide range of experience and expertise. • Life peers specifically appointed for their expertise and experience. • Law lords possess legal expertise. • Bishops can provide expertise on religious matters.
Payment	• Salaried.	• Unpaid except ministers, Bishops and law lords (but peers can claim expenses).
Size of Chamber	• Currently statutorily capped at 646 MPs.	• No fixed cap.
Legislative procedure	• Committee stage taken in general (public Bill) committees. • Use of guillotine. • (Largely) party political/partisan atmosphere.	• Committee stage on the Floor of the House. • No guillotine. • To some extent a less partisan and polemic atmosphere.
Relations with the government	• Responsible for both maintaining and removing the government (vote of confidence).	• No direct responsibility for maintaining or removing a government.

Further reading

Carroll, A, *Constitutional and Administrative Law* (3rd edn, Pearson/Longman, 2003), Chapter 9.

House of Lords Select Committee on the Constitution, 7th Report of Session 2005–06, *Constitutional aspects of the challenge to the Hunting Act 2004*, HL Paper 141 (2006), Appendix 3.

House of Lords Briefing, *The work of the House of Lords – Its Role, Functions and Powers* (Parliamentary Copyright House of Lords, 2005).

Loveland, I, *Constitutional Law, Administrative Law, and Human Rights* (4th edn, Oxford University Press, 2006), Chapter 6.

Royal Commission on the Reform of the House of Lords, *A House for the Future*, Cm 4534 (The Stationery Office, 2000).

Russell, M, and Sciara, M, *The House of Lords in 2005: A More Representative and Assertive Chamber?* (The Constitution Unit, 2006).

The Work of the House of Lords 2005–06 (Parliamentary Copyright House of Lords, 2007).

Website

www.parliament.uk

THE EXECUTIVE

AIMS AND OBJECTIVES

At the end of this chapter you should be able to:

■ Define the term executive

■ Identify the different types of executive

■ Explain the composition of the executive

■ Identify the different functions of the executive

■ Identify and explain the statutory and common law powers of the executive

11.1 Introduction and terminology

11.1.1 Definition of government

As indicated earlier (section 5.3.2), the executive or governmental function is performed by 'Her Majesty's Government' or the administration. It is important to realise that the term 'government' can be used in the following senses:

• Firstly, government can be used in a very broad sense to indicate that an individual is being 'governed' (ie controlled and regulated) by the state and its whole apparatus including, for example, Parliament, the police, the armed forces and the courts.

• Secondly, government can be used in a much narrower sense to indicate government administration, namely, Her Majesty's Government – the government.

• Thirdly, government can be used to denote local government whereby local authorities deliver services (such as housing and libraries) at a local level.

It is with the second definition that we will be particularly concerned with.

11.1.2 The constitutional monarchy and the Crown

The United Kingdom has a constitutional monarchy with an unelected, hereditary sovereign as its Head of State. Republican countries such as the United States and the Republic of Ireland have elected Presidents to act as Head of State. The Queen's role is to a large extent symbolic, comprising ceremonial and formal responsibilities (however, the monarch does have some important residual constitutional powers – see section 11.9.2).

In the British constitution the executive is known as Her Majesty's Government as in constitutional theory the monarch appoints and dismisses government ministers. In addition, civil servants are employed and dismissed by the Crown. Further, in terms of the executive in practice, in a technical sense the Queen is the Commander in Chief of the armed forces.

At this point the term 'Crown' needs to be explained as in the British constitution it can be separated into two elements:

- Firstly, the Crown could be used to signify the monarch herself (the Sovereign),

- Secondly, the Crown can be used to refer to the government of the day or the administration.

In modern parlance, the Crown is typically used in the second sense in order to distinguish between the personal constitutional role of the monarch (who has a largely formal role) from her political government ministers (who make political and executive decisions). This distinction is important because we have a constitutional monarchy, the monarch and her constitutional role being constrained by the uncodified constitution. The reality is that although in strict law the Sovereign enjoys considerable historic constitutional and legal powers, in practice these are either:

- regulated by constitutional convention, or

- are exercised by the Queen's ministers acting on her behalf in the name of the Crown/monarch.

Thus, in a modern democracy it would be considered undemocratic (not to say morally unconstitutional – see section 4.15) for a monarch to exercise personally those powers legally vested in her as her predecessors would have done centuries before.

11.1.3 The different forms of executive

The term executive embraces a number of elements and refers to those who administer and execute the law. A general distinction can be drawn between the following types of executive (drawing upon the terminology used by Heywood, *Politics* (Macmillan, 1997) Ch 16):

- The political executive (Her Majesty's Government – see section 11.2).

- The non-political or bureaucratic executive (the Civil Service – see section 11.3).

- The executive in practical terms (the armed forces and various police forces – see section 11.4).

- Other executives (local authorities, the Scottish Executive, the Northern Ireland Executive Committee, the Welsh Assembly Government, executive power in the European Union – see section 11.5).

- Public authorities/bodies. This is a public law term which we will return to in the context of judicial review (see section 19.3), but for present purposes it essentially refers to a public body performing public functions. It would include, for example, the following:

1. Government ministers.

2. Central government departments.

3. Executive agencies and quangos.

4. Local authorities.

5. Police authorities.

6. Devolved institutions.

7. Non-governmental bodies which perform a public function (eg the Panel on Take-overs and Mergers – see section 19.3.3).

ACTIVITY

Quick quiz

What is meant by the following terms?

- The Crown.

- The government.

- The executive.

11.2 The political executive/Her Majesty's Government

11.2.1 The monarch (see sections 8.3 and 11.1.2)

The political executive is constitutionally Her Majesty's Government and ministers swear an oath of allegiance to the Crown. In practice, the monarch's role is largely formal.

11.2.2 The Prime Minister

Although the monarch is the Head of State and titular head of the executive, the Prime Minister is the effective Head of Government (contrast this with the position in the United States where the elected President is both Head of State and Head of Government). The constitutional office of the Prime Minister has developed historically by constitutional convention (contrast most other Prime Ministers/Presidents which owe their creation to a codified constitutional document) and is the head of the Cabinet (*primus inter pares* – first among equals). By constitutional convention the Prime Minister must be drawn from the House of Commons (see section 4.13.4) so that he can be held directly accountable to the elected representatives of the people (MPs).

The Prime Minister has *inter alia* the following constitutional functions:

- To preside over Cabinet meetings (see section 11.2.3).

- To act as a conduit between the monarch and the government (in this way the Prime Minster can keep the monarch informed of recent political developments).

- To act as the Minister for the Civil Service (he also has the title of First Lord of the Treasury, although in practice the Chancellor of the Exchequer is the acting head of government finance).

- To determine certain appointments. For example, these include, among others, the number of non-party political peers to be appointed to the House of Lords (see section 10.5.4), senior civil servants, the Parliamentary Ombudsman and government ministers.

- To co-ordinate government policy.

- To request a dissolution of Parliament prior to a general election.

- To establish certain non-statutory bodies (eg the House of Lords Appointments Commission in 2000 – see section 10.5.4).

- To issue and revise the *Ministerial Code, A Code of Ethics and Procedural Guidance for Ministers* (Cabinet Office, revised July 2005), which is given to ministers on assuming office and details their responsibilities and expected standard of conduct. It is of interest to note that if the United Kingdom were to adopt a codified constitution, the rules set out in this Code would inevitably form part of it.

The Prime Minister is given advice by the Policy Unit and specialist advisers.

11.2.3 The Cabinet

This body, like that of the office of the Prime Minister, owes its existence to constitutional convention. In constitutional theory, the Cabinet is the most significant political decision-making body in the constitution. The Cabinet comprises the most senior ministers in the government (the head of each government department) who discuss, debate and collectively agree on government policy (eg in relation to prisons or pensions, etc). In this way, the British constitution is hallmarked by Cabinet government with collective decision-making on major state and policy issues being made by a number of senior government ministers. In recent decades, however, the dominance of the office and personality of the Prime Minister has prompted the question as to whether we have 'Prime Ministerial government' instead, whereby the Prime Minister dominates and overshadows the Cabinet. After all, it is the Prime Minister who determines and co-ordinates Cabinet discussion, and 'sums up' Cabinet opinion by determining the Cabinet view on a matter. Moreover, he determines who will be a minister and the government portfolio that they will hold (for example, consider the major Cabinet reshuffle in May 2006). Ultimately, however, the Prime Minister needs the support and confidence of his Cabinet in order to maintain his position. Margaret Thatcher lost the full support of her Cabinet (and party) at the end of her tenure as Prime Minister and resigned.

The Cabinet is supported by the Cabinet Office (a Ministry of State). In addition, the Cabinet Secretariat serves to ensure that Cabinet business is co-ordinated and efficient. It supports and serves both Cabinet ministers (chairing meetings) as well as the Prime Minister.

The Cabinet is regulated by the following conventions:

- As a general rule it is generally composed of around 20 ministers – the exact size of the Cabinet will vary over time as, for example, government departments are not static and will merge with each other from time to time (determined by the Prime Minister).

- Its discussions remain secret (see section 12.2.3).

- Decisions are made collectively and once a decision has been reached all members of the Cabinet (together with the junior ministers) are bound, publicly, to support and endorse this policy. This is known as the constitutional convention of collective responsibility. In this way the Cabinet, together with the rest of Her Majesty's Ministers, present a united front to Parliament and the public (see section 12.2.2).

The Cabinet is supplemented by a number of specialist sub-Cabinet meetings which comprise a number of ministers. According to para 6.4 of the *Ministerial Code* 'they relieve the pressure on the Cabinet itself by settling as much business as possible at a lower level' and also underpin the convention of collective responsibility by making sure that:

Q   'even though an important question may never reach the Cabinet itself, the decision will be fully considered and the final judgment will be sufficiently authoritative to ensure that the Government as a whole can be properly expected to accept responsibility for it'.

Ministerial Code, A Code of Ethics and Procedural Guidance for Ministers
(Cabinet Office, revised July 2005).

The findings of these Cabinet committees will be reported to (and may be endorsed by) the full Cabinet, thereby to some extent undermining the constitutional position of the Cabinet. These committees are established by the Prime Minister and in 2006 there were 32 of them which included, for example, Cabinet committees on:

- Constitutional Affairs (with sub-committees on: *Electoral Policy, Freedom of Information* and *Parliamentary Modernisation*).

- European Policy.

- Defence and Overseas Policy.

- Domestic Affairs.

According to Weir and Beetham:

> 'The fact is that the Cabinet is now the creature of its own cabinet committees. The Cabinet committee structure is now the real 'engine-house' of government policy-making and decision-making. It is there if anywhere, and not in Cabinet, that long-term strategies and policy changes, such as the poll tax, are developed'.

Political power and Democratic Control in Britain (Routledge, 1999) p 128

ACTIVITY

Question

What is the constitutional difference between Cabinet government as opposed to Prime Ministerial government?

11.2.4 Junior ministers

The Cabinet comprises the most senior type of government ministers who head government departments (eg the Secretary of State). Most ministers, however, are junior ministers (Ministers of State or Parliamentary Under-Secretaries of State) and do not form part of the Cabinet, although they are still bound by the convention of collective responsibility.

It is important to note that Her Majesty's Government is supported by a number of parliamentary private secretaries who are not formally part of the government *per se,* but who are each attached to and support a particular minister. The *Ministerial Code* states that they: 'are expected to support the Government in all important divisions' (*Ministerial Code, A Code of Ethics and Procedural Guidance for Ministers* (Cabinet Office, revised July 2005), para 2.9).

ACTIVITY

Problem solving

What is the distinction between a Secretary of State and a junior minister? Find out some examples to illustrate this distinction.

11.2.5 Central government departments headed by a government minister

Central government comprises a number of departments of state, each with a separate and specialist policy responsibility. In March 2007 there were just over 20 departments of state which included, for example:

- The Department for Work and Pensions.
- The Department for Education and Skills.
- The Foreign and Commonwealth Office.
- HM Treasury.

Each department is headed by a senior government minister (typically a Secretary of State) who will be supported by a number of junior ministers. For example, in March 2007 the Home Office comprised the following ministerial hierarchy:

Table 11.1: Ministerial hierarchy in the Home Office

Secretary of State for the Home Department
3 Ministers of State: • Minister of State (Policing, Security and Community Safety) • Minister of State (Immigration, Citizenship and Nationality) • Minister for State (Criminal Justice and Offender Management)
3 Parliamentary Under-Secretaries of State.

Source: www.parliament.uk

As indicated above, government departments are not static institutions, and ministerial policy responsibilities are subject to change, as the Ministers of the Crown Act 1975 enables (in effect) the Prime Minister to:

- Transfer policy responsibilities between ministers – in 2003 specified functions of the Lord Chancellor were transferred to the newly created post of Secretary of State for Constitutional Affairs; this was the case even though the same person held both offices – The Secretary of State for Constitutional Affairs Order 2003 (SI 2003 No 1887). For a more recent example see The Secretary of State for Communities and Local Government Order 2006 (SI 2006 No 1926).

- Dissolve a government department and transfer its responsibilities to another minister.

This is achieved through the passage of a (statutory) Order in Council under the aegis of the 1975 Act.

Central government departments can also be sub-divided into the following two elements:

- **The political element (the temporary government ministers)** – most of whom will be elected politicians, but some will be peers, who will determine the political direction of the department and the policies it will administer.

- **The non-political element (the permanent civil servants)** who carry out and implement the policies as formulated by their government ministers (see section 11.3). It should be noted that, since the 1990s, aspects of government departments have been separated and reconstituted as 'Next Step Agencies', and these are considered at section 11.3.2.

ACTIVITY

Exercise

Explain the different aspects of a central government department. Identify one government department and explain what it does.

11.2.6 The Privy Council

The Privy Council was the precursor to the modern Cabinet and today its executive responsibilities have been eclipsed by it. It does, however, enable the government of the day to pass Orders in Council which, for example, regulate the Civil Service (see section 5.7.7).

KEY FACTS

The political executive is also known as Her Majesty's Government and consists of the following:

- The monarch, who is the titular Head of HM Government. In practice, the monarch's role is largely formal.

- The Prime Minister is the practical Head of Government and of the Cabinet.

- The Cabinet is composed of Cabinet ministers who are senior government ministers who each head a particular government department of state. In theory it is the most important decision-making body in the constitution.

- Junior ministers (eg Ministers of State or Parliamentary Under-Secretaries of State) sit outside the Cabinet.

- Government departments each have a separate and specialist policy responsibility and are typically headed by a Secretary of State. They are staffed by politically impartial civil servants who carry out and implement the policies as formulated by their government minister – see section 11.3.1 below.

11.3 The non-political or bureaucratic executive

11.3.1 The Civil Service

The *Civil Service Code* (as amended in 2006) states that:

> **Q**
>
> 1. The Civil Service is an integral and key part of the government of the United Kingdom. It supports the Government of the day in developing and implementing its policies, and in delivering public services. Civil servants are accountable to Ministers, who in turn are accountable to Parliament.
>
> 2. As a civil servant, you are appointed on merit … and are expected to carry out your role with dedication and a commitment to the Civil Service and its core values: integrity, honesty, objectivity and impartiality.
>
> Source: www.civilservice.gov.uk

Civil servants can be broadly divided into two distinct groups:

- **Senior civil servants** – They have been described as 'Whitehall mandarins' (see Weir and Beetham below) with the most senior civil servant in a department being the Permanent Secretary (not to be confused with political parliamentary private secretaries – see section 11.2.4). Senior civil servants provide information to their respective government minister (their political master) and offer expert advice on policy matters. Civil servants do not control public policy – that is the responsibility of government ministers who are constitutionally accountable to Parliament. Civil servants account directly to their ministerial head and not to Parliament. Instead, it is the minister who as the public face and head of the department who accounts to Parliament for the actions and policies of his department and officials (this is by virtue of the constitutional convention of individual ministerial responsibility – see para 1.5 of the *Ministerial Code*). It should be remembered that it is the case that the courts have sanctioned the practice whereby appropriately qualified civil servants can make decisions on behalf of their ministers (see sections 4.13.12 and 20.2.3).

In terms of determining policy, however, the dividing line between the senior graded civil servants and ministers is a fine one, as the latter necessarily make their policy judgments based (largely) on the information and advice provided by the former. Moreover, it should be pointed out that newly appointed Secretaries of State, who, owing to regular Cabinet re-shuffles, tend to be temporary, will inevitably lack experience and knowledge of the area of administration that they have been assigned. This is in contrast to the permanent, professional and seasoned senior civil servant. In this way, although it is a partnership between the minister and civil servant, it is inevitable that the former will be heavily reliant on the advice and information provided by the latter. It should also be remembered that in addition to their ministerial duties, most government ministers are also elected MPs and will have constituency matters to attend to.

According to Weir and Beetham, the dynamics of the relationship between minister and civil servant is that:

> 'it is the officials who draft the papers ministers see, who filter the information they receive, who define many of the problems, who suggest most of the solutions, who draft the legislation and who ultimately take the great majority of decisions'.

S Weir and D Beetham, *Political Power and Democratic Control in Britain* (Routledge, 1999), p 170.

Senior civil servants must be distinguished from 'special advisers'. In addition to the advice proffered by senior civil servants, ministers may also be given advice by appointed special advisers who are technically temporary civil servants, but who provide advice on a partisan and political basis. In this way they can provide a useful counterpoint to the advice of the senior civil servants. They are appointed by Cabinet ministers, having been sanctioned by the Prime Minister, and are governed by a code of conduct (*Code of Conduct for Special Advisers*). According to para 2.12 of the *Ministerial Code*, ministers are responsible for the actions and decisions of their special adviser. The number of special advisers has grown in the past decade from 38 in 1995/96 to 78 in 2005/06 (O Gay and P Fawcett, 'Special Advisers' (House of Commons Library, 2005) p 8).

- **Lower-ranking civil servants** (the vast majority of the Civil Service) who implement government policy and administration on a daily basis.

The constitutional characteristics of the Civil Service

Civil servants, historically, have been hallmarked by the following principles:

- **Permanence** – In the British constitution government ministers are temporary, whereas civil servants are permanent appointments. This means that a change in government after a general election does not result in a change in the composition of the Civil Service. Civil servants will serve and owe allegiance to the government of the day irrespective of its political colour.

- **Impartiality** – Civil servants are politically impartial in the sense that they must serve all governments equally well (*Civil Service Code*, para 2). This means that whatever their own personal political beliefs, civil servants must serve a government irrespective of its political persuasion (para 13). In addition, in terms of objectivity, para 10 states that civil servants must not 'frustrate the implementation of policies once decisions are taken by declining to take, or abstaining from, action which flows from those decisions'. Moreover, s 1(1)(b) of the House of

Commons Disqualification Act 1975 bars civil servants from becoming MPs. Furthermore, in light of their responsibilities to provide advice etc, the senior grades of the profession are barred from political activity at a national level. There are two categories below this politically restricted category: those who may engage in national and local political activity with permission and those in the lowest category who are free to be involved in such activities.

In terms of integrity, civil servants must not disclose official information without the requisite authorisation (*Civil Service Code*, para 6). In the 1980s a senior civil servant disclosed to an opposition MP information pertaining to the sinking of the Argentine ship the *General Belgrano*. He was subsequently prosecuted under the Official Secrets Act 1911, although at his trial he was acquitted by the jury (*R v Ponting* [1985] Crim LR 318).

Civil servants' appointments are overseen by the Civil Service Commissioners and are selected on merit. Finally, it is pertinent to point out that the *Ministerial Code* imposes a duty on ministers to uphold the political impartiality of the Civil Service (*Ministerial Code*, para 3.1).

- **Anonymity** – As indicated above, government ministers must account to Parliament for the performance and actions of their department, thereby taking constitutional responsibility for their departmental civil servants. In this way the head of the government department (together with his junior ministers) represents the public face of the department with the permanent civil servant remaining anonymous. This in turn allows civil servants to give advice in confidence and enables them to serve successive different governments. The principle of anonymity has, however, been partly eroded by the fact that civil servants appear before select committees to represent their minister (having been appropriately briefed in accordance with the 'Osmotherly Rules' – see section 12.6.5).

The management of the Civil Service

The minister responsible for the Civil Service is the Prime Minister and the employment terms and conditions of civil servants are regulated by Orders in Council (legislation made under the royal prerogative – see *GCHQ* (1985) at section 11.9.6). In recent years, however, there has been a call for a Civil Service Act to be enacted which would regulate civil servants on a statutory basis, because at the moment changes can be made without the support of Parliament. Although in 2004 the government produced a consultation paper, together with a draft Civil Service Bill, and invited comments as to whether legislation was necessary in order to underpin the role and governance of the Civil Service, in early 2007 no government Bill on the matter was forthcoming. In 2006, however, the House of Lords considered Lord Lester's Constitutional Reform (Prerogative Powers and Civil Service etc.) Bill, Pt 2 of which would have created a framework for the Civil Service and placed it on a statutory footing. The Bill, however, did not become law.

ACTIVITY

Question

What do civil servants do? What is their constitutional significance?

11.3.2 Executive agencies/the 'Next Step Agencies'

It is important to note that today the vast majority of civil servants work not in central government departments *per se*, but in executive agencies. The 'Next Step Agencies' (so called because there were named after a Cabinet paper: *Improving Management in Government: the Next Steps* (Cabinet Office, February 1988)) were established in the 1990s in an attempt to make government administration more efficient. In essence, this meant that certain aspects of a government department were separated and reconstituted under a specified agency headed by a Chief Executive. The objectives to be obtained by the agency (thereby in theory ensuring administrative efficiency) would be determined by the relevant government minister. Three examples of executive agencies in early 2007 will suffice:

- The HM Prison Service (with a Director General) under the aegis of the Home Office (the responsible minister is the Minister of State for Criminal Justice and Offender Management) – this agency is concerned with keeping in custody those sentenced by the courts.

- The Driving Standards Agency (with a Chief Executive) under the aegis of the Department for Transport (the responsible minister is the Minister of State) – this agency is responsible for promoting road safety by improving driving standards, which includes the testing of putative drivers.

- The Child Support Agency (with a Chief Executive) under the aegis of the Department for Work and Pensions (the responsible minister is the Parliamentary Under-Secretary of State) – this agency is responsible for the financial maintenance of children where their parents do not live together.

The parent government departmental minister remains constitutionally responsible for these 'hived off' agencies (*Ministerial Code*, para 1.5). There has nevertheless been some constitutional disquiet as to whether ministers in practice take political responsibility for the operation of them (they are, of course, each headed by a Chief Executive who is a specified office holder), leading to a gap in constitutional accountability.

For example, in the mid-1990s when prisoners escaped from Parkhurst Prison, the Home Secretary argued that there was a distinction between operational responsibility (ie being responsible for the day to day security of prisons) and the responsibility for overall general policy. The escapees were considered an operational matter and subsequently the Home Secretary announced that the Director General (Chief Executive) of the Prison Service Agency had left his office.

It is pertinent to mention in the context of the drive for efficiency in government, the development of the *Citzens' Charter* in the 1990s was designed to specify standards in administration.

11.3.3 Quangos

In respect of 'national government' there exist a considerable number of quangos (non-departmental public bodies) for which ministers are constitutionally responsible (although they do not technically form part of the government department). Two examples will suffice:

The Commission for Equality and Human Rights
Under the Equality Act 2006, this body was scheduled in 2007 to take over the responsibilities of the following three bodies:

- The Equal Opportunities Commission which deals with sex discrimination and gender inequality, including, for example, good practice in the equal treatment of men and women.
- The Disability Rights Commission which provides advice, supports disabled people and campaigns to strengthen the law.
- The Commission for Racial Equality which provides advice (similar to the Equal Opportunities Commission above), but in relation to racial issues.

The Electoral Commission
(see section 9.7.1).

KEY FACTS

The non-political or bureaucratic executive comprises the following:

(1) The Civil Service, which can be broadly divided into two distinct groups:

- Senior civil servants who provide information to their respective government minister and offer him expert advice on policy matters.
- Lower-ranking civil servants who simply implement government policy and administration.

Civil servants account directly to their ministerial head and not to Parliament. The Civil Service is characterised by the following principles:

- Impartiality and permanence – civil servants will serve and owe allegiance to the government of the day irrespective of its political colour.

CONTINUED ▶

11.4 The executive in practical terms

11.4.1 The armed forces and police

Both the armed forces and the various police forces (one for each area of the country) form part of the executive in a very general and practical sense. The police, for example, practically enforce the criminal law against those individuals who, *prima facie*, violate it. In short, they carry out and implement the law on a practical basis. They are, nevertheless, barred from membership of the House of Commons (see section 11.6.3).

11.5 Other executive bodies in the British constitution

There are other executive bodies in the British constitution:

Local authorities

From a constitutional perspective, local authorities, technically, form part of the executive. Local councillors are elected by local residents and the political composition of local authorities will, in various parts of the country, be different to that of central government. Local authorities possess both legislative and executive powers (see section 14.2).

Devolution

As part of the devolved settlements, the following executives were established:

- **Scotland** – s 44 of the Scotland Act 1998 established a Scottish Executive (in effect, a Cabinet drawn from the Scottish Parliament). This section further provides that an individual cannot hold national ministerial office at Whitehall whilst being a member of the Scottish Executive.

- **Northern Ireland** – Pt III of the Northern Ireland Act 1998 provided for the establishment of an Executive Committee (analogous to the Scottish Executive). In May 2007 the devolution arrangements pertaining to Northern Ireland were reactivated after a period of suspension.
- **Wales** – s 45 of the Government of Wales Act 2006 established a Welsh Assembly Government.

On all of the above executives see Chapter 14.

The European Community

Although there is no clear separation of powers between the European institutions, historically the European Commission has been regarded as the executive and the Civil Service of Europe. However, both the Council and the European Council also perform executive functions by making executive decisions (see section 15.2.2).

11.6 The statistical breakdown of government ministers

11.6.1 The parliamentary executive

As the United Kingdom has a parliamentary executive system of government, government ministers are necessarily drawn from Parliament. The parliamentary executive can be illustrated by the following two tables:

Table 11.2: The parliamentary executive in March 2007

Parliament (legislature)	
House of Commons (646 MPs)	**House of Lords (744 Peers)**
The Political Executive (113 members) 91 MPs 22 Peers	

Source: www.parliament.uk

Table 11.3: The statistical breakdown of HM Government in March 2007

The Political Executive	
Cabinet ministers	23 (2)
Ministers of State	30 (4)
Under Secretaries of State/Parliamentary Secretaries	34 (6)
Government whips	23 (8)
Law officers	3 (2)
TOTAL	113 (22 peers)

* Figures in brackets represent the number of peers.

Source: www.parliament.uk

It is of interest to point out that in March 2007 almost one third of ministers were female (33 out of 113) which included eight female Cabinet ministers (out of 23). The United Kingdom Cabinet is smaller than in either Canada (36) or Australia (30), but larger than Ireland (15) (S King, *Regulating the Behaviour of Ministers, Special Advisers and Civil Servants* (The Constitution Unit, 2003), p 10). In addition, it should be pointed out that no more than 20 Cabinet salaries, other than the Prime Minister and Lord Chancellor, are payable (Ministerial and other Salaries Act 1975 as amended).

11.6.2 Government ministers in the House of Lords

As is clear from the tables above, the vast majority of ministers are MPs, however, a substantial minority (approximately one fifth) are peers in the House of Lords. In fact, historically, the majority of Cabinet members in the nineteenth century were peers. Although in some countries ministers cannot form part of the upper chamber, the advantages of it are that:

- It ensures that the government has some representation in the upper House.
- The upper House has the opportunity to scrutinise directly some government ministers.
- Government ministers can pilot Bills through the upper House.

11.6.3 The executive and the separation of powers

The House of Commons Disqualification Act 1975 ensures that there is a degree of constitutional separation between certain elements of the executive and the House of Commons.

- Firstly, s 2(1) stipulates that no more persons than 95 can hold ministerial office in the House of Commons at any one time.
- Secondly, s 1 disqualifies the following members of the executive from membership of the House of Commons:

s 1(1)(b) – those employed in the Civil Service
(c) – members of the regular armed forces
(d) – members of any police force.

ACTIVITY

Problem solving

Explain the statistical breakdown of the parliamentary executive. What is the constitutional significance of such data?

11.7 The functions of the executive

The constitutional functions of the executive comprise the following:

- **To formulate domestic public policy.** In short, the constitutional function of the government is to govern the state. The essence of Cabinet government is that a group of senior ministers collectively debate, determine and co-ordinate policies, for example how to address the issues of youth crime or pensions. These policies would be publicly supported by the government as a whole both in and outside Parliament.

- **To formulate and implement foreign policy.** This would include the deployment of troops overseas and responding to an international crisis.

- **To initiate legislative proposals.** Although Parliament is the legislature, it is the government of the day which drafts and introduces most Bills which are laid before Parliament to approve. Government ministers will have the constitutional responsibility to pilot these Bills through Parliament. These Bills will invariably embody certain government policy aims. For example:

  (a) The Terrorism Act 2006 (s 1 makes it a criminal offence to encourage acts of terrorism).

  (b) The Identity Cards Act 2006 (provides the framework for a National Identity Register for the registration of individuals and the issue of identity cards).

- **To implement the law (and policy).** The executive 'executes' and carries out the law. Civil servants will implement the laws in relation to their respective government department. As illustrated in the *Carltona* case (1943) (see section 4.13.12), some senior civil servants will exercise legal powers on behalf of their minister thereby acting as their *alter ego*. The United Kingdom executive, therefore, can both initiate and execute the law. In practical terms, the implementation and enforcement of the law is performed by the police and in emergencies, by the armed forces (thereby ensuring public order).

- **To provide political leadership.** This is performed by the government as a whole, but in recent years has typically focused on the Prime Minister (for example, in the context of summits of the European Council – see section 15.2.1).

- **To make appointments.** For example, the Lord Chancellor will (ultimately) determine the appointments in respect of a range of judicial posts.

ACTIVITY

Essay writing

Consider the different functions of the executive. Are some more important than others?

11.8 The powers of the executive

In order to perform its responsibilities, the executive enjoys both statutory and common law powers.

11.8.1 Statutory powers

Most powers which government exercises are statutory. For example, an Act may:

Confer a power on a minister to pass delegated legislation in order to achieve specified aims:

- Section 47(1) of the Prison Act 1952 empowers the Secretary of State to make rules in order to regulate and manage prisons (see *ex parte Leech* (1993) at section 20.2.2).

- In addition, local authorities can pass delegated legislation in the form of by-laws in order to regulate local matters (eg local parks, or the banning of the consumption of alcohol in specified areas).

Confer a power on a minister to achieve specified purposes:

- Section 1 of the Inquiries Act 2005 empowers a minister to establish a statutory inquiry (see section 21.2.3).

- Section 2 of the Prevention of Terrorism Act 2005 empowers a minister to make a control order in respect of a person who is suspected of being involved in terrorism-related activity. A control order may, for example, restrict their movements within the United Kingdom.

Confer a power on a minister to determine when primary legislative provisions should be brought into force:

- Section 148(4) of the Constitutional Reform Act 2005 authorises the Lord Chancellor to bring into operation the new Supreme Court.

- Section 171 of the Criminal Justice Act 1988 gave the Home Secretary a power to decide when to bring the statutory Criminal Injuries Compensation Scheme into effect (*R v Secretary of State for the Home Department, ex parte Fire Brigades Union* [1995] 2 All ER 244 at section 6.7.10).

Confer a power on a minister to pass delegated legislation which has the effect of amending primary legislation (known as an Henry VIII clause):

- Section 10 of the Human Rights Act 1998 authorises ministers to pass remedial orders in order to render a provision of primary legislation compatible with the European Convention (see section 17.7.3).

- Section 2(2) of the European Communities Act 1972 empowers a minister to implement a European directive into domestic law through secondary legislation.

Impose a duty to achieve a specified purpose:

- Section 7 of the Public Libraries and Museums Act 1964 imposes a statutory duty on all library authorities (in effect local authorities) to provide a comprehensive and efficient library service (see *ex parte Times Newspapers Ltd* (1986) at section 20.2.4).

KEY FACTS

HM Government possesses a number of statutory powers to do the following:

- To pass delegated legislation in order to achieve specified aims (eg s 47 of the Prison Act 1952).

- To achieve specified purposes (eg s 1 of the Inquiries Act 2005).

- To determine when primary legislative provisions should be brought into force. (eg s 171 of the Criminal Justice Act 1988).

- To pass delegated legislation which has the effect of amending primary legislation (eg s 10 of the Human Rights Act 1998).

11.8.2 Common law powers

In addition to statute, government also draws powers from the common law:

- **A residual power to act** – There is a conception that public authorities enjoy a residual freedom to act as evidenced by *Malone v Metropolitan Police Commissioner* (1979) (see section 6.7.7) whereby Sir Robert Megarry VC made it clear that: 'England… is a country where everything is permitted except what is expressly forbidden'. As a result, Malone's telephone line could be tapped because there was no 'positive' law to forbid it (although now see the Human Rights Act 1998 – Chapter 17). According to Le Sueur however, this residual freedom of action would not apply to public authorities established by statute (eg local authorities) whose specific powers would be stipulated in legislation ('The Nature, Powers and Accountability of Central Government' in D Feldman (ed), *English Public Law* (Oxford University Press, 2004) p 226).

• **The royal prerogative** – (see directly below) this is an invaluable power which the government draws from the common law. A number of prerogative powers were abolished as part of the constitutional settlement which led to the Bill of Rights 1689, but a number still remain today.

11.9 The royal prerogative

11.9.1 Definition

In its evidence to the House of Commons Public Administration Select Committee, the Treasury Solicitor's Department provided the following definition of the royal prerogative:

> **Q**
>
> 'There is no single accepted definition of the prerogative. It is sometimes defined to mean all the common law, ie non-statutory powers, of the Crown. An alternative definition is that the prerogative consists of those common law powers and immunities which are peculiar to the Crown and go beyond the powers of a private individual, eg the power to declare war as opposed to the normal common law power to enter a contract … Whichever definition is used there is no exhaustive list of prerogative powers'.
>
> Fourth Report of Session 2003–04, *Taming the Prerogative: Strengthening Ministerial Accountability to Parliament*, HC 422 (2004), Ev 13.

What is clear is that royal prerogative powers, historically, were exercised by successive monarchs over the centuries, but today with a constitutional monarchy those powers have in effect passed in practice to the government of the day (the vast majority of which will have been elected, although some ministers sit in the House of Lords). Indeed, it would be considered (with some exceptions) undemocratic for an hereditary and unelected monarch to exercise personally the executive powers listed below.

The House of Commons Public Administration Select Committee (see directly above) divided the royal prerogative powers into three broad types:

• 'The Queen's constitutional prerogatives' (para 5).

- 'The legal prerogatives of the Crown' (para 7).
- 'Prerogative executive powers' (para 8).

In addition it is also possible to divide broadly, the prerogative powers between:

- Those powers in the domestic sphere (eg dissolution of Parliament, Royal Assent, mercy, etc)
- Those powers relating to foreign affairs (eg ratifying Treaties, declaring war, deploying armed forces abroad, etc).

11.9.2 The Queen's constitutional prerogatives

The Public Administration Select Committee described these as 'the personal discretionary powers which remain in the Sovereign's hands' and would include the following:

To dissolve Parliament – Parliament must be dissolved prior to a general election and as we do not have fixed term Parliaments, the Prime Minister of the day decides when to request a dissolution (see section 8.1.1). The dissolution is a prerogative act technically performed by the monarch, but by constitutional convention, she will accede to such a request, thereby acting on the advice of her Prime Minister.

To appoint the Prime Minister – Although under the prerogative it is the monarch who formally appoints the Prime Minister, the practical reality is that following constitutional convention she will appoint the party leader that has secured the majority of seats in the House of Commons (in other words, he who commands the support of the House). Problems could occur, however, following a general election when no one party has the majority of seats in a 'hung Parliament'. In such circumstances the monarch may have to exercise a personal discretion (no doubt being informed by appropriate political and constitutional advice).

To appoint government ministers – Although the monarch formally appoints government ministers (it is Her Majesty's Government), by constitutional convention she will act on the advice of her Prime Minister who will determine these appointments (eg after a reshuffle in the Cabinet).

To grant the Royal Assent – By constitutional convention the monarch will act on the advice of her ministers and grant Royal Assent to Bills. Such consent has not been refused for three centuries. In modern times the granting of the Royal Assent has not proved controversial,

The right to encourage, warn and advise her government ministers – Bagehot, writing in the nineteenth century, noted that a monarch had the constitutional right to encourage and warn her government ministers (by giving her opinion) as well as to be consulted by them, for example prior to the Budget (W Bagehot, *The English Constitution*, (Oxford University Press, 2001), p 64). Indeed, the current monarch has considerable experience, particularly in relation to the Commonwealth, as she has been Sovereign for over 50 years and has formally appointed a number of different Prime Ministers and numerous ministers over this time.

As noted by the Select Committee, although in normal circumstances the monarch would act on the advice of her ministers in terms of how these powers should be exercised, she also has the power : '(in grave constitutional crisis) to act contrary to or without Ministerial advice' (para 5).

ACTIVITY

Problem solving

Do you think that it would be the monarch's constitutional duty to refuse to grant the Royal Assent (ignoring the advice of her ministers) to the 2011 Abolition of Elections Bill which proposed to abolish parliamentary elections for 30 years? (On acting constitutionally and unconstitutionally – see section 4.15).

11.9.3 The legal prerogatives of the Crown

As noted by the Select Committee these include, for example:

- The principle that the Crown (or the state) can do no wrong – the monarch cannot be sued in her own courts (she is, of course, the fountain of justice as implemented by Her Majesty's judges).

- The Crown is only bound by Acts of Parliament through the use of express words or by necessary implication. For example, s 50 of the Inquiries Act 2005 states that the provisions of the Act bind the Crown.

ACTIVITY

Exercise

Compare and contrast the Queen's constitutional prerogatives with the legal prerogatives of the Crown.

11.9.4 Prerogative executive powers

The Select Committee suggested that the third type of powers should be described as 'ministerial executive' powers, as in practice it is government ministers which exercise these powers in the name of the Crown (as detailed below).

Government ministers' main powers

The Select Committee identified the main 'royal prerogative or Ministerial executive powers exercised by Ministers' to be as follows:

- **A declaration of war** – The decision to go to war is taken not by Parliament but by the government of the day (in effect, the Prime Minister) purporting to do so in the name of the Crown. In contrast, in the United States, Art 1, s 8 of the constitution states that it is Congress which declares war. In 2005 Clare Short MP unsuccessfully introduced a Private Member's Bill: the Armed Forces (Parliamentary Approval for Participation in Armed Conflict) Bill, clause 7 of which would have required that no declaration of war on behalf of the United Kingdom should be made unless the proposal had been laid before each House of Parliament and approved by them.

- **The deployment and use of UK armed forces abroad** – Although the monarch is the titular Commander-in-Chief of the armed forces, as with the declaration of war, it is the government which in effect determines the disposition of troops overseas. In 2003 before the transfer of troops to Iraq the Prime Minister allowed a vote in Parliament on this issue, which in turn has led to the question as to whether this now represents the creation of a constitutional convention which must be followed in future. It is clear that acting under the prerogative, the Prime Minister could have ignored an adverse parliamentary vote in 2003, although this would have raised the issue of whether such conduct would have been construed as unconstitutional (see section 4.15).

Clare Short's 2005 Armed Forces Bill (noted directly above) also proposed that parliamentary approval would be required for Her Majesty's armed forces to participate in armed conflict. In support of her Bill, she argued that the rationale behind it was:

- It was democratically appropriate that Parliament should approve a declaration of war and the deployment of troops in an armed conflict.

- It would help to ensure that such decisions were more effectively scrutinised and informed (*Hansard*, HC Vol 437, cols 1085–90).

Similarly, clause 3 of Lord Lester's 2006 Constitutional Reform (Prerogative Powers and Civil Service etc.) Bill would have enabled Parliament to approve the committal of the armed forces to armed conflict or war. Although neither Bill became law, in 2006 the House of Lords Select Committee on the Constitution issued a report on its review of the government's powers in this context (see section 22.7). In December 2006 another Private Member's Bill on this issue was published: Waging War (Parliament's Role and Responsibility) Bill. The Bill was sponsored by Michael Meacher MP and would require the Secretary of State to lay before the House of Commons a mechanism to obtain the approval of the Commons for the deployment of British troops for armed conflict.

- **The deployment of the armed forces domestically** – As noted by the Select Committee this could involve maintaining the peace of the realm (an executive function) by supporting the police.

- **The ratification of international treaties** – Treaties are typically signed by the Secretary of State for Foreign and Commonwealth Affairs or sometimes by the Prime Minister. There is a practice (the 'Ponsonby rule') whereby the government lays the Treaty before Parliament for at least 21 days before ratification, thereby allowing it be to considered.

The act of treaty-making is a function of the executive and is not susceptible to review by the courts:

> **J** 'The treaty-making power of this country rests not in the courts, but in the Crown; that is, Her Majesty acting on the advice of her Ministers. When her Ministers negotiate and sign a treaty ... they act on behalf of the country as a whole. They exercise the prerogative of the Crown. Their action in so doing cannot be challenged or questioned in these courts'.
>
> Lord Denning MR in *Blackburn v Attorney-General* [1971] 2 All ER 1380.

Similarly, the court dismissed Lord Rees-Mogg's judicial review application regarding the Secretary of State for Foreign and Commonwealth Affairs' decision to ratify the Maastricht Treaty (the Treaty on European Union 1992) signed in 1992 (*R v Secretary of State for Foreign and Commonwealth Affairs, ex parte Rees-Mogg* [1994] QB 552).

In support of his (albeit unsuccessful) 2006 Constitutional Reform (Prerogative Powers and Civil Service etc.) Bill, Lord Lester argued that it was 'anomalous that Parliament has almost no role in the process of the ratification of important treaties' (*Hansard*, HL Vol 679, col 445). Clause 3 of the Bill would have enabled Parliament to approve treaties prior to their ratification.

- **The issuing and revocation of passports** – this is determined by a government minister and has important constitutional implications as it affects an individual's freedom of movement. It is subject to legal supervision by the court:

CASE EXAMPLE

R v Secretary of State for Foreign and Commonwealth Affairs, ex parte Everett **[1989] 1 QB 811**

Everett, a British citizen in Spain, sought a new passport, but was refused one in pursuance of the Secretary of State's policy that passports were not issued where a warrant for arrest in the United Kingdom had been issued (Everett had not been given details of the warrant for his arrest). He sought judicial review of this refusal.

The Court of Appeal held that the judicial review of powers under the royal prerogative depended upon its subject matter. A decision in relation to whether or not a passport

CONTINUED ▶

should be issued was an administrative one which affected the rights of an individual and unlikely to have implications for foreign policy and was reviewable by the courts. On the facts, however, Everett had suffered no injustice or prejudice (he had been given before the court hearing the information which should have been provided, eg the details of the warrant) and there was no suggestion that there were any special circumstances to justify an exception to the policy to issue him a passport.

- **The granting of pardons (the prerogative of mercy)** – This involves the Crown (in effect the Home Secretary advising the monarch) pardoning criminals or reducing their criminal sentences. The exercise of this power is, to some extent, subject to review by the courts:

CASE EXAMPLE

R v Secretary of State for the Home Department, ex parte Bentley [1994] QB 349

The Divisional Court held that the failure of the Home Secretary to appreciate that the royal prerogative of mercy (which was 'a broad and flexible constitutional safeguard against mistakes') could be exercised other than by the issuing of a free pardon (eg a posthumous conditional pardon) was subject to review by the courts. The Home Secretary was, accordingly, required to consider afresh whether it was just to use his prerogative powers so as to recognise the commonly accepted view that Bentley's brother (Derek Bentley who had been executed in 1953) should have been reprieved.

The court stated that decisions taken under the royal prerogative were subject to judicial review where the nature and subject matter of the particular prerogative was amenable to judicial adjudication (ie where it did not necessitate the court reviewing questions of policy).

- **The regulation of the Civil Service** – The management of civil servants is regulated by Orders in Council passed by the Privy Council.
- **The recommendations for honours** (by the defence and foreign secretaries).
- **The Prime Minister's ability to make appointments** – These powers include, *inter alia*, appointing (and thereafter dismissing) government ministers, recommending honours, peerages and a dissolution of Parliament. As pointed out earlier, although the monarch may formally perform these functions, the practical reality is that the Prime Minister of the day will make these decisions in practice.
- **The governance of territories (British) abroad.**

KEY FACTS

The prerogative executive powers comprise the following:

- To declare war and peace.
- To determine the deployment and use of the armed forces abroad.
- To determine the deployment of the armed forces domestically.
- To sign and ratify international treaties.
- To issue and revoke passports.
- To grant pardons (the prerogative of mercy).
- To regulate the Civil Service.

11.9.5 The constitutional relationship between Parliament and the royal prerogative

In the hierarchy of legal sources, as statute law has a higher status than the common law, Parliament can pass Acts of Parliament which eclipse powers under the royal prerogative (see section 7.5.1). In fact, Parliament can:

- expressly limit or abolish prerogative powers (Bill of Rights 1689); or
- pass laws which supersede these powers.

CASE EXAMPLE

Attorney-General v De Keyser's Royal Hotel Limited [1920] AC 508

In 1916 the Crown took possession of De Keyser's Hotel to accommodate the headquarters personnel of the Royal Flying Corps. De Keyser sought compensation for this use and occupation of the hotel. The government argued that the occupation had been exercised under the royal prerogative (the defence of the realm) and so no compensation was payable. De Keyser argued that it was occupied in accordance with the Defence Act 1842 which made provision for compensation.

The House of Lords held that the government occupation of the hotel was under the terms of the Act (and so the powers under the royal prerogative were not available to the

CONTINUED ▸

government) which necessitated compensation. In summary, the Crown could not purport to act under the royal prerogative where the power had been superseded by legislation. (The issue concerning compensation for taking property was decided later in *Burmah Oil* (1965) at section 4.9).

More recently, Lord Browne-Wilkinson, in *R v Secretary of State for the Home Department, ex parte Fire Brigades Union and others* [1995] 2 All ER 244, has noted that royal prerogative powers continue:

'in existence to the extent that Parliament has not expressly or by implication extinguished them.'

In addition to displacing prerogative powers through legislation, Parliament can ensure through the convention of ministerial responsibility that ministers are constitutionally and politically accountable for the use of these powers. With respect to parliamentary questions, generally speaking they can be asked about the prerogative except, for example:

- The advice the Prime Minister had given to the Sovereign in respect of honours.
- The dissolution of Parliament.
- The prerogative of mercy.

Reforms have been suggested periodically, to increase parliamentary control over the use of these powers.

- In March 2004 the House of Commons Public Administration Select Committee attached a draft Bill (supplied by Professor Brazier) to its report to ensure greater scrutiny of the prerogative. Clause 3 of the proposed Ministers of the Crown (Executive Powers) Bill would have imposed a duty on government ministers to lay a statement before Parliament setting out the nature, extent and safeguards in respect of all executive (royal prerogative) powers. Thereafter a joint select committee would review these powers and indicate whether reforms (in the form of draft legislation) should be made for Parliament to consider (Fourth Report of Session 2003–04, *Taming the Prerogative: Strengthening Ministerial Accountability to Parliament* (HC 422, (2004) App 1). The Labour Government, however, in responding to this report remained unconvinced that 'the Committee's proposal to replace prerogative powers with a statutory framework would improve the present position' (*Government Response to the Public Administration Select Committee's Fourth Report of the 2003–04 Session*, 2004).

- Lord Lester's (albeit unsuccessful) 2006 Constitutional Reform (Prerogative Powers and Civil Service etc.) Bill, would have placed executive (prerogative) powers under the authority of Parliament. Clause 4 of the Bill would have established a Joint Committee of both Houses of

Parliament to keep under review, and report to Parliament, the circumstances in which executive prerogative powers were exercised.

ACTIVITY

Exercise

Consider the constitutional advantages of the proposed reforms above.

11.9.6 The constitutional relationship between the judiciary and the royal prerogative

It is clear that owing to their residual nature, new royal prerogative powers cannot be created, as noted by Diplock LJ in *BBC v Johns (Inspector of Taxes)* [1965] 1 CH 32:

> **J** 'it is 350 years and a civil war too late for the Queen's courts to broaden the prerogative. The limits within which the executive government may impose obligations or restraints upon citizens of the United Kingdom without any statutory authority are now well settled and incapable of extension.'

Pre-existing prerogative powers such as keeping the Queen's peace, however, can adapt to the contemporary system of preserving the peace through modern day police forces (*R v Secretary for the Home Department, ex parte Northumbria Police Authority* [1989] 1 QB 26).

In historic terms, the courts supervision of prerogative powers amounted to recognising and demarcating their scope and existence, rather than investigating the manner in which they were used. The *GCHQ* case (1985) (see below), however, made it clear that the courts could legally supervise executive use of the royal prerogative in the same way that they reviewed the manner in which statutory powers were exercised. The *GCHQ* decision followed the earlier cases of *R v Criminal Injuries Compensation Board, ex parte Lain* [1967] 2 QB 864 and *Laker Airways Ltd v Department of Trade and Industry* [1977] 1 QB 643.

CASE EXAMPLE

Council of Civil Service Unions v Minister for the Civil Service [1985] 1 AC 374

This case is commonly known as the *GCHQ* case. In 1983 the Prime Minister (Minister for the Civil Service) issued an instruction pursuant to the Civil Service Order in Council 1982 that staff at Government Communications Headquarters (GCHQ) would no longer

CONTINUED ▶

be permitted to be members of trade unions. No prior consultation had taken place before the instruction was issued and the workers' trade union sought judicial review of the Prime Minister's instruction on the basis that she had a duty to consult those affected by it before issuing it (ie the duty to act fairly).

The House of Lords held that government action was not immune from the jurisdiction of the courts merely because it derived from the royal prerogative. On the facts the claimants would have had a legitimate expectation of being consulted prior to the issuing of the instruction. This was, however, trumped by national security considerations (ie, the risk of industrial unrest had prior consultation taken place). It was for the executive and not the judiciary to decide whether on the facts of the case the requirements of national security outweighed those of fairness.

The *GCHQ* case (1985) represents a watershed in terms of the prerogative as the House of Lords made it clear that the manner in which these common law powers were used was, depending on the subject matter, subject to supervision by the courts. Thus, some uses of the prerogative would be 'justiciable' (reviewable) whilst according to Lord Roskill others would be 'non-justiciable'. For example the latter would include:

- The dissolution of Parliament.
- Ministerial appointments.
- Making treaties (see *Blackburn v Attorney-General* (1971) at section 11.9.4).
- The defence of the realm.
- The granting of honours.
- Mercy (but see *ex parte Bentley* (1994) at section 11.9.4).

The category of 'non-justiciable' prerogatives attempts to ensure a constitutional demarcation between the separate roles of the judge and the politician as the exercise of the above powers have clear political overtones which are considered unsuitable for judicial/legal adjudication. The political and parliamentary supervision over the use of these powers may, however, be considered insufficient (see directly below).

KEY FACTS ☐☐☐☐☐☐☐

Historically, the courts confined themselves to demarcating the scope and existence of royal prerogative powers.

In the *GCHQ* case (1985) the House of Lords made it clear that the courts could supervise the manner of the use of royal prerogative powers providing the subject matter was justiciable (ie reviewable by the courts).

According to Lord Roskill some uses of the prerogative such as the dissolution of Parliament were not amenable to judicial adjudication.

11.9.7 The constitutional significance of the royal prerogative

It is clear that government needs powers which are analogous to the royal prerogative (eg to deploy troops quickly, to respond to international crises, etc). The question is whether there is sufficient constitutional control (legal or parliamentary) over the use of these powers. Royal prerogative powers raise the following issues:

• **The rule of law** – Brazier (the specialist adviser to the Public Administration Select Committee) has stated that:

Q	'Governments should not have imprecise powers. As a matter of basic constitutional principle the user of a power should be able – and if asked should be obliged – to identify the source of that power and to describe its nature and extent. Ministers should be required to do just that.' Fourth Report of Session 2003–04, *Taming the Prerogative: Strengthening Ministerial Accountability to Parliament*, HC 422, (2004) p 24.

The constitutional concern in relation to the royal prerogative is that there is no definitive list of these powers and their precise extent is not always clear.

• **Democracy** – The government of the day can make major political and constitutional decisions (eg declaring war) without approval from the democratically elected House of Commons.

- **Legal accountability** – Although the courts will review the manner in which prerogative powers are used, this is subject to the proviso that such powers are justiciable matters and so suitable for judicial supervision (ie they do not involve issues of political policy). Moreover, as pointed out by the Public Administration Select Committee, challenges in court necessarily come after the event, namely, after the prerogative has been used. Furthermore, s 21(1)(f) of the Human Rights Act 1998 prescribes that an Order in Council made in exercise of Her Majesty's royal prerogative is treated as primary legislation and so cannot be invalidated by the courts under the Act. Other uses of the prerogative (eg other than Orders in Council), however, do have to comply with the strictures of the articles of the European Convention.

- **The separation of powers** – The principle of justiciabilty is a judicial construction. It ensures that the judges act in a self-restrained manner and do not trespass onto the function of the executive who have been constitutionally charged with the responsibility for administering public policy and making executive/political decisions. Justiciabilty, therefore, on the one hand preserves the separation of powers between the executive and the judiciary, but on the other leaves certain uses of the prerogative legally unaccountable to the courts.

- **Political accountability** – Although ministers can be asked to account for the use of the royal prerogative, some aspects are exempt, for example, the dissolution of Parliament. In addition, as with legal challenges, the Public Administration Select Committee has pointed out that accountability to Parliament will come after the event as ministers are not legally required to inform Parliament before such powers are exercised.

The Labour Government's response to the Select Committee's report made the point that government ministers were accountable to Parliament for the use of prerogative powers, in particular through departmental select committees and the Prime Minister appearing before the Liaison Committee (see section 12.6.7). In any event, it noted that the Select Committee had itself recognised that Parliament could overrule a prerogative power with legislation and so 'Parliament is by no means powerless in the face of the prerogative' (*Government Response to the Public Administration Select Committee's Fourth Report of the 2003–04 Session*, 2004).

ACTIVITY

Essay writing

Explain the significance of royal prerogative powers in the context of our uncodified constitutional arrangements. Which aspects should be subject to judicial review?

Further reading

Barnett, H, *Britain Unwrapped* (Penguin, 2002), ch 2.

Benn, A, 'How Democratic is Britain?' in Sutherland, K (ed), *The Rape of the Constitution?* (Imprint Academic, 2000), p 33.

Bradley, A and Ewing, K, *Constitutional and Administrative Law* (14th edn, Pearson/Longman, 2007), chs 12 to 13.

Drewry, G, 'The Executive: Towards Accountable Government and Effective Governance?' in Jowell, J and Oliver, D, *The Changing Constitution* (5th edn, Oxford University Press, 2004), p 280.

Durkin, M and Gay, O, *The Royal Prerogative* (House of Commons Library, 2005).

Fourth Report of Session 2003–04, *Taming the Prerogative: Strengthening Ministerial Accountability to Parliament*, HC 422 (2004).

Nolan, Lord, 'The Executive' in Lord Nolan and Sedley, S, *The Making and Remaking of the British Constitution* (Blackstone Press Limited, 1997), p 33.

Parpworth, N, *Constitutional and Administrative law* (4th edn, Oxford University Press, 2006) ch 4.

Weir, S and Beetham, D, *Political Power and Democratic Control in Britain* (Routledge, 1999) Chs 6–8.

Websites

www.cabinetoffice.gov.uk
www.civilservice.gov.uk

EXECUTIVE/
PARLIAMENTARY RELATIONS ■

AIMS AND OBJECTIVES

At the end of this chapter you should be able to:

■ Understand the nature and constitutional significance of the constitutional convention of ministerial responsibility

■ Understand the role and effectiveness of parliamentary scrutiny of the executive through questioning, debates and committees

Introduction

One of the central constitutional relationships in the British constitution is that between the executive/government and the legislature. As we have a parliamentary executive, one of the constitutional functions of Parliament is to scrutinise government ministers in respect of their policy, administration and actions (whether individually or collectively). In constitutional theory, therefore, ministers are both collectively and individually responsible to Parliament. Government accountability to both Houses of Parliament is secured through various parliamentary mechanisms such as questioning, debates and select committees, all of which are considered below. In short, Parliament acts as a constitutional check on the executive and this is particularly important in the absence of a codified constitution constraining the activities of the executive. The balance between Parliament and the government has been described in the following way by Charles Kennedy MP:

Q	'An effective Parliament should be neither excessively obstructive nor excessively subservient.'
	Hansard, HC Vol 353, col 1109.

12.1 The constitutional convention of ministerial responsibility

12.1.1 Classification

The convention of ministerial responsibility is, arguably, the most important convention in our uncodified constitution, as it purports to hold the government accountable to Parliament (on constitutional conventions in general see section 4.13). In broad terms, the convention can be divided into:

- The convention of *collective* ministerial responsibility.
- The convention of *individual* ministerial responsibility.

Figure 12.1

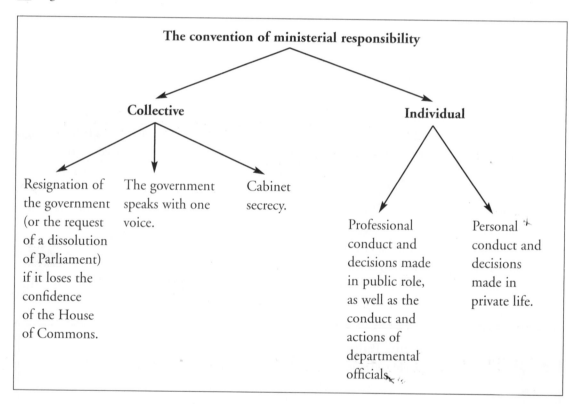

The convention of ministerial responsibility

Collective

- Resignation of the government (or the request of a dissolution of Parliament) if it loses the confidence of the House of Commons.
- The government speaks with one voice.
- Cabinet secrecy.

Individual

- Professional conduct and decisions made in public role, as well as the conduct and actions of departmental officials.
- Personal conduct and decisions made in private life.

12.1.2 The *Ministerial Code*

The *Ministerial Code* sets out clearly the constitutional responsibility of government ministers in relation to the convention of ministerial responsibility:

- Ministers have a duty to Parliament to account, and be held to account, for the policies, decisions and actions of their departments and agencies;

- It is of paramount importance that Ministers give accurate and truthful information to Parliament, correcting any inadvertent error at the earliest opportunity. Ministers who knowingly mislead Parliament will be expected to offer their resignation to the Prime Minister;

- Ministers should be as open as possible with Parliament and the public, refusing to provide information only when disclosure would not be in the public interest.

Ministerial Code, A Code of Ethics and Procedural Guidance for Ministers (Cabinet Office, 2005), para 1.5.

Source: www.cabinetoffice.gov.uk

The convention of ministerial responsibility should be seen in the context of the parliamentary mechanisms for holding the government to account (see sections 12.4 to 12.9).

It is worth noting that the convention of ministerial responsibility also applies to the devolved institutions. For example, in Scotland the Scottish Executive is both collectively and individually responsible to the Scottish Parliament.

12.2 The constitutional convention of collective ministerial responsibility

Geoffrey Marshall (*Constitutional Conventions* (Clarendon Press, 1986), pp 55–61) has noted that in essence this convention is composed of the following three elements:

- The government must resign or advise a dissolution of Parliament if the confidence of the House of Commons is lost (the confidence rule).

- The government is united and speaks with one single voice on policy (the unanimity rule).

- The discussions (and disagreements) within Cabinet should remain secret (the confidentiality rule).

12.2.1 The loss of confidence of the House of Commons

If the government loses a motion of no confidence, then by constitutional convention, the Prime Minister should either recommend dissolution of Parliament in order that a general election could take place (which could, for example, result in a different government taking office as in 1979), or offer his resignation with that of the government. If this were to happen, it might be possible for an alternative government to be cobbled together from the other existing parties in the House without the need for an election. The vote of no confidence is the only parliamentary mechanism for removing an unpopular government mid-term between general elections.

As indicated above, however, the practical reality of the convention is that the motion of no confidence is rarely successful. In fact, in the past 100 years it has been successful only three times:

- 1979 Labour government.
- 1924 (January) Conservative government.
- 1924 (November) Labour government (the very first Labour government).

Three factors can explain why the vote of no confidence is rarely successful:

- The electoral system generally speaking (though not always) will provide the government of the day with the support of the majority of seats in the House of Commons.
- Recalcitrant government backbenchers may vote against their government on various legislative proposals, but would invariably be reluctant to vote against the government on a vote of no confidence leading to the fall of that government.
- As an adjunct to the above point, on a very cynical, but practical, point it is arguable that government backbench MPs may not wish to trigger a general election mid-term, as there is no guarantee that they would be re-elected.

12.2.2 The government speaks with one single voice

It is important that a government is seen to be confident and united over government policy. In contrast, a divided government which is split over major policies will be viewed as weak and lacking clear focus and direction. This principle, therefore, enhances the accountability of the government to Parliament because it avoids ministers disassociating themselves with policies with which they disagree or which have subsequently become deeply unpopular. Speaking with one voice (and voting the same way), therefore, requires individual ministers to defend publicly each others' broad departmental policies, as well as the overall strategy of governmental policy. Paragraph 1.5 of the *Ministerial Code* specifically requires ministers to uphold the principle of collective responsibility.

The convention of presenting a united front raises the following issues

- Although major governmental decisions will be taken in Cabinet, junior ministers not party to these decisions will still be expected to defend them publicly. Further, even Cabinet ministers themselves who were not party to a decision made in a Cabinet sub-committee (see section 11.2.3) will also be expected to support it.
- If a government minister disagrees personally with the policy adopted by the government, he must either:
  (i) resign from office – thereby allowing him to criticise that policy subsequently, from the backbenches. In 2003 Robin Cook MP resigned from the government over foreign policy in respect of Iraq; or

(ii) accept the nature of collective Cabinet decision-making (ie that not all collective decisions made will have universal and total support) and support that policy publicly, even though he has private reservations about it.

• Historically, the principle has been departed from in exceptional circumstances. For example, in 1932 it was set aside in respect of a coalition government over the question of the issue of tariffs. More recently, the convention was departed from in 1975 when the Labour Government was split over its attitude towards continuing membership of the European Economic Community (which the previous Conservative Government had managed to secure). As a result, the incumbent Labour Prime Minister decided to set the convention aside for the purposes of an impending national referendum in 1975 on whether the United Kingdom should remain a member of the EEC. His justification was that this was a unique issue which divided the country as a whole (*Hansard*, HC Vol 884, col 1750). In addition to the above 'agreements to differ', ministers do not have to speak (or vote) the same way on free votes, for example, on moral matters such as the death penalty.

ACTIVITY

Problem solving

Do you think that the Labour Government acted unconstitutionally in departing from the convention in 1975, or does it just demonstrate that constitutional conventions can adapt to exceptional circumstances?

12.2.3 Cabinet discussions remain secret

It is a general principal that discussions within Cabinet remain secret. Paragraph 6.16 of the *Ministerial Code* states that: 'The internal process through which a decision has been made … should not be disclosed'. This buttresses the point made at section 11.2.3, as it enables all shades of opinion within Cabinet to be put forward freely (and without prejudice), safe in the knowledge that the nature and content of this discussion will not subsequently be disclosed publicly. The *Ministerial Code* is quite explicit on this point:

> **Q** 'Collective responsibility requires that Ministers should be able to express their views frankly in the expectation that they can argue freely in private while maintaining a united front when decisions have been reached.'
>
> *Ministerial Code, A Code of Ethics and Procedural Guidance for Ministers*
> (Cabinet Office, July 2005), para 6.17.
> Source: www.cabinetoffice.gov.uk

On the secrecy of Cabinet discussions see *Attorney-General v Jonathan Cape Ltd* (1976) at section 4.13.12.

12.3 The constitutional convention of individual ministerial responsibility

In essence this is composed of two elements:

- Responsibility for conduct in a minister's public role as a minister of the Crown and the actions of his departmental officials.

- Responsibility for conduct in a minister's private life.

12.3.1 Constitutional responsibility for professional conduct and departmental activity

Each Secretary of State will be head of a specific government department. As such, he will represent and defend that department in Parliament. Together with his ministerial team, he will answer questions during ministerial question time (see section 12.4.4) about the operation, policies and decisions made in respect of that department. In this way the Secretary of State will take the blame for errors or mismanagement that occur within his department, and protect the anonymity of his officials (see section 11.3.1). Government ministers, therefore, are not only responsible for their own decisions and actions made as a minister, but also for the actions of their departmental officials (also see *Carltona Ltd* (1943) at section 4.13.12 and 20.2.3).

12.3.2 Resignations due to ministerial decisions or actions made as a minister

Government ministers have to make executive and professional decisions for which they are responsible:

EXAMPLE

In 2002 Estelle Morris MP resigned from office as the Secretary of State for Education. She had previously, and publicly, committed herself to resigning if the government did not reach its literacy and numeracy targets by 2002. In addition, Morris also admitted that she was not as good a Secretary of State as she had been as an Under Secretary of State.

In addition to the above:

- In 1988 the Minister of Health (Edwina Currie MP) resigned after her comments concerning salmonella in eggs.

- In 1990 the Secretary of State for Trade and Industry (Nicholas Ridley MP) resigned for inappropriate remarks made about Germany.

- In 1986 the Secretary of State for Trade and Industry (Leon Brittan MP) resigned following the leaking of a confidential letter from the Solicitor General.

12.3.3 Resignations due to the actions of departmental officials

The classic example traditionally cited in this context is the famous *Crichel Down* Affair:

EXAMPLE

In 1954 Sir Thomas Dugdale MP resigned from office as the Minister of Agriculture. The issue concerned land ('Crichel Down') which had been acquired by the Air Ministry and then transferred to the Ministry of Agriculture (with the Crown Lands Commissioners subsequently administering it). Thereafter, a former landowner was refused permission to buy back the land and other landowners were not permitted to seek tenancies of it. An inquiry was established which criticised the handling by civil servants of this matter.

Dugdale subsequently resigned stating:

Q	'I, as Minister, must accept full responsibility to Parliament for any mistakes and inefficiency of officials in my Department, just as, when my officials bring off any successes on my behalf, I take full credit for them. Any departure from this long-established rule is bound to bring the Civil Service right into the political arena, and that we should all, on both sides of the House, deprecate most vigorously.'
	Hansard, HC Vol 530, col 1186.

Immediately following Dugdale's resignation, the Home Secretary (Sir David Maxwell Fyfe MP) reviewed the convention, which he stated comprised four categories:

- Firstly, a minister must protect a civil servant who has carried out an explicit order.

- Secondly, a minister must protect and defend a civil servant who has acted properly in accordance with a policy which has been set down by the minister.

- Thirdly: 'Where an official makes a mistake or causes some delay, but not on an important issue of policy and not where a claim to individual rights is seriously involved, the Minister

---

CONTINUED ▶

acknowledges the mistake and he accepts the responsibility, although he is not personally involved. He states that he will take corrective action in the Department ... he would not, in those circumstances, expose the official to public criticism.'

- Fourthly, where a civil servant engages in actions which are reprehensible (of which the minister disapproves and had no prior knowledge of), the minister is not obliged to defend what he believes to be wrong, or the errors of his officials. The minister is, however, still constitutionally required to 'account' (ie explain) to Parliament what had transpired 'and render an account of his stewardship'.

Hansard, HC Vol 530, cols 1286–1287.

Crichel Down, historically at least (although it has been subject to different interpretations), is regarded as the seminal case illustrating government ministers being responsible for the actions of their officials, although there have been few examples since of ministers resigning in such circumstances. For example:

- In 1983 James Prior MP the Secretary of State for Northern Ireland did not resign in respect of a break-out of prisoners from the Maze Prison in Ulster.

- In 1982 William Whitelaw MP (the Home Secretary) did not resign when an individual managed to evade palace security and access the Queen's bedroom.

One example where resignations did take place was as follows:

EXAMPLE

In 1982 the Argentine military invaded the Falkland Islands thereby triggering the *Falklands Conflict.* Lord Carrington (the Foreign Secretary and a member of the House of Lords) resigned together with his two junior ministers. Carrington stated that as he was responsible for the conduct of foreign policy, he should resign.

12.3.4 Constitutional responsibility for conduct in a minister's private life

Government ministers are individually responsible to Parliament for personal conduct in their private lives (eg of a financial nature). As noted by the Nolan Committee:

Q 'The public is entitled to expect very high standards of behaviour from Ministers, as they have profound influence over the daily lives of us all … Financial misbehaviour in particular matters to us all, because it strikes at the very heart of that confidence which people must have in Ministers and the motives behind their decisions. The same cannot normally be said of sexual misconduct. It is true that the private lives of Ministers may occasionally be relevant to the performance of their public duties, for example when their private conduct runs directly counter to some public policy, gives rise to embarrassing publicity, or involves a security risk'.

First Report of the Committee on Standards in Public Life,
Standards in Public Life, Vol 1: Report, Cm 2850-I, (1995), pp 47–48.

Following on from the Nolan Committee, the *Ministerial Code* states the following:

- Ministers must ensure that no conflict arises, or appears to arise, between their public duties and their private interests.

- Ministers should avoid accepting any gift or hospitality which might, or might reasonably appear to, compromise their judgment or place them under an improper obligation.

Ministerial Code, A Code of Ethics and Procedural Guidance for Ministers
(Cabinet Office, revised July 2005), para 1.5.

It could be argued that government ministers as individuals should enjoy absolute privacy in their private lives and that private activity should never be subject to public scrutiny. However, it can be argued more persuasively that a government minister's private affairs will be of public interest where these activities have an impact on his public role as a government minister.

Over the years there are a number of examples of government ministers resigning their office owing to their actions in their private life. Below are two examples:

In the context of financial activity

EXAMPLE

In December 1998 the following two ministers resigned:

- Peter Mandelson MP as Secretary of State for Trade and Industry.
- Geoffrey Robinson MP as Paymaster General (Treasury).

The latter had loaned the former money to help support the buying of a house. Mandelson later stated to the Committee on Standards and Privileges that the existence of the loan, which he had registered late, should have been made known to his Permanent Secretary 'so as to avoid the appearance of a conflict of interest' – which is why he resigned. Although he also argued that the House of Commons Register was not the only way to inform his Permanent Secretary (and others) of the loan.

In the context of sexual activity

EXAMPLE

In October 1983 Cecil Parkinson MP, the Secretary of State for Trade and Industry (he was also Conservative Party Chairman) resigned after it became known that he had made his secretary pregnant. Parkinson was a married man.

ACTIVITY

Question

Do you think that a minister's private life should always remain private?

KEY FACTS

Collective responsibility	<ul><li>Governmental resignation (or the request of a dissolution of Parliament) if the confidence of the House of Commons is lost (eg 1979). This is very unlikely in practice.</li><li>The government is united and speaks with one voice on policy.</li><li>Cabinet discussions should remain secret.</li></ul>

CONTINUED ▸

KEY FACTS

Individual responsibility for professional life and actions of officials	• Actions as a minister (Estelle Morris). • Actions of officials (Sir Thomas Dugdale), but few resignations since.
Individual responsibility for personal life	• In the context of financial activity (Peter Mandelson). • In the context of sexual activity (Cecil Parkinson).

12.3.5 Uncertain aspects of individual ministerial responsibility

The following four aspects of the convention are unclear:

- **The reality of modern government**

It is uncertain whether practically, it is possible for government ministers to be fully aware of what is going on inside their departments. Consider, for example:

- The size of modern government departments and complexity of modern day administration.
- Frequent Cabinet reshuffles. Ministers tend to be transient as inevitably they will occupy their ministerial posts for relatively short periods before being moved elsewhere (either in or out of government).

- **Next Step Agencies**

The chain of accountability between government ministers and Parliament has in recent years been undermined somewhat by the emergence of Next Step Agencies (see section 11.3.2), which are aspects of a department (like the Prison Service) which have been separated and reconstituted as an executive agency. These agencies have their own Chief Executives and are semi-autonomous in their affairs. In strict constitutional theory, however, according to para 1.5 of the *Ministerial Code,* ministers are to be held to account for the actions of their respective Next Step Agencies.

- **Resignation**

When should a minister resign? Paragraph 1.5 of the *Ministerial Code* (and the parliamentary resolution which the Code incorporates) makes it clear that a minister who knowingly misleads Parliament should offer their resignation to the Prime Minister. In what other circumstances, however, is it an obligation?

Today this issue is not clear and it has been complicated by the distinctions made below in relation to accountability and responsibility. It seems from the pattern of resignations in recent years that resignations tend to be concerned with personal misconduct in a minister's private sexual or financial life. In any event, the reality is that resignations are ultimately determined by extraneous factors: (the unpopularity of the minister, the lack of support from the party and/or Prime Minister, etc), rather than the actual event/decision/policy in question.

In fact, it is worth remarking that no ministers resigned in respect of the *Arms to Iraq Affair* (which in turn led to the Scott Report). In short, this episode concerned the relaxation in the late 1980s of government restrictions in respect of export controls concerning the selling of equipment (which was indirectly military useful) to Iraq. Parliament, however, had not been informed of this change in policy by the government and the Scott Report concluded that Parliament had therefore been misled. In addition, the whole episode illustrated the limitations of parliamentary mechanisms of scrutiny as, for example, the House of Commons Trade and Industry Select Committee had had difficulty in getting full information from ministers.

In the wake of the *Arms to Iraq affair*, in 1997 the House of Commons passed a resolution (now incorporated within the *Ministerial Code*) setting out the responsibility of ministers to account fully to Parliament.

Two final points to note in relation to resignations are that:

- A minister may be reshuffled to another department before it becomes necessary to seek his resignation.

- Even if a minister does resign from government he may rejoin it at a later date. For example, although Peter Mandelson MP resigned in December 1998 (see section 12.3.4), less than a year later he returned to the Cabinet as Secretary of State for Northern Ireland.

- **A distinction between accountable and responsibility?**

In modern times the following distinction has been drawn (by ministers) between accountability and responsibility:

- Constitutional responsibility concerns ministers being personally at fault and culpable in some way (thereby being constitutionally *responsible* to Parliament).

- Constitutional accountability, in contrast, concerns ministers not being personally responsible (personally culpable), but remaining constitutionally *accountable* to Parliament to account for what has happened (known as explanatory accountability).

Similarly, in recent years a distinction has also been drawn by ministers between:

- Being constitutionally responsible for general policy decisions.

- Not being constitutionally responsible (ie culpable) for their *operation* (ie the carrying out of that policy in a defective way).

For example, James Prior MP in 1984 drew a distinction between being responsible for policy, but not its implementation and so declined to resign for operational failures. Over a decade later, Michael Howard MP as Home Secretary also did not resign over prison escapes as these were considered operational matters in the Prison Service (see section 11.3.2).

This latter distinction is particularly controversial as it begs the question as to who is constitutionally responsible in such circumstances. It leads, arguably, to a gap in constitutional responsibility with the relevant minister merely accounting to Parliament as to what has gone wrong.

ACTIVITY

Quick quiz

1. What is the difference between collective and individual responsibility?

2. What is the difference between individual responsibility for a minister's private life and individual responsibility for a minister's professional decisions?

3. In what circumstances is a minister responsible for the actions of his officials?

4. What factors mitigate against the operation of the convention (both collective and individual responsibility)?

12.4 Parliamentary questions

Introduction

Government ministers are asked parliamentary questions in both Houses and these questions can be either in written form (the overwhelming majority) or asked orally in either chamber:

> **Q** 'The purpose of a question is to obtain information or press for action'.
>
> E May, *Parliamentary Practice* (23rd edn, LexisNexis Butterworths, 2004), p 345.

12.4.1 Oral questions in the House of Commons

Oral questions are questions set down for an oral answer on the Floor of the chamber. In essence, there are two types of oral questions:

- Oral questions to the Prime Minister.
- Oral questions to other government ministers.

12.4.2 Oral questions to the Prime Minister

Prime Minister's Question Time (PMQs) is the most visible and widely published manifestation of Parliament holding the government to account (whether it is actually successful is a moot point). It takes place each Wednesday for 30 minutes. The procedure at PMQs is that MPs can ask the Prime Minister an *open question* (eg 'If he will list his official engagements for that Wednesday'), but the real question is the *supplementary question*. For example, Charles Kennedy MP asked the following supplementary question:

EXAMPLE

'the Prime Minister acknowledged that the state of the railways today is worse than when he became Prime Minister. Will he address the obvious question: why is it that, five years after the shambles of privatisation, a Labour Government have not done more to redress the situation?'

Hansard, HC Vol 385, col 768.

Questions about specific aspects of government departments (as opposed to the general tenor of government policy) should be directed to the relevant Secretary of State, rather than the Prime Minister. In a typical PMQ session only a handful of questions can be asked in 30 minutes. For example, on 28 June 2006 a total number of 29 questions were asked. Moreover, six of these were from the Leader of the Opposition and two from the leader of the second party of opposition (the Liberal Democrats).

12.4.3 The advantages and disadvantages of PMQs

Advantages

- Although the open questions have to be tabled a few days in advance, the supplementary questions do not require notice. In this way PMQs can be highly topical. In the absence of notice, a Prime Minister will be tested on his competence over a wide range of different governmental issues.

- On average the Prime Minister is questioned for two hours a month, in contrast to other government ministers who are questioned on a rota for around one hour per month.

- PMQs are a well-attended televised gladiatorial set-piece at which the Prime Minister is visibly held to account by parliamentarians.

- A very poor performance by a Prime Minister in PMQs could affect his standing and perceived competence to govern both in and out of Parliament.

Disadvantages

- PMQs may be seen simply as a party point-scoring exercise where political comments are exchanged between party politicians. In this light they do not really achieve anything.

- The length of time available for questions is too short, the questions asked are too general and the answers are too brief (in contrast to written questions below).

- Sympathetic questions can be asked which draw attention to a positive aspect of government policy or achievements:

EXAMPLE

Siân C James (Labour): 'Will the Prime Minister join me in congratulating the Swansea division of the South Wales police on its excellent recent crime figures? ... I am sure that he will agree that those figures are worth celebrating'.

Tony Blair: 'I am very happy to congratulate the police in my hon. friend's constituency'.

Hansard, HC Vol 446, col 1477.

- Riddel (*Parliament under Blair* (Politico's, 2000) p 91) has suggested that the consolidation of two PMQ sessions to one (one of the first reforms undertaken by the Prime Minister) has resulted in a reduction in accountability. This is because the Leader of the Opposition can attack the Prime Minister only once a week as opposed to twice (the overall time allocated, however, is still the same as previously).

- The Prime Minister will be fully briefed and informed by civil servants regarding possible and probable supplementary questions which may arise (eg an MP's particular interest).

ACTIVITY

Question
Do you think that PMQs is an effective way of holding the Prime Minister to account?

12.4.4 Oral questions to other government ministers

All heads of government departments will be subjected to an oral question time session on a rota basis. For example, on 24 May 2006 PMQs followed oral questions to the Secretary of State for Northern Ireland. Oral answers can be shared between the team of ministers in the department. All government departments will be subjected to oral parliamentary questions approximately once a month.

The procedure for asking oral questions is to submit them at least three days in advance. These are then shuffled and a number will be randomly selected to be asked. The answers to the main questions will be drafted by civil servants for ministers to approve. The Speaker of the House of Commons plays a pivotal role in oral questions as he determines the pace and the number of supplementary questions (which must be linked to the main one) that can be asked (and by whom). In the questioning session mentioned above, a total of 31 questions were asked.

12.4.5 The advantages and disadvantages of oral questions to ministers

Advantages

- It ensures that each government department (and so the government collectively) is publicly held to account for their actions or omissions each month. It is a direct way of holding the government to account as answers must be given.

- It enforces accountability as government ministers must demonstrate knowledge and competence in respect of their particular department and policies.

- Each oral answer (as with PMQs) is printed in *Hansard* and so is a printed public record which can be referred to in the future.

Disadvantages

- Ministers will be well briefed by their civil servants in respect of the main as well as the anticipated supplementary questions.

- Supplementary questions which are not sufficiently connected with the main question can be ruled out of order (also if they are *sub judice*, etc)

- There is a lack of publicity concerning oral Question Time other than PMQs.

- Answers can be shared within a team of ministers and the rota ensures that they do not answer questions every week.

12.4.6 Written questions in the House of Commons

The vast majority of parliamentary questions are written rather than oral. This is due to the pressure of time on the parliamentary timetable as it would not be practical to expect ministers to provide oral answers to all, or even most, of the questions asked by MPs. The answers to written questions are printed at the back of *Hansard*.

12.4.7 The advantages and disadvantages of written questions

Advantages

- MPs can be more persistent about a particular issue as MPs are permitted to ask more written questions than oral questions.

- Written answers to questions will tend to be more detailed, focused and informative (and arguably less elusive) than terse and somewhat general oral answers. For example, consider the highly detailed table of information provided on supply teachers to MP Sarah Teather's written question: (*Hansard,* HC Vol 447, cols 2005W–2012W).

- It is arguable that written questions are more about seeking information than simply party point-scoring.

- Rogers and Walters (*How Parliament Works* (5th edn, Pearson/ Longman, 2004), p 302) have noted that one advantage of written questions is that it permits MPs to ensure that a substantial amount of information (which we would not otherwise be aware of) is put into the public domain. In this way a valuable bank of public information is created. On this point it is worth recalling one of Parliament's functions as identified by Bagehot, that of educating and informing the public (see section 9.1.1).

- Government departments are monitored by Parliament to ensure that questions are answered within a reasonable time and if not, they can be named and shamed.

Disadvantages

- Although answers are printed in *Hansard*, most people will be simply unaware of their existence.

- There are a number of ways in which an answer can be legitimately refused, for example, if it concerns national security, commercial confidentiality or is simply too expensive to answer:

EXAMPLE

Chris Ruane MP: 'To ask the Minister of State, Department for Constitutional Affairs how many Orders in Council were passed in each of the past 30 years'

Harriet Harman (The Minister) 'The information requested can only be provided at disproportionate cost'.

Hansard, HC Vol 443, col 1368W.

Similarly, in the House of Lords see the government's refusal to answer Lord Lester's written question concerning the pattern of compensation awards under the Human Rights Act 1998: *Hansard*, HL Vol 664, col WA191.

12.4.8 Oral and written questions in the House of Lords

As a number of government ministers sit in the Lords, questioning also takes place in the upper chamber. In this way the government is held to account in both parliamentary chambers. Questions in the Lords are as follows:

- Starred Questions (oral questions) – these consist of a minister answering oral questions together with supplementaries at the start of the day.

- Unstarred Questions (oral questions) – this is in practice a mixture of a question and debate session whereby a minister answers the question in a speech. A recent pertinent example is where Lord Patten asked whether the government considered that Britain needed a written constitution. (*Hansard*, HL Vol 664, col 1242). This was followed by an hour long debate between members and was concluded by the Parliamentary Under-Secretary of State, Department for Constitutional Affairs.

- Written questions – as in the Commons, members of the Lords can request written answers to their questions. Members can ask up to six written questions per day and the answers are published at the back of *Hansard*.

12.4.9 Urgent questions

Both Houses have procedures to enable urgent questions to be asked in exceptional circumstances on matters of public importance such as a major international incident. In the House of Commons the Speaker may allow such a question to be asked. For example, in March 2005 an urgent question was allowed regarding the nature of the Attorney General's legal advice to the government concerning military action in Iraq in 2003 – this resulted in the Foreign Secretary being asked a series of questions on this issue (*Hansard*, HC, Vol 432, col 1003).

Similarly, in the House of Lords such a question can be asked, but historically the Leader of the House (not the Speaker) determines this.

KEY FACTS

Questions		
Type	**House of Commons**	**House of Lords**
Oral questions	<ul><li>Oral questions to the Prime Minister (30 minutes/weekly).</li><li>Oral questions to other government ministers (rota system approximately once a month).</li><li>Urgent questions.</li></ul>	<ul><li>Starred questions.</li><li>Unstarred questions.</li><li>Urgent questions.</li></ul>
Written questions	<ul><li>Answers published in *Hansard*.</li></ul>	<ul><li>Answers published in *Hansard*.</li></ul>

ACTIVITY

Essay writing

Do you think parliamentary questions are effective in holding the government to account? Are written questions more effective than oral ones?

12.5 Parliamentary debates

Introduction

Debates concerning government policy, decisions and future intentions are a major way in which the executive is held to account by Parliament. The two Houses are, after all, debating chambers. In constitutional theory, debates allow members to probe and expose weaknesses in government policy as well as highlighting alternative policies. Ultimately, it forces the government to justify and explain itself in a more detailed way than parliamentary questions.

12.5.1 Debates in the House of Commons

There are various ways in which debates can take place on government policy:

- **Debate on a vote of no confidence** (see also section 12.2.1)

It is a key principle in our uncodified constitution that the government of the day must retain the confidence of the House of Commons. After all, elected MPs represent the people.

If a motion of no confidence in the government (a confidence motion) is set down it will be accompanied by a debate. Owing to the electoral system, which typically confers a government with the support of a majority of seats in the Commons (together with the party machinery which ultimately demands loyalty of MPs), such motions are rarely successful. If a government loses the vote, a general election will generally be expected to follow as the House (as a conduit of the people) has declared that it no longer has confidence in it to govern the country. Not only would the government morally have lost the constitutional right to govern, but in practical terms it would be impossible to govern as it would be unable to secure passage for essential measures such as the Budget.

The last government to fall losing a vote of no confidence was a Labour government in March 1979 (311 votes to 310). This resulted in the May 1979 general election and the election of the Conservative government under Mrs Thatcher (who had tabled the motion). Generally speaking, however, even though the vote of no confidence is one of the most important constitutional checks on the government – as it can remove a government during their term of office – it is rarely successful.

Three other points are also worth noting:

- Firstly, a defeat on a major Bill (eg the Finance Bill encapsulating the Budget) may be considered to be a *de facto* vote of no confidence in the government.
- Secondly, following on from the point above, ironically, a Prime Minister may use the issue of confidence *against* his own backbenchers in order to ensure that they support government proposals. In other words, the Prime Minister could warn that a defeat on a specific Bill would be tantamount to a declaration of a vote of no confidence in the government which would

result in the fall of the government. John Major, when he was Prime Minister, did this in 1992 in respect of the Bill incorporating the provisions of the Maastricht Treaty.

- Thirdly, a motion of no confidence can be directed at a single minister (very unusual) rather than the government collectively. It is highly likely, however, that a minister warranting such attention would have resigned (or been sacked by the Prime Minster) before this became necessary. For a recent example of an (unsuccessful) motion directed at an individual minister (the Chancellor of the Exchequer) see *Hansard*, HC Vol 459, col 165.

- **Set piece debates on the Queen's Speech and the Budget**

The Queen's Speech heralds the start of a new parliamentary session and it will set out the government's proposed legislative programme. This will be followed by a debate of a few days in which the government's proposals in general (precise details will generally not be available at this point) will be debated. Thereafter a vote will take place on the government's intentions and if this were to be lost it would represent a crisis of confidence in the government.

In the context of the Budget (ie the tax proposals for the ensuing year) the Finance Bill will be debated and voted on (as any other Bill) and if the government were to be defeated on this it would be akin to a vote of no confidence as a government cannot govern without tax-raising powers. The House of Lords also debates the Queen's Speech, but no vote is taken.

- **Opposition day debates**

Each parliamentary session, Her Majesty's Opposition is allocated 20 opposition days (these were previously known as Supply days) in which it can select the topic of government policy for debate. In this way the Opposition can dictate the government areas to be scrutinised and they are useful in exposing weaknesses in government policy. A highly pertinent use of one of these days was on 13 July 2000 (*Hansard*, HC Vol 353, col 1084) when the Opposition motion called for the introduction of reforms to re-assert the authority of the House of Commons and reverse the undermining of Parliament. This echoes a prevalent theme in public law that in recent decades the constitutional balance between the executive and legislature has shifted far too much in favour of the former at the expense of Parliament (whose function is to supervise effectively the government of the day).

- **Debates in the context of an Early Day Motion**

Early Day Motions (EDMs) enable a number of like-minded MPs to publicise and canvass further support for specific issues. For example, in June 2006 they embraced such topics as the government restricting funding to the Palestinian Authority (Number 2303).

The parliamentary reality of EDMs is that they will not in general be debated, but merely serve as a mechanism for expressing the views of groups of MPs of varying sizes (who may sign up to the EDMs) on a particular subject.

- **Other debates in the House of Commons**

In the parliamentary timetable there are other opportunities on the Floor of the House of Commons to debate government policy:

- Daily adjournment debates (short debates at the end of the sitting day which involve a response by a government minister). In addition, a recess debate takes place prior to the recess of Parliament.

- Wednesday morning adjournment debates (these take place in Westminster Hall).

- Emergency debates (where a matter warrants urgent discussion, an emergency debate may be held, although it is very unusual).

- Government adjournment debates (here the government may enable a general debate to take place on a topic).

- Government substantive motions for debate (here the government may wish to seek approval for a policy or to allow debate). For example, on 18 March 2003 a substantive motion by the government was approved by the House to, in effect, authorise military action in Iraq. As noted at section 11.9.4, under the British constitution it was not necessary, legally, for the government to seek this approval for the use of military force under the royal prerogative.

- Debates in the context of the scrutiny of legislation – see section 12.7.

12.5.2 Debates in the House of Lords

Debates also take place in the House of Lords and it is often assumed that the quality and standard of these debates is higher than in the House of Commons owing to the existence of a wide range of (unelected) experts on various subjects. In addition, debates tend to be less partisan in the Lords because the party whips have less influence in the second chamber.

Debates in the House of Lords are as follows:

- Unstarred Questions (see section 12.4.8)

- Debates on motions (in effect in three forms):

  (i)   A debate on a motion to seek a resolution (ie to obtain the view of the House on a particular subject).

  (ii) A debate on a motion for papers (a general debate).

  (iii) A debate on a motion 'to take note' – for example, of the publication of a report:

EXAMPLE

Lord Holme of Cheltenham: 'That this House takes note of the report of the Select Committee on the Constitution on Parliament and the Legislative Process'.

Hansard, HL Vol 672, col 728.

Thereafter a two and half hour debate followed on the report which was concerned with improving the legislative process (it should be remembered that most legislative proposals are government Bills).

12.5.3 The advantages and disadvantages of parliamentary debates

Advantages

- They make the government justify their policies and explain their strategies, thereby enabling weaknesses to be exposed. They also provide backbenchers with the opportunity to challenge government ministers directly.

- Government ministers must retain the confidence of Parliament by demonstrating competence in their departmental area.

- They allow the Opposition to raise and explain alternative policies and provide an opportunity to influence government thinking or strategy.

- Debates become a matter of public record (they are printed in *Hansard*) and can inform and educate the public (see Bagehot at section 9.1.1).

Disadvantages

- Where a debate is followed by a vote (eg in the context of legislation, the Queen's Speech or a vote of no confidence), owing to the typical dominance of the government in the House of Commons, it will inevitably win that vote. In this sense it could be argued that debates change nothing as although the Opposition may 'morally' win a debate, they will invariably lose the subsequent vote.

- A number of debates, for example, Daily Adjournment debates, may be sparsely attended. Although all debates will be printed verbatim in *Hansard,* many debates will not be widely reported by the media.

- In terms of information and resources, there is a clear imbalance of power between members (of either House) and government ministers. The latter have civil servants working for them providing them with invaluable information.

- There is limited time within the parliamentary timetable for full debates to take place (less so in the House of Lords, and the use of Westminster Hall has relieved some of the pressure in the Commons). Moreover, in the Commons the length of debate can be curtailed. For example, a guillotine motion can be applied to the time which can be spent discussing and debating a Bill (see section 12.7.4).

- The question remains as to how influential parliamentary debates can be when it is arguable that the only political debate that really matters is the one in Cabinet (or more probably in a sub-committee) where government policy is being crystallised.

- Debates, particularly in the House of Commons, can assume a partisan party point-scoring exercise.

ACTIVITY

Essay writing

Do you think parliamentary debates are effective in scrutinising the government?

KEY FACTS

Debates	
House of Commons	**House of Lords**
• Debate in context of legislation.	• Debate in context of legislation.
• Debate on a vote of no confidence.	• Unstarred Questions.
• Set piece debates on the Queen's Speech and the Budget, etc.	• Debates on the Queen's Speech, etc.
• Opposition day debates.	• Debates on motions.
• EDMs.	
• Other debates in the House of Commons.	

12.6 The parliamentary committee system

12.6.1 Classification

Parliamentary committees are the key way in which Parliament can hold the executive to account. They can be divided into general and select committees. In broad terms, public Bill committees (a type of general committee) scrutinise legislative proposals, whereas select committees are more investigative bodies which produce reports. It should be noted that from the 2006–07 parliamentary session, standing committees were renamed as general committees (with those standing committees scrutinising Bills being renamed public Bill committees).

Figure 12.2

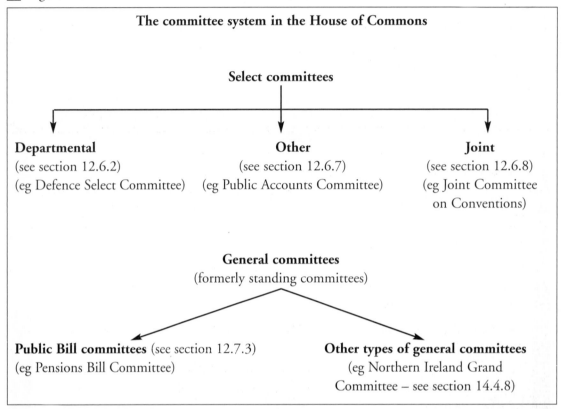

The committee system in the House of Commons

Select committees

Departmental
(see section 12.6.2)
(eg Defence Select Committee)

Other
(see section 12.6.7)
(eg Public Accounts Committee)

Joint
(see section 12.6.8)
(eg Joint Committee
on Conventions)

General committees
(formerly standing committees)

Public Bill committees (see section 12.7.3)
(eg Pensions Bill Committee)

Other types of general committees
(eg Northern Ireland Grand
Committee – see section 14.4.8)

12.6.2 Departmental select committees

Each government department is shadowed by a departmental select committee. In this way the range of government departments can be supervised:

Table 12.1

Government department	Departmental select committee
Ministry of Defence	House of Commons Committee on Defence
Department for Education and Skills	House of Commons Education and Skills Committee
Department of Health	House of Commons Health Committee

12.6.3 The function of select committees

<table>
<tr>
<td>

Q

</td>
<td>

'Select committees shall be appointed to examine the expenditure, administration and policy of the principal government departments'.

Standing Order No 152.

Source: www.publications.parliament.uk

</td>
</tr>
</table>

Select committees investigate issues (including collating evidence) and then issue reports on their findings. Their purpose is to supervise the activities, policies and decisions of their designated government department. In 2002 the Liaison Committee set out the following core tasks which select committees should seek to undertake (Annual Report for 2002, HC 558 (2003) p 9):

Core tasks of select committees

Task 1: To examine policy proposals from the UK Government and the European Commission in Green Papers, draft Guidance etc, and to inquire further where the Committee considers it appropriate.

Task 2: To identify and examine areas of emerging policy, or where existing policy is deficient, and make proposals.

Task 3: To conduct scrutiny of any published draft Bill within the Committee's responsibilities.

Task 4: To examine specific output from the department expressed in documents or other decisions.

Task 5: To examine the expenditure plans and out-turn of the department, its agencies and principal NDPBs.

Task 6: To examine the department's Public Service Agreements, the associated targets and the statistical measurements employed, and report if appropriate.

Task 7: To monitor the work of the department's Executive Agencies, NDPBs, regulators and other associated public bodies.

Task 8: To scrutinise major appointments made by the department.

Task 9: To examine the implementation of legislation and major policy initiatives.

Task 10: To produce Reports which are suitable for debate in the House, including Westminster Hall, or debating committees.

'The overall effect of the core tasks has been to encourage select committees to carry out the full range of activities currently open to them'.

L Maer and M Sandford, *Select Committees under Scrutiny*
(The Constitution Unit, 2004), para 22.

12.6.4 The composition of select committees

As a general rule (as set out in standing orders) the maximum number of MPs permitted to form part of a departmental select committee is 11 (although some, like the select committee on Northern Ireland Affairs, may be larger). By constitutional convention membership is restricted to backbenchers who are proposed by a Committee of Selection (which in itself receives nominations from the various party political whips). As with public Bill committees, select committees will, by constitutional convention, mirror the composition of the Floor of the House. As a result, the governing party will invariably have a majority of supporters on them. Each committee will thereafter choose its Chair and over the range of different select committees these positions will be held by members of the main political parties.

12.6.5 The powers of select committees

- **Specialist support** – Standing orders empower select committees 'to appoint specialist advisers to supply information which is not readily available or to elucidate matters of complexity.'

- **Accessing information** (persons and documents)

  In order to assist them in their work, standing orders enable select committees 'to send for persons, papers and records'. In essence, they have extensive powers of investigation to:

  (i) Request the attendance of a witness to provide evidence directly to the committee.

  (ii) Request that documentary evidence is provided.

Although select committees can compel members of the public to attend and give evidence (it would be contempt of Parliament to fail to do so), they cannot compel government ministers (or members of either House of Parliament for that matter) to attend. In essence, this is really a matter for Parliament as a whole to decide. Moreover, a government minister will determine whether a civil servant will appear, and even then, they will be governed by the 'Osmotherly Rules' whereby:

> **Q** 'Civil Servants who give evidence to Select Committees do so on behalf of their Ministers and under their directions.'
>
> Rule 40, Osmotherly Rules.
> Source: www.cabinetoffice.gov.uk

Furthermore, paragraph 41 reminds us that civil servants are directly accountable to ministers, and not to Parliament.

In general select committees tend to obtain the evidence (orally or in writing) that they seek. Two notable exceptions, however, include:

- Edwina Currie MP – she was initially reluctant to attend the Select Committee on Agriculture to explain her comments concerning the 'salmonella in eggs' issue. Although she did attend eventually, her attendance proved to be of little value.

- The Maxwell brothers refused to give evidence to the Social Services Select Committee in respect of the alleged mismanagement of pensions by their late father.

12.6.6 Select committee reports

Standing orders permit select committees 'to report from time to time'. The report is the essence of the select committee as it critically analyses the evidence before it and makes appropriate recommendations. These reports can be highly critical of government departments and by constitutional convention government should reply to them within two months. There have been concerns identified by the Liaison Committee about the timeliness of government replies to such reports (First Report, *Shifting the balance: Unfinished Business*, HC 321 (2001), paras 108–117.

In spite of the party political composition of select committees, it appears that most reports are unanimous. This makes a critical report of a government department all the more damaging as:

- It has been made on a cross-party basis.
- It is critical of the government notwithstanding that the governing party will ordinarily have a majority of support on the committee.

One problem with reports is that most are not debated on the Floor of the House. This is due to the pressure on the parliamentary timetable: a problem which is common to the other parliamentary mechanisms which aim to scrutinise the government (ie there is not enough time for debates, to ask oral questions, or to consider government legislative proposals in sufficient detail). The use of Westminster Hall has at least partly alleviated this problem. Nevertheless, according to Maer and Sandford there are only 30 opportunities in a parliamentary session to debate these reports: 6 on the Floor of the chamber and 24 in Westminster Hall (L Maer and M Sandford, *Select Committees under Scrutiny* (The Constitution Unit, 2004), p 39).

12.6.7 Other select committees

There are a number of specialised select committees.

- **Liaison Committee** – this comprises the Chairs of the other select committees who meet to consider the work of other select committees. In recent years the Prime Minister has agreed to attend this committee and answer questions twice a year.
- **Public Accounts Committee** – (see section 12.8).
- **European Scrutiny Committee** – (see section 12.9).
- **Public Administration Select Committee** – this considers, *inter alia*, reports of the Parliamentary Ombudsman (see section 21.3.4) and issues concerning the Civil Service.

12.6.8 Joint committees

There are also a number of joint committees which involve members from both Houses of Parliament. For example:

- **Joint Committee on Human Rights** – this considers, *inter alia,* remedial orders made by ministers under s 10 of the Human Rights Act 1998. In addition, it examines the nature and content of Bills with a view to highlighting any issues of human rights which its provisions raise (on the Human Rights Act 1998 see Chapter 17).

- **Joint Committee on Statutory Instruments** – this considers Statutory Instruments (see section 12.7.5).

- **Joint Committee on Conventions** – this was established in 2006 to consider the practicality of codifying the constitutional conventions which regulate the two parliamentary Houses (see section 22.6.2).

12.6.9 Committees in the House of Lords

The House of Lords has its own separate system of committees. For the purpose of scrutinising the government the following are particularly important:

- **House of Lords Select Committee on the Constitution** – This committee is charged with the function of examining the constitutional implications of all public Bills (including, therefore, government Bills).

- **European Union Select Committee** – This committee considers European documents and other European Union matters (see section 12.9).

- **House of Lords Select Committee on the Merits of Statutory Instruments** – (see section 12.7.5).

12.6.10 The advantages and disadvantages of select committees

Advantages

- They allow focused and in-depth examination of government departmental policy and activity in a way which is not possible through parliamentary questions or debates.

- As select committees are appointed for the duration of the parliamentary session (contrast, *ad hoc* public Bill committees), it enables their members to develop specialist knowledge in a specific area of government administration.

- They have discretion as to what they will investigate and how they will do so. Indeed, they can be very useful in investigating topical issues. For example, in August 2006 the Defence Committee issued a report on the situation in Iraq (13th Report of 2005–06, *UK Operations in Iraq*, HC 1241 (2006)).

- Select Committees give backbenchers an enhanced role in holding the government to account and they tend to work on a non-partisan basis so that MPs of all political colours will work together as 'parliamentarians'. The cross-party political consensus of a report can prove particularly embarrassing for a government.

- Their reports, which contain written and oral evidence, provide useful public records of information on aspects of government policy (and other issues) which would otherwise not have been publicised.

- The reports of select committees can be used in the context of the legislative process to help inform and influence debate on the provisions of a Bill. For example, the House of Commons Public Administration Select Committee produced a useful and informative report on the Legislative and Regulatory Reform Bill as it was proceeding through Parliament (Third Report of Session 2005–06, Legislative and Regulatory Reform Bill, HC 1033 (2006)).

- Their reports can inform and influence current political debate concerning, *inter alia,* the exercise of governmental powers and draw media attention to them. For example, in July 2006 the House of Lords Select Committee on the Constitution issued a report reviewing the government's use of the royal prerogative in times of war and put forward a number of recommendations (15th Report of Session 2005–06, *Waging War: Parliament's role and responsibility* HL Paper 236-I (2006)). Also see the criticism of the government made by the Public Administration Select Committee for resisting the findings of the Ombudsman (see section 21.3.4).

- Governments, by constitutional convention, are expected to respond to reports, thereby forcing a government to explain itself in the wake of a highly critical report.

- Finally, according to the Select Committee on Modernisation of the House of Commons:

Q	'Our conclusion is that the select committees have served Parliament and the public well. They have enabled Members of Parliament to hold the Executive to account through more rigorous scrutiny than is possible on the floor of the House and they have brought before the public matters which otherwise might have remained concealed'.
	First Report of Session 2001–02, HC 224 (2002), para 59.

Disadvantages

- In terms of effective powers, they are the poor relation to the United States' Congressional Committees (Appropriation Committees) which can in effect withhold money from the administration if dissatisfied with departmental performance.

- On occasions select committees do not get access to the information that they seek. The *Arms to Iraq Affair* illustrated the limitations of the select committee system to obtain information (see section 12.3.5).

- Its reports are mere recommendations which a very confident government may be able to ignore. Select committees lack teeth because they cannot enforce their findings. Moreover, most select committee reports are not even debated which results in a lack of publicity for their work.

- Although they are empowered to appoint specialist staff, it is arguable that select committees need more resources to assist them in their deliberations. In contrast, government ministers have the full support of their departments. Although in May 2002 the House of Commons did approve a resolution including extra resources for select committees (*Hansard*, HC Vol 385, col 648ff).

- In terms of composition, it is arguable that the party political whips exert too powerful a control over the composition of select committees. Having said that, membership nominations are ultimately approved by the House and in 2001 the House resisted attempts to remove two highly regarded former committee Chairs (Gwyneth Dunwoody and Donald Anderson MPs) from membership of their respective select committees. A revised membership list subsequently included them. This again illustrates that, ultimately, powers lies with the backbenchers, should they choose to exercise it.

ACTIVITY

Quick quiz

1. What do select committees do?

2. What powers do select committees have?

3. What are the advantages and disadvantages of select committees in terms of holding the government to account?

12.7 Scrutiny during the legislative process

Introduction

The vast majority of Bills introduced in Parliament are initiated by the executive (government Bills) and during the course of their various stages they will be subject to scrutiny by both Houses of Parliament. The examination and scrutiny of a government Bill, therefore, necessarily means examining and scrutinising government policy as encapsulated within that Bill. Below is an overview of how the government is scrutinised during the law-making process.

It is worth noting at the outset that one of the criticisms made of primary legislation in recent years is not just the number of Bills which Parliament passes each year, but the cumulative volume of these Bills. For example, the Constitutional Reform Act 2005 is over 300 pages long and contains 149 sections together with 18 Schedules.

12.7.1 Draft legislation

In recent years the government has produced a number of Bills in draft in order that they can be subject to pre-legislative scrutiny. It is argued that this produces better legislation as controversial or technical issues can be identified and discussed at this stage prior to the Bill formally being introduced into Parliament. In fact, it offers the opportunity to influence the government's stance on the Bill. One criticism levelled against the Constitutional Reform Bill in 2003 was that such an important Bill had not been subjected to pre-legislative scrutiny.

12.7.2 The second reading

This permits the first opportunity for Parliament to reject a Bill with its general principles being debated and voted on (the first reading being a mere formality). Owing to executive dominance in the House of Commons, in general it is highly unlikely that a government would lose the vote at second reading. One prominent exception was the Conservative government's defeat on the 1986 Shops Bill concerning Sunday trading. At this time Mrs Thatcher as Prime Minister had a commanding majority of support in the House and her defeat was due to a significant number of her own backbenchers failing to vote in favour of the legislation. This illustrates that no matter the number of seats a government has supporting it, ultimately, it is the government's backbenchers who can break a government. This is the constitutional antidote to the 'elective dictatorship'.

12.7.3 The committee and subsequent stages

The committee stage

In the House of Commons the committee stage will typically take place in a public Bill committee which is composed of a small number of MPs (16–50 MPs). From the start of the 2006–07 parliamentary session the type of committees which were formerly known as standing committees were renamed 'general committees'. In particular, standing committees which were used to consider public Bills are now called 'public Bill committees' named after the Bill they are considering (eg the 2007 Pensions Bill Committee considered the Pensions Bill). The government minister sponsoring the Bill will be expected to defend it as it is considered in detail at this stage, however a number of factors favour him:

- Firstly, by constitutional convention the committee will reflect the composition of the Floor of the House, inevitably therefore, providing the governing party with a numerical advantage when voting takes place.

- Secondly, the imbalance of power between the executive and the MP is illustrated by the fact that the minister will have a supporting team of civil servants to provide information. Indeed, historically such committees, in contrast to select committees, were not ordinarily evidence-taking committees:

> **Q** 'Consideration of a bill is confined to the words in the bill and members who wish to draw on the services of informed and affected bodies do so on a personal basis.'
>
> 14th Report of Session 2003–04, *Parliament and the Legislative Process,*
> Vol 1 Report, HL Paper 173-1 (2004), para 125
> NB: See recent reforms below.

- Thirdly, unlike their departmental select committee counterparts, public Bill committees are selected on an *ad hoc* basis and not for the duration of a parliamentary session.
- Fourthly, only members of the public Bill committee can make amendments at this stage.

As noted by the Select Committee on Modernisation of the House of Commons, standing committees (now public Bill committees) have historically been one of the most criticised aspects of the parliamentary law-making process. Indeed, in its written evidence to the above Committee, the Hansard Society stated that many people argue that standing committees:

> **Q** 'fall badly between several stools: they fail to deliver genuine and analytical scrutiny of the provisions involved, their political functions are neutered, dominated almost exclusively by government ... they fail to engage with the public and the media (in contrast to select committees) and they do not adequately utilise the evidence of experts or interested parties'.
>
> First Report of Session 2005–06, *The Legislative Process* (HC 1097 (2006)), Ev 108.

It should be noted that in November 2006 the House of Commons standing orders were amended with the effect that a public Bill committee to which a Bill has been committed by virtue of a programme order, shall have the power to send for persons, papers and records – this is analogous to the powers of a select committee, see section 12.6.5 (Legislative Process – Standing Orders).

In the House of Lords, the committee stage takes place on the Floor of the House allowing more peers to be involved in scrutinising the Bill.

The committee stage and constitutional Bills

It should be noted that by constitutional convention in the House of Commons a Bill of *first class* constitutional importance would be committed to a Committee of the Whole House, rather than to a smaller public Bill committee. Hazell ('Time for a New Convention: Parliamentary Scrutiny of Constitutional Bills 1997–2005' [2006] PL 247) identified and examined the legislative process for 55 Bills considered to be of constitutional importance between 1997 and 2005 (a period of dramatic reform of the constitution). He noted that there was a strong presumption that Bills of first class constitutional importance (eg those dealing with devolution, referendums, Europe, Parliament and human rights) would be considered on the Floor of the chamber. In contrast, those Bills not counting as first class (eg immigration, the court system, freedom of information, etc.) were referred to standing committees. A second (intermediate) group of Bills (some first class and some not) involving subjects such as elections, emergencies and Northern Ireland, involved a mixture of standing committees and committees of the Whole House (with urgent Bills on these matters being taken on the Floor of the House).

As pointed out by Hazell, the advantages of consideration by a Committee of the Whole House is that it allows more members (and a greater range of them) to contribute to the examination of the Bill. However, committee stages on the Floor tend to be shorter than those in a standing committee and as a result there is a limited number of amendments that can be moved and debated.

Report stage

This provides another opportunity to scrutinise the Bill and influence it by proposing amendments.

Third reading

This is typically a short session with limited opportunities to influence the Bill, although in the House of Lords amendments can be made.

12.7.4 Procedural matters

The following factors favour the government in the legislative process:

- They control the parliamentary timetable and the scheduling of Bills. In recent years, however, there has been the introduction of 'programme motions' – theoretically a more consensual and systematic use of parliamentary time.

- In the House of Commons the government can use, for example, the guillotine motion (an Allocation of Time Motion) to restrict debate and scrutiny of a Bill by providing that proceedings on the Bill end once a stated time has been reached (although now over-taken somewhat by the above motions).

- As noted at section 10.10.1, under the Parliament Acts 1911 and 1949 the House of Commons (controlled by the executive) can in any event ultimately reject any amendments made by the House of Lords.

There are some procedural differences in the way that the two Houses process legislation and these are indicated below:

- The committee stage in the House of Lords is taken on the 'Floor of the House', whereas in the Commons it takes place in a smaller public Bill committee.

- The government has more control over the legislative timetable in the Commons than in the Lords.

- Unlike the Commons, in the Lords all amendments can be (in theory and practice) scrutinised.

- Unlike the Commons, in the Lords debates are not subject to the guillotine.

Overall, it would appear that the balance between the government of the day wishing to see its proposals enacted as law, and Parliament whose role is to subject them to rigorous and detailed scrutiny, still clearly favours the executive. In short, if a government is determined enough, it can ensure that its proposals become law irrespective of the criticism levelled at it.

12.7.5 Delegated legislation

As indicated at section 5.7.2, when government ministers exercise a power to make delegated legislation they violate the principle of the separation of powers. As a consequence of this, there are a number of parliamentary controls over its use. Delegated legislation will typically be made in the form of a Statutory Instrument and so will be governed by the Statutory Instruments Act 1946. It should be pointed out that Statutory Instruments are now accompanied by an explanatory note to explain their nature and aid understanding. This should be seen in the context of the rule of law at section 6.3.2, which requires that law should be accessible and clear.

The enabling Act itself will indicate the type of scrutiny the delegated measure is to receive from Parliament. In essence, the Act may state that the instrument:

- Is simply laid before Parliament. This means that Parliament's attention is simply drawn to it. Alternatively, the instrument may not have to be laid before Parliament at all.

- Is subject to a negative resolution which means that it is laid before Parliament (eg for 40 days) and is subject to annulment by it. In other words, Parliament has to positively object to it or it will become law.

- Is subject to an affirmative resolution which means that it is laid before Parliament, but will not come into force unless it is assented to it. In other words, Parliament has to approve it in order for it to come into effect. A variant on this is that it is laid and comes into effect immediately, but requires positive approval (eg within 28 days) in order to carry on in force.

- Is laid in draft form (with a positive or negative resolution).

- Is subject to what has been termed a 'super affirmative' procedure (involving 60 day periods). For example, see the remedial orders made under s 10 of the Human Rights Act 1998 used in order to remedy an incompatibility with the European Convention on Human Rights (see section 17.7.3).

In addition, the following committees have a role to play in the scrutiny of delegated legislation:

The Joint Committee on Statutory Instruments
This joint committee comprising members of both Houses is responsible for scrutinising all Statutory Instruments. Under Standing Order 151 it can draw Parliament's attention to an instrument which, *inter alia:*

- Imposes a charge tax.
- Purports to have a retrospective effect.
- Appears to be *ultra vires.*
- Exhibits defective drafting.

Those instruments which only have to be laid before the House of Commons are scrutinised by the House of Commons Select Committee on Statutory Instruments.

The House of Lords Select Committee on the Merits of Statutory Instruments

This was established in 2003 and it draws the attention of the House of Lords to a Statutory Instrument (subject to a positive or negative resolution) laid which, *inter alia,* raises issues of public policy or does not perfectly achieve its policy objectives.

The House of Lords Select Committee on Delegated Powers and Regulatory Reform

This committee considers whether:

- any enabling Bill proposes to delegate legislative power inappropriately or
- the proposed parliamentary scrutiny of the delegated legislation to be made under the Act is inappropriate (ie it is insufficient).

Historically, the committee also reported on proposed Regulatory Reform Orders made by ministers under the Regulatory Reform Act 2001. This Act allowed ministers to use delegated legislation to amend primary legislation in order to lessen the burdens on business (see now the Legislative and Regulatory Reform Act 2006 in section 22.2.3). The Commons has a similar committee: the Regulatory Reform Committee.

The constitutional issues raised by delegated legislation

Firstly, Statutory Instruments statistically outnumber Acts of Parliament as over three thousand are passed annually. In 2005 only 42 Acts were passed. Most legislation therefore, is not primary and so is not directly made by the legislature (Parliament).

Secondly, it must be remembered that it is the government of the day which will draft the enabling Bill. This means that (unless the Bill is amended), it will determine the degree of parliamentary control and supervision that is to be exercised over government ministers making Statutory Instruments under the legislation. It is, therefore, not surprising that only around one tenth of Statutory Instruments are the subject of a positive resolution.

Thirdly, parliamentary time is limited and negative resolutions rely on the willingness of parliamentarians to examine these instruments. This is another reason why positive resolutions are not used often.

Fourthly, debates on negative or positive resolutions may take place on the Floor of the House of Commons or in a delegated legislation committee – a type of general committee (formerly known as a standing committee).

Finally, as observed by the Select Committee on Modernisation of the House of Commons:

Q	'To the extent that currently few SIs take up any Parliamentary time and that those that do are generally taken in standing committee, in a debate which may last up to one and a half hours, they have little bearing on Parliament's capacity to consider legislation.' First Report of Session 2005–06, *The Legislative Process*, HC 1097 (2006), p 8.

KEY FACTS

Committees	
Select committees	Appointed for each parliamentary session to supervise the activities, policies and decisions of their designated government department. Investigate issues, collate evidence and issue reports on their findings.
Public Bill committees	Appointed on an *ad hoc* basis to examine in detail, clause by clause, the contents of proposed legislation
Joint committees	Comprising members of both Houses to consider specific issues (eg, the Joint Committee on Statutory Instruments)

ACTIVITY

Essay writing

Compare and contrast how primary and delegated legislation is scrutinised by Parliament. How effective is that scrutiny?

12.8 Scrutiny in the context of finance

Below is a very brief outline of how government is scrutinised in financial matters. It should be noted that financial matters are in essence determined by the House of Commons as it contains elected representatives.

Past expenditure

In terms of public money spent, government departments are monitored by the most important select committee in the House of Commons: the Public Accounts Committee. It scrutinises government expenditure (in terms of value for money) through the examination of audits made by the Auditor-General and Comptroller of the National Audit Office. This scrutiny involves assessing the efficiency of government spending and whether it has been used for the purposes authorised by Parliament. The reports made by the Public Accounts Committee will be subsequently debated in Parliament.

Future expenditure

In particular, this will involve the raising of taxes to pay for government spending in the form of the annual Budget (the Finance Bill) which will be debated and voted on in one of the major set-piece debates in the parliamentary calendar. It should be remembered that under the Bill of Rights 1689, Parliament must authorise the raising of taxation. In addition, the government will supply estimates (requests for specified money) and these are approved annually by Parliament via an Appropriation Act (and on an interim basis via a Consolidated Fund Act).

12.9 Scrutiny in the context of Europe

Government ministers attend meetings of the Council (Council of Ministers – which is the legislature of the European Community) and can commit the United Kingdom to European legislative proposals. Parliament provides extensive provision for the consideration of European law and proposals. In brief, two parliamentary committees perform this function:

- **The House of Commons European Scrutiny Committee** – which considers, *inter alia,* the legal significance of European documents and monitors the activities of British ministers in the Council. Historically, there are three European Standing Committees A-C (now types of general committees) which consider European documents recommended by the European Scrutiny Committee for examination.

- **The House of Lords European Union Select Committee** – which scrutinises European legislative proposals and the reaction of the British government to them. The Committee has a number of sub-committees, for example, Sub-Committee E considers Law and Institutions.

As noted by the Wakeham Commission:

> **Q** 'The United Kingdom Parliament already has one of the most highly developed systems in the EU for considering proposed European legislation and other proposals and for ensuring that Ministers are aware of the balance of opinion within Parliament before they commit the United Kingdom to any significant new position'.
>
> *A House for the Future*, Cm 4534 (2000), p 83.

In particular, the House of Commons European Scrutiny Committee will scrutinise government ministers before and after they attend sessions of the Council (Council of Ministers – see section 15.2). In the Council, ministers are able to commit the United Kingdom to legislative proposals and so it is imperative that government ministers are scrutinised effectively. In 1998 the House of Commons passed the *scrutiny reserve resolution* which constrains a government minister from committing the United Kingdom in the Council, unless the matter has cleared scrutiny by the European Scrutiny Committee (or which is awaiting a resolution by the Commons).

ACTIVITY

Essay writing

Overall, do you think that parliamentary scrutiny of the executive is effective?

Further reading

Hailsham, Lord, 'Elective dictatorship', *The Listener* (1976) 21 October, p 496.

Hazell, R, 'Time for a New Convention: Parliamentary Scrutiny of Constitutional Bills 1997 – 2005' [2006] PL 247.

Gay, O and Powell, T, 'Individual ministerial responsibility – issues and examples', 04/31 (House of Commons Library, 2004).

Gay, O, and Powell, T, 'The collective responsibility of Ministers – an outline of the issues', Research paper 04/82 (House of Commons Library, 2004).

Maer, L and Sandford, M, *Select Committees under Scrutiny* (The Constitution Unit, 2004).

Marshall, G, *Constitutional Conventions*, (Oxford, Clarendon Press, 1986). Chapters 4, 6, 13 and 14.

Sear, C, Strickland, P and Winstone, R, 'Departmental Select Committees', 02/35 (House of Commons Library, 2002).

Winetrobe, B, 'Shifting control? Aspects of the executive-parliamentary relationship', 00/92, (House of Commons Library, 2000).

Factsheet P1, 'Parliamentary Questions' (House of Commons Parliamentary Copyright, 2007).

Factsheet P2, 'Departmental Select Committees' (House of Commons Parliamentary Copyright, 2007).

Factsheet L7, 'Statutory Instruments' (House of Commons Parliamentary Copyright, 2007).

Factsheet L6, 'General Committees' (House of Commons Parliamentary Copyright, 2006).

Weir, S and Beetham, D, *Political Power and Democratic Control in Britain* (Routledge, 1999), Chapters 12–14.

Website

www.parliament.uk

chapter 13 THE JUDICIARY ■

13.1 Introduction and definition

'The public must have confidence in the impartiality, fairness and independence of the judiciary; otherwise they will be less likely to observe the law'.

Lord Woolf, *Shaping the Future*, www.dca.gov.uk 13 October 2004.

The independence and impartiality of the judiciary is a central element of any democratic constitution and as noted at section 3.4.9, it is a key characteristic of Britain's uncodified constitution. The constitutional function of the judiciary is to provide for the resolution of constitutional/legal disputes and determine the law laid down in both statutory and common law sources. Although there is a close connection between the two terms and the two are often used synonymously, it is common to draw a technical distinction between judicial independence and judicial impartiality:

• Judicial independence means that the judiciary is structurally separate from both the legislature and executive. In this way they can perform their judicial function strictly in accordance with the law free from any extraneous pressures (executive or legislative) to determine a case before them in a particular way.

• Judicial impartiality means that judges perform their judicial function in a strictly impartial manner without any preconceptions or prejudgement based on class, sex, education, etc.

In this way judges can make independent and impartial decisions.

13.2 The constitutional dimension of the judiciary

The independence and impartiality of the judiciary must be viewed in the light of the following constitutional principles/concepts:

13.2.1 The separation of powers

As indicated in Chapter 5, the British constitution does not follow a strict separation of powers. In terms of personnel, however, there has been a general separation between the judiciary on the one hand and the executive/legislative arms of the state on the other (s 1 of the House of Commons Disqualification Act 1975 prohibits full-time judges sitting in the House of Commons). Historically, however, there have been two prominent exceptions:

- **The Lord Chancellor** (an overlap of the judiciary, executive and legislature).

Before 2003 the Lord Chancellor sat as a senior judge, was a member of the Cabinet as a senior ranking government minister and (by constitutional convention) was a member of the upper House in Parliament where he performed the functions of both Speaker and a senior government spokesperson. As indicated at section 5.7.9, the Constitutional Reform Act 2005 has now reformed the office so that the Lord Chancellor will no longer:

(i) act as a senior judge (in 2003 Lord Falconer indicated that he would no longer sit as a judge); and

(ii) act as the Head of the Judiciary of England and Wales. Under s 7 of the Constitutional Reform Act 2005 the Lord Chief Justice became President of the Courts of England and Wales as well as Head of the Judiciary and became responsible, *inter alia*, for representing the views of the judiciary in England and Wales (s 5).

- **The law lords** (an overlap of the judiciary and legislature).

Part 3 of the Constitutional Reform Act 2005 (which is currently scheduled to come into effect in 2009) will remove the law lords (who act as our highest judges) from the upper chamber of Parliament and reconstitute them in a constitutionally and physically separate Supreme Court (see sections 5.8.3 and 22.2.1).

In terms of the judicial function, although historically the judges have performed this function exclusively, the following points need to be noted:

- **Tribunals** – The strict, formalised court system is supplemented by a system of tribunals (see section 21.1). These tribunals are not staffed by judges *per se* (although some are), but they do perform an essentially judicial function in applying legal rules to factual disputes (sometimes highly specialised and technical, eg Employment Tribunals). However, it should be noted that appellate tribunals do contain judges, for example, the Employment Appeal Tribunal. On recent and proposed reforms to tribunals see section 22.12.1.

- **The executive performing judicial functions** – The executive, in the form of the Home Secretary, historically has enjoyed powers to determine sentences (a judicial function) to be served by certain categories of prisoners (see section 5.7.6). In modern times, under the European Convention and Human Rights Act 1998, the Home Secretary's powers have been circumscribed, thereby realigning the constitution so as to accord with a stricter separation of powers:

CASE EXAMPLE

R (Anderson) v Secretary of State for Home Department [2002] UKHL 46

Section 29 of the Crime (Sentences) Act 1997 empowered the Home Secretary to determine the tariff (for punitive purposes) to be served by persons convicted of murder. Anderson sought judicial review of the tariff set by the minister under the Human Rights Act 1998.

The House of Lords made a declaration of incompatibility that s 29 of the 1997 Act was incompatible with Art 6 (the right to a fair trial). In brief, the determination of a prison sentence was a judicial function and Art 6 required such a sentence to be decided by an independent and impartial tribunal. The Home Secretary was not independent of the executive (in fact, he was a key member of the Cabinet). Referring to the jurisprudence of the European Court of Human Rights, Lord Bingham observed that:

 'The European Court was right to describe the complete functional separation of the judiciary from the executive as 'fundamental', since the rule of law depends on it.'

As a result of the declaration, the Criminal Justice Act 2003 now provides for the tariff term for those sentenced to life imprisonment by a judge to be exercised by the judiciary, and not the Home Secretary.

In discharging their judicial function, as indicated at section 5.7.10, inevitably judges will also exercise a *de facto* legislative function when they:

(i) develop the common law (which is after all *judge made* law); and

(ii) construe ambiguous and unclear statutory provisions.

ACTIVITY

Essay question

Do you think that the judicial element of the British constitution complies with the separation of powers?

13.2.2 Parliamentary sovereignty

As noted in Chapter 7, it is a central element of the British constitution that the Queen in Parliament is the sovereign law-making body and that the judiciary are subordinate to the will of the legislature. In short, in interpreting and applying legislation, the judiciary must simply give effect to the will of Parliament. Indeed, Lord Diplock in *Duport Steels Ltd and Others v Sirs and Others* [1980] 1 All ER 529 (for the facts of the case, see section 5.8.3), has made it very clear what the constitutional role of the courts is in relation to the provisions of a statute:

> **J** 'Where the meaning of the statutory words is plain and unambiguous it is not for the judges to invent fancied ambiguities as an excuse for failing to give effect to its plain meaning because they themselves consider that the consequences of doing so would be inexpedient, or even unjust or immoral ... It endangers continued public confidence in the political impartiality of the judiciary, which is essential to the continuance of the rule of law, if judges, under the guise of interpretation, provide their own preferred amendments to statutes...'

It has been a hallmark of the British constitution that, unlike in other countries such as the United States of America and Ireland, the United Kingdom judiciary is constitutionally limited. In other words, historically they have been unable to invalidate or challenge Acts of Parliament (but see section 7.7). Indeed, even with the advent of a new United Kingdom Supreme Court scheduled for 2009, this court will not be the constitutional equivalent of the United States' Supreme Court which can invalidate legislation which is inconsistent with the codified constitution (*Marbury v Madison* (1803) 1 Cranch 137). In recent years, however, the traditional judicial deference towards Acts of Parliament has to be revisited in light of European law:

- **European Community law**

As we shall see at section 15.6.2, the European Court of Justice has developed the principle of the primacy of European Community law which states that Community law has primacy over, and is superior to, inconsistent national law. As a result, in *ex parte Factortame* (1991), the House of Lords disapplied provisions of an Act of Parliament as being in conflict with overriding European Community law (see section 15.6.4). The requirements of Community law has also altered statutory interpretation in the United Kingdom with the British judiciary adopting the legal reasoning applied by the Justices in the European Court in Luxembourg (eg the teleological approach to interpreting legislation – see section 15.4.1).

- **European Convention law**

In strict legal terms the Human Rights Act 1998 preserves parliamentary sovereignty. Section 4 does, however, authorise a court to issue a declaration of incompatibility (see section 17.7) which, at least in a moral sense, could be viewed as the courts *questioning* an Act of Parliament for being inconsistent with the provisions of European Convention law. The point must be remembered, however, that Parliament itself has specifically empowered the courts to make such a declaration. In any event, although there may be political pressure to reform the law as a result of a declaration, in law, Parliament is free to accept or ignore such a declaration.

13.2.3 The rule of law and the protection of the individual

> **Q** 'I think the independence of the judiciary and the rule of law are very difficult to sever. It is the role of the judiciary, in practice, to uphold the rule of law, to apply the rule of law, to enforce the rule of law, and to do that they have to be independent of outside influence'.
>
> Lord Phillips (Lord Chief Justice), The House of Lords Select Committee on the Constitution, Fourteenth Report of Session 2005–06, *Meeting with the Lord Chief Justice* HL 213 (2006), Q7.

The judicial arm of the constitution must be independent, because, as they ensure that state bodies act under the law (thereby enforcing the rule of law), inevitably they will come into constitutional conflict with the executive (see section 6.7.10). The independence and impartiality of the judiciary is also inextricably linked to the efficient administration of justice and public confidence in the judicial system to resolve disputes fairly and impartially.

One aspect of the rule of law requires the judiciary to protect the individual. In the absence of a written codified constitution, historically the courts have done so by:

- developing common law remedies such as trespass (see *Entick v Carrington* (1765) at section 4.8.2); and

- interpreting statutory provisions in the light of certain constitutional principles which protect the individual (eg their access to the courts *Chester v Bateson* (1920) at section 5.7.2).

Under the Human Rights Act 1998, the courts are charged specifically with applying and upholding the Convention rights of individuals (see Chapter 17).

13.2.4 Judicial review

Judicial review is inextricably linked with the principles of the rule of law (the courts holding the executive legally to account) and the separation of powers (the courts checking and balancing the actions of the executive – see section 19.2.3). It is of paramount importance, therefore, that the judiciary are independent of the executive. In the absence of a codified constitution limiting the actions of the executive, judicial review helps to fill the void by requiring government officials to exercise their executive powers legally, rationally and fairly (see Chapter 20).

'The claim that the courts stand between the executive and the citizen, and control all abuse of executive power, has been reinvigorated and become a foundation of our modern democracy.'

J Steyn, 'The case for a Supreme Court' (2002) 118 LQR 382.

KEY FACTS

Constitutional principle	Role of the judiciary
The separation of powers	To interpret the law and resolve legal disputes.
Parliamentary sovereignty	To uphold the will of Parliament and give effect to its intention.
Rule of law	To uphold and enforce the rule of law, (particularly against the executive).
Protection of the individual	To protect the individual from state interference.
Judicial review	To hold the executive legally to account for the use of its powers.

13.3 The appointment of the judiciary

13.3.1 Judicial appointments

Historically, a member of the executive (whether the Lord Chancellor or the Prime Minister) has been involved in the appointment of the judiciary with the appointment thereafter being confirmed officially by the monarch. Under the Constitutional Reform Act 2005 (s 61 and Sched 12) a new Judicial Appointments Commission has been established (operational since 2006) to carry out the responsibility of recruiting and selecting candidates for judicial appointments in England and Wales. It is composed of a lay Chairman and 14 members who are as follows:

- 5 judges
- 2 professional members (one practising barrister and solicitor)
- 5 lay members

- 1 lay magistrate

- 1 specified office holder (eg a member of a tribunal)

In particular, special arrangements have been devised for the appointment of the Lord Chief Justice and Heads of Division whereby a panel of four members will be convened to include two judicial members.

In terms of the final court of appeal, when the new Supreme Court is in operation a Supreme Court Selection Commission will be convened by the Lord Chancellor whenever a vacancy occurs (s 26 and Sched 8). The Commission will comprise the following members:

- The President of the Supreme Court;

- The Deputy President of the Supreme Court; and

- One member of each of the following bodies: the Judicial Appointments Commission, the Judicial Appointments Board for Scotland and the Northern Ireland Judicial Appointments Commission.

Although the process is somewhat complex (it can comprise three stages), both the Supreme Court Selection Commission and the Judicial Appointments Commission will consider the suitability of individuals and put forward an appropriate candidate for the Lord Chancellor to accept or reject. Once the Lord Chancellor has agreed to a recommendation, his responsibility (depending on the type of appointment) is to either make the appointment or recommend the appointment to be made. It is of interest to note that there are no parliamentary affirmations of judges as the legislature does not take part in the appointment process.

13.3.2 Arguments against executive involvement in judicial appointments

The system of appointing judges is of immense constitutional importance because the individuals appointed must be considered to be constitutionally acceptable and legitimate. In fact, it is arguable as to whether the executive should have any involvement in this process at all. The arguments against executive participation include the fact that some of the judges appointed inevitably will be involved in reviewing the actions of government ministers at some point in the future (eg in the context of judicial review claims and actions under the Human Rights Act 1998). As a result, it could be suggested that conferring a member of the executive (here the Lord Chancellor who is a Cabinet minister) with the power to determine who is appointed to the judiciary is manifestly inconsistent with the separation of powers.

In 2003 a Bar Working Party noted, in the context of the appointment of High Court judges, that if the judiciary were to perform 'its proper role' this century:

> **Q**
>
> 'It must be protected by constitutional safeguards from the risk or even the perception that its independence might be threatened by the Executive. Put simply, it has become constitutionally unacceptable in our view that the judges should be appointed by the government of the day. We will stress that this is not an attack on the present or any past or future Lord Chancellor. It is a matter of public perception.'
>
> *Bar Council Working Party on Judicial Appointments and Silk Consultation Document*
> (The Bar Council (2003)), p 66.

13.3.3 Arguments in favour of executive involvement in judicial appointments

The arguments in favour of executive involvement include the following:

- It has been commonly said that if the judiciary were to appoint itself, this could amount to a self-appointing (and therefore constitutionally unaccountable) 'judicial oligarchy'.

- The executive (Lord Chancellor) is ultimately accountable to Parliament for any appointments.

- The Commissions established under the Constitutional Reform Act 2005 necessarily fetter the discretion of the Lord Chancellor to that of accepting or rejecting the candidate put forward by the Commission. Indeed, in respect of the Supreme Court, the original version of the Constitutional Reform Bill envisaged the minister selecting a judge from a choice of between two and five candidates. The Bill was amended as it was felt that this conferred excessive discretion onto the minister/executive.

- Other democracies have executive involvement. For example, in the United States the President selects proposed Supreme Court Justices (although these must be confirmed by the upper chamber of Congress: the Senate).

ACTIVITY

Question

Do you think that the executive should be involved in any way with the appointment of the judiciary? If so, why?

13.4 The independence of the judiciary

In the absence of a codified constitutional provision explicitly safeguarding and protecting judicial independence, judicial independence in the British constitution is protected in the following ways:

■ Figure 13.1

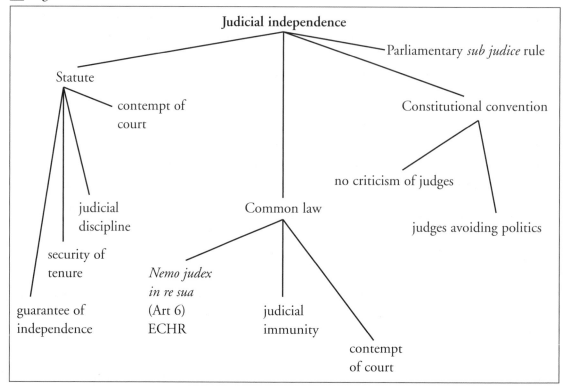

13.4.1 Statutory protection

- **Guaranteed independence**

Section 3(1) of the Constitutional Reform Act 2005 makes specific provision to guarantee the independence of the judiciary:

> **S** **'Guarantee of continued judicial independence** (1) The Lord Chancellor, other Ministers of the Crown and all with responsibility for matters relating to the judiciary or otherwise to the administration of justice must uphold the continued independence of the judiciary'.

This provision presupposes the existence of judicial independence in the British constitution as it refers explicitly to its 'continued independence'. In addition, s 3(5) aims to protect judicial decision-making from the influence of the executive as it states that:

> **S** 'The Lord Chancellor and other Ministers of the Crown must not seek to influence particular judicial decisions through any special access to the judiciary'.

- **Security of tenure**

Judicial independence is enhanced by giving senior judges security of tenure which means that their continued office is not dependent on the favour of the executive. Although the executive is involved in the appointment of the judiciary, they do not remove senior judges as this is achieved by the monarch following an address from both Houses of Parliament:

- Act of Settlement 1700 as amended by s 11 of the Supreme Court Act 1981 in terms of Court of Appeal/High Court judges.
- Section 6 of the Appellate Jurisdiction Act 1876 in respect of law lords.
- Section 33 of the Constitutional Reform Act 2005 in relation to future Justices of the new Supreme Court.

Moreover, as both Houses must act in concert, this serves to emphasise the constitutional significance of the modern House of Lords acting as a constitutional safeguard (see section 10.9.9) by protecting the senior judiciary from the executive. In this context, also see the Scottish case of *Starrs v Ruxton* (2000) (see section 14.3.10).

It should be noted however, that although the senior judiciary are protected, the lower ranks, such as circuit judges, are not as they can be removed by the Lord Chancellor (due to incapacity or misbehaviour), albeit in accordance with prescribed procedures under the Constitutional Reform Act 2005.

- **Judicial discipline**

Under Pt 4 of the Constitutional Reform Act 2005, the disciplining of judges (eg warnings, reprimands) involves the Lord Chief Justice acting with the agreement of the Lord Chancellor.

- **Contempt of Court**

The Contempt of Court Act 1981 preserves the integrity of the administration of justice and the right to a fair trial by prohibiting words which would prejudice court proceedings. For example, a newspaper revealing the previous criminal convictions of a defendant so as to prejudice the jury against him.

13.4.2 Common law protection

- **Judicial immunity**

In order for judges and the administration of justice to perform effectively, it is a common law principle that judges are immune from legal liability for things said during the course of a trial in their judicial capacity (*Anderson v Gorries* [1895] 1 QB 668). If this were not the case, the judiciary would be unable to ensure that the administration of justice was carried out. As pointed out by Lord Denning MR in *Sirros v Moore* [1975] 1 QB 118:

J

'If the reason underlying this immunity is to ensure "that they may be free in thought and independent in judgment", it applies to every judge, whatever his rank. Each should be protected from liability to damages when he is acting judicially. Each should be able to do his work in complete independence and free from fear. He should not have to turn the pages of his books with trembling fingers, asking himself: "If I do this, shall I be liable in damages?" So long as he does his work in the honest belief that it is within his jurisdiction, then he is not liable to an action ... What he does may be outside his jurisdiction – in fact or in law – but so long as he honestly believes it to be within his jurisdiction, he should not be liable.'

Although the House of Lords subsequently overruled this majority decision in relation to magistrates (eg 'it applies to every judge') in *re McC (A minor)* [1985] AC 528, the Court Act 2003 now protects them in terms of acting in or out of their jurisdiction (unless bad faith is shown in the latter).

- **Common law contempt**

Contempt laws protect the administration of justice and the integrity of court proceedings. It includes, for example, contempt in the face of the court which could involve a refusal to answer questions in court.

- *Nemo judex in re sua*

This common law legal maxim means that no man can be a judge in his own cause (see section 20.5.3). It ensures that when the judiciary are hearing cases they remain independent and impartial so that people have confidence in the administration of justice. In modern times the most important case concerning judicial independence is *ex parte Pinochet*:

CASE EXAMPLE

R v Bow Street Metropolitan Stipendiary Magistrate, ex parte Pinochet Ugarte (No 2) [2000] 1 AC 119

In *R v Bow Street Metropolitan Stipendiary Magistrate, ex parte Pinochet Ugarte* [2000] 1 AC 61, the House of Lords held that Pinochet (as the former Head of State of Chile) did not enjoy immunity from extradition proceedings in respect of crimes against humanity (torture and hostage-taking) allegedly committed during his periods of office as Head of State. The judgment was a three to two decision with Lord Hoffmann in the majority. Following the decision, Pinochet discovered that Lord Hoffmann was an unpaid director and chairman of a charity which was controlled by Amnesty International who had joined

CONTINUED ▶

the action in order to seek Pinochet's extradition. As a result, it was alleged that this link gave the appearance that Hoffmann may have been biased against Pinochet.

In the ensuing hearing in the House of Lords, the court set aside their previous decision on the basis that the principle that a man should not be a judge in his own cause applied to the situation where a judge's decision would lead to promoting a cause in which he was involved together with one of the parties to the case. As with the *Dimes* case (see section 20.5.3), there was no suggestion that Hoffmann was actually biased, but instead an appearance of bias.

J 'If the absolute impartiality of the judiciary is to be maintained, there must be a rule which automatically disqualifies a judge who is involved, whether personally or as a director of a company, in promoting the same causes in the same organisation as is a party to the suit' (Lord Browne-Wilkinson).

'One of the cornerstones of our legal system is the impartiality of the trials by which justice is administered ... everyone whom the prosecutor seeks to bring to justice is entitled to the protection of the law, however grave the offence or offences with which he is being prosecuted. Senator Pinochet is entitled to the judgment of an impartial and independent tribunal on the question which has been raised here as to his immunity'. (Lord Hope)

Thereafter, a differently constituted House of Lords decided that Pinochet could be extradited, albeit on narrower grounds (*R v Bow Street Metropolitan Stipendiary Magistrate, ex parte Pinochet Ugarte (No 3)* [2000] 1 AC 147).

As a postscript to *ex parte Pinochet*, in *Meerabux v Attorney General of Belize* [2005] UKPC 12, the Privy Council distinguished *ex parte Pinochet* and held that the *mere* membership of a professional body did not require automatic disqualification. In this case the chairman of the Belize Advisory Council who was also a member of the Bar Association (which was compulsory in this case) considered a complaint against a judge, but automatic disqualification did not apply as the chairman had no financial or personal interest in the outcome of the case. In addition, he had not taken part in the processing of the Bar Association's complaints against Meerabux.

In *Locabail (UK) Ltd v Bayfield Properties Ltd* [2000] QB 451 the Court of Appeal (Lord Bingham CJ, Lord Woolf MR and Sir Richard Scott VC) joined together five cases alleging bias and requesting the disqualification of judges and made it clear that:

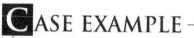

'It would be dangerous and futile to attempt to define or list the factors which may or may not give rise to a real danger of bias. Everything will depend on the facts, which may include the nature of the issue to be decided. We cannot, however, conceive of circumstances in which an objection could be soundly based on the religion, ethnic or national origin, gender, age, class, means or sexual orientation of the judge. Nor, at any rate ordinarily, could an objection be soundly based on the judge's social or educational or service or employment background or history, nor that of any member of the judge's family; or previous political associations or membership of social or sporting or charitable bodies; or Masonic associations; or previous judicial decisions; or extra-curricular utterances ... By contrast, a real danger of bias might well be thought to arise if there were personal friendship or animosity between the judge and any member of the public involved in the case, or if the judge were closely acquainted with any member of the public involved in the case.'

Three other cases are also worth noting:

CASE EXAMPLE

Taylor v Lawrence [2002] EWCA Civ 90

The Court of Appeal held that no observer would consider it conceivable that a judge would favour a party to the case (where no relationship existed), simply because they were represented in the case by solicitors whom the judge was using on a personal matter concerning a will.

CASE EXAMPLE

Lawal v Northern Spirit Ltd [2003] UKHL 35

The House of Lords held that an informed observer would conclude that there was a real possibility that a lay member of an Employment Appeal Tribunal might be biased (subconsciously) where counsel appearing before them had previously sat with them as a part-time judge. As a result, the court noted that this practice should be discontinued.

CASE EXAMPLE

AWG Group Ltd and another v Morrison and another **[2006] EWCA Civ 6**

The Court of Appeal held that a judge should have disqualified himself from presiding over a case where on the eve of the trial he discovered that he was a long-standing family acquaintance of a witness which the claimant wished to call. The judge accepted the claimant's proposal not to call the witness but to call other witnesses instead and he was concerned about the disruption and cost in recusing himself from the case at this late stage. He had concluded that there was too small a risk that the case would change during the trial which would require him not to continue hearing it. In the Court of Appeal Mummery LJ, however, pointed out that:

> 'Inconvenience, costs and delay do not, however, count in a case where the principle of judicial impartiality is properly invoked. This is because it is *the* fundamental principle of justice, both at common law and under article 6 of the Convention for the Protection of Human Rights. If, on an assessment of all the relevant circumstances, the conclusion is that the principle either has been, or will be, breached, the judge is automatically disqualified from hearing the case. It is not a discretionary case management decision reached by weighing various relevant factors in the balance.'

13.4.3 Parliamentary protection

- *The sub judice* resolution

It is a rule of Parliament that members of either House do not discuss or comment on matters which are 'active' in the court system (this includes both civil and criminal matters). This is known as the *sub judice* resolution which has been reaffirmed in 2001 in the House of Commons and 2000 in the Lords. This rule is in practice the parliamentary corollary of contempt of court law as it protects the integrity of the administration of justice and the independence of the judiciary. It should be remembered that parliamentary members are not liable for things said in Parliament and so the contempt laws do not apply to them (see section 8.6).

- **Remuneration**

Judicial salaries are relatively high, which ensures that appropriate candidates will apply and discourages bribery. In addition, judicial salaries are drawn from the Consolidated Fund Service which means that there is constant provision for them. They are also not subject to reduction by the government, acting unilaterally.

- **Constitutional convention** (see directly below).

13.4.4 Protection through constitutional convention

By convention the judiciary are not individually criticised in Parliament as this could lead to an erosion in public respect for, and confidence in, judges. An exception applies where the criticism of conduct is on a substantive motion.

In addition, judges (though obviously having private political views) do not become overtly involved in politics.

ACTIVITY

Essay writing

Explain the different ways in which the independence of the judiciary is secured. Do you think that these methods achieve true independence?

13.5 Judicial accountability

Although judges are independent and impartial in our constitution, this does not mean that they are constitutionally unaccountable (this in itself would violate the rule of law). As indicated above, the senior judiciary can be removed by an address from both Houses of Parliament (the lower ranks by the Lord Chancellor) and they can be subject to disciplinary proceedings. In addition, judicial advancement is dependent upon merit and ability rather than favour. Moreover, as pointed out by Bradley ('The constitutional position of the judiciary' in D Feldman (ed), *English Public Law*, p 343), judges are accountable in the following ways:

- The court process is in public (in general).

- Judges must take cognisance of the submissions made to them during the course of a case.

- In general, their decisions can be appealed against to a higher court (or possibly be subject to judicial review – see section 19.3.2).

- Judges give reasons for their decisions and deliver individual judgments which are a matter of public record.

13.6 The perception of judicial independence, neutrality and impartiality

13.6.1 The composition of the judiciary

The current composition of the judiciary is largely dominated by a socio-economic group comprising largely white men from a narrow social and educational background (a description provided by the Commission for Judicial Appointments – the precursor to the Judicial

Appointments Commission at section 13.3.1). Indeed, in April 2007 in the senior judiciary there was only one female member of the House of Lords, three Justices of Appeal and 10 High Court judges (one of whom was from an ethnic minority). As a consequence, for some commentators this raises concerns about the actual and perceived neutrality of the judiciary. The argument is that owing to their narrow composition there is an inevitability that sub-consciously their judgments will favour the state and the status quo/establishment.

Some counter arguments to this are that:

- As professionals, when judges perform their judicial functions they leave behind them any bias/influences (sub-conscious or not).

- A significant proportion of the judiciary is female if Justices of the Peace (magistrates) are included within the term (in 2005 almost half of magistrates were female). Indeed, Magistrates' Courts process virtually all criminal cases in the legal system.

- The case law detailed in 13.6.2 indicates that the judiciary are prepared rigorously to hold the 'state' and executive to account.

Nonetheless, concern has been raised about composition of the judiciary:

- In 2003 a Bar Council Working Party report made clear the desirability of ensuring that there was greater diversity in the judiciary (*Bar Council Working Party on Judicial Appointments and Silk Consultation Document* (The Bar Council, 2003) pp 12–15).

- In 2003 the government indicated the need to do more to make the judiciary more reflective of the society it serves (*Constitutional reform: a new way of appointing judges* CP 10/03 (2003) p 45).

- In 2004 the Department for Constitutional Affairs issued a consultation paper into the current lack of diversity in the judiciary as a whole (*Increasing Diversity in the Judiciary* CP 25/04 (2004)).

- Baroness Hale (the first and only female member of the House of Lords) has consistently argued for a more diverse judiciary (Lady Hale, 'Making a difference? Why we need a more diverse judiciary' (2005) 56 NILQ 281).

- The Constitutional Reform Bill was amended so that (although selection would continue to be on merit) the Judicial Appointments Commission would be required to:

S s 64 of the Constitutional Reform Act 2005
'have regard to the need to encourage diversity in the range of persons available for selection for appointments'.

For others, however, there is no obligation to appoint judges reflective of the community, Sir Thomas Legg KCB, QC noted that:

> **Q** 'It is no part of the professional judiciary's function to represent anybody or reflect anything. It is different for the lay magistrates, for whom one qualification is, and should be, to reflect the make-up of their local communities. The professional judges, on the other hand, have the unique property of being at once a powerful branch of government and at the same time a highly-skilled professional elite, whose contribution depends essentially on their learning, detachment and wisdom, and not who they are or where they come from in the community. We do not choose brain surgeons to reflect the community. They are chosen on professional merit ... It is, and should continue to be, the same with judges. "Reflection" should not in itself be an aim of the appointments system. Nor do I accept the view that public confidence is undermined by the present composition of the judiciary, or that it could be improved by intervening in appointments policy to change it'.
>
> House of Commons Select Committee on Constitutional Affairs, First Report, *Written Evidence – Volume II* HC 48-II (2004), *Supplementary Written Evidence*, para 6.

ACTIVITY

Question

Do you think that from a constitutional perspective the judiciary should be reflective of society or do you agree with the view of Sir Thomas Legg?

13.6.2 Judges and civil liberties

Historically, the record of the judges in protecting civil liberties and holding the government to account has been variable at times (for example, see *ex parte Hosenball* (1977) at section 6.7.10 and *Liversidge v Anderson* (1942) at section 6.7.10). In recent years, however, there has been a measure of friction between the judiciary and the executive precisely because the courts have held government ministers to account, principally through judicial review proceedings (eg see *Anderson* (2002) at section 13.2.1, *ex parte Venables and Thompson* (1997) at section 5.7.6, *ex parte Fire Brigades* (1995) at 6.7.10 and *M v Home Office* (1994) at section 6.7.6).

All of these decisions indicate that they are prepared to subject the executive to rigorous scrutiny and protect individual rights. In addition to *A and others v Secretary of State* (2004) already considered at section 6.7.4, two other recent examples in the controversial area of terrorism further illustrate this point:

CASE EXAMPLE

A and others v Secretary of State for the Home Department (No 2) [2005] UKHL 71

This case concerned the Special Immigration Appeals Commission (established under the Anti-Terrorism, Crime and Security Act 2001) which processed appeals made by individuals against certification (and detention) by the Home Secretary who, reasonably, believed them to be a risk to national security and reasonably suspected them of being terrorists. The court held that in hearing such appeals the SIAC could not receive evidence against these individuals where it had been obtained by torture.

CASE EXAMPLE

Secretary of State for the Home Department v JJ and others [2006] EWCA Civ 1141

This case concerned the Home Secretary making control orders under the Prevention of Terrorism Act 2005, in respect of six individuals suspected of being involved in terrorism-related activity. The orders, *inter alia*, permitted them to leave their residences (a one bedroom flat) for six hours a day and restricted their movement to specified areas. The Court of Appeal confirmed the decision of the judge of first instance. He had held that the cumulative effect of the orders were that they were contrary to Art 5 of the European Convention as being a deprivation of liberty which resulted in the orders being quashed by him.

According to Dickson:

> 'All in all it has been a busy few years for the Law Lords in the area of human rights. My conclusion is that they have adjusted surprisingly well to the challenge of applying European Convention standards and that they have been supportive of human rights arguments raised in other contexts.'

> 'Safe in their hands? Britain's Law Lords and human rights' (2006) 26 LS 329.

KEY FACTS

Method of protection	Type of protection
Statute	• Constitutional Reform Act 2005 requires government ministers to protect judicial independence. • Act of Settlement 1700/Appellate Jurisdiction Act 1876 provide security of tenure for senior judges. • Contempt of Court Act 1981 protects the administration of justice and the right to a fair trial.
Common law	• Judicial immunity for things said and done in a judicial capacity (*Anderson* (1895) and *Sirros* (1975)). • Contempt of court protects the administration of justice. • *Nemo judex in re sua* – no man should be a judge in his own cause.
Parliament	• *Sub judice* resolution ensures active court cases are not commented on. • Character and motives of individual judges are not commented on. • Salaries drawn from the Consolidated Fund Service.
Constitutional convention	• Judges are not overtly involved in politics and political parties.

Further reading

Bradley, A, and Ewing, K, *Constitutional and Administrative Law* (14th edn, Pearson/Longman, 2007), chapter 18.

Bradley, A, 'The constitutional position of the judiciary' in Feldman, D (ed), *English Public Law* (Oxford University Press, 2004), p 333.

Dickson, B, 'Safe in their hands? Britain's Law Lords and human rights' (2006) 26 LS 329.

Flannery, L, 'In the eye of the beholder?' (2006) 156 NLJ 278.

Griffith, J, 'Judicial decision-making in public law' [1985] PL 564.

Griffith, J, *The Politics of the Judiciary* (5th edn, Fontana, 1997).

Lady Hale, 'Making a difference? Why we need a more diverse judiciary' (2005) 56 NILQ 281.

Lord Nolan, 'The Judiciary' in Nolan, Lord and Sedley, S, *The Making and Remaking of the British Constitution* (Blackstone Press Limited, 1997), p 67.

Lord Woolf 'Judicial review – the tensions between the executive and the judiciary' (1998) 114 LQR 579.

chapter

14 THE DECENTRALISATION OF PUBLIC POWER ■

AIMS AND OBJECTIVES

At the end of this chapter you should be able to:

■ Understand the nature and constitutional significance of local government

■ Understand the nature, type and constitutional significance of the devolved arrangements in Scotland, Wales and Northern Ireland

■ Appreciate the position of England in terms of the overall devolution settlement

14.1 Introduction

The United Kingdom has a unitary state. In constitutional terms this means that power is focused and centralised in the apex of Parliament (which is generally controlled by central government). Historically, however, power has been *decentralised* to local government (local authorities) to carry out governmental functions at a local level. Further, in recent years power has also been *devolved* to regional bodies in Scotland, Wales and Northern Ireland and London. These different levels of government can be illustrated by the following diagram:

■ Figure 14.1: **Tiers of government in the British constitution**

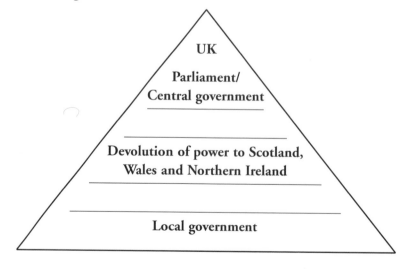

UK

Parliament/
Central government

Devolution of power to Scotland,
Wales and Northern Ireland

Local government

14.2 Local government

14.2.1 Introduction and structure

<table>
<tr>
<td>

Q

</td>
<td>

'Local government is a vital part of our democracy. The vast majority of interactions between citizens and the state take place through local government. It provides leadership for local areas and communities; democratic accountability for a wide range of public services; and is the key to effective partnership working at local level'.

Tony Blair: *Strong and prosperous communities, the Local Government White Paper*, volume 1Cm 6939-I (2006), Foreword p 2.

</td>
</tr>
</table>

Local government is public power which has been decentralised and delegated to directly elected local authorities which administer governmental functions at a local level. Local government has existed for centuries (and certainly precedes modern democracy in Britain). For example, during the nineteenth century local government boroughs exercised responsibility for the sanitation and education of their local inhabitants.

In modern times local government (now in the form of statutory local authorities, which being creatures of statute, are at the mercy of Parliament) has been re-organised a number of times in the past few decades. Indeed, the result is that today the structure of local government is highly complex (not to say confusing for the public) and asymmetrical (ie some areas having two tiers of local government, others having one). A very basic outline of the structure of local government in England and Wales is set out below.

Table 14.1

Structure of local government in the United Kingdom in 2006

England

Non-metropolitan county councils (outside London):

34 county councils

↓

238 district councils
(A tier exists below known as parish councils/meetings)

Note: government functions will be distributed between each tier, for example, social services (county), local roads (district), local footpaths (parish)

Metropolitan and unitary councils (outside London):

36 metropolitan district councils (in urban areas) (Some parish/town councils exist as a tier below)	46 unitary councils/authorities (where single tier councils have been introduced) (Some parish/town councils exist as a tier below)

London:

32 borough councils and the City of London Corporation (The Greater London Authority now exists as a tier above them – see section 14.6.3).

Wales:

22 unitary councils together with a number of community councils/meetings (effectively the equivalent of parish councils)

Scotland:

32 unitary councils together with community councils (effectively the equivalent of parish councils)

Figures drawn and adapted from D Wilson and C Game, *Local Government in the United Kingdom* (4th edn, Palgrave Macmillan, 2006), p 78.

Local government in Northern Ireland takes the form of district councils together with parish councils below them.

14.2.2 The functions of local government

What do local authorities do?

- **The provision of services**

Local authorities, historically, have provided a wide range of different services. For example:

Housing – providing housing in the form of council housing and making provision for the homeless.

Licensing – regulating taxis, cinemas etc.

Planning – making decisions in respect of planning applications.

Environmental health – refuse collection, pollution control, food safety (through inspectors) and consumer protection (trading standards).

Highways – maintaining public roads, traffic management and the provision of street lighting.

Social services – care for the elderly/disabled and provision for the protection of children.

Education – providing and maintaining schools.

Leisure – providing libraries and museums.

ACTIVITY

Problem solving

Find out the type of local government that exists in your area and the various functions that it performs.

- **An administrative role**

As indicated at section 5.3.2, local authorities are constitutionally part of the executive function of government (in a very broad sense of the term) and so therefore carry out government policy as expressed in primary legislation which has been passed in the centre at Westminster. In providing certain services, therefore, local authorities will be implementing government policy determined at the centre. For example, as a result of the National Curriculum introduced in the Education Reform Act 1988, local education authorities were required to publish a general policy statement on the National Curriculum being adhered to by the schools in its area.

In terms of an administrative function, local authorities have to make executive/administrative decisions, for example, in the context of land planning or licensing (see *R v Liverpool Corporation, ex parte Liverpool Taxi Fleet Operators' Association* [1972] 2 QB 299).

- **A discretionary role**

   Local government has been traditionally characterised by the exercise of an element of discretion which allows them to adapt the provision of services to local needs. For example, the needs of an inner city area will not be the same as the requirements of that of a largely rural area. Moreover, in this way local authorities can be innovative as schemes can be tested. For example, under the aegis of the Representation of the People Act 2000, pilot schemes were introduced by various authorities to test strategies aimed at combating voter apathy (eg all postal ballots, extended polling times, touch screen voting).

- **A legislative role**

   In order to carry out their roles, local authorities (like government ministers) are empowered by statute to enact a form of delegated legislation in the form of by-laws which apply to local areas (eg a local by-law concerned with banning alcohol consumption in an area). As local authorities are part of the executive, the enactment of such legislation is theoretically a breach of the separation of powers. However, the following controls do exist on their use:

   (i) They will be subject to ministerial approval.

   (ii) If the by-law is *ultra vires* it can be challenged in the courts by way of judical review proceedings (see Chapters 19 and 20).

- **Raising of revenue**

   Local authorities acquire some of their revenue through taxation (formerly the rates, in modern times: the council tax). Councils also raise money through charges for certain activities (car parks, swimming baths, etc.).

KEY FACTS

The role of local government	
Role	Examples
The provision of services	• Social services. • Street lighting.
Making legislation	• By-laws.

CONTINUED ▶

KEY FACTS

A discretionary role	• Piloting schemes (eg improving voter apathy).
Administrating government functions	• Education.
Raising taxes	• The council tax. • Charges for local services.

14.2.3 The advantages of local government

- In constitutional terms it represents a decentralisation of power from the centre to local areas. In this way it acts as a constitutional counter balance to central government and ensures that public power is not simply focused in government departments.

- Local government is an efficient way of administering government functions. Local authorities exist because central government could not operate without them. It would simply be impracticable for all services to be provided from the centre. As a result, local government prevents central government from being overburdened.

- It allows governmental functions to be specifically tailored to purely local needs and requirements.

- It promotes the constitutional principle of 'participatory democracy' whereby individuals can actively engage in the governmental process. Firstly, local authorities are directly elected and so they will be held directly accountable to local people for the public decisions that they make. This is equivalent to the European Community principle of 'subsidiarity' which is concerned with ensuring that decisions which affect people are taken at the level nearest the people (this ensures greater accountability). Secondly, local government makes the administration more accessible to people in the sense that they have a far higher chance of becoming a local councillor than they ever would have of becoming a member of the government in Whitehall (or even an MP for that matter). It therefore provides an opportunity for groups which are currently under-represented (eg women, ethnic minorities) to become involved in political decision-making. It is certainly the case that in terms of gender, for example, councillors are more representative of the population than MPs are, as almost a third of English councillors are female (contrast section 9.2.2).

- It allows a wider spread of political opinion to be represented, as some elected local councillors will not belong to the main political parties (eg the Green Party).

383

14.2.4 The disadvantages of local government

- The public appear to lack interest in voting at local government elections. Wilson and Game have stated that:

> 'The one thing that everyone thinks they know about local elections is that most people don't vote in them. They are right. Britain's 61.4 per cent in the 2005 General Election put us last among the 'original' fifteen EU countries in a listing of turnouts in most recent parliamentary elections…But that figure was roughly double the recent average for English local elections, and in that league table we are and have long been indisputably at the bottom'.

> *Local Government in the United Kingdom* (4th edn, Palgrave Macmillan, 2006), p 233.

One reason for a poor turnout could be that people are not interested in local affairs or that there is a perception that voting makes no real difference. Another explanation is that as local authorities have been stripped of a number of their powers in recent decades this has led to a misconception that local councils lack real powers. Finally, the cycles of elections can cause confusion with some councils being elected as a whole, whereas other councils are elected one third at a time. As a result of the very poor turnouts at local elections (although turnouts are higher in Scotland, Wales and Northern Ireland), it is possible to argue that local authorities may lack constitutional or political legitimacy to make decisions. Indeed, a similar argument is used in respect of the European Parliament.

- Local government results in a variation in the provision of services around the country. This could lead to a perception of unfairness.

- Local government may actively encourage narrow local attitudes as well as providing a platform for political representatives with extreme political views.

- Local authorities may be viewed as wasteful public bodies. For example, in the 1980s the incumbent Conservative government perceived local government as not providing value for money.

- Where the political colour of central government is different from that of local government (this will always be the case in terms of a number of councils at any one time) political friction may result. In particular, in the 1980s there was a clear ideological divide between the Conservative government and a number of Labour held councils which led to a deterioration in the constitutional relationship between the two arms of the executive (see section 14.2.6).

ACTIVITY

Exercise

Do you think that the advantages of local government outweigh the disadvantages?

14.2.5 The control of local government

Local authorities are controlled in the following ways:

- **Democratically**

  Local councillors are subject to re-election (every four years) and so the actions, decisions and policies of local authorities are accountable directly to the local electorate. The electoral system used in English and Welsh local elections is the 'first past the post' system which as we saw at section 9.4.4 in relation to the House of Commons, is a majoritarian system which can distort the wishes of the electorate. Scotland was scheduled to used the Single Transferable Voting system from 2007.

- **Legally**

  Local authorities, as public bodies, are subject to the law for their actions. They can be held to account in both private (contract, tort, etc) and public law (judicial review). For the purposes of s 6 of the Human Rights Act 1998, local authorities are public authorities and so must not act in a way which is incompatible with the articles of the European Convention.

  In addition, when a local authority enacts delegated legislation which is beyond its legal powers, it can be held accountable in the courts:

CASE EXAMPLE

Arlidge v Mayor, Aldermen, and Councillors of the Metropolitan Borough of Islington
[1909] 2 KB 127

A by-law, made under the aegis of the Public Health (London) Act 1891, by the Council was held to be unreasonable as it would have required a landlord to commit an act of trespass in order to comply with it (ie to clean every part of a lodging house three months a year).

See also *Nicholls v Tavistock Urban District Council* [1923] 2 Ch 18.

- **From the centre**

  Local government is ultimately at the mercy of central government. In short, it is central government (via its control of Parliament) which can set the legal, political and financial context and parameters in which local government must work (as well as providing advice in the form of circulars as to how their delegated powers should be exercised). A government minister will also approve and confirm by-laws made by local government. Moreover, a government minister may well enjoy a 'default power' which authorises him to step in and exercise the decentralised power instead, or transfer it (see *R v Secretary of State for the Environment, ex parte Norwich City Council* [1982] 1 QB 808).

It must be remembered that local government, unlike in other countries with a codified constitution, does not have any legally protected or 'constitutional status'. Local authorities are statutory bodies and they owe their existence to Acts of Parliament and therefore, in constitutional theory, could be extinguished by an Act of Parliament which has been pushed through by a dominant executive (see the Local Government Act 1985 which abolished the GLC, sections 7.5.4 and 14.6.3).

Central government (by virtue of legislation being pushed through Parliament) can re-model local government as it sees fit. For example:

(a) In the 1980s the Conservative government radically reformed the nature of local government whereby, *inter alia*:

- Local government taxation was reformed (the poll tax – Local Government Finance Act 1988).

- Local government became 'enabling authorities' regulating services provided by private bodies, rather than directly themselves. This involved CCT (Compulsive Competitive Tendering) whereby councils which had traditionally provided services would have to compete with private contractors in order to deliver that service in order to secure more efficient services. For example, it applied to:
  - Highways (Local Government Planning and Land Act 1980)
  - Refuse collection (Local Government Act 1988).

(b) Under the aegis of the Local Government Act 1999 the Labour government subsequently replaced CCT with a 'best value concept' (and now Comprehensive Performance Assessment). It also introduced new executive arrangements in relation to how councillors operated (Local Government Act 2000). Historically, the committee system within councils made many decisions, but the new executive arrangements involved making a clear separation between executive councillors (who would make executive policy decisions) and non-executive councillors (who would supervise the executive councillors). The main councils in England and Wales were required to adopt one of the following types of executive models (following consultation with the local population – another example of participatory government):

- Leader and Cabinet (after an election the council would select councillors to act as a Cabinet and elect a Leader).

- Mayor (directly elected by local people) and Cabinet (appointed by the Mayor).

- Mayor (directly elected by local people) and Council Manager (appointed by the council).

Control is also exercised financially as a significant proportion of revenue which local government receives is, ultimately, determined by central government.

* **Audits**

Local authorities will be audited in terms of their financial efficiency.

* **Ombudsman**

Maladministration by local authorities which result in injustice for individuals can be subject to investigation by the Commissioner for Local Administration (see section 21.3.7). Wilson and Game (*Local Government in the United Kingdom* (4th edn, Palgrave Macmillan, 2006), p 163), point out that the local Ombudsman does valuable work (the office received 18,700 complaints in 2004/05). The major complaints related to the following areas: housing, planning, highways, parking and social services.

14.2.6 The relationship between central and local government

* **Juridification**

Relations between the two arms of the executive have historically been characterised by co-operation and an informal partnership (albeit with central government clearly being the dominant partner). Between the 1970s and the 1990s, however, this generally consensual relationship broke down. For example:

CASE EXAMPLE

Secretary of State for Education and Science v Tameside Metropolitan Borough Council **[1976] 3 WLR 641**

A Labour Secretary of State for Education and Science using powers under the Education Act 1944, tried to direct a Conservative council to implement plans (already approved by their Labour predecessors) for the implementation of comprehensive schooling. Thereafter, he unsuccessfully sought an order to compel the authority to comply with his direction.

Loughlin has referred to central-local relations since 1979 as having become 'politicised' and 'juridified' (ie legalised) with the courts being resorted to in order to determine the legal boundary between them (M Loughlin, 'Restructuring of central-local government relations' in J Jowell and D Oliver (eds) *The Changing Constitution* (4th edn, Oxford University Press 2000) p 137). An example is detailed below:

CASE EXAMPLE

***Nottinghamshire County Council v Secretary of State for the Environment* [1986] 1 AC 240**

Nottinghamshire County Council and the City of Bradford Metropolitan Council unsuccessfully sought judicial review of the Secretary of State's guidance determining expenditure targets for local authorities. The councils had contended that the expenditure targets were unfairly low. The House of Lords held that the courts would not intervene on a matter of 'unreasonableness' (in the absence of, for example, bad faith) in respect of public financial administration which had been approved by the House of Commons.

KEY FACTS

Controls on local government	
Control	**Example**
Democratic	• Local electors voting at local elections.
Legal	• Private law. • Public law (including under the Human Rights Act 1998).
Central government/Parliament	• Setting the legal and political parameters in which local government must operate. • Financial control as significant revenue is secured from the centre. • Ministerial approval for by-laws, etc.
Audit	• The auditing of local authority accounts.
Ombudsman	• Maladministration causing injustice to local individuals.

ACTIVITY

Quick quiz

1. What is the constitutional function of local government?

2. Give examples of what it does.

3. How is local government controlled?

4. Explain how central and local government relate to each other.

14.3 Scottish devolution

14.3.1 History

Until 1707 England and Scotland had their own separate Parliaments. The Union with Scotland Act 1706 (passed by the then English Parliament) and the Union with England Act 1707 (passed by the then Scottish Parliament) united the two Parliaments into one single one in Westminster (thereafter the Parliament of Great Britain). After this date the Westminster Parliament legislated for both England (Wales) and Scotland.

Over the course of time, Scotland remained distinctive from the rest of the Union (England, Wales and Northern Ireland), in particular in terms of its different systems of education and law. During the latter half of the twentieth century there was an increasing call from Scottish nationalist politicians for Scotland to be able to direct and govern its own affairs through the re-establishment of a Scottish Parliament. Indeed, in 1978 a Scotland Act was passed which would have provided Scotland with its own elected assembly. The Act, however, did not come into effect (and was repealed) because the Scots voting in the referendum to support devolution did not meet the threshold stipulated in the Act.

The election of the 1997 Labour government placed devolution back on the political agenda. In July 1997 the Labour government issued a White Paper which stated at the outset:

Q	'The Government are determined that the people of Scotland should have a greater say over their own affairs. With their agreement we will change the way Scotland is governed by legislating to create a Scottish Parliament with devolved powers within the United Kingdom'.
	Scotland's Parliament, Cm 3658 (The Scottish Office, 1997), p 1.

Following this, a referendum was held in Scotland in September 1997 for the Scots to either endorse or reject the government's proposals. In constitutional theory this is an example of participatory democracy whereby individuals are given direct influence over proposals which will affect them. At the referendum the Scots were asked two questions:

- Whether the Scottish people wanted a Scottish Parliament? (74 per cent voted Yes).

- Should it have tax-raising powers? (64 per cent voted Yes).

As a result of this endorsement, Parliament duly passed the Scotland Act 1998.

The Scotland Act 1998

This Act devolved powers to Scotland so that for the first time in almost 300 years Scotland had its own Parliament, largely to oversee its own affairs. In fact, the Scotland Act (like the corresponding legislation for Wales and Northern Ireland) can be seen as a type of constitution for Scotland. It should be remembered that the purpose of a constitution (see Chapter 2) is to:

- Establish governmental institutions (eg the Scottish Parliament and Executive).

- Allocate them powers (eg the Parliament is empowered to legislate on health and criminal law, etc.).

- Limit their powers (eg the Scottish Parliament cannot pass legislation for independence).

14.3.2 Arguments for and against Scottish devolution

(It should be noted that some of the arguments from 1997 set out below can, to a greater or lesser extent, apply equally to the other devolved settlements in Wales and Northern Ireland).

Arguments for Scottish devolution

- As Scotland was hallmarked by distinct characteristics (particularly its law), it required a local Parliament to oversee its affairs, rather than a distant Parliament hundreds of miles away.

- In political terms, devolution intensified between 1979 and 1997 when the majority of Scotland had consistently returned non-Conservative MPs (largely Labour) to Westminster, but were governed by an 'English Conservative government'. In particular, it must be remembered that the controversial community charge (colloquially known as the poll tax) was first introduced in Scotland *before* England.

- In constitutional terms, too much power was centralised in London and so devolution to Scotland (and elsewhere) was healthy in a democracy as a way of decentralising and dispersing power.

Arguments against Scottish devolution

- Devolving power would lead to the constitutional anomaly of the 'West Lothian question', whereby Scottish MPs would be able vote on English matters in legislation such as education and crime, but that English MPs would not be able to vote on corresponding Scottish matters as such matters would be devolved to the Scottish Parliament (see section 22.9.1).

- Devolving power to Scotland (and Wales and Northern Ireland for that matter), but not at the same time establishing an 'English Parliament' to oversee and legislate on specifically English affairs, would lead to an imbalance in the constitution.

- Devolving power would inevitably widen the differences between Scotland and the rest of the Union. This would, therefore, lead to the eventual break-up of the Union of the United Kingdom. In essence, once established, a Scottish Parliament would inevitably want more powers ceded to it from Westminster, eventually leading to Scotland becoming a completely separate and sovereign country. In response to this last point it has been argued that providing the Scottish people with devolution and the ability to a large extent to regulate their own affairs would actually stave off political support for complete independence. Indeed, according to the government in its White Paper:

Q	'The Government want a United Kingdom which everyone feels part of, can contribute to, and in whose future all have a stake. The Union will be strengthened by recognising the claims of Scotland, Wales and the regions with strong identities of their own. The Government's devolution proposals, by meeting these aspirations, will not only safeguard but also enhance the Union'.
	Scotland's Parliament, Cm 3658 (The Scottish Office, 1997), p 10.

ACTIVITY

Question

Do you think that the advantages of Scottish devolution (or devolution in general) outweigh the disadvantages?

14.3.3 The Scottish Parliament

Section 1 of the Scotland Act 1998 establishes a Scottish Parliament (to sit at Holyrood in Edinburgh). The Parliament is unicameral consisting of one elected chamber.

Composition and elections

The Scottish Parliament consists of 129 members known as Members of the Scottish Parliament (MSPs). They are elected on the following basis:

- 73 Constituency MSPs elected under the simple majority system (s 1(2)).

- 56 Regional MSPs 'additional members' elected under the Additional Member system of proportional representation (s 1(3)).

Unlike the House of Commons, the Scottish Parliament will not be elected solely on the basis of the 'first past the post' system. This is because this system can distort the wishes of electorate (see section 9.4.4) and the government's White Paper made it clear that the 'electoral arrangements for the Scottish Parliament should reflect the will of the Scottish people'. Instead, there is a combination of MSPs elected by different systems with the majority being elected under the 'first past the post' system, thereby ensuring there is a constituency link between the MSPs and the Scottish people. These are supplemented by additional members (seven members elected from each of the eight European parliamentary constituencies in Scotland). According to the White Paper this will 'bring a closer relationship between votes cast and seats won', thereby injecting greater proportionality which in turn builds stability into the overall devolution settlement. These new electoral arrangements indicate a willingness to move away from the traditional 'first past the post' system in our constitution.

Section 2 states that elections take place every four years and so in this sense (unlike the Westminster Parliament) the Scottish Parliament is a fixed term Parliament with elections at set intervals. Section 3, however, does make provision for extraordinary general elections to take place (for example, if following a general election a First Minister has not been nominated).

The first elections took place in 1999 and the second in 2003. The third set of elections took place in May 2007, the results of which are detailed below, and it produced a Parliament in which no party held a majority of seats. Voters are given two votes: one for a constituency MSP and one for a Regional MSP (cast for a party).

Table 14.2

Elections May 2007			
Main Political Parties	**Constituency MSPs**	**Regional MSPs**	**TOTAL**
Labour	37	9	46
SNP	21	26	47
Liberal Democrat	11	5	16
Conservative	4	13	17
Green	0	2	2
Others	0	1	1
TOTAL	73	56	129

Compiled from www.scottish.parliament.uk

The role of MSPs is similar to that of MPs in the Westminster Parliament:

- Representing constituents.
- Resolving complaints from constituents.
- Holding the Scottish Executive to account.
- Raising issues of public concern.
- Asking questions.
- Participating in debates and the committee system.

The Presiding Officer

Section 19 provides for a Presiding Officer together with two deputies to be elected from the MSPs. In effect the Presiding Officer is the equivalent of the Speaker of the House of Commons as he chairs proceedings in the parliamentary chamber and is required to be impartial. MSPs are also governed by a Code of Conduct and under the Scottish Parliamentary Standards Commissioner Act 2002 an independent Parliamentary Commissioner was created to process complaints.

The committee system

As in Westminster, the Scottish Parliament has a sophisticated committee system. These committees include:

- Subject Committees allocated in respect of government departmental areas (analogous to departmental select committees). For example, the Communities Committee monitors the work of the Communities ministry/department.
- Mandatory committees for the parliamentary term.
- Committees which consider Bills.

14.3.4 The Scottish administration

Section 44 establishes the office of a Scottish Executive known collectively as 'the Scottish Ministers'.

The executive consists of the following:

- The First Minister (analogous to the office of Prime Minister).
- Ministers appointed by the First Minister (analogous to Cabinet ministers), but with the approval of Parliament.
- Lord Advocate and Solicitor-General for Scotland (these law officers, *inter alia*, provide legal advice).

The Executive is effectively the 'Scottish government' and is the equivalent of the British Cabinet in the context of the Westminster Parliament. It is responsible for implementing and developing policies of the Scottish Executive and assumes responsibility in devolved matters. Ministers can also, like British Cabinet ministers, introduce Bills.

The constitutional arrangements in Scotland, therefore, involve a parliamentary executive (as in Westminster) whereby the Scottish Executive is held to account by the Scottish Parliament. For example, as in Westminster, Scottish ministers can be asked oral or written questions with the First Minister having a separate First Minister's Question Time (analogous to PMQs: see section 12.4.2). Furthermore, ss 45 and 47 require the resignation of the First Minister and individual ministers if it is resolved that the Scottish Executive no longer enjoys the confidence of the Scottish Parliament (analogous with the Westminster vote of no confidence: see section 12.2.1).

In terms of political composition, during the 2003–2007 parliamentary session the Scottish Executive comprised a coalition government between the Labour and Liberal Democrat parties. In April 2007 there was a First Minister, Deputy First Minister and ministers for the following governmental portfolios (with their deputy):

- Communities.
- Education and Young People.
- Environment and Rural Development.
- Finance and Public Service Reform.
- Health and Community Care.
- Justice.
- Parliamentary Business.
- Enterprise and Lifelong Learning.
- Tourism, Culture and Sport (no deputy).
- Transport (no deputy).
- Law Officers (see above).

Source: www.scotland.gov.uk

Composition of the Scottish devolved institutions	
Parliament	129 MSPs • 73 Constituency MSPs ('first past the post' system). • 56 Regional MSPs (Additional Member system).
Executive	• The First Minister. • Scottish ministers. • Lord Advocate and Solicitor-General for Scotland.

14.3.5 Legislation

Primary legislation

Scottish devolution involved legislative devolution whereby the Scottish Parliament was empowered to pass primary legislation. Section 28 states that the Scottish Parliament can make laws which are to be known as Acts of the Scottish Parliament. After a Bill has passed through the Scottish Parliament and has obtained the Royal Assent, it becomes an Act of the Scottish Parliament (s 28(2)).

The constitutional standing of these Acts, however, is worth noting as, although these Acts are analogous to primary legislation:

- For the purpose of the Human Rights Act 1998 (s 21) such legislation (as well as any subordinate legislation made by a member of the Scottish Executive) is treated as having the standing of secondary legislation and so amenable to challenge and invalidation under the 1998 Act (see Chapter 17).

- Under the Scotland Act, if the Scottish Parliament passes an Act of Parliament outside of its legal jurisdiction (eg in respect on the British constitution), under s 29 it can be challenged as not being valid law. Contrast the position in respect of Westminster Acts (see Chapter 7).

Secondary legislation

The Scottish Executive can pass delegated/secondary legislation (which is similar to Cabinet ministers enacting Statutory Instruments).

14.3.6 Devolved and reserved matters

Devolution involves devolving powers and responsibility from the centre (Westminster) to the regions (Scotland). The Scotland Act 1998 devolves powers to Scotland (devolved matters), whilst retaining specific powers in the centre (reserved matters).

Reserved matters

These are set out in Sched 5 of the Act and include for example:

- International relations.
- National security.
- Matters affecting the United Kingdom constitution.

The government argued in its White Paper that these sorts of issues 'can be more effectively and beneficially handled on a United Kingdom basis', thereby safeguarding the United Kingdom's integrity and the benefits of a consistent approach in such areas.

Devolved matters

The following are some of the matters over which the Scottish Parliament has legislative competence:

- Education (primary, secondary, further and higher).
- Health.
- Local government.
- Housing.
- Criminal law.
- Criminal justice and prosecution system.
- Civil and criminal courts.
- Economic development.

Since devolution the Scottish Parliament has not been reticent about exercising its legislative powers. Indeed, in its first parliamentary term (1999–2003) the Scottish Parliament passed 62 Bills:

- 50 were executive Bills (eg introduced by the Scottish Executive – similar to a Cabinet minister introducing a Bill in the Westminster Parliament).
- 8 were members' Bills (introduced by an MSP analogous to Westminster Private Members' Bills).
- 3 were committee Bills (introduced by a parliamentary committee – eg the Standards Committee).
- 1 was a private Bill (analogous to a Westminster private Bill).

Source: www.scottish.parliament.uk

Some of these Bills proved to be controversial (for varying reasons) and actually served to widen the difference between Scotland and England in particular. For example:

- The Protection of Wild Mammals (Scotland) Act 2002 (a members' Bill) ended mounted foxhunting and hare coursing in Scotland. This was two years before the Westminster Parliament passed the 2004 Hunting Act (see section 10.10.3).
- The Community Care and Health (Scotland) Act 2002 (an executive Bill). This Act set out the framework for providing, *inter alia*, free personal and nursing care for older people.

14.3.7 Tax-varying powers

In the 1997 referendum the Scottish people endorsed the proposition that the Scottish Parliament should enjoy tax-raising powers. As a result, Pt IV of the Scotland Act 1998 permits the Scottish Parliament to vary central government taxation in Scotland (ie to alter the basic rate of income tax by up to 3 pence in the pound). To date this financial power has not been used, however, this provision sets Scottish devolution apart from the devolution arrangements in both Wales and Northern Ireland.

KEY FACTS

Scottish devolution powers	
Legislative	• Can pass primary legislation (Acts of the Scottish Parliament). • Can pass subordinate legislation.
Financial	• Tax-varying powers.

14.3.8 Legislative competence

In essence, the Scottish Parliament can legislate in respect of devolved matters and such Acts can modify existing primary legislation relating to Scotland. The Scottish Parliament, however, like other legislatures is a *limited* legislature (in contrast to the Westminster Parliament). It cannot pass laws outside of its legislative competence (ie outside of its devolved powers):

s 29(1) Scotland Act 1998

'An Act of the Scottish Parliament is not law so far as any provision of the Act is outside the legislative competence of the Parliament.'

Section 29(2) states that a provision will be outside Parliament's legislative competence if it:

(a) Would form part of the law of another country/territory (eg England).

(b) Related to reserved matters (eg national security).

(c) Breaches the restrictions in Sched 4 – this sets out certain legislation which is protected from being altered by an Act of the Scottish Parliament: (eg the Human Rights Act 1998, etc.).

(d) Is incompatible with the following:

- European Convention rights (under the Human Rights Act 1998)

- European Community law (under the European Communities Act 1972).

(e) Removed the Lord Advocate as the head of the systems of criminal prosecution and the investigation of deaths.

In this way the Scottish Parliament is not legislatively omnicompent, as its Acts can be challenged as *ultra vires* if it legislates outside of its competence.

14.3.9 Ensuring the Scottish Parliament legislates within its powers

Scottish primary legislation can in effect be challenged at two stages to ensure that it is within its legislative competence:

- **The parliamentary stage**

    Section 31 states that a member of the Scottish Executive in charge of a Bill shall at the outset state that in his view the Bill is within Parliament's legislative competence. In addition, the Presiding Officer must also decide whether or not the Bill is within Parliament's legislative competence (ie whether it is *ultra vires* the Scotland Act 1998).

    Under s 33 the Advocate General for Scotland, the Lord Advocate or the Attorney-General may refer to the Judicial Committee of the Privy Council (from 2009 it will be scheduled to be referred to the new Supreme Court) the question as to whether a Bill which has been passed by Parliament, but before Royal Assent has been granted, is within its legislative competence.

Under s 32 if the court determines that such a Bill is outside its powers, the Presiding Officer is unable to submit it for Royal Assent in an unamended form.

Under s 35 the Secretary of State is empowered to prohibit the Presiding Officer from submitting a Bill for Royal Assent if, for example, he has reasonable grounds for believing it would be incompatible with international obligations, etc.

- **The court stage**

  The legal validity of a Scottish Act of Parliament can be challenged in the courts if it is argued that the Act is outside the legal competence of the Scottish Parliament (*ultra vires* – contrast the Westminster Parliament in Chapter 7). This is known as *a devolution issue* and Scottish inferior courts may refer it to the Court of Session or the High Court of Justiciary. Ultimately, the issue may be determined by the Privy Council (scheduled to be the new Supreme Court from 2009).

  Few attempts have been made to challenge Acts of the Scottish Parliament. For example, in *Anderson v Scottish Ministers* [2002] SC (PC) 1, the Mental Health (Public Safety and Appeals) (Scotland) Act 1999 was unsuccessfully challenged as being contrary to Art 5 of the European Convention.

14.3.10 Challenging the actions of the Scottish Executive

In relation to actions of members of the Scottish Executive, s 58 authorises the Secretary of State to direct that such action is not taken if he has reasonable grounds to believe that it would be incompatible, for example, with any international obligations. Similarly, by order he can revoke subordinate legislation made by a member of the Scottish Executive which contains provisions which he has reasonable grounds to believe are incompatible with, for example, the interests of defence. Moreover, s 57 prohibits a member of the Scottish Executive from acting or making subordinate legislation which is incompatible with European Convention rights or European Community law.

In the courts the devolution issues which have been raised to date, have been in the context of the Human Rights Act 1998 and have concerned claims that Convention rights have been violated in Scottish criminal proceedings.

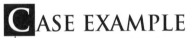ASE EXAMPLE

Starrs v Ruxton 2000 SLT 42

The High Court of Justiciary declared that temporary Sheriffs were incompatible with the right to a fair trial (Art 6) as their appointments lacked security of tenure. As they held office at the pleasure, in effect, of the Lord Advocate (who was part of the Scottish Executive), the appearance of independence was absent.

Following this case, the Scottish Parliament enacted the Bail, Judicial Appointments etc (Scotland) Act 2000 abolishing the office of temporary sheriffs.

CASE EXAMPLE

Brown v Stott (Procurator Fiscal) [2003] 1 AC 681

The Privy Council held that the prosecution could use evidence of Brown's compulsory admission to the police under the 1988 Road Traffic Act (that she had been the driver of a car) against her. Brown unsuccessfully argued that this infringed her right not to incriminate herself under Art 6 of the European Convention (the right to a fair trial).

14.3.11 The relationship with Westminster

Even though Scotland has its own Parliament, this does not mean that it loses its MPs at Westminster (although the recent Scottish Parliament (Constituencies) Act 2004 did reduce the number of Scottish MPs from 72 to 59). Scottish MPs are still needed in Westminster to represent the people of Scotland in respect of reserved matters (ie issues which affect the whole of the United Kingdom). These MPs are entitled (and do) vote on English matters such as English criminal law which has resulted in the 'West Lothian' question (see section 22.9.1).

Scotland is still represented in Cabinet by a Secretary of State (albeit the post is now part-time) and he represents a link between the Scottish Parliament, Westminster, Whitehall and the other devolved areas. In addition, a House of Commons Scottish Affairs Committee examines the administration and policy of the Scotland Office and a Scottish Grand Committee (composed of Scottish MPs) discusses and debates Scottish matters in general (although it has not met recently).

14.3.12 Parliamentary sovereignty and the Scottish Parliament

In strict constitutional theory, parliamentary sovereignty has not been affected by the establishment of the Scottish Parliament. Indeed, on this point the government in its White Paper made it very clear that:

Q
> 'The UK Parliament is and will remain sovereign in all matters ... Westminster will be choosing to exercise that sovereignty by devolving legislative responsibilities to a Scottish Parliament without in any way diminishing its own powers'.
>
> *Scotland's Parliament*, Cm 3658 (The Scottish Office, 1997), p 12.

As a result, the United Kingdom Parliament (in legal theory) could choose to if it wanted:

- To legislate for Scotland in respect of devolved matters without the consent of the Scottish Parliament:

s 28(7) Scotland Act 1998
'This section does not affect the power of the Parliament of the United Kingdom to make laws for Scotland.'

- To revoke the Scotland Act 1998 itself, although according to Laws LJ this would have to be done expressly (see section 4.4.5).

As indicated at sections 7.6.2 and 7.11, however, it would appear to be the case that politically it would be very difficult for the Westminster Parliament to repeal this legislation in practice. Indeed, in its White Paper the government noted that popular support for the Parliament would ensure that its place in our constitution was secure (albeit politically).

Furthermore, a constitutional convention has arisen recently known as the Sewel Convention (named after Lord Sewel who piloted the Scotland Bill through the upper House) which regulates the relationship between the two Parliaments. In essence the convention states that the United Kingdom Parliament will not legislate for Scotland on a devolved matter (or where the competence of the devolved institutions will be altered) without first obtaining the express consent of the Scottish Parliament. This consent is given in the form of a Legislative Consent motion/Sewel motion (eg one was passed endorsing the principle of the putative Supreme Court, which of course would affect Scotland – Official Report, Session 2, col 13661, 19 January 2005). It is worth noting that the House of Commons Scottish Affairs Committee has recommended that the explanatory notes accompanying Westminster Bills should identify more explicitly when a Sewel motion may be triggered (Fourth Report of Session 2005–06, *The Sewel Convention: the Westminster perspective*, HC 983 (2006), para 13).

Legally of course, the Westminster Parliament simply could pass any legislation without consulting the Scottish Parliament, but that action clearly would be regarded as 'unconstitutional' (see section 4.15).

Finally, there has been some academic debate over whether parliamentary sovereignty is fully accepted in Scotland in any event. This is on the basis that the principle was a purely English notion associated with the English, but not the Scottish Parliament, prior to the Acts of Union.

ACTIVITY

Quick quiz

1. What do the Scottish Parliament and Executive do?

2. What is the difference between devolved and reserved matters?

3. How can the actions of the Scottish Parliament and Executive be challenged?

4. What is the relationship between the Scottish and the Westminster Parliaments?

14.4 Northern Irish devolution

14.4.1 History

England had exerted control over Ireland for centuries before the 1800 Act of Union unified the Parliaments of Great Britain with that of Ireland. This Union created the Parliament of the United Kingdom of Great Britain (England, Wales and Scotland) and Ireland. By the beginning of the twentieth century the pressure from Irish nationalist politicians for Home Rule to govern themselves led to the Government of Ireland Act 1914 which aimed to establish an Irish Parliament (it never came into effect owing to the First World War).

In 1920 the Government of Ireland Act was passed which recognised the reality that two separate Parliaments were needed:

- One for the South (overwhelmingly Roman Catholic); and

- One for the North (majority Protestant).

Although the Northern Irish Parliament (Stormont) was established and operated until the 1970s, in contrast, the Southern Irish Parliament was repudiated by Sinn Fein. This in effect led to the creation of the Irish Free State (with Dominion status) in 1922 which thereafter became a Republic (1937) and left the Commonwealth (1949). Northern Ireland with its Stormont Parliament remained part of the United Kingdom (now the United Kingdom of Great Britain and Northern Ireland).

Stormont

The Northern Irish Parliament functioned for five decades and was a bicameral legislature consisting of two chambers:

- House of Commons (directly elected).

- Senate (which was indirectly elected by the lower House).

The executive aspect of the arrangements involved a parliamentary executive comprising a Prime Minister together with a Northern Irish Cabinet. The Parliament was a limited legislature with certain areas (eg defence) excepted from its legislative competence.

The major problem with the Parliament was that in this divided community it continually had a Unionist majority. Civil unrest in the province, fuelled by the grievances of the Catholic minority led eventually in the 1970s to the suspension of Stormont and direct rule being imposed by the United Kingdom government. Thereafter, a Secretary of State for Northern Ireland would make decisions for Northern Ireland and the legislative powers enjoyed by the defunct Stormont would be exercised through Orders in Council.

The 1998 Good Friday Agreement

During the period of direct rule there were various unsuccessful attempts at securing a solution to the 'Northern Ireland problem', but in 1998 in the aftermath of an IRA ceasefire, the Belfast Agreement was signed by all parties ('the Good Friday Agreement'). It endorsed the resumption of devolution of power to Ulster and the establishment of new institutional relationships between the United Kingdom, the Republic of Ireland and Ulster.

The Good Friday Agreement was subsequently endorsed in May 1998 by a vote north and south of the Irish border. Following this, the United Kingdom Parliament passed:

- The Northern Ireland (elections) Act 1998 – to enable elections to take place for the new Northern Ireland Assembly.
- The Northern Ireland Act 1998 – to establish the institutional framework of devolution.

Recent developments

Unfortunately, the actual operation of the devolved arrangements proved to be very problematic as it was not until the end of 1999 that power was finally devolved to the institutions, and in October 2002 the Assembly was suspended. Notwithstanding the resumption of direct rule (with the Northern Ireland Office and Secretary of State exercising powers instead via Orders in Council), elections took place in November 2003 for a new Northern Ireland Assembly to revive devolution. Thereafter, this transitional assembly sat from March 2006 until November 2006 (without law-making powers) and was dissolved to pave the way for fresh elections in March 2007 to endorse the St Andrews Agreement agreed by the Prime Minister and the Irish Taoiseach in October 2006. The results of the March 2007 election are detailed in section 14.4.2 below. At the time of writing devolution in Northern Ireland had resumed in May 2007 with a functioning Executive Committee and Assembly.

14.4.2 The Northern Ireland Assembly

The Northern Ireland Assembly is a legislature which is elected on a four-yearly term (it is interesting to remember that Stormont had been bicameral).

Northern Irish devolution is distinctive in that certain decisions, for example standing orders and the election of First and Deputy First Minister had to be made on a cross-community basis. This involves obtaining the support of the majority of both community representatives (known as parallel consent). Such parallel consent is seen as essential in a divided community.

Composition and elections

The Northern Ireland Assembly consists of 108 Members, who are elected on the basis of STV (Single Transferable Vote) with 18 constituencies returning 6 members each. STV allows voters to indicate their varying preferences for different candidates, thereby maximising consensus amongst voters. The first elections took place in June 1998 and a second set took place in 2003. As a result of the second election the largest unionist party became the Democratic Unionist Party, whilst Sinn Fein became the largest nationalist party. A third election was held in March 2007 and the results are detailed below.

Table 14.3

Northern Ireland Assembly Election 2007	
Political Party	**Seats**
Ulster Unionist	18
Democratic Unionist	36
SDLP	16
Sinn Fein	28
Alliance	7
Others	3

Source: Electoral Office for Northern Ireland

Presiding Officer and committee system

Northern Irish devolution provides for the election from among its membership of a Presiding Officer and Deputies (analogous with the Scottish Parliament). As in Scotland, there is a committee system with committees shadowing the different Northern Irish government departmental portfolios.

14.4.3 The Northern Ireland Executive Committee

Part III of the 1998 Act provides for the establishment of the following ministerial offices (the Executive Committee):

- First Minister and Deputy First Minister (one from the unionist and one from the nationalist community) – under the 1998 Act they are elected jointly by the Assembly through a majority of designated nationalists and a majority of designated unionists. In this way Northern Irish devolution differs from both Scotland and Wales in that it requires 'parallel consent' from both communities for these two officers to assume their ministerial positions. In May 2007 Ian Paisley (DUP) became the First Minister with Martin McGuiness (Sinn Fein) as the Deputy First Minister.

- Northern Ireland ministers – these are determined using the *d'Handt* political system (s 18) based on the proportion of Assembly seats each party has acquired. In this way Northern Ireland devolution is distinctive as its executive reflects the balance of opinion within the Assembly. In short, its *raison d'etre* is power-sharing between the two communities and the various political parties (all of whom will be represented in the Executive Committee).

KEY FACTS

Composition of the Northern Irish devolved institutions	
Assembly	• 108 Members (Single Transferable Vote system).
Executive	• First Minister and Deputy First Minister. • Northern Ireland ministers.

14.4.4 Legislation and legislative competence

Section 5 empowers the Assembly to make primary legislation known as Acts of the Northern Ireland Assembly. As with Scotland, for the purposes of the Human Rights Act 1998 (s 21) such legislation is regarded as secondary and so subject to challenge.

The Northern Ireland Assembly (like its predecessor and the Scottish Parliament) is a limited and subordinate legislature:

S s 6(1) Northern Ireland Act 1998

'A provision of an Act is not law if it is outside the legislative competence of the Assembly'.

Section 6(2) sets out the circumstances which will be outside of the Assembly's legislative competence. These are very similar to those already set out in relation to the Scottish Parliament (see section 14.3.8), however, one additional circumstance which applies specifically to the Northern Ireland Assembly is if its Acts discriminate on the ground of religious belief or political opinion (s 6(2)(e)).

14.4.5 Reserved, excepted and transferred matters

- **Reserved matters**

The Assembly cannot legislate in respect of reserved matters (Sched 3) unless they are allocated the specific responsibility to do so by converting a reserved matter into a transferred one (under s 2 this would require an Order in Council). These areas include, for example, the Post Office and criminal law.

- **Excepted matters**

The Assembly cannot legislate in respect of excepted matters (Sched 2). Excepted matters include, for example, the defence of the realm.

- **Transferred matters**

The Assembly can legislate in respect of transferred matters and these include, for example:

- The Arts.
- Education.
- Agriculture.

14.4.6 Ensuring the Northern Ireland Assembly legislates within its powers

This can be challenged at two stages

- **The parliamentary (Assembly) stage**

  (i) Section 9 requires that a minister in charge of a Bill makes a statement at the outset that in his view it is compatible with the Assembly's legislative competence.

  (ii) Section 10 states that a Bill will not be introduced if the Presiding Officer considers that it is not within the Assembly's legislative competence.

  (iii) Section 11 empowers the Attorney General for Northern Ireland to refer a Bill (which has been passed by the Assembly) to the Judicial Committee of the Privy Council (scheduled to be the Supreme Court in 2009) to determine whether it is within the Assembly's legislative competence. If it is not, the Secretary State (not the Presiding Officer) cannot submit the Bill for Royal Assent in an unamended form (s 14). In addition, the Secretary of State may refuse to submit a Bill which he considers would breach international obligations.

  (iv) Under s 13 the Human Rights Commission (see section 14.4.9) may be asked by the Assembly whether a Bill is compatible with human rights.

- **The court stage**

The legal validity of an Act of the Northern Ireland Assembly can be challenged in the courts (ultimately before the Privy Council – from 2009, before the Supreme Court) on the basis of a devolution issue (ie has the devolved institution acted within its powers?).

In fact, the Assembly in its short period of operation has only produced 36 Acts and none have given rise to a devolution issue: (M Supperstone, J Goudie and Sir P Walker, *Judicial Review* (3rd edn, LexisNexis-Butterworths, 2005), p 627).

14.4.7 Challenging the actions of the Northern Ireland Executive Committee

Under s 24, a Northern Ireland minister or Northern Ireland department has no power to act or to make subordinate legislation which, *inter alia*:

- Is incompatible with European Convention rights.
- Is incompatible with European Community law.
- Discriminates on the ground of religions belief or political opinion.
- Modifies an entrenched enactment (eg modifies the Human Rights Act 1998 or European Communities Act).

Moreover, if such legislation deals with an excepted or reserved matter the Secretary of State may revoke it by order (s 25). Similarly, he may do so where such legislation is incompatible, *inter alia*, with any international obligations (s 26).

KEY FACTS

Northern Irish devolution powers	
Legislative	• Pass primary legislation (Acts of the Northern Ireland Assembly). • Pass subordinate legislation.
Financial	• No tax-varying powers.

14.4.8 The relationship with Westminster and parliamentary sovereignty

As with Scotland, Northern Ireland returns MPs to Westminster. Northern Ireland also retains its Secretary of State whose responsibilities increased when devolution was suspended. At Westminster, like Scotland at section 14.3.11, Northern Ireland has a House of Commons Northern Ireland Affairs Committee (in respect of the Northern Ireland Office) and a Northern Ireland Grand Committee (to debate and discuss the general affairs of Ulster).

As with Scotland, the existence of a Northern Ireland Assembly does not in strict constitutional theory affect parliamentary sovereignty.

> **S** s 5(6) Northern Ireland Act 1998
> 'This section does not affect the power of the Parliament of the United Kingdom to make laws for Northern Ireland'.

Further, the United Kingdom Parliament legally could revoke the Assembly. Indeed, as we have already seen, the previous Stormont Parliament was revoked by the Westminster Parliament in the 1970s.

In terms of sovereignty, however, the Act does make the following declaration at the outset:

> **S** s 1(1) Northern Ireland Act 1998
> 'It is hereby declared that Northern Ireland in its entirety remains part of the United Kingdom and shall not cease to be so without the consent of a majority of the people of Northern Ireland voting in a poll held for the purposes of this section'.

ACTIVITY

> ### Problem solving
> Does s 1 of the Northern Ireland Act 1998 mean that the United Kingdom Parliament could not:
>
> **(a)** legally
>
> and/or
>
> **(b)** politically
>
> legislate to sever Northern Ireland from the rest of the United Kingdom without first obtaining the consent of the Northern Irish people? (See also section 7.10.2.)

14.4.9 Other strands to the Belfast Agreement

These included the following:

- **The North-South Ministerial Council** – composed of ministers from the Irish government and the Northern Ireland Executive Committee to consider matters of mutual interest.

- **The British-Irish Council** – composed of representatives from the British and Irish governments, together with those from the devolved institutions to agree common policies.

Human Rights Commission

Section 68 of the Northern Ireland Act 1998 established a Northern Ireland Human Rights Commission. Its functions include, for example:

- Keeping under review Northern Ireland's law and practice in respect of protecting human rights.

- Advising the Secretary of State and Executive Committee of legislative (and other) measures which ought to be taken to protect human rights.

- Advising the Assembly whether a Bill is compatible with human rights.

ACTIVITY

Quick quiz

1. What do the Northern Ireland Assembly and Executive Committee do?

2. What is the difference between transferred, reserved and excepted matters?

3. How can the actions of the Assembly and the Executive be challenged?

4. How does Northern Irish devolution differ from that in Scotland?

14.5 Welsh devolution

14.5.1 History

For centuries Wales has been closely connected with England as indicated by the 1536 Act of Union between the two countries. Today England and Wales is one single legal jurisdiction. By the second part of the twentieth century, however, there was a growing nationalist call in Wales for it to be able to govern itself. In 1978 the Wales Act was passed which conferred a diluted form of devolution on Wales, but the legislation did not come into effect because only 12 per cent voted in favour of it in a referendum. The Labour Party election manifesto of 1997 was committed to the establishment of Welsh devolution and in July 1997 the government issued its White Paper detailing its proposals (*A Voice for Wales* Cm 3718 (The Stationery Office, 1997)).

As in Scotland, these proposals were endorsed subsequently in a referendum in September 1997 (but only by the narrowest of margins: 50.3 per cent voted yes). Following this the Government of Wales Act 1998 was passed which devolved power to Wales. This Act is now subject to the Government of Wales Act 2006 which re-enacts many of its provisions. The 2006 Act was enacted so as to strengthen and deepen the devolved arrangements in Wales. To a large extent the provisions of this Act will come into effect following the Assembly elections in May 2007. The 2006 Act had been preceded by a White Paper, *Better Governance for Wales* Cm 6582 (Wales Office, 2005).

14.5.2 The National Assembly for Wales

Section 1 of the Government of Wales Act 2006 states that there is to be an Assembly known as the National Assembly for Wales (Cynulliad Cenedlaethol Cymru). Under s 1 of the 1998 Act the Assembly was a corporate body (with executive and legislative arms united) but this will no longer be the case under the 2006 Act.

Composition and elections

The Assembly is composed of 60 Assembly Members (AMs). They are elected on the following basis:

- 40 Assembly constituency members – elected by the 'first past the post' system.
- 20 Assembly regional members – elected by the Additional Member system of proportional representation. (Four from each of the five regional electoral regions).

Section 7 of the 2006 Act prevents a person standing as both a regional and constituency candidate at the same time. As in Scotland, the combination of electoral systems is designed to offset the disproportionate nature of the 'first past the post' system. Elections took place in 1999 and 2003. The third set of elections took place in May 2007:

Table 14.4

2007 Assembly election			
Political Party	**Constituency Seats**	**Regional seats**	**Total**
Labour	24	2	26
Conservative	5	7	12
Plaid Cymru (Welsh Nationalist)	7	8	15
Liberal Democrats	3	3	6
Other	1	0	1
TOTAL	40	20	60

Section 6 provides that voters have two votes:

- A constituency vote – a vote cast for a candidate in their constituency.
- An electoral region vote – a vote cast for a political party or a vote for an individual candidate.

Elections are on a fixed term basis of every four years (s 3), although s 5 permits an extraordinary general election to be held, as is the case in Scotland.

Presiding Officer and committees

Section 25 of the 2006 Act provides for the election by the Assembly of a Presiding Officer together with a Deputy Presiding Officer, similar to the Scottish Parliament. The Assembly operates through a variety of different committees. These include subject committees which are analogous to Westminster departmental committees in shadowing executive policy areas, for example, health and social services (thereby holding the executive to account). In addition, standing committees include for example, the Audit committee which scrutinises the Assembly's resources.

14.5.3 The Welsh Assembly Government

Following the 2003 election the Labour Party operated as a single party Cabinet executive (previously Wales had had a Labour/Liberal coalition administration). Section 45 of the 2006 Act establishes a Welsh Assembly Government (Llywodraeth Cynulliad Cymru) which comprises the following:

- The First Minister – nominated by the Assembly.
- The remaining Welsh Ministers – appointed by the First Minister from among the Assembly members (the arrangements therefore are those of a parliamentary executive and under s 45 of the Act, the First Minister and Welsh Ministers are collectively known as the 'Welsh Ministers').
- The Counsel General to the Welsh Assembly – the government's legal adviser (a new office created by the 2006 Act).
- The Deputy Welsh Ministers – appointed by the First Minister to assist any of the above.

Each minister will be allocated a particular governmental portfolio. For example:

- Education, Lifelong Learning and Skills.
- Local Government and Culture.
- Health and Social Services.

One key change brought about by the 2006 Act was formally to separate the Welsh executive from the Welsh legislature. The 1998 legislation (unlike in Scotland or Northern Ireland) did not separate these constitutional functions as the Assembly was a corporate body exercising both functions. In 2005 the government's White Paper had proposed separating the legislative and executive aspects of the Assembly and this had followed a Commission Report by Lord Richard (*The Report of the Commission on the Powers and Electoral Arrangements of the National Assembly for Wales* (March 2004)) who had recommended that the *status quo* was no longer sustainable. As pointed out in the White Paper:

<table>
<tr><td>

Q

</td><td>

'Often, decisions are made in the name of the Assembly which are in fact, quite properly, the responsibility of one Minster or official, making it hard to know who should be accountable to the public for them.'

Better Governance for Wales, Cm 6582 (Wales Office, 2005), p 3.

</td></tr>
</table>

Under the 2006 Act the Welsh Assembly Government is a separate constitutional entity (although it will sit in the Assembly and will be directly accountable to it), thereby ensuring more transparent accountability for the use of its powers. In fact, under s 48 Welsh Ministers must resign if the Assembly resolves that they no longer enjoy the confidence of the Assembly (similar to a vote of no confidence in the House of Commons). Even before the 2006 Act, however, members of the executive were held accountable to the rest of the Assembly through the committee system, debates and questioning.

KEY FACTS

Composition of the Welsh devolved institutions	
Assembly	• 60 Assembly Members (AMs), comprising: • 40 Assembly constituency members (the 'first past the post' system). • 20 Assembly regional members (the Additional Member system).
Executive	• The First Minister. • Welsh Ministers (including deputies). • The Counsel General to the Welsh Assembly.

14.5.4 Powers and responsibilities

• Under the aegis of the 1998 Act devolved powers included, for example, housing, environment, education and training, sport, transport and culture. Powers were conferred on the Assembly, which in turn in practice were typically delegated to the executive which acted as the delegate of the Assembly. Under the 2006 Act, s 58 permits the transfer of functions directly onto the Welsh Ministers by way of an Order in Council. In this way, the Welsh Ministers will exercise functions in their own constitutional right. They will, therefore, make executive decisions, secondary legislation, etc, albeit they will be scrutinised by the Assembly.

- Under the 1998 Act, the scheme of devolution as applied to Wales was termed '*executive devolution*' as the Assembly was not given powers to make primary legislation (contrast Scotland and Northern Ireland). It was commonly argued that Wales did not need legislative devolution because its arrangements were not sufficiently distinctive (unlike Scotland). Indeed, it was partly due to the diluted form of devolution offered to the Welsh which explains why only 50 per cent voted for devolution in the 1997 referendum. The United Kingdom Parliament, therefore, continues to pass primary legislation affecting Wales (but see below)

The Assembly could, however, make subordinate legislation (which the executive could propose for the Assembly to endorse). In this sense, it did have a law-making role as it must be remembered that in essence, executive devolution involved the Assembly taking over the powers and responsibilities previously exercised by the Secretary of State for Wales. In this way the government, in its 1997 White Paper, argued that:

> **Q** 'By establishing the Assembly, the Government is moving the process of decision-making closer to the citizen: many more decisions about Wales will be made in Wales.'
>
> *A Voice for Wales*, Cm 3718 (The Stationery Office, 1997), p 15.

- Section 93 of the 2006 Act states that the Assembly may make subordinate laws known as Measures of the National Assembly for Wales (although such Measures may affect primary legislation within defined fields). In practice, it appears that typically the Assembly Government will propose Assembly Measures, although this will not preclude other Assembly members from doing so. As a result, the 2006 Act provides an opportunity on a case by case basis (by way of Order in Council approved by Parliament and the Assembly) to enhance the legislative powers of the Assembly.

- In addition, the 2006 Act paves the way in the future for primary legislative powers (to be known as Assembly Acts) to be conferred subsequently onto the Assembly following the support of the Welsh people in a referendum (Pt 4 of the 2006 Act). The conferring of primary legislative powers on the Assembly would bring Welsh devolution more into line with the arrangements pertaining in Scotland and Northern Ireland.

14.5.5 The competence of the institutions

The National Assembly for Wales

 s 94(2) Government of Wales Act 2006
'An Assembly Measure is not law so far as any provision of the Assembly Measure is outside the Assembly's legislative competence'.

Under s 94 a provision will be outside the Assembly's legislative competence if, *inter alia*:

- It extends to a legal jurisdiction other than England and Wales (although England and Wales is a single jurisdiction, the Measures will invariably apply only in Wales).

- Is incompatible with European Convention rights or European Community law.

In addition, the person in charge of a proposed Assembly Measure must state at the outset that in their view it was within the competence of the Assembly, and the Presiding Officer must decide if it is and state his decision (s 97). Further, under s 99 the Counsel General or the Attorney-General can seek a decision of the Supreme Court as to whether a proposed Measure passed by the Assembly is within the Assembly's legislative competence. Under s 101 the Secretary of State also has the power to intervene to prohibit a Measure from being approved by the Crown where, for example, he had reasonable grounds that the measure would have a serious impact on, for example, water resources in England.

The actions of the Welsh Ministers

- Under the 2006 Act, Welsh Ministers have no power to make subordinate legislation or any other act if it is incompatible with European Community law (s 80) or European Convention rights (s 81).

- In addition, s 82 empowers the Secretary of State to direct that the Welsh Ministers do not take proposed action if it would be incompatible with any international obligation. Similarly, he can revoke subordinate legislation on the same basis.

A devolution issue

Schedule 9 of the 2006 Act states that a devolution issue means:

(1) (a) a question whether an Assembly Measure/Act of the Assembly is within the Assembly's legislative competence,

(b) a question whether any function is exercisable by the Welsh Ministers, First Minister or Counsel General,

(c) a question whether an exercise of a function by the above (in b) is within their powers (including ss 80 and 81 – see above),

(d) a question whether the above (in b) have failed to comply with a duty imposed on them (including any obligation under European Community law under s 80),

(e) a question whether a failure to act by the above (in b) is incompatible with the European Convention rights.

The court of last resort in relation to devolution issues, as with Scotland and Northern Ireland, ultimately will be the Supreme Court.

Welsh devolution powers	
Legislative	• Pass subordinate legislation (Assembly Measures).
	• Provision is made in Pt 4 of the Government of Wales Act 2006 for a power to pass primary legislation (Assembly Acts) to be conferred in the future.
Financial	• No tax-varying powers.

14.5.6 The relationship with Westminster and parliamentary sovereignty

Wales returns a number of MPs to Westminster and the country is represented by a Secretary of State (albeit a part-time post). At Westminster, like Scotland and Northern Ireland, Wales has a House of Commons Welsh Affairs Committee (which considers matters within the Secretary of State for Wales' responsibility) and a Welsh Grand Committee. The issue of the 'West Lothian question' does not apply to Wales as, at the time of writing, it does not enjoy primary legislative powers (contrast Scotland). The issue will be raised, however, if primary law-making powers are ever conferred on the Assembly under the 2006 Act.

As with the other devolution arrangements, in legal theory parliamentary sovereignty is unaffected by Welsh devolution as these arrangements could simply be repealed by a Westminster statute. Moreover, the 2006 Act makes it clear that notwithstanding the devolved arrangements, ultimately Parliament can legislate for Wales if it chooses to do so:

S s 93(5) Government of Wales Act 2006
'This Part does not affect the power of the Parliament of the United Kingdom to make laws for Wales'.

ACTIVITY

Quick quiz

1. What is the difference between the two Government of Wales Acts?

2. What powers and responsibilities do the National Assembly and Assembly Government have?

3. How can the actions of the Assembly and the Assembly Government be challenged?

4. How does Welsh devolution differ from that in Scotland?

KEY FACTS

Links between devolved settlements

- **The British-Irish Council** contains representatives from each of the devolved institutions together with the British and Irish governments.

- **The Joint Ministerial Council** contains representatives of all three administrations together with the British government.

- A *Memorandum of Understanding* has been agreed which promotes cooperation and communication between the devolved administrations and the United Kingdom government.

14.6 The position of England

14.6.1 No English Parliament

The devolution arrangements in the British constitution are not symmetrical because whilst Scotland, Wales and Northern Ireland have a tier of government between local government and central government, there is no corresponding tier in England. In short, there is no English Parliament to regulate purely English affairs which means that the vast majority of people in the United Kingdom, who are English, are not regulated by any form of devolved infrastructure (but see below). Instead, England is regulated by the United Kingdom Parliament in Westminster which, of course, includes MPs who are not English (the 'West Lothian question'). It appears, however, that there is little public call or enthusiasm for the establishment of an English Parliament. In recent years, however, the constitutional arrangements of England have seen two changes:

14.6.2 Regional Development Agencies

Although no English Parliament has been created, a new level of strategic administration has been inserted: the Regional Development Agencies (RDAs). These were created under the Regional Development Agencies Act 1998. According to the Prime Minister in 2002:

> **Q** 'We have already done a lot to decentralise decision-making to the English regions. Regional Development Agencies (RDAs) have been established to help strengthen the building blocks for economic growth in all regions, with a network of regional chambers to scrutinise them.'
>
> *Your Region, Your Choice: Revitalising the English Regions*, Cm 5511
> (The Stationery Office, 2002), Preface.

In 2006, there were nine RDAs (West Midlands, North West, etc). In essence they are strategic bodies whose remit includes, *inter alia*:

- improving economic performance, development and regeneration
- promoting employment (and developing employment skills)
- assisting sustainable development.

In this way they provide a strategic and regional approach to these issues, which is specifically tailored for each particular region.

Regional Assemblies

The work of RDAs are scrutinised by corresponding Regional Assemblies. Regional Assemblies are currently voluntary bodies comprising representatives of local government, business and the wider community etc. The Labour government were hopeful that people would vote for elected Regional Assemblies (to whom RDAs would become directly accountable) in their local region. However, the disappointing result of a vote in the North East in respect of a proposed elected North East Regional Assembly indicated a lack of public interest in such bodies. It is somewhat telling that 78 per cent of those that voted in the election in November 2004 voted against the introduction of an elected Assembly.

14.6.3 The London Mayor and Assembly

In 1985 Parliament revoked the Greater London Council (Local Government Act 1985) which meant that London as a large capital city lacked an overall strategic body. The Labour Government elected in 1997 implemented plans for a democratic city government for London by establishing the following under the Greater London Authority Act 1999:

- A directly elected Mayor of London.

- An elected London Assembly.

The next elections are scheduled for 2008.

As in Scotland, Wales and Northern Ireland this legislation followed an endorsement of the government's proposals in a referendum held in 1998.

The London Mayor

The office of Mayor (currently held by Ken Livingstone) represents London. He has an executive role to, *inter alia*, develop transport, environment and planning strategies for London. He also sets a Budget for the Greater London Authority. He is supported by a Deputy (a member of the Assembly).

The London Assembly

This is composed of 25 elected Assembly Members (AMs) whose role, *inter alia*, is to hold the Mayor to account by monitoring, debating and questioning his activities and decisions. In addition, they investigate matters which are of significance to people living in London. The Assembly makes use of an investigative committee system in carrying out its responsibilities.

Elections

As a result of the last election in June 2004 the political makeup of the Assembly in May 2007 was as follows:

Table 14.5

Political Party	Number of AMs
Labour	7
Conservative	9
Liberal Democratic	5
Green Party	2
One London Group	2
TOTAL	25

source: www.london.gov.uk

At the same time Ken Livingstone (the former Labour MP) was re-elected as Mayor of London. Each are elected for a term of four years.

KEY FACTS

	Scotland	Wales	Northern Ireland
Nomenclature **Legislature** **Executive**	Scottish Parliament Scottish Executive	National Assembly Welsh Assembly Government	Northern Ireland Assembly Executive Committee
Size of chamber and electoral system	129 members in total 73 Constituency MSPs (simple majority system) 56 Regional MSPs (Additional Member system)	60 members in total 40 Constituency AMs (simple majority system) 20 Regional AMs (Additional Member system)	108 Members (Single Transferable Vote system)
Primary legislative powers	Yes	No (but the 2006 Act provides for this possibility in the future)	Yes
Subordinate legislative powers	Yes	Yes	Yes
Tax-varying powers	Yes	No	No

Further reading

Scotland's Parliament Cm 3658 (The Scottish Office, 1997).

A Voice for Wales Cm 3718 (The Stationery Office, 1997).

Better Governance for Wales Cm 6582 (Welsh Office, 2005).

Your Region, Your Choice: Revitalising the English Regions Cm 5511 (The Stationery Office, 2002).

Dalyell, T, 'Devolution: The End of Britain' in Sutherland, K (ed), *The Rape of the Constitution?* (Imprint Academic, 2000), p 257.

Leeke, M, Sear, C and Gay, O, 'An introduction to devolution in the UK', 03/84, (House of Commons Library, 2003).

Wilson, D, and Game, C, *Local Government in the United Kingdom* (4th edn, Palgrave Macmillan, 2006), chapters 3, 5, 9, 11 and 12.

Devolution Monitoring Programme (The Constitution Unit). These publications are produced continuously by the Constitution Unit (University of London) and cover all aspect of devolution.

Websites

www.scottish.parliament.uk
www.london.gov.uk
www.wales.gov.uk
www.niassembly.gov.uk

chapter
15 THE EUROPEAN
COMMUNITY

AIMS AND OBJECTIVES

At the end of this chapter you should be able to:

■ Understand the constitutional features of the European Community

■ Appreciate the impact the European Community has had on Britain's uncodified
constitutional arrangements

Introduction

In *Bulmer v Bollinger* [1974] Ch 401 Lord Denning MR observed that:

> J   '... The Treaty is like an incoming tide. It flows into the estuaries and up the rivers. It
> cannot be held back.'

The United Kingdom has been a member of the European Community since January 1973 (via
the European Communities Act 1972). As a result, it is impossible to examine the modern British
constitution without considering the impact of European Community law. In fact, membership of
the Community has had a profound and wide-ranging effect on various different aspects of our
constitutional arrangements. In particular, it has altered our understanding of the lynchpin of the
constitution: parliamentary sovereignty. In addition, it has also affected:

• Individuals (by conferring rights on them).

• Judges (by altering their approach to interpreting legislation).

• Politicians/parliamentarians (who must now work within the constraints of European law).

• The sources of law (the sources of the British constitution now embrace European Treaties,
  secondary legislation and case law decided by the European Court of Justice).

As European Community law is considered in detail in *Unlocking EU Law*, this chapter will simply
highlight the key constitutional aspects raised by joining the European Community.

15.1 The Treaties

15.1.1 A *de facto* constitution?

The Treaty of Rome 1957 (the EC Treaty) established the European Economic Community (called the European Community since 1993) and can be viewed as a *de facto* constitution. It should be remembered that in general terms a constitution will establish the apparatus of the state by creating institutions, allocating them specific responsibilities/powers and providing limitations on them (see Chapter 2). In this way the EC Treaty has many parallels with the constitution of a state. In particular, the Treaty:

- Set out the aims and objectives of the Community which included, *inter alia*, to establish a common market in goods, persons, capital and labour, to raise the standard of living and to develop economic activities (Arts 2 and 3 EC Treaty). Similarly, state constitutions will set out their objectives (eg the protection of human rights). In fact, later revisions of the EC Treaty (ie the Amsterdam Treaty of 1997) do refer to the protection of human rights, democracy and the rule of law.

- Established the Community institutions (see section 15.2) – although it made use of the European Court and Assembly (later to be renamed the European Parliament) which already existed (having been established under the Treaty of Paris 1951 for the European Coal and Steel Community and the European Atomic Energy Community).

- Allocated the Community institutions specific roles. For example, one of the constitutional functions of the European Commission is to enforce European Community law by ensuring that Member States adhere to it (now Art 226). In addition, each institution is equipped with particular powers. For example, under Art 230, as it is now, the European Court of Justice is authorised to review legislation which has been by enacted by the Community institutions. In this respect the European Court is acting in a way which is analogous to a Supreme or Constitutional Court in a state constitution.

- Provided for the European Court of Justice to issue the definitive interpretation of European Community law (now Art 234). This is also similar to state constitutions whereby a Constitutional or Supreme Court (eg the US Supreme Court) will act as the final arbiter as to the meaning of the provisions of the written constitution.

- Has been interpreted (by the European Court) to be regarded as a form of higher and fundamental law which is superior to the law of Member States (see section 15.6.2). This is comparable with state constitutions where the law of the constitution has a special and fundamental legal status.

As indicated in Chapter 2, a codified constitution will usually set out the methods and procedures used to alter the content of the constitution. Similarly, in the context of Europe, the EC Treaty has periodically been revised by the enactment of subsequent Treaties:

- 1986 Single European Act.

- 1992 Treaty on European Union.
- 1997 Treaty of Amsterdam.
- 2000 Treaty of Nice.

In particular, the 1992 Treaty created the European Union which incorporated the existing European Community as one of its three pillars. Moreover, each of the above Treaties has incrementally increased the powers of the European Parliament *vis-à-vis* the other institutions. The procedure used to amend the original EC Treaty involves the unanimous agreement at a summit of the European Council (containing the respective Presidents/Prime Ministers of the Member States) and thereafter being ratified by each Member State.

15.1.2 The European Constitution

Although historically the British constitution has been described as unwritten or uncodified, by virtue of our membership of the European Community/Union, one part of our constitution *is* now written and codified (namely, European Community law and principles). Moreover, Community law is a fundamental law with a higher status than any other Member State law. In this sense, so long as we remain a member of the Community/Union, European Community law will have a special status in our constitutional arrangements.

In 2004 at a European Summit the Heads of State/Government agreed a European Constitution (technically called the Treaty establishing a Constitution for Europe) which was scheduled to be ratified subsequently by all Member States. In order for a Treaty to come into force all Member States must ratify it, but in 2005 both France and the Netherlands rejected the Treaty in separate referenda. In any event, the term *European Constitution* is somewhat of a misnomer. The term European Constitution appears to suggest or presuppose that Europe does not *already* have a constitution of some description, whereas as noted above, the EC Treaty performs many of the functions of a state constitution. In practical terms the European Constitution (if ever enacted in its present, or an amended, form) is effectively a Treaty which 'tidies up' the EC Treaty and its subsequent revisions.

ACTIVITY

Problem solving

Revisit Chapter 2 and then consider whether the EC Treaty represents a constitution for Europe, its institutions and citizens.

15.2 The institutions

15.2.1 An outline of the institutions

The European Community is a supranational body which comprises an institutional structure with each body having a designated role:

- **The European Council** – is composed of the Heads of State/Government which make important decisions concerning the direction of the Community/Union. They also agree new Treaties. Technically the European Council is a body rather than an institution as it is not subject to the jurisdiction of the European Court of Justice.

- **The Council (formerly known as the Council of Ministers)** – is composed of a government minister representing each Member State. It co-ordinates the economic policies of Member States and adopts secondary legislation.

- **The European Commission** – is composed of one nominee from each Member State, but once appointed, they are independent of their respective Member State. The Commission has many roles which include drafting legislative proposals and enforcing European Community law.

- **The European Parliament** – is composed of elected MEPs (Members of the European Parliament) and, *inter alia*, is involved in the process of adopting legislation and acts in concert with the Council to agree the Community Budget.

- **The European Court of Justice** – is composed of one judge from each Member State. The court, together with the Court of First Instance, interprets European Community law (providing definitive interpretations under Art 234) and ensures both Member States and the other Community institutions follow Community law.

15.2.2 The separation of powers in Europe

We saw earlier in Chapter 5 that the British constitution is characterised by the fact that it does not adhere to a strict separation of powers. This is also true in relation to the institutional structure of the European Community as the three government functions are distributed between the various institutions:

The legislative function is performed by:
- The Council in adopting secondary legislation (see section 15.3.2).
- The European Parliament in adopting legislation where the co-decision or co-operation procedure is in use.
- The European Court when it develops principles of European Community law (eg the doctrine of direct effect – see section 15.5).
- The European Council when it agrees Treaty revisions (here it is performing effectively a *de facto* legislative role).

The executive function is performed by:
- The European Council in determining the direction of European policy.
- The Council in co-ordinating the national economies of Member States and making executive decisions.
- The European Commission in enforcing European Community law.

The judicial function is performed by:

- The European Court of Justice and Court of First Instance in providing definitive interpretations of European law and resolving legal disputes

- The European Commission under Art 226 in determining that a Member State has breached European law and issuing a *reasoned* opinion (a non-binding opinion which sets out how the Commission believes that Community law has been violated). In effect, it is performing a *de facto* quasi-judicial function. In addition, in enforcing competition law they can impose a fine on an undertaking (ie a company) for breaching Arts 81–82.

Although there is no clear separation of powers in Europe, the Community institutional infrastructure has the following distinct checks and balances:

- Although the Council adopts legislation, under the co-decision and co-operation procedure, it has to work in concert with the European Parliament.

- Although the Council adopts legislation (analogous to the UK Parliament) it is dependent upon the European Commission to draft proposals to put before it (analogous to the British government drafting a Bill).

- Whilst the European Commission has a degree of discretion in drafting legislative proposals, ultimately it has to make them acceptable to the Council/European Parliament who adopt them.

- The European Parliament can refuse to accept the Council's nominations for a putative President of the European Commission and Commissioners. It can also dismiss the Commission *en bloc*.

- The European Parliament can block the Budget which has been drafted by the European Commission and approved by the Council.

- The European Court of Justice can review the actions and legislation of the Council, Parliament and Commission.

- The European Council can amend the Treaty to increase or decrease the power or responsibilities of any institution (including the European Court of Justice).

15.2.3 Democracy and the European institutions

One charge which has historically been levelled at the European Community/Union has been its 'democratic deficit'. In other words, there was a deficit of democracy in the institutional framework of the Community as most of the institutions were not directly elected, and so lacked democratic legitimacy. Indeed, the body with the most democratic legitimacy (the European Parliament), historically had the least power.

- The European Council is composed of the various Presidents and Prime Ministers who may or may not be directly elected. For example, although the French President is elected by the people of France, neither the British Prime Minister nor the Irish Taoiseach are directly elected *per se*.

Instead, they are drawn from their respective legislatures (United Kingdom Parliament, Irish Oireachtas), albeit they are drawn from the dominant political party within it.

- The Council contains government ministers from each Member State who are not directly elected. In the case of the United Kingdom, government ministers are not elected *per se,* rather they are drawn from the two Houses of Parliament, one of which is not elected at all (see section 11.6.2). Similarly, in the Republic of Ireland government ministers are drawn from the Oireachtas. Both the European Council and the Council represent the interests of the Member States.

- The European Commission is composed of Commissioners who have been in effect, nominated by their respective national governments and approved by the (elected) European Parliament. The latter can also remove Commissioners *en bloc.* The European Commission represents the interests of the European Community which is why once appointed, Commissioners must be independent of their respective Member State.

- The European Parliament is the only wholly directly elected body in the European Community (although it has only been elected since 1979, prior to that representatives of each national Parliament would sit). The European Parliament represents the interests of the people of Europe. In order to address the 'democratic deficit', each revision of the EC Treaty has provided the European Parliament with more powers. The point must be made, however, that the democratic legitimacy of the European Parliament itself has to be questioned when the turnout at European elections (which take place every five years) is poor. For example, at the 2004 election the average turnout for European countries was less than 50 per cent with the United Kingdom registering a turnout of 39 per cent, a British record high for European elections (A Mellows-Facer, R Cracknell and J Yonwin, 'European Parliament elections 2004' 04/50 (House of Commons Library, 2004), p 56).

- The European Court of Justice is composed of a judge being nominated from each Member State.

KEY FACTS

Institution/ Body	Composition	Role	Represents
European Council	Heads of State/government (composed of 27 Heads of State/Government together with each Foreign Minister and the President of the European Commission).	<ul><li>Provides general direction and impetus to the EC.</li><li>Makes political decisions.</li><li>Revises the EC Treaty.</li></ul>	Member States.
Council	Minister from each Member State (Council composed of 27 Ministers).	<ul><li>Adopts legislative proposals.</li><li>Makes executive decisions.</li><li>Co-ordinates national economies.</li><li>Confers powers on the Commission to make legislation.</li><li>Adopts the Budget.</li></ul>	Member States.
European Commission	Nominated from each Member State and approved (and removed) by the European Parliament (27 Commissioners headed by the President of the European Commission).	<ul><li>Initiates and drafts legislative proposals.</li><li>Enforces EC law as a watchdog.</li><li>Exercises powers conferred by the Council.</li><li>Acts as a mediator.</li><li>Drafts Budget.</li></ul>	European Community.
European Parliament	MEPs directly elected by the electorate in each Member State (785 MEPs).	<ul><li>Supervises the other institutions.</li><li>Involved in the legislative process.</li><li>Adopts the Budget with the Council.</li></ul>	European people.

ACTIVITY

Essay writing

To what extent does the institutional structure of the European Community depart from the separation of powers and do you consider that it is democratic?

15.3 Sources of law

Membership of the European Community has widened the legal sources of the British constitution. In broad terms, European Community law can be divided into primary and secondary sources:

15.3.1 Primary sources

These comprise the founding Treaty (Treaty of Rome 1957) together with its subsequent amendment over the years (Single European Act 1986, Maastricht 1992, Amsterdam 1997 and Nice 2000).

15.3.2 Secondary sources

These comprise the legislation (known as Acts – see section 4.7.2) made by the Community institutions.

> **(A)** 'In order to carry out their tasks and in accordance with the provisions of this Treaty, the European Parliament acting jointly with the Council, the Council and the Commission shall make regulations and issue directives, take decisions, make recommendations or deliver opinions'.
>
> Art 249 EC Treaty

- **Regulations** – these are self-executing and of general application (applying to all Member States). They ensure absolute uniformity and exactitude in all Member States. In constitutional terms they by-pass the legislatures of each Member State (including the UK Parliament) as they apply *automatically* in every Member State without the legislature having to endorse it.

- **Directives** – these are more flexible than regulations and are addressed to specific Member States in order to ensure a harmonisation of national laws. For example, it may well be that the law of three Member States are out of kilter with the rest of the Community and so a directive is addressed to them to bring their laws into line. Directives are binding as to the result to be achieved, but leave the Member State with a measure of discretion as to how to implement it.

- **Decisions** – these are binding on those to whom they are addressed (Member States or companies).

These secondary sources enter United Kingdom law via s 2 of the European Communities Act 1972. In addition to the sources above, case law and preliminary rulings of the European Court of Justice also represent a form of secondary source of law (see below).

15.4 The European Court of Justice

The European Court is the judicial arm of the European Community.

15.4.1 The distinctive nature of the court

The European Court is distinctive in constitutional terms (at least from the perspective of a British public lawyer) in the following ways:

- **Composition** – the court (like the European Court of Human Rights in Strasbourg) includes judges who are academics with no direct judicial experience.

- **No public dissent** – the court (unlike the European Court of Human Rights) does not issue dissenting/minority judgments. All judges, whether or not they agreed with the decision, must sign the judgment

- **Advocate General** – the court is assisted by Advocate Generals which have no parallel in the British court system. In brief, after the parties have delivered their submissions, an Advocate General will summarise the legal points in the case (even adding some that have been overlooked so that the court is fully conversant with all relevant information) and put forward a non-binding submission. The court often adopts these submissions.

- **No *stare decisis*** – the court is, technically, not bound by precedent and so does not have to follow its own previous decisions. In practice, however, for legal certainty and practical reasons, the court generally follows its previous rulings.

- **Legal reasoning** – the court's method of interpreting legislation is different from the traditional approach used by the British judiciary (ie a literal/historical method). In contrast, the European Court judges have adopted a more teleological/purposive technique. As a result of the inception of Community law into our constitution and legal system, the United Kingdom judiciary in applying Community law must adopt the legal reasoning employed by the European Court in Luxembourg. As indicated by Lord Denning MR in *Bulmer v Bollinger* [1974] Ch 401:

> **J** 'Beyond doubt the English courts must follow the same principles as the European court. Otherwise there would be differences between the countries ... They must follow the European pattern. No longer must they examine the words in meticulous detail. No longer must they argue about the precise grammatical sense. They must look to the purpose or intent. To quote the words of the European court in the *Da Costa* case ... they must deduce "from the wording and the spirit of the Treaty the meaning of the community rules".'

15.4.2 The role of the European Court of Justice

Under Art 220 of the EC Treaty the European Court of Justice and Court of First Instance:

'shall ensure that in the interpretation and application of this Treaty the law is observed'.

Application of European law

The European Court ensures that the application of European Community law is observed by Member States (Arts 226 and 227 where enforcement proceedings are brought by the European Commission or another Member State, respectively) and the political institutions of the Community under Arts 230 and 232 (excluding the European Council).

Interpretation of European law

Article 234 provides that the European Court (and now the Court of First Instance) shall have the jurisdiction to give preliminary ruling concerning, *inter alia,*

(a) the interpretation of the EC Treaty and

(b) the validity and interpretation of the acts of the institutions (eg regulations, directives see section 15.3.2)

In brief, where a national/domestic court is faced with a provision of either a primary or secondary source of law which is unclear and requires interpretation, Art 234 provides a mechanism whereby that court can make a reference to the European Court which asks it to interpret and clarify the point of law (a preliminary ruling). National courts against which there is no appeal/review *must* make such a reference. The ruling issued by the European Court is binding on the national court and represents *the* definitive interpretation of European law. In this way the European Court is the final arbiter as to the meaning of European Community law.

The Art 234 procedure provides a direct link between the European Court in Luxembourg and the national/domestic courts and tribunals of the Member States. It can be likened to a wheel, with the ECJ as the hub and the national courts and tribunals on the rim. In this way, all domestic courts and tribunals are directly connected to the European Court and it links these Justices with the judges of the Member States.

Figure 15.1

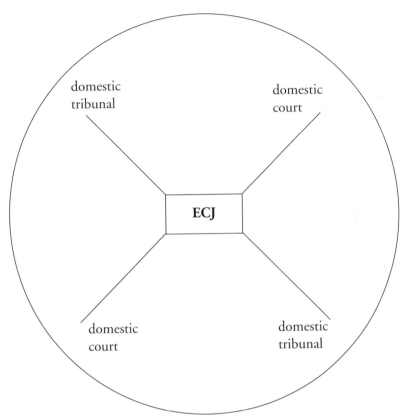

Article 234 is not an appellate system whereby national courts appeal to the European Court. Instead, it is a reference system which involves a partnership between the Justices of the European Court with the respective judges of the Member States. In terms of the British constitution, the preliminary ruling procedure means that the House of Lords is not the ultimate arbiter in respect of European law. This has been specifically authorised by s 3 of the European Communities Act 1972. Indeed, as a court of last resort, our law lords *must* refer ambiguous points of Community law to the justices in Luxembourg.

KEY FACTS

Institution/ Body	Composition	Role
European Court	One judge from each Member State.	• Interprets Community law (Art 234). • Applies and enforces Community law (Art 220) against Community institutions (Arts 230 and 232) and Member States (Arts 226 and 227).

15.5 Individuals

Membership of the European Community has had a direct impact on individuals. Firstly, the Maastricht Treaty of 1992 conferred citizenship of the European Union on individuals in the Member States. Secondly Community law has conferred rights on individuals (eg not to be discriminated against on the grounds of sex) which can be enforced in their own domestic courts. This principle is known as the doctrine of direct effect and it has been developed by the European Court (not having been explicitly set out in the EC Treaty).

CASE EXAMPLE

Marshall v Southampton and South-West Hampshire AHA (No 1) Case 152/84 [1986] ECR 723

Ms Marshall was employed by Southampton and South-West Area Health Authority and was forced to retire at 62 (the authority had a policy which required women to retire earlier than men – 60 rather than 65). She contended that the Sex Discrimination Act 1975 (which did not apply to retirement) contravened Directive 76/207 on the equal treatment of men and women.

The Court of Appeal made a reference to the European Court as to whether Marshall could rely on the directive (the doctrine of direct effect). The European Court issued its preliminary ruling that a policy of different retirement ages contravened the directive and that Marshall could rely on the rights set out in the directive. Thereafter, the Court of

CONTINUED ▸

Appeal applied the ruling to the facts of the case and held that Marshall had been unlawfully discriminated against in being dismissed and she subsequently obtained compensation. This case illustrates an individual using Community law rights (eg the right not to be discriminated against) in a domestic court against a public body (the Area Health Authority being treated as a public body as an emanation of the state).

Similarly, in *Macarthys v Smith* (1981) at section 15.6.3), Mrs Smith relied on the right of equal pay for equal work (Art 119 – now Art 141) with a man whom she had replaced.

15.6 European Community law and parliamentary sovereignty

15.6.1 Introduction

Membership of the European Community has had a profound effect on parliamentary sovereignty. As noted in Chapter 7, the classic and historic doctrine of parliamentary sovereignty is that the Crown in Parliament can pass any law it chooses. This absolute principle, however, is in direct opposition to the principle of the primacy of European Community law as developed and espoused by the European Court of Justice. In short, according to the European Court, where a provision of Community law and national/domestic law conflict, the former must prevail (see *Costa* (1964) below).

15.6.2 The primacy of European law

The doctrine of the primacy (or supremacy) of European Community law, like the doctrine of direct effect, is not expressly set out in the EC Treaty. Instead, it has been developed by the European Court of Justice, thereby illustrating its quasi-legislative role in practice. As an aside it is of interest to note that if the European Constitution ever comes into effect, it provides specifically for the primacy of European law.

The principle was first indicated in *Van Gend & Loos v Nederlandse administratie der belastingen* Case 26/62 [1963] ECR1 where the European Court stated;

> **J** '...the Community constitutes a new legal order of international law for the benefit of which the states have limited their sovereign rights, albeit within limited fields, and the subjects of which comprise not only Member States but also their nationals.'

In the subsequent case of *Costa v ENEL* Case 6/64 [1964] ECR 585 the European Court noted that:

> **J** '...the law stemming from the Treaty, an independent source of law, could not, because of its special and original nature, be overridden by domestic legal provisions, however framed, without being deprived of its character as Community law and without the legal basis of the Community itself being called into question.'

In short, if a provision of domestic law contravenes European law, the latter must prevail, thereby indicating the supreme and fundamental nature of Community law. In the later case of *Internationale Handelsgesellschaft mbH v EVGF* Case 11/70 [1970] ECR 1125 the court made it clear that the principle extended to secondary sources of European law (eg a regulation) and that it prevailed over the constitutional rules of a state (ie its constitutional law):

> **J** '...the law stemming from the Treaty, an independent source of law, cannot, because of its very nature, be overriden by rules of national law ... Therefore the validity of a Community measure or its effect within a Member State cannot be affected by allegations that it runs counter to either fundamental rights as formulated by the constitution of that State or the principles of a national constitutional structure.'

See also *Simmenthal SpA v Amministrazione delle Finanze dello Stato* Case 70/77 [1978] ECR 1453 and *Commission v (French Republic)* Case 167/73 [1974] ECR 359.

ACTIVITY

Question

What is the nature and constitutional significance of the principle of the primacy of directly effective European Community law?

15.6.3 The reception of European Community law in the British constitution

The United Kingdom has a dualist constitution which means that even if a Treaty is agreed to in international law, its provisions do not become legally enforceable in our domestic law unless an Act of Parliament has formally incorporated it. In 1972 Parliament passed the European Communities Act which provided for the reception of Community law into our constitution and legal system. In constitutional terms, it is worth noting that this Act, in spite of its profound constitutional consequences, was passed in the ordinary manner, in the sense that no special majority was needed (although the committee stage was taken on the Floor of the House). In fact, the Bill only narrowly passed its third reading in the House of Commons. This indicates the flexibility of the British constitution as the Republic of Ireland who joined the EEC (as it was then) at the same time was required by their written constitution to hold a referendum.

By virtue of s 2(1) of the European Communities Act 1972, from 1 January 1973, Community law formally became part of the law of the United Kingdom. Section 2(4) is the most controversial aspect of the Act as it deals with the impact of European law on domestic law:

S any such provision (of any such extent) as might be made by Act of Parliament, and any enactment passed or to be passed, other than one contained in this part of this Act, shall be construed and have effect subject to the foregoing provisions of this section.

In constitutional terms s 2(4) means that United Kingdom statutes passed before and after 1972 must be construed and be held subject to Community law:

CASE EXAMPLE

Macarthys Ltd v Smith [1981] 1 QB 180

Mrs Smith replaced a man to manage Macarthys' stockroom but was paid £10 a week less than he had been paid. She claimed equal pay under s 1 of the Equal Pay Act 1970 (although this appeared to be confined to contemporaneous employment) and this raised the issue of whether Art 119 (now Art 141) of the EC Treaty (equal pay for equal work) applied to the situation where a woman replaced a man but who had not worked contemporaneously along side him. The Court of Appeal was uncertain on this point of European law and sent a reference to the European Court asking whether Art 119 was confined to men and women working contemporaneously. The subsequent ruling stated that the principle of equal pay was not so confined but also applied where a woman replaced a man. The Court of Appeal then applied this ruling to the case and held for Mrs Smith. Lord Denning MR stated that.

J 'It is important now to declare – and it must be made plain – that the provisions of article 119 of the EEC Treaty take priority over anything in our English statute on equal pay which is inconsistent with article 119. That priority is given by our own law. It is given by the European Communities Act 1972 itself. Community law is now part of our law: and, whenever there is any inconsistency, Community law has priority.'

Similarly, in *Garland v British Rail Engineering Ltd* [1983] 2 AC 751, the House of Lords, following a preliminary ruling by the European Court of Justice, construed the Sex Discrimination Act 1975 in line with Art 119 (now Art 141) prohibiting discrimination. As a result the court held that British Rail had discriminated against Garland when it provided special travel facilities for the families of retired male employees, but not female ones. The words of the 1975 Act could (without being unnecessarily strained) be interpreted so as to be consistent with Art 119.

In terms of United Kingdom secondary legislation, in *Lister and others v Forth Dry Dock and Engineering Co Ltd and another* [1989] 1 All ER 1134, the House of Lords read and construed a domestic regulation (delegated legislation) so as to conform to a European directive which protected the rights of employees in circumstances when their employer changed. See also *Pickstone v Freemans plc* [1988] 2 All ER 803.

In terms of a conflict between Community law and an Act of Parliament, Lord Denning MR, prior to the reference to the European Court in *Macarthys Ltd v Smith* [1979] 3 All ER 325, made the following *obiter* point concerning the constitutional impact of Community law on United Kingdom statutes:

> **J** 'Thus far I have assumed that our Parliament, whenever it passes legislation, intends to fulfill its obligations under the Treaty. If the time should come when our Parliament deliberately passes an Act with the intention of repudiating the Treaty or any provision in it or intentionally of acting inconsistently with it and says so in express terms then I should have thought that it would be the duty of our courts to follow the statute of our Parliament ... Unless there is such an intentional and express repudiation of the Treaty, it is our duty to give priority to the Treaty.'

In essence, Lord Denning was indicating that the domestic doctrine of implied repeal (see section 7.9.3) does not operate whenever Community law applies. In other words, if domestic legislation passed after 1972 is inconsistent with Community law (which forms part of our law through the European Communities Act 1972), Community law (and so the 1972 Act) will prevail *unless* the later legislation expressly and clearly intends to repudiate Community law. If the legislation violates Community law, but does not do so intentionally, then the courts will apply Community law over the statute. This appears to have been the approach taken by the courts in *ex parte Factortame* which involved a statute which was passed *after* 1972 (ie after the European Communities Act), but which was inconsistent with Community law (eg which forms part of our law through s 2 of the 1972 Act).

15.6.4 The *Factortame* litigation

CASE EXAMPLE

R v Secretary of State for Transport, ex parte Factortame Ltd and others (No 2)
[1991] 1 AC 603

Part II of the Merchant Shipping Act 1988 restricted the number of fishing vessels whose catch could form part of the United Kingdom fishing quota (the European Community had a policy to prevent over fishing of depleted fishing stocks). Under the authority of the Act,

CONTINUED ▶

the Transport Secretary issued the Merchant Shipping (Registration of Fishing Vessels) Regulations 1988 requiring vessels registered as British to re-register. Vessels would only qualify if their owners (or 75 per cent of their company shareholders) were British citizens or lived in Britain. Factortame and others were companies who before the Act had been registered as British, but whose directors/shareholders were Spanish. As they could not meet the new registration requirements, they sought judicial review of the Act and regulations on the basis that they breached Community law, *inter alia*, in terms of discrimination.

The Divisional Court faced with a provision of Community law which required interpretation made a reference to the European Court (the first reference) and pending the receipt of this ruling, provided Factortame with interim relief (thereby protecting their putative Community law rights which had not yet been established) by disapplying Pt II of the Act and preventing the minister from enforcing the legislation against Factortame. The Court of Appeal set aside the order on the basis that the court had no jurisdiction to issue it. The House of Lords confirmed that the court had no power to issue the interim injunction, in terms of either granting an injunction against the Crown or disapplying a statute prior to a ruling of the European Court on a point of Community law. Nevertheless, the House of Lords did refer to the European Court the question (the second reference) as to whether it was a requirement of Community law that a national court should provide a interim remedy in order to protect a party's putative Community law rights whilst waiting for the European Court to issue a ruling on the point.

In June 1990, in response to the second reference, the European Court issued its ruling to the effect that a national court must set aside a rule of domestic law which impeded a national court from granting interim relief to protect Community law rights (otherwise Community law would be undermined).

Thereafter the House of Lords applied the ruling to the facts of the case and reinstated the interim injunction protecting Factortame's putative Community law rights which had not yet been definitely established (ie in advance of the European Court's ruling in respect of the first reference). Lord Bridge noted that:

> **J** 'Some public comments on the decision of the European Court of Justice, affirming the jurisdiction of the courts of member states to override national legislation if necessary to enable interim relief to be granted in protection of rights under Community law, have suggested that this was a novel and dangerous invasion by a Community institution of the sovereignty of the United Kingdom Parliament. But such

CONTINUED ▸

J

comments are based on a misconception. If the supremacy within the European Community of Community law over the national law of member states was not always inherent in the EEC Treaty ... it was certainly well established in the jurisprudence of the European Court of Justice long before the United Kingdom joined the Community. Thus, whatever limitation of its sovereignty Parliament accepted when it enacted the European Communities Act 1972 was entirely voluntary. Under the terms of the Act of 1972 it has always been clear that it was the duty of a United Kingdom court, when delivering final judgment, to override any rule of national law found to be in conflict with any directly enforceable rule of Community law.'

In *R v Secretary of State for Transport, ex parte Factortame Ltd (No 3)* [1992] 1 QB 680 the Divisional Court applied the ruling of the European Court in respect of the first reference, which was issued in July 1991, and declared that the Merchant Shipping Act breached Community law. Thereafter, Parliament passed the Merchant Shipping (Registration) Act 1993, which amended and restated the law relating to the registering of shipping, and in *R v Secretary of State for Transport, ex parte Factortame Ltd (No 5)* [2000] 1 AC 524 Factortame obtained compensation for the loss and expenses incurred by the 1988 Act.

Similarly, in the later case of *Equal Opportunities Commission and another v Secretary of State for Employment* [1994] 1 All ER 910, the House of Lords issued a declaration that provisions of the Employment Protection (Consolidation) Act 1978 were contrary to European Community law (see section 19.4.2).

Also, in *Thoburn v Sunderland City Council* [2002] EWHC 195 (Admin), Laws LJ commented that the European Communities Act 1972 was one of a number of 'constitutional statutes' which were not subject to implied repeal (see section 4.4.5). On the facts of the case, however, the court held that there was no inconsistency between s 1 Weights and Measures Act 1985 and the earlier s 2(2) European Communities Act 1972.

KEY FACTS

- Section 2(1) of the European Communities Act 1972 formally incorporated Community law into the United Kingdom's legal system.

CONTINUED ▶

KEY FACTS

- Section 2(4) of the Act requires the courts to interpret all statutes passed before and after the 1972 Act in line with and subject to Community law.
- In *Garland* (1983) the House of Lords interpreted the Sex Discrimination Act 1975 in line with Art 119 (prohibiting discrimination in retirement).
- In *Lister and others* (1989) the House of Lords interpreted domestic delegated legislation in line with a European directive.
- In *Factortame* (1991) the House of Lords suspended the operation of the Merchant Shipping Act 1988 as it conflicted with the putative Community law rights of Factortame.
- In *EOC* (1994) the House of Lords issued a declaration that the Employment Protection (Consolidation) Act 1978 violated Community law on the basis that it indirectly discriminated against women.

15.6.5 The constitutional impact of *Factortame*

The precise constitutional significance and impact of *Factortame* is not universally agreed upon by academics. Craig, however, has rather usefully summarised how the judgments in *Factortame* (1991), *EOC* (1994) and *Thoburn* (2002) can be conceptualised into three broad themes (P Craig, 'Britain in the European Union' in J Jowell and D Oliver (eds), *The Changing Constitution* (5th edn, Oxford University Press, 2004), pp 103–105):

(i) 'statutory construction':
This approach is a rule of construction which requires any inconsistency between European Community law and a United Kingdom statute to be resolved in favour of the former. This is subject to the United Kingdom Parliament passing legislation which is clearly meant to depart from Community law.

(ii) 'a technical legal revolution':
This approach regards the jurisprudence of the courts as revolutionary in the sense that it affected the traditional view of parliamentary sovereignty. In short, in *Factortame* the courts altered the rule of recognition in respect of statutes with the result that the 1972 Parliament did something which Dicey (see section 7.9) had argued was not possible: it bound its successors. In other words, the 1972 Parliament (which passed the European Communities Act which gave Community law

overriding force in our law) bound the later Parliament of 1988, because the legislation that it had passed (the Merchant Shipping Act 1988) had to be disapplied as being inconsistent with Community law (see H Wade, 'Sovereignty – Revolution or Evolution?' (1996) 112 LQR 568).

(iii) 'normative arguments of legal principle':

Craig argues that the third conceptualisation (and his favoured view) of the above judgments concerning supremacy/sovereignty can be regarded 'as being based on *normative arguments of legal principle the content of which can and will vary across time.*' (sic) In other words, the 'principled consequences' of membership of the European Community entail the United Kingdom being bound by European Community law (and so are reasoned constraints on Parliament's legislative omnipotence).

In any event, the following points are also worth noting:

- It has been suggested that in the *Factortame* case the courts did something which Dicey had argued was impossible, namely the courts challenged and disapplied an Act of Parliament – the Merchant Shipping Act 1988. The constitutional/legal (and moral) authority for the courts to do this came from s 2(4) of the European Communities Act 1972. Indeed, as noted by Lord Bridge, it was Parliament which had voluntarily passed the 1972 Act. Moreover, by virtue of the jurisprudence of the European Court (*Van Gend* (1963) and *Costa* (1964) – see section 15.6.2), in 1972 the United Kingdom would have been fully conversant with the principle of the primacy of Community law.

- It appears that the doctrine of implied repeal does not apply where European Community law operates. In other words, if as a result of, for example, a parliamentary oversight or misunderstanding of the requirements of Community law, an Act of Parliament is passed which is inconsistent with Community law, the UK courts will ensure that Community law prevails over the statute. However, this would not be the case where the violation of Community law is deliberate (see below).

  Notwithstanding the above, Tomkins (*Public Law*, (Oxford University Press, 2003), pp 118–119), along with others, has argued that the *Factortame* case itself did not engage the doctrine of implied repeal as, for one thing, there was no conflict in terms of substance between the Merchant Shipping Act 1988 (dealing with fishing registration) and the earlier European Communities Act 1972 (dealing with the relationship between EC law and domestic law). In short, they were different statutes dealing with different subject matters.

- In *Factortame* although the House of Lords (and the Divisional Court in the earlier stage of the litigation) issued an interim injunction restraining the operation of the 1988 Act, it did not strike it down *per se*. This is not the same, therefore, as a Supreme or Constitutional Court striking down and permanently invalidating legislation.

- It must be remembered that whatever the impact of the decision on parliamentary sovereignty, Community law does not govern every aspect of our lives and so in these contexts the full force of parliamentary sovereignty will continue.

Finally, it seems that if Parliament should decide to do so (and it is highly unlikely that it would do so in the near future), it could legislate to expressly repeal the European Communities Act 1972. In this way it would repudiate European Community law and the jurisdiction and principles of the European Court of Justice. Having said this, we are not exactly sure how the courts would react to such legislation, although it is highly probable that they would accept that Parliament had decided to leave the Community/Union and give effect to the Act repudiating it. Short of this, however, it appears that the courts will continue to construe United Kingdom statutes in the light of Community law (and suspend them if necessary as in *Factortame*) until Parliament makes it clear that it no longer wishes to be governed by Community law and principles (see Lord Denning MR at section 15.6.3).

In the event of the United Kingdom passing legislation which violated or repudiated European Community law, it is inevitable that an investigation would be mounted by the European Commission. It is not without significance to point out that had the (rejected) European Constitution come into force, Member States would have been enabled to withdraw formally from the European Union (Art I-60). Moreover, in 2006 Lord Pearson introduced a Private Member's Bill to consider the consequences of withdrawal from Europe – see section 22.10.1.

In conclusion, Hoffmann J in *Stoke-on-Trent City Council v B & Q* [1991] Ch 48 has provided a useful summary of the constitutional impact of our membership of the European Community:

> **J** 'The EEC Treaty is the supreme law of this country, taking precedence over Acts of Parliament. Our entry into the European Economic Community meant that (subject to our undoubted but probably theoretical right to withdraw from the Community altogether) Parliament surrendered its sovereign right to legislate contrary to the provisions of the Treaty on the matters of social and economic policy which it regulated. The entry into the Community was in itself a high act of social and economic policy, by which the partial surrender of sovereignty was seen as more than compensated by the advantages of membership.'

ACTIVITY

Essay writing

Explain the *Factortame* litigation. What impact has this case had on the nature of the British constitution?

Further reading

Barendt, E, *An Introduction to Constitutional Law* (Oxford University Press, 1998), Chapters 4 and 5 pt 3.

Barnett, H, *Britain Unwrapped* (Penguin, 2002), chapter 4.

Craig, P, 'Britain in the European Union' in Jowell, J and Oliver, D (eds), *The Changing Constitution* (5th edn, Oxford University Press, 2004) p 88.

Ellis, E, 'The legislative Supremacy of Parliament and its Limits' in Feldman, D (ed), *English Public Law* (Oxford University Press, 2004), p 156.

Jenkins, R, 'Britain and Europe: The problem with being half pregnant' in Sutherland, K (ed), *The Rape of the Constitution?* (Imprint Academic, 2000), p 277.

Phillipson, G, 'Parliamentary sovereignty, European Community law and Parliament's ability to bind future parliaments', (2003) 39 *Student Law Review* 11.

Storey, T and Turner, C, *Unlocking EU Law* (Hodder Arnold, 2005), chapters 1, 2, 3 and 8.

Tebbit, N, 'Britain and Europe: The issue of sovereignty' in Sutherland, K (ed), *The Rape of the Constitution?* (Imprint Academic, 2000), p 291.

Tomkins, A, *Public Law* (Oxford University Press, 2003), pp 108–120.

Wade, H, 'Sovereignty – Revolution or Evolution?' (1996) 112 LQR 568.

Website

http://europa.eu.int

chapter 16 THE EUROPEAN CONVENTION ON HUMAN RIGHTS

AIMS AND OBJECTIVES

At the end of this chapter you should be able to:

■ Appreciate the significance of the European Convention on Human Rights both with respect to its contribution to the international protection of human rights and its effect on human rights in the United Kingdom

■ Understand the machinery for the enforcement of human rights laid down in the Convention and administered by the European Court of Human Rights

■ Be aware of the central rights contained in the Convention and how they have been interpreted and enforced by the European Court of Human Rights

■ Appreciate the central principles applied by the European Court which determine the enforcement and restriction of human rights

■ Appreciate the potential effect of the Convention and its case law on the protection of human rights in the United Kingdom

16.1 Introduction and background

The European Convention on Human Rights (1950) is central to the understanding and study of human rights and civil liberties. It is an international treaty for the protection of individual human rights, containing such rights as the right to life (Art 2), freedom from torture (Art 3), liberty and security of the person (Art 5), the right to a fair trial (Art 6), the right to private life (Art 8) and freedom of expression (Art 10). The rights will be discussed in detail later in this chapter (see below).

1. The Convention has its own machinery for enforcing human rights and this machinery has been used on numerous occasions against the United Kingdom government, resulting in changes to domestic law and practice.

2. The Convention and its case law has informed the domestic law of human rights in the United Kingdom, being applied by the domestic courts as an indirect and persuasive source (see below).

3. More specifically, the Convention and its principles are now given effect by the Human Rights Act 1998, allowing the domestic courts to apply Convention principles and case law (see below).

The European Convention on Human Rights was devised by the Council of Europe, which was set up after the Second World War to achieve unity in matters such as the protection of fundamental human rights. It was drafted in the light of the atrocities that took place before and during the Second World War and was signed by the High Contracting Parties in 1950, entering into force in 1953. The United Kingdom ratified the treaty in 1957, and in 1966 it accepted both the compulsory jurisdiction of the European Court and the power of the European Commission (now the Court) of Human Rights to receive alleged violations of Convention rights.

The Convention should not be confused with European Community (Union) law:

- The Council of Europe is separate from the European Communities and has a larger composition than the latter. In 2006 there were 46 member states of the Council of Europe.

- The Convention is enforced by the European Court of Human Rights (ECtHR), whilst community law is enforced by the European Court of Justice (ECJ).

- Whereas European Community law was incorporated via the European Communities Act 1972, the European Convention was given 'further effect' by the Human Rights Act 1998.

- European Community law has supremacy over domestic law via s 2 of the European Communities Act, whilst the Convention is still subordinate to clear contrary domestic law.

- Decisions of the ECJ have direct effect under s 3 of the 1972 Act, whilst the decisions of the ECtHR are binding in international law and can be taken into account by the domestic courts (under s 2 of the 1998 Act).

- The European Convention is not an EU Treaty, but the ECJ can take into consideration the decisions of the ECtHR, and *vice versa*.

- The European Convention on Human Rights should not be confused with the EC Charter of Fundamental Rights 2000, which, when adopted, will seek to protect a wide range of civil and political and social and economic rights within community law.

16.2 The enforcement machinery

The Convention has its own machinery for enforcement in the form of a European Court of Human Rights possessing the power to make judicial decisions, which are then enforceable on the Member States (High Contracting Parties).

Although the Convention is now given effect by the Human Rights Act, this machinery remains important:

- individuals can still petition the European Court of Human Rights if they do not receive a satisfactory remedy in domestic law;

- the domestic courts will apply the same principles and norms used by the European Court of Human Rights when adjudicating on human rights disputes;

- the case law (both former and current) will inform the domestic courts and law.

It should be noted that, under the Convention, the main obligation to protect human rights is placed on the member states.

Art 1
The High Contracting Parties shall secure to everyone within their jurisdiction the rights and freedoms defined in Section I of this Convention.

- This imposes an obligation on the Member State to provide an effective procedure and remedy for protecting human rights, although it is not mandatory to incorporate the Convention.

- Article 1 applies so as to impose a duty towards anyone within the state's jurisdiction, whether a citizen of that state or not.

- The Convention machinery is regarded as subsidiary to the national system for protecting rights and will only be used as a last resort.

- Individuals can only make a claim under the Convention machinery if they have exhausted all effective domestic remedies (Art 35).

- The European Court affords each Member State a certain discretion (A 'margin of appreciation') as to how they protect Convention rights (*Handyside v United Kingdom* (1976) 1 EHRR 737).

16.3 The European Court of Human Rights

Article 19 establishes a European Court of Human Rights to 'ensure the observance of the engagements undertaken by the High Contracting Parties in the Convention and the Protocols thereto'.

Before Protocol 11, the European Commission of Human Rights considered the admissibility of applications, secured friendly settlement and considered the merits of the applications. These roles are now performed by the full-time European Court of Human Rights, although its decisions will still continue to influence the case law of the Convention, and under s 2 of the Human Rights Act 1998 domestic courts are required to take such decisions into account when determining cases raising Convention arguments (see below).

After the ratification of Protocol 11, the Court now functions on a permanent basis and has taken over any adjudicative role formerly carried out by the European Commission of Human Rights and the Committee of Ministers. The former body is now abolished, but their decisions are persuasive authority for both the European Court and the domestic courts under s 2 of the Human Rights Act 1998. The Committee of Ministers (the foreign secretaries of each state) carry out a diplomatic role and ensure that the European Court's judgments are fully and effectively executed (Art 46).

16.3.1 The Composition of the European Court of Human Rights

Under Art 20 the court consists of a number of judges equal to that of the High Contracting Parties, who are elected by the Parliamentary Assembly of the Council of Europe. The procedure of the court is regulated by the Rules of the European Court of Human Rights.

The European Court of Human Rights comprises of

- Committees, consisting of three judges who consider the admissibility of applications (Art 27(1)) and who possess the power (Art 28) to strike out cases from its list;

- Chambers of seven judges who decide on the admissibility and merits of the application (Art 27(2)) combining the roles formerly carried out respectively by the Commission and the old European Court;

- The Grand Chamber, consisting of 17 judges who hear cases referred to them (Art 27(3)).

16.3.2 The Grand Chamber of the European Court

The Grand Chamber of the Court of Human Rights fulfils a number of roles

- Under Art 31 it has the power to determine applications which, under Art 30, have been relinquished by a Chamber of the Court because the case raises a serious issue of interpretation of the Convention (for example, *Goodwin v United Kingdom* (2002) 35 EHRR 18 on the rights of transsexuals).

- It can act as an appeal court by considering referrals by the parties under Art 43 of the Convention (for example, *Hatton v United Kingdom* (2003) 37 EHRR 28, overruling the Chamber's decision on whether night flights violated the right to home and private life).

- It can consider requests for an advisory opinion under Art 47.

Decisions of the Grand Chamber are final and binding.

16.4 The Role of the European Court of Human Rights

The European Court of Human Rights is the judicial arm of the Convention. In addition to considering the admissibility of claims under the Convention and striking out cases (below), the main role of the European Court of Human Rights is to interpret and apply the European Convention with respect to alleged violations brought before it and to make binding judgments. The court is bound to give reasons for its decisions, including its decisions on admissibility (Art 45).

In practice it must decide whether there has been a violation of one of the substantive rights in the Convention and whether there is any justification for any such violation. It will interpret and apply the Convention in the light of both the intention of the drafters and current philosophy on human rights protection (*Selmouni v France* (1999) 29 EHRR 403), and will use various human rights norms during that process – democracy, the rule of law, equality, the protection of human dignity etc.

16.4.1 The effect of the European Court of Human Rights' judgements and their effect

Under Art 46 the decisions of the European Court (subject to any appeal to the Grand Chamber), are binding in international law against that state provided it has accepted the compulsory jurisdiction of the court. The judgment imposes an obligation on that state to comply with judgment (including paying any 'just satisfaction') and to make any necessary changes to domestic law. For example, following the decision in *Malone v United Kingdom* (1984) 7 EHRR 14 Parliament passed the Interception of Communications Act 1985 to regulate telephone tapping.

However, unlike the decisions of the European Court of Justice, the decisions of the Court of Human Rights do not have an overriding force and do not automatically take precedence over inconsistent domestic law.

- The effect of the decision in domestic law will depend on how the Convention and its case law has been incorporated into that system.
- Under s 2 of the Human Rights Act 1998 domestic courts may take the decisions of the European Court into account, but any relevant domestic law remains in force until amended by Parliament.
- The courts can interpret and apply domestic law in the light of the Convention but decisions of the Court of Human Rights cannot override domestic law.

CASE EXAMPLE

R v Lyons and others [2002] UKHL 44

Following the decision of the European Court in *Saunders v United Kingdom* (1996) 23 EHRR 313, a number of individuals sought to have their convictions quashed as violating the rule against self-incrimination and thus in breach of Art 6 of the Convention.

CONTINUED ▶

The House of Lords held that at the time the convictions were lawful under domestic law and that the decision of the European Court could not retrospectively overrule such convictions. Any remedy provided in *Saunders* imposed an obligation in international law and did not overturn domestic law. As the convictions took place before the Human Rights Act 1998 came into force the Act could not be applied to that case and the applicants needed to petition the European Court (*Lyons v United Kingdom* (2003) 37 EHRR 183 CD).

16.4.2 The power to award just satisfaction

Where the European Court finds a violation of the Convention it may under Art 41 award 'just satisfaction' to the injured party. The Member State then has an obligation under the Convention to abide by such a ruling and, for example, pay any compensation awarded by the court.

- The phrase 'just satisfaction' is also used in s 8 of the Human Rights Act 1998 and the domestic courts must ensure that any remedies awarded by them reflect the principles in Art 41 (see below).

- The European Court can award pecuniary damage to compensate for any direct financial loss, including loss, or depreciation of property (*Lopez Ostra v Spain* (1994) 20 EHRR 277), or recovery of any fines or compensation (*Jersild v Denmark* (1994) 19 EHRR 1).

- The court may also award damages for non-pecuniary damage where the applicant has suffered things such as loss of liberty, physical and/or mental distress from a violation the European Convention (see *Smith and Grady v United Kingdom* (2000) 29 EHRR 493).

- The court can compensate for legal costs and expenses actually, necessarily and reasonably incurred by the applicant (*McCann v United Kingdom* (1996) 21 EHRR 97).

- In appropriate cases the court has the power to award no compensation other than costs and expenses (*McCann v United Kingdom* (above)) no compensation awarded for unlawful deaths of suspected terrorists.

ACTIVITY

Quick Quiz

1. Why was the European Convention on Human Rights devised and what does it generally contain?

2. How is the European Convention different from, and related to European Community law?

3. How do the Convention and its case law affect United Kingdom law and its practice?

CONTINUED ▶

ACTIVITY

4. How has the Convention been incorporated into domestic law? (Check your answer once you have studied Chapter 17)

5. What is the role of the European Court of Human Rights, and what powers does the Court have?

16.5 State and individual applications

The European Court has the power to receive applications from either Member States or from individual applicants claiming to be victims of a violation of the Convention.

16.5.1 Inter-State applications

Under Art 33 any High Contracting Party may refer to the court any alleged breach of the provisions of the Convention or the protocols by another High Contracting Party, including claims with respect to victims other than the state's own nationals. Such applications can be brought as part of a political dispute between the states.

CASE EXAMPLE

Ireland v United Kingdom (1978) 2 EHRR 25

The Irish government brought an inter-state case against the United Kingdom in relation to the treatment of suspected terrorists by British authorities detained in army barracks in Northern Ireland. The government claimed that such treatment constituted a violation of, *inter alia*, Art 3 of the European Convention, guaranteeing freedom from torture and inhuman and degrading treatment (the European Court held that there had been a violation of Art 3 in that the interrogation techniques constituted inhuman and degrading treatment, but not torture).

State applications must comply with Art 35, which requires the exhaustion of all domestic remedies and for claims to be brought within six months of the final decision

16.5.2 Individual applications

Under Art 34 the court may receive applications from 'any person, non-governmental organisation or group of individuals' who claims to be a victim of a violation by one of the High Contracting Parties of the rights set forth in the Convention. The individual may bring an application against a state provided he or she was within that state's jurisdiction at the time (Art 1). Applications cannot be brought against another individual or a public authority, although the state can be liable for violations committed by state actors and individuals (*A v United Kingdom* (1999) 27 EHRR 611) and for the violations of another state if it exposes an individual to a risk of violation (*Soering v United Kingdom* (1989) 11 EHRR 439).

Individual applications are made to the Court Registry who will register the complaint and the case will then be referred to the European Court for a determination on admissibility, below. High Contracting Parties must not hinder any individual petition (*McShane v United Kingdom* (2002) 35 EHRR 23).

16.5.3 The requirement to be a victim

Applications under Art 34 may only be brought by persons claiming to be a 'victim' of a breach of the Convention.

- The applicant must normally be directly affected by the alleged violation (*Klass v Germany* (1978) 2 EHRR 214).

- The law or practice must normally be applied to the applicant's disadvantage, although an individual might be directly affected by the mere existence of incompatible law or practice (*Dudgeon v United Kingdom* (1982) 4 EHRR 149 – existence of discriminatory law against homosexuals made the applicant a victim, even though he was never prosecuted).

- The court is also prepared to accept applications from family representatives of the actual victim, particularly in cases of potentially unlawful deaths (*McCann v United Kingdom* (1996) 21 EHRR 97).

The court thus takes a flexible approach to the issue where the applicant is a victim. In *Fairfield v United Kingdom* (Application No 24790/04) it held that the family of a person convicted for using insulting words and behaviour, and who subsequently died, were not victims under Art 34. The court noted that a different, more flexible, test applied in cases under Art 2 of the Convention, because of the importance of that right.

16.5.4 Admissibility of applications

Articles 34 and 35 of the Convention subject applications to an admissibility criteria and the initial role of the European Court is to rule on admissibility of the claim. This will filter out hopeless claims, or claims made in bad faith, and will ensure that the Convention machinery is only used as a last resort. For example, in the United Kingdom citizens will normally be expected to use the machinery under the Human Rights Act 1998 to resolve their human rights disputes

16.5.5 The admissibility criteria

Art 35, which applies to both inter state and individual applications, provides that the court may only deal with the matter after all domestic remedies have been exhausted and within a period of six months from the date on which the final decision was taken.

- The six month rule does not apply to continuing breaches of the Convention, or where the violation shows that there is no effective domestic remedy (*De Becker v Belgium* (1979–80)).

- The applicant is expected to exhaust all *effective* domestic remedies before applying to the court (*Spencer v United Kingdom* [1998] EHRLR 348 – failure to bring confidentiality proceedings for an alleged breach of Art 8).

- Since the passing of the Human Rights Act 1998, applicants would be expected to make full use of that Act in resolving their human rights dispute.

- The exhaustion rule does not apply to inter-state cases where the applicant state alleges widespread breaches (*Ireland v United Kingdom* (1978) 2 EHRR 25) or in individual applications where an administrative practice has rendered remedies ineffective *(Akdivar v Turkey* (1996) 1 BHRC 137).

- An applicant should normally pursue any effective appeal against an initial decision, unless such an appeal would be futile (*Handyside v United Kingdom* (1976) 1 EHRR 737), where the court held that appeal proceedings did not have to be exhausted when the initial court's finding was clearly within domestic law.

In addition to the above rules on time limits and exhaustion of remedies, the court may declare a case inadmissible under Art 35 on the following grounds:

- Where the application is anonymous.

- Where it is substantially the same as a matter that has already been examined by the court, or has already been submitted to another procedure of international investigation or settlement and contains no new information.

- Where the application is incompatible with the provisions of the Convention. In other words, where the claim does not engage a right protected by the Convention – *Bertrand Russell Peace Foundation v United Kingdom* 14 DR 117(1978), no right to diplomatic protection under the Convention.

- Where the application constitutes an abuse of the right of application. For example, where it is brought in bad faith for purely political or personal reasons (*M v United Kingdom* 54 DR 214 (1987)).

- Where the claim is manifestly ill-founded. In other words, where the applicant has failed to show a *prima facie* case against the respondent state, either because the relevant article is not engaged or where the violation is clearly justified.

In addition, under Protocol No 14 (not yet ratified) cases can be declared inadmissible where the applicant has not suffered a serious disadvantage, and where respect for human rights does not require the court to examine the merits of the case (excluding cases where the dispute has not been considered by a domestic tribunal).

16.5.6 Friendly settlements and striking out

Article 38 permits the European Court of Human Rights to effect a friendly settlement between the applicant and the defendant state after deciding on its admissibility. In such a situation the case will be struck out of the court's list (Art 40).

- Some settlements are effected on the basis that the state admits the violation and promises to change its law (*Sutherland v United Kingdom, The Times*, 13th April 2001 – friendly settlement agreed when the UK Government agreed to amend incompatible legislation and to equalise the age of consent for heterosexual and homosexual sex (The Sexual Offences (Amendment) Act 2000)).

- Other settlements do not involve an admission of liability, and are affected by a payment of compensation to the applicant (*Amekrane v United Kingdom* (1974) 44 CD 101 – payment of £30,000 compensation to a relative of a member of the Moroccan Armed Forces who had been sent back to his country to face the death penalty).

16.6 Lawful and permissible interferences with Convention rights

Many Convention rights may be interfered with in particular circumstances, provided that interference has certain qualities. In particular, the 'conditional rights' contained in Arts 8–11 of the Convention, contain a particular mechanism for testing the legality of any interference:

- any such interference must be prescribed by, or in accordance with the law;
- it must relate to a legitimate aim listed in the qualifying part of the article;
- it must be necessary in a democratic society for the protection of one of a number of those aims.

This mechanism can also be used to test the legality of interferences with other rights, such as the right to a fair trial under Art 6 (*Osman v United Kingdom* (2000) 29 EHRR 245), the right to liberty of the person under Art 5 (*Steel v United Kingdom* (1998) 28 EHRR 603), and freedom from discrimination under Art 14 (*Pretty v United Kingdom* (2002) 35 EHRR 1).

The Human Rights Act 1998 adopts these principles and thus the domestic courts must subject any interference under domestic law to an equivalent test when adjudicating upon Convention rights.

16.6.1 Prescribed by law/in accordance with law

Any interference of Convention rights must comply with the rule of law and thus must derive from some legal provision.

- For example, under Art 2 of the Convention the death penalty is provided for, but only for a crime for which the penalty is *prescribed by law*.

- Art 5 of the Convention allows interference with a person's liberty, but only in accordance with a procedure *prescribed by law*.

- The 'conditional rights' contained in Arts 8 to 11 provide that any interference with those rights are '*prescribed by law*' or '*in accordance with law*'.

The meaning of 'in accordance with law' was considered in *Malone*, below, and the phrase 'prescribed by law' (used in Arts 9, 10 and 11), is interpreted and applied identically (*Silver v United Kingdom* (1983) 5 EHRR 347).

CASE EXAMPLE

Malone v United Kingdom (1984) 7 EHRR 14

The applicant's telephone had been tapped in the course of criminal investigation and the applicant claimed that the tapping was not authorised by law as the rules for interception were contained in administrative guidance.

The European Court held that for a measure to be prescribed by law it had to have a legal basis (in other words the law must be identified and established), the rule had to be accessible, and such a rule should be formulated with sufficient certainty to enable people to understand it and to regulate their conduct by it.

The court concluded that it could not be said what elements of the power to intercept communications were incorporated in legal rules and what elements remained within the discretion of the executive. Accordingly the tapping was not in accordance with law and was thus in violation of Art 8.

In *Malone* the European Court insisted that there is a measure of legal protection against arbitrary interference by public authorities and that provisions must exist which are sufficiently independent of those who administer them. This law can be either in statutory or common law form (*Sunday Times v United Kingdom* (1979) 2 EHRR 245).

In addition, the rule has to be accessible, so that those who are likely to be affected by it can access and understand it (*Silver v United Kingdom* (1983) 5 EHRR 347 – the regulation of prisoners' correspondence via administrative guidance produced by the Secretary of State was not prescribed by law because such guidance was only available to the prison authorities).

Finally, the provision should be sufficiently clear to allow individuals to govern their future behaviour. This was explained by the European Court of Human Rights in *Sunday Times v United Kingdom* (1979) 2 EHRR 245:

> **J** 'a law has to be formulated with sufficient precision to enable the citizen to regulate his conduct: that person must be able – if need be with appropriate advice – to foresee, to a degree that is reasonable in the circumstances, the consequences which a given action may entail. Those consequences need not, however, be foreseeable with absolute certainty. Whilst the Court noted that certainty is desirable, it also accepted that excessive rigidity should be avoided and that laws are inevitably couched in terms which, to some extent, are vague and whose interpretation and application are questions of practice. Similarly, although the law itself may be vague, its meaning and scope may become apparent after it has been construed and applied by the courts.'

The law's meaning and extent must, therefore, be capable of reasonable prediction, even though the European Court accepts that many laws are inevitable vague and open to flexible interpretation. For example, in *Hashman and Harrap v United Kingdom* (1999) 30 EHRR 241 when the applicants were ordered to desist in conduct that was *contra bones mores* (conduct which is seen as wrong in the eyes of the majority of contemporary citizens) the court held that the offence failed to give sufficient guidance to the applicants as to what conduct they were not allowed to carry out in the future.

16.6.2 Legitimate aims

Not only should any restriction of a Convention right be based in law, it must pursue a legitimate aim. These aims are expressly mentioned in the qualifying paragraphs of Arts 8–11 of the Convention, but also constitute implied restrictions of other Articles, such as freedom from discrimination (Art 14), the right to marry (Art 12) and the right to vote (Art 3, Protocol 1).

For example, Art 10, guaranteeing the right to freedom of speech and expression, refers to a host of legitimate aims

> **A** Art 10(2)
> 'The exercise of these freedoms … may be subject to such … restrictions, conditions and formalities as are prescribed by law and necessary in a democratic society, in the interests of national security, territorial integrity, public safety, the prevention of disorder or crime, the protection of health or morals, the protection of the reputation and or rights of others, the prevention of the disclosure of information received in confidence and the maintenance of the authority and impartiality of the judiciary'.

The Member State must then satisfy the court that the restriction pursued one of those aims and was genuinely applied to the applicant in a particular case. Thus, in *Handyside v United Kingdom* (1976) 1 EHRR 737 the court accepted that the applicant had been prosecuted and convicted under the Obscene Publications Act 1959 for the legitimate purpose of protecting health and morals and the rights of others (the right of young, vulnerable individuals not to be corrupted).

16.6.3 Necessary in a democratic society

In addition to the restricting being legal and related to a legitimate aim, the Convention (and now the Human Rights Act 1998) guards against excessive or unnecessary interferences by insisting that a restriction is 'necessary in a democratic society' for achieving its legitimate aim.

The phrase 'necessary in a democratic society' was defined in *Handyside v United Kingdom* (1976) 1 EHRR 737:

> J   'the word "necessary" does not mean "absolutely necessary" or "indispensable", but neither does it have the flexibility of terms such as "useful" or "convenient". Instead there must be a 'pressing social need' for the interference. The Court must ask whether is there a pressing social need for some restriction of the Convention and whether the particular restriction corresponds to that need, including whether it a proportionate response to that need, and whether the reasons advanced by the authorities are relevant and sufficient.'

The court has also stressed that it is not faced with a choice between two conflicting principles, but with a principle of, for example, freedom of expression subject to a number of exceptions, which must be narrowly interpreted (*Sunday Times v United Kingdom* (1979) 2 EHRR 245). However, the principle of necessity, and proportionality, are linked to the doctrine of the margin of appreciation (see directly below).

16.6.4 The doctrine of proportionality

The doctrine of proportionality (now part of domestic law after the Human Rights Act 1998 was passed – see Chapter 17) ensures that there is a fair balance between pursuing a legitimate aim and the protection of Convention rights.

Thus the European Court insists that any restriction should be strictly proportionate to the legitimate aim being pursued and that the authorities can show that it does not go beyond what is strictly required to achieve that purpose (*Barthold v Germany* (1985) 7 EHRR 383). In doing so the court can consider the following factors:

- The importance of the right that has been interfered with.
- The extent to which the right was violated, including the level of the sanction or penalty.
- The nature and importance of the legitimate aim (*Handyside v United Kingdom* (1976) 1 EHRR 737 – protection of morals best decided by national authorities).

- Whether there was a less restrictive alternative available to the domestic authorities (*Goodwin v United Kingdom* (1996) 22 EHRR 123 – disclosure of press source not necessary in addition to an injunction to prohibit disclosure of confidential information).

- Whether the restriction destroys the very essence of the Convention right in question (*Hamer v United Kingdom* (1979) 24 DR 5 – complete prohibition of the prisoner's right to marry disproportionate).

16.6.5 The margin of appreciation

In deciding whether there has been a violation of the Convention, and in determining whether the Member State has achieved a correct balance, the European Court is prepared to give the state a level of discretion. This is known as the 'margin of appreciation'.

The doctrine was first used in the context of Art 15, allowing derogation in times of war or other emergency, and where the European Court gives the state a margin of error in deciding how to compromise Convention rights in such circumstances. The margin is offered by the European Court because it recognises that its role under the Convention is subsidiary to the system of rights protection adopted by each Member State (Art 1 of the Convention):

> **J** 'the machinery of the Convention is subsidiary to the national systems safeguarding human rights, and consequently the Convention leaves to each state a margin of appreciation, given both to the domestic legislature and to the bodies called upon to interpret and apply the laws. This margin of appreciation goes hand in hand with the Court's power to give the final meaning on whether a restriction is compatible with the Convention right in question.' (*Handyside v United Kingdom* (1976) 1 EHRR 737)

The doctrine is flexible, and the court will offer a wide or narrow margin depending on the circumstances. A wide margin will be offered in cases where free speech conflicts with public morality. Thus, in *Handyside v United Kingdom* (above) the European Court stated that it was not possible to find a uniform conception of morals within the Council of Europe, and that states were in a better position than the international judge to give an opinion on the exact content of the requirements of morals.

However, a narrower margin may be offered where the restriction in question impinges on the enjoyment of the individual's right to *private* life (*Dudgeon v United Kingdom* (1982) 4 EHRR 149).

CASE EXAMPLE

Smith and Grady v United Kingdom (2000) 29 EHRR 493

The applicants had been dismissed from the armed forces because of their homosexuality and claimed that their right to private life had been violated.

The court held that the restriction placed on homosexuals from remaining in the armed forces was not necessary for the purpose of achieving national security and public order. The negative attitudes of heterosexuals towards homosexuals could not, of themselves, justify the interferences in question.

A similarly narrow margin may be offered in cases where the restriction impinges on press freedom. Thus, in *Sunday Times v United Kingdom* (1979) 2 EHRR 245 the court held that the laws protecting the laws of contempt of court displayed a much more common European approach, allowing the court to more easily judge the necessity of any particular interference. In addition, the publication in question (an article on the ongoing Thalidomide disaster) reported on a matter of great public interest, and an injunction should not be granted unless it was *absolutely certain* that the publication would hinder the due administration of justice.

The doctrine of margin of appreciation does not, theoretically, apply to domestic proceedings under the Human Rights Act 1998. However, it is clear that the domestic courts will show Parliament and public authorities a good deal of deference in cases where human rights have to be balanced with other rights and interests (see Chapter 17).

ACTIVITY

Problem Solving

Consider the following hypothetical case and answer the questions that follow it.

In November 2010 Parliament passed the (imaginary) Public Offices Act 2010, which regulated the conduct of those who hold public office and which encouraged responsible government. Under s 60 of the Act it is an offence for any person to use grossly offensive words either in describing a person who holds a public office, or to criticise such a person with respect either to the performance of his public duties or to the conducting of his or her private life; under s 60(4) 'grossly offensive words' are defined as those which relate to an individual's reputation or integrity and which a reasonable person would regard as highly indecent or improper'. The maximum fine for committing an offence under the Act is £2,000.

CONTINUED ▸

ACTIVITY

In March 2006, Lionel, a local councillor, was convicted under s 60 of the Act by Birdchester Magistrates when he distributed leaflets in Birdchester city centre, which criticised the local Member of Parliament for his recent speech on immigration and asylum seekers. In the leaflet Lionel described the MP as 'a bloody Nazi and a hypocrite' stating that the MP and those who subscribed to his views were as dangerous as sex offenders. Lionel was fined £1,000 and the conviction and fine was upheld by the Court of Appeal.

Lionel now brings an application under the European Convention.

1. Have any of L's Convention rights been interfered with?

2. If so, is that restriction been 'prescribed by law'?

3. Do the Act and the conviction pursue a legitimate aim?

4. In your view, was the conviction and fine necessary in a democratic society?

5. What level of margin of appreciation would the European Court give to the UK authorities in such a case?

16.7 Derogations and reservations

The Convention recognises that a state might not always be able to fully comply with its obligations under this treaty and allows it to compromise those rights in certain cases. Accordingly, Art 15 allows derogation in times of war or other emergency, and Art 57 permits the state to make a reservation with respect to a particular Convention right and its application within that jurisdiction.

16.7.1 Derogation in times of war or other public emergency

Article 15 of the Convention provides as follows:

(A) In times of war or other public emergency threatening the life of the nation any High Contracting Party may take measures derogating from its obligations under this Convention to the extent strictly required by the exigencies of the situation, provided that such measures are not inconsistent with its other obligations under international law.

The right to derogate under Art 15 is qualified in a number of respects:

- The High Contracting Party can only take such measures as are *strictly required* by the exigencies of the situation.

- The measures must not be inconsistent with the state's other obligations under other treaties.

- Article 15(2) provides that no derogation is allowed in respect of certain Convention rights: no derogation is possible in relation to Art 2 (the right to life), (excluding deaths resulting from lawful acts of war), Art 3 (prohibition of torture etc.), Art 4(1) (prohibition of slavery or servitude) or Art 7 (prohibition of retrospective criminal law).

- The High Contracting Party must keep the Secretary General of the Council of Europe informed of the measures which it has taken and when such measures have ceased to operate, including the reasons for such action.

Derogation measures can be challenged under the European Convention and the court can adjudicate on their compatibility. In doing so, the Court will provide the state with a wide margin of error.

CASE EXAMPLE

Lawless v Ireland (No 3) (1961) 1 EHRR 15

Although the court found that the detention of the applicant without trial for a period of five months was in violation of Art 5(3) of the Convention, it held that the Irish government was entitled to derogate from its obligations by virtue of the existence of a public emergency.

The court stressed that the measures governments can take when derogating are strictly limited to what is required by the exigencies of the situation and must not be in conflict with other international law obligations. However, the court was satisfied that those strict limitations were met in the present case. The court held that the respondent government should be afforded a certain margin of error or appreciation in deciding what measures were required by the situation, and it was not the court's function to substitute for the government's assessment any other assessment of what might be the most prudent or most expedient policy to combat terrorism.

Moreover, the court must arrive at its decision in the light of the conditions that existed at the time that the original decision was taken, rather than reviewing the matter retrospectively.

A similarly wide discretion has been given to the UK Government with respect to provisions intended to deal with terrorism in Northern Ireland.

CASE EXAMPLE

Brannigan and McBride v United Kingdom (1993) 17 EHRR 539

The United Kingdom Government lodged a derogation after the European Court's decision in *Brogan v United Kingdom* (1989) 11 EHRR 117, where it was held that detention provisions in the Prevention of Terrorism (Temporary Provisions) Act 1984 were in contravention of Art 5(3) of the Convention, guaranteeing the right to be brought promptly before a judge or other officer.

The European Court held that the derogation was lawful. The derogation was not invalid merely because the government had decided to keep open the possibility of finding a means in the future of ensuring greater conformity with Convention obligations. In addition there were effective measures in domestic law to challenge the use of the provisions and thus to safeguard against arbitrary action.

Note, the *domestic* courts have shown less deference with respect to the compatibility of anti-terrorism measures: *A and others v Secretary of State* (see 17.11.1).

16.7.2 Reservations

Article 57 of the Convention allows a state to make reservations to specific provisions of the Convention when ratifying the Convention. The reservation must be in respect of laws in existence at the time of ratification and the article does not allow reservations of a general character. For example it would not be possible to make a reservation of an entire Convention right.

The United Kingdom made a reservation with regard to Art 2 of the First Protocol to the Convention, which imposes a duty on each state to respect the rights of parents to ensure education and teaching in conformity with their own religious and philosophical convictions. This duty is only accepted in so far as it is compatible with the provision of efficient instruction and training and the avoidance of unreasonable public expenditure. The reservation is contained in Sched 3 of the Human Rights Act 1998 and thus has effect in domestic law.

KEY FACTS

Principle	Legal Authority
The European Convention imposes an obligation on each state to ensure the observance of Convention rights within its own jurisdiction.	Art 1, ECHR

CONTINUED ▸

KEY FACTS

Principle	Legal Authority
The UK has given effect to the Convention via the Human Rights Act 1998 and thus the principles of the Convention and the court can be used in domestic proceedings.	s 2, HRA 1998
In addition, the Convention machinery can be used by victims who have exhausted all effective domestic remedies.	Art 34, ECHR
The European Court was set up to ensure the observance of the Convention and can receive inter state or individual applications.	Arts 19, 33 and 34, ECHR
A full-time European Court decides on the admissibility and of all applications, which must be received within 6 months of the act and the applicant must have exhausted all effective domestic remedies.	Art 34, ECHR
A Grand Chamber of the European Court hears appeals and referrals from the European Court of Human Rights and its decisions are final.	Arts 43 and 44, ECHR
Individual applications are subject to further tests of admissibility and must not be manifestly ill-founded.	Art 35, ECHR
The court has the power to strike out cases and to secure friendly settlements between the parties.	Art 38, ECHR
The court has the power to make awards of 'just satisfaction', including granting pecuniary and non-pecuniary loss and costs and expenses.	Art 41, ECHR

CONTINUED ▸

KEY FACTS

Principle	Legal Authority
Certain Convention rights can be interfered with provided the restriction is in accordance with or prescribed by law and necessary in a democratic society for the pursuance of a legitimate aim.	*Malone v United Kingdom* (1984) and *Handyside v United Kingdom* (1976)
The European Court adopts the concept of proportionality to judge the necessity of restrictions but also offers the state a margin of appreciation when they pass and maintain laws that interfere with Convention rights.	*Barthold v Germany* (1985) and *Handyside v United Kingdom* (1976)
The standard of review, and the width of the margin of appreciation, depends on the nature of the legitimate aim and the importance of the right.	*Handyside v United Kingdom* (1976) and *Smith and Grady v United Kingdom* (1999)
States can derogate from their Convention obligations under and can make reservations with respect to specific aspects of a Convention rights under Art 57. Derogations are subject to regulation by the Council of Europe and the European Court, but the court offers a wide margin of error to the sates.	Arts 15 and 57, ECHR and *Brannigan and McBride v United Kingdom* (1993)

16.8 The rights guaranteed under the European Convention on Human Rights

The substantive rights guaranteed under the European Convention are contained in Section One of the Convention, in Arts 2–14 and a number of optional protocols. Most of these rights (excluding Art 13, guaranteeing an effective remedy in domestic law for violation of these rights) are contained in s 1 of the Human Rights Act 1998.

16.8.1 Absolute and conditional rights

Some Convention rights are absolute rights, whilst some are conditional. An absolute right is not capable of derogation under Art 15, and their violation cannot generally be justified. A conditional right, however, can be violated provided that interference is lawful and necessary.

For example, Art 2 (the right to life), Art 3 (prohibition of torture etc), Art 4(1) (freedom from slavery), and Art 7 (no punishment without law) cannot be derogated from under Art 15. Additionally, in the case of an absolute right such as freedom from torture, there can be no justification for a violation, whereas for conditional rights (such as freedom of expression), interference is allowed provided the restriction was prescribed by law and was necessary for the purpose of achieving a legitimate aim (see below).

The Convention also makes certain rights subject to express restrictions:

- Article 4 excludes work done in the course of detention from the term 'forced or compulsory labour'.

- Article 5 lays down a number of specific circumstances where it is permissible to interfere with liberty of the person.

- Article 2 provides that deprivation of life will not be unlawful where it results from the use of absolutely necessary force during, for example, a lawful arrest.

- Article 7(2) states that prohibition against retrospective criminal law does not apply to behaviour that is criminal according to the general principles of international law.

16.9 Article 2 – The Right to Life

The fundamental right to life is protected by Art 2 of the Convention, which seeks to protect a person's right to life under the law.

 Law shall protect everyone's right to life. No one shall be deprived of his life intentionally save in the execution of a sentence of a court following his conviction of a crime for which the penalty is provided by law.

16.9.1 The scope of Article 2

The right to life cannot be derogated from even in times of war and other public emergency (apart from lawful acts of war), but intentional deprivation of life is allowed in exceptional cases listed in Art 2(2) (see directly below).

Article 2 imposes an obligation on the state to preserve life, but does not extend to the right to die (*Pretty v United Kingdom,* (2002) 35 EHRR 1). Neither does Art 2 extend to protect the right to life of the unborn child (*Vo v France* (2005) 40 EHRR 12).

Article 2 imposes a negative duty not to interfere with a person's right to life, but also places a positive duty on the state to ensure that an individual's life is not taken unnecessarily. The duty applies where the act is one of a state official (*McCann v United Kingdom* (1996) 21 EHRR 97), and the state can also be responsible where the death is caused by a private individual and the state has not taken due care to safeguard the victim's life.

 ASE EXAMPLE

Osman v United Kingdom (2000) 29 EHRR 245

The applicants, the wife and son of the deceased, brought a claim under Art 2 after one of the son's teachers had killed the husband after forming an attachment to the son.

The European Court held that under Art 2 the state must take appropriate steps to safeguard the lives of those within its jurisdiction, including the duty to put into place effective criminal law provisions backed up by law-enforcement machinery for preventing and sanctioning such deaths. This would also include a positive (although not an impossible or disproportionate) obligation on the authorities to take preventive operational measures to protect an individual whose life is at risk from the criminal acts of another individual. (On the facts, the court held the police could not be criticised for attaching greater weight to the presumption of the teacher's innocence, and accordingly there had been no violation of Art 2.)

That decision can be contrasted with a recent domestic decision in *Van Colle v Chief Constable of Hertfordshire, The Times,* 28th March 2006, where the High Court held that there had been a violation of Art 2 when the police had taken inadequate steps to safeguard the life of a prosecution witness from a real risk of attacks by suspects in a forthcoming trial.

The state will owe a specific positive duty to safeguard the lives of those in detention, either from the actions of fellow inmates, or themselves (*Edwards v United Kingdom* (2002) 35 EHRR 19 – a cellmate posed a real and serious risk to the applicant's son and the prison authorities had not been properly informed of the cellmate's medical history and perceived dangerousness). Article 2 might also be engaged where the individual has taken his or her own life, provided there was a *clear risk* of such - *Keenan v United Kingdom* (2001) 33 EHRR 38, no breach of Art 2 when a vulnerable prisoner had committed suicide whilst under supervision by the prison authorities.

16.9.2 The duty to carry out an effective investigation

In addition to the substantive duty under Art 2, the article imposes a procedural duty on every Member State to carry out a proper investigation into any death that may be in violation of Art 2. In the case below, the court established some guidelines for establishing a violation of this procedural duty.

CASE EXAMPLE

Jordan and others v United Kingdom (2003) 37 EHRR 2

The court held that Art 2 required that there had to be some form of effective official investigation when individuals had been killed as a result of the use of force. The state must take the initiative in conducting the investigation and it should be carried out by someone independent from those involved in the events. It should lead to a determination of whether the force used in such circumstances was justified, and to the identification and punishment of those responsible. The authorities must take reasonable steps to secure the necessary evidence and the investigation should be carried out with reasonable promptness.

Article 2 also gives the victim's relatives the right to effectively participate in the investigation (*Edwards v United Kingdom* (above)) and, in conjunction with Art 13 of the Convention, the right to effective compensation, where appropriate (*Keenan v United Kingdom* (above)).

The procedural right has also been upheld by the domestic courts under the Human Rights Act 1998. In *R (Amin) v Secretary of State for the Home Department* [2003] UKHL 51 the House of Lords held that an internal investigation into the killing of a prisoner by his racist cellmate did not fulfill the requirements of Art 2, and that a full independent public investigation had to be held.

16.9.3 The exceptions under Article 2.2

Article 2(2) provides exceptions to the general right to life where the intentional deprivation of life will not constitute a violation of that right.

(A) The deprivation of life shall not be regarded as inflicted in contravention of Art 2 when it results from the use of force which is no more than absolutely necessary … in defence of any person from unlawful violence, in order to effect a lawful arrest or to prevent the escape of a person lawfully detained, or in action lawfully taken for the purpose of quelling a riot or insurrection.

For the exceptions in Art 2(2) to come into play the force used must be no more than absolutely necessary.

CASE EXAMPLE

McCann v United Kingdom (1996) 21 EHRR 97

Three suspected IRA terrorists were seen near a car. Members of the SAS, believing that the car contained a bomb and that it was to be detonated, shot them dead. The families brought a claim under Art 2 of the Convention.

The European Court held that although the SAS members had used no more force than was necessary in the circumstances, there had been a violation of the right to life through the careless planning of the operation by the administrative authorities. The authorities had been negligent in the planning of the operation and the soldiers had been provided with misinformation.

Despite this decision, the court will normally afford the authorities and individual officers a wide area of discretion where they have acted in good faith and with reasonable diligence (*Bubbins v United Kingdom* (2005) 41 EHRR 24).

16.9.4 Article 2 and the death penalty

The first sentence of Art 2 provides for the death penalty, provided it takes the form of an execution of a sentence of a court following a person's conviction of a crime for which the penalty is provided by law. However the death penalty may be unlawful in a number of cases.

- Optional Protocol No 6 of the Convention provides that the death penalty shall be abolished in peacetime and that no one shall be condemned to such penalty or executed. In addition optional Protocol No 13 abolishes it in all circumstances. The UK has ratified both protocols and thus any execution within its jurisdiction would be contrary to its Convention obligations. This would include executions in other jurisdictions where there was a real risk of such a penalty (*Soering v United Kingdom* (1989) 11 EHRR 439).

- In *Ocalan v Turkey* (2005) 41 EHRR 45, the Grand Chamber of the European Court held that the second sentence in Art 2 might now have been amended by state practice and that accordingly states would now regard it as an unacceptable form of punishment in peacetime. However, as not every state had signed Protocol No 13 it could not be concluded that the death penalty was automatically in violation of Art 3.

- The circumstances of a death penalty may constitute a violation of Art 3 of the Convention (*Soering v United Kingdom* (1989) 11 EHRR 439).

- Any execution not proceeded by a fair trial would not come within Art 2(1).

16.10 Article 3 – Prohibition of torture and inhuman and degrading treatment and punishment

 No one shall be subject to torture or to inhuman or degrading treatment or punishment

16.10.1 The scope of Article 3

The Article imposes an absolute prohibition on such treatment, even in times of war or other public emergency (see above). Thus once a violation of Art 3 has been found, there can be no justification for that breach (*Chahal v United Kingdom* (1997) 23 EHRR 413).

The role of the European Court of Human Rights in such cases is, thus, to define the terms 'torture' and 'inhuman and degrading treatment or punishment' and to assess whether the applicant has been subjected to treatment in violation of the article.

Under Art 3 Member States owe a positive, yet limited, duty to ensure that a person does not suffer ill treatment at the hands of others, whether state actors or public or private individuals.

CASE EXAMPLE

A v United Kingdom **(1999) 27 EHRR 611**

The applicant, a young boy had been beaten with a cane by his step-father, who was then acquitted after relying on the defence of reasonable chastisement.

The European Court held that the United Kingdom government was held liable for the ill treatment of the applicant because domestic law provided him with inadequate protection against treatment which was contrary to Art 3 (see now s 58 of the Children Act 2004).

Also in *Z v United Kingdom* (2002) 34 EHRR 3 the European Court held that the state (via social services) had a duty to take such measures to provide effective protection against long-term abuse and neglect in the home.

16.10.2 Definition of torture, inhuman and degrading treatment or punishment

The terms used in Art 3 were explored in the inter-state case of *Ireland v United Kingdom.*

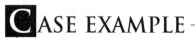

CASE EXAMPLE

Ireland v United Kingdom (1978) 2 EHRR 25

The applicants had been the victims of the 'Five Techniques' interrogation measures, involving being subjected to intense noise, wall-standing, and deprivation of food and sleep.

The European Court defined torture as treatment constituting deliberate inhuman treatment causing very serious and cruel suffering; inhuman treatment as causing if not bodily injury, at least intense physical and mental or psychiatric suffering; and degrading treatment as that which would arouse in victims feelings of fear, anguish and inferiority capable of humiliation, or taking away one's physical or moral resistance.

On the facts the court found that the techniques were inhuman and degrading, but were not severe enough to constitute torture.

A finding of torture is, therefore, reserved for treatment constituting an aggravated and deliberate form of inhuman treatment or punishment; although the court has stressed that Art 3 must be interpreted in the light of present-day conditions. As a result certain acts (in this case, the deliberate, serious and prolonged assault of a detainee) which in the past were classified as inhuman and degrading as opposed to torture, might now be classified as torture (*Selmouni v France* (1999) 29 EHRR 403).

For a breach to take place the treatment or punishment must cross the threshold set by Art 3. Accordingly the humiliation or debasement must reach a particular level, and the European Court has stressed that such an assessment is relative and depends on all the circumstances of the case, including the victim's age (*Tyrer v United Kingdom* (1978) 2 EHRR 1).

16.10.3 Article 3 and corporal punishment

Not all forms of corporal punishment will necessarily be in violation of Art 3, although judicial corporal punishment appears to be outlawed by the European Court.

CASE EXAMPLE

Tyrer v United Kingdom (1978) 2 EHRR 1

A 15-year-old boy in the Isle of Man had been found guilty of assault and birched on his bare buttocks in accordance with Isle of Man law. The government argued that the punishment was an effective deterrent and that in all the circumstances was not inhuman or degrading.

CONTINUED ▶

The European Court described the punishment as institutionalised violence and held that the applicant had been subjected to an assault on his dignity and physical integrity and that it was immaterial that the punishment was an effective deterrent, or that the majority of society in the Isle of Man approved it as a punishment.

Corporal punishment in schools was abolished in the United Kingdom by the Schools Standard and Framework Act 1998, although the European Court has never outlawed the practice *per se* (*Costello-Roberts v United Kingdom* (1993) 19 EHRR 112). However, corporal punishment of a child against the parent's wishes would be in breach of Art 2 of the First Protocol, which gives them the right to have their children educated in conformity with their philosophical and religious convictions (*Campbell and Cosans v United Kingdom* (1982) 4 EHRR 293).

Whether parental chastisement is in breach of Art 3 depends on all the circumstances and the severity of the punishment. Thus, in *A v United Kingdom* (1999) 27 EHRR 611, when a nine-year-old boy had been repeatedly and severely beaten by his stepfather with a garden cane it was held that the threshold in Art 3 of the Convention had been satisfied.

16.10.4 Article 3 and deportation and extradition

Deportation or extradition may expose a person to a real risk that they will face treatment or punishment in breach of Art 3. In such a case the state which deports or extradites may be liable for the violation committed by the receiving state.

CASE EXAMPLE

Soering v United Kingdom (1989) 11 EHRR 439

A young German national was to stand trial in the USA for the murder of his girlfriend's parents. The UK Government agreed to his extradition having been assured that the prosecutors would argue that he should not face the death penalty.

The European Court held that the UK Government could be liable for a violation by the USA if it exposed the applicant to a real risk of a violation of Art 3. In this case, the death row phenomenon constituted a breach of Art 3 and extradition would constitute a violation of that article by the UK Government as there was a real risk that he would be exposed to those conditions.

The *Soering* principle applies even though there may be good national or other security reasons for deportation. Thus, in *Chahal v United Kingdom* (1997) 23 EHRR 413 the European Court held that the prohibition under Art 3 is absolute and the activities of the person, however undesirable, cannot be a material consideration in deciding whether Art 3 has been breached.

However, the court must be satisfied that the facts reveal a real risk of ill treatment in violation of Art 3, as opposed to a *mere possibility* (*Vilvarajah v United Kingdom* (1991) 14 EHRR 248).

The *Soering* principle can also apply even where the receiving state would not be in violation of Art 3, but nevertheless the applicant would be subjected to inhuman or degrading treatment (*D v United Kingdom* (1997) 24 EHRR 423 – return of applicant to the West Indies where there would be inadequate medial treatment to deal with his condition (he had contracted AIDS) constituted a violation of Art 3 by the UK). However, the court stressed that the decision was based on the very exceptional facts of the case and the domestic courts have also applied that case cautiously (*N v Secretary of State for the Home Department* [2005] UKHL 31, not allowing the claim unless the suffering is intense).

ACTIVITY

Quick Quiz on the Right to Life and Freedom from Torture

1. What obligation does Art 2 impose on states with respect to the right to life?

2. Does the right to life include (a) the right to die, (b) the right to life of the unborn child?

3. When is it lawful under Art 2 for life to be intentionally taken away?

4. How has the European Court defined the terms 'torture' and 'inhuman and degrading treatment?'

5. What is the '*Soering*' principle and what is its importance with respect to the protection of human rights?

16.11 Article 4 – Prohibition of slavery and forced labour

 No one shall be held in slavery or servitude. No one shall be required to perform forced or compulsory labour.

Article 4(1) prohibits slavery and servitude in absolute terms and no derogation is allowed under Art 15.

16.11.1 The prohibition of slavery and servitude

CASE EXAMPLE

Siliadin v France **(2006) 43 EHRR 16**

The applicant had been used as unpaid help by a French couple for four years. She claimed that this constituted slavery and servitude under Art 4.

The European Court held that this did not amount to 'slavery'; although she had lost her autonomy, there was insufficient evidence that her employers had exercised a genuine right of ownership over her. However, the court found that as she was a vulnerable and unofficial immigrant entirely dependant on her employers for all assistance, she had been held in servitude. The failure of domestic law to create a specific criminal offence against slavery, and the failure to secure a criminal conviction against her abusers for wrongfully using the services of a dependent person, meant that the state were in violation of its positive duty under Art 4.

16.11.2 Prohibition of forced or compulsory labour

Article 4(2) then guarantees freedom from forced or compulsory labour, which has been defined as unjust or oppressive work done against the will of the person causing avoidable hardship (*X v FRG* (1974) 46 CD 22). This aspect of Art 4 can be derogated from and is subject to a number of exceptions listed in Art 4(3).

- 'forced or compulsory labour' does not include work required to be done in the ordinary course of detention or during conditional release from such detention.

- Article 4(3) excludes any service of a military character, or in the case of conscientious objectors, service instead of such service (*Johansen v Norway* (44 DR 155 (1985)).

- Article 4(3) exempts service exacted in the case of an emergency or calamity threatening the life or well-being of the community, and any work or service which forms part of normal civic obligations.

16.12 Article 5 – Liberty and security of the person

 Everyone has the right to liberty and security of the person. No one shall be deprived of his liberty save in … accordance with a procedure prescribed by law.

16.12.1 Scope of the article

Article 5 is concerned with the protection of an individual's liberty as opposed to a right of free movement, guaranteed under Art 2 of the Fourth Protocol (not ratified by the UK). However, a curfew or house arrest may amount to a deprivation of liberty (*Secretary of State for the Home Department v JJ and others* [2006] EWCA Civ 1141). Also Art 5 is not engaged by a claim relating to the conditions of lawful detention (*Winterwerp v Germany* (1979) 2 EHRR 387).

The right under Art 5 is subject to a number of exceptions contained in Art 1(a)–(f), below. Under Art 5(1) any interference will only be lawful if it is 'in accordance with a procedure prescribed by law' so must comply with principles of fairness and legality (see above).

16.12.2 Lawful detention after conviction

Art 5(1)(a) provides for the lawful detention of a person after conviction by a competent court. Under this provision, any conviction must have a sufficient basis under domestic law (*Tsirlis and Kouloumpas v Greece* (1997) 25 EHRR 198) and there must be a sufficient connection between a finding of guilt by a competent *court* and any subsequent detention.

The European Court allows some exercise of administrative involvement in the detention process (*Van Droogenbroek v Belgium* (1982) 4 EHRR 443) provided there is a sufficient link with the original sentence.

CASE EXAMPLE

Stafford v United Kingdom (2002) 35 EHRR 32

The applicant had been sentenced to life imprisonment for murder and after release committed a number of property offences. The Home Secretary refused to release him on the grounds that there was a risk of him committing property offences in the future.

The European Court held that there was an insufficient connection between imposing a mandatory life sentence for murder, and the subsequent recall and detention of that prisoner on the basis of perceived fears that he would commit crimes of a non-violent nature. Accordingly, there was a violation of Art 5(1).

Such executive involvement may also constitute a violation of Arts 5(4) and 6, below.

16.12.3 Lawful arrest or detention for non-compliance of a lawful court order

Article 5(1)(b) permits the arrest or detention of a person who has not complied with a court order when such arrest or detention is required for the fulfilment of an obligation that is prescribed by law.

This normally requires that a specific legal obligation has been, or is danger of being, breached (*Engel v Netherlands* (1976) 1 EHRR 647), although in *McVeigh, O'Neill and Evans v United Kingdom* (1981) 25 DR 15 it was held that a duty to submit to an examination on entering the country (in order to determine whether he should be subject to an exclusion order) satisfied Art 5, even though it was not a general obligation arising under criminal or disciplinary law. Similarly, in *Steel v United Kingdom* (1998) 28 EHRR 603, the European Court held that the power to bind over an individual in order to keep the peace was compatible with Art 5, provided the applicant's conduct displayed some threat to the peace.

A detention by a court will not be unlawful simply because the decision to detain is overruled on appeal provided the initial court acted in good faith (*Benham v United Kingdom* (1996) 22 EHRR 293, unless it did not properly consider the law (*Beets and others v United Kingdom, The Times,* 10th March 2005).

16.12.4 Lawful detention following arrest

Article 5(1)(c) allows for the lawful arrest or detention of a person for bringing them before a competent legal authority; either on reasonable suspicion of them having committed an offence, or when it is necessary to prevent them committing an offence or fleeing after having done so.

Any arrest or detention must be in accordance with clear domestic law (*K-F v Germany* (1997) 26 EHRR 390), and in particular any arrest must be made on *reasonable* suspicion. This does not require evidence that would justify a conviction at trial or the bringing of a criminal charge (*O'Hara v United Kingdom* (2002) 34 EHRR 32), but the European Court has laid down strict requirements in order to justify deprivation of liberty on such grounds.

CASE EXAMPLE

Fox, Campbell and Hartley v United Kingdom (1990) 13 EHRR 157

The applicants were arrested under s 1 of the Northern Ireland (Emergency Provisions) Act 1978 on suspicion of being terrorists and then released without charge.

The European Court held that 'reasonable suspicion' under Art 5(1)(c) presupposes the existence of facts that would satisfy an objective observer that the person might have committed the offence. However, in respect of terrorism the test differs from that involved in conventional crime, provided the essence of reasonableness is not impaired. The government must provide at least some facts or information which were capable of showing that the arrested person was reasonably suspected of having committed the offence. (In this case the only evidence was that they had committed offences seven years previously, which was insufficient for the purposes of Art 5.)

16.12.5 Other lawful restrictions

Article 5 also provides for lawful detention in the following cases:

- The detention of a minor for the purpose of educational supervision or for the purpose of bringing him before a competent legal authority (Art 5(1)(d)).

- For the prevention of the spreading of infectious diseases, of persons of unsound mind, alcoholics or drug addicts or vagrants (Art 5(1)(e) and *Winterwerp v Germany* (1979) 2 EHRR 387).

- For the lawful arrest or detention of a person to prevent him from effecting an unauthorised entry into the country or to facilitate a person's deportation or extradition (Art 5(1)(f) and *Chahal v United Kingdom* (1997) 23 EHRR 413).

16.12.6 Right to be informed of reasons for arrest and charge

Article 5(2) provides that everyone who is arrested shall be informed properly, in a language which he understands, of the reasons for his arrest and of any charge against him. An individual need not be supplied with full reasons for arrest at the actual time of that arrest provided it is done promptly in all the circumstances.

CASE EXAMPLE

Murray (Margaret) v United Kingdom (1994) 19 EHRR 193

The applicant was arrested under s 14 of the Northern Ireland (Emergency Provisions) Act 1978 on suspicion of having committed a terrorist offence and informed of the fact and reasons of arrest after two hours.

It was held that although the reasons for her arrest had not been brought to her attention at the time of her arrest, she had been sufficiently notified during her subsequent interrogation and an interval of a few hours did not fall outside the definition of promptness as required by Art 5(2).

16.12.7 The right to be brought promptly before a judge for trial or release

Article 5(3) provides that everyone arrested or detained under Art 5 must be brought *promptly* before a judge or other officer authorised by law to exercise judicial power, that person then being entitled either to trial within a reasonable time, or to release (either absolutely or on conditions) pending trial.

The relevant 'officer' must be independent of the executive and of any parties to the action (*Assenov v Bulgaria* (1999) 28 EHRR 652), and the person must, in all the circumstances, be brought before the relevant judicial authority 'promptly'.

CASE EXAMPLE

Brogan v United Kingdom (1989) 11 EHRR 117

The applicants had been arrested on suspicion of terrorism and had been detained for periods between four and a half days and six days and eventually released without charge.

The European Court held that even the shortest of the periods in this case was inconsistent with the notion of promptness as required by Art 5(3). Even in the context of terrorism, such a period seriously weakened the essence of the procedural right guaranteed by that provision.

Article 5(3) does not preclude pre-trial detention provided there are sufficient safeguards (*Caballero v United Kingdom* (2000) 30 EHRR 643).

16.12.8 Right to challenge lawfulness of detention

Article 5(4) of the Convention provides that everyone deprived of their liberty by arrest or detention shall be entitled to take proceedings by which the lawfulness of their detention shall be decided speedily by a court and his release ordered if the detention is not lawful. This is the case even if the original detention was lawful, and for Art 5(4) to be complied with the original court order must be linked sufficiently with any subsequent detention (*De Wilde, Ooms and Versyp v Belgium* (1971) 1 EHRR 373).

Where a person is deprived of their liberty by the executive that person has a right of access to a court or court-like body in order to question the legality of that detention, including the evidence on which the decision was made (*Chahal v United Kingdom* (1997) 23 EHRR 413). Further, any review must not be limited to judging simple legality, and must assess the necessity and proportionality of the detention (*Winterwerp v Netherlands* (1979) 2 EHRR 387).

Article 5(4) has been used to challenge the legality of domestic law allowing the Home Secretary to determine the release of life sentence prisoners and the European Court has held that such powers were incompatible with both the separation of powers and the Convention (*Thynne, Wilson and Gunnell v United Kingdom* (1990) 13 EHRR 666 (discretionary lifers); and *Stafford v United Kingdom* (2002) 35 EHRR 32 – mandatory lifers). In addition, such prisoners are entitled to a review of their detention by a court like body at reasonably regular intervals (*Oldham v United Kingdom* (2001) 31 EHRR 34).

16.12.9 Right to compensation for breach of Article 5

Article 5(5) provides that everyone who has been the victim of an arrest or detention in contravention of Art 5 shall have an enforceable right to compensation. The provision is contained within s 9(3) of the Human Rights Act 1998 (see Chapter 17).

The provision guarantees compensation whether the detention was lawful or otherwise under domestic law (*Brogan v United Kingdom* (1989) 11 EHRR 117) and is supplemented by Art 13, which guarantees an effective remedy for violation of Convention rights (see below).

16.13 Article 6 – The right to a fair and public hearing

In the determination of his civil rights and obligations or of any criminal charge against him, everyone is entitled to a fair and public hearing within a reasonable time by an independent and impartial tribunal established by law.

16.13.1 The scope of Article 6

Article 6 guarantees the right to a hearing before an impartial and unbiased court or tribunal, and specifically a number of procedural rights before and during the trial.

Article 6 applies to all proceedings where the applicant is either facing a 'criminal charge', or where that person's 'civil rights and obligations' are subject to determination.

With respect to the term 'civil rights and obligations' it is not necessary that both parties to the proceedings are private individuals (or that the proceedings are classed as public – for example judicial review proceedings), provided the result of the proceedings were decisive of private rights and obligations (*Ringeisen v Austria* (1971) 1 EHRR 455). For example, in *Tinnelly v United Kingdom* (1998) 27 EHRR 249 the European Court held that a right not to be discriminated against in the provision of contracts under domestic legislation was a 'civil right' even though the source of the right was statutory.

Whether the proceedings constitute a criminal charge will depend on how the offence has been classified in domestic law, the nature of the offence, and the severity of the punishment (*Engel v Netherlands* (1976) 1 EHRR 647). Prison disciplinary proceedings amount to a criminal charge where the penalty is sufficiently serious and the offence sufficiently criminal in nature (*Ezeh and Connors v United Kingdom* (2004) 39 EHRR 691).

16.13.2 The right of access to the courts

The European Court held in *Golder v United Kingdom* (1976) 1 EHRR 524, that the right of access to the courts is implicit in Art 6:

J 'Article 6(1) of the Convention was not limited to guaranteeing the right to a fair trial in legal proceedings that are already pending, but secures in addition a right of access to the courts to every person wishing to commence an action in order to have his civil rights and obligations determined … the Court could scarcely conceive of the rule of law without there being a possibility of having access to the courts.'

This includes the obligation of the state to provide facilities so to allow individuals to seek legal redress, for example, legal aid (*Airey v Ireland* (1979) 2 EHRR 305). The right may be restricted to certain persons and on grounds of security (*Campbell v United Kingdom* (1992) 15 EHRR 137).

In addition, domestic law must not place procedural obstacles in the way of the parties, precluding claims irrespective of their merits.

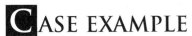

CASE EXAMPLE

Osman v United Kingdom (2000) 29 EHRR 245

The applicants brought civil proceedings against the police in negligence but the domestic courts held that no action could lie against the police with respect to the investigation and suppression crime.

The European Court held that the blanket application of that rule unjustifiably deprived the applicants of their right to have the merits of her civil action tried before a court. The application of the rule in this case constituted a disproportionate restriction on the applicant's rights under Art 6.

However, it is not unlawful for *substantive* domestic law to limit the success of a particular legal action (*Z and others v United Kingdom* (2002) 34 EHRR 3, and *Brooks v MPC* [2005] UKHL 24), although such a rule might violate Art 13 (see below).

16.13.3 The right to a public hearing before an impartial court or tribunal

Under Art 6 an individual is entitled to a trial before an impartial and unbiased court and this means a court that is free from the *appearance* of bias (*Findlay v United Kingdom* (1997) 24 EHRR 221). This includes freedom from the appearance of executive and political bias.

CASE EXAMPLE

McGonnnel v United Kingdom (2000) 30 EHRR 289

The Deputy Bailiff of Guernsey, a senior judge and President of a number of state committees, adjudicated on the applicant's planning permission application.

It was held that there had been a violation of Art 6. That person's direct involvement in the passage of legislation or of executive rules was capable of casting doubt on his impartiality and thus was in violation of Art 6.

- Executive adjudication is not incompatible with Art 6 provided such decisions are subject to appropriate judicial review (*Bryan v United Kingdom* (1995) 21 EHRR 342).

- Article 6 can be violated where there is evidence of bias from a jury (*Sander v United Kingdom* (2001) 31 EHRR 44).

- Article 6 guarantees the right to a fair sentence (*V and T v United Kingdom* (2000) 30 EHRR 121, and *R (Anderson) v Secretary of State for the Home Department* [2002] UKHL 46).

- Article 6 states that everyone is entitled to a fair and *public* hearing and that judgment shall be pronounced publicly, although it is lawful to limit the open and public nature of the proceedings in order to protect the rights of the participants, of justice in general (*V and T v United Kingdom* (2000) 30 EHRR 121).

- Article 6(1) guarantees that an individual receives a fair trial within a *reasonable time*. This applies to the length of the judicial proceedings, including appeals, and what amounts to a reasonable time depends on all the circumstances of the case. (*Robins v United Kingdom* (1997) 26 EHRR 527.)

16.13.4 The right to effective participation in the trial

Article 6(1) implicitly guarantees the right to put legal arguments before the court in support of one's case. This right is supplemented by the right of legal assistance, contained in Art 6(3)(c) (see directly below).

Any restriction of this right must be proportionate and necessary and ensure a basic right to a fair trial.

CASE EXAMPLE

P, C and S v United Kingdom (2002) 35 EHRR 31

The applicants (a mother and father of a child who was felt to be in danger from the mother) were not legally represented in the relevant care order or adoption proceedings.

CONTINUED ▸

> The European Court held that although courts had to strike a balance between the interests of the parents and the welfare of the child, the refusal of the domestic courts to defer the proceedings and to allow the applicants to obtain legal representation prevented the applicants from putting forward their case in a proper and effective manner.

Equally, *both* parties should be able to present any relevant evidence before the court in an equal manner (*Rowe and Davis v United Kingdom* (2000) 30 EHRR 1 – refusal to order disclosure of a document that the prosecution had provided to the court during a murder trial was in violation of Art 6). However, exclusionary rules are not unlawful provided they do not interfere with the basic right to a fair trial (*Jasper and Fitt v United Kingdom* (2000) 30 EHRR 97).

The use of unlawfully obtained evidence may lead to a violation of Art 6, but will not do so in all cases. Accordingly, in *Khan v United Kingdom* (2001) 31 EHRR 45 the European Court held that the admission of evidence obtained in breach of Art 8 did not violate the applicant's right to a fair trial within Art 6 because the applicant had been given an opportunity to question the admissibility of the evidence and the domestic courts had considered whether its inclusion would cause substantive unfairness.

For Art 6 to be complied with the individual should be aware of the nature of the charge or other proceedings and must be allowed to participate constructively in them (*V and T v United Kingdom* (2000) 30 EHRR 121 – subjection of 11-year old defendants to an adult trial violated Art 6). Specifically, Art 6(3)(a) provides that every person has the right to be informed promptly, in a language which he understands and in detail, of the nature and cause of the accusation made against him (*Broziek v Italy* (1989) 12 EHRR 371), and Art 6(3)(e) guarantees right to have the free legal assistance of an interpreter if he cannot understand or speak the language used in court.

16.13.5 The presumption of innocence and the rule against self-incrimination

Article 6(2) states that everyone charged with a criminal offence shall be presumed innocent until proved guilty according to law and in conjunction with in Art 6(1) protects an individual from self-incrimination.

CASE EXAMPLE

Saunders v United Kingdom (1996) 23 EHRR 313

The applicant had been required to answer questions put to him by the Department of Trade and Industry in the course of their administrative investigations. The answers were used as evidence in a subsequent criminal trial where he was found guilty.

CONTINUED ▶

> The European Court held that the use of such evidence by the prosecution infringed the applicant's right against self-incrimination. In this case the prosecution had made use of these statements to question the applicant's honesty and integrity and it was irrelevant that the statements were not self-incriminating.

Although Art 6(2) implicitly recognises the right to silence, that right is not absolute (*Murray v United Kingdom* (1996) 22 EHRR 29), provided the applicant receives a fair hearing in all the circumstances (*Condron v United Kingdom* (2001) 31 EHRR 1 – violation of Art 6 when the trial judge had impliedly directed the jury to draw an adverse inference form the applicant's silence).

16.13.6 The right to legal assistance

Article 6(3)(c) states that everyone has the right the right to defend themselves against any criminal charge in person or through legal assistance of one's own choosing. In addition, if the defendant has not got sufficient means to pay for such assistance, he has the right to be given it free where the interests of justice demand it. Whether the defendant is entitled to free legal assistance depends on all the circumstances, including the complexity of the case (*Benham v United Kingdom* (1996) 22 EHRR 293, and *Steel and Morris v United Kingdom* (2005) 41 EHRR 22).

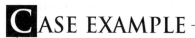

CASE EXAMPLE

Granger v United Kingdom (1990) 12 EHRR 469

The applicant, a man of limited intelligence, had been charged with a criminal offence and had been refused legal aid and thus not provided with counsel on appeal. The applicant had notes from his solicitor but he clearly did not understand them when he read them out in court.

The European Court held that Art 6(1) and 6(3)(c) should be read together, and where it was apparent that a fair hearing could not take place without legal advice, then both provisions would be violated. In the present case, having regard to the applicant's intelligence and the complexity of the case he should have been given legal aid.

Article 6(3)(c) also guarantees the right to legal assistance during detention and interrogation where justice so requires (*Brennan v United Kingdom* (2002) 34 EHRR 18).

16.13.7 The right to call and question witnesses

Article 6(3)(d) gives an individual the right to examine, or have examined, witnesses against him and to obtain the attendance and examination of witnesses on his behalf. This includes the right to confront witnesses (*Saidi v United Kingdom* (1993) 17 EHRR 251).

Article 6 does not guarantee an unlimited right to call and ex... remains within the discretion of the domestic courts provided th... the round (*Van Mechelen v The Netherlands* (1997) 25 EHRR 647).

16.14 Article 7 – Prohibition of retros... criminal law and penalties

(A) No one shall be held guilty of any criminal offence on account of any act or om... which did not constitute a criminal offence under national or international law at th... time when it was committed. Nor shall a heavier penalty be imposed than the one that was applicable at the time that the criminal offence was committed.

16.14.1 The scope of Article 7

Article 7 prohibits retrospective criminal law and penalties, and is fundamental to the rule of law and due process. Accordingly, under Art 15(2) a state cannot derogate from Art 7.

The article only applies where the applicant is found guilty of a criminal offence (see *Engel v Netherlands* (1976) 1 EHRR 706, discussed above), and lays down two basic principles:

- No person shall be guilty of an offence for an act which at the time of its commission was not an offence in domestic or international law.

- No person should be subjected to a heavier penalty than the one which existed at that time.

CASE EXAMPLE

Welch v United Kingdom (1995) 20 EHRR 247

The applicant was convicted of drug offences and as part of the sentence the trial judge imposed a confiscation order under the Drug Trafficking Act 1986, which came into force after the applicant's arrest but before his conviction.

The European Court held that the confiscation was clearly retrospective as it was made in respect of offences committed before the relevant provision came into force. Whether the confiscation proceedings constituted a 'penalty' depended on whether the measure was imposed following conviction for a criminal offence, the nature and purpose of the measure; its characterisation, and its severity. Taking into account a combination of punitive elements involved in this measure, the proceedings came within Art 7.

16.14.2 The exceptions to Article 7

Article 7 will not be violated where the relevant law has been developed in a foreseeable manner and then applied to the detriment of the defendant.

THE EUROPEAN
CONVENTION ON
HUMAN RIGHTS

...pective

...amine witnesses, the number of which
...e applicant receives a fair trial in

...ssion

404

...sult of the domestic courts' ruling that a
...arital rape' (*R v R* [1991] 4 All ER

...iolation of Art 7. The development of the
...had been foreseeable and consistent
...t was unlawful at the time they

...e the trial and punishment of any person
...itted, was criminal according to the general
...mple torture or 'war crimes').

ACTIVITY

Quick Quiz on Due Process Rights

1. What rights does Art 5 of the Convention provide to the individual and what is the importance of those rights?

2. What exceptions to the right to liberty does Art 5 allow, and what are the restrictions on those exceptions?

3. What values does Art 6 of the Convention seek to uphold?

4. Name five specific rights that Art 6 bestows on the individual.

5. What does Art 7 of the Convention prohibit, and why?

16.15 Article 8 – Right to private and family life

 Everyone has the right to respect for his private and family life, his home and his correspondence.

16.15.1 The scope of Article 8

Article 8 provides the right to *respect* for private and family life, home and correspondence, including freedom from interference of those rights by both state actors and, in certain cases, private individuals (*X and Y v Netherlands* (1985) 8 EHRR 235). Thus, Art 8 can have a 'horizontal' effect, and the domestic courts have adopted this approach in developing the private law of confidentiality (*Douglas v Hello! Ltd* ([2001] 2 WLR 992).

- Article 8 imposes a positive obligation on the state to ensure the enjoyment of those rights (*Marckx v Belgium* (1979) 2 EHRR 330).

- The right to private life includes the right to physical integrity, to private space, to communicate privately with others, to access personal information, and the right to private sexual life.

- In particular Art 8 provides freedom from press and other intrusions into privacy (*Von Hannover v Germany* (2005) 40 EHRR 1 and *Peck v United Kingdom* (2003) 36 EHRR 31).

- Article 8 is a conditional right and interferences are permitted under Art 8(2) provided they are in accordance with law and necessary in a democratic society in the interests of national security, public safety or the economic well-being of the country, for the prevention of disorder or crime, for the protection of health or morals, or for the protection of the rights and freedoms of others.

- Such restrictions will be invalid if they lack a proper legal basis (*Malone v United Kingdom* (1984) 7 EHRR 14).

16.15.2 The right to respect of private life

Article 8 covers privacy and confidentiality and the right to be let alone, but the European Court has also recognised the right to develop and establish relationships with others (*Niemietz v Germany* (1992) 16 EHRR 97). The court has also accepted that a private life can be enjoyed in the employment sphere (*Halford v United Kingdom* (1997) 24 EHRR 523).

Article 8 protects a person's right to physical and moral integrity, and a state owes a positive duty to protect those interests from attack from both state officials and other individuals (*X and Y v The Netherlands* (1985) 8 EHRR 235). Equally, the European Court has also held that the term private life protects an individual's health (*McGinley and Egan v United Kingdom* (1998) 27 EHRR 1).

There has also been much case law on the individual's right to a private sexual life.

CASE EXAMPLE

Dudgeon v United Kingdom (1982) 4 EHRR 149

The applicant was a practicing homosexual in Northern Ireland and complained that the existence of criminal laws prohibiting homosexuality violated his Art 8 rights

The European Court held that the right to private life included the right to enjoy one's private *sexual* life and the existence of domestic laws prohibiting certain sexual activity

CONTINUED ▸

> between men was in violation of Article 8. In addition, strong justification would be required to allow interference with such intimate aspects of a person's right to private life; in this case there was not a pressing need for such a blanket prohibition.

The European Court will thus be reluctant to allow interference with private sexual life on the grounds of public morality or disapproval (*Smith and Grady v United Kingdom* (2000) 29 EHRR 493), but will permit it in cases where there is a sound reason for enforcing morality and protecting the rights of others (*Laskey, Jaggard and Brown v United Kingdom* (1997) 24 EHRR 39 – conviction of voluntary sado-masochistic acts permitted by Art 8(2)).

The court has also used Art 8 (and Art 12) to recognise the private rights of transsexuals (*Goodwin v United Kingdom* (2002) 35 EHRR 18), leading to the passing of the Gender Recognition Act 2004.

16.15.3 The right to respect of family life

Along with Art 12, guaranteeing the right to marry, Art 8 protects the right to *family* life and the European Court has extended the meaning of family beyond the marriage relationship (*X, Y and Z v United Kingdom* (1997) 24 EHRR 143 and *Goodwin v United Kingdom*, above). However, Art 8 does not guarantee the right to divorce (*Johnston v Ireland* (1986) 9 EHRR 203).

Although restrictions are permitted under Art 8(2), the European Court will have to be satisfied that there are pressing reasons for such interference and that such reasons are not discriminatory.

CASE EXAMPLE

Abdul Aziz, Cabales and Balkandali v United Kingdom (1985) 7 EHRR 471

UK immigration authorities refused to allow the applicants' foreign husbands entry into the country.

The European Court held that although Art 8 did not impose an obligation to respect the choice by married couples of the country of their matrimonial residence, the applicants had been discriminated against on grounds of their gender. Accordingly there was a breach of Art 8 in conjunction with Art 14.

16.15.4 The right to respect for the home

Article 8 guarantees the right to respect for the home, protecting that right from intrusions by the state (*Akdivar v Turkey* (1996) 1 BHRC 137). The right is also related to Art 1 of the First Protocol (see directly below) protecting the right to property.

Such a right can be breached in the public interest, although the European Court will require a strong justification for any violation (*Gillow v United Kingdom* (1986) 11 EHRR 335). Thus any planning laws must strike a correct balance between the public interest and the enjoyment of private and family life (*Buckley v United Kingdom* (1996) 23 EHRR 101).

Despite the fundamental character of this right, the European Court will offer each state a wide margin of appreciation in balancing these respective rights.

CASE EXAMPLE

Hatton v United Kingdom (2003) 37 EHRR 28

Residents living on the flight path of Heathrow airport complained that the introduction of a scheme to regulate flights had increased night-time noise and interfered with their private and family lives and their homes.

The Grand Chamber of the European Court held that the authorities had achieved a proper balance between the rights of the residents to peaceful enjoyment of their homes and their family lives in allocating the number of night flights at Heathrow. Only a limited number of people were affected by the noise and house prices had not devalued, thus giving those people the opportunity to move.

16.15.5 The right to respect for correspondence

Article 8 protects the right to communicate with others, including correspondence with friends and family (*Silver v United Kingdom* (1983) 5 EHRR 347) and in a business context (*Halford v United Kingdom* (1997) 24 EHRR 523).

The European Court has afforded special protection with respect to legal correspondence, which also engages the right of access to the courts (*Golder v United Kingdom* (1976) 1 EHRR 524 – refusal of permission for prisoner to contact a solicitor for the purpose of bringing a civil action against a prison officer constituted a disproportionate interference with the prisoner's Art 8 rights and also constituted an impermissible breach of the his right of access to the courts under Art 6).

16.16 Article 9 – Freedom of thought, conscience and religion

(A) Everyone has the right to freedom of thought, conscience and religion; this right includes freedom to change his religion or belief and freedom, either alone or in community with others and in public or private, to manifest his religion or belief, in worship, teaching, practice and observance.

16.16.1 The scope of Article 9

The right to freedom of thought, conscience and religion is an absolute right in the sense that it is not subject to the restrictions laid down in para 2 of the article, which only apply to the manifestation of those beliefs.

Article 9 protects an individual from persecution on grounds of his beliefs and is not limited to religious beliefs or convictions (*Arrowsmith v United Kingdom* (1978) 3 EHRR 218 – pacifism was protected by Art 9). However Art 9 does not apply to every individually held opinion or conviction.

CASE EXAMPLE

Pretty v United Kingdom (2002) 35 EHRR 1

The applicant claimed that the state had interfered with her beliefs under Art 9 by denying her the right to die with the assistance of her husband.

The European Court held that the applicant's views on euthanasia did not involve a manifestation of a 'religion or belief, through worship, teaching, practice or observance'. The term 'practice' did not cover each act that was motivated or influenced by a religion or belief. (The applicant's views related to her ideas of personal autonomy, under Art 8, but such a right was overtaken by the need to protect the rights of others.)

Article 9 imposes a positive obligation on the state to allow individuals to enjoy their beliefs peacefully and without interference (*Dubowska and Skup v Poland* (1997) 24 EHRR CD 75), including enjoying these rights in employment, subject to necessary restrictions on the manifestation of such rights (*Ahmed v United Kingdom* (1981) 4 EHRR 126).

Although the European Court has accepted that freedom of expression may be compromised to ensure religious observance, it has not insisted that domestic law pass and maintain a law of blasphemy (*Choudhury v United Kingdom* (1991) 12 HRLJ 172).

16.16.2 Permissible restrictions

The right to manifest one's religion or beliefs is subject to limitations that are prescribed by law and necessary in a democratic society in the interests of public safety, for the protection of public order, health or morals, or for the protection of the rights and freedoms of others.

CASE EXAMPLE

Sahin v Turkey (2004) 19 BHRC 590

The applicant had been refused permission to wear a Muslim headscarf and was
suspended from University for non-compliance of that order.

The Grand Chamber of the European Court held that the ban was proportionate to the
protection of the rights of others and of public order, being necessary to preserve
secularism in the country's educational institutions. Article 9 did not always guarantee the
right to behave in a manner governed by religious beliefs and did not confer a right to
disregard justifiable rules.

See also *(R) Begum v Denbigh High School* [2006] UKHL 15 (see below), where the House of a
Lords held that a school uniform policy banning full Muslim dress was not in breach of a
schoolgirl's Convention rights.

16.17 Article 10 – Freedom of expression

 Everyone has the right to freedom of expression. This right shall include freedom to
hold opinions and to receive and impart information and ideas without interference by
public authority and regardless of frontiers

16.17.1 The scope of Article 10

Article 10 guarantees the right to impart information and ideas, and the right of others to receive
them. It is viewed as fundamental to both democracy and individual freedom by the European
Court of Human Rights (*Handyside v United Kingdom* (1976) 1 EHRR 737).

Article 10 covers both commercial speech (*Markt Intern Velag Gmbh and Klaus Beermann v
Germany* (1989) 12 EHRR 161) and obscene and indecent speech (*Handyside* (above)), although
the European Court has accepted that the state will be given a wider margin of appreciation to
regulate such speech.

In contrast, the European Court places greater significance on the dissemination of information
and ideas in the public interest (*Sunday Times v United Kingdom* (1979) 2 EHRR 245, protecting
such speech in particular from prior restraint (*Observer and Guardian v United Kingdom* (1991) 14
EHRR 153)).

The European Court has also given greater weight to press and media freedom.

CASE EXAMPLE

Jersild v Denmark (1994) 19 EHRR 1

A broadcasting company had been fined for aiding and abetting the dissemination of unlawful racist speech by broadcasting their views as part of a documentary.

The European Court held that although the views of the group were not protected by Art 10, punishing the applicant for statements made by that group during an interview was a serious restriction on the duty of the press to discuss matters of public interest.

Article 10 applies to restrictions on freedom of expression and does not provide a general right of freedom of information (*Leander v Sweden* (1987) 9 EHRR 343). However, refusal of access to private information could constitute a violation of Art 8.

16.17.2 Restrictions on freedom of expression – Article 10(2)

Article 10(2) provides that the exercise of the rights contained in para 1 carry with it duties and responsibilities and is therefore subject to restrictions and penalties that are 'prescribed by law,' and necessary in a democratic society for the furtherance of a number of listed legitimate aims.

In such cases, therefore, the court has to consider whether the need for the legal restriction is sufficiently pressing and whether any penalty or condition is reasonable and proportionate.

CASE EXAMPLE

Von Hannover v Germany (2005) 40 EHRR 1

The former Princess Caroline of Monaco complained that persistent photographs taken of her by the 'paparazzi' was in violation of her rights under Art 8.

The European Court held that there had been an interference with the applicant's privacy rights and that there was no overriding public interest in the photographs so as to justify that violation on grounds of freedom of expression and the public right to know.

16.18 Article 11 – Freedom of assembly and association

 Everyone has the right to freedom of peaceful assembly and to freedom of association with others, including the right to form and to join trade unions for the protection of his interests.

16.18.1 The scope of Article 11

Article 11 of the European Convention provides that everyone has the right of association with others (including the right to join a trade union) and of *peaceful* assembly. The Article is conditional and subject to restrictions provided they are prescribed by law and necessary in a democratic society in the interests of national security or public safety, for the prevention of disorder or crime, for the protection of health or morals or for the protection of the rights and freedoms of others (Art 11(2)).

In addition, Art 11(2) allows lawful restrictions on members of the armed forces, of the police or of the administration of the state (*Council of Civil Service Unions and others v United Kingdom* (1987) 50 DR 228).

16.18.2 Freedom of association

The right of association specifically includes the right to form trade unions and the state has an obligation to ensure that this right is enjoyed by individuals even against private employers (*Swedish Engine Drivers' Union v Sweden* (1976) 1 EHRR 617). Although there is no right to insist on collective bargaining with employers, union members are entitled not to be discriminated against on grounds of their membership (*Wilson and others v United Kingdom* (2002) 35 EHRR 20).

Article 11, together with Art 9, also provides the negative right not to join a trade union (*Young Webster and James v United Kingdom* (1982) 4 EHRR 38), thus protecting non-unionists from discriminatory treatment.

The European Court has also held that the term 'association' covers various groups, including political parties (*United Communist Party of Turkey v Turkey* (1998) 26 EHRR 121). However, it does not include gatherings for entirely social purposes (*Anderson v United Kingdom* (1998) 25 EHRR CD 172).

The right of association is conditional and subject to lawful and necessary restrictions. However, proscription of a group would only be allowed in the most exceptional cases (*United Communist Party of Turkey v Turkey* (1998) 26 EHRR 121) – the banning of a group merely because it used the word communist in its name could not be justified in relation to any legitimate aim.

CASE EXAMPLE

Refha Partisi Erbakan Kazan and Tekdal v Turkey (2003) 37 EHRR 1

The applicant's party had been dissolved by the Turkish Constitutional Court on the ground that it had become a centre of activities against the principles of secularism.

CONTINUED ▸

> The European Court held that political parties who incite others to use violence or support political aims that were inconsistent with democracy and the rights and freedoms of democracy could not rely on Art 11. In this case the measure was necessary and proportionate.

Such a finding may be strengthened by the state's reliance on Art 17 of the Convention, which provides that nothing in the Convention gives any person or group any right to engage in any activity or perform any act aimed at the destruction of any of the rights and freedoms in the Convention.

16.18.3 Freedom of peaceful assembly

Article 11 of the European Convention contains both a negative right not to have one's peaceful assembly interfered with, but also imposes a positive obligation on the state to ensure that everyone can enjoy that right (*Platform Arzte fur dan Laeben v Austria* (1988) 13 EHRR 204).

The Convention protects the right to *peaceful* assembly, excluding assemblies that use, advocate or incite violence. Such assemblies would also conflict with Art 17 of the Convention, above. Moreover, the alleged restriction must actually interfere with the right of assembly, as opposed to curtailing one of its activities (*R (Countryside Alliance) v Attorney-General* [2006] EWCA Civ 817 – the ban on hunting did not stop the group assembling, but simply outlawed a particular activity of that assembly).

As Art 11 is a conditional right, Art 11(2) also allows restrictions on peaceful assemblies, provided those restrictions are legal, necessary and proportionate to legitimate aims such as the preservation of public order, the protection of the rights of others and the prevention of crime. In this respect the European Court has given the domestic law and authorities a wide margin of appreciation in balancing the right of peaceful assembly with those aims, and may even permit the banning of meeting in advance (*Rai, Allmond and Negotiate Now v United Kingdom* (1995) 19 EHRR CD 93).

The European Court will give the police authorities a wide discretion when dealing with alleged breaches of the peace (*Chorherr v Austria* (1993) 17 EHRR 358), although interferences must not be disproportionate to achieving any legitimate aim.

CASE EXAMPLE

Steel v United Kingdom (1998) 28 EHRR 603

Two demonstrators had been arrested and bound over for breach of the peace when handing out leaflets outside a conference.

CONTINUED ▶

The European Court held that on the evidence the police had no grounds for believing that the applicant's conduct would cause a breach of the peace. Consequently their arrest and subsequent restraint was an unlawful and disproportionate interference with their right to liberty and freedom of expression and assembly.

16.19 Article 12 – The right to marry

Men and women of marriageable age have the right to marry and found a family, according to the national laws governing the exercise of that right.

16.19.1 The scope of Article 12

Article 12 complements Art 8 of the Convention (the right to private and family life), and imposes a negative duty on the state not to interfere with the enjoyment of the right to marry. It does not guarantee the right to divorce (*Johnston v Ireland* (1986) 9 EHRR 203), but if national law does allow divorce, it must not place unreasonable restrictions on a person's right to remarry (*F v Switzerland* (1987) 10 EHRR 411).

Although Art 12 leaves the right to marry and found a family at the discretion of national law, any conditions or restrictions on such a right must be necessary and proportionate (see below).

16.19.2 Restrictions on the right to marry

The European Court will offer Member States a reasonably wide margin of appreciation with respect to an individual's right to marry, although any restriction must not be arbitrary or destroy the essence of that right (*F v Switzerland* (1987) 10 EHRR 411).

CASE EXAMPLE

B and L v United Kingdom (2006) 42 EHRR 11

The applicants – former father and daughter-in law – were prohibited by domestic law from marrying unless both former spouses were deceased and claimed that this contravened Art 12.

The European Court held that the legal prohibition of such marriages was a disproportionate interference with the right to marry. Although there was a legitimate aim – the protection of family life and of children's interests – the fact that such relationships did not establish criminal liability suggested that there was no pressing need for such prohibition.

Domestic law prohibiting prisoners from marrying whilst incarcerated was held to destroy the essence of Art 12 (*Hamer v United Kingdom* (1982) 4 EHRR 139) and in *Goodwin v United Kingdom* (2002) 35 EHRR 18 the European Court recognised the right of transsexuals to marry in accordance with their new gender.

16.20 Article 1 of the First Protocol – the right to property

Every natural or legal person is entitled to the peaceful enjoyment of his possessions. No one shall be deprived of his possessions except in the public interest and subject to the conditions provided for by law and by the general principles of international law.

16.20.1 The scope of the right to property

This article guarantees the right to peaceful enjoyment of possessions (both real and personal property), and complements Art 8 of the Convention, guaranteeing respect for family life and the home.

The article makes the enjoyment of this right subject to the rules of domestic law and further states that it does not impair the right of a state to enforce such laws as it deems necessary to control the use of property in accordance with the general interest or to secure the payment of taxes or other contributions or penalties.

16.20.2 Lawful restrictions on the right to property

Any such restriction must be in accordance with law and constitute a necessary and proportionate measure, and the court will attempt to strike a fair balance between the interests of the community in general and the protection of the individual's property rights (*Sporrong and Lonnroth v Sweden* (1982) 5 EHRR 35).

The court will provide each state with a wide margin of appreciation in this respect (*James v United Kingdom* (1986) 6 EHRR 123; *National and Provincial Building Society v United Kingdom* (1997) 25 EHRR 127), but will protect the individual from arbitrary or unfair interferences.

CASE EXAMPLE

Pye (Oxford) Ltd v United Kingdom (2006) 43 EHRR 3

Landowners had lost possession of their land by virtue of the domestic rules on adverse possession.

The European Court held that the law at that time provided inadequate protection to the true owners, particularly as there was no statutory right for them to be notified of the possessor's intention to claim those rights.

16.21 Article 2 of the First Protocol – the right to education

(A) No person shall be denied the right to education. In the exercise of any functions which it assumes in relation to education and to teaching, the State shall respect the right of parents to ensure such education and teaching in conformity with their own religious and philosophical convictions.

Article 2 of the first protocol provides the individual with the right to enjoy the means of instruction that is provided by the state at any given time. The right is limited and there is no obligation on the part of the state to establish or fund any particular type of educational institution (*The Belgian Linguistic Case* (1968) 1 EHRR 252). The UK Government has made a reservation with respect to guaranteeing parents' rights, restricting its obligations to the provision of efficient instruction and training and the avoidance of unreasonable public expenditure.

In addition, the Article complements the rights to private and family life (under Art 8) and the right to religion (under Art 9) by providing parents with the right to have their children taught in conformity with their religious and philosophical convictions.

CASE EXAMPLE

***Campbell and Cosans v United Kingdom* (1982) 4 EHRR 293**

The applicants' claimed that the threat of corporal punishment to their children constituted a violation of their Convention right to respect of their philosophical convictions.

The European Court held that although there had been no breach of Art 3 (because the children had not been punished or threatened with punishment), there had been a violation of Art 2 of the First Protocol by subjecting the children to the regime of corporal punishment against the wishes of the parents.

(Note, there is no corresponding right to insist that one's child is subjected to corporal punishment (*R (Williamson) v Secretary of State for Employment* [2005] UKHL 15), see section 17.10.)

16.22 Article 3 – the right to free elections

(A) The High Contracting Parties undertake to hold free elections at reasonable intervals by secret ballot, under conditions which will ensure the free expression of the people in the choice of the legislature.

16.22.1 The scope of the right to vote

The article imposes an obligation on each Member State to hold free elections, and thus provides a right to the general public to have such elections. Also, the European Court has held that the article provides individuals with the right to vote and the right to stand for election to the legislature (*Mathieu-Mohin and Clerfast v Belgium* (1988) 10 EHRR 1).

An individual also has the right to vote in non-national elections (*Matthews v United Kingdom* (1999) 28 EHRR 361 – exclusion from voting in the elections to the European Parliament violated Art 3).

16.22.2 Limitations on the right to vote

The right to vote and stand for election is subject to implied limitations and domestic law can restrict it provided the very essence of the right to free elections is not undermined (*Mathieu-Mohin v Belgium* (1988)). Recently, the European Court has considered the legality of depriving prisoners of the right to vote (see section 9.6.3).

16.23 Articles 13 and 14 – the right to an effective remedy and freedom from discrimination

To facilitate the enjoyment of the above rights the European Convention guarantees the right an effective remedy for their breach (Art 13) and that the rights are enjoyed free from discrimination (Art 14).

16.23.1 The Right to an Effective Remedy – Article 13

(A) Everyone whose rights and freedoms as set forth in this Convention are violated shall have an effective remedy before a national authority notwithstanding that the violation has been committed by persons acting in an official capacity.

Article 13 complements Art 1 of the Convention, which places a duty on Member States to secure the rights and freedoms laid down in the Convention. Article 13 does not place a duty on the state to incorporate the Convention into domestic law, but domestic law should ensure that a person can enjoy his or Convention rights in reality rather than theory. Article 13 is not 'incorporated' by the Human Rights Act 1998, but the government argue that the passing of the Act in itself satisfies Art 13.

In *Silver v United Kingdom* (1983) 5 EHRR 347 the European Court laid down the following principles with respect to Art 13:

- Where individuals have an arguable claim of a violation of their Convention rights, they should have a remedy before a national authority to have the claim decided and to obtain redress.

- The authority should normally be a judicial one, and if it is not then its powers and the guarantees should be as effective.
- The aggregate of remedies provided under domestic law must provide effective redress for the individual.

There will be a violation of Art 13 if domestic law fails to recognise a Convention right (*Malone v United Kingdom* (1984) 7 EHRR 14), or if proceedings are struck out, precluding the court from determining whether there has been a violation, and if so what compensation should be granted (*Z v United Kingdom* (2002) 34 EHRR 3).

Domestic law should allow individuals to argue their case in accordance with principles such as proportionality (*Smith and Grady v United Kingdom* (2000) 29 EHRR 493), to air their complaint before a sufficiently independent body (*Khan v United Kingdom* (2001) 31 EHRR 45), and to be awarded compensation for breach of Convention rights in appropriate cases (*Edwards v United Kingdom* (2002) 35 EHRR 19).

16.23.2 Prohibition of discrimination – Article 14

(A) The enjoyment of the rights and freedoms set for the in this Convention shall be secured without discrimination on any ground such as sex, race, colour, language, religion, political or other opinion, national or social origin, association with a national minority, property, birth or other status.

As with Art 13, above, Art 14 complements the substantive Convention rights and prohibits discrimination in the enjoyment of such rights.

16.23.3 The scope of Article 14

Unlike Art 26 of the International Covenant on Civil and Political Rights 1966 – which ensures equality under the law – Art 14 does not provide a 'free-standing' right against discrimination. Thus, any complaint under Art 14 must be related to a violation of another Convention right. Note, Protocol No 12, as yet not ratified by the United Kingdom Government, imposes a general prohibition on discrimination, thus establishing a general right of freedom from discrimination.

Thus, Art 14 is used in addition to (or in conjunction with) a claim under another article of the Convention (*Smith and Grady v United Kingdom* (2000) 29 EHRR 493 – dismissal from the armed forces on grounds of sexual orientation a breach of Arts 8 and 14; and *ADT v United Kingdom* (2001) 31 EHRR 33 – conviction of homosexual men for gross indecency a violation of Arts 8 and 14 as the law discriminated against homosexuals).

Accordingly the court can not find a violation of Art 14 unless it establishes first that the Convention right in question is engaged.

CASE EXAMPLE

Choudhury v United Kingdom (1991) 12 HRLJ 172

The applicants complained that the absence of a law of blasphemy to protect the Muslim faith was in breach of Art 9 and was discriminatory under Art 14.

The European Commission held that freedom to manifest one's religion under Art 9 of the Convention did not include a duty on the state to pass specific blasphemy laws. Accordingly, even though the domestic law discriminated in favour of the Anglican faith, the claim under Art 14 failed as Art 9 was not engaged.

However, the court may find a breach of a Convention right on the facts because of the evidence of discrimination (*Abdulaziz Cabales and Balkandali v United Kingdom* (1985) 7 EHRR 471).

16.23.4 Justifiable discrimination

Article 14 is not an absolute right and the European Court recognises that discrimination in the enjoyment of Convention rights is legitimate where there is objective or reasonable justification for such treatment. In such a case any difference must not only pursue a legitimate aim, but the measure must also be reasonably proportionate (*'Belgian Linguistic' case* (1968) 1 EHRR 252).

CASE EXAMPLE

Willis v United Kingdom (2002) 35 EHRR 21

The applicant applied for the equivalent of a widow's payment and Widowed Mother's Allowance when he was forced to leave his employment to care for his children after his wife died. No such payments were available to him as a widower.

The European Court held that there had been a violation of Art 14 taken in conjunction with Art 1 of the First Protocol to the Convention; the only reason for being refused the benefits was that he was a man; a female in the same position would have had a right to such payments, and the difference in treatment between men and women was not based on any objective and reasonable justification.

Similarly, in *PM v United Kingdom* (2006) 42 EHRR 45, where the applicant had been denied tax relief in respect of maintenance payments made to his daughter because he had not been married to the girl's mother the European Court held that there was no justifiable reason to treat him differently from a married father, who would have been eligible for relief.

However, the European Court might be prepared to offer a wide margin of appreciation in some cases (*Pretty v United Kingdom* (2002), see section 16.16.1 – subjection of the applicant to a uniform law prohibiting assisted suicide was reasonably justifiable).

KEY FACTS

The substantive Convention rights are contained in both Part One of the Convention and various protocols	Arts 2–14 and Arts 1, 2 and 3 of the First Protocol, ECHR
The rights (apart from Art 13) are 'incorporated' into domestic law via the Human Rights Act 1998	s 1 and Sched 1, HRA
Some rights are absolute (for example, freedom from torture) and cannot be compromised, whilst others (for example, freedom of expression) are conditional and can be interfered with under specific conditions	Arts 3 and 10, ECHR
Under the Convention a state must protect life and must conduct effective investigations into deaths	Art 2, ECHR, *Osman v United Kingdom* (2000) and *Jordan v United Kingdom* (2003)
The Convention prohibits torture and inhuman and degrading treatment or punishment in absolute terms and irrespective of any public good	Art 3, ECHR and *Chahal v United Kingdom* (1997)
States can be liable under Art 3 for violations committed by other states	*Soering v United Kingdom* (1989)
The Convention guarantees due process by safeguarding liberty of the person and the right to a fair trial	Arts 5 and 6, ECHR
The Convention complements the above rights by prohibiting retrospective criminal law or penalties	Art 7, ECHR

CONTINUED ▸

KEY FACTS

The Convention rights of private and family life, freedom of religion, free speech, freedom of association and assembly, and the right to marry are conditional rights and can be restricted provided the interference is prescribed by law, has a legitimate aim, and is necessary in a democratic society	Arts 8–12, ECHR
The Convention protects the rights to property, education and the duty to hold free elections. These rights can be interfered with by legitimate and proportionate measures	Arts 1, 2 and 3 of the First Protocol, ECHR (ratified by the UK and included in the 1998 Act)
The Convention guarantees access to an effective remedy when Convention rights have been violated	Art 13, ECHR and *Silver v United Kingdom* (1983)
The Convention guarantees the enjoyment of all Convention rights free from discrimination	Art 14, ECHR
Article 14 does not provide a 'free-standing' right against discrimination	*Choudhury v United Kingdom* (1991)

Further Reading

Amos, M, *Human Rights Law* (Hart 2006), Pt II.

Cavanaugh, K, 'Policing the Margins: Rights Protection under the European Court of Human Rights' [2006] EHRLR 422.

Foster, S, *Human Rights and Civil Liberties* (Longman, 2003), chs 2 and 3.

Gearty, C, 'The European Court of Human Rights and the protection of civil liberties: an overview' (1993) 52 CLJ 89.

Harris, D, O'Boyle, M and Warbrick, C, *The Law of the European Convention on Human Rights* (2nd edn, OUP, 2007).

Mowbray, A, *Cases and Materials on the European Convention on Human Rights* (2nd edn, Butterworths, 2001).

AIMS AND OBJECTIVES

At the end of this chapter you should be able to:

■ Appreciate the constitutional and legal significance of the Human Rights Act
1998 and why it was passed

■ Appreciate the role of the law in protecting human rights before the Act was
passed and how the Act has impacted on that role

■ Understand the central provisions of the Act and appreciate how the Act impacts
on the protection of human rights in the United Kingdom

■ Be aware of the essential case law decided under the Act and appreciate
whether and how such case law has achieved the Act's purpose

17.1 Introduction

The Human Rights Act 1998 came into effect on 2nd October 2000 and while it does not strictly
incorporate the European Convention into domestic law, it allows the courts to give 'further effect'
to the Convention and to take Convention rights and case law into account when interpreting and
developing domestic law. As a consequence individuals can now rely *directly* on Convention rights
in the domestic courts.

Before the Act the courts could only give indirect effect to the Convention (eg where an Act of
Parliament was ambiguous (*R v Home Secretary, ex parte Brind* [1991] 1 AC 696)), and they could
not apply Convention rights where the domestic law did not recognise that right (*Malone v
Metropolitan Police Commissioner* [1979] Ch 344 – an individual could not claim that telephone
tapping was in violation of Art 8 of the Convention, guaranteeing the right to private life).

The Act builds on and enhances the traditional method of protecting civil liberties (see section
17.2). Thus, the courts can still apply traditional constitutional principles such as the presumption
of innocence, the control of arbitrary power and the rules of natural justice. However, the doctrine
of Parliamentary sovereignty is retained – the courts still cannot refuse to recognise an Act of
Parliament and Parliament retains the right to pass incompatible legislation.

17.2 Pre-Human Rights Act 1998 position

In the absence of a written constitution and a Bill of Rights, individual human rights were protected by the courts, Parliament and the democratic process, including public support and opinion.

Dicey distinguished the British method from other countries by stating that our constitution was not the *source* but the *consequence* of the rights of individuals, as expounded by the common law courts (see Chapter 6). Thus individual rights resulted from court decisions, applying the traditional private law to which all, including the government, were subject to. For example in *Entick v Carrington* (1765) 19 St Tr 1030 the court upheld the individual's right to property and person by applying the traditional law of trespass against government officials.

17.2.1 The role of the courts in protecting civil liberties

By the above methods and through the formal procedure of judicial review (see Chapters 18 and 19) the courts could safeguard against arbitrary and unreasonable interference with human rights. Thus the courts could:

- Interpret legislation in the light of constitutional fundamentals, ensuring a human rights friendly interpretation (*Waddington v Miah* [1974] 2 All ER 377).

- Assume Parliament did not intend to interfere with fundamental rights (*Raymond v Honey* [1984] AC 1).

- Subject executive decisions to stricter review where human rights were violated (*R v Ministry of Defence, ex parte Smith* [1996] 1 All ER 257).

- Apply the principles of natural justice to ensure a fair and impartial hearing (*Ridge v Baldwin* [1964] AC 40 and *R v Bow Street Metropolitan Stipendary Magistrate, ex parte Pinochet Ugarte (No2)* [2000] 1 AC 119).

17.2.2 The role of Parliament in protecting civil liberties

In addition, Parliament could pass legislation securing the rights and freedoms of its citizens.

- Statutes such as the Race Relations Act 1976 and the Sex Discrimination Act 1975 protect individuals from unlawful discrimination and safeguard the right to equality.

- The Police and Criminal Evidence Act 1984 provides safeguards against arbitrary police powers with respect to arrest, detention and search and entry.

- The Data Protection Acts 1984 and 1998 safeguard the right to privacy with respect to personal information.

However, Acts of Parliament could take away or interfere with rights without challenge from the courts on human rights grounds.

- The War Damage Act 1965 retrospectively took away the individual's right to compensation for war damage.

- The Public Order Act 1986 contained restrictions on the right of peaceful protest.

- Anti-terrorism legislation (for example the Terrorism Acts 2000 and 2006) provided wide powers to the authorities to control terrorist activities and association.

17.2.3 The criticisms of the traditional system

However, the 'common law' method was subject to a number of criticisms:

- The common law courts did not recognise all rights, for example the right of privacy (*Malone v Metropolitan Police Commissioner* [1979] Ch 344).

- The courts were powerless to challenge primary legislation which clearly violated individual rights (*Rossminster Ltd* (1980) – see section 6.7.5).

- The courts were not willing to apply 'European' principles of necessity and proportionality when challenging executive actions (*R v Home Secretary, ex parte Brind* [1991] 1 AC 696).

- The courts could not take the European Convention on Human Rights into account as a direct source of rights (*Brind* (1991) and *Malone* (1979)).

- Acts of Parliament enjoyed sovereignty and could not be questioned by the courts.

As a consequence of these defects individuals very often had to take direct cases under the European Convention on Human Rights 1950. This resulted in a number of high profile (and dozens of other) defeats for the United Kingdom Government before the European Court of Human Rights:

- *Malone v United Kingdom* (1984) 7 EHRR 14 – where the European Court held that unregulated telephone tapping was contrary to the right to private life and correspondence under Art 8 of the Convention.

- *Sunday Times v United Kingdom* (1979) 2 EHRR 245 – where domestic contempt laws were held in violation of Art 10, guaranteeing freedom of expression and press freedom.

- *Smith and Grady v United Kingdom* (2000) 29 EHRR 493 – where the European Court held that the dismissal of homosexual armed forces personnel was both contrary to Art 8 and discriminatory under Art 14.

- *Chahal v United Kingdom* (1997) 23 EHRR 413 – where it was held that the deportation of the applicant on grounds of national security violated Arts 3 and 5 of the Convention (freedom from inhuman treatment and liberty of the person).

17.3 The passing of the Human Rights Act 1998

The passing of the Human Rights Act 1998 was intended to rectify these deficiencies and to allow the domestic courts to directly apply Convention principles and case law, thus improving our human rights record in Strasbourg and reducing the need for citizens to seek the assistance of the European Court.

> **Central aims and provisions of the Act**
>
> - To give effect to the rights contained in Part 1 of the European Convention (s 1).
> - To allow victims of violations of human rights to rely on their Convention rights in domestic proceedings (ss 7–9).
> - To make it unlawful for public authorities to violate Convention rights (s 6).
> - To allow the domestic courts to take into account Convention case law when determining human rights cases (s 2).
> - To give the courts greater powers to interpret legislation in line with the Convention (s 3).
> - To allow the courts to declare domestic legislation incompatible with the Convention (s 4).
> - To make provision for the government to initiate legislation repealing or amending incompatible legislative provisions (s 10).
> - To make special provision for the protection of freedom of expression and freedom of religion (ss 12 and 13).
> - To require the government to make statements of compatibility with respect to new legislation (s 19).

The basic aim of the Act is to bring the European Convention rights 'home' to domestic law and allow its provisions to be applied in the domestic courts. This will mean that individuals will not in most cases be required to use the Convention machinery in Strasbourg, although the individual is still entitled to petition the European Court after exhausting domestic remedies (s 11).

17.3.1 Retrospective effect of the Act

The provisions of the Act generally only apply to acts or decisions of public authorities taking place after the coming into operation of the Act. Thus violations taking place before this time are subject to the general principles of judicial review and legality.

CASE EXAMPLE

Secretary of State for the Home Department v Wainwright [2003] UKHL 53

The claimants brought a case against the Prison Service alleging that they had been subjected to unlawful searches. Part of their claim was that this had violated their right to privacy under Art 8 of the Convention.

The House of Lords held that as the alleged violation took place before the Act came into force the claimants could not rely on the Act and the right to private life under Art 8.

ASE EXAMPLE ─────────────────────────────

Wilson v First County Trust Ltd (No 2) [2003] UKHL 40

The Court of Appeal had held that provisions of the Consumer Credit Act 1974 were incompatible with Article 6 of the Convention because they prevented credit companies from enforcing agreements unless specific procedures had been followed in the making of such agreements.

The House of Lords held that the Court of Appeal had been wrong in making a declaration of incompatibility in respect of a cause of action that arose before the Act came into operation; the Court of Appeal were wrong to find that the original court's order in refusing to enforce the agreement was the relevant act for the purpose of s 6 of the Act.

Neither does the Act apply to appeals against criminal convictions that took place before the Act, even where the appeal takes place after the Act's operation. Thus, in *R v Lambert, Ali and Jordan* [2001] UKHL 37 the House of Lords held that the Act does not have such retrospective effect and that such effect only applied to proceedings brought by a public authority. An unsuccessful appeal, brought by the defendant, was not to be treated as proceedings brought by or at the instigation of a public authority.

The decision in *Lambert* was reluctantly accepted by the House of Lords in *R v Kansal* [2001] UKHL 62, and the individual in such a case would need to petition the European Court: see now *Kansal v United Kingdom* (2004) 39 EHRR 31, finding a violation of Art 6.

Neither can the domestic courts overrule a court decision made before the Act, which has now become inconsistent with a decision of the European Court.

ASE EXAMPLE ─────────────────────────────

R v Lyons and others [2002] UKHL 44

The defendant had been convicted of fraud, which the European Court held was in violation of Art 6 of the Convention (*Saunders v United Kingdom* (1996) 23 EHRR 313). He now claimed that that conviction should be overturned.

It was held that held that the decision of the European Court could not disturb a conviction before the Human Rights Act had come into force and which was quite clearly lawful in domestic law.

Again the individual in such a case would need to petition the European Court.

Also, the courts have not allowed the Act to have retrospective effect with respect to their powers of statutory interpretation.

CASE EXAMPLE

R (Hurst) v HM Coroner for Northern District Council [2007] UKHL 13

The applicants claimed that a coroner was bound to construe the Coroners Act 1988 so as to order the resumption of an inquest into a death, even though the death had taken place before the Human Rights Act came into force.

The Court of Appeal held that in appropriate circumstances a court could give a Convention compliant interpretation to any legislation even though the dispute in the case related to an act committed before the Act came into effect. Whether an Act could be interpreted in such a way as to bestow individual rights and public duties with respect to pre-Act actions depended on the circumstances, and in this case public policy dictated that Art 2 should inform the duty of the coroner and that would not cause unfairness to the public body. The House of Lords overturned this decision and held that Art 2 could not be employed retrospectively.

17.3.2 The rights guaranteed under the Act

Section 1(1) of the Human Rights Act 1998 gives effect to the Convention rights contained in Arts 2 to 12 and 14 of the main Convention, Arts 1 to 3 of the First Protocol and Arts 1 and 2 of the Sixth Protocol (see Chapter 16 for details on the individual rights).

The rights that can be relied on are as follows:
- Article 2 – The Right to Life.
- Article 3 – Freedom from Torture and Inhuman and Degrading Treatment and Punishment.
- Article 4 – Freedom from Slavery and Forced Labour.
- Article 5 – Liberty and Security of the Person.
- Article 6 – The Right to a Fair Trial.
- Article 7 – Prohibition on Retrospective Criminal Law and Penalties.
- Article 8 – The Right to Private and Family Life, Home and Correspondence.
- Article 9 – Freedom of Religion, Thought and Conscience.
- Article 10 – Freedom of Expression.
- Article 11 – Freedom of Association and Peaceful Assembly.
- Article 12 – The Right to Marry.
- Article 1 of the First Protocol – The Right to Peaceful Enjoyment of Possessions.
- Article 2 of the First Protocol – The Right to Education.
- Article 3 of the First Protocol – The Duty to Hold Free Elections and the Right to Vote.

The Act omits Art 1 of the European Convention (Member States must ensure that the rights laid down in Part One of the Convention are guaranteed to everyone within the state's jurisdiction) and Art 13 of the Convention (which guarantees an effective remedy for breach of a person's Convention rights). This was because the government felt that the passing of the Human Rights Act 1998 in itself would provide the individual with a satisfactory remedy and thus comply with its obligations under the Convention.

These rights are subject to any designated derogation or reservation made under ss 14 and 15 of the Act (see section 17.11).

17.4 Use of Convention case law by the domestic courts

Section 2 of the Act allows domestic courts to consider the relevant case law of the European Convention when determining disputes that raise Convention rights.

S When a court or tribunal is determining a question involving any Convention right, it must take into account any judgment, decision, declaratory or advisory opinion of the European Court of Human Rights, any opinion of the European Commission given in a report, any decision of the European Commission, and any decision of the Committee of Ministers whenever made or given, so far as, in the opinion of the court and tribunal, it is relevant to the proceedings in which that question has arisen.

The section does not state that the courts have to *apply* such decisions, but as the main aim of the Act is to avoid individuals having to petition the European Court, the domestic courts are unlikely to refuse to apply any case law favourable to the claimant. In addition the courts are unlikely to depart from such case law and replace it by a more generous interpretation of the Convention, as seen in *Anderson and Taylor* (2001), below.

CASE EXAMPLE

R v Secretary of State for the Home Department, ex parte Taylor and Anderson [2001] EWCA Civ 1698

The Court of Appeal were asked to declare the Home Secretary' power to set tariffs for mandatory life sentence prisoners incompatible with Art 6, even though the European Court had stated that such powers were not in breach of the Convention.

The Court of Appeal held that it would be improper for the domestic courts to decide a case in a way that was contrary to the application currently being applied by the European

CONTINUED ▶

Court of Human Rights. The Home Secretary's power to set tariffs for mandatory life sentence prisoners had clearly been accepted by the European Court of Human Rights (*Wynne v United Kingdom* (1995) 12 EHRR 333) and thus it would not be proper to act in a manner which was inconsistent with that approach.

NB When the European Court overruled *Wynne* in the later case of *Stafford v United Kingdom* (2002) 35 EHRR 32, the House of Lords in *Anderson and Taylor* (2002) declared the Home Secretary's powers as incompatible with Art 6 and the government accordingly introduced new legislation in this area (see section 13.2.1).

Also, the courts may choose to follow binding domestic law, where the European Court has not ruled directly on the legal issue.

CASE EXAMPLE

Kay v Lambeth LBC; Price v Leeds County Council [2006] UKHL 10

Here the Court of Appeal ([2004] EWCA Civ 926) held that when faced with a House of Lords' decision that was inconsistent with a decision of the European Court of Human Rights it should follow the decision of the House of Lords and refer the case to the House of Lords. As the domestic decision was on a particular statutory scheme it would subvert legal certainty if the European decision was followed.

In the House of Lords it was held that the European Court accorded a generous margin of appreciation to the national authorities, attaching much importance to the facts of the case. Thus, it was for the courts to decide how in the first instance the principles expounded in Strasbourg should be applied in the special context of national legislation, practice and social and other considerations.

17.5 The doctrine of proportionality

Section 2 allows the courts to employ the doctrine of proportionality, which had been rejected by the domestic courts before the Act (*R v Home Secretary, ex parte Brind* [1991] 1 AC 696). Interference with a Convention right, such as freedom of expression, must correspond to a pressing social need and be proportionate to the aim that the restriction was seeking to achieve.

The effect of the doctrine on the court's review powers, and the distinction between proportionality and the traditional *Wednesbury* unreasonableness principles, were explained by Lord Steyn in *R v Secretary of State for the Home Department, ex parte Daly* [2001] UKHL 26:

> **J** 'There is a material difference between the *Wednesbury* and *Smith* grounds of review
> and the approach of proportionality applicable in respect of review where Convention
> rights were at stake. Most cases would be decided in the same way whichever
> approach were adopted. But the intensity of review is somewhat greater under the
> proportionality approach … First, the doctrine of proportionality may require the
> reviewing court to assess the balance which the decision-maker has struck, not merely
> whether it is within the range of rational or reasonable decisions. Secondly … it may
> require attention to be directed to the relevant weight accorded to interests and
> considerations. Thirdly, even the heightened scrutiny test developed in *R v Ministry of
> Defence, ex parte Smith* [1996] 1 All ER 257 is not necessarily appropriate to the
> protection of human rights … The intensity of the review … is guaranteed by the twin
> requirements that the limitation of the right was necessary in a democratic society, in
> the sense of meeting a pressing social need, and the question whether the interference
> was really proportionate to the legitimate aim being pursued.'

After the Human Rights Act 1998 the courts do not have to show that the decision affecting the enjoyment of a Convention right was outrageous or irrational, but can conduct a balancing exercise to see whether the interference was necessary and proportionate. This new power has been used in a number of high-profile cases.

CASE EXAMPLE

R (A and others) v Lord Saville of Newdigate and Another [2001] EWCA Civ 408

The chairman of the 'Bloody Sunday' inquiry had refused requests from a number of soldiers to give their evidence at a venue other than Londonderry, believing that this would increase public confidence in the inquiry and concluding that there was no real and immediate risk to the soldiers' lives.

Held – the decision-maker had to consider whether interference with fundamental human rights was a serious or real possibility and it was for him to find compelling justification for any interference. The tribunal should have asked whether it had exposed any of the soldiers to the real possibility of a risk to life. In this case the tribunal had used public confidence as the determinative factor, and accordingly its decision was wrong.

See also *A and others v Secretary of State for the Home Department* [2004] UKHL 56. In that case the House of Lords had to decide whether the detention of foreign nationals suspected of terrorism under s 21 of the Anti-Terrorism, Crime and Security Act 2001 was a disproportionate response to the threat of terrorism and strictly required by the exigencies of the situation so as to allow the government's derogation under Art 15 of the Convention.

The House of Lords held that while any decision of a representative democratic body commanded respect, the degree of respect would be conditioned by the nature of the decision made. The traditional *Wednesbury* approach was no longer appropriate and the domestic courts themselves had to form a judgment whether a Convention right was breached. Even in terrorist situations the Convention organs were not willing to relax their supervisory role. Given the importance of Art 5, judicial control of the executive's interference with individual liberty was essential; although the judiciary must keep to their proper limits, the courts possessed an express role under the Act to interpret legislation compatibly with Convention rights. On the facts, the House of Lords held that the detention provisions contravened Arts 5 and 14 of the Convention (see section 17.11.1).

The doctrine of proportionality increases the review powers of the courts and raises concerns about whether it is proper for the courts to interfere with the decisions of government, or Parliament. In response the courts often show deference towards the executive and, in particular, to Parliament and in *Edore v Secretary of State for the Home Department* [2003] EWCA Civ 716, the Court of Appeal held that given the margin of discretion available to decision-makers, there was often room for two possible proportionate outcomes in a particular situation. Within that margin, a decision-maker may, in some circumstances, fairly reach one of two opposite conclusions. However, both decisions would strike a fair balance between the competing claims and be proportionate.

In some cases, the courts will show deference to the decision-maker and offer a wide margin of discretion to government and Parliament, either because the decision maker has an area of expertise or because the issue is policy-based and sensitive.

CASE EXAMPLE

R (British American Tobacco and others) v Secretary of State for Health **[2004] EWHC 2493 (Admin)**

The High Court had to consider the proportionality of regulations banning the advertising of tobacco products and their compatibility with Art 10 of the European Convention and the applicant's right to commercial speech. It was held that although any restriction on freedom of expression had to be proportionate, there were areas in which the courts had to be particularly wary of imposing its own value judgments upon a legislative scheme. The protection of health was a far-reaching aim and the objective of the regulations was much wider than the protection of children and was sufficiently important to justify limiting a fundamental right. Thus, the measures were rationally connected and were proportionate to promoting health by restricting advertising at the point of sale.

CASE EXAMPLE

R v Secretary of State for the Home Department, ex parte Farrakhan [2002] EWCA Civ 606

The Home Secretary had excluded F from entering the country because the claimant's presence would not be conducive to the public good and that he was likely to threaten public order and commit offences of racial hatred. The High Court held that the Home Secretary had failed to produce any evidence so as to justify his decision. The Court of Appeal held that the Secretary of State had struck a proportionate balance between the legitimate aim of the prevention of disorder and freedom of expression. The fact that the decision was personal to the Secretary, who was far better placed to reach an informed decision than the court, and that the Secretary was democratically accountable for his decision, made it appropriate to give him a particularly wide margin of discretion.

ACTIVITY

Quick Quiz

1. Why was the Human Rights Act 1998 passed?

2. What were the deficiencies of the traditional method of protecting human rights in the UK and how does the Act address those issues?

3. What is the importance of s 2 of the Human Rights Act 1998?

4. What is the doctrine of proportionality and how important is it to the resolution of human rights disputes?

5. Do you think the decision in *A and others v Secretary of State* (2004) (above) displayed too much judicial power?

17.6 Interpreting statutory provisions in the light of the Convention

Under the Act the courts are given increased powers of statutory interpretation to allow them to reach a Convention-friendly result wherever that is possible. Even before, the courts could interpret legislation in the light of the European Convention when the statute was ambiguous (*Waddington v Miah* [1974] 2 All ER 377).

Section 3 of the Act provides that *so far as is possible*, primary and subordinate legislation must be read and given effect in a way that is compatible with Convention rights.

(1) So far as it is possible to do so, primary legislation and subordinate legislation must be read and given effect in a way which is compatible with the Convention rights

(2) This section – does not affect … (b) the validity, continuing operation or enforcement of any incompatible primary legislation; and (c) does not affect the validity, continuing operation and enforcement of any incompatible subordinate legislation if … primary legislation prevents removal of the incompatibility.

- Courts are now allowed to adopt a different interpretation to statutory provisions than applied by the courts before the Act and to disregard any previous interpretation of a higher court.

- The doctrine of parliamentary sovereignty is preserved because the section does not affect the validity etc of any incompatible primary legislation or any incompatible subordinate legislation where the parent Act clearly allows interference with Convention rights.

- Thus, the courts have no power to set aside an Act of Parliament and must follow it even where it is not possible to interpret it in a Convention-friendly manner.

- Under section 3 the court does not have to find a true ambiguity in the statute, provided the Convention interpretation is 'possible'.

In addition, in *Wilson v First County Trust Ltd (No 2)* [2003] UKHL 40 the House of Lords held that courts were entitled to have regard to the policy objectives behind the legislation by looking at ministerial statements at the time the Bill was proceeding through Parliament.

17.6.1 The scope of section 3

The scope of s 3 depends on the extent to which the courts are prepared to interpret legislation in the light of Convention rights – in other words what the courts regard as a 'possible' interpretation.

CASE EXAMPLE

***R v Offen* [2001] 1 WLR 253**

Section 2 of the Crime (Sentences) Act 1997 imposed a duty on the courts to grant an automatic life sentence to defendants who have committed two serious offences, unless there were 'exceptional circumstances'. The defendant was sentenced to life imprisonment despite the fact that the trial judge conceded that the offences were at the lower end of the scale and had been committed using a toy gun.

The Court of Appeal held that a court was entitled to decide that there existed exceptional circumstances if an offender did not constitute a significant risk to the public. An alternative interpretation would have made the sentence arbitrary and thus in violation of Art 5 of the European Convention Human Rights. The word 'exceptional' must be given its ordinary meaning and Parliament could not have intended that the section apply to someone who did not pose a future risk.

A more radical approach was taken by the House of Lords in *R v A* (2001), below, and thus the courts were accused of legislating rather than interpreting existing legislation passed by the democratically elected Parliament.

CASE EXAMPLE

R v A (Complainant's sexual history) [2001] UKHL 25

Section 41 of the Youth Justice and Criminal Evidence Act 1999 provides that evidence of the complainant's sexual behaviour can only be allowed with leave of the court in express circumstances. The defendant wished to use the section in circumstances that appeared outside its terms

The House of Lords held that the interpretative obligation placed on the courts under s 3 of the Human Rights Act 1998 applied even where there was no ambiguity and the court must strive to find a possible interpretation compatible with Convention rights. Section 3 required the courts to proceed on the basis that the legislature would not, if alerted to the problem, have wished to deny the right to an accused to put forward a full and complete defence by advancing truly probative evidence. Thus, the section should be read as being subject to the implied exclusion that evidence required to secure a fair trial under Art 6 of the Convention should not be inadmissible.

Section 3 thus allows the courts to depart from traditional principles of statutory interpretation and to assume, wherever possible, that legislation is not intended to conflict with the 1998 Act.

CASE EXAMPLE

Sheldrake v DPP: Attorney-General's Reference (No 4) [2004] UKHL 43

The House of Lords interpreted s 11(2) of the Terrorism Act 2000 as imposing an evidential rather than legal burden on the defendant so as to make that provision compatible with Art 6 of the Convention and to avoid a finding that that provision was disproportionate and incompatible.

The House of Lords held that even though Parliament had intended to impose a legal burden in such cases when passing the 2000 Act; having regard to its intention in passing s 3 of the Human Rights Act 1998 it was possible to read s 11(2) down in such a way as to avoid a legal burden.

However, s 3 does not allow the courts to read words into a statute that are clearly not there, and in *Poplar Housing and Regeneration Community Association Ltd v Donoghue* [2001] EWCA Civ 595 Lord Woolf CJ stressed that the courts must not radically alter a statute in order to achieve compatibility.

The House of Lords sounded a clear warning against 'judicial legislation' in the case below:

CASE EXAMPLE

In Re W and B (children: Care Plan); In Re W (Child: Care Plan) [2002] UKHL 10

The Court of Appeal ([2001] EWCA Civ 757) had authorised a system under the Children Act 1989 which allowed courts to star essential milestones in the care plan of a child so that action had to be taken by a local authority if they were not achieved within a reasonable time.

The House of Lords held that the 1998 Act maintained the constitutional boundary between the interpretation of statues and the passing and repeal of legislation, and that a meaning that departed substantially from a fundamental feature of an Act of Parliament was likely to have crossed the boundary. Further, in using their powers of interpretation under s 3 the courts should be able to identify clearly the particular statutory provision or provisions whose interpretation led to that result.

The distinction between robust interpretation and judicial legislation is often difficult to make and will often depend on whether the courts are prepared to leave Parliament with the task of amending incompatible legislation. Thus, in *Bellinger v Bellinger* [2003] UKHL 21 the House of Lords held that it was not possible to use s 3 to interpret the words 'man and woman' to include a person who had undergone gender reassignment. However, in *Mendoza v Ghaidan* [2004] UKHL 40 the House of Lords held the words 'living together as husband and wife' could be interpreted to mean as if they were living together as husband and wife. In *Mendoza* Lord Millett dissented on the grounds that it was for Parliament to change a law that was quite clearly not intended to cover same sex relationships.

In some cases (such as *Bellinger*) the courts might feel that certain changes in the law should be carried out by Parliament rather than the courts: the decision in *Bellinger* was followed by the passing of the Gender Recognition Act 2004.

ACTIVITY

Quick Quiz

1. How does s 3 of the Act change the courts' role with respect to statutory interpretation?

2. Does the Act threaten Parliamentary Sovereignty in any respect?

3. What is the difference between statutory interpretation and 'judicial legislation?

CONTINUED ▶

ACTIVITY

Quick Quiz

4. Do you think the House of Lords were guilty of 'judicial legislation in *R v A* (2001), above?

5. Should the courts use s 3 to 'change' incompatible law, or should it make a declaration of incompatibility (below) instead?

17.7 Declarations of incompatibility

Under s 4 of the Act courts are allowed to declare both primary and secondary legislation incompatible with the substantive rights of the European Convention.

Section 4(2) 'If the court is satisfied that the provision (of primary legislation) is incompatible with a Convention right, it may make a declaration of incompatibility'.

Section 4(4) 'If the court is satisfied that that the provision (of secondary legislation) is incompatible with a Convention right and that the primary legislation concerned prevents removal of the incompatibility it may make a declaration of incompatibility'.

Section 4(6) 'A declaration ... does not affect the validity, continuing operation or enforcement of the provision in respect of which it is given and is not binding on the parties to the proceedings in which it is made'.

- Section 4 applies where the court has not been able to use its powers of interpretation under s 3 of the Act.
- Section 4 restricts the power to issue such declarations to courts including the High Court and above.
- Section 5 of the Act gives the Crown the power to intervene where a court is considering making a declaration of incompatibility.
- Section 4 does not include the right to strike down incompatible, but clear legislation.
- Incompatible legislation must be addressed and amended by Parliament, see s 10 of the Act, below.

Declarations cannot be granted in respect of violations of human rights caused by the application of incompatible legislation that took place before the Act came into operation: *Wilson v First County Trust Ltd (No 2)* [2003] UKHL 40 (see section 17.3.1).

It is not possible to use the powers under s 4 where the relevant legislation has not, or is not likely to, personally affect any particular person. Thus, the claimant must prove that they are a 'victim' of the violation.

CASE EXAMPLE

R v Attorney-General, ex parte Rushbridger and another [2003] UKHL 38

The House of Lords were asked to declare s 3 of the Treason Felony Act 1848 as incompatible with Art 10 of the European Convention.

It was held that the courts would refuse to make such a declaration without proof that there was any victim of the legislation. In this case there was no real risk of anyone being prosecuted under the legislation for non-violent conduct and thus no real risk of any interference with free speech. It was for the legislature and not the courts to keep the statute book up to date.

Similarly, in *Taylor v Lancashire CC* [2005] EWCA Civ 284 it was held that a person who was not affected by a provision allegedly incompatible with Art 14 of the European Convention could not seek a declaration of incompatibility of that provision. In this case the claimant had been affected by a different (and compatible) provision of the relevant legislation (Agricultural Holdings Act 1986) and could not thus rely on the possible incompatibility of another provision of that Act.

Courts will not issue a declaration of incompatibility merely because a statute contains a gap, which, if included, would make it compatible with the Convention; *In Re S; Re W* (section 17.6.1). The relevant 'victim' would then have to pursue an action in Strasbourg. Following the decision of the House of Lords in *Re S; Re W* an application was lodged before the European Court of Human Rights, alleging a violation of Arts 6 and 8 of the Convention: *S v UK* (Application No 34407/02, 31 August 2004).

In *Wilson v First County Trust Ltd (No 2)* [2003] UKHL 40 (section 17.3.1 above) the House of Lords held that in assessing the compatibility of primary legislation, a court was entitled to have regard to the policy objectives behind the legislation by looking at ministerial statements at the time the Bill was proceeding through Parliament. However, the content of parliamentary debates had no direct relevance to the issues the court was called upon to decide in compatibility matters and those matters were not a matter for investigation or consideration by the courts.

17.7.1 Declarations of incompatibility in practice

Since the Act has come into force, the courts have issued a number of declarations, some of which have resulted in legislative change. For example, in *R v Mental Health Tribunal ex parte H* [2001] EWCA Civ 415 the Court of Appeal held that ss 72 and 73 of the Mental Health Act 1983 were incompatible with Art 5 of the European Convention because they placed the burden of proof on a restricted patient to show that he no longer warranted detention. Following this decision the Mental Health Act 1983 (Remedial) Order 2001 amended the offending legislation.

The courts will declare legislation incompatible if it imposes excessive or unfair penalties.

CASE EXAMPLE

International Transport Roth GMBH and others v Secretary of State for the Home Department [2002] EWCA Civ 158

Drivers and owners of vehicles had all been subjected to penalties for effecting clandestine entrants to the United Kingdom contrary to s 32 of the Immigration and Asylum Act 1999. They claimed that the penalties were contrary to Arts 5 and 6 of the Convention and to the right of property under Art 1 of the first protocol.

Held – the penalty regime did not adequately protect the rights of those alleged to be responsible for clandestine entrants. The scheme was unfair in imposing strict liability and in imposing so high a fixed penalty without the possibility of mitigation.

Also, a court is likely to declare legislation as incompatible if it is clearly out of line with the case law of the European Court of Human Rights.

CASE EXAMPLE

Bellinger v Bellinger [2003] UKHL 21

Here the House of Lords held that the refusal of domestic law to recognise a marriage celebrated between a man and a transsexual born a male was contrary to Arts 8 and 12 of the European Convention and in particular, the decision of the European Court of Human Rights in *Goodwin v United Kingdom* (2002) 35 EHRR 18.

Similarly, in *Anderson* (2002) (see section 13.2.1), the House of Lords declared the Home Secretary's sentencing powers incompatible with both Art 6 of the Convention and the decision of the European Court in *Stafford v United Kingdom* (2002) 35 EHRR 32.

The courts have issued a number of declarations of incompatibility where the relevant provisions are discriminatory:

CASE EXAMPLE

R (Morris) v Westminster City Council [2005] EWCA Civ 1184

The Court of Appeal held that s 185(4) of the Housing Act 1996 was incompatible with Art 14, taken with Art 8, of the Convention because it required a dependent child of a British citizen to be disregarded when determining priority needs, when that child was

CONTINUED ▸

515

subject to immigration control. Thus, the applicant had been discriminated against in the enjoyment of her family and home life on the grounds of her daughter's national origin. The measures were not a proportionate and reasonable response to discouraging overstaying tourists

See also the decision of the House of Lords in *A and others v Secretary of State* (2004) (see section 17.5) with respect to the detention without trial of foreign terrorist suspects. The decision in *A* also shows the courts' insistence that individual liberty and due process are not unduly interfered with. However, see the case of *Re MB*, below

CASE EXAMPLE

Re MB [2006] EWCA Civ 1140

Here the Court of Appeal held that the procedures in s 3 of the Prevention of Terrorism Act 2005 relating to supervision orders under that Act (passed in response to the House of Lords' decision in *A and others v Secretary of State* (above), were compatible with Art 6 of the Convention.

The High Court ([2006] EWHC 1000 (Admin)) held that as the procedure only allowed the court to review the legality of the secretary's decision to make a detention order the individual's rights were being determined by the executive and not by an independent court. However, the Court of Appeal held that the court could review the secretary's suspicion to ensure it was made on reasonable grounds and thus Art 6 was complied with.

On the other hand, the domestic courts are unlikely to interfere with legislation that appears consistent with European Convention case law and principles

CASE EXAMPLE

R v Secretary of State for the Environment, Transport and the Regions, ex parte Barnes [2001] UKHL 23

The courts considered the compatibility with Art 6 of the Secretary of State's statutory power to determine planning applications that had not been determined by the local authority and to determine appeals against refusal of planning permission. The High Court held that such powers were incompatible as interfering with the claimants' right to an independent and impartial tribunal.

CONTINUED ▸

> The House of Lords held that the planning laws were not incompatible with Article 6. Although the Secretary of State was not an independent and impartial tribunal, the power of the High Court in judicial review proceedings to review the legality of the decision and the procedures followed was sufficient to ensure compatibility with Art 6(1). Where the decision at issue was a matter of administrative policy, the European Court of Human Rights in *Bryan v United Kingdom* (1995) 21 EHRR 342 had accepted that the court's powers of appeal and review were sufficient to ensure that the decision-making process, as a whole, complied with Art 6.

The courts have also shown a good deal of deference to Parliament in deciding whether to grant a declaration of incompatibility.

CASE EXAMPLE

Brown v Stott (Procurator Fiscal) [2003] 1 AC 681

The Privy Council had to consider whether s 172(2)(a) of the Road Traffic Act 1988, which compelled a person to answer the question whether he or she had been driving a car, was compatible with the rule against self-incrimination as guaranteed by Art 6 of the Convention.

It was held that although the right to a fair trial is an absolute right that cannot be compromised, there might be exceptional cases in which the defendant's procedural rights have to give way to the greater interests of the public that justice be done. Consequently national courts should give weight to the decisions of the representative legislature and the democratic government within the discretionary area of judgment accorded to such bodies. In this case, therefore, it was held that the provision was proportionate and compatible with Art 6.

See also *R v Shayler* [2002] UKHL 11 where the House of Lords held that ss 1 and 4 of the Official Secrets Act 1989 were compatible with Art 10 of the European Convention. See section 18.3.6.

CASE EXAMPLE

R v DPP, ex parte Pretty and another [2001] UKHL 61

The House of Lords had to decide whether the DPP had the power to give an undertaking that the applicant's husband would not be prosecuted under s 2(1) of the

CONTINUED ▸

Suicide Act 1961 if he assisted her in taking her own life, and whether that provision was incompatible with her rights under the European Convention.

The House of Lords held the right to life under Art 2 did not include the right to die. Further, although the case engaged the claimant's right to private and home life, and her right to enjoy her Convention rights free from discrimination, any interference with those rights was necessary and proportionate to meet the aims of the Suicide Act 1961. This decision was upheld by the European Court of Human Rights in *Pretty v United Kingdom* (2002) 35 EHRR 1 it was held that it was within the state's discretion to impose a blanket ban on assisting suicide.

17.7.2 Statements of compatibility

Under s 19(1) a Minister of the Crown in charge of a Bill in either House must, before the Second Reading of the Bill, either make a statement of compatibility to the effect that in his view the provisions of the Bill are compatible with the Convention rights, or make a statement to the effect that the government nevertheless wishes the House to proceed with the Bill.

- Because an Act of Parliament cannot bind future Parliament as to the manner in which legislation is passed, a bill that did not contain such a declaration could not be invalidated by the courts.

- A declaration that a bill is Convention compliant would not bind the courts and prevent them from subsequently declaring legislation incompatible with Convention rights.

Thus far, only one statement of incompatibility has been made. This was in respect of s 321(2) of the Communications Act 2003, which makes political advertising unlawful. As the provision may be inconsistent with the European Court's decision in *VgT Verein gegen Tierfabriken v Switzerland* (2002) 34 EHRR 4 the responsible Minister made a declaration under s 19(1) that he intended to proceed with the Bill. Subsequently the provision was declared compatible with Art 10: *R (Animal Defenders International) v Secretary of State for Culture and Media and Sport* [2006] EWHC 3069 (Admin).

17.7.3 Remedial action

The Act leaves the ultimate power of deciding the compatibility of domestic legislation with Convention rights with the democratically elected legislature. Thus, where a court had declared a statutory provision as incompatible with the Convention, it has no power to disapply the provision and the ultimate decision of whether the provision remains on the statute books rests with the law-makers. Thus, Parliament can either leave the provision on the statute books, risking an application under the European Convention by a relevant victim, or alter that provision in line with the court's finding.

Specifically, s 10 of the Human Rights Act 1998 provides that where legislation has been declared incompatible under s 4 of the Act (or it appears to a Minister of the Crown that a finding of the European Court of Human Rights against the United Kingdom makes such legislation appear to be incompatible with the Convention) the Minister may make such amendments to the legislation as he considers necessary to amend that incompatibility.

Under s 10(3) a similar power is created in the case of subordinate legislation, where a Minister considers it necessary to amend the primary legislation under which the subordinate legislation was made. This will allow an incompatibility between the provision and the Convention right to be removed. In such a case he may order such amendments to that primary legislation, as he considers necessary.

- Under Sched 2, para 2 of the Act no remedial order can normally be made unless a draft of the order has been approved by a resolution of each House of Parliament made after the end of the period of 60 days beginning on the day that the draft was laid.

- Under para 3(1) of the Schedule no draft can be laid unless the person proposing to make the order has laid a document before Parliament containing a draft of the proposed order and the required information, explaining the reasons for the order, and a period of no less than 60 days has expired.

- In emergency cases where the order is made without being approved in draft, para 4 provides that the person making the order must lay it before Parliament, accompanied by the required information, after it is made.

KEY FACTS

Issue	Effect	Provision
European Case Law	Domestic courts can now have direct reference to the articles, principles and case law of the European Convention on Human Rights	s 2, HRA

CONTINUED ▶

KEY FACTS

Issue	Effect	Provision
Employing Convention principles	Domestic courts must now inquire whether domestic law and decisions are prescribed by law, have a legitimate aim, and are necessary in a democratic society (including whether the measure is proportionate)	ss 2 and 6, HRA
Following Precedent	The courts must merely take the case law of the European Convention into account when determining disputes raising Convention rights, it is not bound to follow it	s 2, HRA
Statutory Interpretation	Courts must interpret all legislation, wherever possible, in a way that is compatible with Convention rights	s 3, HRA
Parliamentary Sovereignty	Courts not able to legislate or to strike down incompatible legislation	ss 3 and 4, HRA
Declarations of Incompatibility	Where it is not possible to achieve a Convention-friendly result, the higher courts can declare inconsistent legislation as incompatible, leaving the government to initiate any relevant legislative changes	s 4, HRA
Amending incompatible legislation	Minister empowered to make remedial orders, amending incompatible legislation	s 19, HRA
Ministerial Declarations of incompatibility	Relevant Minister to make a statement of compatibility or incompatibility when introducing legislation before Parliament	s 10, HRA

ACTIVITY

Problem Solving

In 2010 Parliament passed the (imaginary) Public Order Act 2010. Section 1 of that Act allows the Home Secretary to pass such regulations as he thinks fit to secure public order. Acting under that provision, the Home Secretary passed a regulation in June 2010 that provided that if the Secretary of State is of the opinion that the formation of any group or society poses a serious threat to public order, he may order the proscription of that group, in which case it will be unlawful to join or take part in the activities of that group or society.

1. What Convention rights does s 1 potentially threaten?

2. Could the courts interpret s 1 in such a way that it would not conflict with any Convention rights?

3. In particular, could the courts interpret 'group or society' to exclude groups or societies who have a political message or mandate?

4. Do you think that the power of the Home Secretary under that section is compatible with those Convention rights?

5. How could the doctrine of proportionality be used to ensure that the section, and its use by the Minister, is not excessive?

17.8 Liability of public authorities under the Act

The Act applies principally with respect to violations committed by public authorities, although the act can also operate in a 'horizontal' fashion and be applied in private proceedings.

Section 6 of the Act imposes an obligation on public authorities not to violate Convention rights.

(1) It is unlawful for a public authority to act in a way that is inconsistent with a Convention right.

(2) Section 6(1) does not apply ... if as the result of one or more provisions of primary legislation, it could not have acted differently, or in the case of a provision of, or made under, primary legislation which cannot be read or given effect in a way which is compatible with Convention rights, the authority was acting so as to give effect to or enforce those provisions.

- Section 7 then provides a remedy to a person who claims that a public authority has acted (or proposes to act) in a way that is unlawful under s 6 (see section 17.9).

- An act includes a failure to act but does not include a failure to introduce in, or lay before, Parliament a proposal for legislation, or make any primary legislation or remedial order (s 6(6)).

521

- Section 6 retains parliamentary sovereignty by providing that the duty does not apply where the authority could not have acted differently having regard to the power granted by Parliament.

- In such a case the court is limited to making a declaration of incompatibility under s 4 (see section 17.7).

17.8.1 Definition of 'public authority'

The term public authority is not defined under s 6, however:

- it includes a court or tribunal, and does not include either House of Parliament or a person exercising functions in connection with proceedings in Parliament (s 6(3));

- 'public authority' includes any person certain whose functions are functions of a public nature (s 6(3)(b));

- in relation to a particular act a person is not a public authority if the nature of the Act is private (s 6(5));

- thus the act preserves the distinction between public and private bodies, and public and private law issues, employed formerly in judicial review proceedings (see Chapter 19).

In the post-HRA era the courts have had to distinguish between public and private bodies and acts. Contrast the cases of *Heather* and *Poplar,* below

CASE EXAMPLE

Heather, Ward and Callin v Leonard Cheshire Foundation **[2002] EWCA Civ 366**

A housing foundation had closed a care home, allegedly in violation of Article 8 of the Convention.

The Court of Appeal held that the housing foundation was not a public authority and did not exercise a public law function within the meaning of s 6. Before the 1998 Act it had been established that such bodies were not susceptible to judicial review, and the Human Rights Act had not done anything to alter that. The foundation was essentially private and carrying out private functions, despite the fact that it received public funding, was state regulated, and, had it not existed, its functions would have been provided by the state.

CASE EXAMPLE

Poplar Housing and Regeneration Community Association Ltd v Donoghue [2001]
EWCA Civ 595

The applicant argued that a possession order executed by the defendants, an association set up by the local authority to take over its housing stock, was in breach of her Convention rights.

The Court of Appeal held that the defendant housing association was a public authority under s 6. The court held that the fact that the association provided a public service and was regulated by the local authority, which would have exercised its powers had the association not existed, were relevant, yet not decisive, factors. However, in this case the role of the of the association was so closely connected to that of the local authority that *in this case* it was performing public rather than private functions.

The body in question thus has to have *sufficient* governmental links and public status.

CASE EXAMPLE

Parochial Church Council of the Parish of Aston Cantlow and others v Wallbank
[2003] UKHL 37

The applicants had been required by the defendants to pay for the repair of the chancel of a church they had bought and claimed this was in violation of their right to property. The Court of Appeal held that the Parochial Church Council was a public authority because it was created and empowered by the law and its notice to repair had statutory force.

On appeal the House of Lords held that a parochial church council was essentially a religious body and not a governmental one. It was not a 'core' public authority under the Act and its duty in this case was private rather than a public function. (The House also agreed that there was no violation of article 1 of the first protocol to the Convention simply because the owners of property acquired a very expensive duty to repair.)

17.8.2 The 'horizontal' effect of the Human Rights Act 1998

Although the Act applies directly to public authorities, it can, to a limited extent, impose obligations on private persons and thus be used in private proceedings. As courts are public authorities under s 6, and it is unlawful for them to act in a way that is incompatible with Convention rights, they will have a duty to develop the law, including the private law, consistently with Convention rights.

The Act will, therefore, have a 'horizontal' effect. This has been most evident in the area of the law of confidentiality, where that law has been applied and expanded so as to afford an individual a right of privacy consistent with Art 8 of the European Convention (see *Douglas and others v Hello! and others* [2001] 2 WLR 992 and *Venables and Thompson v Associated Newspapers* [2001] 1 WLR 1038) – where the courts accepted that confidentiality could be expanded to accommodate the claimants' Art 8 privacy rights).

The Act can also be applied to other areas of private law, such as the law of defamation (*Reynolds v Times Newspapers* [2001] 2 AC 127) and the law of employment, below:

CASE EXAMPLE

In X v Y [2004] EWCA Civ 662

An employee claimed that his dismissal for receiving a caution for an indecency offence committed in a public toilet with another man was in breach of his Convention rights under Arts 8 and 14 of the Convention and that the test of unfairness should be interpreted in the light of those rights.

The Court of Appeal held that the 1998 Act might have an effect on unfair dismissals in the private sector in appropriate cases. It would not normally be fair to dismiss an employee in violation of the enjoyment of his Convention rights, although if there was a justifiable reason for his dismissal under the Employment Rights Act 1996 the tribunal should consider (Art 8) in the context of the application of s 3 of the 1998 Act to the provisions of the 1996 Act (on the facts Arts 8 and 14 were not engaged because the act in question was not part of his private life and that the real reason for the dismissal was his failure to disclose the criminal caution).

The 1998 Act is thus used as a guiding principle for the main substantive law and the case below illustrate the courts' reluctance to give the Act full horizontal effect.

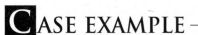

CASE EXAMPLE

Wainwright v Home Office [2003] UKHL 53

The applicants claimed that their search by prison officer violated their right to privacy, even though it occurred before the 1998 Act came into force.

The House of Lords confirmed that there was no common law tort of invasion of privacy and that it was not necessary to develop such a general tort: the gap in the law had been filled by the passing of the Human Rights Act 1998, and it was not necessary to develop a law of privacy to apply to actions which occurred before the passing of the Act. The development of the law of privacy in accordance with Art 8 has been realised through the law of confidence and not by creating a separate tort of privacy.

17.9 Remedies under the Act

As we have seen, s 6 makes it unlawful for public authorities to act in a way that is incompatible with a person's convention rights. Further, under s 7(1) a person who claims that a public authority has acted (or proposes to act) in a way which is made unlawful by s 6 may either bring proceedings against the authority under this Act in an appropriate court or tribunal, or may rely on the Convention right or rights concerned in *any legal proceedings* – such as during a criminal trial or in judicial review proceedings.

In the case of judicial review proceedings, the applicant may now take advantage of the 1998 Act where he is, or would be, a victim of that Act (s 7(3)). Thus, such an applicant could use the grounds of proportionality and breach of a Convention right, established under the 1998 Act. Other affected persons, such as representative groups, would bring proceedings on traditional grounds of review (*R v Secretary of State for the Environment, ex parte Greenpeace Ltd* [1994] 4 All ER 352).

Section 7(5) imposes a time limit and provides that proceedings must be brought before the end of the period of one year with the date on which the act complained of took place, or such longer period as the court or tribunal considers equitable having regard to all the circumstances. This provision is made subject to any rule imposing a stricter time limit in relation to the procedure in question, such as the time limit imposed under the Civil Procedure Rules 1998, where an application for judicial review must normally be brought within three months of the decision against which review is sought.

17.9.1 Victims of a Convention violation

Section 7(1) limits the Act to those who are 'victims' of a violation of Convention rights. Further, a person is only a victim of an unlawful act if he would be regarded as such for the purposes of Art 34 of the European Convention (s 7(7)) (see Chapter 16). This will cover anyone directly or potentially affected by the act as well as relatives and dependants of such persons (*R (Holub and another) v Secretary of State for the Home Department* [2002] EWHC 2388, and *R (Amin) v Home Secretary* [2003] UKHL 51).

However for the person to be a victim there must be a real risk that the relevant legal provision be applied against them (*Rusbridger v Attorney-General* [2003] UKHL 38). The court will not thus decide a hypothetical case and will *generally* wait for a substantive decision.

CASE EXAMPLE

R (Hirst) v Parole Board [2002] EWHC 1592 (Admin)

Here it was held that a prisoner could not bring an application for a declaration that the Crime (Sentences) Act 1997 was incompatible with Art 5 of the European Convention until the Parole Board had considered his case for release. It would not be proper for it to rule on the question of compatibility until the Board had considered the claim, because until that time it would not be apparent that the statutory power was capable of impacting on the prisoner's case.

The Convention accepts that a person can be a victim if the individual is affected by the mere existence of the restriction (*Dudgeon v United Kingdom* (1982) 4 EHRR 149), and where there is an anticipated and real risk of a breach (*Soering v United* Kingdom (1989) 11 EHRR 439).

17.9.2 Power to award an appropriate remedy

Section 8 of the Act bestows on the courts the power to grant remedies for breach of the victim's Convention rights:

S Where a court finds that an act (or proposed act) of a public authority is (or would be) unlawful, it might grant such relief or remedy, or make such order, within its powers as it considers just and equitable.

Section 8 applies directly to violations committed by public authorities, but as that term includes courts and tribunals, victims will be able to rely on the principles and case law of the European Convention in all types of legal proceedings, including those taken against private individuals (see, for example, *Campbell v MGN Ltd* [2004] UKHL 22, where damages for breach of confidence included a claim for breach of the right to private life).

The courts' liability for violating Convention rights is limited and s 9(1) provides that the remedy for such a breach will be via judicial review or by appeal. Under s 9(3) of the Act damages are not generally awarded in respect of a judicial act done in good faith, although s 9(3) makes an exception in cases where there is a violation of Art 5(5) of the European Convention. This provision guarantees an effective remedy when a person's right to liberty has been violated.

17.9.3 Damages and the Human Rights Act 1998

The courts' power under s 8 includes the power to award damages, although only where the court has a power to award damages or order the payment of compensation in civil proceedings (s 8(2)).

Under s 8(3) no award of damages shall be made unless the court is satisfied in the circumstances that the award is necessary to afford 'just satisfaction' to the person in whose favour it is made. In deciding whether to award damages, or in deciding the amount of any award, the court must take into account the principles applied by the European Court of Human Rights in relation to the award of compensation under Art 41 of the Convention (s 8(4)) (see Chapter 16).

The domestic courts have taken a flexible approach to the award of damages under the Act, taking into account factors such as the type of right that has been violated, the effect of the violation on the victim and the conduct of the public authority

CASE EXAMPLE

R (Bernard and others) v Enfield LBC [2002] EWHC 2282 (Admin)

The local authority had failed to find suitable accommodation for the claimant (who was disabled) and her husband and six children.

The High Court held that damages for breach of human rights under the Act should be no lower than for a comparable tort and should, as far as possible, reflect the English level of damages. Also, awards recommended by the Local Government Ombudsman were a helpful guide. Awards should not be so minimal so as to diminish the policy that public authorities should respect Convention rights. Given the conduct of the authority and the humiliation suffered by the victim the award should be at the top end of the scale, in this case £10,000 (£8,000 to the wife and £2,000 to the husband).

CASE EXAMPLE

R (KB) v Mental Health Review Tribunal [2003] EWHC 193 (Admin)

The court held that damages would not be granted automatically for violation of Art 5, and that the courts should follow the principle of just satisfaction as practiced by the European Court. Mental patients should not automatically receive damages for a violation of their rights, but the courts should recognise their vulnerability in assessing any damages. In this case the court awarded damages of between £750 and £1,000 to patients whose release had been delayed in breach of Art 5(4) of the Convention.

CASE EXAMPLE

Van Colle v Chief Constable of Hertfordshire [2006] EWHC 360 (QB)

The High Court held that that there had been a violation of Arts 2 and 8 when the defendant had taken inadequate steps to safeguard the life and private and family life of a prosecution witness (G).

CONTINUED ▶

It was held that in deciding the level of damages the court should consider the character and conduct of the parties and the extent and seriousness of the breach. Taking into account the negligence of the police officer, the distress suffered by the death victim and the mother, and the fact that there had been no apology from the force or the individual officer, who had faced minor disciplinary charges, the court awarded £15,000 for G's distress suffered before his death. In addition the court found that the death had resulted in the complete destruction of family life and awarded £35,000 for the distress suffered by his mother and father.

However, some cases have taken a more cautious approach and have limited the right to claim damages for breach of Convention rights.

ASE EXAMPLE

R (N) v Secretary of State for the Home Department; Anufrijeva v London Borough of Southwark [2003] EWCA Civ 1406

The High Court in N had granted damages when the Home Office had mishandled the claimant's asylum application, thus depriving him of income support and related benefits. On appeal the Court of Appeal held that although Art 8 of the Convention was capable of imposing positive obligation to provide such support, maladministration on the part of an authority would only infringe Art 8 where the consequences were serious.

The Court of Appeal also held (in A) that damages for breach of Art 8 of the Convention were not recoverable automatically, and would only be awarded when necessary to give just satisfaction. Breach of a public law duty would not be sufficient on its own and for an award to be made there would have to be a degree of culpability together with foreseeable harm.

Also, in *Secretary of State for the Home Department v Wainwright* [2003] UKHL 53 the House of Lords held that it was doubtful whether damages could be claimed under the Human Rights Act 1998 for invasion of privacy by a public authority which had caused distress to a person, where that act was merely negligent.

In some cases a finding of a violation in itself is just satisfaction, especially if there is insufficient causal connection between any violation and the victim's loss.

CASE EXAMPLE

R (Greenfield) v Home Secretary **[2005] UKHL 14**

A prisoner had been refused legal representation during prison disciplinary proceedings, in violation of article 6 of the European Convention.

The House of Lords held that when domestic courts are considering awarding compensation under s 8 of the Human Rights Act 1998 they should take into account the case law of the European Court, although they are not bound to follow such decisions. In particular, the courts should apply the principle applied by the European Court in cases where there has been held to be a breach of Art 6, to the effect that a finding of a violation of Art 6 is normally just satisfaction in itself, and that it was not appropriate for such awards to be comparable to tortuous awards.

In the present case it would not be appropriate to speculate whether the procedural defect would have influenced the outcome of the proceedings and the prisoner's guilt or sanction.

KEY FACTS

Issue	Effect	Authority
Liability for breaching Convention rights	It is now unlawful for a public authority to violate the Convention rights listed in the 1998 Act	s 6, HRA
Convention rights and parliamentary sovereignty	Section 6 preserves parliamentary sovereignty, allowing public authorities to violate Convention rights with the clear authority of Parliament	s 6(2), HRA
Definition of Public authority	'Public authority' includes the courts, who have a duty to uphold Convention rights	s 6(3), HRA

CONTINUED ▸

KEY FACTS

Issue	Effect	Authority
Application to private law	The Act has a limited horizontal effect, allowing the principles of the Act to be applied in proceedings of a private nature	*Douglas v Hello!* (2001)
Who can use the Act and where?	The Act can be used in any proceedings by anyone who is a 'victim' of any alleged violation	s 7, HRA
Time limit for bringing proceedings	Proceedings under the Act must be brought within one year, or via other proceedings in line with the appropriate time limit for such proceedings	s 7, HRA
Remedies	The courts have the power to grant appropriate remedies to those whose Convention rights have been violated	s 8, HRA
Just satisfaction, including damages	The courts may award 'just satisfaction' to the victim, in line with the principles applied by the European Court of Human Rights. 'Just satisfaction' includes the power to award damages to compensate for pecuniary and non-pecuniary loss suffered by the victim	s 8, HRA
Availability of damages	The courts will not automatically grant damages for breach of Convention rights	*Greenfield v Home Secretary* (2005)

17.10 Freedom of expression and freedom of religion

Because of fears that the Act might interfere unduly with free speech, press freedom and freedom of religion organisations, it makes specific provision to protect freedom of expression (s 12) and freedom of religion (s 13).

Section 12 applies whenever a court is considering granting relief which might affect the right of freedom of expression. The section then lays down three rules:

- Any such relief should not normally be granted where the respondent is neither present or represented (s 12(2)).

- Where such relief would have the effect of restraining publication before trial, no such order should be given unless the applicant is likely to establish that publication should not be allowed (s 12(3) – see *Cream Holdings v Banerjee* [2004] UKHL 44).

- Where the proceedings relate to material which is journalistic, literary or artistic, the court must have regard to the extent to which the material has, or is about to become available to the public, whether it is, or would be, in the public interest for the material to be published, and any relevant privacy code (s 12(4)).

During the passage of the Human Rights Bill church organisations were concerned that the right to employ suitable teachers in religious schools and to impose requirements for religious marriages would be threatened by actions under the 1998 Act. Under s 13, if a court's determination of any question arising under the Act might affect the exercise by a religious organisation of its right to freedom of thought, conscience and religion, it must have particular regard to the importance of that right. Thus, the courts will be obliged to take this right into account in developing the law in favour of the enjoyment of the rights contained in Art 9, including allowing interferences with other Convention rights.

Despite s 13, the right to religion may be outweighed by other interests and rights.

CASE EXAMPLE

R (Williamson) v Secretary of State for Employment [2005] UKHL 15

Teachers and parents claimed that the prohibition of corporal punishment in schools interfered with their Convention rights to have their children educated in conformity with their religious convictions (under Art 2 of the First Protocol) and was in violation of Art 9 of the European Convention, guaranteeing freedom to manifest religion.

CONTINUED ▸

The House of Lords held that although the articles were engaged, Parliament was entitled to make an exception to those rights on the basis that they interfered with the child's rights not to be subject to inhuman and degrading treatment under Art 3. Parliament was entitled to have a broad blanket rule on prohibition and the domestic legislation was thus not incompatible.

CASE EXAMPLE

R (Begum) v Denbigh High School [2006] UKHL 15

A school had insisted that a student wear school uniform, which precluded the wearing of the full Muslim 'jilbab'. The student claimed that she had been excluded from the school in breach of her Convention rights to manifest her religion.

The House of Lords held that there had been no interference with her right to manifest her religion as she had chosen a school where such a policy existed; the two-year disruption to her schooling was the result of her unwillingness to comply with a rule to which the school was entitled to adhere. In any case the school was fully justified in acting as it had as it had, after full consultation with parents and religious bodies, designed a flexible and fair uniform policy.

17.11 Derogations and reservations

Article 15 of the European Convention allows member states to lodge a formal derogation in respect of a state of war or other public emergency. Article 16 also allows a state to place a reservation on its commitment to a specific Convention right.

17.11.1 Derogations

Article 15 allows a Member State to 'derogate' from its obligations under the Convention in times of war or other public emergency threatening the life of the nation (see Chapter 16), and under s 14 of the Human Rights Act United Kingdom derogations existing at the time of the Act's implementation are contained in Sched 3.

This included the government's derogation notices of 1988 and 1989, which were made after the European Court's decision in *Brogan v United Kingdom* (1989) 11 EHRR 117, where the court found that domestic provisions allowing extended detention of suspected terrorists were in violation of Art 5 of the Convention.

This derogation was withdrawn by an order made under the Human Rights Act (Human Rights Act (Amendment) Order 2001 SI 2001/1216) when the relevant statutory provisions were replaced by the

Terrorism Act 2000. The Secretary of State then made The Human Rights Act 1998 (Amendment No. 2) Order 2001, derogating from Art 5(1) of the European Convention and providing for an extended power to arrest and detain foreign nationals, whom it is intended to remove or deport from the United Kingdom, but where such removal would be in violation of the Convention if a person has returned to that particular country (*Chahal v United Kingdom* (1997) 23 EHRR 413).

These powers were challenged in *A and others v Secretary of State for the Home Department* [2004] UKHL 56 where it was alleged that the detention provisions contained in s 23 of the Anti-Terrorism, Crime and Security Act 2001 were in violation of Arts 5 and 14 of the Convention. The House of Lords held that the detention of foreign nationals suspected of terrorism under s 21 of the Anti-Terrorism, Crime and Security Act 2001 was a disproportionate response to the threat of terrorism and not 'strictly required by the exigencies of the situation'. The fact that the provisions did not apply to British terrorists and failed to adequately safeguard against the threats from foreign terrorists (deported suspects could be deported and continue their activities) made those provisions discriminatory under Art 14, and a disproportionate interference with liberty of the person.

17.11.2 Reservations

Article 57 of the European Convention on Human Rights allows each Member State to make reservations in connection with its obligations under the Convention (see Chapter 16) and s 15 of the Human Rights Act 1998 incorporates any designated reservation that has been lodged under the Convention. If a designated reservation is withdrawn wholly or in part it ceases to have effect, (s 15(3)) and reservations cease to have effect five years after the Act came into force, or five years after the designation order (s 16(1)). The Secretary may extend that period by a further five years, under s 16(2).

ACTIVITY

Quick Quiz

1. What constitutes a 'public authority' under the Act, and how have the courts interpreted that term?

2. Who can claim to be a 'victim' under the Act? Give real and hypothetical examples.

3. Explain the term 'just satisfaction' with respect to the courts' powers to grant remedies under the 1998 Act.

4. In what circumstances may damages be granted by the courts and on what basis are they assessed?

5. How are freedom of expression and freedom of religion given specific protection under the 1998 Act?

6. Explain the powers of derogation under s 14 of the Act and explain how the government's derogation was successfully challenged in *A and others v Secretary of State* (2004)?

Further reading

Amos, M, *Human Rights Law* (Hart 2006), Pt I.

Clayton, R, 'The Human Rights Act six years on: where are we now?' [2007] EHRLR 11.

Feldman, D, *Civil Liberties and Human Rights in England and Wales* (2nd edn, Oxford University Press 2002), Chapter 2.

Foster, S, *Human Rights and Civil Liberties* (Longman, 2003), Chapters 4 and 5.

Feldman, D, 'The Human Rights Act and Constitutional Principles' (1999) 19 *Legal Studies* 165.

Klug, F and Starmer K, 'Standing Back from the Human Rights Act: how effective is it 5 years on?' [2005] PL 716.

Wadham, J and Mountfield, H, *Blackstone's Guide to the Human Rights Act 1998* (4th edn, Oxford University Press, 2006).

chapter 18 FREEDOM OF SPEECH ■

AIMS AND OBJECTIVES ☐☐☐

At the end of this chapter you should be able to:

■ Appreciate the constitutional importance of freedom of expression and its position within the British constitution

■ Appreciate the impact of the Human Rights Act 1998 on such a right

■ Explain some of the circumstances in which the criminal law can interfere with freedom of expression

■ Explain some of the circumstances in which the civil law can interfere with freedom of expression

18.1 The constitutional importance of free speech

18.1.1 Introduction

Freedom of expression is a central aspect of all democratic states. In most countries this right is constitutionally ring-fenced and protected by being incorporated into a Bill or Charter of Rights. For example, the First Amendment of the United States constitution (ie the 1791 Bill of Rights) declares that:

 Congress shall make no law … abridging the freedom of speech, or of the press.

Similarly, Pt III, Art 19 of the Indian constitution states that:

 All citizens have the right to freedom of speech.

Freedom of speech, therefore, is one of the most important constitutional rights that an individual enjoys. The overriding constitutional significance of freedom of expression has been consistently re-affirmed by the European Court of Human Rights in *Handyside v United Kingdom* (1976) 1 EHRR 737 as it represents:

J '… one of the essential foundations of society, one of the basic conditions for its progress and for the development of every man. Subject to Article 10(2) [see section 18.2.4], it is applicable not only to "information" or "ideas" that are favourably received or regarded as inoffensive or as a matter of indifference, but also to those that offend shock or disturb the state or any sector of the population. Such are the demands of that pluralism, tolerance and broadmindedness without which there is no "democratic society".'

Finally, two further points need to be made.

Firstly, although the terms freedom of expression and free speech are used interchangeably, the former is more inclusive than the latter. In short, whereas speech is typically associated with the written and spoken word, expression can be broader and includes artistic expression (eg a sculpture in an art gallery).

Secondly, the media have a particular role to play in a democracy in advancing freedom of expression interests and this function has been recognised by the European Court of Human Rights (*Lingens v Austria* (1986) 8 EHRR 407). In particular, the media can impart information which informs political debate and the political decision-making process.

18.1.2 The justification for the principle of free expression

Fenwick has drawn attention to four main justifications widely advanced in favour of free speech (H Fenwick, *Civil Liberties and Human Rights* (3rd edn, Cavendish, 2002) at pp 200–205):

- **Moral autonomy**
  The argument under this heading is that freedom of expression supports an individual's moral autonomy by permitting him to make choices for himself as to what he reads, sees or hears. In other words, the individual chooses the information which he receives, rather than this being decided by the state.

- **Self-fulfilment**
  The argument in relation to self-fulfilment is based on the notion that freedom of expression advances the growth of an individual. In short, free access to information can stimulate and foster an individual's intellectual and moral growth.

- **Democracy**
  This argument is based on the inherent connection between free speech and the democratic process. In order for a democracy to function and flourish, it necessitates that individuals (and in particular the press) have the freedom to disseminate information concerning governmental and public affairs. In this way free speech informs political debate, discussion and the electoral process. Indeed, the European Court of Human Rights has repeatedly emphasised the importance of political speech. In *Castells v Spain* (1992) 14 EHRR 445:

> **J** 'The limits of permissible criticism are wider with regard to the Government than in relation to a private citizen, or over a politician. In the democratic system the actions or omissions of the Government must be subject to the close scrutiny not only of the legislative and judicial authorities but also of the press and public opinion.'

- **Truth**
  The argument under this heading is that freedom of speech leads ultimately to the discovery of the truth. In other words, the danger with limiting free speech is the possibility that the truth is being suppressed.

ACTIVITY

Question

Why do you think that freedom of expression is considered to be one of the most important human rights enjoyed by an individual?

18.2 Freedom of expression in the British constitution

18.2.1 The liberty of expression

Prior to the enactment of the Human Rights Act 1998, the British constitution was hallmarked by providing negative, residual liberties, rather than positive human rights (see Dicey's views on the role of the judiciary being to protect the liberties of the individual at section 6.7.8). Historically, in the United Kingdom individuals have not (as in the United States) enjoyed a positive *right to free speech* per se; instead they had the *residual liberty of expression*. In other words, an individual could write or say whatever they liked provided they did not infringe a law (statutory or common law). See Sir Robert McGarry in *Malone v Metropolitan Police Commissioner* (1979) at section 6.7.7.

In this sense, therefore, provided an individual did not violate the laws of defamation, obscenity, indecency, contempt of court, etc, everything else was permitted (ie the residue left when all the laws have been identified). This is illustrated by the Figure below:

Figure 18.1

	Contempt of Court	Defamation
Obscenity		
	RESIDUAL LIBERTY OF EXPRESSION	Inciting racial and religious hatred
Blasphemy	Indecency	Confidentiality

There were a number of difficulties with residual liberties:

- Firstly, it presupposed that an individual was aware of the laws (and their parameters) which restricted their liberty of expression.

- Secondly, Parliament (through the enactment of statutes), the executive (through the enactment of delegated legislation) and the courts (through the development of the common law) could incrementally reduce the residue of liberty. In this sense, residual liberties were vulnerable in a way that positive rights were not.

18.2.2 The interplay of freedom of speech with other competing interests

Notwithstanding the above, historically the courts, indirectly, have tried to protect residual liberties (such as the liberty of expression) from unnecessary interference. In other words, in interpreting, applying and determining the parameters of laws such as defamation and confidentiality, the courts, indirectly, could determine the extent to which these laws impinged on the residue of freedom of expression.

For example, in the context of the law of libel, the wider the defences to this tort are drawn the more difficult it will be for an individual to sue for libel. This in turn gives greater protection to freedom of expression. For example, in *Reynolds v Times Newspapers* [2001] 2 AC 127 the House of Lords developed the common law defence of qualified privilege to enable the press, in appropriate circumstances, a defence (albeit restricted) of qualified privilege where the publication of information is in the public interest. This restricted defence depended on factors such as, for example, the seriousness of the allegation, public concern in respect of the subject matter, together with whether the claimant had been given an opportunity to explain or comment on the allegations. On the facts, however, the allegations made by the press were not considered to be information which the public had a right to know (The Times had failed to mention Reynolds' explanation). On defamation see section 18.4.1.

Conversely, the narrower these defences are drawn, the easier it is to sue for libel, and this necessarily impacts on free speech. In this way, the courts, in determining the parameters of laws which aim to protect other interests (eg defamation serves to protect reputations, confidentiality aims to protect secret information) can indirectly protect freedom of expression. In *R v Home Secretary, ex parte Brind* [1991] 1 AC 696 in the House of Lords, Lord Bridge stressed that there had to be a strong justification for interfering with free speech:

> **J** 'this surely does not mean that in deciding whether the Secretary of State, in the exercise of his discretion could reasonably impose the restriction he has imposed on the broadcasting organisations, we are not perfectly entitled to start from the premise that any restriction of the right to freedom of expression requires to be justified and that nothing less than an important competing public interest will be sufficient to justify it.'

At times, however, judges have disagreed with each other over the weight that should be attached to competing interests (eg the conflicting interests of protecting an individual's reputation with the principle of freedom of speech of the press). Another set of competing interests involve the freedom of speech of the press and national security/the administration of justice.

CASE EXAMPLE

Harman v Secretary of State for the Home Department [1983] 1 AC 280

Harman, a solicitor (legal officer of the National Council for Civil Liberties – now LIBERTY), was acting for a person taking legal action against the Home Office. In the context of the litigation the latter disclosed documents and after the court hearing Harman allowed a journalist access to documents which had already been read out in court. The journalist then wrote an article and the Home Office sought an order against Harman for contempt of court. The House of Lords (dismissing Harman's appeal) held by three to two that a solicitor gave an implied undertaking not to use the information obtained on discovery during the course of litigation for a purpose other than for her client's action. The court confirmed that Harman had been guilty of a (civil) contempt of court.

Their Lordships, however, opined different views over whether the case engaged freedom of expression. Lord Diplock (in the majority) stated that:

> **J** 'I start by saying what the case is *not* about. It is *not* about freedom of speech, freedom of the press, openness of justice or documents coming into "the public domain".'

Conversely, Lord Scarman (in the dissenting minority) commented that:

CONTINUED ▸

> **J** 'A balance has to be struck between two interests of the law – on the one hand, the protection of a litigant's private right to keep his documents to himself notwithstanding his duty to disclose them to the other side in the litigation, and, on the other, the protection of the right, which the law recognises, subject to certain exceptions, as the right of everyone, to speak freely, and to impart information and ideas, upon matters of public knowledge.'

Similarly, see the different judicial attitudes exhibited by the majority on the one hand, and Lords Scarman and Fraser (in the minority) on the other, in relation to the issue of national security impinging upon the freedom of the press and compelling journalists to disclose their sources in *Secretary of State for Defence v Guardian Newspapers* [1985] 1 AC 339.

Fenwick has stated that before the Human Rights Act 1998 'the judiciary did not seem to be united around a clear conception of their role' and 'that common practice as regards fundamental freedoms did not emerge'. In effect, the British courts, unlike in other countries, lacked a Bill or Charter of Rights to 'anchor', and so help shape, their decisions (H Fenwick, *Civil Liberties and Human Rights* (3rd edn, Cavendish, 2002) pp 110–111). The existence, however, of such a Charter or Bill of Rights which protects freedom of expression has not prevented judicial inconsistency in, for example, the United States Supreme Court.

Finally, it should be noted that the balancing of freedoms/rights/liberties is achieved sometimes by Parliament in enacting legislation. For example, the Obscene Publications Act 1959 makes it a criminal offence to publish an obscene article, however, s 4 of the Act protects freedom of expression where the article is in the interests of the public good (eg literature) (see section 18.3.3).

18.2.3 The Human Rights Act 1998

The passing of the Human Rights Act 1998 resulted in negative residual liberties being converted into positive rights which can be directly asserted in domestic courts. Moreover, the Human Rights Act 1998, together with the European Convention on Human Rights with its voluminous European Court of Human Rights case law, provide the modern judiciary with an established set of principles concerning the protection of human rights and how they interrelate with other competing rights and interests. Indeed, s 2 of the Human Rights Act 1998 places a statutory obligation on our judges to have regard for the jurisprudence of the European Court in Strasbourg.

18.2.4 Article 10

Article 10 of the European Convention states that:

'Everyone has the right to freedom of expression. This right shall include freedom to
hold opinions and to receive and impart information and ideas without interference by
public authority and regardless of frontiers.'

Article 10 is a conditional right and can be legitimately interfered with by other competing
interests. The corollary of this right is the recognition that the right carries with it certain
responsibilities and duties. The primary right of freedom of expression is thus not an absolute right
(as it conflicts with other interests and carries with it responsibilities) and therefore can be
restricted by the following wide range of interests as set out in Art 10(2):

 'national security, territorial integrity or public safety, for the prevention of disorder or
crime, for the protection of health or morals, for the protection of the reputation or
rights of others, for preventing the disclosure of information received in confidence, or
for maintaining the authority and impartiality of the judiciary.'

Under the Human Rights Act 1998, if individuals contend that the state (public authority) has,
without lawful justification, interfered with their right to freedom of expression, they can petition a
domestic court and seek a remedy. In such circumstances the court must follow the legal reasoning
adopted by Strasbourg and will, therefore, have to determine:

- Whether there has been an interference with the primary right under Art 10.
- Whether the interference (ie the restriction) can be justified as:
  (i)   having a legitimate aim (ie seeking to achieve one of the objectives set out in Art 10(2)
        above),
  (ii) being prescribed by law (ie being sufficiently clear and certain),
  (iii) being necessary in a democratic society (ie there is a pressing social need for it and it is
        not disproportionate).

In this way the courts will balance competing interests, but will have the advantage of the
jurisprudence of the European Court to assist them in determining this. In domestic law the
Human Rights Act 1998 makes particular provision for Art 10 and freedom of expression: s 12 of
the Act applies to a situation where a court is considering to grant relief that will impact on
Art 10. In particular, a temporary injunction which restrains an article from being published
pending the full trial on the matter will only be granted if the court is satisfied that the applicant
(at the full trial) is likely to prove that the article should not be published. Section 12(2) also
prevents *ex parte* applications (ie those where the other party is not present) being made, although
they could be made in exceptional circumstances.

It should be noted that s 12 is peculiar to the Human Rights Act 1998 (ie the provision is not
drawn from a corresponding European Convention article) and it is clear that the domestic judges
have differed over its requirements (ie whether Art 10 should be given an elevated weighting). In

Cream Holdings v Banerjee [2004] UKHL 44, the House of Lords held that in applying s 12(3), when an applicant sought an interim injunction (which if granted would infringe Art 10), the test which the court should employ was to consider whether the applicant's prospect of success at the full trial was sufficiently favourable to justify the granting of the interim injunction.

ACTIVITY

Essay writing

Compare and contrast how freedom of expression was protected by the British courts before and after the passing of the Human Rights Act 1998.

KEY FACTS

Freedom of expression is one of the most important constitutional rights that an individual enjoys and it is recognised by all democratic states.

Article 10 of the European Convention states that: Everyone has the right to freedom of expression. This is, however, a conditional right which can be legitimately interfered with to secure a wide range of competing interests.

Under the Human Rights Act 1998 individuals can now raise Art 10 directly in domestic courts and the judiciary are required to take cognisance of the case law of the European Court of Human Rights and adopt the legal reasoning that it employs in determining whether Art 10 can be legitimately interfered with.

18.3 Free speech and the criminal law

Introduction

Although freedom of expression is of fundamental constitutional importance, as indicated above, it is not (and cannot be) an absolute right. As free speech comes into conflict with other competing interests (eg national security, public decency and the administration of justice), it is necessarily a conditional right which can be legitimately interfered with to protect these other interests. There are a wide variety of ways in which the criminal law (whether statutory or common law) can legitimately interfere with an individual's freedom of expression.

18.3.1 Protecting religious sensibilities

Blasphemy is a common law criminal offence which in effect outlaws the scurrilous treatment and vilification of matters which are sacred to Christians and which is likely to outrage and shock their feelings. A few points should be noted about this offence. Firstly, it is confined to the Anglican version of Christianity. Secondly, it criminalises the publication of matters (blasphemous libel if in written form) for which a convicted person could (in theory) endure life imprisonment. Thirdly, blasphemy does not apply to other religions (*R v Chief Metropolitan Stipendiary Magistrate, ex parte Choudhury* [1991] 1 All ER 306 – see section 4.8.2). Fourthly, there is no 'public good' defence available to a defendant (contrast obscenity in section 18.3.3). Fifthly, in modern times prosecutions for blasphemy have been very rare. The only prosecution since the early twentieth century was *Lemon* and this was a private prosecution instigated by Mary Whitehouse:

 ASE EXAMPLE

Whitehouse v Lemon [1979] AC 617

Lemon was the editor of *Gay News* which in 1976 published a poem (together with a drawing) which, among other things, purported to describe acts of sodomy with Christ following his death as well as attributing homosexual practices to him with his Apostles. Mary Whitehouse successfully instituted a private prosecution against Lemon and Gay News Ltd for blasphemous libel. The House of Lords upheld the conviction by a majority on the basis that it was not necessary for the prosecution to prove an intention to blaspheme, merely an intention to publish a matter which was blasphemous.

Gay News Ltd subsequently unsuccessfully petitioned the European Commission of Human Rights on the basis that blasphemy violated freedom of expression (*Gay News Ltd and Lemon v United Kingdom* (1982) 5 EHRR 123).

The law of blasphemy could be justified under Art 10(2) of the European Convention as a legitimate interference with free speech as protecting the *rights of others* (ie Christian believers not to be outraged, see *Wingrove v United Kingdom* (1996) 24 EHRR 1). In this case the European Court afforded the United Kingdom a measure of discretion (ie the margin of appreciation – see section 16.6.5) because on matters of morality and the significance of religion, there was no uniform conception across European countries.

LIBERTY has questioned the need for the law of blasphemy:

> **Q**
>
> 'Blasphemy law as it stands is both outmoded and illiberal, and should be abolished. Similar concerns have been voiced by commentators and the Law Commission recommended abolition as far back as 1985. The offence has no true value or purpose in society today … There is no need for the law in modern society'.
>
> *Racial and Religious Hatred Bill, Liberty's briefing for Second Reading in the House of Commons*
> (Liberty, June 2005), paras 13–14.

In 2003 a House of Lords select committee identified the main options available in respect of the offence of blasphemy:

- Leave blasphemy as it stands.

- Repeal it without replacing it.

- Repeal it, but replace with a statute which covered all religious faiths/beliefs and the rejection of religion.

(The Select Committee on Religious Offences in England and Wales, HL Paper 95-1 (2003), para 31).

18.3.2 Protecting the public from indecent material

- **Common law indecency**

  It is a common law offence to commit an act to outrage public decency (to protect the public from outrage). As with blasphemy above, there is no public good defence to this offence.

CASE EXAMPLE

R v Gibson and another [1991] 1 All ER 439

Sylveire ran an art gallery. In the gallery's catalogue was an exhibition entitled 'Human Earrings' which was a work (made by Gibson) which consisted of a model's head to which a freeze-dried human foetus had been attached to each ear lobe. Both Gibson and Sylveire were convicted of outraging public decency. The Court of Appeal dismissed their appeals against conviction on the ground, *inter alia*, that the prosecution did not have to prove that the appellants had intended to outrage public decency.

- **Statutory indecency**

  A number of statutory offences outlaw indecency. For example, s 1 of the Indecent Displays (Control) Act 1981 makes it a criminal offence (punishable by up to two years' imprisonment) publicly to display an indecent matter. The Act is essentially designed to deal with nuisance public displays and there is no public good defence.

The laws of indecency could be justified under Art 10(2) of the European Convention as a legitimate interference with free speech as serving the legitimate objective of protecting the *rights of others* (ie individuals not be offended by, or subject to, nuisance material) and *the protection of health or morals.*

18.3.3 Controlling material which depraves and corrupts

The Obscene Publications Act 1959 (as amended in 1964) makes it a criminal offence, punishable by up to three years' imprisonment, for a person to publish an obscene article (or one who has such an article in his possession for publication for gain).

The definition of obscenity is set out in s 1 namely that the effect of the article is such as (taken as a whole) *to tend to deprave and corrupt* those persons who are likely to see, read or hear the matter. In this context, therefore, the Act is not concerned with articles which shock or offend, but instead with something more pernicious: corruption. It should be recalled that Handyside (a publisher) was convicted under the Act for having in his possession for gain an obscene article: copies of a reference book called *Little Red Schoolbook* (see section 6.6.2 above). This was aimed at children and adolescents (12–18 years) and it contained topics such as masturbation, pornography, etc.

He was convicted and a forfeiture order was issued which resulted in the destruction of these books. Handyside subsequently unsuccessfully petitioned the European Court of Human Rights contending that this violated Art 10, however, the court held that it was a legitimate and proportionate interference with Handyside's right to freedom of expression.

The Obscene Publications Act 1959 aims to strike a balance between protecting the public from being depraved and corrupted and freedom of expression. Section 4 states that a person has a defence (the defence of public good):

'if it is proved that publication of the article in question is justified as being for the public good on the ground that it is in the interests of science, literature, art or learning, or of other objects of general concern.'

In this context, it is of interest to note that Penguin Books were unsuccessfully prosecuted under the Act in relation to the publication of DH Lawrence's *Lady Chatterley's Lover* (*R v Penguin Books* [1961] Crim LR 176). The defence made use of expert witnesses to testify to the literary importance of the book and the jury acquitted, evidently on the basis that the book fell within s 4 as being justified in the interests of literature.

The law of obscenity could be justified under Art 10(2) of the European Convention as a legitimate interference with free speech as serving the legitimate objective of *the protection of health or morals* (ie preventing the corruption of individuals) – see *Handyside* (1976)).

ACTIVITY

Exercise

Do you think that the laws of blasphemy, indecency and obscenity are necessary in a democratic society and achieve a proper balance between free speech and public morality?

18.3.4 Protecting public order

There are a number of offences which restrict free speech in order to preserve public order. For example, s 18 of the Public Order Act 1986 makes it a criminal offence for a person to use threatening, abusive or insulting words/behaviour in order to intend to stir up racial hatred (or where it is likely to be stirred up). The Racial and Religious Hatred Act 2006 was scheduled to come into force in 2007 (and amend the Public Order Act 1986) and make it unlawful to stir up hatred against persons on religious grounds. However, as a concession to free speech s 29J (as incorporated into the 1986 Act) provides that:

> **S** 'Nothing in this Part shall be read or given effect in a way which prohibits or restricts discussion, criticism or expressions of antipathy, dislike, ridicule, insult or abuse of particular religions or the beliefs or practices of their adherents, or of any other belief system or the beliefs or practices of its adherents, or proselytising or urging adherents of a different religion or belief system to cease practising their religion or belief system'.

The law of inciting racial hatred could be justified under Art 10(2) of the European Convention as a legitimate interference with free speech as serving to prevent *disorder or crime.*

18.3.5 Protecting the administration of justice

Under s 1 of the Perjury Act 1911 it is an offence for a person sworn in as a witness to make a statement during judicial proceedings which he knows to be false (or does not believe to be true). The law of perjury could be justified under Art 10(2) of the European Convention as a legitimate interference with free speech as serving to maintain *the authority and impartiality of the judiciary.*

In addition, the Contempt of Court Act 1981 provides criminal strict liability 'whereby conduct may be treated as a contempt of court as tending to interfere with the course of justice'. The Act, therefore, is designed to protect the integrity of court proceedings. Section 2(2) states that:

> **S** 'The strict liability rule applies only to a publication which creates a substantial risk that the course of justice in the proceedings in question will be seriously impeded or prejudiced'.

18.3.6 Protecting national security

Section 1 of the Official Secrets Act 1989 makes it a criminal offence for a member of the security/intelligence services to disclose information (without lawful authority) relating to security or intelligence:

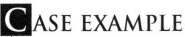**ASE EXAMPLE**

> **R v Shayler [2002] UKHL 11**
>
> Shayler had been charged with unlawfully disclosing information contrary to ss 1 and 4 of the 1989 Act. As the Human Rights Act 1998 was in force, he contended that the 1989 Act should be interpreted with a public interest defence (ie that Shayler was acting in the public interest in disclosing such information). The House of Lords dismissed Shayler's appeal and held that the Official Secrets Act 1989 was consistent with the requirements of Art 10 of the Convention. It was noted that Shayler could have sought internal authorisation for the disclosure of the information.

The Official Secrets Act could, therefore, be justified under Art 10(2) of the European Convention as a legitimate interference with free speech as serving *the interests of national security*.

18.4 Free speech and the civil law

In addition to the restrictions imposed by the criminal law, free speech can be legitimately interfered with by the civil law with the intention of protecting private interests such as reputation and confidential information.

18.4.1 The protection of reputation

The law of defamation serves to provide protection for a person's reputation from false statements which damage it, or which are capable of doing so. There are a number of defences to an action for defamation which serve to protect free speech. These are:

- **Justification** – that the impugned statement was true (or substantially true).
- **Fair comment** – that the statement was simply a fair comment on an issue of public interest.
- **Absolute privilege** – immunity from legal liability for things said during the proceedings in court (see section 13.4.2) or Parliament (see section 8.6).
- **Qualified privilege** – this defence (providing there is no malice) is available in certain situations, for example, where one party has a duty to inform another who has a corresponding interest/duty to receive such information. In *Reynolds v Times Newspapers* (2001) (see section 18.2.2), the House of Lords held that although the press did not have a defence of public

interest *per se*, in certain circumstances the defence of qualified privilege might be available to the press to justify information published in the public interest.

- **Innocent dissemination** – this is particularly relevant to broadcasters.

As noted above, the judges, in interpreting and applying the law of defamation and its defences determine its impact on freedom of expression. For example, in *Derbyshire County Council v Times Newspapers Ltd* (1993) (for the facts see section 4.8.2) the House of Lords held that under the common law a local authority could not sue in defamation. Lord Keith stated that:

> J
>
> 'It is of the highest public importance that a democratically elected governmental body, or indeed any governmental body, should be open to uninhibited public criticism … I regard it as right for this House to lay down that not only is there no public interest favouring the right of organs of government, whether central or local, to sue for libel, but that it is contrary to the public interest that they should have it. It is contrary to the public interest because to admit such actions would place an undesirable fetter on freedom of speech.'

The law of the defamation could be justified under Art 10(2) of the European Convention as a legitimate interference with free speech as serving to protect *the reputation of others*.

18.4.2 The protection of confidential information

The law of confidentiality seeks to protect the confidentiality of private/secret information (including information held by the state).There are a number of defences to an action for confidentiality which serve to protect free speech. One such defence is that such information is already in the public domain as demonstrated in the '*Spycatcher*' case:

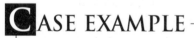

CASE EXAMPLE

Attorney-General v Observer Ltd and others **[1988] 3 WLR 776**

Peter Wright (a former member of MI5) wrote *Spycatcher*, a book which detailed alleged unlawful activities of members of MI5. In 1985 in Australia, the Attorney General sought to prevent the book being published on the ground of confidentiality (eg a duty to the Crown not to disclose information).

Thereafter, the Attorney General obtained interlocutory (temporary) injunctions against *The Guardian* and the *Observer* until trial from publishing any information from Peter Wright in his role as a member of MI5. The Attorney General also subsequently secured an

CONTINUED ▶

interlocutory injunction restraining *The Sunday Times* from publishing further extracts from its serialisation of *Spycatcher.*

The House of Lords held that the world-wide publication of *Spycatcher* (it had been published in the United States) had destroyed the secrecy of its contents (hence its confidentiality) and as a consequence, the injunctions against the newspapers were not necessary and should be discharged. In essence, for a public body to override freedom of expression in the context of confidentiality, a clear public interest of non-disclosure must be demonstrated.

As a postscript to this case, the newspapers subsequently successfully petitioned the European Court of Human Rights on the basis that the continuation of the injunctions after the book was freely available (having been published in America) violated Art 10 (*Observer and Guardian v United Kingdom* (1991) 14 EHRR 153).

The law of confidentiality could be justified under Art 10(2) of the European Convention as a legitimate interference with free speech as serving to protect the *rights of others* (ie a private life/privacy). This is illustrated by the following case which involves a balance between privacy (private life) and the exercise of freedom of expression by the press:

CASE EXAMPLE

Campbell v MGN Ltd [2004] UKHL 22

Naomi Campbell (a model) sued MGN Ltd for breach of confidentiality for publishing details of her therapy for drug addiction at a self-help group meeting, together with photographs of her leaving a meeting.

The House of Lords held that the Convention right of Art 8 (the right of Campbell to a private life – including details of her therapy which was private and confidential information) outweighed the competing right under Art 10, the freedom of expression of the press. As a consequence Campbell was entitled to damages.

KEY FACTS

As a conditional right, freedom of expression can be legitimately interfered with by both the criminal and civil law.

The criminal law

Free speech can be infringed in order to secure the following legitimate objectives:

- The protection of national security (Official Secrets Act 1989).
- The protection of public order (Public Order Act 1986).
- The protection of the administration of justice (Perjury Act 1911/Contempt of Court Act 1981).
- The protection of the public from indecent material (common law and statutory indecency).
- The protection of religious sensibilities (blasphemy).
- The prevention of corruption (Obscene Publications Acts 1959 and 1964).

The civil law

Free speech can be infringed in order to secure the following legitimate objectives:

- The protection of reputation (defamation).
- The protection of confidential information (confidentiality).

Further reading

Amos, M, 'Can we speak freely now?' [2002] EHRLR 750.

Barendt, E, *Freedom of Speech* (2nd edn, Oxford University Press, 2005).

Bradley, A and Ewing, K, *Constitutional and Administrative Law* (14th edn, Pearson/Longman 2007), Chapter 23.

Fenwick, H, *Civil liberties and Human Rights* (3rd edn, Cavendish, 2002) Pt II, pp 199–214 and Chapters 5 to 7.

Klug, F, Starmer, K and Weir, S, *The Three Pillars of Liberty* (Routledge, 1996), Chapter 9.

Foster, S, *Human Rights and Civil Liberties* (Longman, 2003), Chapters 6 to 8.

chapter 19 JUDICIAL REVIEW I (RATIONALE AND PROCEDURE)

AIMS AND OBJECTIVES

At the end of this chapter you should be able to:

■ Define and understand the nature of administrative law

■ Understand the nature and constitutional significance of judicial review

■ Understand who can seek judicial review and which bodies are subject to it

■ Appreciate the general public law procedure of judicial review

19.1 Administrative law

19.1.1 Introduction

As noted earlier at section 1.2.2, in broad terms administrative law concerns the principles relating to executive/governmental powers. Government officials and agencies are conferred with extensive powers (typically by statute) to provide public services (social security, housing, etc). Administrative law focuses specifically on the powers and responsibilities exercised by governmental bodies and how they are regulated and controlled by both legal and extra-judicial means. Although there is no clear demarcation between constitutional and administrative law (due largely to the absence of a codified constitution), the latter is particularly concerned with how the executive/administration uses and misuses its public law powers. In short, administrative law is concerned with ensuring that government and public law decision-makers are accountable for their actions.

Public lawyers are particularly interested in the following:

● The methods by which the exercise of public powers and duties may be controlled by the courts or by other extra-judicial bodies (eg the Ombudsman).

● The ways in which the government/administration in exercising its public law powers and duties facilitates the following constitutional principles (justice, participation in public affairs, open government).

An overview of the regulation of governmental power

Although administrative law primarily concerns the legal regulation of the exercise of public power by governmental bodies, it also embraces non-legal controls outside the strict court system. In general terms, government power is regulated in the following ways:

■ Figure 19.1

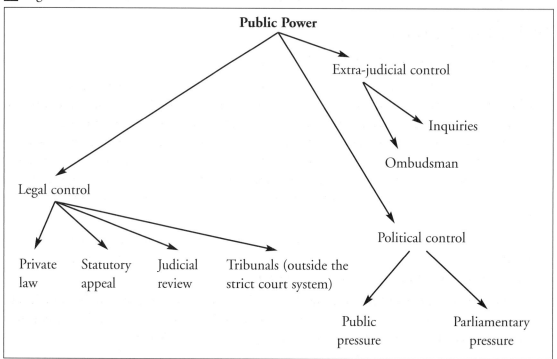

19.1.2 Political control

The government is politically controlled in the following ways:

(i) Public pressure – Government is influenced by public pressure and may therefore react to public opinion (for example, the replacement of the controversial community charge 'the poll tax' with the council tax by virtue of the Local Government Finance Act 1992). Sometimes by reacting to public opinion, the government may act illegally (see *ex parte Venables and Thompson* (1997) at section 5.7.6 where the Home Secretary acted unlawfully in taking into account public concern regarding the length of Venables and Thompson's detention for killing James Bulger). Ultimately, of course, governments (or more accurately, MPs in the government) need to seek re-election at least every five years and obtain the support of the electorate (the notion of political sovereignty – see section 7.2.2).

(ii) Parliamentary pressure – In constitutional theory, government ministers are controlled and regulated in Parliament through the following devices:

- Parliamentary questions (see section 12.4).

- Parliamentary debates (see section 12.5).

- Parliamentary committees (see section 12.6).

In fact, two of the most fundamental constitutional conventions underpinning our constitution are the conventions of collective and individual responsibility (see sections 12.2 to 12.3).

19.1.3 Legal control

The government is legally controlled in the following ways:

- **Private law remedies** – In general terms, government bodies, like private individuals, are subject to the private laws of tort and contract, etc. In other words, should a local authority fail to fulfill its obligations under a contract made with a private citizen, the latter may sue for breach of contract. In private law, however, public bodies are treated differently in two respects. Firstly, for public interest reasons they may have defences to private law actions which private individuals do not. Secondly, the courts may apply constitutional principles of acting fairly (and not capriciously) to public bodies when they act in a purely private way, for example, in contract law.

- **Statutory appeal** – Appeals are statutory mechanisms which Parliament has specifically legislated for and so it may be possible, for example, to appeal against the decision of an administrative officer (in particular, see tribunals below).

- **Judicial review** – This is the cornerstone of administrative law and will be considered in detail here and in Chapter 20. In essence, judicial review is the legal mechanism whereby a claimant can seek to judicially review the decision-making process of a public body.

- **Tribunals** – In essence, tribunals are a grievance mechanism which are an alternative to the strict formal court system. For example, an appeal concerning a social security officer's decision to refuse eligibility in respect of a particular benefit would proceed not to a court, but instead to a more informal (and cheaper) specialist tribunal (see section 21.1).

19.1.4. Extra-judicial remedies

The government is regulated also by a number of supplementary non-judicial remedies:

- **Ombudsman** – There are a number of different Ombudsmen who supervise and regulate the activities of the administration (see section 21.3). The first, and most constitutionally significant, is the Parliamentary Commissioner for Administration who investigates complaints that government departments have engaged in maladministration (in effect, faulty administration) which has resulted in injustice to the complainant.

- **Inquiries** – There are a number of different types of inquiries which include, for example, a land inquiry concerning the decision of a local authority to refuse planning permission. Further, a public inquiry can be held in respect of, for example, the siting of a new airport. From a constitutional perspective, this permits individuals to influence the decision-making process of a public official.

19.2 Judicial review

19.2.1 Definition

> 'Judicial review represents the means by which the courts control the exercise of governmental power. Government departments, local authorities, tribunals, state agencies and agencies exercising powers which are governmental in nature must exercise their powers in a lawful manner'.

> H Barnett, *Constitutional and Administrative Law* (6th edn, Routledge-Cavendish, 2006) p 719.

The High Court historically has exercised an inherent power to supervise the actions of public bodies, as well as inferior courts, to ensure that these bodies act strictly within their legal powers and thus act legally. For the purposes of judicial review, the part of the High Court which processes these cases is now known as the Administrative Court. The following examples illustrate the nature of judicial review acting as a check on the following bodies:

- **Government ministers** – In *R v Secretary of State for Foreign and Commonwealth Affairs, ex parte World Development Movement Ltd* [1995] 1 WLR 386 the pressure group WDM successfully challenged the Foreign Secretary's decision to grant funding for the construction of a Malaysian hydro-electric power station on the Pergau river under the Overseas Development and Co-operation Act 1980 on the basis of it being economically unsound.

  In relation to delegated legislation, in *R v Secretary of State for Health, ex parte United States Tobacco International Inc* [1992] 1 QB 353 the court quashed the Oral Snuff (Safety) Regulations 1989 made by the Secretary of State for Health, on the basis that the claimants had not been given the opportunity to make representations before they were enacted.

- **Local authorities** – In *R v Wear Valley District Council, ex parte Binks* [1985] 2 All ER 699, a street trader successfully sought judicial review of the Wear Valley District Council's decision (without prior notification or reasons) to give her notice to quit her hot food take-away caravan.

- **Parole Board** – In *R (West) v Parole Board* [2005] UKHL 1, prisoners successfully challenged the procedural fairness of the Parole Board in respect of revoking their licences (they had been released on licence) as they had not been offered oral hearings (see section 20.5.4).

- **Inferior courts** – In *R (DPP) v South East Surrey Youth Court* [2005] EWHC 2929 Admin the Director of Public Prosecutions sought judicial review of the decision of the South East Surrey Youth Court not to commit a defendant for trial at Crown Court. On the facts the court did not quash the decision of the Youth Court, but noted that its approach had been flawed when it had declined to consider certain statutory provisions.

These cases illustrate a number of points concerning judicial review:

(i) Firstly, judicial review can be brought against a disparate number of different public bodies (from a Secretary of State to a Parole Board). In fact, judicial review can be used against bodies which are not, in a strict sense, part of the government at all (see the *Panel on Take-overs and Mergers* case at section 19.3.3).

(ii) Judicial review can be sought by a number of different claimants (from individual street traders and pressure groups through to the DPP acting in the public interest).

(iii) Judicial review is not confined to supervising the actions of government bodies *per se*, as it can include reviewing the decision-making process of judicial bodies (eg inferior courts, which are those ranking lower than the High/Administrative Court).

19.2.2 A review and not an appellate jurisdiction

In *Chief Constable of the North Wales Police v Evans* [1982] 1 WLR 1155, Lord Brightman stated that:

'Judicial review is concerned, not with the decision, but with the decision-making process. Unless that restriction on the power of the court is observed, the court will in my view under the guise of preventing the abuse of power, be itself guilty of usurping power.'

The constitutional function behind judicial review is to supervise the decision-making process of public bodies and not to act as an appellate court which questions the decision itself. In short, the Administrative Court is concerned with the legality and lawfulness of the actions taken by the public authority, rather than the merits of the decision. Judicial review, therefore, is concerned with the nature of the decision-making process and with asking the following questions:

In reaching its decision (as part of the decision-making process) did the public body:

- Misinterpret its legal powers?
- Take into account an irrelevant matter?
- Ignore a relevant matter?
- Act with an improper purpose in mind?
- Act in a procedurally unfair way by either ignoring a statutory requirement or by failing to follow the common law rules of natural justice?

By asking these sorts of questions, in constitutional theory, the court is in effect questioning the *process* of making the decision and *not* the decision itself. In other words, the reviewing court is not questioning the merits or quality of the decision made (eg was it qualitatively a good or bad decision), which is an exercise carried out by an appellate court, but rather was the process lawful? It is in this way that judicial review can be constitutionally justified. It must be noted that this is an inherent remedy which the courts themselves have developed rather than Parliament. Appeals, on the other hand are statutory, whereby Parliament has decided that in a particular set of circumstances, where a person disagrees with the decision made by a public body, it can be appealed against. As Lord Greene MR has made clear in *Associated Provincial Picture Houses Ltd v Wednesbury Corporation* [1948] 1 KB 223, the role of the court in judicial review proceedings (in the context of a local authority):

> J 'is not as an appellate authority to override a decision of the local authority, but as a judicial authority which is concerned, and concerned only, to see whether the local authority have contravened the law by acting in excess of the powers which Parliament has confided in them.'

The following points need to be noted in this context:

(i) The constitutional theory set out above is more readily applicable to some grounds of judicial review than to others. For example, in relation to the ground of irrationality, the courts are, in effect, questioning the quality of the decision made (albeit, for the court to intervene the decision must be so irrational that no reasonable decision-maker could have arrived at it). Moreover, today in the context of the Human Rights Act 1998, the courts may have to consider whether an interference with human rights is proportionate.

(ii) The traditional view that a reviewing court has a supervisory role only, is now subject to the new Civil Procedure Rules which (in limited circumstances) permit the reviewing court to *substitute* a decision for the one that the court has quashed. Part 54.19(3) provides that:

> 'Where the court considers that there is no purpose to be served in remitting the matter to the decision-maker it may, subject to any statutory provision, take the decision itself'.

ACTIVITY

Exercise

What is the constitutional distinction between a review and an appeal?

19.2.3 The constitutional dimension of judicial review

Judicial review is a central component of Britain's uncodified constitution and is inextricably linked with the following constitutional principles:

The rule of law

Judicial review can be viewed as the rule of law in operation (see Chapter 6). In short, it ensures that public bodies act strictly within their legal powers and do not exceed them. As indicated earlier, the rule of law necessities that government acts within the law and judicial review can provide a remedy if a public body misuses or exceeds its public law powers. In particular, the court will ensure that public decision-makers do not abuse their public law discretion. There is a clear public policy case for conferring discretion on government officials and administrators (see section 6.7.5) and the process of judicial review aims to control and regulate the use of that discretion. In essence, judicial review underpins the rule of law in our uncodified constitution.

The separation of powers

As noted at section 5.8.4, from one perspective judicial review can be seen as an illustration of the separation of powers with the judicial arm of the constitution (the Administrative Court) checking and balancing the actions of the executive (the government/administration). In this way the executive is held legally to account. Moreover, the courts have used the principle of the separation of powers as justifying their somewhat limited constitutional role as a reviewing court. Thus, in constitutional theory the judges confine themselves simply to reviewing the decision-making process of public bodies, whilst leaving the latter to make the actual decision themselves. After all, it is the public bodies which have been specifically charged with the responsibility to make the decision (a specialist executive/administrative role). In this way, the courts avoid trespassing on the constitutional role of the executive, which is to administer the law and take decisions. The courts will intervene via judicial review proceedings only when, for example, a public body misunderstands or misuses its powers, or adopts a faulty decision-making process.

Parliamentary sovereignty

As government derives many of its public law powers from Parliament, judicial review can be viewed as simply upholding parliamentary sovereignty by ensuring that public bodies act strictly within their allocated statutory powers. If these authorities were permitted to exceed their legal powers as conferred by Parliament, they would undermine the legal authority and status of Acts of Parliament. Judicial review ensures that public decision-makers act within the legal parameters set by Parliament.

One difficulty with this point is that government also enjoys substantial common law powers in the form of the royal prerogative and some uses of this power have been held subject to judicial review (see section 11.9). Clearly in these cases, the justification for judicial review in this context cannot be to uphold the will of Parliament. A second problem concerns the judicial attitude to ouster clauses (see section 19.2.4).

The protection of human rights

Judicial review is a procedural remedy in the sense that it challenges the decision-making process, and in this way it is a somewhat limited remedy. In recent decades however, the human rights context of a judicial review application has assumed increasing significance. In other words, the more a decision has impacted adversely on human rights, the more justification would be required by the court for the public body to be able to make it (see *ex parte Smith* (1996) at section 20.3.2). Today the Human Rights Act 1998 is in operation and the Convention rights can be upheld through an action in judicial review. Under s 6 of the Act, public authorities must act in accordance with the rights set out in the European Convention and if they do not their actions can now be subject to judicial review for breaching them.

The control of the exercise of public law powers

Judicial review can be constitutionally justified as a legal control on the misuse of public law powers (including both statutory and common law prerogative powers). In the absence of a formal codified constitution which constitutionally constrains the actions of the executive, judicial review provides a mechanism whereby the abuse of public law powers (which can affect millions of people) can be legally constrained. In fact, it could be observed that the dramatic growth of judicial review in the past 30 years has coincided with the overwhelming dominance of the executive in the legislature and so has, therefore, re-balanced the constitution. It is true to say that although in the past 30 years there has been less *political* control over the executive, there has, however, been a significant increase in the *legal* control over it via judicial review proceedings.

19.2.4 The controversial nature of judicial review

Judicial review has a number of controversial and/or disputed elements.

An inherent and unelected jurisdiction

Judicial review is in effect a judge-driven process as it stems from the common law. In other words, it is the courts themselves which have developed, expanded and refined the principles, grounds and remedies available in judicial review proceedings. In effect, the courts determine who can seek judicial review, against whom and on what grounds. The judges are, of course, unelected and largely unrepresentative of society (see Chapter 13) and therefore would appear to lack a democratic mandate for their actions in supervising the executive.

This common law basis of judicial review can, however, be justified as upholding the constitutional principles set out in section 19.2.3 and in particular, controlling the abuse of public law powers. Moreover, it should be remembered also that the executive itself is not elected *per se*, it is merely drawn (largely though not exclusively) from the elected House of Commons. In *ex parte Witham* (1997), for example, the courts declared secondary legislation passed by the *unelected* Lord Chancellor to be unlawful and *ultra vires* (see section 4.8.3). In a democracy it is paramount that the executive does not exceed its legal powers, thereby upholding the rule of law.

Controlling ultra vires action?

There is debate concerning the constitutional justification for judicial review, namely whether it is, in essence, concerned with questioning actions which are *ultra vires* (beyond the powers conferred). On the one hand, it has been argued traditionally that the courts are simply upholding the will of Parliament as by challenging *ultra vires* action they ensure that public bodies act *intra vires* (within the powers conferred). As noted earlier, however, judicial review also regulates the exercise of the royal prerogative which is a common law power. In addition, the courts imply certain principles (eg the need to use powers rationally and fairly) into the statutory powers conferred on public bodies.

According to Barnett the principle of *ultra vires*:

> 'is nowadays too limited a term to encompass the whole ambit of judicial review. It may be preferable, therefore, to regard judicial review as the control of discretion and the regulation of the decision making process by the courts.'

H Barnett, *Constitutional and Administrative Law* (6th edn, Routledge-Cavendish, 2006) p 750.

The ground of irrationality

As will be indicated below, irrationality (historically) is the second ground on which judicial review can be sought (see section 20.3). The difficulty with this ground is that it is difficult to reconcile with the principle that judicial review is concerned simply with review rather than appeal. When a court decides that a decision is irrational, in practice this comes close to questioning the *quality* of the decision made.

Red light/green light theories

Leyland and Anthony, *Textbook on Administrative Law* (5th edn, Oxford University Press, 2005), pp 4–9) have drawn attention to the following theories (the so-called red/green light models as set out by C Harlow and R Rawlings in *Law and Administration* (Weidenfeld & Nicolson, 1984)) which have been associated with judicial review:

- The red light theory is that the function of the courts in judicial review is to act as a clear brake on the administration (hence the red light). This places restrictions on the executive and limits its impact on individuals and society. In effect, it limits state interference.

- The green light theory, in contrast, facilitates administrative action by limiting judicial intervention with it on the basis that it is in the public interest that public decision-makers make decisions which benefit the public. In short, administrators should be enabled to administrate without fearing that every action will be legally challenged (which in itself causes administrative paralysis in decision-making).

- Leyland and Anthony note that the amber light theory is a compromise between the two opposed views above. In other words, this essentially balances the need to control public bodies so that public power is not abused (red), with the recognition that the state must be permitted to make decisions for the benefit of society (green).

Ouster clauses

Ouster clauses are provisions in legislation which specifically exclude the jurisdiction of the courts. The judiciary have historically resisted such clauses, and it could be argued therefore, that in these circumstances, strictly speaking, the courts are not really upholding the plain will of Parliament. For example, in *Anisminic Ltd* (1969) at section 20.2.6, the relevant statutory provision stated explicitly that the determination of the Commission 'shall not be called in question in any court of law'. The court nevertheless held that this provision did not apply where the Commission had acted beyond its jurisdiction and so had not made a determination at all.

The controversial nature of total ouster clauses (which are arguably contrary to the principles underpinning the rule of law, as they aim specifically to exclude the supervisory remedy of judicial review) was demonstrated when the government was persuaded to drop such a clause from the Asylum and Immigration Bill in 2004. This episode also raises the issue of the role of the Lord Chancellor whose function (which has now been codified in the Constitutional Reform Act 2005) is to defend rigorously the rule of law (including within the Cabinet) and in doing so, prevent such legislative provisions from being put forward (see section 5.7.9).

The courts are, however, willing to accept clauses which restrict court jurisdiction to a limited time (*Smith v East Elloe RDC* [1956] AC 736 and *R v Secretary of State for the Environment, ex parte Ostler* [1977] 1 QB 122). A recent example of such a clause is s 38 of the Inquiries Act 2005 which states that:

An application for judicial review of a decision made-

(a) by the Minister in relation to an inquiry, or
(b) by a member of an inquiry panel,

must be brought within 14 days after the day on which the applicant became aware of the decision, unless that time limit is extended by the court.
(The rationale behind this provision is to prevent delays to inquiries).

An uneven remedy?

In some respects judicial review can be seen as lacking a clear overall uniform pattern. This is partly due to the fact that the court is a *reactive* body simply processing judicial review claims as and when they are brought before them. Thus, their ability to develop overarching judicial review principles is dependent upon the type and nature of the case brought before them at any one time.

In addition as indicated at section 18.2.2, the courts historically have lacked an authoritative set of clear and agreed constitutional guidelines and so judicial review has developed in an *ad hoc* fashion. The modern courts do at least now enjoy the benefit of the principles espoused in the European Convention when processing human rights cases (see s 2 of the Human Rights Act 1998 at section 17.4).

The following points suggest judicial review lacks uniformity:

- The courts will determine, on a case by case basis, which bodies will be subject to judicial review. For example, in terms of two non-governmental bodies: the Panel on Take-overs and Mergers and the Jockey Club, the former was subject to judicial review whilst the latter was not (see section 19.3.3).

- Claimants seeking judicial review need to demonstrate that they have sufficient interest in the matter. For example, in terms of organisations seeking review, Greenpeace was permitted to do so, whilst *Rose Theatre Trust Company* (1990) was not (see section 19.4.2).

- The courts will deem certain executive actions to be *non-justiciable* (ie owing to its subject matter, it is not suitable for judicial resolution) and so not subject to judicial review. Historically, the *non-justiciable* subjects have included national security and national finance (see respectively: *R v Secretary of State for Home Affairs, ex parte Hosenball* (1977) (see section 6.7.10) and *Nottinghamshire County Council* (1986) at section 14.2.6).

- The remedies in judicial review are discretionary and so even though an individual may succeed in demonstrating that a public body has acted illegally, the court may nevertheless decline to give a remedy on the basis that if, for example, it quashed the decision it would cause administrative chaos.

Conflict between the judicial and executive arms of the constitution

Judicial review has inevitably increased constitutional tension between the judiciary and government ministers (see, D Blunkett, 'I won't give in to the judges', *Evening Standard*, 12th May 2003). In recent years, this has been further heightened with the passage of the Human Rights Act 1998 which has provided a further ground of review, namely that a minister has breached the European Convention. This is particularly ironic given that it was a Labour Government that drafted and oversaw the passage of the Human Rights Bill through Parliament.

ACTIVITY

Question

To what extent do you think that judicial review is controversial? Re-visit this question after you have completed Chapter 20.

19.2.5 A special 'administrative court'?

In the context of the rule of law (see section 6.7.6), it was pointed out that Dicey contrasted our constitution with that of France where disputes between French citizens and government officials were processed in special tribunals (*tribunaux administratifs*) which were separate from the main court system. Instead, Dicey preferred our constitutional arrangements whereby state officials were held to account before the ordinary courts like any other individual. This view, however, must be revised in the light of the modern development and nature of judicial review proceedings which in the following respects is similar to the French system of administrative law (*droit administratif*):

- In 2000, a Practice Direction was issued in which the Crown Office List was renamed the Administrative Court in the context of judicial review proceedings. This court is staffed by specialist judges conversant with the principles of judicial review and administrative law. Judicial review is a highly specialist field of law.

- Under the 'exclusivity' principle (see section 19.5) if a claimant wishes to challenge the misuse of public law powers by a public body, they must use the exclusive judicial review procedure set out in the Civil Procedure Rules and the Supreme Court Act 1981. In other words, an individual will not be permitted to use the ordinary court system in order to assert public law rights.

- In judicial review proceedings the courts apply special administrative principles (eg the responsibility of the public body to act rationally and to follow the precepts of natural justice). These are principles which purely private bodies and individuals do not generally have to follow (but note section 19.3.4).

KEY FACTS

Constitutional concept	The connection with judicial review
The rule of law	It upholds the rule of law by ensuring that public bodies do not exceed their legal powers.
The separation of powers	It forms part of the checks and balances on the actions of the executive.
Parliamentary sovereignty	It upholds parliamentary sovereignty by ensuring that public bodies act within their powers allocated by Parliament.

CONTINUED ▸

KEY FACTS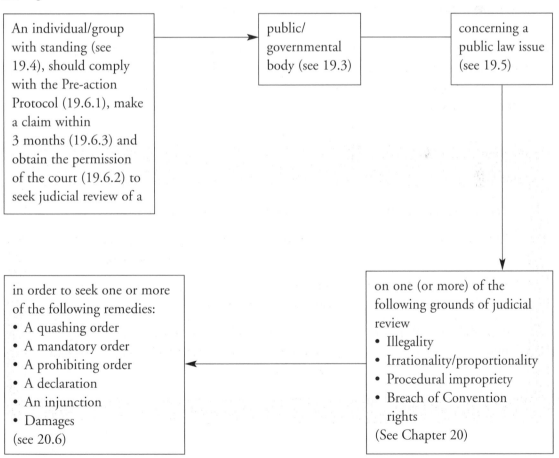

The protection of human rights	Under the Human Rights Act 1998 public authorities can be subject to judicial review if they disregard Convention rights.
The control of the exercise of public law powers	It is a legal control on the misuse of public law powers.

19.2.6 The mechanics of judicial review

The basic mechanics of judicial review are illustrated by the following figure:

■ Figure 19.2

An individual/group with standing (see 19.4), should comply with the Pre-action Protocol (19.6.1), make a claim within 3 months (19.6.3) and obtain the permission of the court (19.6.2) to seek judicial review of a

→ public/ governmental body (see 19.3)

→ concerning a public law issue (see 19.5)

↓

on one (or more) of the following grounds of judicial review
• Illegality
• Irrationality/proportionality
• Procedural impropriety
• Breach of Convention rights
(See Chapter 20)

←

in order to seek one or more of the following remedies:
• A quashing order
• A mandatory order
• A prohibiting order
• A declaration
• An injunction
• Damages
(see 20.6)

19.3 Bodies subject to judicial review

Which bodies are subject to judicial review? In essence, judicial review is aimed chiefly at controlling government bodies/public authorities (public law bodies); although both non-governmental and inferior courts are also subject to review proceedings.

▇ Figure 19.3

Bodies subject to judicial review

governmental/public   some judicial   some non-governmental

19.3.1 Government/public bodies

The following governmental/public bodies are subject to judicial review:

- **Government ministers/departments:** In *ex parte Venables and Thompson* (1997) (see section 5.7.6) the House of Lords held that the Home Secretary had acted illegally by abusing his public law discretion. In fact, government ministers are regularly subject to challenges in judicial review.

- **Local authorities:** In *ex parte Times Newspapers Ltd* (1986) (see section 20.2.4) the court held that the banning of *The Times* newspaper from the libraries of three councils was unlawful.

- **Parole Board:** For an example, see section 19.2.1.

- **Devolved institutions/bodies**: The devolved institutions set up under the various devolution settlements are subject to judicial review proceedings – see Chapter 14.

19.3.2 Judicial bodies

The following inferior courts and tribunals are also subject to judicial review by the higher Administrative Court:

- **The Crown Court:** providing the issue is unconnected with a trial on indictment.

- **Magistrates' Court:** (*R v Hereford Magistrates' Court, ex parte Rowlands* [1998] 1 QB 110).

- **The Coroners' Court:** (*R v Greater Manchester Coroner, ex parte Tal* [1985] 1 QB 67).

- **Tribunals**: (*R v Immigration Appeal Tribunal, ex parte Singh* [1986]1 WLR 910 – see section 20.2.5).

NB The High/Administrative Court and above are not subject to judicial review.

19.3.3 Non-governmental bodies

Judicial review is also available to challenge certain non-governmental bodies. These are bodies which are not part of the government/administration *per se*, but which exercise *de facto* public law powers. In practice, therefore, although these bodies have not been established by the government or Parliament, they do nevertheless exercise powers which are analogous to governmental powers. The courts, therefore, in determining who is subject to review do not merely confine themselves to looking at the source of power (statutory or royal prerogative), but also consider the nature of it (ie is the power *de facto* governmental in nature?).

CASE EXAMPLE

R v Panel on Take-overs and Mergers, ex parte Datafin PLC [1987] 1 QB 815

Datafin PLC sought judicial review of the actions of the Panel on Take-overs and Mergers. The panel was not a government body and had not been established by an Act of Parliament or under the royal prerogative. In effect, it had been set up in the City of London in order to regulate the City Code on Take-overs and Mergers of companies (a system of self-regulation).

The Court of Appeal held that judicial review was adaptable. Its jurisdiction could be extended to a body which operated as part of a system which performed public law duties. The panel, though not a government body, was a powerful body which made important decisions in regulating the financial activity in the City of London. In this way the panel was treated as a *de facto* public body, although on the facts, however, there were no grounds in this case to judicially review its actions.

Contrast *ex parte Datafin* with the following cases where judicial review was denied:

CASE EXAMPLE

R v Disciplinary Committee of the Jockey Club, ex parte Aga Khan [1993] 2 All ER 853

The disciplinary committee of the Jockey Club disqualified the Aga Khan's horse which had won a major race. The latter sought judicial review of the committee's decision.

The Court of Appeal held that although the Jockey Club regulated horse racing in Britain which affected the public (eg race meetings had to be licensed by the Jockey Club and people connected to racing had to be licensed by, or registered with it), nevertheless, it was not subject to judicial review. According to the court the club was not a public body (in terms of its history, constitution or membership) and the powers it exercised were not governmental

CONTINUED ▶

in nature. In this case the powers of the Jockey Club derived from the agreement between the parties (ie with the Aga Khan) which gave rise to private rights which were enforceable by private law remedies. It should be noted that judicial review is a remedy of last resort, so the courts may decline judicial review where another legal remedy exists.

See also *R v Football Association Ltd, ex parte Football League Ltd* [1993] 2 All ER 833.

ASE EXAMPLE

R v Chief Rabbi of the United Hebrew Congregations of Great Britain and the Commonwealth, ex parte Wachmann [1993] 2 All ER 249

The High Court refused to subject the functions of the Chief Rabbi to the jurisdiction of judicial review. The court indicated that his functions were in essence spiritual and religious and were such that the government would not seek to discharge them in his absence.

A recent case in the context of the Human Rights Act 1998 is:

ASE EXAMPLE

R (on the application of West) v Lloyd's of London [2004] EWCA Civ 506

The Court of Appeal held that the actions of the Business Conduct Committee of Lloyd's were not amenable to judicial review. The decisions made by Lloyds were of a private nature and in terms of s 6 of the Human Rights Act 1998 it was not exercising public or governmental functions (contrast with *ex parte Datafin* (1987) above).

In short, if a non-governmental body exercises powers which are of a public nature and which are sufficiently governmental in nature (eg the government would have to exercise those powers if the body did not exist), then the court is more likely to declare that body is susceptible to judicial review. Where, however, the relationship between the claimant and the non-governmental body is essentially a commercial one governed, for example, by contract law, the court may decline the claim for judicial review on the basis that an alternative remedy in private law is open to the claimant.

19.3.4 Private bodies and administrative principles

Even if a (powerful) private non-governmental body is not held to be subject to judicial review, there appears to be some evidence that the courts in the context of private law proceedings may nevertheless subject these bodies to certain administrative principles (eg to act fairly and not capriciously). This appears to be the case in the context of some sporting activities: *Nagle v Feilden* [1966] 2 QB 633.

KEY FACTS

Bodies subject to judicial review:

- **Government bodies**

Government ministers, government departments, local authorities, devolved institutions, police authorities, etc are subject in principle to judicial review.

- **Non-governmental bodies**

These may be subject to judicial review providing their *de facto* powers are essentially governmental in nature and no other reasonable alternative remedy is available to the claimant (*ex parte Datafin* (1987)).

- **Purely private bodies/individuals**

These are not subject to judicial review, however, some powerful private bodies which effectively enjoy monopolistic power in an area affecting the public (eg sport) may well be subject to the administrative principles of acting fairly and not capriciously even in an area of private law (*Nagle v Feilden* (1966)).

19.4 Standing in judicial review

Who or what can seek judicial review? For a claimant (individual or group) to claim judicial review they must have sufficient interest (formerly known as *locus standi*) in the matter. In other words, there must be a connection between the claimant and the contested action of the public law body. From a constitutional perspective this ensures that those not affected by the action (eg 'mere busybodies') cannot seek judicial review as such claims would necessarily inflate the volume of claims and in doing so obstruct the process of administration.

The following have standing to seek judicial review:

■ Figure 19.4

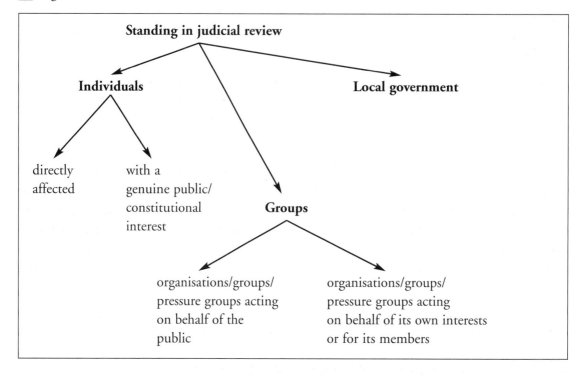

The following categories of standing draw upon those used in M Supperstone, J Goudie and Sir P Walker (eds) *Judicial Review* (3rd edn, LexisNexis Butterworths, 2005) Ch 17.

19.4.1 Individuals

- **Individuals directly affected by a public law decision**

Individuals have standing to seek judicial review where they have been directly or indirectly affected (financially or otherwise) by the actions of a public law body. For example, in *ex parte Binks* (1985) (see section 19.2.1), Binks was directly affected by the decision of the Wear Valley District Council to issue her with a notice to quit her take-away food caravan without prior notice or any accompanying reasons. In contrast, individual 'busybodies' (for example, a well meaning citizen who is upset on Binks's behalf) would not be able to apply for judicial review to challenge the District Council as they had not been directly affected.

- **Individuals with a genuine public/constitutional interest**

An exception to the 'mere busybody' rule above is that individuals who have a genuine constitutional interest in the actions of a public body may have standing to challenge it in judicial review.

CASE EXAMPLE

R v Secretary of State for Foreign and Commonwealth Affairs, ex parte Rees-Mogg
[1994] QB 552

Lord Rees-Mogg unsuccessfully sought judicial review of the Foreign Secretary seeking a declaration that the United Kingdom could not lawfully ratify the Maastricht Treaty. Although on the facts his claim failed, Lloyd LJ noted that there was no dispute as to standing: 'we accept without question that Lord Rees-Mogg brings the proceedings because of his sincere concern for constitutional issues'.

See also *R (Feakins) v Secretary of State for the Environment, Food and Rural Affairs* [2003] EWCA Civ 1546 which concerned a challenge to the Secretary of State's decision not to incinerate the residue of Feakins' burnt carcasses and those of other farms (burnt as a result of foot and mouth disease), but instead to dispose of them by landfill elsewhere. The Court of Appeal considered that on the facts Feakin had standing to challenge this decision as he was acting in the public interest and his motive was not improper.

Notwithstanding *ex parte Rees-Mogg* (1994), the line between a person with a genuine constitutional interest and a 'mere busybody' necessarily will be a fine one at times.

19.4.2 Organisations/groups/pressure groups

- **Organisations/groups/pressure groups acting on behalf of the public**

Groups/pressure groups or organisations may seek judicial review if they are a recognised body acting in the interests of the wider public (analogous to *ex parte Rees-Mogg* (1994) above). In essence, they are not acting in their own interest *per se,* but rather for the general public interest. As indicated at section 19.2.1, the pressure group World Development Movement Ltd successfully challenged the Foreign Secretary's decision to issue a grant to fund the Pergau Dam.

An early (rather restrictive) case involving groups is the following case:

CASE EXAMPLE

R v Secretary of State for the Environment, ex parte Rose Theatre Trust Co **[1990] 2 WLR 186**

A trust company (the Rose Theatre Trust Company) was established to preserve the remains of an historical theatre which were discovered during a development in London. They sought judicial review of the Secretary of State who had declined to register the theatre in the schedule of monuments pursuant to the Ancient Monuments and Archaeological Areas Act 1979. The court held that the company did not have standing in respect of the matter as members of the public had insufficient interest to be entitled to apply for judicial review.

The case of *ex parte Rose Theatre Trust Co* (1990) should be contrasted with the following two later cases:

CASE EXAMPLE

Equal Opportunities Commission and another v Secretary of State for Employment [1994] 1 All ER 910

The Equal Opportunities Commission was successful in obtaining a declaration that provisions of the Employment Protection (Consolidation) Act 1978 were contrary to European Community law as they indirectly discriminated against women. The House of Lords (by a majority) accepted that the EOC had standing as its statutory responsibility was to work towards eradicating sex discrimination.

CASE EXAMPLE

R v Inspectorate of Pollution and another, ex parte Greenpeace Ltd (No 2) [1994] 4 All ER 329

Greenpeace (a well known and respected pressure group on environmental issues) was granted standing to challenge the Inspectorate of Pollution's decision to vary authorisations concerning radioactive waste (although on the facts their claim failed). The court recognised that Greenpeace was a well established and respected pressure group with concern for the environment. It should also be noted that a number of Greenpeace members lived in the Sellafield area.

- **Organisations/groups/pressure groups acting on behalf of their own membership**

These groups would include for example, professional bodies and Trade Unions. See for example *R (Montpeliers and Trevors Association) and another v Westminster City Council* [2005] EWHC 16 Admin, where an association representing the residents of two squares in London successfully challenged a traffic order made by Westminster City Council which affected their residential areas.

Finally, in terms of groups, historically, one of the most significant cases concerning standing is *National Federation of Self-employed and Small Businesses*:

CASE EXAMPLE

IRC v National Federation of Self-employed and Small Businesses Ltd **[1982] AC 617**

The National Federation (representing small businesses and the self-employed) sought judicial review of the Inland Revenue in respect of its treatment of casual workers in Fleet Street (ie giving them an amnesty in terms of past tax which had not been paid). The National Federation sought a declaration that this was unlawful (as it differentiated between tax payers) and an order of mandamus to compel the Inland Revenue to assess and collect this outstanding income tax.

The House of Lords held that the National Federation did not have standing (the Court of Appeal had said that they did) as it was merely a body of taxpayers. One taxpayer (or group of tax payers like the Federation) did not have sufficient interest in asking the court to investigate the tax affairs of another.

The above case is also notable as the House of Lords made clear that although in obvious ('simple') cases the issue of standing could be definitively decided at the leave stage (when permission is being sought from the court to apply for judicial review – see section 19.6.2), standing should be decided at the substantive hearing where full (factual and legal) information would be available. As a result, although standing may be initially granted, it may be subsequently refused at the main hearing in the context of the merits of the case as a whole.

19.4.3 Local government

It must be remembered that judicial review also can be used by one aspect of the executive against another. For example, in *Nottinghamshire County Council v Secretary of State for the Environment* (1986), Nottinghamshire County Council sought (albeit unsuccessfully on the facts) judicial review of the Secretary of State's guidance in respect of local authority expenditure targets (see section 14.2.6).

ACTIVITY

Quick quiz

1. Who is subject to judicial review?

2. Who can seek judicial review?

19.5 A public law issue

19.5.1 Public law issues

Judicial review is concerned with public law issues and the enforcement of public law rights. It is not concerned with private matters and private law rights (eg contract and tort).

Not every action of a public body falls within the ambit of judicial review. In order to seek judicial review a claimant must raise an issue of public law. In essence, this will relate to how public law powers have been misused, misunderstood or misapplied. The Civil Procedure Rules, Pt 54.1(2)(a) states that judicial review is concerned with the lawfulness of:

(i) an enactment; or

(ii) a decision, action or failure to act in relation to the exercise of a public function.

For example, should a local authority breach its contract with an individual, the remedy lies in private contract law (a *private law* matter). Should the local authority, however, revoke a market licence without any prior notification or reasons etc, then the remedy lies in asserting a public law right (namely that of the requirement in natural justice to be treated fairly) in judicial review proceedings (a *public law* matter). In other words, the mere fact that the defendant is a public body is not sufficient on its own to bring the matter within the ambit of judicial review. The issue at stake has to involve a public law issue. As a result, in general terms the exercise of a statutory public law function will involve a public law issue.

19.5.2 Exclusive proceedings

If a claimant can demonstrate that a public law issue is at stake, in general terms he must use the special judicial review procedure (formerly under Order 53 and now governed by Pt 54 of the Civil Procedure Rules) to enforce this public law right. This procedure (see section 19.6) is hallmarked by certain characteristics, for example:

• The requirement of permission to seek judicial review.

• Short time limits.

It protects public law bodies by limiting the number of judicial review claims made and also prevents 'busybodies' from engaging in this process.

CASE EXAMPLE

O'Reilly v Mackman [1983] 2 AC 237

Four prisoners were charged with disciplinary offences in Hull Prison. The Board of Visitors found the charges proved and imposed penalties. The prisoners sought to challenge the Board alleging that it had breached the rules of natural justice, the fourth prisoner alleged bias. The prisoners did not use the judicial review procedure, but instead used private law proceedings (writ and originating summons).

The House of Lords confirmed the order to strike out these proceedings as they had used the wrong procedure. It would be contrary to public policy as well as an abuse of the court process for an individual to seek redress by ordinary private law action when it was contended that his public law rights (eg a breach of natural justice) had been violated. Lord Diplock stated:

> **J** 'My Lords, I have described this as a general rule … there may be exceptions, particularly where the invalidity of the decision arises as a collateral issue in a claim for infringement of a right of the plaintiff arising under private law, or where none of the parties objects to the adoption of the procedure by writ or originating summons.'

In essence, *O'Reilly* stands for the principle that the enforcement of public law rights should be through the judicial review procedure which, of course, protects the administration. This is known as the *exclusivity* principle. There are, however, some exceptions which are illustrated in the diagram below:

■ Figure 19.5

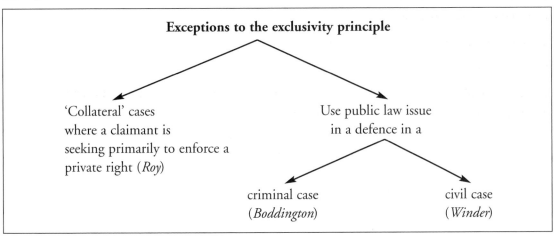

Exceptions to the exclusivity principle

'Collateral' cases where a claimant is seeking primarily to enforce a private right (*Roy*)

Use public law issue in a defence in a

criminal case (*Boddington*)

civil case (*Winder*)

19.5.3 Collateral cases

The judicial review procedure need not be used where the questioning of a public law decision is a collateral issue (ie incidental) to the enforcement of a private right.

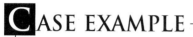ASE EXAMPLE

Roy v Kensington and Chelsea and Westminster Family Practitioner Committee [1992] 1 AC 624

Roy was a general practitioner who brought a private action against the Family Practitioner Committee for withholding payment of part of his basic practice allowance. The Committee sought to have the action struck out as an abuse of process on the basis that the challenge should have been made by way of judicial review. The House of Lords held that the bringing of an ordinary action to enforce a private law right was not an abuse of the court, even though it would involve a challenge to a public law decision.

In this case, Roy's purpose was to enforce a private law right to compensation and it was merely collateral that this also involved considering the validity of a public law decision (eg the Committee's finding that Roy had failed to devote a substantial amount of his time to general practice).

19.5.4 The use of a public law issue in an individual's defence

In *Roy* (1992) above, the claimant had initiated legal action. Sometimes however, an individual will be the defendant in legal proceedings commenced by another body. In these circumstances it appears that the validity of a public law decision/act (a public law issue) can be questioned in their defence.

- **A criminal prosecution**

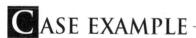ASE EXAMPLE

Boddington v British Transport Police [1999] 2 AC 143

Boddington was prosecuted under byelaw 20 of the Railways Byelaws 1965 (made under the Transport Act 1962) for smoking in a train carriage. The House of Lords stated that he was not prevented from raising in his defence the contention that the byelaw was *ultra vires* and unlawful (on the facts it was held that the railway company had not acted unlawfully in bringing into operation the byelaw as it did).

- **A civil case**

 ASE EXAMPLE

Wandsworth London Borough Council v Winder **[1985] 1 AC 461**

Wandsworth Council commenced legal proceedings in the County Court against Winder (a council tenant) for arrears of rent and possession of the flat. Winder had considered recent rent increases excessive and refused to pay these increases. In his defence he argued that the resolutions to increase the rents were *ultra vires* and void.

The House of Lords stated that (in the absence of clear words to the contrary) an individual had a right to challenge a local authority's decision in his defence. Winder had not, after all, initiated the action.

ACTIVITY

Quick quiz

1. What is a public law issue?
2. What is meant by the principle of exclusivity?
3. What is the purpose of this rule?

19.6 Procedure

In seeking judicial review special rules and principles apply. Formerly, judicial review was regulated by Order 53 Rules of the Supreme Court and the Supreme Court Act 1981. The former has now been replaced by Part 54 of the Civil Procedure Rules which came into force in 2000 and were added to in 2002 by the Pre-action Protocol.

The basic outline of the procedure is as follows:

19.6.1 The Pre-action Protocol and claim

Before commencing proceedings the claimant (formerly the applicant) should write to the public body identifying the issues at stake to which the defendant should reply. The purpose of the Pre-action Protocol is to avoid litigation and achieve a settlement. One of the problems with judicial review in recent years has been its popularity, which in turn has lengthened the time the court takes to process a claim. For example, in 2005 there were 5,381 applications for permission to apply for judicial review (*Judicial Statistics (Revised) England and Wales for the year 2005*, Cm 6903 (DCA, 2006) p 23). The Protocol can be departed from in a very urgent case.

Judicial review claims are brought before the Administrative Court. The claim form should state the action being challenged and the remedy sought.

19.6.2 Permission to apply for judicial review

Judicial review is not available as of *right* to a claimant, as the permission of the court is required to commence the action (formerly known as seeking leave to apply). This is one way in which judicial review differs from private law actions. This acts as a filter system whereby the courts can weed out vexatious claims with no foundation. This protects public bodies and facilitates good administration whereby the government is not unnecessarily hampered by unarguable/unrealistic claims. Judicial review is also a remedy of last resort so that if a claimant has an alternative remedy (eg a statutory appeal), he should avail himself of it instead.

Permission was formerly sought *ex parte* (in the absence of the other side), but today it is dealt with *inter parties* (both sides are present). This enables the court to be better informed about the whole nature of the matter.

> 'The precise test as to when permission should be granted has been variously stated but there is no doubt that at bottom the question is as to whether there is an arguable case, which merits full consideration at a substantive hearing'.
>
> R Drabble and T Buley in M Supperstone, J Goudie, Sir P Walker (eds),
> *Judicial Review* (3rd edn, LexisNexis Butterworths, 2005), p 551.

19.6.3 The time limit

Claims for judicial review must be made *promptly*. In any event, they must be made 'not later than three months after the grounds to make the claim first arose' (Pt 54.5(1)). This is another hallmark of judicial review which distinguishes it from private law actions as the time to make a claim is very short. The purpose of this is twofold:

- It protects public bodies (and the administrative process) as such bodies know three months after their action/decision it will not ordinarily be subject to judicial review.

- If a public body is acting illegally (which has consequences for the public), then in accordance with the rule of law it is of paramount importance that it is legally constrained from doing so as soon as is possible.

19.6.4 The substantive hearing

At the substantive hearing the court will determine whether or not the defendant has infringed one or more of the grounds of judicial review (see Chapter 20 for the grounds). At this stage it can also reconsider whether the claimant has standing. The substantive hearing typically involves the consideration of documentary evidence, and the burden (civil burden of proof) rests on the claimant to prove unlawful action. If proven, the court may or may not issue a remedy (see section 20.6.2).

KEY FACTS

An overview of the judicial review procedure	
Pre-action Protocol	This must be complied with before a claim is made.
The claim	Is brought before the Administrative Court.
Permission required	Judicial review is not a remedy as of right.
Time limit	The claim must be made promptly (within three months).
Standing	The claimant must have sufficient interest in the matter.
Public body	The claim must be sought against a public body.
Public law issue	The claim must concern a public law issue (public law rights).
Substantative hearing	The Administrative Court will determine whether a public body has acted unlawfully and if so, may provide a remedy (see Chapter 20).

Further reading

Barnett, H, *Constitutional and Administrative Law* (6th edn, Routledge-Cavendish, 2006), Chapter 26.

Budge, I, Crewe, I, McKay, D and Newton, K, *The New British Politics* (Addison Wesley Longman, 1998), Chapter 11.

Forsyth, C, 'Of fig leaves and fairy tales: The ultra vires doctrine, the sovereignty of parliament and judicial review' [1996] CLJ 122.

Horne, A and Berman, G, 'Judicial Review: A short guide to claims in the Administrative Court', 06/44, (House of Commons Library, 2006).

Laws, Sir J, 'Is the High Court the Guardian of Fundamental Constitutional Rights?' [1993] PL 59.

Leyland, P and Anthony, G, *Textbook on Administrative Law* (5th edn, Oxford University Press, 2005), Chapter 9.

Oliver, D, 'Is the ultra vires rule the basis of judicial review?' [1987] PL 543.

Weir, S and Beetham, D, *Political Power and Democratic Control in Britain* (Routledge, 1999), Chapter 15.

Woolf, Lord 'Judicial review – the tensions between the executive and the judiciary' (1998) 114 LQR 579.

chapter
20 JUDICIAL REVIEW II (GROUNDS OF REVIEW AND REMEDIES) ■

AIMS AND OBJECTIVES □□□

At the end of this chapter you should be able to

■ Identify and explain the different grounds of judicial review

■ Distinguish between those grounds

■ Identify those remedies that are available for a successful judicial review claim

■ Assess the effectiveness of judicial review as a public law remedy

20.1 Grounds for judicial review

Judicial review can be sought on a number of different grounds. In *Council of Civil Service Unions v Minister for the Civil Service* [1985] 1 AC 374 (commonly known as the *GCHQ* case) Lord Diplock took the opportunity to re-classify the existing grounds of review in the following terms (in doing so he, in effect, provided a codification of them):

> J   'Judicial review has I think developed to a stage today when without reiterating any analysis of the steps by which the development has come about, one can conveniently classify under three heads the grounds upon which administrative action is subject to control by judicial review. The first ground I would call "illegality", the second "irrationality" and the third "procedural impropriety".'

According to Lord Diplock there were essentially three different grounds of judicial review, although he noted that proportionality may be developed at a later date (this has now occurred with the advent of the Human Rights Act 1998 – see section 20.4). It must be emphasised that these three grounds should not be viewed as rigid categories which are mutually exclusive from each other as it is possible for a claimant to argue that the actions of a public law body involve more than one ground of review.

In 2007, the different grounds of judicial review can be illustrated as follows:

■ Figure 20.1

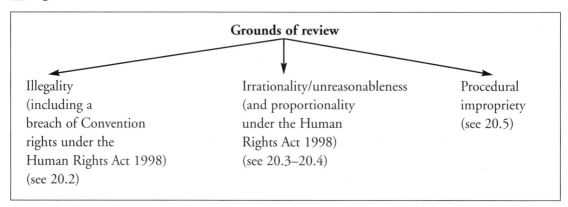

20.2 The ground of illegality

20.2.1 Definition and classification

The ground of illegality has a number of different aspects to it and was defined by Lord Diplock in *Council of Civil Service Unions v Minister for the Civil Service* [1985] 1 AC 374 in the following way.

> **J** By 'illegality' as a ground for judicial review I mean that the decision-maker must understand correctly the law that regulates his decision-making power and must give effect to it.

Illegality can be further broken down into the following elements – the decision-maker has acted illegally because he has:

- Acted in an *ultra vires* way, that is beyond his powers (simple *ultra vires*).
- Misinterpreted his public law powers (excess of jurisdiction).
- Wrongly delegated his legal powers (wrongful delegation).
- Acted for an improper purpose (improper/ulterior purpose).
- Abused his discretion by failing to exercise it at all, or he has considered irrelevant factors and/or ignored relevant ones (an abuse of discretion).
- Acted in a way which is incompatible with the rights in the European Convention on Human Rights (the Human Rights Act 1998).

In essence, the ground of illegality is concerned with the misinterpretation or wrongful application of public law powers. These categories are not rigidly demarcated however, for example, a public body which takes into account an irrelevant factor may also act for an improper purpose at the same time.

■ Figure 20.2

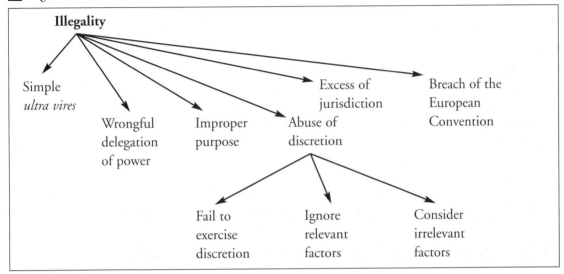

Illegality

Simple *ultra vires*

Wrongful delegation of power

Improper purpose

Abuse of discretion

Excess of jurisdiction

Breach of the European Convention

Fail to exercise discretion

Ignore relevant factors

Consider irrelevant factors

20.2.2 Simple *ultra vires*

The principle of *ultra vires* means acting beyond and exceeding legal powers. For example, if A has been conferred with the legal power to do X, when he does X he acts *intra vires* (within his powers), but if he does Y instead, he acts *ultra vires*. The concept of *ultra vires* is associated with the intention of Parliament and so an action not authorised by the statute (eg Y above) is unlawful. As indicated previously (see section 19.2.4), however, the concept of *ultra vires* alone cannot explain the ambit and nature of judicial review.

CASE EXAMPLE

R v Secretary of State for the Home Department, ex parte Leech [1993] 4 All ER 539

Under s 47(1) Prison Act 1952 the Secretary of State could make rules in order to regulate and manage prisons. Leech (a prisoner) successfully sought judicial review of r 33(3) of the Prison Rules 1964 which enabled a prison governor to read letters to and from a prisoner and stop any letter which was of inordinate length or objectionable. Leech argued that this rule allowed the reading and stopping of correspondence between a prisoner and his legal adviser where no legal proceedings were pending.

CONTINUED ▶

The Court of Appeal granted a declaration that r 33(3) was *ultra vires* the enabling Act (s 47(1) of the Prison Act 1952). It could not have been Parliament's intention to impede a prisoner's right of access to the courts (via his legal adviser).

CASE EXAMPLE

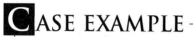

***Attorney-General v Fulham Corporation* [1921] 1 Ch 440**

Fulham Corporation, purporting to act under powers under the Baths and Wash-houses Acts 1846–78, established a laundry which involved customers bringing their clothes to the wash-house to be washed. These clothes were then washed by the employees of the Corporation and returned to the customers.

It was held that this scheme was *ultra vires* as it was not authorised by the Baths and Wash-houses Acts 1846–78. These Acts authorised the establishment of wash-houses whereby people could use the facilities to wash their own clothes. Instead, Fulham Corporation had created a laundry which was an entirely different enterprise and not authorised by the 1846–78 legislation.

See also *London County Council v Attorney-General* [1902] AC 165.

In addition, earlier examples of the use of *ultra vires* which we have already encountered in the text include the following:

* *Chester v Bateson* (1920) – where reg 2A(2) was held *ultra vires* the Defence of the Realm (Consolidation) Act 1914 for obstructing access to the courts (see section 5.7.2).

* *Commissioners of Customs and Excise v Cure & Deeley Ltd* (1962) – where reg 12 was held *ultra vires* the Finance (No 2) Act 1940 as it, in effect, purported to confer on to the Commissioners of Customs and Excise the powers of a judge and which ousted the courts' jurisdiction (see section 6.7.5).

* *R v Lord Chancellor, ex parte Witham* (1997) – where the Supreme Court Fees (Amendment) Order 1996 was held *ultra vires* the Supreme Court Act 1981 for precluding a person's access to the courts (see section 4.8.3).

The 'fairly incidental rule'

Although the *ultra vires* principle states that a public body may not do that which is not *expressly* authorised, in practice the courts have also permitted actions which are 'fairly incidental' to these expressly authorised powers.

CASE EXAMPLE

Attorney-General v Crayford Urban District Council [1962] 2 All ER 147

Crayford UDC made arrangements with an insurance company for council tenants to be able to insure their effects. This sum was collected at the same time as the council rent.

The Court of Appeal upheld the scheme as *intra vires* as acts of general management within s 111 of the Housing Act 1957. In short, if council tenants were uninsured, should they suffer loss (ie by virtue of fire or storm) then they were more likely to default on their council rent to make up the loss, than if they were insured against such loss. As a result, the council was helping to ensure the payment of council rents and so by implication were allowed to act as they did.

Furthermore, Parliament has recognised that local authorities should not be confined strictly to only those actions explicitly authorised – s 111 Local Government Act 1972 states that local authorities shall be empowered to do anything:

… which is calculated to facilitate, or is conducive or incidental to, the discharge of any of their functions.

CASE EXAMPLE

McCarthy & Stone Ltd v Richmond Upon Thames London Borough Council [1992] 2 AC 48

Richmond Borough Council levied a charge on developers in respect of inquiries concerning speculative development proposals.

The House of Lords held that the above charge for pre-application advice was unlawful. In terms of s 111 of the Local Government Act 1972, the charge for such advice did not facilitate (nor was it conducive or incidental to) the council's functions of considering and determining applications for planning.

See also *Hazell v Hammersmith and Fulham London Borough Council* [1992] 2 AC 1.

20.2.3 Wrongful delegation of power

As a general constitutional principle, if public law powers are conferred on A (eg delegated to A by Parliament), they should not be delegated (or sub-delegated) to B.

■ Figure 20.3

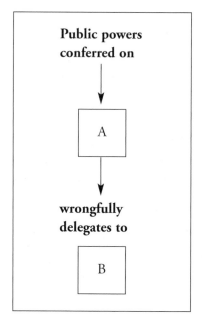

The constitutional consequences of this is twofold:

• A does not fulfill his public law obligation to exercise the power conferred on him (he may well have been delegated that power because of his expertise).

• The wrong person in law (ie B) is exercising public law powers.

This principle is encapsulated in the legal maxim: '*delegatus non potest delegare*' (the delegate is not permitted to delegate).

CASE EXAMPLE

Allingham and another v Minister of Agriculture and Fisheries [1948] 1 KB 780

A county war agricultural executive committee (which itself had been lawfully delegated powers by the Minister of Agriculture and Fisheries) decided that a number of acres of sugar beet should be grown by the owners of certain land. The committee, however, delegated to its executive officer the selection of the exact field on which to grow the sugar beet. It was held that the committee could not delegate its power to determine the land to be used and cultivated.

Whether a body can delegate powers is a matter of statutory construction for the court to determine. For example, the Act may expressly authorise delegation. Where, however, the Act is silent as to delegation, the courts will consider the nature, purpose and context of the powers. For example:

- Is the power a judicial or quasi-judicial one?
- Is the power purely administrative (eg involving simply the collation of information)?
- Has the power been conferred on a government minister?
- Would delegation be in the public interest and would it cause injustice?

Judicial/quasi-judicial powers

Where the power is essentially a judicial or quasi-judicial power, the courts are reluctant to allow delegation. Lord Parker CJ, in *R v Governor of Brixton Prison, ex parte Enahoro* [1963] 2 QB 455 stated that:

> **J** 'It is well settled that certainly no person made responsible for a judicial decision can delegate his responsibility.'

 CASE EXAMPLE

Barnard and Others v National Dock Labour Board and Another [1953] 1 All ER 1113

The Dock Workers (Regulation of Employment) Order 1947 established the National Dock Labour Board which in turn was authorised to delegate specified disciplinary functions, including the power of suspension, to local dock boards (an example of an express authorisation to delegate). The secretary of a local board suspended Barnard and others with the power to do so being purportedly delegated by the local board. The Court of Appeal held that the power of suspension was a judicial/quasi-judicial function (it affected a person's rights) which could not be delegated by the local board. The suspensions were declared a nullity.

See also *Vine v National Dock Labour Board* [1957] AC 488, where a local dock labour board wrongfully delegated their disciplinary powers to a disciplinary committee which had terminated Vine's employment. This dismissal was therefore invalid due to the delegation of a quasi-judicial function.

Administrative powers

Where a power is not judicial, but merely consists of, for example, the collection of evidence, fact-finding or a preliminary investigation, then the courts have held delegation to be permissible (in this context see: *Jeffs v New Zealand Dairy Production and Marketing Board* [1967] AC 551 and *R v Race Relations Board, ex parte Selvarajan* [1975] 1 WLR 1686).

Government ministers

The courts have recognised the practical reality of government administration, that it is not practically possible for a government minister to exercise every single power conferred on him. Lord Greene MR, in *Carltona Ltd v Commissioners of Works* [1943] 2 All ER 560 (see section 4.13.12), stated that:

> J 'the functions which are given to ministers … are functions so multifarious that no minister could ever personally attend to them … The duties imposed upon ministers and the powers given to ministers are normally exercised under the authority of the ministers by responsible officials of the department. Public business could not be carried on if that were not the case.'

In fact, for the purposes of the decision the official becomes the *alter ego* of the minister and therefore in reality there is no real delegation. Moreover, the minister must select an appropriate official of sufficient experience and expertise:

CASE EXAMPLE

R v Secretary of State for the Home Department, ex parte Oladehinde [1991] 1 AC 254

The Home Secretary delegated to officials (of not less than inspector level) the power to make decisions, on his behalf, to deport persons under the Immigration Act 1971. Oladehinde was served with a notice of an intention to deport and he sought judicial review to quash the decision on the basis that the Home Secretary had wrongfully delegated his power under the Act to immigration inspectors.

The House of Lords held that the minister was entitled to authorise responsible officials to exercise his powers. The officials (immigration inspectors) were of suitable grading and experience to exercise these powers.

It should also be remembered that the minister will remain constitutionally accountable to Parliament for his decisions (whether or not he took them personally). Furthermore, in some cases delegation may be prohibited where a statute specifically requires the minister personally (and no other person) to take the decision. For example, s 13(5) of the Immigration Act 1971 refers to directions having 'been given by the Secretary of State (and not by a person acting under his authority)'.

ACTIVITY

Self-test questions:

1. What is meant by action which is *ultra vires*?

2. What is meant by unlawful delegation of power?

3. When is it permissible to delegate a power?

20.2.4 Improper purpose

A public law power should be exercised for the purpose that it has been conferred. If a power has been conferred in order for a public body to achieve purpose X, it will be unlawful for that power to be used to achieve purpose Y. In short, public power should not be used with an ulterior motive/purpose in mind, as this is an abuse of power (this area, therefore, could arguably also fall under section 20.2.5).

CASE EXAMPLE

Congreve v Home Office [1976] 1 All ER 697

In 1975 the cost of a colour television licence was increased from £12 to £18. In order to avoid paying this increase Congreve (along with others) renewed his licence early. The Home Office became aware of this and with the anticipated loss of revenue, Congreve and others were informed that unless they paid the £6 difference, their licences would be revoked.

The Court of Appeal held that the licence which Congreve had obtained lawfully was valid and the demand for payment was an unlawful exercise of power. Lord Denning MR held that the Home Secretary must use his statutory power to revoke licences under the Wireless Telegraphy Act 1949 in accordance with the law, that is to say not being influenced by ulterior/improper motives (eg want of money). It would be different if an individual had breached the conditions of the licence (a proper purpose).

Similarly, in *Porter v Magill* [2001] UKHL 67, the House of Lords held that a local authority could dispose of land under s 32 of the Housing Act 1985 to achieve proper housing objectives, but not for promoting an electoral advantage of a party on the council (an improper purpose). The case concerned the sale of council houses and the belief that owner-occupiers were more likely to vote Conservative as a result of these sales.

CASE EXAMPLE

R v Ealing London Borough Council, ex parte Times Newspapers Ltd and others (1986) 85 LGR 316

Under the Public Libraries and Museums Act 1964 it is the duty of a library authority to provide a comprehensive and efficient library service. As a result of an industrial dispute between *The Times* newspaper and their former employees, three councils banned copies of these newspapers in their library. *The Times* successfully sought judicial review of these decisions. The court held that the ban was imposed for an ulterior object (to be used as a weapon against *The Times* in their industrial dispute) and so declared it to be unlawful.

In *Wheeler v Leicester City Council* [1985] 1 AC 1054 Leicester City Council passed a resolution which prevented Leicester Football Club from using the council's recreational grounds for one year (the council considered that Leicester Football Club had failed to discourage three of its players from playing in an England Rugby tour of South Africa during the apartheid era and should have condemned the tour). The House of Lords held that the council had *inter alia*, misused its powers, as although under s 71 of the Race Relations Act 1976 it had the power to consider race relations when exercising its powers, Leicester Football Club had not acted improperly or broken any law. In this context also see *R v Lewisham London Borough Council, ex parte Shell UK Ltd* [1988] 1 All ER 938. An interesting case involving the rule of law is detailed below:

CASE EXAMPLE

R v Coventry City Council, ex parte Phoenix Aviation and others [1995] 3 All ER 37

Judicial review applications were sought against public authorities operating air and sea ports as to whether lawfully, they could ban the transportation of livestock so as to avoid the consequences of unlawful protests by animal rights protestors. It was held that the air and sea ports had to remain open to traffic and the trade in livestock. In terms of their concern about the actions of the protestors, Simon Brown LJ commented:

> J
>
> 'One thread runs consistently throughout all the case law: the recognition that public authorities must beware of surrendering to the dictates of unlawful pressure groups. The implications of such surrender for the rule of law can hardly be exaggerated ... Tempting though it may sometimes be for public authorities to yield too readily to threats of disruption, they must expect the courts to review any such decision with particular rigour.'

20.2.5 Abuse of discretion

A public law discretion (the conferment of a power to act) should not be abused by a public law decision-maker. Abuse of discretion is a generic term which covers a number of unlawful actions which include:

- Failing to use or fettering a discretion.

- Ignoring relevant factors.

- Taking irrelevant factors into consideration.

In fact, it could also be argued that acting for an improper purpose (see section 20.2.4) is also an abuse of discretion. As indicated earlier, there are no rigid sub-categories within illegality. For example, it could be argued that by wrongfully delegating a power (section 20.2.3), a public decision-maker has failed to exercise his public law discretion because he has divested himself of it altogether.

Although a statute may provide that a public body can make a decision *as it thinks fit* the courts have adopted the approach that this does not mean that the public body can make *literally any* decision *it thinks fit*. Instead, the courts will imply certain limitations, as they do not accept the notion of an absolute or complete discretion. This is consistent with the rule of law (see section 6.7.5) as although public law discretion is a valuable tool in public administration, if the use of the discretion is not structured and controlled, it is akin to an arbitrary power.

Failing to use (or fettering) a discretion

If a public decision-maker has been conferred with a public law discretion he should consider whether to exercise it:

CASE EXAMPLE

Padfield v Minister of Agriculture, Fisheries and Food [1968] AC 997

Under the Agricultural Marketing Act 1958 the minister had a power/discretion to send (in any case he so directed) complaints arising out of the operation of the milk marketing scheme to a committee of investigation. Padfield, and others, asked the minister to appoint a committee to investigate their complaint (ie to refer their complaint to a committee of investigation) but the minister refused.

The House of Lords held that an order of *mandamus* should be made directing the minister to consider Padfield's complaint according to the law. The minister had argued that under the Act he had, in effect, a complete discretion in respect of whether or not to refer a complaint. The House of Lords held, however, that his discretion was not unlimited as it was conferred on him so that he could promote the policy of the Act (ie substantial and genuine complaints concerning the milk marketing scheme were to be investigated). Furthermore, the minister had been concerned about the political repercussions of referring this complaint (according to Lord Upjohn a 'fear of parliamentary trouble') thereby also indicating an ulterior motive (see section 20.2.4).

This case illustrates that the courts will not recognise absolute discretion. It should be remembered that public decision-makers are exercising public law powers which can directly or indirectly affect millions of people. The *Padfield* case was, however, a somewhat pyrrhic victory as although following the court case the complaint was referred, the minister subsequently disregarded the recommendations of the committee.

For another example of a minister failing to use his discretion see *ex parte Fire Brigades Union* (1995) (see section 6.7.10).

Public law decision-makers can also abuse their discretion if they unnecessarily restrict the circumstances in which they will use it (eg they adopt an overly-rigid or blanket policy which affects an individual). In this way the decision maker is fettering his discretion by refusing to exercise it when new or exceptional circumstances arise. Lord Reid, in *British Oxygen Co Ltd v Minister of Technology* [1971] AC 610 stated that:

> **J** 'What the authority must not do is to refuse to listen at all. But a Ministry or large authority may have had to deal already with a multitude of similar applications and then they will almost certainly have evolved a policy so precise that it could well be called a rule. There can be no objection to that, provided the authority is always willing to listen to anyone with something new to say.'

The point here is that it is common in public administration for administrators to adopt general guidelines to assist them in making decision-making more efficient (this is a 'structuring' of a discretion – see section 6.7.5). However, the adoption of an over-rigid policy, excluding any exceptions in any circumstances, could be challenged by a claimant affected by it.

Relevancy and irrelevancy

In making public law decisions a public decision maker will necessarily have to consider a number of different factors. In public law a decision-maker must:

- Consider *relevant* factors and
- Disregard *irrelevant* factors.

Relevant factors

A decision-maker must consider relevant factors:

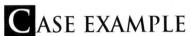

ASE EXAMPLE

R v Immigration Appeal Tribunal, ex parte Singh [1986] 1 WLR 910

The House of Lords held that an immigration adjudicator in deciding whether or not to deport Singh had ignored a relevant factor: that third party interests might be relevant. Singh was a talented musician who had performed the functions of a priest in the Sikh community and so his deportation would have had an impact upon that community.

Similarly, in *Bromley London Borough Council v GLC* [1983] AC 768 the House of Lords held that the Greater London Council (GLC) should have had regard to the interest of ratepayers in implementing its reduced fares scheme.

Irrelevant factors

In some respects the issue of a public body taking into account irrelevant factors can blur into the ground of acting for an improper purpose. For example, if a public decision-maker in exercising a discretion has an ulterior motive in mind, he is also necessarily taking into account an irrelevant factor (eg the ulterior motive).

Below are some examples involving the consideration of irrelevant factors:

ASE EXAMPLE

R v Somerset County Council, ex parte Fewings [1995] 3 All ER 20

The council passed a resolution banning deer hunting over its land as the majority of councillors viewed the activity as morally repulsive. In the Divisional Court Laws J held that the council could not ban hunting on the basis that it was morally repugnant, as this was a free-standing moral perception and not an objective judgment as to what would 'conduce to the better management' of their lands as required by s 120 of the Local Government Act 1972. According to Laws, the councillors' moral view on hunting had 'nothing whatever to do with such questions' (ie it was an irrelevant factor).

The Court of Appeal affirmed Laws' decision that the hunting ban was unlawful (albeit on other grounds). The court held that the council had not exercised its power in order to promote the benefit of its area as, for one thing, it had not even considered the statutory provision of s 120. It is of interest to note that Sir Thomas Bingham MR and Simon Brown LJ indicated that it could not be said that the 'cruelty' argument was necessarily irrelevant to the question as to what is for the benefit of the area.

In addition, as noted earlier in *ex parte Venables and Thompson* (1997) at section 5.7.6, the House of Lords held that the Home Secretary had misdirected himself in law by considering an irrelevant consideration (public protest concerning the sentences to be imposed in respect of these two particular individuals). Moreover, he had ignored relevant factors (ie the progress and development of Venables and Thompson whilst they were detained).

This aspect of judicial review can be somewhat controversial as the judges are, in effect, determining which factors are relevant. As noted by Forbes J, however, judges are not concerned with whether due or proper weight is given to any particular material consideration/factor (*Pickwell v Camden London Borough Council* [1983] 1 All ER 602). Nevertheless, the controversial nature of this ground is illustrated by the area of financial considerations concerning the 'duties' of local authorities to provide services:

CASE EXAMPLE

R v Gloucestershire County Council, ex parte Barry [1997] AC 584

Barry's cleaning and laundry services had been withdrawn because of financial resources. The House of Lords held (by a majority) that, in effect, financial considerations (ie the cost of care and the availability of resources) might be proper factors for a local authority to consider in assessing an individual's need for a service under the Chronically Sick and Disabled Persons Act 1970.

In contrast, however, in *R v East Sussex County Council, ex parte Tandy* [1998] 2 All ER 769, the House of Lords held that the availability of resources was *not* a consideration in the context of the provision of suitable education (in the case – special educational needs) under the Education Act 1993.

20.2.6 Excess of jurisdiction

Jurisdiction refers to the power of a body to act, for example, if a local authority is empowered to provide a service or exercise a discretion. In terms of jurisdiction it is possible for a public body to make either a:

- Mistake of fact or a
- Mistake of law.

Mistake of fact

In broad terms the courts in judicial review proceedings will not interfere when a body makes a mistake of fact (ie they get factual details wrong). This is because

- They take the view that the specified public body has been conferred with the responsibility of determining facts.
- Judges are experts in law and not facts.
- Judicial review would become overwhelmed with cases involving public bodies that had made factual errors.

- The nature of judicial review proceedings is not particularly amenable to investigating disputed facts (eg there is a limited use of cross-examination).

There are, however, some mistakes of fact that the courts will subject to review:

- Precedent facts.
- Facts which have no supporting evidence.

Precedent facts

The courts will interfere where the fact is a 'precedent fact' or 'jurisdictional fact' in that its existence is necessary in order for the public body to act. In other words, certain facts must be correctly established before the body can act, as these facts are central to the decision-maker's power.

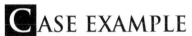

CASE EXAMPLE

R v Secretary of State for the Home Department, ex parte Khawaja [1984] 1 AC 74

The House of Lords held that the existence of the power to detain Khawaja (with a view to deportation) under the Immigration Act 1971 depended upon him being an 'illegal entrant'. This was a precedent fact which had to be satisfied and it was the duty of the court to inquire whether there had been sufficient/adequate evidence to justify and support the immigration officer's belief that entry into the United Kingdom had been illegal.

In other words, the existence of some facts are so fundamental that they trigger the public law power of a public body to act. Similarly, in *White and Collins v Minister of Health* [1939] 2 KB 838 a local authority was not permitted to compulsorily purchase land which was part of a park. In this case the land was factually held to be part of a park and so the compulsory purchase order was quashed.

Facts which have no supporting evidence

This concerns the position whereby a public body makes a decision regarding a fact for which there is objectively no supporting evidence to support that factual finding. Lord Denning MR, in *Ashbridge Investments Ltd v Minister of Housing and Local Government* [1965] 3 All ER 371 stated that:

> J 'the Minister must himself decide the question of 'house or not a house', just as he must decide 'fit or unfit'. The legislature has entrusted it to the Minister for decision … it seems to me that the court can interfere with the Minister's decision if he has acted on no evidence; or if he has come to a conclusion to which, on the evidence, he could not reasonably come.'

Mistake of law

The courts are less reluctant to review errors of law. An error of law refers to a body misinterpreting its legal powers by misunderstanding the statutory provisions which enable it to act. It should be noted that not every interpretation of a word will involve an error of law. Lord Reid, in *Brutus v Cozens* [1973] AC 854 noted that:

> J
> 'The meaning of an ordinary word of the English language is not a question of law. The proper construction of a statute is a question of law. If the context shows that a word is used in an unusual sense the court will determine in other words what that unusual sense is.'

According to Barnett (*Constitutional and Administrative Law*, 6th edn, Routledge-Cavendish 2006, p 758) one form of an error of law is the wrongful interpretation of a word to which a legal meaning has been attached. Historically, the issue of the court reviewing errors of law has generated some highly complex case law with the seminal case being *Anisminic Ltd* (1969):

CASE EXAMPLE

Anisminic Ltd v Foreign Compensation Commission [1969] 2 AC 147

Under the Foreign Compensation Act 1950 the Foreign Compensation Commission was charged with the responsibility of determining claims of compensation in respect of British property which had been seized or destroyed during the Suez crisis in 1956. Anisminic was a British company (whose property had been sequestrated by the Egyptian authorities) which appeared to satisfy the criteria required to claim compensation (in 1957 Anisminic sold the sequestrated property to an Egyptian organisation). The Commission rejected Anisminic's claim. Section 4 of the Act stated that a determination of the Commission could not be called into question by a court of law. In other words, this was an 'ouster clause' (which ousted the jurisdiction of the courts) which left the final decision with the Commission.

The House of Lords, however, held that the Commission had, in determining Anisminic's claim, asked itself in law the wrong question by misconstruing its responsibilities. In short, the Commission had asked whether the successor in title to Anisminic's property was British (on the facts it was an Egyptian organisation), rather than simply: was the applicant (and original owner of Anisminic) British? Thus, the court held that the Commission had gone outside its jurisdiction and as a result the ouster clause of s 4 did not apply as the Commission had not made a 'determination', but had merely purported to do so.

The case indicates that the courts will intervene where a public decision-maker has misunderstood its legal powers. In addition, it indicates the courts' resistance to 'ouster clauses' (see section 19.2.4).

Following *Anisminic Ltd* (1969) a number cases (eg *Pearlman v Keepers and Governors of Harrow School* [1979] 1 QB 56, *Re Racal Communications Ltd* [1981] AC 374 and *R v Lord President of the Privy Council, ex parte Page* [1992] 3 WLR 1112) clarified the courts' position in respect of errors of law. Today the courts are concerned that public bodies properly interpret their public law powers. It may well be that a statutory appeal may be available where a body commits an error of law, but failing that, the courts will now review an error of law regarding them as 'jurisdictional errors of law'.

Craig (*Administrative Law* (5th edn, Sweet & Maxwell, 2003), pp 499–500) helpfully has set out the modern position as follows:

- The courts will review an error of law although the error must be a relevant/material one.
- If a tribunal/administrative body has made an error of law, the courts adopt the presumption that Parliament did not intend that body to be the definitive arbiter in respect of an issue of law and so will subject it to review. After all, such bodies are not necessarily experts in the law (however, tribunals may contain experts which routinely deal with specialist areas).
- If an inferior court (eg Magistrates' Court or County Court) has made an error of law, there is no presumption that Parliament did not intend the issue of law to be left to the inferior court.

It should be remembered that in terms of the higher courts, these are not subject to judicial review in any case.

Mistake of law and fact

In terms of a mistake of a mixture of law and fact, the courts will be unlikely to interfere unless it is an aberrant interpretation. For example, in *South Yorkshire Transport Ltd* (below) the House of Lords held that the Monopolies Commission's interpretation of the term 'in a substantial part of the United Kingdom' in the context of s 64 of the Fair Trading Act 1973 (a mixture of law and fact) would be upheld as it was within the permissible field of judgment open to it. Lord Mustill, in *South Yorkshire Transport Ltd and another v Monopolies and Mergers Commission and another* [1993] 1 All ER 289 noted that:

> J 'the criterion so established may itself be so imprecise that different decision-makers, each acting rationally, might reach differing conclusions when applying it to the facts of a given case. In such a case the court is entitled to substitute its own opinion for that of the person to whom the decision has been entrusted only if the decision is so aberrant that it cannot be classed as rational.'

ACTIVITY

Self-test questions

1. What is meant by a decision-maker abusing his discretion?

2. What is the difference between a mistake of:
   - fact
   - law or
   - a mixed question of fact and law?

20.2.7 Breach of the European Convention on Human Rights

As a result of the Human Rights Act 1998, it is now possible for a claimant to seek judicial review of a public law body on the basis that they have violated the rights set out in the European Convention. Under s 6 of the Act, a new statutory obligation is placed on public bodies that they must act consistently with the Convention rights. Any discretion a public decision-maker has must now be exercised in line with the Convention (see Chapter 17).

If a public body infringes the Convention, the claimant (as a victim under s 7) can seek judicial review on the ground of illegality; namely, that the public body has acted illegally by infringing the European Convention. Although in general terms the Human Rights Act 1998 has added a new aspect of illegality, where Art 6 and the right to a fair tribunal is raised, this will be subsumed under the third ground of review: procedural impropriety.

KEY FACTS

The ground of illegality	
Simple *ultra vires*	Acting beyond and exceeding legal powers (*Fulham Corporation (1921), ex parte Witham* (1997)).
Wrongful delegation of power	Public law powers should not be unlawfully delegated (*Vine* (1957)). Government ministers, however, typically confer power on officials to take decisions on their behalf (*Carltona Ltd* (1943)).

CONTINUED ▸

KEY FACTS

Improper purpose	Powers should be used for its proper and lawful purpose (*Congreve* (1976)).
Abuse of discretion	A public law discretion should not be fettered (*Padfield* (1968)).
	Irrelevant factors must not be taken into consideration (*ex parte Venables* (1997)).
	Relevant factors must be considered (*ex parte Singh* (1986)).
Excess of jurisdiction	Generally the courts will not interfere with a mistake of fact unless it is a precedent fact (*White and Collins* (1939)) or lacks supporting evidence (*Ashbridge Investments Ltd* (1965)).
	Today the courts will intervene in order to rectify a mistake of law (*Anisminic Ltd* (1969)).
Breach of the European Convention on Human Rights	Section 6 of the Human Rights Act 1998 requires public bodies to act in line with the European Convention on Human Rights.

20.3 The ground of irrationality

20.3.1 Origins and definition

An Act of Parliament will not state expressly that a statutory power conferred on a public law body must be exercised rationally. The courts, however, imply that Parliament never intended such a power to be used unreasonably or in an irrational way. The ground of irrationality, therefore, is concerned with a public body acting strictly within its legal powers (ie within the four corners of its powers), but arriving at a decision which is totally unreasonable. In his re-classification of the grounds of review, Lord Diplock, in *Council of Civil Service Unions v Minister for the Civil Service* [1985] 1 AC 374, described irrationality as follows:

'By "irrationality" I mean what can by now be succinctly referred to as "Wednesbury unreasonableness" … It applies to a decision which is so outrageous in its defiance of logic or of accepted moral standards that no sensible person who had applied his mind to the question to be decided could have arrived at it.'

Lord Diplock's reference to Wednesbury unreasonableness is derived from the following case:

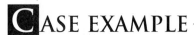ASE EXAMPLE

Associated Provincial Picture Houses Limited v Wednesbury Corporation [1948] 1 KB 223

Under s 1 of the Sunday Entertainments Act 1932 a local authority had the power to grant licences for cinema performances on a Sunday 'subject to such conditions as the authority think fit to impose'. Wednesbury Corporation granted Associated Provincial Picture Houses Ltd a licence to give Sunday performances subject to the condition that 'no children under the age of fifteen years shall be admitted to any entertainment whether accompanied by an adult or not'. The claimants sought a declaration that this condition was unreasonable and *ultra vires*.

The Court of Appeal held that Wednesbury Corporation had not acted *ultra vires* or unreasonably in setting this condition. Lord Greene MR noted that:

 'It is true to say that, if a decision on a competent matter is so unreasonable that no reasonable authority could ever have come to it, then the courts can interfere. That, I think, is quite right; but to prove a case of that kind would require something overwhelming and, in this case, the facts do not come anywhere near anything of that kind.'

In other words, acting unreasonably (Wednesbury unreasonableness) means that a body has come to a decision which no reasonable body could have come to. It is often forgotten in this case the court held that Wednesbury Corporation had imposed a condition which a reasonable corporation could have imposed. In *GCHQ*, Lord Diplock re-defined this narrow form of unreasonableness (Wednesbury unreasonableness) as 'irrationality'.

ACTIVITY

Question

Do you think that a modern court would hold the condition set by Wednesbury
Corporation to be rational?

20.3.2 The controversial nature of irrationality

Irrationality is, historically, the most controversial ground of judicial review because, as indicated
earlier at section 19.2.2, the nature of judicial review is that it concerns the decision-making
process rather than the decision itself:

■ Figure 20.4

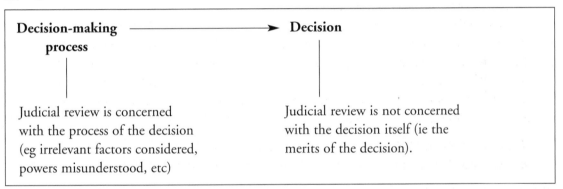

The difficulty with irrationality, however, is that in essence it challenges the *decision* itself: namely *a
decision which no reasonable decision-maker could have made.* Thus, it could be argued that this
infringes the separation of powers as Parliament had conferred the power to make the final decision
on the public body and not the courts.

The justification for irrationality is on the following basis:

(i)   For a decision to be irrational, by definition, the decision-making process is likely to have
      been faulty.

(ii) The courts set a very high threshold for irrationality. A court cannot interfere with a decision
      with which they simply disagree, but only if *no* reasonable body could have come to that
      decision. As an irrational decision needs to be, in effect, an absurd one, there are few examples
      of successful challenges on this ground.

(iii) The courts, in interfering with an irrational decision are only exercising a secondary judgment.
      The public body exercises the primary judgment and is only subject to a 'second look'
      (secondary judgment) by the courts in the event that the decision is absurd.

- It appears that historically the level of judicial intensity in looking at 'irrational decisions' depended on the context. For example, in the context of politically controversial policy areas such as national security or national economic considerations, the courts would be reluctant to interfere short of a minister *taking leave of his political senses: Nottinghamshire County Council v Secretary of State for the Environment* (1986) (see section 14.2.6). Indeed as noted by Sir Thomas Bingham MR in *R v Ministry of Defence, ex parte Smith* [1996] 1 All ER 257:

> J   'The greater the policy content of a decision, and the more remote the subject matter of a decision from ordinary judicial experience, the more hesitant the court must necessarily be in holding a decision to be irrational ... Where decisions of a policy-laden, esoteric or security-based nature are in issue even greater caution than normal must be shown in applying the test, but the test itself is sufficiently flexible to cover all situations.'

In contrast, in respect of human rights, the courts provided a more intensive look. Lord Bridge in *Bugdaycay v Secretary of State for the Home Department* [1987] 1 AC 514 pointed out:

> J   'The most fundamental of all human rights is the individual's right to life and when an administrative decision under challenge is said to be one which may put the applicant's life at risk, the basis of the decision must surely call for the most anxious scrutiny.'

Similarly, in *ex parte Smith* (see above and section 20.4.2) the Court of Appeal stated that the human rights context of a judicial review application was important and that the greater the interference with human rights, the more justification the court would require on the part of the decision-maker (see also *R v Secretary of State for the Home Department, ex parte McQuillan* [1995] 4 All ER 400).

In either case, however, according to Sir Thomas Bingham MR in *ex parte Smith*, the test of irrationality was sufficiently flexible to adapt to the context of the application (whether this involved a policy matter or fundamental human rights).

- Today in the light of the operation of the Human Rights Act 1998 there is some debate over whether the ground of irrationality still exists as a separate free-standing ground of review, or whether it has been subsumed under the doctrine of proportionality (see section 20.4.5).

20.3.3 Irrationality in practice

Although the ground of irrationality has historically been raised by claimants, it is rarely successful. This is because the threshold which needs to be crossed is set at a very high level by the courts.

Indeed, Lord Greene MR in *Associated Provincial Picture Houses Ltd* (1948) made reference to the example provided by an earlier judge which indicates the level of absurdity required. Warrington LJ, in *Short v Poole Corporation* [1926] 1 Ch 66 commented that:

> 'I suppose that if the defendants were to dismiss a teacher because she had red hair, or for some equally frivolous and foolish reason, the Court would declare the attempted dismissal to be void.'

An unsuccessful example of the ground being raised is as follows:

CASE EXAMPLE

R v Home Secretary, ex parte Brind [1991] 1 AC 696

The House of Lords held that the minister's decision to direct broadcasters to refrain from broadcasting words spoken by individuals representing organisations proscribed under terrorism legislation was not unreasonable/irrational.

Similarly, the argument of irrationality failed in *ex parte Smith* (1996) (see section 20.4.2).

There are however, two recent cases where the ground of irrationality was successful. In *R (Rogers) v Swindon NHS Primary Care Trust* [2006] EWCA Civ 392, the Court of Appeal held that the Trust's policy in relation to the availability of a drug was irrational. Similarly, in *R (Technoprint Plc & ANOR) v Leeds City Council* [2007] EWHC 638 (Admin), the granting of retrospective planning permission relating to industrial filters with noise attenuators was deemed irrational by the Administrative Court.

20.4 The ground of proportionality

20.4.1 Origins and definition

In 1984 when Lord Diplock re-classified the grounds of judicial review he confined them to three grounds in *Council of Civil Service Unions v Minister for the Civil Service* [1985] 1 AC 374:

> 'That is not to say that further development on a case by case basis may not in course of time add further grounds. I have in mind particularly the possible adoption in the future of the principle of "proportionality".'

A test of proportionality is as follows:

> 'Proportionality works on the assumption that administrative action ought not go beyond what is necessary to achieve its desired result (in everyday terms, that you should not use a sledgehammer to crack a nut) and, in contrast to irrationality, is often understood to bring courts much closer to reviewing the merits of a decision.'

P Leyland and G Anthony, *Textbook on Administrative Law*
(5th edn, Oxford University Press, 2005), p 331.

In other words, proportionality considers the aims of the decision-maker and whether the means to achieve that objective are proportionate.

For example, suppose with the aim of maintaining public order under the (imaginary) Public Order Act 2010, the Home Secretary chooses to ban *all* public demonstrations for two years. Although the government would inevitably succeed in securing the maintenance of public order (the objective), at what cost to human rights (eg the right to protest) has this been achieved? In short, the Home Secretary would be acting disproportionately (ie using a hammer to crack a nut).

Although historically proportionality has not been a ground of judicial review, it is a principle well known in other European countries (eg Germany) as well as in international law (both European Community and Convention laws – Chapters 15 and 16, respectively).

20.4.2 Proportionality and irrationality compared

The tests of proportionality and irrationality are different legal tests. This is neatly illustrated in the *ex parte Smith* litigation:

CASE EXAMPLE

R v Ministry of Defence, ex parte Smith [1996] 1 All ER 257

The Ministry of Defence had a policy which prevented homosexual men and women from serving in the armed forces. This policy required the discharge of those of homosexual orientation. As a result three gay men and a lesbian were discharged and they sought judicial review of the policy on, *inter alia*, the ground that it was irrational.

The Court of Appeal held that in terms of irrationality the greater the interference with human rights, the more justification would be required. Nevertheless, it could not be said that the policy was irrational – for one thing Parliament had supported the policy.

Although the claimants were unsuccessful domestically, subsequently they petitioned the European Court of Human Rights:

CASE EXAMPLE

Smith and Grady v United Kingdom (2000) 29 EHRR 493

Lustig-Prean and Beckett v United Kingdom (2000) 29 EHRR 548

The claimants successfully contended that the MOD policy violated Art 8 – the right to a private sexual life. The European Court held in both cases that the blanket policy which required automatic discharge on the basis of sexual orientation could not be justified as it was a disproportionate interference with their right to private life.

In short, the domestic and international tests were different:

- In the Court of Appeal the issue was one of irrationality:

  Could a reasonable body have come to that policy?

- In the European Court of Human Rights the issue was one of proportionality:

  Was the interference with the claimants' right of private life justified and in proportion?

Thus, the proportionality test is much stricter and more exacting than the irrationality test. It is easier for a public body to show that their decision was not irrational (as such a decision needed to be perverse), rather than to show that their decision was in proportion (ie it was a balanced one which was a proportionate method of achieving a lawful objective).

The test of proportionality, therefore, has a controversial element to it as it requires the court, in effect, to *assess the quality* of the decision made and to determine if the appropriate balance between means and objective has been achieved. It is for this reason, that Lords Ackner and Roskill were particularly averse to the introduction of proportionality as a ground of review in *ex parte Brind* (1991) (see section 20.3.3). Nevertheless, as a result of the Human Rights Act the principle of proportionality is now a part of judicial review.

20.4.3 Proportionality pre-Human Rights Act?

Although historically the courts were unwilling to establish a separate ground of review labelled proportionality, to some extent the concept was not unknown in our law *before* the advent of the Human Rights Act 1998.

- European Community law used the principle and so our judges were required to apply it in the context of European law:

CASE EXAMPLE

> **R v Chief Constable of Sussex, ex parte International Trader's Ferry Ltd [1999] 2 AC 418**
>
> Animal rights groups protested against ferry operators carrying livestock cargo on their ferries. Due to resource implications, the Chief Constable of Sussex Police decided to reduce the level of policing provided. International Trader's Ferry Ltd sought judicial review on the ground, *inter alia*, that it violated European Community law (Art 34 of the EC Treaty as being a quantitative restriction on exports between Member States).
>
> The House of Lords held that assuming Art 34 could be enforced by the claimant, the actions of the Chief Constable were not disproportionate to the restrictions which they imposed. The actions were therefore within the public policy exemption of Art 36.
>
> It is interesting to note that a claim that the Chief Constable had acted irrationally also failed.

- It was accepted that if a decision was lacking any proportionality at all, it was likely to be irrational in any event. Furthermore, in *R v Barnsley Metropolitan Borough Council, ex parte Hook* [1976] 3 All ER 452, the majority of the Court of Appeal held that the punishment imposed on a market trader (the loss of his licence) was altogether excessive and out of proportion.

- In *ex parte Leech* (1993) (see section 20.2.2) the Court of Appeal held that the more fundamental the right interfered with by a rule (in this case r 33) and the more drastic that interference, the stronger the justification would have to be. This is, in effect, a kind of proportionality in practice. Similarly, see *ex parte Smith* (1996) (section 20.4.2).

20.4.4 Proportionality and the Human Rights Act 1998

The Human Rights Act 1998 gave further effect to the rights of the European Convention in domestic law. This meant that the domestic courts must follow the legal reasoning adopted in Strasbourg which includes the principle of proportionality. For example, as indicated earlier (sections 6.7.4, 17.5 and 17.11.1), in *A and others v Secretary of State for the Home Department* (2004), the House of Lords held that part of the Anti-Terrorism, Crime and Security Act 2001 was a disproportionate response and not strictly required by the exigencies of the situation.

In *R v Secretary of State for the Home Department ex parte Daly* [2001] UKHL 26 Lord Steyn made the following comments concerning proportionality:

> **J** 'First, the doctrine of proportionality may require the reviewing court to assess the balance which the decision maker has struck, not merely whether it is within the range of rational or reasonable decisions. Secondly, the proportionality test may go further than the traditional grounds of review in asmuch as it may require attention to be directed to the relative weight accorded to interests and considerations.'

NB: for the full quotation see section 17.5.

ACTIVITY

Exercise

Define the terms irrationality and proportionality and explain the difference between them.

20.4.5 The demise of irrationality?

There is currently a debate over whether irrationality continues to exist as a ground of review, or whether with the establishment of the Human Rights Act 1998, it has been overtaken by (and subsumed under) proportionality. In *Association of British Civilian Internees* (below) the Court of Appeal held that the principle of proportionality had not replaced irrationality where no European Community or Convention issues were raised. In this context, however, Dyson LJ giving judgment for the court made the following comments in *R (Association of British Civilian Internees: Far East Region) v Secretary of State for Defence* [2003] EWCA Civ 473:

> **J** 'The *Wednesbury* test is moving closer to proportionality and in some cases it is not possible to see any daylight between the two tests ... Although we did not hear argument on the point, we have difficulty in seeing what justification there now is for retaining the *Wednesbury* test. But we consider that it is not for this court to perform its burial rites. The continuing existence of the *Wednesbury* test has been acknowledged by the House of Lords on more than one occasion.'

In conclusion, although it appears that irrationality is still a free-standing ground of review, to what extent this will be the case in the near future remains to be seen.

KEY FACTS

The ground of irrationality/proportionality	
Irrationality	A decision which no reasonable body could have come to: *Associated Provincial Picture Houses Limited* (1948). Historically, the test was flexible to involve: • a less intense review in the context of politically controversial policy areas (*Nottinghamshire County Council v Secretary of State for the Environment* (1986)) • a more intensive review in the context of human rights (*ex parte Smith* (1996)).
Proportionality	Proportionality considers the aim of the decision-maker and whether the means to achieve that objective are proportionate (the Human Rights Act 1998).

20.5 The ground of procedural impropriety

20.5.1 Definition

Lord Diplock in *Council of Civil Service Unions v Minister for the Civil Service* [1985] 1 AC 374:

'I have described the third head as "procedural impropriety" rather than failure to observe basic rules of natural justice or failure to act with procedural fairness towards the person who will be affected by the decision. This is because susceptibility to judicial review under this head covers also failure by an administrative tribunal to observe procedural rules that are expressly laid down in the legislative instrument by which its jurisdiction is conferred, even where such failure does not involve any denial of natural justice.'

Procedural impropriety can be sub-divided into the following:

■ Figure 20.5

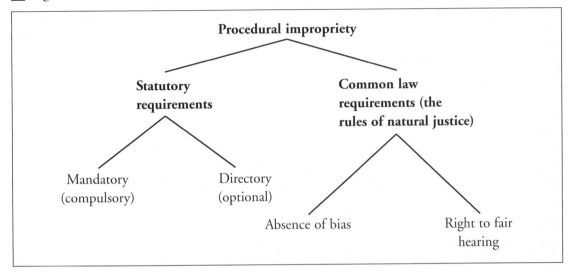

In other words, a public decision-maker will breach this ground of review if he ignores either the requirements of a statute or the principles of natural justice.

20.5.2 Statutory requirements

The courts can subject a public body to review if it has failed to comply with statutory procedural requirements (eg before X can take a decision, X must consult A, B and C). The point must be made at the outset, however, that not all breaches of statutory requirements are the same. Some, for example the failure to consult interested parties, will be clearly more significant than others (eg a public body required to act within 28 days but instead does so within 29).

Historically, therefore, the courts have distinguished between two types of statutory requirements:

- a mandatory requirement (an essential requirement which will invalidate action if not followed).
- a directory requirement (a less important requirement which is not fatal, as it is a minor technical defect).

In a sense this is analogous to the classification of contractual terms into conditions (very important) and warranties (less important).

The above dichotomy begs the question as to which statutory requirements are mandatory and which are directory? This is essentially a question of statutory interpretation for the courts to determine using the following factors:

- The Act itself (rather unusually) may expressly state the consequences of a breach of a statutory requirement.

- Failing the above, what did Parliament intend to be the result in the event of a failure to follow a procedural requirement?

- Were obligatory terms such as 'must' used?

- What is the purpose of the requirement? Who or what is it intended to protect and for what reason?

- What is the nature of the breach?

In *London & Clydeside Estates Ltd v Aberdeen District Council* [1980] 1 WLR 182 Lord Hailsham LC stated that although the terms mandatory and directory may be helpful, he emphasised that the courts should not adopt an overly rigid set of legal categories in this regard. In recent years, Lord Woolf MR has noted that the question of whether a requirement was mandatory or directory was only at most a first step before, in the majority of cases, the following questions were likely to be asked (*R v Secretary of State for the Home Department, ex parte Jeyeanthan* [2000] 1 WLR 354):

> **J**
>
> '1. Is the statutory requirement fulfilled if there has been substantial compliance with the requirement and, if so, has there been substantial compliance in the case in issue even though there has not been strict compliance? (The substantial compliance question).
>
> 2. Is the non-compliance capable of being waived, and if so, has it, or can it and should it be waived in this particular case? (The discretionary question) …
>
> 3. If it is not capable of being waived or is not waived then what is the consequence of the non-compliance? (The consequences question).
>
> Which questions arise will depend upon the facts of the case and the nature of the particular requirement.'

Historically the case law has indicated the following principles:

- **A requirement to consult**

  This is generally viewed as a mandatory and important requirement:

CASE EXAMPLE

Agricultural, Horticultural and Forestry Industry Training Board v Aylesbury Mushrooms Ltd [1972] 1 WLR 190

As the Industrial Training Act 1964 provided for prior consultation by the Ministry of Labour with interested organisations, and the Mushroom Growers' Association had not actually been consulted, a 1966 Order (establishing a training board imposing a levy) had no application to them. Consultation was treated as a mandatory requirement in relation to the Mushroom Growers' Association.

- **A requirement to notify of the right to appeal**

  In *Agricultural, Horticultural and Forestry Industry Training Board v Kent* [1970] 1 All ER 304 the Court of Appeal held that the provisions of the Industrial Training Levy (Agricultural, Horticultural and Forestry) Order 1967 were mandatory. As a consequence, in the interests of fairness, an assessment notice (indicating a levy to be paid) must state the address of the training board in order that an individual may make a notice of appeal.

20.5.3 Common law requirements: *Nemo judex in re sua*

The rules of natural justice (also known as the duty to act fairly) can be sub-divided into the following:

- *Nemo judex in re sua* (directly below).
- *Audi alteram partem* (see section 20.5.4).

Natural justice is a substantial area in its own right and accordingly below is a very basic outline of the subject.

Nemo judex in re sua

(No man should be a judge in his own cause/the decision-maker must be unbiased)

For constitutional reasons a public decision-maker must be unbiased in the sense of having no vested interest in the outcome of the case/decision or any other pre-judgment. The rule against bias applies to both judicial and disciplinary/administrative functions and it is not just confined to the area of public law as the principle is also found in both civil and criminal proceedings. In essence, the rule against bias can be sub-divided in the following way:

■ Figure 20.6

Actual bias

It is self-evidently a breach of natural justice if the decision-maker is *actually* biased. For example, an immigration official deports X because he has taken a personal dislike to him. Cases of actual bias are, for obvious reasons, rare.

The appearance of financial bias

The decision-maker must not (or objectively appear to) have a financial interest in the outcome of either judicial or quasi-judicial proceedings. The appearance of a pecuniary interest will (automatically) disqualify the presiding judge.

CASE EXAMPLE

Dimes v The Proprietors of the Grand Junction Canal (1852) 3 HLC 759

In this case the Lord Chancellor (Lord Cottenham) affirmed on appeal the Vice-Chancellor's decree that Dimes could not obstruct the Grand Junction Canal's land. It transpired that the Lord Chancellor held shares in the Grand Junction Canal, and so had a financial interest in it. The House Lords reversed the Lord Chancellor's decree and Lord Campbell stated that:

> **J** 'No one can suppose that Lord Cottenham could be, in the remotest degree, influenced by the interest that he had in this concern; but, my Lords, it is of the last importance that the maxim that no man is to be a judge in his own cause should be held sacred.'

The courts have more recently reaffirmed this principle. Slade J in *R v Camborne Justices, ex parte Pearce* [1955] 1 QB 41:

> **J** 'It is, of course, clear that any direct pecuniary or proprietary interest in the subject-matter of a proceeding, however small, operates as an automatic disqualification. In such a case the law assumes bias.'

The appearance of non-financial bias

The appearance of non-pecuniary bias can take many forms (eg a connection which is personal, a professional link, a mingling of functions, etc). Below are a few examples to illustrate this ground.

A professional/family link

CASE EXAMPLE

Metropolitan Properties Co (FGC) v Lannon [1969] 1 QB 577

In this case, landlords, Metropolitan Properties Co contended that the chairman of a rent assessment committee should be disqualified on the ground of bias. In short, the chairman had acted for and advised Regency Lodge tenants in dispute with their landlords (who were a company in the same group as Metropolitan Properties). He had also advised his father, a Regency Lodge tenant, about a fair rent.

CONTINUED ▶

The Court of Appeal held that decision of the committee must be quashed (and remitted to another committee) because of the connection between the chairman and Regency Lodge tenants. This connection was such as to give the reasonable impression that the chairman was biased – though this was an appearance of bias as there was no actual bias.

A dual-involvement/intermingling of functions

CASE EXAMPLE

Hannam v Bradford City Council [1970] 2 All ER 690

Hannam was a schoolmaster who absented himself and refused to return to work. In December 1967 his employment was terminated by a meeting of the school governors. In January 1968 a council staff sub-committee met to consider whether the council should prohibit the dismissal. It decided not to do so. Three of the members of the sub-committee were governors, although they had not attended the meeting in December 1967.

The Court of Appeal held that as the three governors had sat on the staff sub-committee this gave rise to the possibility of bias. They did not cease to be part of the school governors when they sat on the sub-committee and it did not matter that they had not personally attended the meeting of the governors.

A connection with a party to the case

The seminal case in this respect (though now since refined through a later decision) is *ex parte Pinochet Ugarte* (2000) (see section 13.4.2). This case concerned the connection between one of the judges in the case (Lord Hoffmann) and Amnesty International who had joined the case as a party seeking Pinochet's extradition for alleged human rights violations. To avoid the appearance of bias, the House of Lords set aside its own decision and re-heard the matter because of this connection.

Finally, it should be noted that the modern test for the appearance of non-financial bias is as follows (Lord Hope in *Porter v Magill* [2001] UKHL 67):

> **J** 'The question is whether the fair-minded and informed observer, having considered the facts, would conclude that there was a real possibility that the tribunal was biased.'

ACTIVITY

Questions

1. What is the consequence of failing to follow the procedural requirements of a statute?

2. Explain the different ways in which a decision-maker could be biased.

20.5.4 Common law requirements: *Audi alteram partem*

Audi alteram partem

(Hear the other side/the right to a fair hearing.)

Natural justice (and now Art 6 of the European Convention) provides minimum standards of fairness in respect of public decision-making. Historically, *Ridge v Baldwin* (below) acted as a watershed in indicating that the right to a fair hearing/duty to act fairly was to be universally applied (ie to judicial and administrative bodies affecting individual rights).

CASE EXAMPLE

Ridge v Baldwin [1964] AC 40

Ridge, a Chief Constable, had been dismissed from his office by a watch committee. The House of Lords held that this decision was null and void as the committee had not followed the rules of natural justice. They had not informed Ridge of the charges against him nor had they given him the opportunity to be heard.

The exact requirements of natural justice will vary according to the context:

- the body involved
- the nature of the decision and
- the issue at stake.

NB Article 6 applies only to 'criminal charges' or 'the determination of civil rights'.

In essence, the requirements of a fair hearing embody the following elements:

- The knowledge of the charge/allegations.
- An indication of adverse evidence.
- Notice of the hearing.
- The right to submit a defence (in writing or orally).
- The right to challenge adverse evidence (in writing or orally).

- The right to submit evidence.
- The right to legal representation.
- The right to reasons for a decision.

The right to a fair hearing (or fairness / the duty to act fairly in modern parlance) is variable depending upon the context and so its requirements may include all or a number of the features set out directly above. Sir Robert Megarry VC in *McInnes v Onslow-Fane* [1978] 1 WLR 1520 rather usefully identified the following categories:

- **Forfeiture cases** – where a decision takes away an existing position or right (eg a licence is revoked).

- **Application cases** – where the decision refuses the position or right that the applicant seeks (eg admission to a club).

- **Expectation cases** – where the applicant has a legitimate expectation that his application will be accepted (on the basis of what has already happened). For example, Megarry referred to an existing licence holder seeking renewal of it.

Three examples of legitimate expectation cases are:

- *ex parte Liverpool Taxi Fleet Operators' Association* (1972) – Taxi drivers had a legitimate expectation – based on past history and an undertaking given by the council – to make representations before more licenses were issued (see section 20.6.1).

- *GCHQ* (1985) (see section 11.9.6) – civil service unions had a legitimate expectation based on previous practice to be consulted prior to their employment conditions being changed (in the event trumped by national security).

- *R v North and East Devon Health Authority, ex parte Coughlan* [2001] 1 QB 213 – a number of disabled people had a legitimate expectation that a Heath Authority would keep the assurance that it had given to them that their move to an NHS facility would be for life.

Megarry made the point that in forfeiture cases more can be expected in terms of natural justice (the right to unbiased tribunal, notice of charges and to be heard in respect of them), than in contrast to mere application cases (as in the actual case at hand where the body should act honestly and without bias, but there was no expectation of an oral hearing). In other words, there is a sliding scale of natural justice: the nearer the case is towards the forfeiture scenario, the more rights can be expected (akin to the characteristics of a criminal court hearing). In contrast, the nearer to the mere application scenario, the less can be expected (in effect the obligation/duty to be fair). In terms of natural justice, legitimate expectation cases would be nearer the scenario of a forfeiture case.

It has been pointed out that although the *McInnes* case 'should not be read as establishing rigid categories to which different templates of fairness apply, it usually indicates some of the factors which help determine where on the scale particular cases will be located' (M Elliott, *Administrative Law, Text and Materials* (3rd edn, Oxford University Press, 2005) p 365). Indeed, as noted by Lord Bridge in *Lloyd v McMahon* [1987] 1 AC 625:

> J '... the so-called rules of natural justice are not engraved on tablets of stone. To use the phrase which better expresses the underlying concept, what the requirements of fairness demand when any body, domestic, administrative or judicial, has to make a decision which will affect the rights of individuals depends on the character of the decision-making body, the kind of decision it has to make and the statutory or other framework in which it operates.'

The case law of natural justice is voluminous and below is a selection of some examples to suggest an outline of this area:

- **The right to know adverse evidence**

Lord Denning in the Privy Council in *Kanda v Government of the Federation of Malaya* [1962] AC 322 commented that:

> J 'If the right to be heard is to be a real right which is worth anything, it must carry with it a right in the accused man to know the case which is made against him. He must know what evidence has been given and what statements have been made affecting him.'

Although it may appear axiomatic that a person should know the exact particulars of the case against them, this principle can be modified by national security. In *ex parte Hosenball* (1977) at section 6.7.10, Hosenball had a deportation order issued against him under the Immigration Act 1971. The Court of Appeal held there had been no breach of natural justice as the Secretary of State had considered personally Hosenball's request for further particulars of the allegations. Hosenball's request had been denied as it was not in the interests of national security to provide further information. The court noted that on occasions natural justice had to give way to considerations of national security. See also *R v Secretary of State for the Home Department, ex parte Cheblak* [1991] 1 WLR 890.

- **The right to have sufficient time to prepare a defence/answer the case against him**

In order for an individual to defend himself, he must be given a reasonable time to defend himself in answer to a charge:

CASE EXAMPLE ————————————————————

R v Thames Magistrates' Court, ex parte Polemis [1974] 2 All ER 1219

Polemis was served with a summons at 10.30am concerning an alleged breach of the Prevention of Oil Pollution Act 1971. At 4.00pm that day a stipendiary magistrate heard

CONTINUED ▸

the case and convicted him. Polemis's conviction was quashed by an order of *certiorari* on the basis that natural justice required that a party should have a reasonable opportunity to prepare his case. Lord Widgery CJ stated that:

> J
>
> 'nothing is clearer today than that a breach of the rules of natural justice is said to occur if a party to proceedings, and more especially the defendant in a criminal case, is not given a reasonable chance to present his case ... it necessarily extends to a reasonable opportunity to prepare your case before you are called on to present it.'

- **The right to make representations**

In *ex parte Binks* (1985) (see section 19.2.1) the council's decision to issue Binks with a notice to quit was quashed. It was held that as her livelihood was at stake (a street trader selling hot food under an informal arrangement), the council had denied her natural justice because:

1. she had not been given prior notification before the issuing of its decision giving her notice to quit;

2. she had not been given an opportunity to be heard;

3. it had not given any reasons for its decision.

In *ex parte Doody* (1994) (see below) the House of Lords held that the Home Secretary was required to provide a mandatory life sentence prisoner with the opportunity to make written representations concerning the period he should serve (to satisfy deterrence and retribution) in advance of the date being set by the Home Secretary for the first review of that prisoner's sentence.

- **The equality of treatment between the parties**

The parties to a case should be treated equally:

CASE EXAMPLE

R v Barnsley Metropolitan Borough Council, ex parte Hook [1976] 3 All ER 452

The court held that the rules of natural justice had been breached when a local authority committee considered a complaint about Hook's (a market trader) behaviour in allegedly urinating in a side street. The committee heard the oral evidence (by the market manager) against Hook in the absence of Hook himself. He could not therefore challenge or orally cross-examine this evidence. The court quashed the decision of the committee.

Similarly, in *Errington v Minister of Health* [1935] 1 KB 249 the court held that one side should not be heard in the absence of the other.

- **The right to an oral hearing**

The right to a hearing does not necessarily mean the right to an oral hearing, as (depending on the circumstances and what is at stake) the right to a hearing may only mean that written representations can be put forward. In any event, in a written hearing an individual can still submit evidence which he wishes the decision-making body to see.

CASE EXAMPLE

R (West) v Parole Board **[2005] UKHL 1**

The House of Lords held that an oral hearing before a Parole Board, in respect of prisoners who had had their licences revoked, might be necessary where, for example, facts were at issue (ie were in dispute) which could affect the outcome (such issues, of course, could be better resolved in person than on paper). Although the court held that whether an oral hearing was necessary depended on the circumstances of each particular case, on the facts it was held that the Parole Board had breached their common law duty of procedural fairness by failing to offer the prisoners an oral hearing.

In *R v Army Board of the Defence Council, ex parte Anderson* [1992] 1 QB 169, the court held that the Army Board had been wrong to adopt an inflexible policy where it did not permit oral hearings before it.

The disadvantage of oral hearings are that they are much more time consuming than paper hearings. The advantage of an oral hearing is, of course, the possibility of cross-examining evidence and witnesses (thereby allowing adverse evidence to be tested orally). In *R v Hull Prison Board of Visitors, ex parte St Germain and others (No 2)* [1979] 3 All ER 545 the court noted that in terms of hearsay evidence, a fair hearing might involve the prison board informing prisoners (accused of breaching Prison Rules) of the hearsay evidence against them and could also involve allowing them the opportunity to cross-examine witnesses whose evidence was before the decision-maker as hearsay. In addition, the board had improperly failed to allow witnesses to be called in defence (eg the right to submit evidence).

- **The right to legal representation**

When appearing before a criminal court a person will expect to enjoy legal representation, but whether this is applicable in respect of administrative decisions will depend on the facts. The advantage of legal representation is that it enables individuals lacking specialist knowledge or competence to present their case. The disadvantage of legal representation is that lawyers inevitably lengthen and complicate proceedings. Indeed, Lord Denning MR in *Enderby Town Football Club Ltd v Football Association Ltd* [1971] 1 Ch 591 noted that it may be a good thing for a domestic body not to involve legal representation (although the domestic tribunal in the case – the Football Association – must not fetter its discretion by making it an absolute rule that legal representation will never be permitted).

CASE EXAMPLE

R v Secretary of State for the Home Department, ex parte Tarrant [1985] 1 QB 251

The court held that the Board of Visitors had a discretion as to whether prisoners should be granted legal representation. In this case, it would be fair in all the circumstances for a prisoner to be allowed to be legally represented (here the charge of mutiny was an especially grave offence).

See also Art 6 of the European Convention on Human Rights which specifically states that everyone charged with a criminal offence has, *inter alia*, the following rights:

(A) Article 6(3)(c)
To defend himself in person or through legal assistance of his own choosing or, if he has not sufficient means to pay for legal assistance, to be given it free when the interests of justice so require.

In *Ezeh and Connors v United Kingdom* (2004) 39 EHRR 691 the European Court of Human Rights held that the right to a fair trial had been breached when prisoners (who had been sentenced to extra days under Prison Rules) had been denied legal representation. For the purposes of Art 6, the court considered the charges against the prisoners under the Prison Rules as criminal.

- **The right to reasons for a decision**

Although there is no general common law duty for a decision-maker to provide reasons for a decision (in contrast, the judiciary give reasons in court), in modern times it is the hallmark of good administrative practice. Lord Mustill in *R v Secretary of State for the Home Department, ex parte Doody* [1994] 1 AC 531 stated that:

J 'the law does not at present recognise a general duty to give reasons for an administrative decision. Nevertheless, it is equally beyond question that such a duty may in appropriate circumstances be implied.'

The following case is interesting as it concerns the provision of information during the decision-making process.

CASE EXAMPLE

R v Secretary of State for the Home Department, ex parte Al Fayed and another
[1997] 1 All ER 228

The Fayed brothers applied for naturalisation as British citizens under the British Nationality Act 1981. Their applications were refused and no reasons were given for this refusal. They sought judicial review of the Home Secretary's failure to give reasons and that there had been a breach of natural justice.

The Court of Appeal held that although the Home Secretary was not (owing to s 44 of the 1981 Act) required to give reasons when an application was refused, he still had to act fairly in arriving at a decision. As a result, the Home Secretary should have given the Fayeds information (ie the right to notice) in respect of the area of his concern. This in turn, would then have allowed them to make representations on this issue to the Home Secretary before he made his decision. In the case, the decision of the Home Secretary was quashed. Lord Woolf MR, stated that:

> **J**   'I appreciate that there is also anxiety as to the administrative burden involved in giving notice of areas of concern. Administrative convenience cannot justify unfairness but I would emphasise that my remarks are limited to cases where an applicant would be in real difficulty in doing himself justice unless the area of concern is identified by notice.'

ACTIVITY

Exercise

Explain the different aspects of *audi alteram partem*. Why do such rules exist?

KEY FACTS

The ground of procedural impropriety	
Statutory requirements	A failure to comply with statutory procedural requirements: • A mandatory requirement is an essential requirement which will invalidate action if not followed (*Aylesbury Mushrooms Ltd* (1972)). • A directory requirement is a minor technical defect. See now Lord Woolf's analysis (*ex parte Jeyeanthan* (2000)).
Nemo judex in re sua	• Actual bias where a decision-maker is actually biased. • The appearance of financial bias where the decision-maker has a financial interest in the outcome of either judicial or quasi-judicial proceedings (*Dimes* (1852)). • The appearance of non-financial bias – (*Metropolitan Properties Co (FGC)* (1969) and *ex parte Pinochet Ugarte* (2000)).
Audi alteram partem	Decision-makers must respect all or most of the following requirements which protect the right to a fair hearing: • An awareness of the charge/allegations and notice of the hearing. • The right to submit a defence and evidence (in writing and/or orally). • An indication of adverse evidence and the right to challenge it (in writing and/or orally). • The right to legal representation. • The right to reasons for a decision.

20.6 Remedies

20.6.1 The different remedies available

If a claimant can demonstrate that a public body has breached one of the grounds of judicial review, he *may* obtain a remedy. There are six remedies available:

■ Figure 20.7

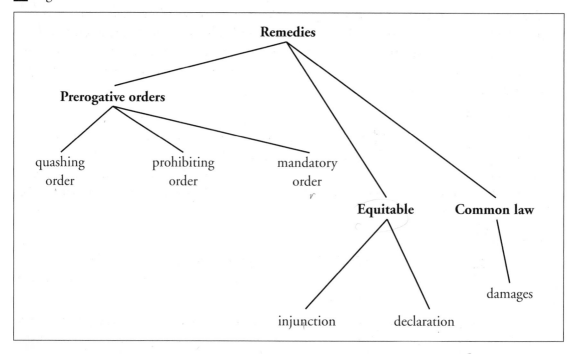

It should be noted that a combination of remedies may be appropriate. For example, a quashing order combined with a mandatory order would compel a public body to take the decision again (after the original decision had been quashed by a quashing order), but this time in accordance with the law.

- **A quashing order**

  This order (formerly known as *certiorari*) quashes an unlawful decision. For example, in *ex parte Binks* (1985) (see sections 19.2.1 and 20.5.4). Binks successfully obtained an order to quash an unlawful decision of Wear Valley District Council that she should cease trading. Similarly, in the context of delegated legislation see *R v Secretary of State for Health, ex parte United States Tobacco International Inc* [1992] 1 QB 353 at section 19.2.1.

- **A prohibiting order**

  This order (formerly known as *prohibition*) is pre-emptive in the sense that it prevents a body from acting unlawfully in the future (see *R v Liverpool Corporation, ex parte Liverpool Taxi Fleet Operators' Association* [1972] 2 QB 299 – preventing a council from granting further taxi licences without first hearing the representations of interested parties).

- **A mandatory order**

  This order (formerly known as *mandamus*) compels a body to act (eg to perform a statutory function). In *Padfield* (1968) (see section 20.2.5) the court directed the Minister of Agriculture to consider a complaint submitted to him according to the law.

- **An injunction**

   This equitable remedy can compel a body to perform an act or restrain it from doing so. In *ex parte Factortame* (1991) at section 15.6.4 the House of Lords issued an interim injunction which prevented the Secretary of State from enforcing provisions of the Merchant Shipping Act 1988. An injunction is a useful remedy because it can be obtained in a temporary form as in the *Factortame* litigation.

- **A declaration**   ~~Judicial statement of legal position of the parties.~~

   This equitable remedy is non-coercive as it represents a formal statement of the law by the courts. For example, in *Equal Opportunities Commission* (1994) (see section 19.4.2) a declaration was issued stating that provisions of domestic law indirectly discriminated against women and so were contrary to European Community law. This is also a remedy which can be obtained on an interim basis.

- **Damages**

   This common law remedy has historically not been a free-standing remedy as it had to be combined with another. In practice, to claim damages a claimant was required to show that the unlawful public decision was also, for example, negligent.

   Today a breach of the European Convention by a public body may result in damages, however, the awards will be relatively modest as they will be in line with awards in the European Court in Strasbourg (see section 17.9.3).

20.6.2 The discretionary nature of remedies

The above remedies are discretionary. Even though a claimant can demonstrate that a public body has acted unlawfully, the court may nevertheless decide to provide no remedy at all (or may provide a different one from the one sought). A remedy may be refused on *inter alia* the following change to bases:

- The behaviour of the claimant in the case (eg an ulterior motive in seeking judicial review).

- If change to the claimant has delayed in processing a claim (see section 19.6.3).

- A remedy would result in an adverse effect on either (a) general administration or (b) third parties.

- The remedy would provide no tangible benefit.

20.7   The effectiveness of judicial review

How effective is judicial review?

20.7.1 Factors which support its effectiveness

Lord Scarman in *Nottinghamshire County Council v Secretary of State for the Environment* [1986] 1 AC 240:

> **J** 'Judicial review is a great weapon in the hands of the judges: but the judges must observe the constitutional limits set by our parliamentary system upon their exercise of this beneficial power.'

- The existence of judicial review necessarily improves good administration. It encourages administrators and public decision-makers to exercise their powers in accordance with the law as they are aware that otherwise they will be subject to review. Indeed, government officials have been issued with the booklet 'The Judge Over Your Shoulder: A Guide to Judicial Review for UK Government Administrators' (4th edn, Crown Copyright, 2006) which has been revised to take into account the Human Rights Act and which reminds officials of their public law responsibilities. As a preventative measure, we will never know how many illegal public law decisions judicial review has prevented.

- Judicial review has caused friction between the courts and the executive in the past two decades, as successive ministers, of whatever political colour, have been subject to judicial review. In fact, it is arguable that it is actually healthy in a democracy for there to be some friction between the two arms of the constitution as it suggests that the courts are successfully holding the executive to account and restraining their actions. This is particularly important in the light of the modern executive's domination of the legislature.

- Judicial review claims can be used to highlight a particular issue (homelessness, prisoners' rights, etc).

20.7.2 Factors which question its effectiveness

- It must be remembered that judicial review is in essence a procedural remedy whereby the courts have historically confined themselves to questioning the decision-making process, rather than the decision itself. The result of this is that judicial review may be in some cases a rather pyrrhic victory. Although the court may quash the offending decision of a public body, it will not replace it with another one, but instead may require the body to take the decision again, but this time in accordance with the law (eg this time by considering relevant considerations that were previously ignored). This could still result in the decision-maker making the same decision, and provided it was taken legally, rationally and fairly, it will stand.

- Some areas of public law decision-making such as national security and national economic consideration are not susceptible to judicial review.

- The remedies available are discretionary and may be denied even though it has been demonstrated that a public body has acted unlawfully.

- Judicial review is necessarily a reactive jurisdiction in which its ability to develop administrative principles is subject to claimants initiating actions.

- As noted by the Democratic Audit of the United Kingdom, in terms of the effectiveness of judicial review, it is clear that the few thousand of judicial review claims made each year 'are infinitesimal when compared with the millions of decisions taken every year by public bodies'. (S Weir and D Beetham, *Political Power and Democratic Control in Britain* (Routledge, 1999), p 446). Indeed, in 2005 a total of 5,381 applications were made for permission to apply for judicial review (of which 744 were granted) and of the 281 substantive applications for judicial review decided that year, 42% were allowed (*Judicial Statistics (Revised) England and Wales for the year 2005*, Cm 6903 (2006), p 23).

- Judicial review is a remedy of last resort to be used when there are no other (or reasonable) remedies available.

ACTIVITY

Essay writing

Do you think that judicial review is effective?

20.8 Judicial review checklist

Judicial review examination questions are particularly amenable to problem-solving questions. One useful way of approaching such questions is to list each ground (and sub-division) of judicial review and work down this checklist in order to determine which issues are raised by the scenario:

Judicial review checklist

Procedural issues:

Is the decision-maker a public body (or one which the courts would regard as performing governmental functions)?

Is the decision/action complained about a public law issue?

Does the claimant have standing?

Has the complaint complied with the public law procedure?

Grounds of review:

Has the decision-maker acted illegally? Has he:

- Acted *ultra vires* the parent Act?
- Wrongfully delegated public law powers?
- Acted for an improper purpose?
- Abused his discretion by (a) fettering his discretion (b) ignoring relevant factors (c) considering irrelevant factors?

CONTINUED ▸

- Acted in excess of his jurisdiction by misinterpreting his legal powers?
- Breached a European Convention right (and acted disproportionately)?

Has the decision-maker acted irrationally?

- Has the decision-maker made a decision which no reasonable decision-maker would have made?

Has the decision-maker acted in a procedurally unfair manner? Has he:

- Breached a statutory requirement?
- Demonstrated bias or an appearance of bias?
- Ignored the rules concerning the right to a fair hearing?

Further reading

Bailey, S, 'Grounds for Judicial Review: Due Process, Natural Justice and Fairness' in Feldman, D (ed), *English Public Law* (Oxford University Press, 2004), p 775.

Barnett, H, *Constitutional and Administrative Law* (6th edn, Routledge-Cavendish, 2006), Chapter 27.

Bradley, A and Ewing, K, *Constitutional and Administrative Law* (14th edn, Pearson/Longman, 2007), Chapter 30.

Craig, P, 'Grounds for Judicial Review: Substantive Control Over Discretion' in Feldman, D (ed), *English Public Law* (Oxford University Press, 2004), p 831.

Horne, A and Berman, G, 'Judicial Review: A short guide to claims in the Administrative Court' 06/44 (House of Commons Library, 2006).

Leyland, P and Anthony, G, *Textbook on Administrative Law* (5th edn, Oxford University Press, 2005), Chapters 10 to 16.

Parpworth, N, *Constitutional and Administrative Law* (4th edn, Oxford University Press, 2006), Chapters 13 and 14.

Sunkin, M, 'Grounds for Judicial Review: Illegality in the Strict Sense' in Feldman, D (ed), *English Public Law* (Oxford University Press, 2004), p 715.

Turner, I, 'Judicial Review, Irrationality and the Review of Merits' (2006) 15(2) *Nottingham Law Journal* 37.

Walker, P, 'What's Wrong with Irrationality?' [1995] PL 556.

Weir, S and Beetham, D, *Political Power and Democratic Control in Britain* (Routledge, 1999), Chapter 15.

GRIEVANCE MECHANISMS ◼

AIMS AND OBJECTIVES ☐☐☐

At the end of this chapter you should be able to:

- Appreciate the role of grievance mechanisms (other than the courts) in the British constitution

- Understand the nature and constitutional role of the tribunal system

- Understand the nature and constitutional role of inquiries

- Appreciate the role, workings and constitutional importance of the system of Ombudsmen

Introduction

As government officials and agencies exercise disparate and wide-ranging powers to provide services and discharge responsibilities, it is inevitable that the actions and decisions of state officials will come into conflict with individuals. As a result, a number of different grievance mechanisms (both legal and non-legal) are available to individuals who feel aggrieved by the actions of the state. In brief, tribunals provide individuals with a legal form of redress which is an alternative to the strict formal court system. In contrast, inquiries are an extra-judicial grievance mechanism which permit individuals to challenge, for example, the decision of a local authority to compulsorily purchase their land. A further (extra-judicial) form of redress is the Ombudsman which investigates an injustice caused to an individual by maladministration (ie faulty administration) by the state. This chapter will provide a very general overview of all three grievance mechanisms against the state.

21.1 Tribunals

21.1.1 Definition and history

In historical terms, the powers and responsibilities of the state increasingly have impacted on the lives of individuals (for example, whether it was the collection of taxes or the entitlement of a social security benefit). In the light of the volume of millions of decisions made by state officials and administrators each year, mistakes and discrepancies are inevitably going to cause injustice to particular individuals. As a consequence, tribunals have been established on an *ad hoc* basis (mainly by Parliament, although some under the royal prerogative) to enable individuals to challenge the decisions of state officials in these areas in a forum which is outside the formal court system. In essence, tribunals are adjudicative bodies which apply laws and rules to a case in order to resolve disputes between the individual and the state.

In 1957 the Franks Committee (*Report of the Committee on Administrative Tribunals and Inquiries* Cmnd 218 (1957)) examined the network of tribunals. This in turn led to the passing of the 1958 Tribunals and Inquiries Act (as subsequently consolidated in the Tribunals and Inquiries Acts 1971 and 1992) which, among other things, established the Council on Tribunals whose responsibility was to oversee and report on the operation and workings of tribunals (as well as inquiries). A further review of tribunals was undertaken by Sir Andrew Leggatt whose report in 2001 (*Tribunals for Users: One System, One Service* (The Stationery Office, 2001) indicated that at this point in time (and for the purposes of its terms of reference) there were 70 different types of administrative tribunals in England and Wales which processed one million cases between them. The network of these tribunals, however, lacked co-ordination and needed to be rationalised. The government has now responded to the Legatt Report (see sections 21.1.6 and 22.12).

21.1.2 Types of tribunals

There are a wide variety of different types of tribunals ranging from immigration (the Asylum and Immigration Tribunal), mental health (the Mental Health Review Tribunal) and education (the Special Educational Needs and Disability Tribunal). In broad terms, however, a clear distinction can be drawn between:

- those which resolve disputes between the individual and the state (eg the Social Security and Child Support Appeals Tribunal); and

- those which regulate disputes between private parties, for example, employee and employer in the context of employment law issues such as redundancy (Employment Tribunals).

Below are three brief examples of tribunals in operation:

- A has a dispute with the state concerning his entitlement to social security payments and to which social security officials have decided that he is no longer entitled. A can appeal against this decision to the Social Security and Child Support Appeals Tribunal.

- B has made a claim under the criminal injuries compensation scheme but it was rejected by the Criminal Injuries Compensation Authority as being insufficiently serious. B can appeal against this decision to the Criminal Injuries Compensation Appeals Panel.

- C claims that he has been unfairly dismissed by his employer. He can seek redress in an Employment Tribunal.

(Examples adapted from Tribunals Service website: www.tribunals.gov.uk.)

21.1.3 The constitutional position of tribunals

Tribunals are fact-finding bodies which apply legal principles and administrative rules in order to adjudicate on legal disputes (largely between an aggrieved individual and the state). In constitutional terms tribunals are impartial grievance mechanisms which are distinct from both the government as well as the ordinary court system.

Independent of the government/state

The existence of tribunals necessarily raises the constitutional question as to whether such bodies are part of the administration (executive) or the judicial arm of the state. In countries such as Australia, the tribunal system is considered to be part of the administration because as noted by Leggatt, they are specifically charged with administrative duties and 'putting themselves in the shoes of the relevant Government official'. In Britain, however, the 1957 Franks Committee plainly refuted the view that tribunals were part of the administration:

Q

'Tribunals are not ordinary courts, but neither are they appendages of Government Departments ... We consider that tribunals should properly be regarded as machinery provided by Parliament for adjudication rather than as part of the machinery for administration.'

Report of the Committee on Administration Tribunals and Inquiries
Cmnd 218 (1957) para 40.

Notwithstanding this, historically there has always been a necessarily close connection between a tribunal and the arm of the state which it regulates. This is due to the fact that the government department invariably provided the former with support. As a result, there has been concern that in terms of 'appearance', tribunals were not independent of the administration. Indeed, the Leggatt Report noted that were significant doubts as to whether the current arrangement of tribunals provided individuals with 'the necessary confidence in their independence and effectiveness'.

Moreover, the report commented that:

<table>
<tr><td>

Q

</td><td>

'There is no question of the Government improperly attempting to influence individual decisions. In that sense, tribunal decisions seem to us clearly impartial. But it cannot be said with confidence that they are demonstrably independent. Indeed, the evidence is to the contrary. For most tribunals, the departments provide administrative support, pay the salaries of members, pay their expenses, provide accommodation, provide IT support … are responsible for some appointments, and promote the legislation which prescribes procedures to be followed. At best, such arrangements result in tribunals and their departments being, or appearing to be, common enterprises.'

Tribunals for Users: One System, One Service, (The Stationery Office, 2001), para 2.20.

</td></tr>
</table>

As a result of the Leggatt Report, the government in an effort to protect the independence of tribunals, has announced reforms in this direction (see section 21.1.6).

Distinct from the court system

Tribunals are part of the justice system, but are outside the formal court structure. They are similar to courts in the sense that they act fairly, impartially, decide facts and apply legal rules to resolve legal disputes. Sometimes these are highly complex rules, for example, Employment Tribunals will apply convoluted employment and European law. Tribunals however, are broadly speaking less formal and less concerned with procedural/evidential rules than the courts. Indeed, in many cases, they do not require the participation of paid lawyers to represent complainants and they lack their own enforcement powers. In general terms, therefore, tribunals can be viewed as less adversarial than the formal court system.

Tribunals and courts are nevertheless connected in the sense that both are governed by an appellate system. In fact, a number of appeals from tribunals can ultimately end up being resolved in a court. For example, an appeal can progressively be made from the Employment Tribunal to the Employment Appeal Tribunal through to the Court of Appeal and the House of Lords. The government is committed to rationalising the tribunal appellate system and in 2006 unveiled legislative proposals to do so (see section 22.12.1).

21.1.4 Advantages of tribunals

There are a number of distinct advantages to tribunals:

- **Volume of cases**

  State officials take millions of decisions annually and it is not practicable to process all challenges to official decisions in a court as this inevitably would overload the court system. For example, in 2003–04 the Appeals Service – the precursor to the Social Security and Child Support Appeals Tribunal – received 235,657 appeals and the Mental Health Review Tribunals 20,408 (*Transforming Public Services: Complaints, Redress and Tribunals*, Cm 6243 (DCA, 2004), para 3.28). As the Leggatt Report pointed out, an individual is more likely to appear before a tribunal than a court.

- **Cost and efficiency**

  The court system involves lawyers and so is necessarily expensive. In contrast, tribunals are more efficient and cost effective as typically, they operate without paid legal representation and the awarding of costs. As a result, they provide swifter resolution of disputes which is consistent with the principle that *justice delayed is justice denied*. It should be noted, however, that in some tribunals such as Mental Health Review Tribunals, parties do use lawyers.

- **Specialism**

  Tribunals are subject specific so that they process cases involving a highly specialist aspect of the administration (eg social security benefits) and they are accordingly staffed by experts in that particular area. For example, Mental Health Review Tribunals will involve a medical expert. Similarly, whenever a Social Security and Child Support Appeals Tribunal is processing an appeal involving a disability living allowance, in determining the case a lawyer will be supplemented by a medical practitioner and a disability expert. In contrast, where specialist knowledge is required in the court system, an expert witness will be called. Some tribunals are composed of single lawyers whilst others may sit as Chairman accompanied by experts with appropriate expertise or other skills.

- **Formalism and accessibility**

  Tribunals are intended to be more accessible and user-friendly than courts and so do not necessarily follow strict procedural (eg evidential) rules. As noted by the Leggatt Report, the procedure in tribunals (both pre and during hearings) is generally simpler and more informal than the court system. In fact, the government in its 2004 White Paper (see above) has commented that, in general terms, individuals should be able to deal with public officials without the need to study voluminous information or seek professional/legal help. Not only are tribunals less formal than courts, they also tend to be less adversarial and so more inquisitorial.

- **Good governance**

  As pointed out in the Leggatt Report, in the light of the volume and variety of cases that they process, tribunals are in the invaluable position of being able to identify and highlight systematic administrative problems in departmental decision-making.

21.1.5 Disadvantages of tribunals

A number of problems are associated with tribunals:

- **Haphazard nature of the tribunal system**
  The Leggatt Report described the network of tribunals as incoherent and ineffectual with different procedures and rules applying to different tribunals. This is due to tribunals having being established in an *ad hoc* fashion responding to specific needs at the time. In fact, the report argued that in view of this lack of coherence: 'It is obvious that the term "tribunal system" is a misnomer' (see now the reforms section 22.12.1).

- **Independence**
  As indicated above, historically there has been concern that tribunals were not necessarily seen to be independent, however impartial they were. The Leggatt Report stated that: 'plainly they are not independent. Even in tribunals which are no longer paid for by "their" departments, there can be an unhealthy closeness' (para 1.10).

- **Legal representation**
  Research conducted in this area has indicated that individuals are likely to be more successful if they are represented. The Leggatt Report recognised that although legal representation can be beneficial, such representation inevitably drives up costs and works against tribunals being accessible. In any event, as suggested by the report, individuals could be better informed through the provision of more advice and assistance from the tribunal itself.

- **Delay**
  The Leggatt Report identified some unacceptable delays in processing cases, thereby mirroring the problems associated with the modern and overloaded court system.

ACTIVITY

Essay writing

Explain the constitutional and practical advantages and disadvantages of tribunals. Do the former outweigh the latter?

21.1.6 Reform

In 2001 the Leggatt Report made a number of recommendations which included:

- Rationalising the structure of the network of tribunals (bringing them together under one system) and its appellate system, thereby ensuring common structural arrangements.

- Enhancing the position of 'users' of the tribunal system.

Following the report the government issued its White Paper (*Transforming Public Services: Complaints, Redress and Tribunals* Cm 6243 (DCA, 2004)) in which it stated, *inter alia*, that it intended to:

- Place the system of tribunals on an unified and cohesive basis (including appeals).
- Rename the legal members of a tribunal 'Tribunal Judges'.
- Create the post of a Senior President of Tribunals.

In April 2006 the Tribunals Service became operational, providing administrative support to the major tribunals of central government. At this time the Tribunals Service included the tribunals for which the then Department for Constitutional Affairs was responsible (eg asylum) and these were added to with other major central government tribunals such as Social Security and Child Support Appeals Tribunal, the Criminal Injuries Compensation Appeals Panel and the Special Educational Needs and Disability Tribunal (others were scheduled to be added periodically). In this way, the independence of tribunals would be enhanced by removing them from their associated departments (ie the Mental Health Review Tribunal was transferred from the Department of Health and the Social Security and Child Support Appeals Tribunal from the Department for Work and Pensions).

In the Queen's Speech in November 2006 it was announced that the government intended to make further reform to tribunals (see the 2006 Tribunals, Courts and Enforcement Bill at section 22.12.1).

KEY FACTS

1. Tribunals are a grievance remedy which enables individuals to challenge decisions made by state officials in a forum which is outside the formal court system.

2. Tribunals can be divided into those which resolve disputes between the individual and the state (eg the Mental Health Review Tribunal), and those which regulate legal disputes between individuals and companies (eg Employment Tribunals).

CONTINUED ▶

KEY FACTS □ □ □ □ □ □ □ □

3. Tribunals are impartial decision-making bodies which are not part of the government department which it oversees.

4. They are also separate and distinct from the formal court system.

5. They are intended to be more accessible and user-friendly than the courts.

6. They do not necessarily follow strict procedural rules.

7. Generally they do not involve paid legal representatives.

21.2 Inquiries

Introduction

In very broad terms inquiries can be divided into two types:

- Those which investigate and report on local land issues (eg the refusal of a local planning authority to grant planning permission). This concerns an individual's dispute with the state.

- Those which investigate and report on specific events/scandals (eg the Bloody Sunday inquiry into the shooting of civilians in Londonderry). Such inquiries can be established either under statute (Inquiries Act 2005) or are non-statutory inquiries.

21.2.1 Land inquiries

When a local planning authority refuses to grant planning permission, an individual may seek to challenge such a decision and appeal to the Secretary of State. In such circumstances, under the Town and Country Planning Act 1990 the Secretary of State (part of central government) may enable a public local inquiry to be held, although this only happens in a small minority of cases. Indeed, in the vast majority of cases the issue is resolved by way of written submissions/ representations, although in approximately one-fifth of cases, a less formal (eg private) hearing is held

Public local inquiries generally will be ultimately decided by an inspector (drawn from the Planning Inspectorate – an executive agency) who will oversee the conduct and proceedings of such an inquiry. The interested parties (eg individual and planning authority) can call evidence and cross-examine witnesses. Following the inquiry, the inspector will issue a report making a recommendation to the Secretary of State, who will ultimately determine the issue. However, in the vast majority of cases, in practice, the final decision will have been delegated to the inspector himself. On the compatibility of the powers of the Secretary of State with Art 6 of the European Convention, see *R v Secretary of State for the Environment, Transport and the Regions, ex parte Barnes* [2001] UKHL 23.

As noted by Leyland and Anthony (*Textbook on Administrative Law* (5th edn, Oxford University Press, 2005) p 198), it could be argued that these inquiries are part of the constitutional principle of participatory democracy in that the individual is informing the decision-making process of the administration. In other words, the individual is to some extent influencing the ultimate decision to be taken by the minister or, more likely, the inspector. This is particularly the case in the context of objections to the citing of a controversial public development (eg road, airport, etc) whereby a public inquiry may be convened allowing the affected public to have the opportunity to raise their concerns and introduce supporting evidence/witnesses opposing the development. In this way individuals can actively influence and help shape governmental policy on this issue.

21.2.2 Inquiries into national events/scandals

The second type of inquiry investigates and makes recommendations in respect of a national event (eg the Scarman Report into the riots and disorder in Brixton in the early 1980s) or a public scandal (eg the Denning report into the Profumo affair). There are two categories of these types of inquiry:

- A statutory inquiry.

- A non-statutory inquiry.

In both cases these inquiries are not courts and their findings do not have legal effect:

Q	'Inquiries are designed to establish facts through an inquisitorial, investigatory process … inquiries are not courts and are not designed to determine criminal or civil liability or to settle disputes between parties'. Department for Constitutional Affairs Consultation Paper, *Effective Inquiries* (DCA, 2004), para 81.

In the context of statutory inquiries this point is reaffirmed by s 2 of the Inquiries Act 2005.

The constitutional purpose of both types of inquiries is to investigate issues of national concern, evaluate the evidence and make recommendations. In doing so, as noted by the government's consultation paper, these inquiries can restore public confidence, provide some benefit for those affected by the event in question and identify lessons that can be learnt.

21.2.3 Statutory inquiries into national events

Historically, there have been two types of statutory inquiries:

- A statutory inquiry under subject specific legislation, for example, the Stephen Lawrence inquiry established under the Police Act 1996.

- A statutory inquiry under the Tribunals of Inquiry (Evidence) Act 1921, for example, the (first) Bloody Sunday inquiry under Lord Widgery.

Today, statutory inquiries are held under the Inquiries Act 2005. This Act repealed the Tribunals of Inquiry (Evidence) Act 1921 together with other statutory provisions authorising inquiries (eg s 49 of the Police Act 1996). Under s 1 of the 2005 Act a government minister can establish an inquiry and set out its terms of reference:

 where it appears to him that –

 (a) particular events have caused, or are capable of causing, public concern, or

 (b) there is public concern that particular events may have occurred.

Formerly, under the 1921 Act such inquiries were relatively rare, although two recent examples were the Shipman Inquiry (into the deaths of a number of elderly women) and the (second) Bloody Sunday inquiry. Section 21 of the 2005 Act empowers the Chairman of the inquiry to compel evidence (witness or documents) and under s 35 it is a criminal offence not to comply with a notice issued by the Chairman under the Act.

The Act enables a minister to appoint a judicial figure to act as a panel member or Chairman (though there would be consultation with, for example, the Lord Chief Justice or senior law lord). In constitutional terms the involvement of the judiciary in high profile inquiries can raise questions as to whether it (ultimately) undermines their constitutional independence. In other words, as the subject matter of such inquiries can be overtly politically charged (eg into the events of Bloody Sunday), and as the government set out the terms of the inquiry, it can be argued that whatever recommendations are made, the judge involved inevitably will be subject to criticism. The government, however, has defended the use of judges:

> **Q**
>
> 'The Government believes that it can be appropriate for judges to chair inquiries, because their experience and position make them particularly well suited to the role. The judiciary has a great deal of experience in analysing evidence, determining facts and reaching conclusions … The judiciary also has a long tradition of independence from politics, and judges are widely accepted to be free from any party political bias.'
>
> Department for Constitutional Affairs Consultation Paper,
> *Effective Inquiries* (DCA, 2004), para 46.

21.2.4 Non-Statutory inquiries into national events

The government has regularly established non-statutory inquires to consider major national events. For example:

- The Hutton inquiry into the circumstances surrounding the death of Dr David Kelly.
- The Scott inquiry into the export of equipment to Iraq (see section 12.3.5).
- The foot and mouth inquiry into the lessons to be learned from the epidemic.

Such inquiries are more flexible than statutory inquiries, although they lack enforcement powers to compel evidence (witnesses or documents). Under s 15 of the 2005 Act, however, a government minister can convert such an inquiry into a statutory one. For example, where it was considered that enforcement powers were required.

KEY FACTS

Inquiries are an extra-judicial grievance mechanism which permit individuals to challenge, for example, the decision of a local authority to compulsorily purchase land or to refuse planning permission.

A second type of inquiry investigates and reports on major public events. Such inquiries are either:

CONTINUED ▸

KEY FACTS

Statutory inquiries – historically the following were established under statute:
- Stephen Lawrence inquiry under the aegis of the Police Act 1996.
- Bloody Sunday inquiry under the aegis of the Tribunals of Inquiry (Evidence) Act 1921.

These have now been replaced by the Inquiries Act 2005. Under the 2005 Act a government minister can establish an inquiry into events which have, or are capable of, causing public concern.

Non-statutory inquiries
- Hutton inquiry.

ACTIVITY

Essay writing

In terms of their nature and constitutional role, compare and contrast inquiries with tribunals.

21.3 Ombudsmen

Introduction

Q

'The activities of the Ombudsmen are concerned with holding public bodies to account and exposing maladministration where it has occurred. In so doing, part of their function is to encourage best practice in public administration'.

Reform of Public Sector Ombudsmen Services in England
(Cabinet Office, 2005), para 45.

The British constitution has a number of different public sector ombudsmen which cover central and local government, the National Health Service and the devolved administrations in Wales,

Scotland and Northern Ireland. The function of these ombudsmen is to investigate complaints relating to maladministration – in other words, faulty government/administration. This section will focus on arguably the most constitutionally significant of the Ombudsmen: the Parliamentary Commissioner for Administration (hereafter the Ombudsman).

21.3.1 Origins

Prior to the creation of the Ombudsman, there were essentially two main remedies available to an individual who was aggrieved by the actions of the officials of government departments:

- **The parliamentary remedy** – individuals could consult their constituency MP in order to resolve their grievance. The effectiveness of this remedy depended upon the tenacity and ability of the MP accessing governmental information.

- **The legal/judicial remedy** – individuals could seek justice before the courts by suing the government department concerned in public or private law. This was (as it is today) necessarily expensive and in any event, the action causing the grievance may not even be illegal as not falling within a recognised legal category (eg negligence, breach of contract).

The *Whyatt* Report (The Citizen and the Administration: the Redress of Grievances (JUSTICE, 1961)) noted the limitations of the then 'existing means of seeking redress' and recommended the creation of an independent officer of Parliament to investigate such grievances against the state. There was concern that the creation of the Ombudsman independently examining departmental issues, would undermine the constitutional convention of ministerial responsibility. It is clear, however, that the office has enhanced the operation of the convention by requiring ministers to explain publicly and account for maladministration found in their department. In 1967 Parliament established the Parliamentary Commissioner for Administration under the Parliamentary Commissioner Act 1967 (as amended). Under s 1 the Ombudsman (currently Ann Abraham) is appointed by the Crown. The constitutional function of the Ombudsman is to independently investigate complaints of injustice caused by maladministration by government and public bodies.

21.3.2 Maladministration

Maladministration is referred to in the 1967 Act, but it is not specifically defined. As a consequence, historically it has been apposite to refer to the famous '*Crossman Catalogue*' to indicate the type of behaviour that maladministration covers:

> **Q** 'bias, neglect, inattention, delay, incompetence, inaptitude, perversity, turpitude, arbitrariness and so on. It would be a long and interesting list.'
>
> *Hansard* HC Vol 734, col 51.

Latterly the Ombudsman's website has indicated that maladministration also embraces, *inter alia,* the following types of behaviour:

- A faulty procedure.
- Rudeness.
- Avoidable delay.
- A refusal to answer reasonable questions.
- A failure to indicate a right of appeal.

Three points can be made in relation to maladministration:

Firstly, maladministration is concerned essentially with the procedure (behaviour) of the state officials as apposed to the actual decision itself. In other words, it is concerned, for example, with how a person's claim for a social security benefit was processed by the department (eg was there an avoidable delay? Were forms lost? Were officials rude?), rather than whether they are legally entitled to a particular benefit (which is a legal question). In this way maladministration focuses on the decision-making process rather than the actual decision itself. However, the select committee supporting the Ombudsman has urged the office to infer an element of maladministration where a decision is *thoroughly bad* (as this presupposes an element of maladministration).

Secondly, although maladministration is broader than illegality, the precise dividing line between maladministration and illegality may well on occasions be a very fine one. For example, avoidable delay or the provision of inadequate advice could well be considered to be legally actionable for negligence.

Thirdly, although the lists above suggest behaviour which to an objective observer may appear to be somewhat trivial and unimportant (eg discourtesy by a public official), nonetheless, to the individual concerned, such behaviour inevitably will leave them feeling that they have a grievance against the state.

Under s 5 of the Act individuals must claim 'to have sustained injustice in consequence of maladministration in connection with the action so taken'. The cases indicate that injustice can embrace financial hardship/loss or even distress.

21.3.3 Jurisdiction

The bodies subject to the investigations of the Ombudsman are set out in Sched 2 of the Act and include:

- Central government departments of state (eg the Home Office).
- Bodies performing a public function and quangos (eg the Arts Council of England).

In terms of the number of complaints, according to figures for the 2005–06 session the Ombudsman accepted for investigation a number of complaints against the following (selected) bodies:

- HM Revenue and Customs (tax credits) (404 complaints)
- Jobcentre Plus (263)
- Child Support Agency (209)
- HM Revenue and Customs – other matters – (144).

It is not altogether surprising that these types of bodies should have the most complaints registered against them given that the public have regular contact with them. In contrast, there was only one complaint accepted for investigation in respect of the Arts Council of England (Annual Report 2005–06, *Making a difference*, HC 1363 (2006), figure 4).

A number of matters are excluded from the Ombudsman's remit and these are detailed in Sched 3 and include, *inter alia,* investigations relating to:

- Foreign relations.
- Contractual/commercial matters.
- The investigation of crime.

In addition, the Ombudsman is precluded from investigating where the individual has a legal remedy available to them in a court or tribunal. This is subject to the proviso that the Ombudsman *can* investigate such a compliant if satisfied that it would be unreasonable for that person to resort to such a remedy (eg it is too expensive or the law is unclear on the point). In the context of the *Debt of Honour case* (see below), the House of Commons Public Administration Select Committee made the following point:

<table>
<tr>
<td>

Q

</td>
<td>

'The entire basis of the 1967 Parliamentary Commissioner for Administration Act is that it is possible for a measure to be legal, and yet to be maladministered. The fact that legality has been established through Judicial Review may be irrelevant to maladministration. There may even be circumstances where the Ombudsman feels it is appropriate to conduct an investigation while Judicial Review proceedings are taking place, so that she can subsequently report without delay'.

First Report of Session 2005–06, *A Debt of Honour*, HC 735 (2006), para 20.

</td>
</tr>
</table>

In fact, the overlap between the Ombudsman and the courts can be illustrated by the *Congreve* case (see section 20.2.4) in which the court decided that the Home Secretary had acted illegally by threatening to revoke television licences purchased early in order to avoid paying an increased licence fee. This court ruling followed an earlier investigation by the Ombudsman which had held that maladministration had occurred, but had not recommended a remedy.

21.3.4 The investigation process

In broad terms the three stages are as follows:

- **The first/screening stage**

  This is known as the filter or screening stage whereby an aggrieved person must first send their complaint to an MP (generally their own, but other MPs can deal with it) who in turn may pass it on to the Ombudsman. The complaint must be given to the MP within 12 months of the individual having notice of the grievance, however, although the Ombudsman has a discretion to accept a complaint outside the time limit, the limit is usually applied. In short, complainants cannot complain directly to the Ombudsman, instead the MP referral system operates, which has proved controversial.

  In fact, this filter system is unusual amongst the different public sector Ombudsmen and it can be seen to act as a barrier preventing access to the Ombudsman. On the other hand, the rationale behind the referral system was to protect the constitutional position of the MP, one of whose functions is to resolve the problems of constituents. A further problem with removing the filter is the argument that direct access would overwhelm the Ombudsman with complaints. In any event, over the years there have been attempts at removing this filter. In fact, in July 2001, the government indicated that it supported its removal.

- **The investigation stage**

  On receipt of a referral by an MP, under s 5 of the Act the Ombudsman has a discretion as to whether or not to investigate a complaint and how an investigation is conducted. Moreover, the Ombudsman can also discontinue an investigation once commenced. She has wide-ranging powers of investigation which enable her to require any government minister, officer or member of the department (or other person) to furnish information or documents apposite to the investigation. The Act states that for the purpose of the investigation the Ombudsman:

> **S** s 8(2)
>
> 'shall have the same powers as the Court in respect of the attendance and examination of witnesses ... and in respect of the production of documents'.

Furthermore, it will amount to contempt to obstruct the work of the Ombudsman (s 9). Although the Ombudsman has powerful investigatory powers, she operates in a more inquisitorial way than the courts, which employ an adversarial approach. Investigations are carried out in private and she can go directly to the heart of the government department or public body and obtain information. On completion of the investigation, a report will be issued.

- **The report stage**

  Under s 10 of the Act, a report of the investigation is sent to the MP who referred the complaint, and to the principal officer of the government department. Where the report indicates a finding of maladministration resulting in injustice, generally speaking the department/authority concerned will comply with the recommendations for remedial action. Below are the percentages of complaints which were upheld (in full or part) against some of the bodies investigated during the 2005–06 session:

  - HM Revenue and Customs – tax credits (90%).

  - HM Revenue and Customs – other (30%).

  - Jobcentre Plus (52%).

  - HM Driver and Vehicle Licensing Agency (21%).

  - HM Prison Service (60%).

  - Legal Services Commission (44%).

  (Source: Annual Report 2005–06, *Making a difference*, HC 1363 (2006), figure 4).

It should be noted, however, that despite the Ombudsman's wide-ranging investigatory powers, her recommendations are not legally binding. In other words, although she can invite a department to, for example, award compensation, alter its administrative procedures or offer an apology, she cannot legally insist on it. Having said this, in general terms (although see below) the Ombudsman's recommendations are accepted as indicated by the Barlow Clowes affair, where the government paid out *ex gratia* payments even though they did not accept the findings of maladministration. The Ombudsman is supported in her work by a select committee: the House of Commons Public Administration Select Committee.

Under s 10(3) of the Act, if after conducting an investigation the Ombudsman believes that the injustice she has identified will not be remedied, a special report can be issued which will draw the attention of Parliament (and the wider public) to this deficiency. The second of these reports to be issued occurred in relation to the Channel Tunnel Link which resulted in the 'blighting' of houses which could not be sold whilst the exact route was being determined and in the event, the government proposed compensation. More recent examples of two special reports being issued are detailed below (these represent the third and fourth special reports issued by the Ombudsman in four decades):

CASE STUDY 1

Debt of Honour – ex-gratia payments to former civilian internees in the Far East **(2005)**

The Ombudsman held that injustice, in the form of distress, had been caused as a result of maladministration by the Ministry of Defence in respect of the operation of its *ex-gratia* payments for British internees held by the Japanese during the Second World War. The government refused (at least initially) to accept two of the recommendations made: (i) to review the scheme in light of the investigation and (ii) to reconsider the position of those denied payment owing to the government's 'bloodline' criterion. Thereafter, in July 2005 the Ombudsman issued a special report and this was followed by a report by the House of Commons Public Administration Select Committee in January 2006 which was critical of the Ministry of Defence:

First Report of Session 2005–06, *A Debt of Honour*, HC 735 (2006)

One interesting point to note about this case was that there was a delay in processing this complaint because the Association of British Internees Far Eastern Region challenged the Secretary of State in judicial review proceedings. They contended that the civilian eligibility criterion which meant that for the purposes of the scheme being British meant being a civilian who had been born in Britain or whose parent or grandparent had been, was disproportionate and or/ irrational and defeated a legitimate expectation. The Court of Appeal dismissed their appeal and held, *inter alia,* that it was not irrational for the Secretary of State to limit the application of the scheme to those individuals with close links to the United Kingdom at the time of their detention as an internee or to introduce the birth criteria (*R (Association of British Civilian Internees: Far East Region) v Secretary of State for Defence* [2003] EWCA Civ 473).

CASE STUDY 2

Trusting in the Pensions Promise **(2006)**

The Ombudsman found injustice caused by maladministration in terms of information provided by the government in respect of the security of members' final salary occupational pension schemes. The government rejected the finding that maladministration had occurred and the Ombudsman's recommendation. As a consequence in March 2006 a special report was issued and in July 2006 the Public Administration Select Committee in support of the Ombudsman made the following constitutional point:

CONTINUED ▸

Q

'this system will only work if the Parliamentary Ombudsman, the
Government and Parliament share a broad common
understanding of what maladministration might be and who
should properly identify it (para 76) ... We share the
Ombudsman's concern that the Government has been far too
ready to dismiss her findings of maladministration ... It would be
extremely damaging if Government became accustomed simply to
reject findings of maladministration, especially if an investigation
by this Committee proved there was indeed a case to answer. It
would raise fundamental constitutional issues about the position
of the Ombudsman and the relationship between Parliament and
the Executive (para 78). We trust that this Report will act as a
warning to the Government ... The Parliamentary Commissioner
is Parliament's Ombudsman: Government must respect her'
(para 79).

Sixth Report of Session 2005–06, *The Ombudsman in Question: the Ombudsman's
report on pensions and its constitutional implications,* HC 1081 (2006).

As an interesting postscript to this case, in *R (Bradley and others) v Secretary of State
for Work and Pensions* [2007] EWHC 242 (Admin), the Administrative Court quashed
the Secretary of State's rejection of the Ombudsman's finding of maladministration.

In addition to the periodic special reports above, the Ombudsman is required to provide an annual
report detailing her activities.

21.3.5 Ombudsman or Ombudsmouse?

There has always been academic debate over the effectiveness of the Ombudsman. On the one
hand the Ombudsman has wide-ranging investigatory powers, but on the other, she has no legal
powers of enforcement. As noted by the Public Administration Select Committee in the context of
the report on pensions (see above), however, historically even when government departments have
denied maladministration found by the Ombudsman, they have 'ultimately been willing to offer
some recompense out of respect for the Ombudsman's office' (para 67). In addition, in her speech
to the Constitution Unit in December 2006 the Ombudsman made it clear that in relation to the
majority of complaints where maladministration is found, the government accept these findings
and then comply with her recommendations. As a consequence, she noted that she could not see

the need for legal enforcement powers, although she added that this was subject to a proviso that if government departments systematically ignored her findings then she 'might begin to see some role for legal enforceability'.

In addition, it must be remembered that the Ombudsman also performs a *de facto* preventative role in that the very existence of the office acts to some extent as a deterrent to government departments to avoid engaging in behaviour which could be deemed as maladministration. In this way the Ombudsman promotes good governance. Indeed, according to her 2005–06 annual report one of the aims for the 2006–09 period was: 'To contribute to improvements in public service delivery by being an influential organisation, sharing our knowledge and expertise (p 59). Indeed, in 2007 the Ombudsman, after consultation, produced a document on developing '*Principles of Good Administration*'. It set out in broad terms the Ombudsman's view as to what the organisations and bodies subject to her jurisdiction should be doing in order to deliver good administration/customer service. These principles will help to clarify the meaning of maladministration (see section 21.3.2).

The following two case studies illustrate the effectiveness of the Ombudsman:

CASE STUDY 3

Sachsenhausen (1967)

The Ombudsman found maladministration by the Foreign Office in the way that it had distributed money supplied by the German Government to compensate British citizens who had suffered persecution under Nazi rule. As a result, the Foreign Office provided compensation to the aggrieved individuals who had been affected.

CASE STUDY 4

Child Support Agency (2001–02) Case No C.1685/00

The Ombudsman found injustice caused by maladministration by the Child Support Agency when they unreasonably demanded payment of arrears as well as failing to reply to correspondence. This indicated that the CSA had consistently failed to handle this case in a satisfactory fashion. The complainant was awarded £900 by the Child Support Agency.

21.3.6 Accountability

Under the rule of law all bodies are subject to the law. Although the Ombudsman is an independent officer of Parliament she is still accountable to:

- **The courts** – s 5 of the 1967 Act confers a broad discretion on the Ombudsman in terms of deciding whether to investigate a case (see *Re Fletcher's Application* [1970] 2 All ER 527) and the conduct of that investigation (*R v Parliamentary Commissioner for Administration, ex parte Dyer* [1994] 1 All ER 375). In December 2006 in her speech to the Constitution Unit, the Ombudsman noted that although the number of applications for judicial review of the Ombudsman was increasing, they were generally rejected by the courts. However, in a series of cases involving Balchin, the courts did review (and overturn) the decisions of the Ombudsman: *R v Parliamentary Commissioner for Administration, ex parte Balchin* [1997] COD 146, *R v Parliamentary Commissioner for Administration, ex parte Balchin (No 2)* [2000] JPL 267, *R (Balchin) v Parliamentary Commissioner for Administration (No 3)* [2002] EWHC 1876 (Admin).

- **Parliament** – under s 1 of the 1967 Act, the Ombudsman is removable by both Houses of Parliament (analogous to senior judges – see section 13.4.1). In addition, the Ombudsman also provides Parliament with an annual report of her workload.

KEY FACTS

The Ombudsman is an extra-judicial form of redress who investigates complaints of maladministration (eg poor government) against:
- Central government departments of State (Department for Work and Pensions).
- Bodies performing a public function and quangos (eg the Arts Council of England).

Individuals must have sustained injustice in consequence of maladministration and this can take the form of financial hardship or distress.

The Ombudsman (after being contacted by an MP) works in an inquisitorial manner and has wide investigatory powers to ascertain whether maladministration has occurred.

On conclusion of the investigation a report will be issued detailing the maladministration found (or otherwise) together with recommendations for remedial action.

Although the Ombudsman cannot legally enforce her recommendations, she can issue a special report where she considers that the maladministration will go unremedied.

ACTIVITY ☐ ☐ ☐

Essay writing

Explain the constitutional purpose of the Ombudsman, her jurisdiction and how she operates. Do you feel that the Ombudsman is an effective constitutional tool?

21.3.7 Other Ombudsmen

The system of public sector ombudsmen embraces the following:

- **Health Commissioner** – This Ombudsman was established under the National Health Service Reorganisation Act 1973 (as amended), and investigates complaints concerning unfair or improper services provided by the NHS in England. Traditionally the office holder also operates as the Parliamentary Commissioner for Administration, hence references to the Parliamentary and Health Service Commissioner (PHSO).

- **Local government** – The three local government Ombudsmen for England (established under the Local Government Act 1974) investigate complaints of maladministration in the context of local councils. It should be noted that in 2005 the government recommended streamlining the constitutional relationship of the parliamentary, health and local commissioners (*Reform of Public Sector Ombudsmen Services in England* (Cabinet Office: 2005).

- **Scotland** – The Scottish Public Services Ombudsman Act 2002 (a Scottish statute) rationalised the different ombudsmen under one organisation. The Scottish Public Services Ombudsman considers complaints of maladministration in relation to, among others, the:
  - Scottish Executive.
  - NHS.
  - Local government and housing associations in Scotland.

- **Wales** – The Public Services Ombudsman for Wales was established under the Public Services Ombudsman (Wales) Act 2005. It considers maladministration in the context of:
  - Local government.
  - NHS.
  - Devolved government (National Assembly for Wales).

- **Northern Ireland** – The Northern Ireland Ombudsman considers complaints in respect of:
  - Northern Ireland government departments and agencies (as the *Assembly Ombudsman for Northern Ireland*).
  - Local councils and Health and Social Services boards/councils/trusts (as the *Northern Ireland Commissioner for Complaints*).

- **Europe** – Under the Maastricht Treaty a European Ombudsman was established to inve maladministration by the institutions of the EC (except the judicial bodies acting in the judicial capacity).

- **Judges** – Under s 62 of the Constitutional Reform Act 2005 a Judicial Appointments and Conduct Ombudsman has been created to investigate complaints of maladministration in the context of the judicial appointments process.

Further reading

Beatson, J, 'Should judges conduct public inquiries?' (2005) 121 LQR 221.

Craig, P, *Administrative Law* (5th edn, Sweet & Maxwell, 2003), Chapter 9.

Leyland, P and Anthony, G, *Textbook on Administrative Law* (5th edn, Oxford University Press, 2005), Chapters 6 and 7.

Purdue, M, 'Investigations by the Public Sector Ombudsmen' in Feldman, D (ed), *English Public Law* (Oxford University Press, 2004), p 1019.

Purdue, M, 'Public Inquiries as a Part of Public Administration' in Feldman, D (ed), *English Public Law* (Oxford University Press, 2004), p 1059.

Richardson, G, 'Tribunals' in Feldman, D (ed), *English Public Law* (Oxford University Press, 2004), p 985.

Scorer, R, 'Modern Inquiries and the public purse' (2005) NLJ 61.

Wade, H and Forsyth, C, *Administrative Law* (9th edn, Oxford University Press, 2004), Chapters 23 and 24.

Websites

www.ombudsman.org.uk
www.tribunals.gov.uk

CONSTITUTIONAL DEVELOPMENTS AND REFORM

AIMS AND OBJECTIVES

At the end of this chapter you should be able to:

- Appreciate the nature of constitutional reform in the British constitution

- Identify and summarise the main constitutional developments which have taken place in recent years

22.1 The process of constitutional change

The purpose of this chapter is to provide a summary of the principal constitutional reforms and developments which have taken place since 1997 (a period of unprecedented change). It will highlight such changes on a themed basis thereby providing the pattern of constitutional development in this period.

22.1.1 A snapshot of constitutional reform in Britain

> **Q**
>
> 'In some respects, the constitution is like the English language – it is not preserved in aspic, requiring an academy, a two-thirds majority or a referendum to authorise variation; it is a living organism, adapting to change as evolutionary circumstances require. It is almost infinitely flexible …'.
>
> House of Lords Select Committee on the Constitution 15th Report of Session 2005–06,
> *Waging war: Parliament's role and responsibility*, HL Paper 236-I (2006) para 97.

The above quote highlights that the rules of the constitution have not historically been codified in a single authoritative document, but instead are found in a mixture of statutory and common law sources which are supplemented by constitutional conventions. As parliamentary sovereignty is the dominant feature of the British constitution, the sources of the constitution (see Chapter 4) are at the mercy of Parliament and can be altered (or abolished) with the passing of a statute. As a consequence, these sources are constantly being added to. For example, the Electoral Administration Act 2006 altered the arrangements in terms of the electoral process. Indeed, it should also be remembered that historically, 'constitutional' statutes have had no special legal status or protection from repeal (but see Laws LJ at section 4.4.5).

It is for these reasons that the British constitution is described as highly flexible where the process of constitutional change can at times, be remarkably swift. In particular, since the Labour Government came to power in 1997, Parliament has passed a wide-ranging raft of legislation which collectively has radically altered the content and form of the British constitution.

22.1.2 Constitutional reform elsewhere

In contrast, the process of constitutional reform in other countries with a codified constitution (such as the United States or Republic of Ireland) is more sedate and measured. For example:

- **United States** – In 1951 a restriction was placed on the number of terms of office which an American President could serve (the 22nd Amendment). This change to the constitution was achieved via Art V which required the reform to have the support of two-thirds of both Houses of Congress, together with three quarters of all the states.

- **Ireland** – In 1995 divorce was introduced (the 15th Amendment) following the passage of legislation through the Irish Parliament and approval by the people in a referendum (Art 46).

- **Germany** – In 2006 a constitutional measure was passed (in force in 2007) by the two Houses of the German Parliament (Bundestag and Bundesrat – lower and upper chambers, respectively) which rebalances the constitutional power between central (federal) and local (Länder) governments.

ACTIVITY

Exercise

In terms of constitutional reform, what are the advantages and disadvantages of the British constitution being flexible?

22.2 The separation of powers

As indicated in Chapter 5, the British constitution is typically described as one which fails to adhere to the principle of the separation of powers with the position of the law lords (see section 5.7.4) and the Lord Chancellor (see section 5.7.9) among the most obvious violations. In recent years however, the passing of the Constitutional Reform Act 2005 has, to some extent, realigned the constitutional arrangements of Britain in line with a stricter form of separation of powers.

22.2.1 The Supreme Court

Part 3 of the 2005 Act establishes a Supreme Court (to replace the existing Appellate Committee of the House of Lords) which will be legally, constitutionally and physically separate from Parliament. The law lords will become Justices of the Supreme Court and they will exercise the same powers as the existing judges of the Appellate Committee with the exception that they will also process 'devolution' issues (see Chapter 14). The Supreme Court is scheduled to become operational in 2009 with the Middlesex Guildhall being earmarked as the building to house it. During the parliamentary debates on the creation of a new Supreme Court, the following arguments were made for and against this proposal.

The arguments for the removal of the law lords from Parliament

- It was part of the government's drive to modernise a constitution which was antiquated in a number of ways.

- It would realign the constitution in accordance with a purer separation of powers. As noted by the Lord Chancellor:

Q	'The Law Lords are judges and not legislators: the separation between those two roles should be made explicit. That principle of separation is already established in many other democracies'. House of Lords Select Committee on the Constitutional Reform Bill, *Constitutional Reform Bill (HL)* Volume 2: Evidence, HL Paper 125-II (2004), p 9.

In this way, separating the judges from Parliament would enhance their independence.

- As a result of other constitutional reforms (in particular, the Human Rights Act 1998), it was important to separate clearly the law lords from Parliament.

- It would be consistent with Art 6 of the European Convention which prescribes a right to a fair trial.

- The self-denying ordinance (see section 5.7.4) was no longer sustainable. A complete separation from the legislature would avoid law lords having to 'recuse' themselves from court cases in relation to legislation which they had previously had a role in scrutinising/passing.

- On a pragmatic and practical level, in terms of accommodation, the law lords could be better catered for in a new Supreme Court building specifically equipped for that purpose.

It should be noted that the proposal for a Supreme Court had significant support including the senior law lord, Lord Bingham, the Bar, the Law Society and a number of academics. There were, however, a number of arguments levelled against the creation of a new Supreme Court.

The arguments against removal

- As noted by Lord Norton, the law lords were already considered to be independent, therefore separation could hardly 'enhance' their independence (*Hansard*, HL Vol 657, col 1269).

- If the argument for a Supreme Court was based solely on the principle of the separation of powers, it foundered because according to a former law lord (Lord Lloyd): 'the separation of powers is not part of our constitution'. (*Hansard*, HL Vol 665, col 57).

- Article 6 of the European Convention does not require an institutional separation of powers (see *Pabla Ky* (2006) at section 5.7.4).

- No practical benefit would result from the separation. Instead, the new Supreme Court Justices could become constitutionally isolated without the protection of Parliament. Moreover, not only would the judges lose out on the benefit of working with parliamentarians (eg non-lawyers), but Parliament itself would lose the advantage of the input of their judicial wisdom. It should be noted, however, that both Houses already contain a number of lawyers.

- The cost would not justify the reform. In 2004 it was estimated by the Lord Chancellor that it would cost £30 million to renovate Middlesex Guildhall and £15 million to relocate its existing courts. Furthermore, the operational annual costs of the new Supreme Court would be approximately £5.2 million more than the existing Appellate Committee.

It is not without significance that at the time of the 2005 Act, the law lords themselves were roughly divided on the issue (the senior law lord, Lord Bingham in favour, the second senior law lord, Lord Nicholls, against it). On the Supreme Court see: M Ryan, 'The House of Lords and the Shaping of the Supreme Court' (2005) 56 NILQ 135.

22.2.2 The Lord Chancellor

The Lord Chancellor is historically cited as the quintessential violation of the separation of powers as he has had a role in all three functions. As indicated above (see section 5.7.9), although he will remain a government minister, his role has now changed. For example, he no longer acts as the Speaker of the House of Lords (see section 10.7.4) and even though by constitutional convention he has historically been a peer, in future he may not even be a member of the upper House (s 2 of the Constitutional Reform Act 2005). In fact, in June 2007 Jack Straw MP became Lord Chancellor.

Under the Constitutional Reform Act 2005, the Lord Chancellor is under a statutory duty to respect the rule of law (s 1), protect the independence of the judiciary (ss 3 and 17) and ensure that the courts are supported in terms of resources (s 17). Moreover, the Lord Chancellor is no longer the Head of the Judiciary in England and Wales. This position is now held by the Lord Chief Justice who also assumes many of the judicial functions formerly exercised by the Lord Chancellor. In terms of judicial appointments under the Act, in essence the Lord Chancellor either approves or rejects candidates nominated by an independent Appointments Commission (see section 13.3.1).

22.2.3 The Legislative and Regulatory Reform Act 2006

As indicated above (see section 5.7.2), delegated legislation is a clear violation of the separation of powers, however, it is a practical necessity as Parliament cannot pass all the law that is required. Under the Legislative and Regulatory Reform Act 2006 a government minister is empowered to legislate by making an order (this replaces the power to make Regulatory Reform Orders under the Regulatory Reform Act 2001). The rationale behind this legislation (and its predecessors in 2001 and 1994) is to enable a minister to remove unnecessary red tape and regulation (ie to remove outdated legislation).

The 2006 Act empowers a minister to make an order in order to serve the following purpose:

 s 1(2)

That purpose is removing or reducing any burden, or the overall burdens, resulting directly or indirectly for any person from any legislation.

Section 1(3) of the Act defines a burden in the following ways:

(a) financial cost,

(b) administrative inconvenience,

(c) obstacle to efficiency, productivity or profitability, or

(d) a sanction which affects the carrying on of any lawful activity.

Due to the broad power conferred on a minister, s 3 requires him to be satisfied of the following preconditions before making an order:

(a) the policy objective intended to be secured by the provision could not be satisfactorily secured by non-legislative means;

(b) the effect of the provision is proportionate to the policy objective;

(c) the provision, taken as a whole, strikes a fair balance between the public interest and the interests of any person adversely affected by it;

(d) the provision does not remove any necessary protection;

(e) the provision does not prevent any person from continuing to exercise any right or freedom which that person might reasonably expect to continue to exercise;

(f) the provision is not of constitutional significance.

In addition, an order cannot be made in relation to tax (s 5) or to create a new criminal offence (or increase the penalty for an existing offence) which imposes a punishment exceeding two years' imprisonment on indictment or exceeding the normal maximum term of imprisonment (or a fine exceeding level 5) on summary trial (s 6). Moreover, a minister must consult when proposing to make an order (s 13) and lay the draft order and explanatory document before Parliament (s 14). The minister will recommend the level of parliamentary scrutiny which the order will receive (negative, affirmative or super-affirmative resolutions), although either House can stipulate a higher level of scrutiny.

The advantages levelled in favour of this legislation (and its predecessors in 2001 and 1994) is that unnecessary legislative provisions can be efficiently removed without following the alternative long-winded route of a Bill. Moreover, before the measure is made there is a specific requirement for consultation to take place with relevant parties.

The constitutional disadvantages are, however, that this measure permits primary legislation to be altered by the means of secondary legislation (ie by an Order). In short, this measure, like the preceding Acts of 2001 and 1994, is an 'Henry VIII clause' which enables a minister to alter primary legislation by means of secondary legislation.

At its second reading, however, in the House of Commons the Parliamentary Under-Secretary of State for the Cabinet Office stated that:

Q	'I am giving a clear undertaking today that orders will not be used to implement highly controversial reforms … key procedural safeguards have been retained and I have given clear undertakings on the appropriate use of these powers.'
	Jim Murphy MP, *Hansard* HC, Vol 442 cols 1058–59.

22.3 The rule of law

22.3.1 Statutory recognition

The Constitutional Reform Act 2005 gave statutory recognition to the 'existing constitutional principle of the rule of law'. Section 1 states that the Act does not adversely affect this pre-existing principle, or the Lord Chancellor's responsibility towards it. Moreover, s 17 details the oath to be taken by a Lord Chancellor which specifies that the incumbent must respect the rule of law. The question remains whether s 1 is merely declaratory (ie aspirational), rather than actually enforceable and *justiciable* in a court of law.

22.3.2 Clear laws

In recent years the following developments have been made to make legislation clearer and thus more accessible:

- **Explanatory notes** – these notes which accompany Bills and Acts are prepared to make legislation more intelligible to individuals. These explanatory notes have been made available to the public since 1998. Furthermore, in 2006 the Coroner Reform: The Government's Draft Bill, Cm 6849 (DCA, 2006) was published which included detailed passages explaining each aspect/clause of the Bill in alternative pages. This was specifically designed to make the draft Bill as intelligible (and so accessible) to the public as possible.

- **Explanatory memorandum** – are now available in respect of Statutory Instruments. Such notes explain the purpose, objective and application of the measure.

22.3.3 Excessive state power?

The past few years have been punctuated by the successive passage of legislation designed to counter terrorism. These Acts have cumulatively increased the power of the state to interfere with the rights of the individual with the public policy intention of combating terrorism. For example:

- **The Terrorism Act 2000** – this Act, in effect, placed counter-terrorist powers on a permanent basis (ie not annually reviewed).

- **The Anti-Terrorism, Crime and Security Act 2001** (passed in the aftermath of the terrorist attacks of 9/11) – increased police stop and search powers and authorised the indefinite detention of individuals suspected of international terrorism. The latter was subsequently (and successfully) challenged in the House of Lords in *A and others v Secretary of State* (2004) (see section 6.7.4) which in turn led to the following Act:

- **The Prevention of Terrorism Act 2005** – the Act authorised control orders on individuals which could be used for example to restrict their movements (eg a curfew). These control orders were introduced as a result of the successful challenge (above) to the indefinite detention of suspects. Control orders made under the 2005 Act were then successfully challenged in *Secretary of State for the Home Department v JJ and others* [2006] EWCA Civ 1141 (see section 13.6.2).

- **The Terrorist Act 2006** – this Act, *inter alia*, extended the length of time that terrorist suspects could be held from 14 to 28 days. As indicated earlier (see section 6.7.5), the government had originally sought a period of detention of 90 days, but the House of Commons refused to accept this. The Act also created an offence of encouraging terrorism (s 1) and one relating to the sale or distribution of terrorist publications (s 2), both of which raise issues of an interference with freedom of speech.

According to LIBERTY (an organisation dedicated to the protection of human rights), although a government has a responsibility to take steps to protect individuals from terrorism, this does not justify encroaching unnecessarily on individual rights and freedoms. The concern of LIBERTY is that legislative measures (for example, such as above) which confer excessive powers on the state are counter productive as they risk alienating individuals (thereby acting as a 'recruiting sergeant' for terrorism) and in fact threaten the values which we should be striving as a society to protect.

22.4 Parliamentary sovereignty

Two interesting developments have occurred in this area in recent years:

22.4.1 Implied repeal

As indicated earlier at section 4.4.5, in *Thoburn v Sunderland City Council* (2002) Laws LJ commented (albeit *obiter*) that the time had come for the recognition of a category of statutes (eg Human Rights Act 1998, devolution Acts) which were not subject to implied repeal (on this doctrine see section 7.9.3). Under the constitution, statutes have, historically, been held to be subject to repeal both expressly (see section 7.9.2) and impliedly.

22.4.2 Challenging an Act of Parliament

The principle of parliamentary sovereignty concerns the relationship between Parliament and the courts with the effect that (at least historically) the latter did not question Acts of Parliament (see section 7.8.1). In *R (Jackson) v Attorney-General* [2005] UKHL 56 (for the facts see section 10.10.3), Jackson unsuccessfully tried to challenge the Hunting Act 2004 on the basis that it was not valid as it had been passed without the consent of the House of Lords under the Parliament Act 1949.

The main thrust of the argument was that the 1949 Parliament Act was itself invalid as it had been passed without the consent of the House of Lords, thereby rendering any Act passed under this legislation invalid. One line of argument which Jackson tried to deploy was that the Parliament Act 1949 was not primary legislation, but delegated legislation as it had been passed under the aegis of the Parliament Act 1911. As such, it is a constitutional principle that a delegate (here the House of Commons and the Crown acting in the absence of the House of Lords) could not increase its own powers (ie increase its capacity to pass legislation at the expense of the House of Lords).

The House of Lords rejected Jackson's submissions and affirmed that the 1949 Act was valid and so by implication therefore was the 2004 Act. They held that it was possible to amend the 1911 Act so as to reduce the delaying power of the House of Lords without the consent of the upper chamber. Lord Steyn made some interesting (albeit *obiter*) observations concerning the ultimate relationship between Parliament and the courts:

> J
>
> 'If the Attorney General is right the 1949 Act could also be used to introduce oppressive and wholly undemocratic legislation. For example, it could theoretically be used to abolish judicial review of flagrant abuse of power by a government or even the role of the ordinary courts in standing between the executive and citizens. This is where we may have to come back to the point about the supremacy of Parliament. We do not in the United Kingdom have an uncontrolled constitution as the Attorney General implausibly asserts. The classic account given by Dicey of the doctrine of the supremacy of Parliament, pure and absolute as it was, can now be seen to be out of place in the modern United Kingdom. Nevertheless, the supremacy of Parliament is still the *general* principle of our constitution. It is a construct of the common law. The judges created this principle. If that is so, it is not unthinkable that circumstances could arise where the courts may have to qualify a principle established on a different hypothesis of constitutionalism.'

It is of interest to note that the Lord Chancellor rejected Lord Steyn's analysis when being questioned by the House of Lords Select Committee on the Constitution in 2005 (see section 7.7).

As a postscript to this case, in *R (Countryside Alliance) v Attorney-General* [2006] EWCA Civ 817, the Court of Appeal rejected claims that the Hunting Act 2004 violated European Convention law (Arts 8, 11 and Art 1 of Protocol 1 of the Convention) or European Community law (Arts 28 and 49 of the EC Treaty).

ACTIVITY

Essay writing

Explain the significance of the developments that have made been in recent years to the fundamental principles that underpin the British constitution.

KEY FACTS

Fundamental elements of the British constitution: constitutional developments and reforms	Source
The separation of powers	
• A new Supreme Court to replace the existing Appellate Committee of the House of Lords	Pt 3, Constitutional Reform Act 2005
• Reform of the office of the Lord Chancellor	Pt 2, Constitutional Reform Act 2005
The rule of law	
• Statutory recognition of the 'existing principle of the rule of law'	ss 1 and 17, Constitutional Reform Act 2005
• Explanatory notes for Bills and memorandum for Statutory Instruments	Change in practice and notes prepared by the relevant government department
• Draft bills	Change in practice and drafts prepared by the relevant government department
Parliamentary sovereignty	
• No implied repeal of constitutional statutes (ie devolution statutes, Human Rights Act 1998)	Laws LJ, *Thoburn v Sunderland City Council* (2002)

22.5 The House of Commons

22.5.1 Modernisation

The Labour Party came into power in 1997 with a manifesto commitment to reform the arcane procedures of Parliament. In June 1997 the House of Commons Select Committee on the Modernisation of the House of Commons was established to examine how such practices/procedures should be modernised. In the ensuing years the following reforms have been made:

- **Westminster Hall** – Since 1999 Westminster Hall has operated as a parallel debating chamber to the Commons (analogous to the main Committee in the Australian House of Representatives). This has enabled backbenchers to raise issues which would not have found time in the Commons chamber. In so doing it has further held the government to account by allowing, for example, 'cross-cutting' questions which are answered by disparate departmental ministers on a common theme.

- **Liaison Committee** – This committee consists of the Chairs of the other select committees and since 2002 has taken evidence from the Prime Minister, thereby increasing scrutiny of his actions and policies.

- **Working hours** – The House of Commons traditionally has had late sitting hours (eg to 10pm), but these have been modified by reducing the number of daily late sittings (which were not conducive to family life or, arguably, productive in any event) and bringing the parliamentary day forward. In addition, the parliamentary calendar has piloted September sittings.

In terms of the legislative process the following reforms have been made:

- **Explanatory notes** – (see section 22.3.2).

- **Programme motions** – In order to modernise and provide more certainty to the law-making process, programming of bills has been introduced. This is a more formal procedure than the parliamentary timetable being agreed through the '*usual channels*' between the front benches.

- **Pre-legislative scrutiny** – Although Bills have been published in draft since the early 1990s, this process has been slightly accelerated since 1997. Indeed, in the period between 1992 and 1997 there were 18 Bills published in draft, whereas, for example, in the 2002–03 session there were 10 such Bills (source: The House of Commons Select Committee on Modernisation of the House of Commons, First Report of Session 2005–06, *The Legislative Process*, HC 1097 (2006), p 10). The advantage of this process is that it allows interested parties and parliamentarians the opportunity to influence a Bill in draft before it takes final shape.

- **The carry-over procedure** – this allows a Bill to be carried over between parliamentary sessions, thus saving the Bill from abandonment. In constitutional terms this mitigates the effect of the Parliament Acts of 1911 and 1949 as such Bills are not lost at the end of a session. The

Constitutional Reform Bill was a high profile Bill which was carried over from one parliamentary session to the next (from the 2003–04 to the 2004–05 session).

Finally, Parliament is in the process of trying to improve the connection between itself and the people, particularly younger people: First Report of Session 2003–04, *Connecting Parliament with the Public*, HC 368 (2004). This paper, produced by the House of Commons Select Committee on the Modernisation of the House of Commons, was an attempt to explore ways in which Parliament could 're-connect' with the public through improved facilities (eg use of information technology).

22.5.2 Elections

Reform of the electoral system

The 1997 Labour Party manifesto committed the incoming government to establish an independent commission on the voting system for the House of Commons and thereafter hold a referendum on the system. As indicated earlier, one of the perceived difficulties with the present 'first past the post' system (see section 9.4.4) is that as a majoritarian system, it can distort the wishes of the electorate. In 1998 the Jenkins Commission delivered its report (*The Report of the Independent Commission on the Voting System*, Cm 4090-I (1998)) which recommended a highly convoluted system. It involved providing each elector with two votes:

- One vote for a constituency MP (this would involve single member constituency MPs being elected by the Alternative Vote system).

- One vote for an individual or party (this would involve additional or top up members which would correct the disproportionality of the above constituency MPs).

The first vote would result in the election of 80–85 per cent of MPs of the House of Commons, who would be supplemented by MPs being elected by virtue of the second vote. Since the report, no referendum has taken place.

Reform of the electoral process and enfranchisement

The Electoral Administration Act 2006 was passed in order to increase turnout at elections, enable more people to vote and to combat electoral fraud. It must be remembered that this legislation was passed in the context of allegations of fraud in the general election of 2005. A few of the measures are detailed below:

- The Act was concerned to improve the electoral registration process to ensure that electoral registers are as accurate as possible (Pt 2). In addition, in an attempt to ensure that voting more accessible to the public, a framework is provided so that local authorities regularly r the accessibility of their polling stations (Pt 4). Moreover, in order to encourage public participation in elections, s 69 requires that:

A local electoral officer must take such steps as he thinks appropriate to encourage
the participation by electors in the electoral process in the area for which he acts.

- In an attempt to combat electoral fraud, the Act requires postal and proxy voters to provide
  their signature and date of birth (Pt 3). Part 7 regulates political parties (for example, the
  regulating of loans to political parties).

- Section 17 reduces the age of candidates who wish to stand for election to the House of
  Commons (and local authority, etc) from 21 to 18 years. Furthermore, s 73 removes any
  common law rule which provided that individuals who owing to their mental state were subject
  to a legal incapacity to vote in an election (illustrating how Parliament can over-ride the
  common law – see section 7.5.1).

Finally, it is worth noting that in December 2006 the Department for Constitutional Affairs
initiated a consultation process in respect of the enfranchisement of prisoners (*Voting Rights of
Convicted Prisoners Detained within the United Kingdom – The UK Government's response to the
Grand Chamber of the European Court of Human Rights judgment in the case of Hirst v The United
Kingdom*, CP 29/06 (2006)). In the *Hirst* case (see section 9.6.3) the court had held that a blanket
ban on prisoners voting violated Art 3 of Protocol No I which protects the right to free and fair
elections. The government recognised that the enfranchisement of prisoners was a contentious issue
and sought the views of respondents on the potential options available: These included:

- Continuing with the total disenfranchisement, notwithstanding the court's judgment as the
  government wanted to include views in favour of this position 'in deciding the extent of any
  reform to the UK's current position'.

- To enfranchise those prisoners who had been sentenced to less than a specified period.

- To enable those sentencing prisoners (the judiciary) to determine disenfranchisement.

- To consider two specific issues: 'Namely, the franchise of prisoners convicted of an offence
  relating to an election, and the enfranchisement of different categories of offenders detained in
  mental hospitals'.

In the context of the disenfranchisement of prisoners see also: I White, 'Convicted prisoners and
the franchise', SN/PC/1764 (House of Commons Library, 2007).

22.6 The House of Lords

22.6.1 Composition

1997 Labour Party manifesto gave a commitment to reform the House of Lords by removing
hereditary peers and establishing a joint parliamentary committee to consider long-term
reform. As indicated earlier (see section 10.6.3) the House of Lords Act 1999 removed all but 92 of
the hereditary peers. In tandem with the introduction of 1999 House of Lords Bill, the

government issued a White Paper (*Modernising Parliament, Reforming the House of Lords* Cm 4183 (The Stationery Office 1999)). This set out the various options for long-term reform to be considered by a Royal Commission, and its proposals for an independent Appointments Commission to select non-party political peers (a power previously exercised by the Prime Minister). This Appointments Commission was established in 2000 and has been operational ever since and in 2007 it recommended another six non-party political peers to sit in the House in addition to the previous 36 that it had recommended in previous years. Significantly in 2006 it declined to approve a handful of nominations for party political peerages (a second of its functions), which in turn led to an investigation into the nomination of putative peerages.

In January 2000 the Royal Commission under Lord Wakeham issued its report on future reform of the upper chamber (*A House for the Future* Cm 4534 (The Stationery Office, 2000)). In short, it recommended a mixed House with a largely appointed membership with a minority of members (65, 87 or 195) being elected as regional members.

In 2001 the government issued another White Paper on Lords reform (*The House of Lords – Completing the Reform*, Cm 5291 (2001)). This paper reaffirmed the government's commitment to removing the remaining hereditary peers and in terms of composition proposed a House of 600 members:

- One fifth elected.
- One fifth independents.
- The remainder being nominated by political parties.
- The law lords and bishops to remain.

This proposal proved unpopular and in 2002 in order to achieve parliamentary consensus on a reformed composition, a Joint Committee on House of Lords Reform was established. In 2003 both Houses voted on the different options put forward by the Committee:

- Wholly elected chamber.
- Wholly appointed.
- 80% appointed.
- 80% elected.
- 60% appointed.
- 60% elected.
- 50% appointed/50% elected.

The Commons did not approve any of the options, although they came closest (281 votes in favour to 284 against) to endorsing the option which proposed an 80 per cent elected House. The House of Lords, rather predictably, approved the fully appointed option. In addition to the above options, the House of Commons voted on, and rejected (by 390 to 172 votes), a further option of the abolition of the House of Lords thereby leading to a unicameral Parliament. For an analysis of these votes see: M Ryan, *'Parliament and the Joint Committee on House of Lords reform'* (2003) 37 Law Teacher 310.

In September 2003 the government issued a consultation paper (*Constitutional reform: next steps for the House of Lords* – CP 14/03 (DCA, 2003)) in which it stated that in the absence of consensus on composition it nevertheless proposed to:

- Remove the remaining hereditary peers.
- Place the Appointments Commission on a statutory basis.

In 2005 an all-party group of MPs published a paper in which it tried to show that party political consensus was possible and recommended a 70 per cent elected House (K Clarke, R Cook, P Tyler, T Wright and G Young, *Reforming the House of Lords: Breaking the deadlock* (Constitution Unit, 2005). Thereafter, the 2005 Labour Party general election manifesto stated that it would:

- Remove the remaining hereditary peers.
- Legislate to place reasonable limits on the time the House of Lords could delay legislation.
- Seek agreement on codifying the conventions between the two Houses following a review.

In June 2006 a Cross-Party Working Group on Lords Reform, consisting of members from both Houses and the main political parties, began the first of a number of meetings to discuss the future of reform.

In the 2006 Queen's Speech the government stated that it would work towards cross-party consensus on Lords reform and remove the remaining hereditary peers and in February 2007 another White Paper was issued (*The House of Lords: Reform*, Cm 7027 (The Stationery Office, 2007)). For its part, the government in the White Paper suggested that the reformed House should be a partly elected/partly appointed chamber containing 540 members. Moreover, no political party should have a majority of party political members and at least 20 per cent of the chamber's membership should be made up of non-party political members. It also recommended retention of the spiritual element. In essence, the White Paper paved the way for the following debates and votes to take place in the House of Commons in March 2007:

- The retention of a bicameral Parliament (Yes 416 votes, No 163 votes)
- No 1 – wholly appointed chamber (Yes 196, No 375)
- No 2 – 20% elected/80% appointed no vote
- No 3 – 40% elected/60% appointed no vote
- No 4 – 50% elected/50% appointed (Yes 155, No 418)
- No 5 – 60% elected/40% appointed (Yes 178, No 392)
- No 6 – 80% elected/20% appointed (Yes 305, No 267)
- No 7 – wholly elected chamber (Yes 337, No 224)

- The removal of the remaining hereditary peers (Yes 391, No 111).

R Cracknell, 'Commons divisions on House of Lords Reform: March 2007', SN/SG/4279

(House of Commons Library, 2007), p 2.

The overall result, therefore, was that the Commons supported the principle of retaining a second chamber, removing the remaining hereditary peers and having an upper House which was either fully or overwhelming elected (the former having the support of a majority of 113 MPs and the latter 38). One week later, informed by the votes taken in the Commons, the House of Lords voted overwhelmingly in favour of (rather unsurprisingly) a fully appointed House by 361 votes to 121. The other options were rejected with the 50 per cent elected House being decisively dismissed by 409 votes to 46 (see *Hansard*, HL Vol 690, cols 741–759).

22.6.2 Conventions in the House of Lords

In 2006 the Joint Committee on Conventions was established to examine the practicality of codifying the conventions which regulate the constitutional relationship between the two Houses of Parliament. Its report (Joint Committee on Conventions, First Report of Session 2005–06, *Conventions of the UK Parliament*, HL Paper 265-I, HC 1212-I (2006)) concluded that the term codification was unhelpful as it implied rule-making and an enforcement mechanism, whereas by their nature, constitutional conventions were unenforceable. As a consequence, to codify a constitutional convention was a contradiction in terms:

> **Q**
>
> 'far from reducing the risk of conflict, codification might actually damage the relationship between the two Houses, making it more confrontational and less capable of moderation through the usual channels. This would benefit neither the Government nor Parliament (para 279) … However, we offer certain formulations for one or both Houses to adopt by resolution. In our view, both the debates on such resolutions, and the resolutions themselves, would improve the shared understanding which the Government seek (para 280) … all recommendations for the formulation or codification of conventions are subject to the current understanding that conventions as such are flexible and unenforceable, particularly in the self-regulating environment of the House of Lords' (para 281).
>
> Joint Committee on Conventions, First Report of Session 2005–06,
> *Conventions of the UK Parliament*, HL Paper 265-I, HC 1212-I (2006).

The formulation suggested by the Committee included the following:

- The primacy of the House of Commons over the House of Lords was a fact which did not require codification.

- The convention that a manifesto Bill should not be opposed at the second or third reading by the House of Lords (the Salisbury-Addison Convention – see section 10.11) should be described as the *Government Bill convention*. The House of Lords should debate and set out the terms of this convention for the Commons subsequently to debate and note. The Committee pointed out that in practice there was little likelihood that the upper chamber would breach the Salisbury-Addison Convention.

- The existing convention that the government should have its business considered in a reasonable time in the upper chamber could be adopted by the House of Lords by way of a resolution. In addition, a new symbol could appear on the Lords' order paper indicating a Bill which had spent more than a certain period in the upper chamber (a period of 80 days was suggested).

- Although neither House rejects secondary legislation (Statutory Instruments) on a regular basis, in exceptional circumstances this may be appropriate and a statement to this effect could be approved by both Houses (or either House):

Q	'There are situations in which it is consistent both with the Lords' role in Parliament as a revising chamber, and with Parliament's role in relation to delegated legislation, for the Lords to threaten to defeat an S.I.'. Joint Committee on Conventions, First Report of Session 2005–06, *Conventions of the UK Parliament*, HL Paper 265-I, HC 1212-I (2006), para 229.

- It was universally recognised that there was no need to legislate on these matters.
- It was made very clear that the courts should have no role in relation to determining whether a parliamentary convention has been breached.

In December 2006 the government issued its Formal Reply to this report in which it accepted the Committee's conclusions and recommendations (*Government Response to the Joint Committee on Conventions' Report of Session 2005–06: Conventions of the UK Parliament*, Cm 6997 (Crown Copyright, 2006)).

22.6.3 Other constitutional developments

Two other constitutional developments in the Lords are worth noting:

- **The Speaker** – following the reform of the office of the Lord Chancellor, in July 2006 the House of Lords elected Baroness Hayman as Lord Speaker (see section 10.7.4).
- **Constitution Committee** – A House of Lords Constitution Committee has been established whose remit includes considering every Bill which has constitutional implications and keeping the constitution under review.

- **Select Committee on the Merits of Statutory Instruments** – this committee provides additional scrutiny of Statutory Instruments.

ACTIVITY

Problem solving

With your knowledge of the constitution, how do you think the two Houses of Parliament should be reformed to make a more effective and accountable Parliament?

22.7 The executive

22.7.1 Recent developments

In 2005 the Prime Minister issued a new edition of the *Ministerial Code* which details the constitutional roles and responsibilities of government ministers. (At the time of going to print, the code had been reissued again.) In addition, in 2006 a new edition of the *Civil Service Code* was published. Also in that year, a Private Member's Bill in the House of Lords – the Constitutional Reform (Prerogative Powers and Civil Service etc) Bill – was unsuccessful in attempting to put the Civil Service on a statutory footing.

As has always been the case, government departments and their associated ministers have not remained static. For example, in 2003 the Lord Chancellor's Department was replaced by the Department for Constitutional Affairs. Moreover, in 2006 the combined new office of the Secretary of State for Communities and Local Government, and Minister for Women was established. Executive Agencies have also been added to with, for example, the Tribunals Service becoming operational in 2006.

In terms of the royal prerogative there have been two recent unsuccessful legislative attempts to reform prerogative powers:

- The Armed Forces Bill 2005 proposed that parliamentary approval would be required for the armed forces to participate in an armed conflict (see section 11.9.4).
- The Constitutional Reform (Prerogative Powers and Civil Service etc) Bill 2006 proposed to codify the various prerogative powers exercised by the government.

In addition, in 2006 the House of Lords Select Committee on the Constitution issued its report on the government's powers under the prerogative to declare war and deploy armed forces. It is of constitutional interest to note its conclusion:

Q 'the exercise of the Royal Prerogative by the Government to deploy armed force overseas is outdated and should not be allowed to continue as the basis for legitimate war-making in our 21st century democracy. Parliament's ability to challenge the executive must be protected and strengthened'.

House of Lords Select Committee on the Constitution, 15th Report of Session 2005–06
Waging war: Parliament's role and responsibility, HL Paper 236-I (2006), para 103.

It recommended that a constitutional convention should be developed which would require the government to seek parliamentary approval (except in emergency situations) prior to the deployment of troops outside the United Kingdom in an armed conflict.

KEY FACTS

Parliament and the executive: constitutional developments and reforms	Source
The House of Commons Modernisation in terms of working hours, carry-over procedure, programme motions, pre-legislative scrutiny and the use of Westminster Hall	House of Commons resolutions
The House of Lords • The removal of the hereditary peers (with the exception of 92) • Elected Speaker	House of Lords Act 1999 House of Lords resolution

CONTINUED ▸

665

KEY FACTS

Parliament and the executive: constitutional developments and reforms	Source
The House of Lords • Continuous debate over the reform of the composition, role and powers of the upper chamber (most recent voting on composition taking place in March 2007)	Government White/consultation Papers: • *Modernising Parliament, Reforming the House of Lords,* Cm 4183 (1999) • *The House of Lords – Completing the Reform,* Cm 5291 (2001) • *Constitutional reform: next steps for the House of Lords* – CP 14/03 (2003) • *The House of Lords: Reform*, Cm 7027 (2007) Royal Commission: • A *House for the Future*, Cm 4534 (2000) Parliamentary committees • Public Administration Select Committee, *The Second Chamber: continuing the reform* HC 494-I (2002) • Joint Committee on House of Lords Reform, *Second Report* HL Paper 97, HC 668 (2003) • Joint Committee on Conventions, *Conventions of the UK Parliament*, HL Paper 265-I, HC 1212-I (2006)

CONTINU

KEY FACTS

Parliament and the executive: constitutional developments and reforms	Source
The executive	
• New editions of the *Ministerial Code* and *Civil Service Code*	Issued by the Prime Minster
• Continual restructuring of departments by transferring policy areas and altering the titles of government ministers	Ministers of the Crown Act 1975

22.8 The judiciary and judicial review

22.8.1 Judicial appointments and independence

In 2002 in order to improve the judicial appointments process, the independent Commission for Judicial Appointments assumed responsibility for making recommendations for appointments to the Lord Chancellor. In 2006 this body was superseded by the statutory Judicial Appointments Commission established under the aegis of s 61 of the Constitutional Reform Act 2005 (see section 13.3.1). These independent bodies have given more transparency to the process of appointing judges. The Supreme Court Selection Commission (set out in Sched 8 of the Act) will become active when the court becomes operational and a vacancy arises.

The Constitutional Reform Act has also afforded statutory protection for the principle of judicial independence:

• Section 3 places a statutory obligation on the Lord Chancellor and other ministers to uphold this principle and expressly prohibits government ministers from seeking to influence particular judicial decisions by having 'special access' to the judiciary. Under the Tribunals, Courts and Enforcement Bill, the legal members of tribunals (as Tribunal Judges) would also be afforded protection.

• Section 17 stipulates that the oath to be taken by a Lord Chancellor charges him to defend the independence of the judiciary.

• Section 7 provides for the Lord Chief Justice to replace the Lord Chancellor as Head of the Judiciary in England and Wales and under Pt 4 the administering of judicial discipline is performed in concert with the Lord Chancellor.

In addition, in giving effect to the government's consultation paper: *Increasing Diversity in the Judiciary* (DCA, 2004), Pt 2 of the 2006 Tribunals, Courts and Enforcement Bill proposed to amend the eligibility requirement for judicial office to widen the pool of those candidates eligible for judicial office.

22.8.2 Judicial review

In 2000, for the purposes of processing applications for judicial review proceedings, the Crown Office List was renamed the Administrative Court as it was recognised by Sir Jeffrey Bowman (Chairman of the Review of the Crown Court Office List) that there was a need for a specialist court to process public and administrative law cases. In doing so it has recognised the growing influential body of a separate system of administrative law and principles. It is worth recalling Dicey's antipathy towards the French system of administrative tribunals (see section 6.7.6).

The principles of judicial review, as common law principles, have continued to evolve and to be refined by the courts. One particularly significant area of development in terms of the constitution has been that of the right to a fair trial and judicial impartiality. After the *Pinochet* litigation the courts have refined what constitutes judicial bias (see section 13.4.2).

Also, the Tribunals, Courts and Enforcement Bill 2006 proposed to allow the Upper Tribunal to exercise a judicial review jurisdiction (see section 22.12.1).

22.9 The decentralisation of power

22.9.1 Devolution

The devolved institutions of the Scottish Parliament, National Assembly for Wales, Northern Ireland Assembly, London Mayor and Assembly have all been created since 1997 (following approval in referenda). Indeed, the Labour Party was elected with a manifesto commitment to implement devolution and the decentralisation of power away from the centre. The following developments are worth mentioning briefly:

- **The 'West Lothian question'**

One of the constitutional consequences which has resulted from devolution is the 'West Lothian question' (raised in the 1970s by Tam Dayell MP for the constitutency of West Lothian). In short, the 'West Lothian question' raises the issue as to whether it is constitutionally, or politically proper, to allow Scottish MPs to vote on purely English legislative matters (such as education and health), whilst English MPs cannot vote on the equivalent Scottish education and health issues, as they have been devolved to the Scottish Parliament. In order to address this question, Lord Baker introduced a Private Member's Bill: The Parliament (Participation of Members of the House of Commons) Bill 2006. This Bill successfully passed through the House of Lords, but foundered in the Commons. This legislation proposed to enable the Speaker of the House of Commons to certify the territorial extent of a Bill (eg a Bill affecting only England) on which only designated groups of MPs (eg MPs representing English constitutuencies) would be entitled to vote.

It is pertinent to point out that the 'West Lothian question' also means, of course, that ironically MPs representing Scottish constituencies (such as the Prime Minister Gordon Brown MP) could not vote on those Scottish issues which had been devolved to the Scottish Parliament. In any event, in recent years Scotland has had a reduction in the number of its Westminster MPs from 72 to 59 (Scottish Parliament (Constituencies) Act 2004).

- **The Government of Wales Act 2006 and the Greater London Authority Bill 2006**

These measures demonstrate the common constitutional belief that devolution is a *process* rather than a single static event, in that further powers, roles and responsibilities can be continually devolved and *rolled out* (rolling devolution).

In respect of Wales, as indicated earlier (section 14.5), Welsh devolution was a much weaker from of devolution than that of Scotland or Northern Ireland as the National Assembly lacked the power to make primary legislation. The changes brought about by the Government of Wales Act 2006 included, formally separating the Welsh executive from the National Assembly, enhancing the powers of the Assembly and paving the way for it to exercise a primary law-making power (following support for this in a referendum).

In relation to London, the Greater London Authority Bill 2006 proposed, *inter alia*, to expand the London Mayor's powers in respect of the London Fire and Emergency Planning Authority, impose a duty on him to publish a housing strategy for London and confer additional powers on him in relation to his spatial development strategy (planning).

- **Northern Ireland**

Powers were devolved to the Northern Ireland institutions in May 2007 following an election in March 2007.

22.9.2 Local government

In terms of local government, a number of reforms have taken place in recent years, arguably one of the most interesting being the requirement under the Local Government Act 2000 for local councils to adopt executive arrangements (eg the introduction of a Leader and Cabinet, Mayor and Cabinet or Mayor and Council Manager). It should be noted that in order to increase voter turnout at local and European Parliamentary elections (MEPs), Parliament passed the Local Government Act 2003 which enabled the holding of local and European elections at the same time.

The most recent government White Paper (*Strong and prosperous communities, The Local Government White Paper* Volume 1, Cm 6939-I (2006), pp 8–9) put forward, *inter alia*, the following proposals in order to make local government more accountable and responsive:

- Executive powers to be vested in the council leader.

- Councils will have three choices of leadership models involving a directly elected mayor, directly elected 'executive of councillors' or a leader elected by the other councillors.

- A review to be conducted in order to consider the barriers (and incentives) to people serving their local communities as councillors.

- By-laws no longer being subject to ministerial approval.

- Council scrutiny committees to be strengthened.

Finally, although in the past decade a new level of strategic administration has been inserted in the form of Regional Development Agencies (the Regional Development Agencies Act 1998); there has been no success in terms of introducing elected Regional Assemblies. In 2004 the North East overwhelming voted against the introduction of an elected Regional Assembly.

22.10 The European Community/Union

22.10.1 Constitutional changes

Since 1997 the United Kingdom, as part of the European Council, has agreed to three highly significant European Treaties. In 1997 the Treaty of Amsterdam was signed which, *inter alia*, expanded the competencies of the communities, altered the law-making process and re-numbered the Treaty Articles. This was formally incorporated into United Kingdom law via the European Communities (Amendment) Act 1998. In December 2000 the Treaty of Nice was signed which reformed the European institutional structure (eg reduced the number of Commissioners, capped the European Parliament and re-weighted the votes in the Council). This was formally incorporated into United Kingdom law via the passing of the European Communities (Amendment) Act 2002.

In recent years, arguably the most significant development in the European Community/Union was the signing in October 2004 by the Heads of State/Government of the Treaty establishing a Constitution for Europe (the European Constitution). This Treaty would have reformed the Community by, for example, reforming the institutional structure and legislative measures, and allowing Member States an exit strategy. Due to successive rejections in referenda in France and the Netherlands, the Treaty has been suspended as it requires all Members States to endorse it. It should be noted that the British Government had committed itself to holding a referendum on whether to approve the Constitution (an example of participatory government). In 2006 Parliament passed the European Union (Accessions) Act which paved the way for Romania and Bulgaria to join the Union/Community in 2007. These two countries joined in January 2007 making 27 Member States in total.

Finally, note the publication of the 2006 European Union (Implications of Withdrawal) Bill introduced by Lord Pearson in the House of Lords. Its purpose was to establish a committee to inquire into the implications (economic, constitutional, etc) of the United Kingdom withdrawing from the Union. This Bill presupposes, of course, that under parliamentary sovereignty, Parliament could repeal the European Communities Act 1972 (see section 15.6.5).

KEY FACTS

The judiciary, decentralisation and Europe: constitutional developments and reforms	Source
The judiciary	
• Renamed High Court the Administrative Court	Practice Direction
• Reformed the judicial element of the office of the Lord Chancellor	Pt 2, Constitutional Reform Act 2005
• Reformed the Judicial appointments system	s 61, Constitutional Reform Act 2005
Decentralisation of power	
• Devolved power to Scotland (Scottish Parliament)	Scotland Act 1998
• Devolved power to Wales (National Assembly for Wales)	Government of Wales Act 1998 as amended in 2006 (separating the Assembly from its executive body)
• Devolved power to Northern Ireland (Northern Ireland Assembly)	Northern Ireland Act 1998 (devolution reactivated in 2007 after a period of suspension)
• Devolved power to London (London Mayor and Assembly)	Greater London Authority Act 1999 (proposed to be amended in 2007 by conferring additional powers)
Europe:	
• Successive revisions of the 1957 Treaty of Rome	1997 Treaty of Amsterdam (incorporated by European Communities (Amendment) Act 1998)
	2000 Treaty of Nice (incorporated by European Communities (Amendment) Act 2002)
• Proposed European Constitution	2004 Constitutional Treaty

22.11 Free speech and civil liberties

22.11.1 Civil liberties

The Human Rights Act 1998 is a constitutional watershed in terms of the protection of civil liberties in the United Kingdom. In short, it has transformed negative, residual liberties (such as the freedom to protest providing this is not against the law) into positive human rights (eg the right to peacefully protest).

In essence, the constitutional effect of the Act is that it imposes a new statutory obligation on the courts to interpret all legislation in line with the Convention rights whenever it is possible to do so (s 3), and empowers them to issue a declaration of incompatibility where a statute cannot be construed as such (s 4). Public authorities are now under a new statutory obligation to act consistently with the Convention (s 6). Victims can seek redress in the domestic courts where they claim that their Convention rights have been violated by a public authority (s 7), and the courts are empowered to award damages where the Convention has been infringed (s 8).

In 2007 the Commission for Equality and Human Rights was scheduled to become active under the aegis of the Equality Act 2006. This Commission will not only bring together existing Commissions on Racial Equality, Disability Rights and Equal Opportunities, but will also promote awareness of, and good practice in relation to, the requirements of the Human Rights Act. One criticism of the Human Rights Act has been that historically it has not been accompanied by a Human Rights Commission to support it.

22.11.2 Free speech

Two recent developments which involve restricting freedom of expression are worth drawing attention to:

- **The Racial and Religious Hatred Act 2006** – this Act amends the Public Order Act 1986 by creating new offences of stirring up hatred on religious grounds. The government was particularly concerned about protecting the Muslim community from religious hatred.

- **The Terrorism Act 2006** – s 1 creates a criminal offence of encouraging terrorism (including statements which glorify the commission or preparation of acts of terrorism). Section 2 criminalises the dissemination of terrorist publications (eg booksellers).

22.12 Grievance mechanisms

22.12.1 Tribunals

In recent years the organisation of the network of tribunals has been revamped with the creation of the Tribunals Service (operational in April 2006) which provides common administrative support to a number of central government tribunals. This development had been preceded by the Leggatt

Report (*Tribunals for Users One system, One Service* (2001) and government White Paper (*Transforming Public Services: Complaints, Redress and Tribunals,* Cm 6243 (DCA, 2004)). Following this, the Tribunals, Courts and Enforcement Bill 2006 was announced in the Queen's Speech of November 2006. This Bill sought to reform further the tribunal system. Its proposals included the following:

Two tribunal system

The Bill proposed a simplified two-tier system of tribunals which would be composed of the following:

- A First-tier Tribunal.
- An Upper Tribunal.

The Lord Chancellor would specify existing tribunals to be transferred to this structure, for example, the Mental Health Review Tribunal. In addition, the two tribunals would be organised into 'Chambers' (headed by a President) so that similar jurisdictional areas could be grouped together. This would allow more efficient organisational use of tribunal members and resources.

In general terms, the Upper Tribunal would act as an appellate tribunal (on a point of law) for the First-tier Tribunal, thereby rationalising the appeals process for tribunals. Thereafter, appeals would be possible from the Upper Tribunal to the Court of Appeal. Note that the Bill proposed to confer on the Upper Tribunal a power of judicial review of certain classes of cases either specified by the Lord Chief Justice or particular cases transferred from the High (Administrative) Court. It would be highly unlikely for the Upper Tribunal to review immigration or nationality issues. In this jurisdiction the Upper Tribunal would have similar powers to those exercised by the existing Administrative Court.

The Lord Chancellor would be under a statutory obligation to ensure an effective and efficient tribunal administration.

Personnel

Legal members of tribunals (ie legally qualified members) would be designated as Tribunal Judges. In addition, a new statutory office would be created that of the Senior President of Tribunals which would provide leadership to the Tribunal Judges and oversee the tribunal system. The Constitutional Reform Act 2005 would be amended to provide for the Lord Chancellor and other ministers to protect the independence of the Tribunal Judges.

The Administrative Justice and Tribunals Council

The Bill proposed to replace the existing Council on Tribunals (which oversees tribunals and inquiries and makes appropriate recommendations) with an Administrative Justice and Tribunals Council. This new body would not only oversee the new tribunal system and its arrangements, but would also have a wider remit to review the whole administrative justice system (including, how government departments, the Ombudsmen, etc relate to the public).

Procedures and rules

At present the rules and procedure governing tribunals are generally composed by the Lord Chancellor or relevant government minister. The Bill proposed that a Tribunal Procedure Committee would assume responsibility for making these rules and in doing so would provide consistency in the procedural rules operated by the tribunal system. Moreover, the Senior President of Tribunals would be able to issue practice directions (analogous to those in a court).

22.12.2 Inquiries and Ombudsmen

In terms of inquiries, statutory inquiries have been reformed through the passing of the Inquiries Act 2005, having been preceded by a consultation paper (Department for Constitutional Affairs Consultation Paper, *Effective Inquiries* (DCA, 2004)).

In terms of the various different Ombudsmen in the United Kingdom, recent reforms have rationalised the ombudsmen system by creating single bodies in Scotland (The Scottish Public Services Ombudsman), Wales (The Public Services Ombudsman for Wales) and Northern Ireland (Assembly Ombudsman and Commissioner for Complaints).

In terms of the Westminster Ombudsman (the PHSO), she still retains the MP filter as to date this has not been reformed despite the government's support in 2001 for its abolition. It should be noted that in a 2005 consultation paper the government recommended streamlining the constitutional relationship of the parliamentary, health and local commissioners (*Reform of Public Sector Ombudsmen Services in England* (Cabinet Office, 2005).

Also note that s 62 of the Constitutional Reform Act 2005 established a Judicial Appointments and Conduct Ombudsman whose role would involve investigating complaints of maladministration in the context of the judicial appointment process.

Recent developments

At the time this book was going to press, the newly appointed Secretary of State for Justice and Lord Chancellor (Jack Straw MP) published a Green Paper on the government's vision and proposals for constitutional renewal (*The Governance of Britain*, Cm 7170 (2007)).

KEY FACTS

Civil liberties and grievance mechanisms: constitutional developments and reforms	Source
Civil liberties:	
• Conversion of negative residual liberties into positive human rights whereby Convention rights can be raised directly before domestic courts and all legislation to be interpreted in line with them (whenever possible to do so)	Human Rights Act 1998
• Commission for Equality and Human Rights to be established in 2007	Equality Act 2006
• Recent restrictions of free speech including: the outlawing of the glorification of terrorism and inciting religious hatred	Terrorism Act 2006 and Racial and Religious Hatred Act 2006, respectively
Grievance mechanisms:	
• Establishment in 2006 of the Tribunals Service providing common support for specified tribunals	Administrative action
• Proposed restructuring of tribunal system into a First-tier Tribunal and an Upper Tribunal	Tribunals, Courts and Enforcement Bill 2006
• Reform of ministerial statutory inquiries	Inquiries Act 2005

ACTIVITY

Essay writing

Do you think that the above reforms and developments improve the British constitution? As a result of these changes, does the British constitution accord more with the principles underpinning constitutionalism?

Further reading

Maer, L, 'Modernisation of the House of Commons 1997–2005' 05/46 (House of Commons Library, 2005).

Oliver, D, 'The Modernisation of the United Kingdom Parliament' in Jowell, J and Oliver, D (eds), *The Changing Constitution* (5th edn, Oxford University Press, 2004), p 256.

Oliver, D, *Constitutional Reform in the United Kingdom* (Oxford University Press, 2004).

Russell, M, *Reforming the House of Lords, Lessons from Overseas* (Oxford University Press, 2000).

Ryan, M, 'The House of Lords and the Shaping of the Supreme Court' (2005) 56 NILQ 135.

Ryan, M, 'Parliament and the Joint Committee on House of Lords reform' (2003) 37 Law Teacher 310.

Website

www.ucl.ac.uk/constitution-unit

INDEX ▪

Locators in italics indicate Key Facts, f indicates figures and t, tables